THE YALE EDITIONS OF
The Private Papers of James Boswell

Boswell

LAIRD OF AUCHINLECK

1778-1782

EDITED BY JOSEPH W. REED

PROFESSOR OF ENGLISH

WESLEYAN UNIVERSITY

AND FREDERICK A. POTTLE

STERLING PROFESSOR OF ENGLISH, EMERITUS

YALE UNIVERSITY

McGRAW-HILL BOOK COMPANY

NEW YORK   TORONTO   LONDON

Library of Congress Cataloging in Publication Data

Boswell, James, 1740–1795.
  Boswell, Laird of Auchinleck, 1778–1782.

  (The Yale editions of the private papers of James Boswell)
  Includes index.
  1. Boswell, James, 1740–1795—Biography. 2. Authors, Scottish—Biography. I. Reed, Joseph W., 1932–   II. Pottle, Frederick Albert, 1897–   III. Title. IV. Series.
PR3325.A795 1977   828'.6'09 [B]   76-44502
ISBN 0-07-051520-4

      1 2 3 4 5 6 7 8 9 BPBP 7 6 5 4 3 2 1 0 9 8 7

This book was set in Baskerville with display lines in Stationer's Semiscript by The Book Press and was printed and bound by The Book Press. The editors were Nancy Frank and Cheryl Hanks. The copy editor was Seymore Copstein. The designer was Christine Aulicino. Milton Heiberg supervised the production.

To the memory of

FREDERICK W. HILLES,

mentor, colleague, benefactor, friend,

this volume is affectionately dedicated

by its editors.

The Yale Editions of the Private Papers of James Boswell will consist of two independent but parallel series. One, the "research" edition, will give a complete text of Boswell's journals, diaries, and memoranda; of his correspondence; and of the *Life of Johnson*, from the original manuscript: the whole running to at least thirty volumes. It will preserve the spelling and capitalization of the original documents, and will be provided with extensive scholarly annotation. A large group of editors and a permanent office staff are engaged in this comprehensive undertaking, the first, second, and third volumes of which appeared in 1966, 1969, and 1976, respectively. The other, the reading or "trade" edition, will select from the total mass of papers those portions that appear likely to be of general interest, and will present them in modern spelling and with appropriate annotation. The publishers may also issue limited de luxe printings of the trade volumes, with extra illustrations and special editorial matter, but in no case will the trade volumes or the de luxe printing include matter from Boswell's archives that will not also appear in the research edition.

The present volume is the eleventh of the trade edition.

The preparation of *Boswell, Laird of Auchinleck* for publication in 1977 was made possible in part by the generous support of the Editing Program of the National Endowment for the Humanities.

CONTENTS

ILLUSTRATIONS

following page 250

Alexander Boswell, Lord Auchinleck, artist unknown, from the collection of Mr. and Mrs. Paul Mellon, Upperville, Virginia. Reproduced by permission.

Martha Ray, a magazine print. Courtesy of the Lewis Walpole Library, Farmington, Connecticut.

Robert Macqueen, Lord Braxfield, painting by Sir Henry Raeburn. Courtesy of the Faculty of Advocates, Edinburgh.

The Hon. Topham Beauclerk, water-colour drawing probably by G. P. Harding. Courtesy of the Lewis Walpole Library, Farmington, Connecticut.

A note, in Samuel Johnson's hand, 4 April 1781, now in the Boswell Papers at Yale.

Charlotte Ann Burney, miniature by Charles Jagger, whereabouts unknown. Photograph reproduced by permission of the National Portrait Gallery, London.

Sir John Pringle, Bt., painting by Thomas Gainsborough, now in the possession of W. R. Rees Davies, Q.C., M.P., London. Reproduced by permission.

An Excellent New War Song, by Boswell, now in the Boswell Papers at Yale.

INTRODUCTION

§ I

The present volume ends with the death of Boswell's father and Boswell's long anticipated inheritance of Auchinleck, so we have called it *Boswell, Laird of Auchinleck*. But the inheritance, when it comes, seems more an incidental event than the climax to the clear and constant development of this portion of the journal. Boswell has not cast himself in the role of laird in the way he formerly cast himself in his momentary roles of rake, disciplined student, foreign correspondent, ardent suitor, advocate. His continual daily problems are too pressing and immediate for him to define any such long-range decision or role. The earlier journal was stronger in what, if it were fiction, would be called plot, but this one is richer in developed instant and incident. If this journal has a major theme, it is the persistence of problems: the problem for Boswell of seeing clearly the themes of his life at present, the problem of sorting out the problems; if it has a clear shape, it is organic rather than architectonic: a welter of themes and immediate quandaries, interacting, separating, and then combining again in permutation.

Boswell is clearly "in the middle of life's journey." He pauses to reflect on his fortieth birthday: "I hoped to live better from this day, being now forty years of age," and again, a few weeks later, "How insignificant is my life at present! How little do I read! I am making no considerable figure in any way, and I am now forty years of age. But let me not despond. I am a man better known in the world than most of my countrymen. I am very well at the bar for my standing. I lead a regular, sober life. I have a variety of knowledge and excellent talents for conversation. I have a good wife and promising children." The despair of the opening sentence leads finally into reassuring summary. But for each reassurance there is a corresponding doubt or despair recorded elsewhere. Boswell's consistency and his literary power come from honest immediacy, so it is perhaps to be expected that the middle of his life would not be blessed by unqualified assurance or ruled by a determined plan so much as it might be continually marked by shifting and even contradictory characterizations of his standing at this moment or that.

Lack of plot, in other words, is no proper criticism for this text. Theme it has and wealth of rumination and self-knowledge, to say nothing of that rich welter of perfectly rendered momentary detail. And if its development is perhaps obscure, constant thematic concerns clarify the momentary contradictions. Each element of Boswell's birthday assessment defines an area of concern for this stretch of journal, and from these an order emerges without forcing the material to take on what might be a largely synthetic "plot."

§ II

"I have a good wife and promising children." Boswell's family, here cited by him rather dutifully, are, as our epigraph [1] demonstrates, central to his existence. In these pages Boswell appears continually as a devoted and happy paterfamilias to his expanding family. James and Elizabeth ("Betsy"), the last two of his five children, are born in this period. Boswell's wife is now clearly consumptive, sometimes near death, not in a continual decline to which Boswell might resign himself, but rather intermittently waning and blooming, leaving him in a state of watchful doubt. At one point he contemplates her death as a coming certainty: "The apprehension of losing her and being left with five young children was frightfully dreary. All my affection for her and gratitude to her, and the consciousness of not having acted as her husband ought to do, overwhelmed me." But at another point he observes she looks better than she has since she first came to him, and at yet another contemplates her illness with "a sort of agitation that rather gave a kind of pleasure." Death and the threat of death are a constant theme of these years: his father and wife are ill, Dr. Johnson is aging; Edward Dilly, Dr. Boswell, Sir George and Lady Preston, Sir John Pringle, James Boswell of Balbarton, and "poor Annie Cuninghame" all die in these pages. Earlier deaths have loaded Boswell with the responsibilities for his wife's sisters' children, the orphaned broods of Treesbank and Lainshaw. A man as devoted to heritage and family history as Boswell's family catechism shows him to be cannot define only his wife and children as his family. But Boswell, the centre of responsibility for the larger family (at least as he views it), confronts each death as an individual shock, not as an occasion for the realization or contemplation of his own advancing journey. That contemplation is evident only disguised as ancestral piety when Boswell views the vault at Auchinleck: "Beheld with solemn emotion our family vault, my *long home*."

There is a balance here: Boswell's care for his immediate family, generally a source of joy and tender concern, has come into apparent conflict with his responsibilities for more distant family and especially what he felt to be the selfishness of his father's separate establishment. "My dear wife's illness was more distressing to me that I reflected she had never had the advantages to which the match she made entitled her, my father

[1] Below, p. [xxxvi].

having kept me upon a small allowance, and he and his women having treated her with shameful coldness. When I thought she might perhaps die before my coming to the estate of Auchinleck, which would place her in a situation which she so well deserves, I was grievously vexed; and as a wife is to be preferred to a father, especially when he lives only to continue the harsh and unjust power of a stepmother, I could not help viewing his death as a desirable event. I know not what to think of this. Certainly the death of a father *may* be a desirable event. It is nice to determine in what cases. A son should be able to give strong reasons. I have given mine, and I do not see as yet that I am in the wrong."

Boswell's relationship with his father has been a constant throughout these volumes: here Lord Auchinleck becomes Boswell's chief antagonist. Probably he was a good man, faithful to his duties as a judge, guardian of the name, and preserver of the estate. But he was cold and harsh, and sometimes cruel. Certainly his mad son John was disagreeable, but had Boswell not interfered, Lord Auchinleck would have been content to have had him sent off to Inveresk to be beaten and caged like an animal. James Boswell gave his father ample cause for harshness, and Lord Auchinleck disapproved of his choice in a wife, but there is no evidence for his father's dogged belief that she encouraged Boswell in extravagance, and no reason for him to extend to Margaret Boswell and her children his animosity toward his son and heir or for him to continue to snub her long after he should have known her better. Lord Auchinleck has talked to Boswell as he might to a recalcitrant child and treated him as such. He has listened to Boswell's arguments much as he might have heard from the bench a badly prepared brief, so Boswell is doubly insulted, as neglected son and rejected advocate. "I went to my father's at night. He spoke of poor John with contemptous disgust. I was shocked and said, 'He's your son, and God made him.' He answered very harshly, 'If my sons are idiots, can I help it?' I supped with him and was patient."

As Lord Auchinleck sees it, there has been no progress in Boswell beyond 1763. "My father has not treated me as a man should be treated, but has looked on me as a mere dependant on him. This has, I dare say, prevented me from making a greater figure in the world than I do. Though it may be it has secured me from splendid ruin." Perhaps it is clearer to us than to Boswell that his father has, in the worst possible way, stretched his admittedly irresponsible youth into his fortieth year. The clearest moment of this antagonism appears at a dinner in the last month of his father's life. Boswell knew of his father's "meanness at his table in grudging claret," but Lord Auchinleck always supplied a bottle for Dr. Webster. When Boswell asks for a glass and Dr. Webster hands him the bottle, his father says "with a snarl, 'That's Dr. Webster's bottle, man.' "

Boswell, attempting to shame him, replies, " 'I know . . . but the Doctor makes me welcome, and I like to take a glass of claret when I'm with a man who can afford it.' " Then he persists, " 'If it is disagreeable to you that I should drink claret, I shall let it alone.' " Lord Auchinleck, anxious to conceal his meanness, replies, " 'Never fash your head.' " But when Lady Auchinleck calls for another bottle of claret, she rouses the old man, and "with a vengeance" he fills Boswell's glass with sherry. "I was stunned. . . . I once thought of instantly leaving the company, but . . . said, 'It's all one,' and then putting some claret into my glass, said, 'I'll make burgundy of it.' . . . It was really wretched treatment."

Boswell sees himself in these years as very much his own man, as well he might. Yet he must campaign through intermediaries just to get a necessary increase in his annual allowance to support his expanding family. He feels under obligation to ask parental permission for any jaunt which carries him away from Scotland for very long. His father settles more and more on his second wife and grants a lifetime pension to his physician. Boswell's family is treated shabbily while the old man sequesters himself more and more with his household of women.

Of course there is another side to all this. Lord Auchinleck is slowly and painfully dying and is miserably ill. His wife looks after him and protects him from a son and heir he suspects may be trying to ruin him and from other such bothersome intrusions on the privacy of his suffering. Dr. Gillespie does for Lord Auchinleck what he can no longer do for himself—empty his bladder three times a day—and settling a pension on him is Lord Auchinleck's prudent Scots solution to the continuing expense of the physician's constant faithful attendance which has curtailed his regular practice.

Boswell is too close, of course, to see this. But his frustration at his father's neglect, cruelty, and lack of trust is as real and as constant as his father's suffering. There is dramatic illumination of this when David Boswell returns. Boswell's junior by eight years, his brother David had left home in 1767 when only nineteen to live in Spain. The prospect of his return fills Boswell with eager anticipation and hope. Perhaps he may provide the occasion for a firm decision to remain in Scotland, to stick by the rock of Auchinleck. Short of that, David might at least take the side of Boswell's young family against Lord Auchinleck, take the offensive where Boswell cannot—return, see what is happening, point out directly to his father his senseless cruelty toward the heir to Auchinleck.

David comes and fails Boswell completely. He goes through with an elaborate pageant at the Old Castle of swearing to stand by Auchinleck with heart, purse, and sword, but David, the straightforward, no-nonsense businessman, cannot conceal from Boswell for a minute how silly he thinks

all this is. Boswell is disappointed. "He talked *rationally* of my *flights.* . . .
I . . . now think him a good deal more agreeable than I did at Edinburgh,
though his cool, attentive conduct to the *noverca* [Lady Auchinleck], and
insensibility to her sour, resentful behaviour to a brother who had been
all along warmly kind and generous to him, could not but give me uneasiness." David tempers his coolness enough to say that "though he had
not much affection, he felt it" for Boswell's children, but Boswell still is
not sure of him. "But," as he says, "I study character too closely." Their
return to Edinburgh ends in a violent dispute and sarcastic epithets fly
about ("He said we should not travel together. I said I would not travel
with him for five guineas a day"). Once again Boswell has anticipated that
some outside event will come along and bring him dramatic release from
his problems; but again he is thrown back upon himself and the necessity
to resolve his own dilemmas. His father's death is similar. Boswell has
contemplated it in the abstract rather coldly; when it finally comes he is
dissolved in grief. Long anticipated as a release from the perpetual conflict, the death resolves nothing.

§ III

"*I am very well at the bar for my standing.*" Boswell's practice declines
as his father appears less and less frequently on the bench in the Court of
Session, which makes him "uneasy," not just financially, but because he
knows that the two facts can hardly be unconnected. "Mr. Lawrie was of
opinion with me that my father's absence from the House did me hurt.
. . . I knew not how to raise £200." Boswell wants very much to be a good
advocate and he is, in his own way, devoted to the law. But it has not
advanced him very rapidly. "I . . . dreaded insignificance, while at the
same time I had all this year as yet been so averse to the business of the
Court of Session that I had no keenness for it, as I once had, and wished
always to have anything I had to do decently over. I saw no opportunity
for ambition in this narrow sphere. What practice I had, I had with the
dignity of a gentleman, not having used the artifices which many advocates
have done." The law keeps him in Scotland, and at least part of the time
(when he is not seeing it as the land of his fathers, his Rock), he sees
Scotland as what hems him in, what keeps him from London. "I languished for London; yet feared I should not be able to rise to any
eminence there. Sir John Pringle said to me one day this summer, 'I know
not if you will be at rest in London. But you will never be at rest out
of it.' I felt a kind of weak, fallacious attachment to Edinburgh. But I
considered, 'I hope to be in Heaven, which is quitting Edinburgh. Why

then should I not quit it to get to London, which is a high step in the scale of felicity?' " In these pages there are many fits and starts about resolving this tension, but again, no resolution. For the journal Boswell continually describes the tension as a choice, but this is self-delusion. He cannot move to London. As it is, his income from all sources is barely sufficient to meet the needs of his family. Yet were he to leave Scotland, he would sacrifice all his income except the £100 a year his father has bound himself to.

This does not, of course, mean that there is no uncertainty, for the idea that the choice of Scotland or London is his to make is a potent fantasy. If only, if only. If only there were some way to transfer his professional duties to London, joining "felicity" to destiny and necessity. He spends most of the year in Scotland and two or three months (when he can get there at all) in London. Could he but exchange the proportions, combine profession with his strange penchant for recording scenes and conversations (hardly to be understood or even mentioned in Edinburgh), restore some of that agonizing loss of conversation, encounter, scene: neither London nor Edinburgh to be abandoned, but their claims reversed. Fantasy again, but the kind of eddying fantasy which mid-life uncertainty feeds on. Boswell wants to be laird of Auchinleck. But he also wants to go to London, to sit in Parliament, or at least to have a good appointment under Government. Here in the middle of his life he sues for cordial relations with Henry Dundas; eighteen months later he makes similar overtures to the Lord President. He begs Edmund Burke (in a tone totally uncharacteristic of their close, punning relationship) to ask for an appointment for him. He has to ask out of friendship because he has never supported Burke's party. The most risky of several impossible possibilities is practice at the English bar.

The call never comes. Boswell ends this volume with his life still split. He couldn't have gone had it come. But this impossibility does not properly represent the continual anguish of argument, of fantasy and necessity, of advance and retreat and fluctuation.

§ IV

"I am making no considerable figure in any way. . . . I am a man better known in the world than most of my countrymen." Despair and self-assurance merge here in the birthday assessment. Boswell has reason to pride himself on his reputation: his acquaintance includes the first company of the land. In 1781 he has a considerable conversation with George III (whom he had previously met), and it seems likely that he

meets more important and famous people in this stretch of journal than in any previous volume. Boswell's literary reputation now certainly makes him "a considerable figure." He writes many things and is publishing now more than at any earlier period of the decade: an essay for the *London Magazine* every month; a pamphlet addressed to Lord Braxfield; a series of letters to the *Public Advertiser* about the mutiny of the Seaforth Highlanders (his equally vivid account of the anti-Catholic riots in Edinburgh apparently remained unpublished till our time); a major encounter with a romantic felon, James Hackman; a New Year's editorial for the *Caledonian Mercury*. He is writing occasional verse—its quality is no more remarkable than it ever was, but his best poem is produced at this time, the deplorable epithalamium for the supposed nuptials of Dr. Johnson and Mrs. Thrale. He is writing up from his notes and memory some concluding entries (22–26 October 1773) of his tour to the Hebrides with Johnson.

And there are projects aplenty—projects he is always starting gathering materials for and never finishing: a life of his London friend General Oglethorpe, a life of Lord Kames, a history of the Union, a life of James IV. For Kames and Oglethorpe he gathers materials, probably never intending to do more in their lifetimes. But he asks Lord Hailes to put him on a "plan of writing" for the history of the life and reign of James IV of Scotland "from whom our family got Auchinleck," and Lord Hailes puts him on a plan not at all to his taste: "Abridging everything in *Foedera* concerning that period, carefully marking pages and dates . . . the same as to all our Scottish and English writers about that period. . . . If you cannot submit to the toil of abridging the *Foedera*, you will certainly produce an imperfect work." [2] Boswell could have submitted to the toil—under other circumstances he had enjoyed abstracting and digesting legal and legislative records—but this is perhaps irrelevant. He starts with not much more than an enthusiasm and to go farther would be to yoke no more than an enthusiastic impulse to certain drudgery.

Boswell's best writing involves no such yoking because there is no such separation between impulse and result. The *Life of Johnson* has never been such a "project," a task requiring a plan. He works on it, inasmuch as he works on the journal, and works very hard, but it is not a project to labour through, an assignment to complete. It is the journal, that certain and confident life's work, pursued with unquestioning lack of doubt and unselfconscious ease that only genius can provide. An all-

[2] From Lord Hailes, 22 November 1778. "*Foedera*" is the collection of treaties and documents on English diplomacy in twenty volumes, compiled by Thomas Rymer (1641–1713): *Foedera, Conventiones, Literae, et Cujuscunque Generis Acta Publica* (*Treaties, Compacts, Edicts, and Other Such Public Acts*), 1703–1735.

important remark here shows he has thought more about what lies ahead for the *Life* than he has heretofore recorded: "I told Erskine I was to write Dr. Johnson's life in scenes. He approved."

There are three important events in the journal's "biography" in this volume: the disjointed 1779 London journal, Boswell's re-reading of an earlier journal, and his wife's discovery and reading of a passage (perhaps just as painful to her as the earlier reading is to Boswell) of the more recent journal. The 1779 London journal is a patchwork—detached fragments, jumps, gaps, unexpanded notes—perhaps as difficult a text for editors to make readable as any the journal contains. Boswell's explanation for this in the *Life* is candid enough: "During my stay in London this spring, I find I was unaccountably negligent in preserving Johnson's sayings, more so than at any time. . . . There is no help for it now. . . . But I am nevertheless ashamed and vexed to think how much has been lost. It is not that there was a bad crop this year, but that I was not sufficiently careful in gathering it in." "Not sufficiently careful" does not give any idea of the chaotic confusion of the record. Many days are noted twice or even three times; he loses notes or is unable later to apply himself to the task even to fill in the gaps of his jotted headings. The explanation for this is obscure, but one that can be easily rejected is that Boswell has lost faith in his task.

The re-reading of earlier journals is a greater test of faith. He looked back "into my journal in 1762, that I might console myself in Edinburgh by being reminded that I had been as weary and melancholy in London as here. And I was so engaged . . . that I read on all the time that I had appropriated to the Memorial. This was wrong. I was sickened in mind by reviewing my own sickly weakness. Yet I thought that it was not fair to judge of London now to me by what it was when I had a narrow acquaintance in it." Good reading, but painful remembering leading to an ultimate reassurance. Earlier, in comparing his journal to someone else's, it had not been so easy to ward off his doubts about the whole question of journal-keeping. In 1779 he had been reading a journal kept by a John Bogle of Hamilton Farm: "In that diary his acts of profligacy were recorded in plain terms, and his folly and vanity set down, while at the same time there were several reflections on his own insignificancy and on the unhappiness of life, which I excerpted. Reading this journal made me uneasy to think of my own. It is preserving evidence against oneself; it is filling a mine which may be sprung by accident or intention. Were my journal to be discovered and made public in my own lifetime, how shocking would it be to me! And after my death, would it not hurt my children? I must not be so plain. I will write to Dr. Johnson on the subject."

It is, as it turns out, his wife who springs the mine he has filled: he had left the journal lying open in the dining-room while he went downstairs to look for something, "and my dear wife having taken it up, read the account of my life on Monday the 18, with which she was shocked, and declared that all connexion between her and me was now at an end, and that she would continue to live with me only for decency and the sake of her children. I was miserably vexed and in a sort of stupor, but could say nothing for myself. I indulged some glimmering of hope, and just acquiesced in my fate for the present." Boswell doesn't offer to burn the offensive writing (as he burned some of his early letters returned by James Bruce earlier in this volume) or even think of giving over that honest immediacy which so upsets his wife but so gratifies us as readers. Instead this crisis for the journal simply becomes a little more grist for its mill.

§ V

"I lead a regular, sober life. I have a variety of knowledge and excellent talents for conversation." Boswell the paterfamilias is balanced by Boswell the man of the world. "I had a fine letter this week from my friend Temple which humbled me. For it showed me that he continued constant to literature, so that *in himself* he was much my superior. But then as a social being I had the advantage of him." The finest proof of Boswell's force as a social being, the charm of his person, is offered in this volume, an account by Charlotte Ann Burney here published for the first time. If a reader has had trouble believing Johnson's praise for Boswell's social presence, he need only refer to this remarkable account. For believers it offers satisfying corroboration; for non-believers a persuasive case.

But Boswell is himself in the present volume from time to time one of the non-believers. There are doubts, enforced by terrible mornings-after, about his drinking. He swore off time and again: the present volume opens with a sober interlude which seems to have begun in January 1778 and to have lasted seven months and more. His birthday assessment is quite true: he *does* lead a regular, sober life, and has done for three months together now. But for the bulk of the journal the assessment will seem to readers to be outrageously false. Boswell never drank in the morning, he never drank secretly, he did not drink alone. It was sociability that ruined him: "*Why* wish to entertain everybody?" "If I can once get free of a notion that my company is dissatisfied when I do not drink with them, I shall do well." One does not know whether to rate as comic or pathetic his fall from sobriety when in the fulness of his heart, he resolved to "indulge . . . in liberal moderation" at the meeting of particular friends after Jamie's christening. There is now a fine line between easy sociability ("I drank some cider and Madeira, which warmed my animal spirits and made me think for the time of good social inter-course as the most valuable employment of time") and excess ("I *must* pull the reins. But I feel my dull insignificance in this provincial situa-tion. I have even little employment as a lawyer and my mind is vacant and listless till quickened by drinking"). Swearing off was the only sure pre-ventive, because "I was at this time conscious of what is the state of a man who has a craving for strong drink; and I dreaded being perhaps at some future period of my life a wretched sot. However, I persisted." Boswell strove for regularity and sobriety; frequently he succeeded for stretches of time, but he too confidently confused three months of success at water-drinking with a more general reform.

We know a great deal about Boswell's struggles with drink because he writes very freely about them at all periods of his life: we know very little about his struggles with sexual temptation in these later years because he has pretty much stopped recording them. That there were struggles is evident: he had picked up a venereal infection on 14 July 1780 when "in a wild desperation," he had resorted to the Pleasance "for the last time." His avowed belief in concubinage never helped him much. He con-fessed, he left his journal lying about so his wife could find it, he was ashamed, he was deeply contrite, he vowed lasting reform, two days or so later he was headed back to Portsburgh or the Pleasance. Boswell felt ambivalent about chastity, as he did about temperance, and his practice wavered even more than his theory.

§ VI

We have confronted the specific reassurances of Boswell's birthday assessment with corresponding doubts and despairs. We could use these to trace an ominous pattern of doubts leading to a distressing conclusion, Boswell's thought of suicide in August of 1782, one of the very few such thoughts entrusted to his journal that we can recall. But we might as easily take the opposite course leading through reassurances towards the heights: the joyous jaunt to Chester "where I declare I passed my time more happily than I ever did in any place—I know not if I should even except London —for the same portion of time." The reader of this volume will look in vain for Boswell's day-by-day account. The Chester journal, that "log-book of felicity," as Boswell styled it, is unaccountably missing. But there are other such exaltations scattered throughout these pages, for almost every despair a high hope: "I was active and animated and full of hope. How very different from the dreary metaphysical wretch that I have been!" "I relished everything, even the Court of Session."

But to impose either synthesis would be an injustice to the material. Boswell's journal is autobiography only if viewed from a much greater distance than just the few years represented here: these incidents and moments are as brush-strokes to a finished painting, and many of the most memorable passages are matter for his biography only in the sense that Reynolds's portraits are matter for Reynolds's biography. We read Boswell's journal primarily not for what we can learn there of one man, or for the "plot" or even primarily for what it can teach us of the eighteenth century, but because it is art. Its honest immediacy transforms a generally ordinary sequence of day-to-day events into a series of achieved literary moments, a narrative of literary effect, quite frequently a narrative of genius. The ups and downs are not only inevitable because this is also a life, they are necessary for the literary structure of the narrative. A life maintained at a consistent pitch of involvement, vivacity and satisfaction would not only be impossible to live, it would not be worth the reading. And a life of perpetually consistent development and climax would not be capable of supporting the intense belief we grant so easily to Boswell's journal. Our involvement as we read on is not the same as what we might grant to a novel, an involvement in consistent development and a coherent world, but rather an involvement in process, a whole rendered moment-to-moment as it develops, the immediate responses of a mercurial consciousness, fortunately also a consummate artist.

This present portion of the journal is powerful, with passages as good as Boswell ever wrote: the argument between Beauclerk and Johnson about Hackman, settlement of wine dues at The Club, a meeting between Langton and Beauclerk. Along with brilliant scenes are less developed but fully rendered moments: Boswell dreams of his great toe, that his wife has married somebody else, of a long conversation with "a steady English counsellor," of a visit to a mosque in Constantinople. We have Boswell's distress to thank for all these moments, for without that, without frustration and fluctuation, the eddying doubts, ups and downs, we would not have the Boswell we value.

Two such moments, quite dissimilar, might be evidenced as examples of the delight this journal offers. One comes in the jaunt to the Carlisle Assizes which opens this volume: "I am wonderfully fond of all processions and ceremonies, and I felt myself very happy in the midst of the hurry and crowd and noise and dust, rousing always up in my mind ideas of Old England. It was in vain to ask myself, '*Why* or *how* does this please?' I *felt* it, as one does the heat of a fire when cold, or the sensation of pleasure

from any agreeable object." No thought of the necessary return to Edinburgh and Auchinleck can intrude on this. Boswell feels released because
he knows who he is in the crowd. At dinners at Carlisle he can put on his
London persona. When he says, "I find myself always easiest among
strangers, unless indeed among my very intimate acquaintance," the
strangers come first because they permit him to use the invented, the
earned persona. As he says at a somewhat elevated moment in the midst
of Edinburgh gloom, he is "in better humour than ordinary; something
in London spirits."

The second moment is in a coach returning to London in April 1781.
"A well-looked, stately woman who sat on the coach-box begged as a
favour we would make room for her in the coach. I told her all the seats
were filled. But if she chose to sit on my knee, she was heartily welcome.
This being agreed, in she came, and I had a very desirable armful. She was
a widow with three children. . . . I grew very fond of her, cherished her in
the coach, and when she went from us, kissed her repeatedly and warmly,
and wished to be better acquainted with her. Such incidents are marrow
to my bones." Boswell need hardly add the final sentence; we know the
incident is dear to him because he has rendered it with that immediacy
which so frequently endows his journal with genius. He has for the
widow become that person Johnson described, "Mr. Boswell never was in
anybody's company who did not wish to see him again." This is the
Boswell of "London spirits," the Boswell he has made himself and re-
makes moment by moment, the Boswell Charlotte Ann Burney meets and
describes, the one Lord Auchinleck could never know: the Boswell Boswell
believes in, even in the midst of all his doubts.

Believe is not too strong a word. For it is Boswell's belief in himself
and his journal that affords this volume its secret "plot." One of his
infrequent moments of satisfaction with David triggers a bit of immediacy
and in turn raises a question: "Little circumstances present him to my
mind in the most lively manner, as I believe is the case with everything. I
mark then my sitting in his room with him, he intense upon some calculation, I reading his Spanish almanac or calendar and having foreign ideas.
It is impossible to record fully one's *life* if all such sensations are to be
minutely described." What is one to settle for in the journal? Docket of
events or living moments, clear development or the organic welter of what
Boswell elsewhere calls *"realities* and activity?" In the moment with
David, Boswell seems to be risking a loss of faith in his task and his
chosen life work. He is tempted to settle for something less.

But he weathers this as he does all such fleeting doubts. He knows that
the real enemy he and his journal confront is far more significant than
any doubt or despair of the moment: "Was saddened by speculative

clouds composed of the uncertainty of life, the forgetfulness of things years after their happening, and such dreary truths." The moments his journal preserves, not its dutiful record, the sum of that journal as endeavour and not its high or low points, are his attack upon this enemy, and the means of sure victory over uncertainty, forgetfulness, and such dreary truths. "It is unpleasing to observe how imperfect a picture of my life this journal presents. Yet I have certainly much more of *myself* thus preserved than most people have."

DOCUMENTATION

A. In this section are listed the manuscripts and printed documents used to make the text of the present book. The separate manuscripts of Boswell's journal for the period are very numerous, but the narrative of Boswell's life which they provide is much less disjointed than a hasty reading of the following list might suggest. Boswell's shifts from bound notebook to loose leaves and back again to bound notebook generally entail some change in fulness and formality of style, but they need not indicate any gap in chronology, and in this case generally do not. *Boswell in Extremes* ended on 28 May 1778; the journal in the present volume ends on 4 September 1782. Of the 1,560 days between and including these dates Boswell originally left some kind of record (journal, note for journal, or review) for all but at most a mere 55. Unexplained losses, mildew, and family censorship have sadly increased the gaps, but even so the journal of 1778–1782 remains the most fully written and most complete four-year stretch in the entire record. To signalize this, we have departed from the former practice of this series and have printed the text continuously, distinguishing the London journals only in the page-heads.

The bibliográphical list follows. Unless notice is given to the contrary, all the manuscripts in Section A are at Yale and are printed in full in this book.

1. Journal of Jaunt to the Assizes at Carlisle, 19 to 25 August 1778. Octavo notebook, pages numbered 1–46, plus an unpaged memorandum of expenses on the inside of the back cover.

2. Journal in Edinburgh and at Auchinleck, 15 September to 11 November 1778, review of 12 November–31 December 1778. Quarto notebook, pages numbered 51–108. (Pp. 1–50, journal 1 to 21 March 1778, are printed in *Boswell in Extremes, 1776–1778*.)

3. Journal in Edinburgh, 1 to 3 January 1779. Quarto notebook, pages numbered 109–110.

4. Journal in Edinburgh, 1 to 14 February 1779. Quarto notebook, pages numbered 111–125.

5. Journal of Jaunt to London, 10 to 12 March 1779. Quarto notebook, pages numbered 127–129 (p. 126 is blank).

6. Notes for Journal in London, 15 to 30 March, 14 to 29 April 1779. 6 leaves, mainly duodecimo, 7 sides written on, loose. Extensive defects caused by crumbling of the paper. Recovered from Malahide in August 1960 after vol. 13 of *Private Papers of James Boswell* was printed. Some of these Notes are summarized in Editorial Notes, some conflated with the corresponding entries of A7. The entries for 28, 29, 30 March are printed at length, omission of one very obscure bit apparently peculiar to A6 being indicated by an ellipsis (. . .). To report all the new bits presented piecemeal in conflated entries is not practicable in an edition like the present, but we have signalized in the text this one considerable continuous passage peculiar to these Notes.

7. Journal and Notes for Journal in London, 16, 26, 31 March; 1–6, 8–21, 24–26 April 1779. (26 March consists only of Johnsonian conversation.) 33 leaves, 45 sides written on, loose, extensive defects caused by crumbling. Some of the leaves and many scraps not included in the above enumeration were recovered from Malahide in August 1960 after vol. 13 of *Private Papers of James Boswell* was printed. There are two entries for 11 and 16 April and three for 18 April; 14 and 16 April have dated supplements limited to Johnsonian matter. Parts of the existing entries are clearly missing, but it is by no means certain that Boswell ever expanded all the entries of A6. The duplicated entries (including duplications from A6) have been conflated. To report all the new bits in the conflated entries or those recovered from small scraps is not practicable in this edition, but we have signalized in the text all the continuous and extended new matter which these leaves furnish. The occasional ellipses indicate omission of undeciphered or extremely obscure bits.

8. Notes on the Meeting between Johnson and Lord Marchmont, 1 May 1779. Written on a blank side of Boswell's draft or copy of a letter to Johnson, 29 April 1779.

9. Notes for Journal and Journal: Return from London and Life in Scotland, 4 May to 11 June 1779. 6 octavo, 8 quarto leaves, 17 sides written on, loose. Up to 25 May summarized in the Editorial Note following 1 May 1779.

10. Journal of the Summer Session, 12 June to 11 August 1779. Quarto notebook, pages numbered 131–175 (p. 130 is blank).

11. Journal in Edinburgh, 12 August to 26 September 1779. Quarto notebook, pages numbered 1 to 24.

12. Journal in Edinburgh, 19 December 1779 to 6 May 1780, pre-

ceded by a "Review" of the period from 9 November to 18 December 1779. Quarto notebook, 154 pages, numbered 25–53, 53–58, 60–178, but continuous and complete.

13. Journal in Edinburgh, 7 May to 18 June 1780. Quarto notebook, originally 42 numbered pages, but pp. 11–12, 19–20, 27–32, and 37–40 have been torn out and are now missing.

14. Notes for Journal in Edinburgh, Journal in Edinburgh, Journal at Auchinleck. Originally, it would appear, 19 June to 13 September 1780, plus a Paper Apart for 4 September, but the Notes for 3 to 13 July are now missing. 31 octavo leaves of various sizes, 61 sides written on, loose. 4 leaves have been added since vol. 14 of *Private Papers of James Boswell* was published. 2 leaves containing a Paper Apart for 4 September were recovered from Malahide in 1950. 2 leaves, containing the record of 29, 30 August and parts of 28, 31 August were recovered in 1963 by Mr. E. D. Buchanan from the files of a firm of accountants in Edinburgh which had once handled the accounts of the Auchinleck estate. These new leaves are now printed for the first time. The entries for 20 June–29 July are summarized in an Editorial Note.

15. Journal in Edinburgh, 14 September to 31 December 1780. Quarto notebook, pages originally numbered 43–135, but pages 83–88, 91–92, 97–102, and 111–128 have been torn out and are now missing. Between this journal and No. 16 a leaf paged 137–138 has also been removed.

16. Journal in Edinburgh, 16 February to 12 March 1781, with a "Review" of the period from 1 January to 15 February. Quarto notebook, pages originally numbered 139–167, but pages 141–148 have been torn out and are now missing.

17. Journal in London, 13 March to 1 April 1781. Octavo notebook, 58 sides written on.

18. Journal in London, Notes for Journal in London, and Papers Apart giving a fuller account of particular days, 3–15, 20, 24 April–31 May; 2–5 June 1781. 93 leaves of various sizes, 110 sides written on, loose. Two of the leaves were recovered from Malahide Castle in March 1937 after vol. 14 of *Private Papers of James Boswell* was printed. Notes for 7, 8, 9, ?13 April and 1, 5, 6, 7, 8, 22, 27, 30 May are duplicated or supplemented; 8 and 13 May have three entries each. The portion assigned to 13 April is a fragment, and the lower halves of the leaves bearing 1 and 22 May have been cut away and are now missing. Entries for 16–19, 21–23 April and 1 June, if ever made, are now missing, and the conversation at the dinner at Dilly's on 8 May 1781 at which Johnson met Wilkes for the second time is now represented by no more than the notation "Dined Dilly's." As explained under A6 and A7 we have silently conflated the duplicated entries so as to

include all the information they contain, but have called attention by a foot-note to the one continuous and extended new portion of journal (5 May).

19. Journal in Edinburgh, 10 June to 10 July 1781. Quarto notebook, originally numbered 167–180 (the conclusion of No. 16 occupies a few lines at the top of p. 167), but pages 171–172 have been torn out and are now missing.

20. Journal in Edinburgh, 11 July to 9 September 1781. Quarto notebook, pages numbered 1–32.

21. Journal at Auchinleck, 10 September to 5 October 1781. 6 quarto leaves, 10 sides written on, loose.

22. Journal in Edinburgh, 6 October 1781 to 1 March 1782. Quarto notebook, pages originally numbered 33–111, but pages 65–70, 79–86, 101–102 have been torn out and are now missing.

23. Notes for Journal and Journal in Edinburgh; Journal at Auchin· leck, 2 March to 11 June 1782. 12 leaves, mainly quarto, 24 sides written on, loose. The entries for 16 May–9 June 1782 are summarized in an Editorial Note.

24. Journal in Edinburgh and at Valleyfield, 12 June to 28 August 1782. Quarto notebook, originally 60 pages numbered 111–125, 124–151, 52–63, 164–168, though continuous, but about three-fourths of the leaf bearing the pages numbered 55–56 has been torn away and is now missing.

25. Notes of Journal at Valleyfield, in Edinburgh, and at Auchinleck, 29 August to 4 September 1782. 2 quarto leaves, 4 sides written on, loose.

26. Manuscript of the *Life of Johnson* as first drafted by Boswell, narrative for the dates 7 April; 4, 10, 12 (and other unspecified dates in the period 4–18) October 1779; 1–4, 6, 13 April; 8 May, 4 June 1781. In all, 28 quarto leaves, loose, at the stage of the first draft blank on the versos and numbered on the rectos 775, 776, 787–798, 816, 818, 820–822, 833–839, 852, 853. The narrative for 1–4 April 1781 is abridged. Also portion (last paragraph) of a Paper Apart keyed to p. 839 of the main draft (*second* page so numbered), account of an evening at Miss Monckton's, undated but shown by the journal entry of 29 April 1781 (below) to be 22 April 1781: 1 quarto leaf, both sides written on, loose.

27. David Boswell's Family Oath, 19 October 1767 and 11 September 1780, 2 unpaged quarto leaves, all 4 sides written on. Oath in Boswell's hand, Ratification in T. D. Boswell's. A few lines are omitted at the end.

28. Entry from a Journal-Letter by Charlotte Ann Burney, British Library, Egerton MSS. 3700B, ff. 34–36, dated Tuesday 10 April 1781, reporting events of Saturday 7 April. 3 quarto leaves, 6 pages, numbered

by Miss Burney 18 (a recto) to 23 (a verso). Now first printed, with permission of the British Library. It was most kindly called to our attention by Professor James L. Clifford.

29. Extracts from newspapers: (*a*) *Public Advertiser*, 8 April 1779, letter by Boswell dated April 6, signed "Tantalus." (There is among Boswell's papers at Yale an off-print of this on a long narrow slip with blank verso. Boswell has entered a marginal gloss or correction to a Scotticism: "discharged" meaning "forbid.") (*b*) *London Evening Post*, 8–10 April 1779, account of the murder of Miss Ray by the Rev. James Hackman. (*c*) *Public Advertiser*, 19 April 1779, two paragraphs by Boswell relating to his report of Hackman's trial to Hackman's brother-in-law. (*d*) *St. James's Chronicle*, 15–17 April 1779, letter about Hackman signed "J.B." (Yale has an off-print of this, in two columns with blank verso.) (*e*) *Lloyd's Evening Post*, 16–19 April 1779, account of Hackman's execution, erroneously reporting that Boswell accompanied him to the scaffold. (*f*) *Public Advertiser*, 21 April 1779, paragraph by Boswell correcting (*e*).

30. No. 39 of Boswell's essay series *The Hypochondriack, London Magazine*, December 1780, text as corrected by Boswell in a set of the papers prepared by him for collection in a book.

31. Boswell's *Epithalamium on Dr. J. and Mrs. T.*, 12 April 1781, afterwards published by him as *Ode by Dr. Samuel Johnson to Mrs. Thrale upon Their Supposed Approaching Nuptials*, London, Faulder, 1784 (for 1788). Written on 3 sides of 3 leaves, the first a discarded wrapper addressed to Sir Joshua Reynolds. We have gone to the printed *Ode* for stanzas not in the draft.

32. Various letters, printed in whole or in part, as indicated in the text: Boswell to Samuel Johnson, 29 April 1779, 2 leaves, 2 sides written on, a draft or abbreviated copy; Boswell to Johnson, 22 October 1779 (from the *Life of Johnson*); extract from Boswell to Bennet Langton, 23 December 1779, 2 quarto leaves, 3 sides written on, copy by Boswell's clerk, John Lawrie; Boswell to Edmund Burke, 18 March 1782, 4 quarto leaves, 7 sides written on (Sheffield City Libraries, Fitzwilliam Papers); Boswell to Burke, 18 April 1782, 2 quarto leaves, 2 sides written on (Sheffield City Libraries, Fitzwilliam Papers); Burke to Boswell, 23 April 1782, 2 quarto leaves, 2 sides written on; copy, Burke to Conway, 23 April 1782, 1 quarto leaf, 1 side written on, somewhat abridged; Conway to Burke 23 April 1782, 2 folio leaves, 1 side written on, wrapper; Boswell to Burke, 30 April 1782, 2 quarto leaves, 3 sides written on (Sheffield City Libraries, Fitzwilliam Papers), two slight omissions; Johnson to Boswell, 7 September 1782 (*Life of Johnson*), one brief paragraph omitted; Boswell to Johnson, 1 October 1782, 4 quarto leaves, 8 sides

written on, one brief omission. The letters to Burke of 18 March, 18 April, and 30 April 1782 are printed with permission of the Earl Fitzwilliam and the Director of the Sheffield City Libraries.

33. Bill at the Shakespeare, Covent Garden, 31 May 1781; bills in connexion with Lord Auchinleck's funeral: Alexander Allan, cloth merchant, Edinburgh; George Jolly, tailor, Edinburgh; Alexander Stoddart & Co., cloth merchants, Edinburgh; Hart & Co., presumably Edinburgh; Robert Hart, presumably Edinburgh; John Hendrie, cloth merchant, Ayr; James Bruce, overseer, at Auchinleck; William Gibb, merchant, Mauchline; Robert Wharton, vintner, Ayr; James Cummyng, herald-painter, Edinburgh; Young & Trotter, cabinet-makers, funeral undertakers, Edinburgh.

B. Other Boswellian documents, as follows, have been available for editorial links and annotation. They are all at Yale unless statement is made to the contrary.

1. Journal and Notes for Journal in London, Yorkshire, and Scotland, 20 March to 28 June 1778. 105 leaves, 204 sides written on, loose. Printed to 28 May in *Boswell in Extremes*. The Sketch of Boswell's Life to 18 August 1778 with which the present volume opens summarizes the remainder.

2. Notes for Journal in Edinburgh, 5 July to 15 August 1778. 2 leaves, 4 sides written on, loose. Entirely in the hand of John Lawrie, Boswell's clerk. Little more than a dated list of Boswell's professional and social engagements. Summarized in the Sketch of Boswell's Life to 18 August 1778.

3. Notes for Journal in Edinburgh, 12 November to 31 December 1778. 3 leaves, 8 sides (after folding) written on, loose. Summarized by Boswell himself at the end of A2.

4. Notes for Journal in Edinburgh, 12 to 31 January 1779. 2 leaves, all 4 sides written on, loose. Partly in Lawrie's hand. Summarized in the Editorial Note following A3.

5. Notes for Journal in Edinburgh, 15 February to 9 March 1779. 2 leaves, 3 sides written on, loose. Partly in Lawrie's hand. Recovered from Malahide in 1950, after vol. 13 of *Private Papers of James Boswell* was printed. Summarized in the Editorial Note following A4.

6. Notes on Conversation with Dr. Johnson, 10 October 1779. 1 quarto leaf, a torn letter to Boswell from Charles Dilly. Boswell has written the note in a space that Dilly had left blank. We use instead the entry for 10 October 1779 from the manuscript of the *Life of Johnson*.

7. Notes for Journal, 9 November to 18 December 1779. 4 leaves, 4

sides written on, loose. Partly in Lawrie's hand. Slight defects caused by crumbling of the paper. Summarized by Boswell at the beginning of A12.

8. Memoranda in Edinburgh and Notes for "Boswelliana," 27–29 September 1780. 1 leaf, both sides written on, loose.

9. More than 350 letters sent and received by Boswell have been reported for the period 18 June 1778 to 1 October 1782. For 54 of these— Boswell's letters to and from Johnson—the manuscripts of only 4 (all by Boswell and all at Yale) are known to exist. We print 2 of the 4 in the text (29 April 1779, 1 October 1782: see A32 above); otherwise it may be assumed that when we draw on this correspondence we are using the texts which Boswell printed in the *Life of Johnson*. (He usually printed Johnson's letters in full, but he often excerpted or summarized his own.) Of his voluminous correspondence during this period with his intimate friend William Johnson Temple, Temple's side (18 letters) is at Yale, while all of Boswell's that is known to exist (3 long letters, 1 mutilated) is in the Pierpont Morgan Library. Besides these and the other letters at Yale for the period, 30 miscellaneous letters by Boswell and 4 to him have been reported, nearly all of them accessible in other collections or known from printed texts. When quotation is made from this miscellaneous group, the present location of the manuscript will be stated. Yale has about 265 manuscripts of letters by and to Boswell for the period, most of them unpublished. (The manuscripts of letters by Boswell recovered from Malahide and Fettercairn and now held by Yale, as one would expect, are generally drafts or file copies.) Boswell's Register of Letters fails frequently during this period to report letters received but, in spite of its gaps, it is very useful in providing summaries of letters which have perished or dropped out of sight.

10. Legal documents. Boswell's own papers at Yale contain very full manuscript documentation of the cause Craufurd v. Gemmill, and a copy of his printed Petition for Patrick Douglas of Garallan in Earl of Dumfries v. Douglas. We have obtained from the Advocates' and the Signet Libraries, Edinburgh, photocopies of printed pages by Boswell and others in Alexander-Shaw v. Kerr, Crosse v. Marshall, Duff and Mercer v. Mercer and others, and Walker v. Young. (All Boswell's printed legal papers in the Signet Library, Harvard Library, Yale Library, and the Hyde Collection have now been indexed, and indexing of those in the Advocates' Library is proceeding. So far, ignoring duplications, we have located 273 papers. The total will surely run over 300 when the search in the Advocates' Library has been completed.) Mrs. Jean Munro searched the processes of causes in the Scottish Record Office, Edinburgh, and provided us with materials which enabled us to give some account of Carruthers v. Douglas and Roberton v. Dundonald. Yale has a manuscript copy from

Auchinleck of the Declaration amending the Auchinleck Entail, 8 March 1781, and photocopies from the Scottish Record Office of all the other testamentary documents mentioned in the present volume: the Auchinleck Entail, 7 August 1776; Lord Auchinleck's Bond of Liferent and Disposition in favour of Lady Auchinleck, 8 August 1776, which summarizes and augments the provisions of his Contract of Marriage, 25 November 1769, with subsequent Dispositions to Lady Auchinleck, 24 March 1779 and 21 February 1782; Lord Auchinleck's Trust Disposition of 1 March 1782, putting his personal estate in the hands of trustees for the implementation of his various bequests; and Boswell's Nomination of Tutors and Curators for his children, 4 and 8 January 1780.

11. Miscellaneous: Accounts, memoranda, Boswelliana, Uxoriana, manuscript verses, notes on reading, hints for *The Hypochondriack*, newspaper cuttings, broadsides, newspapers at Yale and elsewhere.

C. Boswell's minor published works, when cited, will be identified at the places where they are quoted or referred to. References to the text of the *Life of Johnson* are made by date, enabling the reader to use whatever edition he has at hand. Because of the wealth of its annotation and its remarkable index, scholars use the edition by G. B. Hill, 6 vols., Clarendon Press, 1887, revised by L. F. Powell, 1934–1964. The fifth volume of this edition is Boswell's *Journal of a Tour to the Hebrides with Samuel Johnson*, the text as published by Boswell himself in 1785 and 1786. The text of the Hebridean journal as actually written by Boswell on the tour was published in 1936 by the Viking Press and William Heinemann, Ltd., under the editorship of F. A. Pottle and C. H. Bennett; a new impression with additional notes by F. A. Pottle appeared in 1961 with the imprint of the McGraw-Hill Book Company, and in 1963 with that of William Heinemann, Ltd. Professor Chauncey Brewster Tinker's *Letters of James Boswell*, 2 vols., Clarendon Press, 1924, the only printed general collection, contains 24 letters from Boswell for our period, 14 of them not derived from the *Life of Johnson. The Correspondence of James Boswell and John Johnston of Grange*, edited by R. S. Walker, McGraw-Hill and Heinemann, 1966 (the first volume of Yale's Research Edition of the Correspondence for the period), contains a letter by Mrs. Boswell and 2 letters by Boswell, and *The Correspondence of James Boswell with Certain Members of The Club* edited by C. N. Fifer, McGraw-Hill and Heinemann, 1976 (third volume of the Research Edition), contains 22 by and to Boswell, none of them duplicated in Tinker. The great majority of the letters from summer 1778 to autumn 1782 will appear in a chronological volume of the Research Edition not yet on the stocks. Nearly all the journal printed in *Boswell, Laird of Auchinleck* was published by F. A. Pottle without annotation in 1932 in the thirteenth, fourteenth, and fifteenth volumes of *Private Papers of James Boswell from Malahide Castle in the Collection of Lt.-Colonel Ralph H. Isham*, 1928–1934, an expensive privately printed edition in 18 volumes limited to 570 sets. The present edition is the first to make this matter available to the general reader. Some interesting bits (see above, A6, A7, A9, A14, A18) of the journal now appear in print for the first time.

Spelling, capitalization, and punctuation of text and notes (including quotations in the notes from all sources) have been brought close to modern norms, Boswell being allowed to retain a few idiosyncrasies. The standard of spelling for all but proper names is *The Concise Oxford Dictionary* (1964). For place names, F. H. Groome's *Ordnance Gazetteer of Scotland*, J. G. Bartholomew's *Survey Gazetteer of the British Isles*, and *London Past and Present* by Peter Cunningham and H. B. Wheatley have been followed. Family names have been conformed to the usage of *The Dictionary of National Biography*, Mrs. Margaret Stuart's *Scottish Family History*, G. E. Cokayne's *Complete Baronetage* and *Complete Peerage*, Sir James Balfour Paul's *Scots Peerage*, and various other special books of reference. Abbreviations and contractions have been silently expanded at will. Names of speakers in conversations cast dramatically are set in small capitals. Names of speakers in conversations cast dramatically which Boswell failed to provide are supplied silently when there is no doubt as to who is speaking; otherwise, all words whatever added by the editors where the documents show no defects are enclosed in square brackets. Words or parts of words missing from the manuscripts through crumbling are restored silently when the sense (not necessarily the exact words or order of words) seems certain; restorations involving any considerable degree of conjecture are enclosed in angular brackets. Omissions, apart from those resulting from the conflation of duplicate entries (see above, A6, A7, A18) are indicated by ellipses. Omissions so indicated in the documents from which the text is composed (A1 to A24) are always slight, and usually mean that transcription at that point is highly uncertain or that the omitted words would require a forbidding amount of annotation to make them intelligible. A few clear inadvertencies in the manuscripts have been put right without notice.

Continuing the practice of *Boswell in Extremes*, we provide somewhat fuller annotation of Boswell's legal causes than was attempted in the earlier volumes. As remarked above, 273 different printed legal papers by Boswell have now been located, besides many related papers by other advocates. These papers always provide a narrative (*ex parte*, to be sure) of the cause to the date of writing.

The index to this volume is intended to serve not merely as a finding tool but also as a supplement to the annotation. Readers should normally consult the index for Christian names, professions, and titles of persons whom Boswell mentions only casually.

ACKNOWLEDGEMENTS

The preparation of the text and its annotation owe much to earlier studies in Boswell and Johnson. The *Private Papers of James Boswell*, Tinker's edition of Boswell's *Letters*, and the Hill-Powell edition of the *Life of Johnson* have already been mentioned. To these should be added R. W. Chapman's edition of the *Letters of Samuel Johnson*, 3 vols., Clarendon Press, 1952; F. A. Pottle, *The Literary Career of James Boswell*, Clarendon Press, 1929, 1965, 1967; the catalogue of the Isham Collection as it stood at the end of 1930 (*Private Papers of James Boswell* by F. A. and Marion S. Pottle, Oxford University Press, New York); and *A Catalogue of Papers Relating to Boswell . . . Found at Fettercairn House*, by C. Colleer Abbott, Clarendon Press, 1936. A great deal of unpublished research was also available in the Boswell Office, Yale, which has been in operation since 1931. Mrs. Pottle's great catalogue, combining the two earlier catalogues and incorporating descriptions and minutes of content of the many papers found at Malahide after 1930, long since available at Yale in typescript, is now ready to go to press. The late Dr. Charles H. Bennett in the 1930s reviewed the text and prepared systematic research annotation for all the journal in the present volume except for the "new" bits listed above (Documentation under A6, A7, A9, A14, and A18). Drawing on Dr. Bennett's collections and his own researches, F. A. Pottle some thirty years ago prepared for a reading or trade edition a text and notes of all the fully-written journal in the present volume. As is well known, Colonel Isham in 1948 acquired the Fettercairn papers by judicial award and purchase, and in the next year allowed the reunited Boswell papers to be purchased by Yale University.

Since the publication of our last trade volume, we have added to the Editorial Committee Professor Frank Brady, co-editor of *Boswell on the Grand Tour: Italy, Corsica, and France* and *Boswell in Search of a Wife*, and Professor Marshall Waingrow, editor of the *Correspondence and Other Papers of James Boswell Relating to the Making of the "Life of Johnson."* We have suffered severely through the loss by death of one of the Committee's most active and useful members, Professor Frederick W. Hilles. Professor Brady has succeeded him as General Editor of Boswell's

Correspondence, Professor Waingrow is General Editor of the *Life of Johnson*. Frank E. Taylor having left the employ of the McGraw-Hill Book Company, his place on the Editorial Committee was first taken by Dan Lacy, Senior Vice President, and then by Thomas H. Quinn, Publisher, Scholarly Books Division of McGraw-Hill. From the Advisory Committee we have also lost by death C. Colleer Abbott, the Earl of Crawford, L. P. Curtis, Sir Gavin de Beer, Sir James Fergusson of Kilkerran, L. F. Powell, and William K. Wimsatt. Professor Abbott, the discoverer of the Boswell papers at Fettercairn was to have edited for our research edition the correspondence of Boswell with Sir William Forbes. Lord Crawford, with whom the elder editor of the present volume was in correspondence on Boswellian subjects for more than thirty-five years, was always prompt and generous with answers to questions dealing with a wide range of antiquarian topics. Professor Curtis was one of our referees in British history of the eighteenth century. Sir Gavin de Beer was especially helpful on all questions dealing with Switzerland, Voltaire, and Rousseau. Sir James Fergusson was for years our expert on Ayrshire and on the papers in the Records of which he was Keeper. Dr. Powell remained interested in our work to the end of a life longer than is granted to most men. Professor Wimsatt, co-editor of *Boswell for the Defence*, had only just accepted appointment at the time of his unexpected death. We have added to the Committee Alan Bell, John Brooke, Sheila Lambert, Roger Lonsdale, James N. M. Maclean of Glensanda, David Musto, Martin Price, Fred C. Robinson, and Charles Ryskamp. Because of stringency of funds, we regretfully accepted the resignation of Mrs. Helen A. Cooper, Secretary to the Editorial Committee, and for some time were reduced to a single salaried worker, Harriet Chidester, editorial assistant, who doubled as typist and office secretary. Dr. Irma S. Lustig having drawn up a persuasive application for us to the National Endowment for the Humanities, we received as of 1 January 1975 a generous grant for a period of twenty-seven months which has enabled us to appoint Dr. Lustig Managing Editor and Secretary to the Editorial Committee, to make Miss Chidester Chief Copy Editor, and further to expand our staff by Mrs. Rachel E. McClellan, Copy Editor and Assistant in Research, and Mrs. Caterina Kazemzadeh, Secretary. All the members of the office staff have worked in various ways in preparing copy for the present volume, which Mrs. McClellan prepared for the printer. Two student volunteers, Joanne Conroy, Yale Ph.D. in English, 1976, and Mark Vamos, Yale College, 1976, prepared an index of names which was very useful in checking proofs. John P. Crigler helped to verify the annotation. The index has been compiled by Rachel McClellan, Delight Ansley, Harriet Chidester, Caterina Kazemzadeh, and Irma Lustig, under the direction of Mrs. McClellan.

The proofs for this volume were read by the office staff, by Professor Brady, Mr. Liebert, and Professor Waingrow of the Editorial Committee, and by Professor Bergin, Mr. Brooke, Professor Clifford, Miss Lambert, and Dr. Lonsdale. Of the Advisory Committee, Dr. Beattie, Mr. Bell, Mr. Brooke, Sir James Fergusson, Sheriff Ireland, Dr. Lewis, Dr. Maclean, Professor Musto, Professor Peyre, and Professor Robinson have answered queries on particular points. We have had constant help from Mrs. Marion S. Pottle, Cataloguer of the Boswell Papers at Yale, and the only person who holds in her head the contents of all of them. Grace Bacon, Michael Durkan, Sister M. Ian, S.S.N.D., Sylvia Joan Jurale, and Wyman W. Parker of the Olin Library, Wesleyan, have aided us, as have our neighbours in the Walpole Office: George L. Lam, John C. Riely, and Warren H. Smith.

We also acknowledge various kinds of expert assistance from Henry D. Abelove, Donald H. Allen, William W. Appleton, Jean Archibald, William J. Barber, Gerald E. Bentley, Jr., Carole Berman, Richmond P. Bond, Jeffrey E. Butler, J. Menzies Campbell, Garland Cannon, William B. Coley, W. Wistar Comfort, Janet Dick-Cunyngham, Robert Donaldson, the Hon. David H. Erskine, Elspeth A. Evans, Joseph and Nesta Ewan, E. Stuart Falconer, Olof von Feilitzen, Joseph Foladare, Joyce Hemlow, C. Beecher Hogan, Benjamin F. Houston, Harold Hugo, J. W. Irvine-Fortescue, Lewis M. Knapp, Stanley Lebergott, Angus McIntosh, Dougald MacMillan, John Morris, David D. Murison, John Peckham, Henry Pettit, John M. Pinkerton, John Craig Reed, Edmund A. Rubacha, Antony P. Shearman, T. B. Simpson, Robert N. Smart, George W. Stone, and Joan H. Sussler.

Middletown, Connecticut   J. W. R.
and New Haven, Connecticut   F. A. P.
5 August 1976

BOSWELL
LAIRD OF AUCHINLECK

1778-1782

I insisted with her [Mrs. Boswell] that she ought in duty as a wife to be ever attentive, ever ready to soothe my temper and be complaisant. She said very sensibly that she had been educated without that timorous restraint in which I had been kept, and that it was much easier for me not to insist on subjection than on her to submit to it. But she was certainly wrong in contradicting my favourite notions and partialities. In particular, she was much to blame in endeavouring to counteract the principle of family which has prevailed in the family of Auchinleck from generation to generation. She said, and perhaps with some truth, that our pride and high estimation of ourselves as if German princes (my phrase) was ridiculous in the eyes of other people. ...But as I have great enjoyment in our fancied dignity...I wish to encourage it; and my wife therefore should at least not oppose it. My son Sandy seems to imbibe it as I could desire. I cathechize him thus: "What is your first duty?" "My duty to GOD." "What is your second duty?" "My duty to the family of Auchinleck." "Who was the first laird of Auchinleck?" "Thomas Boswell." "From whom did he get the estate?" "From his king." "Who was his king?" "King James the IV of Scotland." "What became of Thomas Boswell?" "He was killed at Flodden Field fighting with his king against the English, for Scotland and England were then two kingdoms." "Who was Thomas Boswell's son?" "David." "What became of him?" "He fought for his sovereign, Queen Mary, at the Battle of Langside, lived a worthy gentleman, and died at Auchinleck." He seems much pleased with this genealogical instruction. I shall go on with it and habituate him to think with sacred reverence and attachment of his ancestors and to hope to aggrandize the family.

[6 JANUARY 1780]

Boswell, Laird of Auchinleck

1778–1782

SKETCH OF BOSWELL'S LIFE TO AUGUST 1778. James Boswell was born in Edinburgh on 29 October 1740, the eldest son of Alexander Boswell, Lord Auchinleck, one of the fifteen judges of the Court of Session, Scotland's highest tribunal for civil actions. The title was not a peerage, but the Boswells had owned their estate of Auchinleck since 1504 and were related to many of the noble families of Scotland and to the royal House of Stuart. Boswell's parents being cousins, Boswell claimed the blood of the Bruces on both sides. Some of his strong notions of feudal honour were instilled from birth—blood, connexions, the ruins of Auchinleck Castle on the family's extensive Ayrshire property—but he also cultivated feudal notions on his own with a powerful romantic imagination.

He was educated in a manner befitting the eldest son of such a family: private school, lessons with a domestic tutor, and university studies in law at Edinburgh and Glasgow. After passing the Civil Law examination in July 1762, he resumed legal studies in Holland at Utrecht in 1763–1764, and then was launched upon a Grand Tour of the German courts and Switzerland, Italy, Corsica, and France.

A proper education for a gentleman of property, or at least a gentleman in expectation of property. But there was also an informal education acquired by the way which was to prove more significant to Boswell. An early enthusiasm for playgoing and actors led to a temporary conversion to Roman Catholicism and a runaway trip to London in 1760. He sought a commission in the Guards in London in 1762 (as an escape from his father's insistence on a career in the law), and this resulted in a heady initiation into the exciting world of the metropolis and an introduction to Samuel Johnson which was to ripen into a lifelong friendship. Boswell recorded these formative experiences in a brilliant journal of a young man's fancy and imagination.[1] On the Tour Boswell alternated sightseeing

[1] *Boswell's London Journal, 1762–1763*, published by the McGraw-Hill Book Company (New York) and William Heinemann, Ltd. (London). See page i for the titles of subsequent volumes in this series continuing Boswell's journal to 1778.

about the courts, cathedrals, and ruins with the almost systematic collection of further distinguished acquaintance: in Switzerland Rousseau and Voltaire; in Corsica the great patriot and leader, General Pasquale Paoli. On later visits to London he continued to collect acquaintance and to cultivate friendship with the worthy and the great, acquaintance with nobility and condemned felons alike, friends ranging from John Wilkes to Edmund Burke. Boswell sought out remarkable men for his own delight; later they profited with posterity from their encounters with this determined, eager, curious, methodical literary artist and his pursuit of immediacy—at once chronicler and participant, instigator and observer.

For Boswell's informal education had evolved into a second career as a determined and conscious literary artist. He had not only written for newspapers, published poems, pamphlets, and a chatty volume of letters, but in 1768 had turned his experiences in Corsica into a literary event in *An Account of Corsica, the Journal of a Tour to That Island; and Memoirs of Pascal Paoli*.

He had married his first cousin, Margaret Montgomerie, in 1769, and they now had three surviving children: Veronica, six years old, Euphemia four, Alexander almost three. Mrs. Boswell is pregnant with another son, James, born 15 September 1779. It is an essentially happy marriage and an essentially happy family, but Boswell is not happy enough always to perceive this. This family is (at least as he sees it) vying with his father's family: Lord Auchinleck is ill and Boswell must put up with his nagging, scolding, and sometimes his undisguised contempt. Yet he loves his father and is overcome with grief when he dies. This apparent contradiction is the heart of the present journal.

August of 1778 finds Boswell headed off on a jaunt to the Carlisle Assizes. His companion is John Christian, a young man with estates at Milntown in the Isle of Man and Ewanrigg in Cumberland. Earlier this month a letter from William Douglas, Esq. (presumably Boswell's cousin, William Douglas, Younger of Kelhead), had introduced this young companion. Christian's wife had died this year; he later married Isabella Curwen of Workington (1782) in whose right he then assumed the name and arms of Curwen. He was High Sheriff for Cumberland in 1784 and was M.P. (first for Carlisle and then for Cumberland) for most of the period from 1786 to his death in 1828. Lord Ellenborough was his first cousin, as was Fletcher Christian, the *Bounty* mutineer; his granddaughter, Isabella Curwen, married Wordsworth's eldest son.

Journal in Scotland and England

19 August 1778–4 September 1782

WEDNESDAY 19 AUGUST. Set out from Edinburgh with Mr. Christian in his phaeton after breakfast. A very warm day. Dined at Bank House. Lay at Selkirk. Mr. Christian made me observe how very well cultivated the country was. Saw remarkably good thorn hedges at Bowland, quite a strong, thick fence, which one seldom sees.[1] The bridges over all the brooks upon the road today had instead of the usual *ledges*, as we call them, or low parapet walls on each side, walls of six feet in highth at least. We could not guess the reason of this seemingly superfluous labour and cost. We asked masons at two different places, and were informed that it was to prevent mischievous people from breaking the walls and tumbling them down, which indeed is often done when they are low. But this is a clumsy preventative.

THURSDAY 20 AUGUST. Set out between seven and eight. Driving with horses that were to take us all the journey seemed to me unpleasantly slow. But I knew use would reconcile me to the motion. It was a good deal cooler than yesterday. Breakfasted at Hawick. Mr. Christian showed me there an inscription upon a house which he had observed in coming to Scotland:

> All was others.
> All will be others.
>
> 1775

We could not explain the meaning of this. We applied to the proprietor, who was standing in his shop, in which he seemed to have variety of goods for sale but chiefly candles; and with some wonder at our slowness of understanding he told us the meaning was the great truth that property changes from one to another. "One generation cometh and another goeth," said he, "but the earth abideth." [2] He said the inscription was originally

[1] Bank House was an inn about three miles north-west of Stow. Bowland is three miles south-east of Stow on Gala Water.
[2] Paraphrase of Ecclesiastes 1. 4.

put on in 1688, when there were troubles in the country, and that when he rebuilt the house, he *"renewed the moral."* Between Hawick and Langholm I met Langton's Lady Rothes and her children driving down to Scotland, an agreeable unexpected interview.[3] We got on very well. Dined at Langholm very well. A servant of Lord Surrey's who had passed us on the road had ordered dinner for us, which was ready when we arrived. We were but poorly accommodated at Bank House, and still worse at Henderson's at Selkirk. We got a good breakfast at Hawick. But though the house is large, and Stephenson, an Englishman, is the landlord, it is not in good order. We walked out and looked at the village of Langholm, which is prettily situated, and at the Duke of Buccleuch's residence about half a mile from it. The Senhouse family and Miss Fleming came up with us at this place, and we drank coffee and tea together.[4] I was glad to hear of my wife and children a few hours after I had left them. I had been disturbed with anxiety about my wife, lest she should be taken ill in my absence. We had rather a tedious drive to Longtown, as we were in the dark for several miles. But we were solaced with an admirable inn built by Mr. Graham of Netherby. Time had passed on very well with moderate conversation, looking at a Scotch atlas and a book of the roads, and the newspapers at the inns.

FRIDAY 2 1 AUGUST. While we were at breakfast the Senhouse coach came up again. But we did not unite, for they, having post-horses, got away before us. We arrived at Carlisle before twelve. The weather was still fine, and the situation and environs of this first English town that I saw appeared to me as pretty as ever; though to be sure I had not the same vivid sensations as I had one-and-twenty years ago when I rode to Carlisle from Moffat.[5] My spirits were now a good deal better. Mr. Christian made me observe that the land about Carlisle was not so well cultivated as about Edinburgh. He introduced me to Mr. Brisco the High Sheriff, Mr. Fletcher, one of the Members for the county, and several more gentlemen; and at two o'clock we dined by invitation with the High Sheriff on a cold collation. I was here introduced to Lord Surrey, whom I found to be a lively, affable, talking man, with very good sense and competent knowl-

---

[3] Bennet Langton, an original member of The Club, had married the widow of the tenth Earl of Rothes (a Scottish peer) in 1770, and at this time had five children. Two other women with the title of Lady Rothes were living in 1778.

[4] "The Senhouse family" was probably the family of Humphrey Senhouse of Netherhall, later M.P. for Cockermouth and Cumberland. Humphrey Senhouse's mother was a Fleming, daughter of Sir George Fleming, second Baronet. This Miss Fleming had supped with Boswell at Edinburgh the previous Friday.

[5] Boswell is not known to have kept a journal before the autumn of 1758. In his later journal he makes surprisingly few references to this first visit to England.

edge.[6] He observed that all animal pleasure consists in heating and cooling ourselves. We take exercise to heat us. We drink fermented liquors for the same reason; and we enjoy various modes of relieving ourselves from heat.

It is the custom for the High Sheriff to ride to [Irthing bridge],[7] seven miles from the town, to meet the judges; and he is accompanied by as many gentlemen as choose to attend him. Formerly, and till within these few years, he used to go to the extremity of the county. The Sheriff has as many servants of his own as he pleases to bring, and his friends send every one a servant. These used formerly to be dressed in the Sheriff's own livery, so that there were new liveries every year, which was a great expense. But now one livery serves year after year till the clothes are worn out. The livery on this occasion was brown faced with red. Each servant carries a long pole with a javelin of gilt at the end of it and a bunch of red fringe round the pole where the javelin joins it, and they are called javelin-men. This Sheriff was not a popular man, so was but poorly attended. He had not twenty javelin-men, and few gentlemen. An old gentleman of the county, Mr. Appleby Dacre, told us that when he was Sheriff he was attended by two hundred and fifty javelin-men whose liveries cost £3 apiece, so that the cost of that alone was seven hundred. But he had a numerous body of relations and friends, several out of Scotland.

I was determined to see everything, since I had come to see an English assizes for the first time. So I mounted a hack and rode out with the Sheriff. I am wonderfully fond of all processions and ceremonies, and I felt myself very happy in the midst of the hurry and crowd and noise and dust, rousing always up in my mind ideas of Old England. It was in vain to ask myself, "*Why* or *how* does this please?" I *felt* it, as one does the heat of a fire when cold, or the sensation of pleasure from any agreeable object. At the little public *hut* (for I cannot call it *house*) where we waited, there was wine for anybody who chose to take it. In a little the judges arrived in a post-chaise and four, upon which the Sheriff with his white rod approached the carriage, the other gentlemen following, and all paid their compliments to the judges; and then the Sheriff conducted them to his coach and four, which had followed the riders empty, together with two or three chaises with gentlemen in them. The Sheriff sat back-

[6] Charles Howard, later eleventh Duke of Norfolk, renounced the Roman Catholic faith at the time of the Gordon Riots (1780) and was elected M.P. for Carlisle. He was a Whig (as were most of the gentlemen Boswell met in Carlisle), and a violent opponent of the Lowther interests.

[7] Boswell's blank filled by the editors.

wards, and the judges fronted him. The judges were Willes and Hotham. Willes had a countenance a good deal like Charles MacDowal of Crichen: the same clear eye and perpetual smile of good humour.[8] He was all bustle and talk and laugh, and by no means answered the notion which I had formed of an English judge. Hotham was a decent, grave, polite young man.

Willes, in the hearing of all round, begged the Sheriff to order his servants to drive as fast as they could. There was a levity in this. The Sheriff gratified him and kept us at a hard canter, I may say a gallop, till we were within a quarter of a mile of the town. The Sheriff told me Willes said, "I don't love to go jigmagowe," [9] and several times repeated his request to be driven fast. He asked the Sheriff if he was a married man and whom he married, which was questioning him "only by way of conversation," pretty much with equal propriety that a good country squire, of whom Willes himself afterwards told me, questioned a judge: "Pray, my Lord, have you been to see the rhinoceros?" (a show then in the assize town.) "No indeed, Sir," said the judge. " 'Tis true we both travel with trumpets. But we have not yet settled which of us shall pay the first visit." (This I find is a circuit joke which is told by judges and counsel over and over again and always laughed at.) I should have mentioned that the Under-Sheriff goes forward to where the judges dine and comes up with them. Willes stopped the coach a little bit from the town and made it drive in more composedly. They drove to the Town Hall, and there their commission was read; that is to say, *read short*, as Willes called out to do, so that a word here and there only was uttered. The Sheriff then conducted their Lordships to lodgings provided for them at his expense. And there the Mayor, Aldermen, and Recorder, preceded by their mace, waited on their Lordships.[1]

Christian secured quiet lodgings for him and me at a house in Fisher Street belonging to Lupton at the King's Arms, with nobody but a servant-maid in it. I should have noted that I saw counsel and their servants travelling along, and that I got acquainted with Dr. Carlyle, physician, nephew to Old Lymekilns, my grandfather's great friend, and himself my uncle the Doctor's companion at Leiden.[2] When my mind is

---

[8] Edward Willes (d. 1787), the son of a Chief Justice, had been justice of the King's Bench since 1768. Sir Beaumont Hotham was one of the barons of the Exchequer. MacDowal was an Edinburgh friend of Boswell's.

[9] That is, jogging along.

[1] At this time Jeremiah Wherlings was Mayor and Andrew Huddleston Recorder. Boswell himself became Recorder of Carlisle in 1788.

[2] George Carlyle had received his M.D. at Leiden in 1736. "Old Lymekilns" was John Carlyle of Lymekilns, an Edinburgh solicitor.

not sick or sore with some gloomy oppression or irritating fretfulness, I have great satisfaction in such circumstances of connexion. Time was tedious a little in the evening while Christian was engaged among his friends. But afterwards he and I and the High Sheriff and a Mr. Hicks of Whitehaven played whist at the Bush, and the three first supped there.

SATURDAY 22 AUGUST. In the morning breakfasted at the Bush with Christian. Had almost the very same sensations as on the first morning of a circuit in Scotland. Went to the *Nisi Prius* Court,[3] where Hotham sat, and saw the form of proceeding. Heard Wallace (the Solicitor-General), Lee, Bolton, and Davenport perform a little. Thought I could do very well as a counsel here. Saw a numerous body of barristers. Archie Macdonald as soon as he saw me sent me a polite note to dine with the counsel.[4] I sat upon the bench, just next to Mr. Graham of Netherby, with whom I had a good deal of chat, and he asked me to his house. Whether he knew who I was, so that my character procured me this, or my manners as a stranger, my vanity was pleased. I dined at the counsel's mess, and found them social but not elegant. Macdonald and I took a walk, and then I drank tea at his lodgings. He talked of the severe affliction of his mother, Lady Margaret, in losing Sir James and having such a being as Sir Alexander to come after him. I said it was having salt and vinegar applied to a sore-wounded back. Sir Alexander was a sad brine.[5]

There is not a good coffee-house in Carlisle. Beck's, which takes the name, is rather a brandy-house. Here however I wrote to my dear wife, which was a pleasing imaginary intercourse; and then I went to the card assembly, where I met Miss Gilpin, with whom I had been very merry sixteen years ago at Springkell and had not seen her since.[6] I was glad to find her looking plump and cheerful and (in my opinion) better than when I saw her formerly. My spirits were calm, and I made no effort to agitate them, thinking it as well to be like any other gentleman, without being con-

---

[3] Essentially, the court directed to try matters of fact in a county. The term comes from the phrasing of old court writs: a given trial was set for Westminster in the superior court "unless" the justices shall "first" come into the county to take assizes.

[4] Macdonald later became Lord Chief Baron of the Exchequer and was created a baronet.

[5] Lady Margaret's eldest son, Sir James, who had died in 1766 at the age of twenty-four, had been so impressive in learning and character as to win the appellation "the Marcellus of the North." His brother, Sir Alexander, stands convicted by his own letters of being rather silly. He had won Boswell's and presumably his mother's displeasure by the meanness with which he discharged the duties of his hereditary office of chieftain of a great clan.

[6] Boswell had met her at the seat of his kinsman Sir William Maxwell in 1762, and had exchanged with her impersonations of their acquaintances (Journal, 12 Oct. 1762, quoted in *Boswell's London Journal*, p. 338 n. 4).

spicuous. I had been introduced the day before to Miss Bell Waugh. To-night I got acquainted with her four sisters, with a Miss Dacre, at whose father's Miss Gilpin was staying, and with Archdeacon Law, the Bishop's son. I played whist. There was some lively dancing, and I was in good humour and liked the English cheerfulness. Christian and I supped by ourselves at Lupton's.

I have omitted to observe that at one o'clock I went into the court on the Crown's side held by Judge Willes,[7] and heard first the Justices of Peace of the county called over, each of whom that was present put a shilling into a little bag held out by the crier, who said to each, *"Vous avez."* The Judge asked all of them to dine with them.[8] Then the Grand Jury were called over. Sir James Lowther was their foreman. It was agreeable to see a man of his great fortune appear doing his duty to his country, both as a Justice and a Grand Juryman. He had travelled night and day from London to be present at the assizes. There was a swarthy, Turk-like stateliness in his looks and manner. They speak very differently of him in the county. It seems to be universally agreed that he is a humourist.[9] But some say that he is capricious and proud and dis-obliging, and does not choose to have interest by making himself agree-able, but by compulsion—by means of his immense wealth. Others say that he is very friendly where he takes a regard.[1] Judge Willes read a charge to the Grand Jury, neat but commonplace, blaming neither min-isters nor generals for our bad success in America, but the profligacy of the nation, and recommending reformation.

In the afternoon I heard a trial for sheep-stealing: John Forrest, com-monly called Jack of the Forest, a tenant of Mr. Graham of Netherby's and a noted thief, indicted upon the Act of Parliament which makes it felony to steal a sheep or kill a sheep with intention to steal it. He was a big, strong, resolute fellow. Three witnesses swore to the sheep's being newly killed (one of them said its flesh was still palpitating); that Forrest was standing close to it, and that he run away when they came up; and the witnesses whom he called to his character could only say he had never done *them* any harm. His character was, it seems, notoriously bad. However, the same excuse might be made for him as a sheep-stealer that Garrick in one of his Jubilee songs

---

[7] "Crown side" designates the prerogative and criminal jurisdiction, as distinguished from the plea side, which transacts civil business.

[8] That is, with himself and Baron Hotham.

[9] One subject to humours or fancies; a fantastical or whimsical person.

[1] Sir James was a Member of Parliament from 1757 until he was created Earl of Lonsdale in 1784, and a powerful political force. He controlled as many as nine seats in Parliament, the Members he controlled being known as his ninepins.

makes for Shakespeare as a deer-stealer, only changing *venison* into *mutton*, and *our Bard* into *poor John*:

> As mutton is very inviting,
> To steal it poor John took delight in;
> To make his friends merry he never was lag, etc.[2]

For John was acknowledged to be a good neighbour. Willes puzzled himself a good deal with the account which the witnesses gave of the sheep: that its head was cut off, and that they did not see that it had been killed any other way. He thought this very improbable, for that a man could hardly cut off a live sheep's head. It would struggle and get away. He was too jocular in examining the witnesses; for instance, asking for his amusement if they eat of the flesh of the sheep? and how it was dressed? and observing with a laugh, "I should think it would be very bad meat"; and then all the audience laughed too. But I was much pleased with his humanity in favour of the prisoner, so very different from the disposition of our Scotch judges, who are always for hanging, seeming to think that sitting for hours without a condemnation is like hunting without catching anything.[3] I was much afraid for *Jack.* For there was only such *suspicion* against my client *John Reid.*[4] However, Willes, in his charge to the jury, told them that the prisoner certainly did not steal the sheep; and although he might intend to carry off its carcass, there was no evidence that he killed it. He was standing by it. But the time was five o'clock in the afternoon in May, when it was not probable that a man in the next farm would kill the sheep. He desired them to consider that a verdict against the prisoner would be death, and he thought they should bring him in *"Not guilty."* The jury were so well acquainted with John's bad character that they hesitated a long time between conviction and want of evidence. I was surprised to observe the Judge call up to them after they had been a good while enclosed in the box or loft where they were placed: "Gentlemen, you must not mind the prisoner's general character, but

[2] "Ye Warwickshire lads and ye lasses," the sixth stanza.

[3] The final song of the *Justiciary Opera*, composed by Boswell, John Maclaurin, and Andrew Crosbie in 1776 and 1778, contains a similar sentiment. The Lord Justice Clerk is angry at the jury's verdict:

> Our duty, believe us,
> Was not quite so grievous
> While yet we had hopes for to hang 'em up all;
> But now they're acquitted,
> O how we're outwitted!
> We've sat eighteen hours here for nothing at all.

[4] The principal matter of *Boswell for the Defence.*

consider if there is evidence against him. The man's life is at stake." He grew very impatient and said, "I cannot sit here all night. Mr. Sheriff, will you order your coach?" (For the High Sheriff carries the judges to and from court in his coach.) At last the jury turned about in readiness to deliver their verdict, which was *"Not guilty."* Willes seemed pleased, and said to them, "I don't say he is innocent. But there was not evidence to convict him."

SUNDAY 23 AUGUST. Christian went with me to pay a visit to Mr. Archdeacon Law, son to the Bishop of Carlisle, who I found had an elegant house with many pictures and prints, and I was told was a very ingenious man but somewhat odd.[5] We breakfasted at the King's Arms, and then went to the cathedral. Willes was indisposed and did not attend. But Hotham was there both forenoon and afternoon. I thought the chanting here more agreeable than usual. I know not if I was right in thinking the music peculiar to the choir here. It was a good decent *show* to me to see the Judge in his robes, scarlet faced with black, at public worship. I did not hear one sentence of the sermon, the crowd made such a disturbance. But although that disturbance somewhat hindered my devotion, I had it tolerably well excited by the service and by recollecting that *here* I first heard cathedral worship. I walked about and went with Christian and waited on Lord Surrey; and then Christian and I met his Lordship and Mr. Wallace, the Solicitor-General, and some more company at dinner at the Miss Waughs', where we had a very handsome entertainment. It was a singular group: five unmarried ladies with better than £500 a year apiece. Their grandfather was Bishop of Carlisle and their father one of the prebendaries there and Dean of Worcester; and their brother, who was also high in the Church, was killed by a fall from his horse not two years ago;[6] so that they became ladies of great fortune late in life, the youngest of them being above thirty.[7] Lord Surrey is a jovial companion, and when I mentioned my having drank only water for more than two months, he said the sooner I was reformed the better, and asked me to drink a glass of claret with him. I told him that I had said before I left home that if the Earl of Surrey should ask me, I should

[5] John Law, later a bishop in the Irish church, holding successively the sees of Clonfert (1782), Killala (1787), and Elphin (1795), was Christian's first cousin.

[6] Grandfather, father, and brother were all named John Waugh. The first (?1655–1734) was Dean of Gloucester before he became Bishop of Carlisle; his son (c. 1703–1765) was a prebendary of Carlisle, married a daughter of a dean of Carlisle, and was Dean of Worcester; his son (1730–1777) was a prebendary of Carlisle and Vicar of Bromsgrove.

[7] The great fortunes of the five ladies failed to procure them husbands. Not one of them married, and they became known as "the five famous Miss Waughs of Carlisle."

comply; for could I refuse a Howard? And I accordingly drank one glass. But I drank one only.

The judges came to coffee and tea here, and it was just a Sunday afternoon at a circuit in Scotland, when the judges pay an afternoon visit to some family of consideration in the place. I was presented to their Lordships. Willes was all brisk volubility and hearty laughter. He received me thus: "Mr. Boswell, your servant. You're acquainted with my friend Mr. Symonds. I believe you and he know Corsica better than anybody else." [8] He said that, of nineteen whom he had charged juries to bring in not guilty, he believed seventeen were guilty. But there was not evidence against them. He was certainly in the right. For *belief*, without being able to tell *why*, or in other words without evidence, should not take away a man's life. Hotham, after I had sitten some time, most courteously rose and came up to me and began a conversation by putting some question, such as, "Have you been at Carlisle before?" upon which I rose, and we talked together some time on the floor, till I said, "Had not your Lordship better sit down?" And then we talked on the settee. He was the nephew of the elegant Earl of Chesterfield, so might well be graceful. [9] Archie Macdonald said he had the most perfect propriety without any stiffness. I was in complete comfortable spirits this evening, and felt that England and dignity of office and real affairs had full effect upon my mind.

I had supposed that the English judges lived quite abstracted at the assizes. But Baron Hotham told me that they entertained every day, sometimes fifty at table, and that they have no allowance for their expenses on the circuits as our judges have. He told me that the English judges have the choice of their circuits according to seniority, and he, being a young judge, has hitherto gone upon the longest circuits, so that his expenses have been near £400 a year. He explained to me the power which the judges upon the circuit have of reprieving. If they think the case dubious, they reprieve till a certain day, perhaps at a month's distance, that the convict may have time to apply to the King for a pardon; and whenever application is made, the judge must transmit a report of the trial, a copy of the evidence which he has taken down, and his opinion upon it. If he thinks the case clear, he

[8] John Symonds had succeeded Thomas Gray as Professor of Modern History at Cambridge. Boswell met him in Genoa in 1765, and, having just arrived from Corsica, aroused Symonds's interest in the island to such an extent that Symonds also visited it, two years later. His journal of this visit, translated into Italian, was published in London in 1768.
[9] Nephew only by marriage, his uncle, Sir Charles Hotham, having married Chesterfield's sister.

reprieves without fixing a day, and the convict lies in prison till next circuit; when the judge who inspects the criminal calendar and finds a man
reprieved *sine die*, applies for a pardon to him. Or perhaps the judge who
tried him applies before that time. He said it never happened that a man
was executed when the judge reported he should be pardoned. But he told
me the reverse sometimes happened. For instance, he condemned a man
to be hanged for robbing a wreck. On a petition to the King, a report was
desired and the Baron gave it as his opinion that the man should be
executed, for the proof was very clear, the crime was heinous, and there
was not the excuse of want for the convict, because he was a man of £200
a year. The late Chancellor told the Baron that he had declared his perfect
approbation of the Baron's opinion. Nevertheless the man was pardoned,
and the Baron had the curiosity to find out why; and he discovered that
the man was a voter of Lord Talbot's.[1] The Baron said to me he was very
well pleased the man escaped, since it did not lie upon him. This was
humanely and conscientiously spoken.

Judge Willes asked me to dine with him next day, Hotham being to sit
from morning to night upon a long cause about a right over a common.
Hotham told me that he supposed it was understood amongst robbers to be
quite fair for one to be evidence against another to save himself, for he never
knew an instance of any one of them expressing any resentment upon such
an occasion; nay, if the prisoner has been acquitted, he has gone out that very
afternoon with the accomplice that was evidence against him. He said it
seemed to him that there was a certain crop of criminals every year for the
Old Bailey. Christian and I supped with the counsel at their mess.

MONDAY 24 AUGUST. Breakfasted at Mr. Dacre's, where Miss Gilpin
lodged. Christian was one of the jury upon a dull cause of *common* before
Baron Hotham in the *Nisi Prius* Court, and was kept there till next morning between two and three. The duty of an English judge is very severe.
He must give unremitting attention during the longest trial, must take
down the evidence in writing, and then sum it up with observations upon
it in a charge to the jury. I felt a high respect for the office. I was in Judge
Willes's court this forenoon and heard a man charged with highway
robbery tried and acquitted, and sentence of death pronounced on Joseph
McGhee, a young sailor convicted of highway robbery on Saturday. I had
heard Mr. Dun, my governor, describe the solemnity of this ceremony,
which I now saw for the first time.[2] And indeed the judge's putting on a

---

[1] Boswell first wrote, "a voter of Lord Talbot's, and could give him a good deal of
assistance." He seems to have deleted the concluding phrase immediately.
[2] The Rev. John Dun, later Minister of Auchinleck, together with the Rev. Joseph
Fergusson, had complete charge of Boswell's education from the age of eight to the
age of thirteen.

black cap, as if to hide his face during the awful and affecting scene, makes a great impression on the imagination. Willes behaved with more composure and gravity than I could have believed him capable of assuming. I must do him the justice to observe that notwithstanding the levity of his *manner* he appeared to understand his business very well, and to go through it with accuracy.[3] I paid a visit to the Miss Waughs and walked with some of them in their garden and eat wall fruit.[4] Though I did not find any high or exquisite enjoyment in life, it was a very tolerable thing. I dined with Judge Willes and drank three glasses of wine. We were eight at table. The name of *Willes* roused my spirits, having from my earliest youth associated it with high office in England, this Judge's father having been Lord Chief Justice of the King's Bench. This gentleman said his father was Chief Justice (I think) twenty-six years and lived to the age of seventy-six.[5] He said he was lively to the last.

"The very day he died," said he, "I dined with him, and he eat heartily of the first course. He then called to me, 'Ned, shall I eat of the second course?' 'Why, yes,' said I, 'if your Lordship has an appetite.' 'I don't think I have,' said he. 'Why then,' said I, 'you had better not.' However, after dinner he took what he used to take every day: a piece of toasted cheese and a brown toast, which he dipped in his wine, and he was quite cheerful. But I saw he was dying. His lip was fallen. His two physicians said he'd be dead by twelve o'clock at night. I did not imagine it would happen so soon. At ten at night he called me to his bedside and talked very well, and had another brown toast and a pint of wine. The physicians were right. He was dead by twelve. But they carried me out of the house. I could not stand it. For I loved him much." The affection of this judge for his father, though volatile, pleased me. He gave us coffee and tea, and he showed me a curious inscription on Burkitt's commentary on the New Testament which belonged to his landlady here, who it seems had been Lord Mansfield's landlady, and it seems a great crony from the connexion of political principles. As I was going away, Willes said, "I am sorry I have not seen more of you. I go tomorrow." I begged to look again at the inscription

---

[3] Boswell's respect for Willes increased with the passage of time. When Willes died, Boswell inserted the following anonymous paragraph in the *Public Advertiser*: "The late Judge Willes was not only one of the honestest and most constitutional judges that ever sat in Westminster Hall, but was distinguished upon all occasions for his humanity. When Skinner had resigned, and Willes was dead, a gentleman at the bar observed that the Court of Exchequer had lost its *head*, and the Court of King's Bench its *heart*." (9 February 1787, cutting with Boswell's mark of authorship among the Boswell Papers at Yale.)

[4] The fruit of trees grown or espaliered against a wall.

[5] Sir John Willes was Chief Justice of the Court of Common Pleas, not of King's Bench. He held the office not quite twenty-five years.

that I might remember it. Said he: "Will you take a copy of it? I know you love to take copies." I said I was obliged to him. So he gave me pen, ink, and paper, and I copied as follows: "Ann Lowry's book, given to me by my brother Edward Lowry in Great Queen Street, Lincoln's Inn Fields, merchant in London, in the year of our Lord 1745; given to comfort me at the time when Carlisle was besieged." [6] It will be remembered that Carlisle was besieged by the Duke of Cumberland, so that it was during an attack from the House of Hanover that she required comfort. She had dined with Willes one day, and I was told she has a glass out of which Lord Mansfield and she drank a certain health.[7]

In the evening I went to the dancing assembly, where I reckoned forty ladies. There was an ease here which I liked much. During the intervals of dancing, we walked from one end of the room to the other without any formality or restraint. But I find myself always easiest among strangers, unless indeed among my very intimate acquaintance. It was pretty to see the company seated in different parties at tea round the room, light tables having been shuffled up and chairs brought. There was a very good card-room adjoining to the assembly room. I played at whist. They played whist very well, and danced with uncommon vivacity. I paid two shillings the card assembly night, and four shillings this night. Cards and tea are furnished without any additional charge. The Miss Waughs asked me to sup with them tonight. But as they did not go home till between two and three, I chose rather to go quietly to bed. They sat till past five.

TUESDAY 25 AUGUST. Christian and I were to have set forward this day for Keswick to see the Lakes, and then to have gone to Cockermouth and Whitehaven and his seat at Ewanrigg. But he was so desirous to be at the ball this evening that I could not press him to go. I however was now so anxious lest my wife might be seized with her pains in my absence, and be uneasy or perhaps in danger, that I did not like to go farther from home, as I saw that Christian was of that sort of disposition that we might be kept much longer than we intended; and therefore I stipulated with him that we should set out for Scotland again next morning, as I could see the Lakes at another time, and the truth being that I have little or no pleasure from seeing beautiful natural scenes. I breakfasted with the High

[6] The city and Castle, which had been surrendered to the rebel army in the '45, were besieged by the Duke of Cumberland's forces from 21 to 30 December, when the rebels surrendered.

[7] That is, to King James. Lord Mansfield came of a Jacobite family and his brother and sister were prominent in the Old Pretender's court. Stories of his own Jacobite leanings were constantly in circulation, and in 1753 he was examined before the Cabinet and in the House of Lords on the charge that he had toasted the Pretender years before in the house of a mercer in London. He denied the charge, and his denial was accepted.

Sheriff and his lady. I was now tired of Carlisle, and in that uneasy state of indecision what to do which I have often experienced. Once I had my boots on to go out that night to Netherby. I was fretful, I must confess. Then I resolved to weather out another day. I had great pleasure in reading Dr. Johnson's *Journey* again, which Christian had with him. I read I fancy about a half of it, and wondered at the variety of observations, many of which seemed new to me for as often as I had read the book.

I heard Hotham giving a charge to the jury in a dreary common cause after I had dined with the counsel at their mess. I drank three glasses of wine with them. The counsel have an excellent way. The first time a stranger dines at their mess, he pays nothing. If he does not like them, he does not come back again, and he has had his dinner. If he comes back, he is considered to be of the mess, and pays like the rest. The mess is very moderate. Supper on Sunday was half a crown in all. Dinner today four shillings. There was little drinking at the lawyers' mess. There were four- or five-and-twenty counsel at Carlisle. Lee, a curious rough fellow, respected for his abilities and encouraged in his peculiarities, Mr. Serjeant Walker, Wilson, Bolton, etc., etc. One of them was Mr. Arden, who has, besides the Christian name of Richard, the name also of *Pepper* from his mother's family, and as he is smart and warm, the name of *Pepper* suits him well; so he is always called *Pepper Arden*, the sound of which combination brings the Carlisle Assizes into my mind in the liveliest manner.[8] It seems that once, before a Committee of the House of Commons, when Arden was very warm, Lee, who was on the other side, called to him, "Master *Pepper*, don't be so hot." Upon which the Chairman signified that it was not decent to give nicknames before the Committee, whatever liberties might be taken in private company. "Sir," said Lee, "I am giving no nickname. *Pepper* is the gentleman's name." "Oh, then," said the Chairman, "I have no objection."

After sauntering about, by no means in very good humour, I waited on Judge Hotham, whom I found sitting after dinner late in the evening, with the Solicitor-General and several more of the counsel taking a glass of wine with him. I was very politely received, and drank one glass. His conversation put me in spirits again. He had so manly and yet so gentle a manner that I was quite pleased. Wallace said to me he was sorry I stayed so short a while in that country, for he should have been glad to see me at his house. I had resolved not to go to the assembly tonight. I however went with him and Archie Macdonald, and was in pretty good humour, and played at whist two rubbers, so as neither to . . .

---

[8] Richard Pepper Arden was created Baron Alvanley in 1801, when he succeeded Eldon as Lord Chief Justice of the Common Pleas.

[EDITORIAL NOTE: The journal was never carried further. The next words would probably have been "win nor lose." On the inside of the back cover of the notebook appears the following memorandum of expense:]

EXPENSE OF JAUNT TO CARLISLE ASSIZES, ETC.
1778

		£	s.	d.
August 20.	Maid, Selkirk	—	1	—
21.	Maid, Longtown	—	1	—
	Barber	—	—	6
	Invalid, Carlisle Castle	—	1	—
22.	Breakfast, Christian and self	—	1.	6
	Capillaire [9] and paper	—	—	7
	Assembly	—	2	—
	Supper	—	2	—
23.	Breakfast, Christian and self	—	1.	6
	Supper	—	2.	6
	Charity	—	1	—
24.	Guide to the Lakes	—	2.	6
	Cup and ball [1]	—	—	6
	Paper	—	—	3
	Postage	—	—	4
	Assembly	—	4	—
25.	Assembly	—	4	—
	Dinner	—	4	—
	Lodgings during the Assizes	1.	10.	6
	Horse when I rode with Sheriff	—	2.	6
	Barber	—	3	—

[EDITORIAL NOTE: Boswell appears to have started back for Edinburgh on 26 August. So far as is known, he kept no journal for 26 August–14 September.]

TUESDAY 15 SEPTEMBER. (Writing Thursday the 17th.) The birth of another son is a new era in my life; and I flatter myself that I may continue my journal from this day on which my son *James* was born, with more constancy than I have done for some time past. I had rested ill all night, having been disturbed by being raised from bed with my

[9] An infusion of the maidenhair fern, sometimes flavoured with orange-flower water, to which a great many medicinal properties were ascribed. Boswell used it for a hangover cure, and Johnson (according to Mrs. Thrale) poured it into his port.
[1] A toy for Veronica.

wife, and having more than ordinary anxiety about her, as she had been very ill and apprehensive of being in a consumption at the time she fell with child. I rose between nine and ten. She was in great distress all the forenoon. I prayed earnestly for her to GOD and to Jesus Christ, and I addressed myself (if I could be heard by them) to the Virgin Mary, to my dear mother, to my grandfather and hers, and to her father and mother for their intercession.[2] About ten minutes after two she was safely delivered of a fine, big, stout boy, and she herself was better than ever she had been on such an occasion. She however had suffered so severely that she told me she had now for the first time expressed a wish that she might have no more. I was satisfied to think she should not. Dr. Young and Grange dined with Miss Cuninghame and me.[3] In the evening arrived little James's nurse, ———, wife of ———, a day-labourer at Gilmerton, a strong, brown-coloured woman. I wrote letters to my father and several friends, with the good news. Grange supped.

WEDNESDAY 16 SEPTEMBER. I had pleased myself with thinking that I should drink no wine since the birth of my son James. But I dined today with Mr. Donaldson, the bookseller, and tasted some whisky; and then being pained with the toothache, took two half glasses of port, which excited in me the desire of drinking, and I resolved to indulge myself in liberal moderation this evening with my friends after the christening, for which purpose I brought up a bottle of old Malaga for myself. I drank tea at my wife's bedside, and between six and seven little James was baptized by Dr. Webster in presence of Miss Cuninghame, Balbarton, Mr. Alexander Boswall, who had arrived from England the night before, Grange, George Campbell and David, and my other three children.[4] I was

[2] Boswell had been briefly a Roman Catholic in 1760, and his final religious position was "a Christian orthodoxy which repudiated the exclusive claims of Rome, but accepted nearly everything else in the dogma and practice of Western Catholicism" (F. A. Pottle, *James Boswell, the Earlier Years*, 1966, p. 52). In 1774 he was prepared to disenfranchise himself rather than swear that a belief in the invocation of saints was unscriptural (*Ominous Years*, p. 31, *sub* 31 Oct. 1774).

[3] Thomas Young, Professor of Midwifery in the University of Edinburgh, had delivered the baby. John Johnston of Grange, writer (solicitor) in Edinburgh, a very early acquaintance and Boswell's most intimate friend in Scotland, occupied a flat in James's Court just downstairs from the Boswells. Annie Cuninghame, the orphaned daughter of Mrs. Boswell's eldest sister by her first marriage to Captain Alexander Montgomerie-Cuninghame, had been living with the Boswells off and on for some years.

[4] Dr. Alexander Webster, Minister of the Tolbooth Church in Edinburgh, was a close family connexion (he had married the sister of Boswell's mother but was now a widower). James Boswell of Balbarton was a very distant cousin, as was also Alexander Boswall, a surgeon who had gone to India, served the Nawab of Arcot as medical adviser, and returned home with a fortune. George and David Campbell,

more impressed with religious faith by the ceremony tonight than I had felt myself for some time. The gentlemen and I passed a couple of hours most agreeably. I drank all the Malaga but one glass which Grange took, and which I supplied with a glass of Madeira. I was sedate; yet my heart was very warm, and as the child was named for my worthy grandfather, Mr. James Boswell, I had peculiar satisfaction. It was curious to compare the ages of the oldest and youngest James Boswell: Balbarton, seventy-eight years; my James, two days. I had good steady views of real life while I drank. But I felt the inflammation rise too high.

THURSDAY 17 SEPTEMBER. (Writing Saturday the 19 September.) I had been restless and uneasy all night, and in the morning I was very sick and had a violent headache. I lay till past one o'clock and should have lain longer. But this was the last day on which I could send *The Hypochondriack* No. 12 to be in time for this month's *London Magazine*, and only three pages of it were as yet done.[5] I set myself steadily to it, and by taking some good onion soup I made it out wonderfully well. My wife continued to recover well. At night I read some of the *Histoire philosophique, etc.*[6] Dr. Boswell had sat by me awhile in the forenoon.[6a]

FRIDAY 18 SEPTEMBER. I was very ill with a colic and looseness all the forenoon. However, I was amused by taking care of myself, drinking a great deal of beef tea, which cured me. My mind was in a state of unpleasing indifference, and I was fretted to think that I had neither solid science nor steady conduct, and that my two daughters were under no awe of me. I read some of the *Biographia Britannica*. How insignificant is my present existence![7]

Mrs. Boswell's nephews and Boswell's cousins, sons of Mrs. Boswell's sister Mary and the late James Campbell of Treesbank, were respectively ten and seven years of age. Boswell was one of their guardians. Boswell's other three children were Alexander (three), Euphemia (four), and Veronica (five).

[5] The *London Magazine* for any given month was published about the first of the month following. Boswell generally had his essays in the post by the sixteenth of the month, but once apologized to Dilly for being as late as the twentieth; Dilly on one occasion offered to hold the issue open until the twenty-seventh. That Boswell was pressed for time on this essay is perhaps demonstrated by the fact that he quotes sixteen lines from Brome's *Jovial Crew* near the end of the piece.

[6] Guillaume-Thomas-François Raynal, *Histoire philosophique et politique des établissements et du commerce des Européens dans les deux Indes*, 1770.

[6a] Dr. John Boswell, Lord Auchinleck's brother, was one of the leading physicians in Edinburgh. He and Boswell were much alike in temperament.

[7] "The uneasiness occasioned by languor is doubtless very great. But there is a worse state of hypochondria, when the mind is so tender and sore that everything frets it. When a man is in that state, he is not only harassed by the same pieces of business which when in a sound state afford rather an agreeable exercise to his faculties, but even the company of those whom he loves and values is a burthen to him, and

SATURDAY 19 SEPTEMBER. (Writing on Monday 21 September.)
Paid a visit to Robert Boswell, and saw Mr. Alexander Anderson, merchant in London, and his wife, who were with him. Anderson's activity,
compared with my own relaxation, was unpleasingly wonderful to me.
Sir Alexander Dick was here. I engaged to dine with him, which I did. I
was in a tolerable state of spirits; drank some cider and three glasses of
port. Nobody there but Mr. Bennet [8] and Alison of the Excise, who walked
in with me part of the way and told me that he remembered to have seen
my grandfather, a big, strong, Gothic-looking man; and that he was present in the General Assembly when patronages began first to have a party
for them, and some of the young clergy spoke very slightingly of the common people as unfit to judge of their teachers, there being a cause under
consideration in which the people were concerned. That my grandfather
got up and said, "Moderator, I am an old man; and I remember the time
when the Gospel was not so easy as it is now. But those who wished to
hear it according to their conscience were subject to persecution. Several
of those I myself have seen. But amongst them were not many rich, not
many noble. They were mostly common people, whom we have heard
treated with much contempt this day." [9] Mr. Alison said *"a vote"* was
immediately called, and it was carried for the people by a great majority.
He said what my grandfather spoke had a great effect. He was a man of
weight. I was pleased thus accidentally to hear another good anecdote in
addition to many which I have heard of my grandfather. I came home

---

affects him with irritation.... In such a state books, which have been well called
silent friends, afford a kindly relief. Every man should then read what he likes best
at the time. I have generally found the reading of lives do me most good, by with-
drawing my attention from myself to others, and entertaining me in the most satisfactory manner with real incidents in the varied course of human existence. I look
upon the *Biographia Britannica* with that kind of grateful regard with which one
who has been recovered from painful indisposition by their medicinal springs be-
holds Bath, Bristol, or Tunbridge" (*The Hypochondriack*, No. 6, conclusion).

[8] Sir Alexander, a retired physician, was Boswell's close friend, though nearly forty
years his senior. The Rev. William Bennett was minister of Sir Alexander's parish
(Duddingston).

[9] Patronage (the right of landowners who built and endowed churches, and of their
heirs and assigns, to present ministers of their choice to the congregations) had been
a vexed question in the Church of Scotland since the sixteenth century, and successively contradictory acts of Parliament in the seventeenth century had only ag-
gravated the problem. Boswell's grandfather no doubt spoke in the General Assembly
as ruling elder, not as counsel, on a disputed settlement—a conflict between appointment by patron and election by congregation not previously settled by the presbytery or synod—some fifty of which were referred to the General Assembly in the
1740's. Patronage "began first to have a party" when the issue became a point of
antagonism between the moderates and the popular party in the church.

and drank coffee in my wife's bedroom. It is wonderful how uneasy sleeping in solitude has been to me upon this occasion. Though the dining-room where I lie is agreeably spacious, I have an unwillingness to go to bed.

SUNDAY 20 SEPTEMBER. Was too late for church in the forenoon. Read the *Critical* and *Monthly Reviews* for August. Between sermons walked down to Belleville and paid a visit to Lady Elizabeth Heron, who was indisposed. Heron had paid me a visit yesterday.[1] Lady Dundonald talked keenly of planting, and said she would plant on the very day that she was sure to die. "Yes," said I. "With my very last grasp I would put an acorn into the ground." Grange was kind enough to walk down with me and wait in the King's Park till I came from my visit. I was languid, but pretty well. I heard Dr. Blair preach on rejoicing in the Lord in the New Church in the afternoon. Both my own children and Sir George Campbell and David did very well in little religious exercises.[2] I read Mr. Carr's ———— sermon twice: once to my wife and once to Grange, who supped with me. I drank cider both at dinner and supper. I read at night in the *Biographia Britannica*.

MONDAY 21 SEPTEMBER. When I do not mention the day on which I write, it is always on the day recorded, or the day after. This day I indulged my two daughters and Sandy and the two Campbells with a visit to Prestonfield [3] in the forenoon. Grange accompanied us. Everything appeared pleasing. The day was beautiful. They got fruit (the children, I mean), and my daughters and son rode up and down the garden on a sheltie. Grange dined with me, and in the afternoon he and I walked down to the country-house of M. Dupont and Miss Scott at the foot of Leith Walk and drank tea.[4] I never felt a more delightful day. The sun shone so bright and benignant that existence was a pleasure. It was a calm and comfortable scene at tea. M. Dupont, who was seventy-nine last

[1] Lady Elizabeth was a daughter of the eighth Earl of Dundonald and a cousin of Boswell's mother. She had married in 1775, as his second wife, Patrick Heron, of Kirroughtrie, a wealthy man with a seat in Kirkcudbrightshire. Belleville, in the environs of Edinburgh between Holyrood House and Abbey Hill, was the town residence of her mother, Lady Dundonald, now a widow.

[2] George Campbell was heir male to Sir Hugh Campbell of Cessnock, who had died almost a century before (1686). Boswell's insistence upon a title for him (here and in three other places in this portion of the journal) is an honest mistake: until some time late in 1778 he thought George was heir to a baronetcy. He wrote to Bruce Campbell on 18 December, "Now . . . we find our pupil is not Sir George, his ancestors having been only knights" (Register of Letters).

[3] Sir Alexander Dick's seat in the eastern environs of Edinburgh.

[4] The Rev. Pierre Loumeau Dupont was pastor of the French Protestant congregation in Edinburgh and Magdalen Scott was his housekeeper.

March, was quite entire and even lively. At night I read part of Young *On Opium*.[5] I have not had so agreeable a day of a long time.

TUESDAY 22 SEPTEMBER. (Writing Saturday 26 September.) This day being the anniversary of His Majesty's coronation, there was a good deal of bustle in the town, the Duke of Buccleuch's Fencibles having marched into the Castle and Lord Seaforth's Highlanders being to march out. A large body of the private Highlanders with a few sergeants were dissatisfied to such a degree that they resolved not to allow themselves to be embarked at Leith as ordered. They complained of being cruelly treated, of having large arrears both of levy-money and pay owing to them, and they had a notion that they were to be sold to the East India Company. Above a hundred of them were on the Castle Hill with loaded muskets when I walked there about twelve. It was as fine weather as yesterday. The mutineers marched down to the Canongate, and when the regiment marched down the street, seemingly in good humour, they met it at the entry to the New Bridge, and a strange tumultous [6] struggle took place. It was offensive during the commotion to see Harriet Powell in the rear in Lord Seaforth's chaise with the coronet.[7] It was so unsuitable to a Highland chieftain on command, and such an outrage against decorum. The mutineers carried several more of the regiment back to the Canongate with them. But I shall not fill my journal with this mutiny, as I am to write a particular account of it. I shall however set down some incidents.

I dined with Dr. Young (his lady in the country), with several physicians, and Mr. Cruickshanks, a popish priest. There was no valuable conversation, though we were cheerful enough. I drank only cider. When we went to coffee, we were informed that the mutinous Highlanders were on Arthur's Seat. Dr. Monro, Dr. Home, and I walked down to the King's Park, where crowds were gathered. It was truly picturesque to see the Highlanders in arms upon that lofty mountain. Several people had been up amongst them, and bread and beer had been carried to them. They were quite irregular, and they fired many shot. It was supposed they would march off for the Highlands by Stirling in the night. I was wonderfully animated by this extraordinary scene, and came home and wrote

---

[5] *A Treatise on Opium, Founded upon Practical Observations*, by George Young, M.D. (1753).

[6] Boswell's more usual spelling of adjectives in *-uous*, indicating a common eighteenth-century pronunciation concerning which dictionaries are strangely silent.

[7] Boswell clearly considers Harriet Powell, an apothecary's daughter, singer, and actress, to be Lord Seaforth's mistress. She may however already have been entitled to the coronet, for in his will, executed in the following April, Seaforth refers to her as "Harriet, Countess of Seaforth, my wife."

some account of it in a great hurry for the *Public Advertiser*. But was too late for the post.

WEDNESDAY 23 SEPTEMBER. (Writing Thursday 1 October.) The weather had been very fine all night, and continued to be so. The mutineers kept possession of their hill. I walked up to the Castle Hill after breakfast and found Lord Loudoun entering the Castle.[8] I attended his Lordship. He told me he would have gone into it last night, but thought it might give an alarm. He would give no opinion what should be done with the mutineers, which I imputed to his being dissatisfied that he was not Commander-in-Chief. He said, "If I defend this castle, I do my duty." Plomer of the Southern Fencibles told me that it was thought the mutineers could not be reached with any kind of artillery from the Castle while they remained on the top of Arthur's Seat, but that one of the engineers had talked of throwing a shell amongst them while they were upon a lower part of the hill. I walked down to the King's Park with young Robert Syme, and walked a part of the way up the hill. Then Grange and I walked out to Sir Alexander Dick's, where we dined upon invitation of last Monday. Mr. Bennet and Mr. Mercer were there, and we had much conversation about the men on the hill.[9] I was much too violent for them. Worthy Grange did his best to moderate me. I drank cider and a little port.

THURSDAY 24 SEPTEMBER. (Writing Thursday 1 October.) Carried Sir George Campbell and David to wait on Lord Loudoun. Waited on Lord Eglinton and engaged him to sup with me tonight. The election of a peer was this day.[1] There was a wonderful animation in the town from there being a Highland camp on Arthur's Seat. I was in admirable spirits. Loch of Drylaw and I walked to the top of the hill. I do not insert particulars in my journal, as I write a separate account of all that I observed or heard about the singular event of the mutiny. I read, I think, nothing at present but newspapers. I wrote a little yesterday and more today about the mutiny for the *Public Advertiser*, and sent it off tonight.[2] Lord Eglinton came very cordially and visited my wife before supper, and then Miss

---

[8] John Campbell, fourth Earl of Loudoun (an Ayrshire peer), had been the ineffective Commander-in-Chief of the British forces in America, 1756–1757. He held the rank of general (from 1770), and was Governor of Edinburgh Castle.

[9] Boswell quotes Mr. Bennet in his final letter to the *Public Advertiser*. See the second note following this.

[1] The Act of Union (1707) abolished the Scottish Parliament, but did not give all Scottish peers the right to sit in the House of Lords of Great Britain. Instead they were empowered at each general election to elect sixteen peers from their number to represent them. This was a by-election to fill a vacancy; the Marquess of Lothian was elected.

[2] Boswell's serial account, dated 22, 23, 24 September, appeared in the *Public Ad-*

Cuninghame and he and I supped.[3] I drank one glass of Sitges [4] with him, and after supper we had a bowl of brandy punch and I drank fair with him, as he was now upon a sober regimen.

He told me tonight, upon my questioning him earnestly, the mysterious story which I have often heard of his having seen a vision. I wished to hear it from himself, and it was as follows: his Lordship, then Captain Montgomerie of Lord Robert Manners's regiment, and another officer of the same corps, Rubens Green (writing Saturday 3 October), were walking out one forenoon at Aberdeen, when they saw Captain Veale of their regiment distinctly before them, and he, as they thought, hid himself in a field of cabbages. They sought for him as good as half an hour, but could see no appearance of him. Colonel James Seton, who married Miss Moray of Abercairney, came up to them and asked what they were about, which they told him. Veale was at this time insane and under the care of a keeper. They inquired at his lodgings, and were told he had not been out above five minutes, and then his keeper was with him. They observed he had on the same dress which they imagined they saw him have on in the field: viz., a thick greatcoat, though it was warm weather. He died some time after this. But his death did not coincide with the vision, or follow it so soon as to make a connexion between the two circumstances, as is usual in such cases whether true or false. It is the best-attested story of the kind that I have been able as yet to obtain. Why there should be such a vision without any purpose that we can perceive, not even that of a warning that a person was to die, I cannot tell. It is remarkable that the name of the officer whose vision Lord Eglinton saw, was *Veale*—the same with that of the lady of whose apparition an account is prefixed to the translation in English of Drelincourt *On Death*. I have heard Dr. Johnson controvert the truth of that famous story and Mrs. Williams defend it.[5] The Earl did not sit late, and would not even finish the bowl; so I got off very well.

---

vertiser for 29 September; a fourth instalment dated 25 September, which he does not mention, appeared in the *Public Advertiser* for 1 October.

[3] Archibald Montgomerie, eleventh Earl of Eglinton, was an Ayrshire peer and Mrs. Boswell's chief. A professional soldier (at this time lieutenant-general), he was also a representative peer. Boswell had been fond of his older brother, the tenth earl, but generally found cause for irritation in his dealings with Archibald. As Boswell hints below, he was usually a hard drinker.

[4] Wine from Sitges, near Barcelona. Boswell's brother, Thomas David, a merchant at Valencia, had probably sent it over.

[5] Reported in *Boswell for the Defence*, 28 March and 9 April 1772. Defoe's *True Relation of the Apparition of Mrs. Veal to Mrs. Bargrave* (apparently a journalistic rendering of a ghost-story which was circulating in London in 1705) was prefixed to the fifth (1707) and subsequent editions of an English translation of Charles Drelincourt's treatise, *Les Consolations de l'âme fidèle contre les frayeurs de la morte*.

FRIDAY 25 SEPTEMBER. (Writing Saturday 3 October.) This morning the Highlanders marched down from Arthur's Seat. Luckily Grange and I just reached the King's Park in time to see the singular scene. He dined with me, and I drank a little; I forget whether wine or cider. I had my pocket-book stolen in the crowd, which vexed me. Dr. Young drank tea with us. I supped at the French tavern with Lord Eglinton, Lord Cassillis, Sir Patrick Warrender, and Commissioner Brown. I was glad to find that I had been mistaken in thinking that Lord Cassillis had not answered a letter from me asking an ensigncy for Sandy Cuninghame, for he had not received it.[6] So he assured me, and I could not reasonably disbelieve him. I resolved to see if he would call on me, which he had not done for two times that he had been in town, which was very ungrateful. I was in excellent health and spirits, eat heartily, drank cider, two glasses of wine, and some brandy punch. We were exceedingly merry. I was quite sober, but sat till two. I had now for (I think) two nights slept in my wife's room.

SATURDAY 26 SEPTEMBER. (Writing Sunday 4 October.) Passed the forenoon at the Court of Inquiry in the Canongate court-house to hear the complaints of the mutineers against their officers. Dined at Prestonfield. Nothing to remark.

SUNDAY 27 SEPTEMBER. (Writing Sunday 4 October.) Was at the New Church in the forenoon and heard Dr. Blair. In the afternoon took the young Campbells to the English Chapel.[7] At night walked down to the Abbey Close with Lieutenant Farquharson of Gordon's Highlanders to hear what particulars he could tell about the mutineers. But I could not trust to his authenticity. After I parted with him, a wanton-looking wench catched my eye in the street. I accosted her, but without intention to transgress. She endeavoured to hold me, and named me, *"Mr. Boswell."* This was a proof to me that I must not suppose I am not known by such creatures in Edinburgh, so that if other motives fail, a regard to my reputation as a man of some decency may restrain me. Grange supped in my wife's room. I now slept with her.

MONDAY 28 SEPTEMBER. (Writing Sunday 4 October.) Called on General Skene and wished him joy on having settled the mutiny so agree-

6 David Kennedy, tenth Earl of Cassillis, a member of the Faculty of Advocates, was one of the representative peers. Alexander Cuninghame (Annie's brother) was Mrs. Boswell's nephew.

7 The New English Chapel in the Cowgate, opened in 1774, was the principal place of worship of Episcopalians in Edinburgh who did not wish to be associated with congregations served by the non-juring priests of the Episcopal Church in Scotland. Its clergy were in English or Irish orders and read the English Book of Common Prayer.

ably. My spirits were now as good as when I am in London, such is the effect of agitation upon me. I called on Maclaurin and talked over the mutiny with him. He took a sufficient interest in it. He and I went and called on Mr. Robertson, minister of the Erse congregation, and got him to engage to have Sergeant Robertson and some of the most sensible of the mutineers to drink a bowl of punch with us at a tavern at six this evening.[8] I called a little at home, Maclaurin waiting for me; and then I went and dined with him on a leg of his own mutton, and drank half a bottle of old hock. We were really social. At six we went to the Cross, where Mr. Robertson was to meet us. We drank tea in the Exchange Coffee-house. But our curious interview did not hold, the Highlanders having been prevented from coming, either by suspicion or some other reason.

TUESDAY 29 SEPTEMBER. (Writing on Monday 5 October.) Called on Dr. Bosvile, son of a gentleman of our clan in Monmouthshire, a Roman Catholic, who had taken his degree at Louvain and had come to pass a winter at our university. He was recommended to me by Squire Godfrey Bosville and had been with me on Saturday. He dined with me today with Grange; and then he and I drank tea at Lord Macdonald's, where was Young Lady Wallace (Eglinton Maxwell) with whom I went home, being asked by her.[9] She was charming. I twice tasted her delicious lips, and did not mind the reproof which she gave or affected to give me. I was quite free of *love* in the *tender* sense. I was a *hearty* admirer.

WEDNESDAY 30 SEPTEMBER. (Writing Monday 5 October.) My time passed away at present, I cannot tell how. But I was easy and cheerful. Grange dined with me; I drank cider. After dinner we walked to Leith. He returned with me and drank tea. I ought not to be satisfied with living thus ingloriously.

THURSDAY 1 OCTOBER. (Writing Thursday 8 October.) Mrs. Dr. Grant and Mr. James Baillie dined with me; I drank cider. Sir George Campbell and his brother had been with us for a month. They slept in Grange's. I made them read each a chapter every day, and made Sir

---

[8] John Maclaurin (later Lord Dreghorn) was one of Boswell's most intimate friends in the Faculty of Advocates. The Rev. Joseph Robertson MacGregor (who resumed his rightful name in 1784 after the repeal of the proscriptive act against the Mac-Gregors) was the first minister of the Gaelic Chapel on the Castle Hill.

[9] Formerly wife of Thomas Dunlop-Wallace, self-styled baronet of Craigie. She had divorced him earlier this year on grounds of various adulteries, and had launched herself upon a single life of wandering about the British Isles and the Continent (and of incidental playwriting) which was to bring her a measure of notoriety and a niche in the *Dictionary of National Biography*. She apparently called herself "Eglantine," but Boswell's "Eglinton" is much more plausible. Women of family in eighteenth-century Scotland were not given baptismal names like "Eglantine."

George say a lesson in Corderius, and David in the Rudiments; [1] and on Sundays say psalms and the Lord's prayer. I believe I did not omit my task above three days all the time. They were to return to school at Lanark next day. It was comfortable to accustom them to a kindly connexion with their aunt and me and our children.

FRIDAY 2 OCTOBER. (Writing Thursday 8 October.) Robert Boswell went to Lanark with the young Campbells. I rose between six and seven and saw them in the chaise.[2] I had rashly engaged to dine with Sir James Foulis at Colinton today.[3] I thought it better to breakfast with him. So I rode out and had my servant with me. It was wonderful to see what a large collection of Gaelic words he had made in the form of a dictionary of that language. But I was dissatisfied with the wild vivacity of his conversation. Lord Covington paid a visit at Colinton while I was there. It was a charming day. My wife, for the first time since her last in-lying, dined upstairs. Grange was with us at dinner. I drank cider and wine, but in fine moderation.

SATURDAY 3 OCTOBER. (Writing Thursday 8 October.) I walked out and breakfasted with Sir Alexander Dick, whom I found much better than he had been for some time. I went out an airing with him in his chaise, and then walked into town before dinner, as I did not like to walk in after dinner.

SUNDAY 4 OCTOBER. (Writing Friday 9 October.) Was at home all day, I know not how, and did very little good except reading one of Mr. Carr's sermons and hearing my children say psalms. Veronica could say two: the 23 and ———; and part of the first, and the Lord's prayer quite well. Poor Effie could say only a little of the 23 imperfectly. But what was wonderful, Sandy could say the Lord's prayer down to "daily bread" very distinctly, and could say more of it imperfectly. Mr. James Baillie dined with us.

MONDAY 5 OCTOBER. (Writing Friday 9 October.) Saw eight companies of the Glasgow Volunteers reviewed on Leith Links. Was much pleased with their appearance, and wondered to see a young corps have so soon a veteran look. At dinner I was seized with a fit of ill-humour and eat nothing but potatoes. Charles Preston and Mr. Wellwood drank tea with us. My ill-humour did not last. Mr. Robert Boswell, his friend Mr. Anderson of London, and Welsh Dr. Boswell supped with me.[4] My wife

---

[1] Latin primers by Mathurin Cordier and Thomas Ruddiman.

[2] Boswell's first cousin, Robert Boswell, W.S. (son of Dr. John Boswell), was another of the guardians of the Campbell boys.

[3] Boswell considered Sir James to be "without either dignity or elegance" (Journal, 4 January 1776).

[4] The "Welsh" Dr. Boswell was the "Dr. Bosvile" mentioned above, 29 September.

kept her room and Miss Cuninghame attended her. My spirits now were so sound that I was easy in all companies. I drank wine.

TUESDAY 6 OCTOBER. (Writing Friday 9 October.) I intended this day to begin to write an Information for Marshall against Crosse.[5] But I was idly lively and sauntering all the morning. Before two, Lady Rothes and her three eldest children paid us a visit with Miss Wauchope of Niddrie, her Ladyship being on a visit to that family. Then came Maclaurin, whom I asked to take a dinner with me today as I had done with him last week, and we should drink just one bottle of my old hock. He agreed. We first drank cider and Sitges, and then the hock. I did not feel myself comfortable, as he has no congenial religious dispositions; and what I had drank made me unfit to write my Information, I was so fretted with a sort of irritability of blood which wine sometimes produces in me.

WEDNESDAY 7 OCTOBER. (Writing Saturday 10 October.) This morning I had a message from Mr. William Wilson[6] begging that I would send him by the bearer the Information, Marshall against Crosse. This roused me. I sent for answer it should come in the evening. I fell to work after breakfast, but was volatile. Walked out as far as Portsburgh.[7] Called on Mr. Wilson and talked a little on the cause; came home, and went on very well. Charles Preston and Mr. Wellwood dined with us. I drank a little wine. I laboured assiduously and had fifteen pages finished before I went to bed.

THURSDAY 8 OCTOBER. (Writing Saturday 10 October.) Finished my Information this forenoon, and was pleased with my work. Kept the house all day, the weather being very rainy and windy. Supped at Dr. Young's with Lord and Lady Linton and Sir Philip and Lady Ainslie.

FRIDAY 9 OCTOBER. (Writing Tuesday 13 October.) Grange dined with us. I drank cider. I have nothing more to mention. Yet strange as it may seem, I really had not to complain of a *taedium vitae.*

SATURDAY 10 OCTOBER. (Writing Tuesday 13 October.) The Miss

Godfrey Bosville in a letter to Boswell (3 May 1778) refers to "the Welsh Bosville of Monmouthshire." Monmouthshire, included among English counties for Parliamentary purposes, was still commonly considered Welsh.

[5] A written pleading ordered by the Lord Ordinary when he took a cause to report to the Inner House. It meant in effect that the cause in question (a most ridiculous one) was being carried by appeal to the highest court in Scotland. For a summary see Appendix A.

[6] A Writer to the Signet who had given Boswell his first fee.

[7] This word, in the entries for 7 and 11 October, is followed by private symbols too uncertain to be reproduced typographically (the first something like an 8 with a vertical stroke through it, the other a "b" crossed by two horizontal strokes). Boswell's reason for using a symbol to record his activities in Portsburgh will soon become apparent (see below, Editorial Note, 30 January 1779).

McAdams, Craigengillan's daughters, dined with us. I drank only water. Lord Macdonald drank tea with us.

SUNDAY 11 OCTOBER. (Writing Tuesday 13 October.) In the morning before breakfast I walked out as far as Portsburgh. Heard Dr. Blair in the forenoon and Mr. Walker in the afternoon. Between sermons sat awhile with Maclaurin, whom I found reading the Sixth Book of the *Aeneid* with Warburton's commentary upon it in his *Divine Legation of Moses*. In the evening made my children repeat psalms and the Lord's prayer. Lady Colville and Lady Anne Erskine called and sat some time. Sir Thomas Wallace called and stayed supper.[8] I drank two bumpers of raspberry brandy which had been set down by mistake for Madeira, and half a bottle of Madeira. I was so much intoxicated as to be fiery and passionate. V.[9]

MONDAY 12 OCTOBER. (Writing Tuesday 13 October.) Got up not at all well. Sat a while in the forenoon with Grange. Walked a little in the street. Grew worse; went to bed at three and lay all the rest of the day in great distress with a headache and sickness. My mind just acquiesced.

TUESDAY 13 OCTOBER. (Writing Wednesday 21 October.) Nothing particular to remark, but that at night I had a severe toothache after I was in bed. My wife took the most affectionate care of me by rising and getting me tincture of myrrh, etc. V. At last I fell asleep.

WEDNESDAY 14 OCTOBER. (Writing Wednesday 21 October, and till another date is mentioned, it is to be understood I write on that day.) Finished *The Hypochondriack* No. 13.[1] I have nothing else to mention.

THURSDAY 15 OCTOBER. Went to Valleyfield.[2] Found Sir George

---

[8] Sir Thomas was the ex-husband of "Eglantine" Wallace (see above, 29 September).

[9] That is, *voluptas*, "enjoyment."

[1] "Marriage is unquestionably the great support of civil society; and in so far as love conduces to the advancement of that state, it is beneficial. . . . We must keep in mind that as a storm sometimes drives ships from their moorings into the ocean, so love not unfrequently loosens the conjugal anchors, and sets its victims adrift upon the waves of licentiousness. . . . Whatever respect I have for the institution of marriage, and however much I am convinced that it upon the whole produces rational happiness, I cannot but be of opinion that the passion of love has been improperly feigned as continuing long after the conjugal knot has been tied. . . . There is no doubt that experience affords sufficient conviction that all the rapture, when rapture has been felt, is very transient. I do not limit its existence to any precise portion of time, either with the French poet 'que le jour du mariage fut le tombeau de l'amour,' that the day of marriage was the tomb of love; or with the proverbial expression, that it lasts no longer than the honeymoon. But it is surely very short" (*The Hypochondriack*, No. 13).

[2] Valleyfield House, Fife, near Culross, was the seat of Sir George Preston. This was a jaunt of some thirty miles, involving a ferry crossing. Lady Preston was aunt to Boswell's mother.

"wearing away," as he said himself, but without pain. He however could not read now, which was a great loss to him. Yet he seemed to be free from discontent, and was satisfied with eating, drinking, sleeping, sitting close to a great fire, and hearing news of any sort. Lady Preston was pretty well, but dull of hearing. I was in a good comfortable frame. Drank a little wine, both at dinner and supper.

FRIDAY 16 OCTOBER. (Writing at Auchinleck, Saturday 24 October.) Rode three miles to Luscar to breakfast with Mr. Stobie.[3] He was gone to Auchinleck. But I was entertained by his wife and two daughters. The day was afterwards passed at Valleyfield very comfortably. The power of association of ideas appears every day stronger to me. Had I been at most country seats, I should have wearied sadly. But my mind was so much pleased with thinking of Valleyfield as the place where I had been happy in my early days, where my dear mother had been often, and where the gallant old General Preston had lived, that I was not only easy but happy.[4] I must add that Sir George and Lady Preston had been like parents to my wife and me ever since our marriage; and Charles, who now had the estate, was a worthy, decent, fine-tempered man. These circumstances were truly agreeable. We had whist every night between tea and supper. I drank a little wine today, both at dinner and supper. I walked out a little each afternoon. I read in the *Annual Register, London Magazine,* and Douglas's *Baronage.*[5]

SATURDAY 17 OCTOBER. (Writing as per last notandum, and it shall be mentioned when the day of writing is changed.) I was refreshed by receiving a kind letter from my dear wife, absence from whom is really an immediate uneasiness to me, though perhaps that is balanced by the joy of meeting her again after each period of separation. Colonel Preston walked down with me to Culross, that I might pay my respects to Archibald, Earl of Dundonald. He was quite engrossed with coal concern, the

---

[3] Lord Auchinleck's clerk.

[4] George Preston (?1659–1748), great-uncle of Sir George, had been Governor of Edinburgh Castle and at one time Commander-in-Chief of the forces in Scotland. He was active in defence during the rebellion of 1745, although he had been relieved of the command of the garrison of the Castle, and was crippled. According to family report he had himself carried in an armchair round the guards, that he might personally see if all were on the alert; and when the Jacobites threatened to burn Valleyfield if the Castle were not surrendered, he countered with a threat to have the Royal Navy destroy Wemyss Castle, to which one of the Jacobite generals was heir. In the event, Edinburgh Castle was not surrendered.

[5] Sir Robert Douglas's *Baronage of Scotland,* though in print to p. 562 when he died in 1770, was not published till 1798. From a remark that Boswell made on 10 June 1782 (see below) it appears that Sir George had a set of the unpublished sheets up to about p. 400.

sea having broke into a pit on which he had great dependence; so we did
not accept of his invitation to dinner. I felt all my old sensations of
grandeur from seeing Culross, which was a proof that my mind was clear.[6]
So free from melancholy was I at present that worthy Sir George Preston's
visible approach to death did not make me gloomy. I viewed the ordinary
course of nature with tranquillity. As I have experienced such variety of
states of mind, I can fully conceive the multiplicity of characters amongst
mankind. I drank after dinner today some old Malaga of the year 1749,
brought from Gibraltar. It was either this day or the next that I drank it.
I relished it highly; and I felt for a moment an inclination to indulge in
intoxication, but checked it. At night I drank some admirable cider.

SUNDAY 18 OCTOBER. Went to Culross Church with Mr. and Miss
Preston. Mr. Rolland preached from John, 3 Epist.,[7] 3 Chap., 3 verse:
"And every man that hath this hope," etc. He was very orthodox. But he
could give no clear ideas of the hope, but just mentioned happiness in
general. And to be sure, the happiness of a future state is quite incon-
ceivable by us at present. We came home to dinner. I read to Lady Preston
in her own room a letter of Mrs. Rowe's to an infidel, who was supposed
to be estimable in every respect but one.[8] We came home to dinner, after
which I drank some wine. Mr. Rolland came in the evening and said
prayers, but Sir George was gone to bed. I drank one glass of cider after
supper, and nothing else but water. I found I had been living too full.

MONDAY 19 OCTOBER. Left Valleyfield after breakfast. It had been
for some days frosty weather. It was milder today. I had a pleasant journey
home. I rode on both sides of the firth, and really felt the motion of the
horse and the inhaling of fresh air sensibly refreshing and invigorating.
Had a most agreeable meeting with my wife and children. Worthy Grange
dined with us. I drank some cider. I drank tea at Robert Boswell's. The
Doctor came home after it. I sat a long time and was cheerfully comfortable. Was happy to find myself at home at night. V.

TUESDAY 20 OCTOBER. (Writing Sunday 25 October.) I intended to
have set out for Auchinleck next day, but was detained till a new frock-

[6] Culross Abbey Church and Culross Abbey House are intrinsically grand, but they
caused especially affecting sensations in Boswell because his mother had grown up in
Culross. The Abbey House was at that time owned and occupied by her grandmother,
Lady Mary Cochrane, Lady Preston's mother. Archibald Cochrane, ninth Earl of
Dundonald, Lady Mary's grandson and first cousin to Boswell's mother, was Boswell's junior by several years. A gifted inventor and engineer, he was engaged in
chemical and manufactory experiments aimed at the production of sailcloth, carbonate
of soda, and coal tar; thus he had a special interest in the coal-fields of Culross.

[7] Properly "1 Epist."

[8] Presumably the first letter of *Letters from the Dead to the Living* (1728), but Boswell's description is inexact.

suit should be made for me. I passed the day very idly, but was in good spirits. I received an excellent letter from my friend Temple, which made me think favourably of myself, without which I never am happy.* ⁹ In the forenoon I called on Dr. Blair at his country-house between Edinburgh and Leith, and, at Mr. Charles Dilly's desire, made him an offer of £300 for a second volume of his sermons. The Doctor said Strahan had behaved so handsomely to him that he could not but give him the first offer, but he would let me know before a bargain was concluded, that Messieurs Dilly might treat either with himself or with Strahan.¹ I was disgusted with the Doctor's vanity, burring pronunciation, and drawling manner with the Lothian tone. It is in vain to attempt to break associations of ideas. Let a man, instead of losing time in the attempt, choose companions who present to his mind pleasing ideas, unless it be his duty to reconcile himself to those who disgust him, or other companions cannot be had. I dined quietly at home and drank small beer. Lord Advocate's lady's (writing Tuesday 27 October) intrigue with Captain Fawkener was now the great topic of discourse. I went and sat an hour with Maclaurin, who had been with her, and heard all the particulars. I then drank tea with Mr. George Wallace, knowing that he would relish with me this first rub in the prosperous career of the overbearing Dundases.² He read to me part of an essay on the ancient Scottish peerage which he was preparing for the press.³ I liked it well. (From the * on [this] page is all recollected after my marking that I passed the day very idly, which was not a just confession. Perhaps I have written too strongly of my dissatisfaction with

⁹ "Balance your advantages against what you consider in a different light: your wife's equal and cheerful disposition, the name you have got, your well-grounded hopes, etc. Can you think of any better philosophy than this?" (From Temple, 3–5 October). The asterisk at the end of this sentence is explained at the end of the entry.

¹ Strahan, who had published the first volume of the Rev. Hugh Blair's sermons the previous year, bought the second also, for £300, thus meeting Dilly's offer.

² Boswell's dislike of Henry Dundas (later Lord Melville) was of long standing, and may even have gone back to the days when they were class-mates in Edinburgh College. In 1776 he had almost challenged him to a duel for a supposed insult to Lord Auchinleck. He wrote to Temple in 1775 that he was "angry and fretful" at Dundas's promotion to Lord Advocate: "He has, to be sure, strong parts. But he is a coarse, unlettered, unfanciful dog. Why is he so lucky?" (22 May 1775). But his most bitter resentment, which included the whole family, went back to their management of Lord Auchinleck in the Ayrshire election of 1774. Fawkener, later a commissioner of stamps, was at this time a lieutenant in the 11th Dragoons. Dundas secured a divorce from his wife the next month. Sir Alexander Dick says in his diary (29 November 1778) that she was soon after married to Fawkener.

³ Published in 1783 under the title *Thoughts on the Origin of Feudal Tenures and the Descent of Ancient Peerages in Scotland.*

Dr. Blair. But the truth is that the conversation which I enjoy in London has made me very difficult to be pleased.)

WEDNESDAY 21 OCTOBER. Breakfasted at Lady Colville's, and was more upon my guard than usual, being more swift to hear and more slow to speak.[4] Grange dined with us. I drank some cider. I was uneasy from a very trifling cause: want of power of mind to decide whether I should ride or take post-chaise to Auchinleck. I was quite fretted to find myself so weak. Worthy Grange bid me consider how unhappy I was this time twelvemonth when my valuable wife was so ill.[5] This did me good. V.

THURSDAY 22 OCTOBER. It would be ridiculous to mark down the waverings of my mind between riding and taking a chaise. My wife and Grange determined for the latter. I breakfasted early and set out at nine. Poor little Sandy cried to go to Auchinleck with me. It was painful to think that he would not be welcome. But I did resolve to take him next year. I was somewhat uneasy at going from home, because my wife and Veronica and little James had all the cold, and I feared they might grow worse. However, I thought it was a duty to pay a visit to my father, and I had to inquire about setting [6] Dalblair and several other things. I stopped at Corsethill and dined on eggs and tasted some shocking porter and good whisky.[7] I was curious to see this house at which my father in his early years had so often put up, and where I had not been, I believe, for about two-and-twenty years. It seemed to be as bad as it was then. But I kept my mind unruffled, and found it not so soft and spongy as formerly, so as to suck in all ideas that come near it. Ideas must now for the most part have a good deal of spirit in them to penetrate into my mind, to such firmness hath it attained. I found here to my surprise a number of books. The *Rambler* soon attracted me, and I read several papers in the ———— volume. Now that I have written several numbers of a periodical paper myself, I did not regard even the *Rambler* with quite so much mysterious reverence as formerly. I imagined that I had written some sentences as well as some that I now read. I got to Douglas Mill at night, had Mr. Gillespie, the landlord, to sup with me, and drank a little small beer and port. I have a desire to be popular at inns which is disproportionate to the object. My father by his example taught me this.

[4] Elizabeth, Lady Colville, now widowed for the second time, was perhaps Boswell's closest female friend in Edinburgh.

[5] Mrs. Boswell had been seriously ill in July 1777 and in October 1777 had had a nearly fatal attack (probably a haemorrhage).

[6] "Letting" or "leasing": a Scotticism.

[7] "Corsethill" is an old variant name of Crosswood Hill, seventeen miles from Edinburgh on the Ayr road, one mile before the road enters Lanarkshire.

FRIDAY 23 OCTOBER. Had saddle-horses ready for me at half an hour after four, when I rose. But the day grew so wet that I was glad of my chaise. I was uneasy to think of poor Gillespie the landlord's distress by being a partner of Douglas, Heron, and Company.[8] Pity, when one cannot reasonably help, is sad. I breakfasted at Muirkirk, and got to Auchinleck between one and two. My father gave me a pretty good reception. But his indifference about my wife and children hurt me. The ladies did well enough.[9] Mr. Stobie's rental book helped to amuse me. I found that the ladies had brought my father to play every night at whist, to amuse him and themselves. I played in the evening. I drank two glasses of sherry after dinner. Supped on porridge and milk. It was a storm of wind and rain. My mind was quite sound; and what is curious, the restraint here did me good. The coldness checked fretful fancies as frost kills weeds. I was glad to find honest James Bruce very well. Had my room sufficiently warmed, and was comfortable.

SATURDAY 24 OCTOBER. (Writing Wednesday 28 October.) The weather was still rainy. I passed the most part of the morning with my father in the library. In the afternoon it was fair, and I had Sandy Bruce to walk down with me to the Old Garden, surveyed the wall-fruit trees which I sent from Edinburgh, and the bank at the old washing-green which my father had now repaired. I sat a little in James Bruce's house, and viewed Sandy's own house, which had been made a very good dwelling last summer out of the stable, by building a cross wall and vents, etc.[1] Drank only water today; played whist at night.

SUNDAY 25 OCTOBER. It was a fine day. My father and the ladies stayed at home. Mr. Stobie and I rode to Auchinleck Church and heard Mr. Bain, Mr. Dun's assistant. We came home between sermons, to comply by desire with the present practice of the family. I felt uneasy after I was upon the road for giving so bad an example, and I thought that doing thus was worse than staying all day at home; for in that case I might be supposed to be sick, whereas my absenting from afternoon service was open and deliberate. At night I read a good many chapters of the Bible to my father, the ladies, and Mr. Stobie; and I read by myself some of Fénelon's *Education of a Daughter*, which Lady Auchinleck put

[8] The failure (in 1772) of this banking company (of which Archibald Douglas and Patrick Heron were the principal partners) spread financial ruin far and wide in Scotland.

[9] Lady Auchinleck's two unmarried sisters, Margaret and Marion ("Menie"). Margaret lived with her.

[1] James Bruce was Lord Auchinleck's overseer. Alexander (Sandy), his son, assisted his father in his duties.

into my hands; also part of the life of Fraser of Brea, which, though clouded with puritanical scrupulousness, has a good deal of thought in it. I had read some of it at Corsethill, particularly a very good account of the Bass, in which he had been imprisoned.[2]

MONDAY 26 OCTOBER. It was a hard frost. I walked with James Bruce along with me round the march of Roadinghead, of which a tack was proposed, and then up the avenue at the head of the west park, in which I saw larixes growing wild, that is to say, sown by the planted trees.[3] My father showed me a strange notion in Carolus Stephanus *De Re Rustica* that larix would not burn by itself.[4] This has been copied into all the writers on trees, or many of them at least. Yet it is quite without foundation, as my father has proved by experience. We went into the Tenshilling-side and Little Hern parks, in the middle of each of which I, in the year ————, planted five fir trees, with intention that when they were grown up a little I might choose the best and give it full room to grow and spread so as to be like any of the large forest trees with bushy and extending heads, which a fir will be if not crushed in a crowd as it generally is, so that firs are just like may-poles. I once saw one full-spread fir in a field at Kilravock, and Dr. Walker at Moffat showed me a pretty good one in his garden. He was much pleased to hear that I had resolved to have firs in their natural growth. I pruned a great deal off the four in each group which were to stand only to shelter the best one for some years. I had a good deal of satisfaction in seeing the progress of my scheme. I believe I shall come to delight in country affairs. We next went into the Hill avenue and walked round by the Little Hern park, then to the Grotto, and then home. Mrs. Blair (widow) of Dunskey came before dinner. I drank water and played at whist at night, after having read some of the *Education of a Daughter*. My mind was now so very sound that I was constantly serene. I find that I am easiest when not agitated. But at this time I had no lively thoughts, no aspiring hopes of felicity in a better world. I existed in present tranquillity and in calm Christian patience, or rather composure, without any fervency or anxiety. I wonder how long this frame will last.

TUESDAY 27 OCTOBER. (Writing on Saturday 31 October.) Dined at Mr. Dun's. Proposed to myself to have revived my youthful ideas and to have talked with him confidentially of some particulars. But I was kept in

---

[2] *Memoirs of the Life of the Very Reverend Mr. James Fraser of Brea, Written by Himself*, was published at Edinburgh in 1738. He had been apprehended in 1674 as a preacher at conventicles, and was imprisoned on the Bass Rock for two years.
[3] A tack is a lease, larixes are larches.
[4] Charles Estienne's *Praedium Rusticum*, 1554, a collection of tracts compiled from ancient writers on various branches of agriculture.

the town of Auchinleck so long by different people talking of getting feus and leases [5] that it was just upon dinner-time when I got to the manse, and his assistant dined with us; and immediately after dinner came in Knockroon and his father; [6] so that I was called off from gentle recollection and private consultation to general talk. I drank a dram of brandy after eating goose, and two glasses of wine. I stayed and drank tea. At night Mrs. Blair was still at Auchinleck. I played a little at whist.

WEDNESDAY 28 OCTOBER. Immediately after breakfast I got on horseback, and, accompanied by Mr. Stobie and James Bruce, rode to the Trabboch and surveyed the greatest part of that barony, but particularly the farm of Hoodston upon the march, between which and Chipperlaigan it was proposed by James Bruce to make a belt of planting, as also on the march between it and Lord Glencairn's farm called Tarelgin. I approved much of both. I really felt myself take an interest in improving the estate. John Hood, the tenant in Hoodston, was not at home. He is the fourth from father to son in that farm, proved by the Session records of Ochiltree, and it is not known how far back his family has been there. Perhaps they have been proprietors. Mr. Reid, the Minister of Ochiltree, by lending his credit, kept the family in possession in this man's minority, when my Uncle James had the administration of the estate and was rigorous. The rent is now neat [6a] £20.12.6 sterling. It is very pleasing to think of such an ancient race in a farm. I made his three sons come out of his house that I might see them. I am anxious that the family should continue in the farm from age to age. I was glad to see John Hood's brother ———, tenant in Loudieston, who told me he had two sons, so that the family was strong. We called at George Henry's at Gibston and saw his wife, Betty Bruce, James's daughter, and three children. George was not at home. I wished much that my father would buy Trabboch Mains,[7] a beautiful farm now offered to sale by Sir John Whitefoord, as it was the very manor-

[5] In effect, long-term and short-term leases of land in Auchinleck village for purposes of building. Strictly speaking, feus were perpetual grants of land in return for fixed periodic payments, and Lord Auchinleck could no longer make such grants, for they involved a disponing or transfer of title and the estate was now under entail. He could, however, grant leases of land for building in Auchinleck village for any period of years not exceeding ninety-nine, and popular usage (which Boswell here follows) gave the name of feus to these long-term leases. In a Deed of Declaration signed 8 March 1781 (see that date below) Lord Auchinleck and Boswell extended the permitted period to nine hundred and ninety-nine years.

[6] Boswells of the Auchinleck line both named John. The son but not the father was heir to the large farm of Knockroon which had once been part of the estate of Auchinleck.

[6a] Net, after all deductions.

[7] Scots term for a farm attached to a mansion-house.

place of the barony of Trabboch, and has the *vestigia* of the old house still to be seen. We next fixed on Creochhill grassyard for making a plantation, which I had promised to Sundrum [8] to do for a view from his house. It had been planted round. But the trees were so much exposed they did not rise. But they would serve as a screen to a plantation with which all the space (about an acre) would be filled. We got home just in time to dinner; found Mrs. Blair gone and Bruce Campbell come. I had tasted whisky at Gibston, and I drank two glasses of wine after dinner. Bruce Campbell went home in the evening. I studied the rental book with Mr. Stobie.

THURSDAY 29 OCTOBER. Had James Bruce with me to look at Mount James, which I planted with my own money in 175–; found the trees wonderfully advanced. Marked some firs to be given to Andrew Morton to be part of the timber of a new house he was to build in Church Street, Auchinleck town; and James Bruce bought two from me for a shilling, that I might say I sold firs of my own planting at sixpence apiece. He said they were worth the money. Thus was my mind amused with little particulars. It is not impossible but I may grow very fond of the country. We came in by the Know, and went into the house and talked a little with Sanders Pedin, the tenant. Hallglenmuir,[9] Knockroon, and Dr. Johnston at Cumnock dined. I drank one glass of wine. I had been ill with a headache all day. It continued for the evening, so that I was able to do nothing but sit by the fire. But my mind was tranquil. I had the pleasure to receive a letter from my dear wife. I went to my room early, cleansed my stomach with warm water, and went to bed.

FRIDAY 30 OCTOBER. (Writing on Sunday 1 November.) After we had done with breakfast, Lord Justice Clerk [1] arrived, and, I dare say, was surprised to find the table clear ten minutes before ten. He had breakfast by himself, and was in such good spirits and talked so heartily that I liked to contemplate him. My father had appeared to me to be greatly better than he had been for more than two years past. But when I saw him with Lord Justice Clerk, his failure was very visible. He lagged sadly upon recent topics. Lord Justice Clerk said to me when my father was out of the room that I should buy Trabboch Mains, as it lay quite into our lands; and that he would not interfere against us, though he should get it to buy at twenty years' purchase. This was genteel. I regretted that there was an unhappy coolness between him and me. I hoped to bring about better terms in time, though I own I did not wish for an intimacy with so

[8] John Hamilton of Sundrum, a college chum of Boswell's.

[9] Alexander Mitchell of Hallglenmuir.

[1] Thomas Miller, Lord Glenlee, later Lord President of the Court of Session and a baronet. His residence, Barskimming House on the Ayr, was nearer to Auchinleck than any other gentleman's seat.

near a neighbour. I am not fit for such intimacies, nor do I enjoy them.
Dr. Young has two lines which suit me excellently:

> My time my own,
> My faults unknown.[2]

After Lord Justice Clerk went away, I walked down to the Old House and
had James Bruce to attend me to the top of the Old Castle. I then gathered
nuts and pears in the garden for my children. Sat a good while in the
evening with Mr. Stobie studying the *Constitution of the Estate*.[3] Played
a little at whist.

SATURDAY 31 OCTOBER. It was one of the wettest days that I
ever saw. My father and I sauntered a good while in the dining-room,
and I listened to his stories, which really entertained me in a peculiar way.
I then began in the library to read Erasmus *De Praeparatione ad Mortem*,
which I have long intended to read and translate, from the satisfaction
which I had many years ago in reading a little of it, where he recommends
pictures of pious subjects to dying people.[4] Mr. Stobie had informed me
where my mother's contract of marriage lay. I had often wanted to see it,
but my father evaded it, which was not right. He seemed now to acquiesce
in my looking through all the family papers; so I got it this forenoon and
found that for all the work that my father had made about the order of
succession of the estate, it never had been in his power, even with my
consent, to alter the destination to heirs male. I observed a marginal note
which confounded me very much, so that it required a good deal of presence of mind to show no agitation. Perhaps I was mistaken in the opinion
which I formed, and I certainly shall not here put it in writing. When I
mentioned to my father the entail in his contract of marriage, he said he
had another paper from his father giving him power to settle the estate.
But I imagine he was in a mistake; and besides, both of them could not
hurt the provision in the contract.[5] I laid it again into the place where I

[2] Opening of last stanza but one of *Ocean: An Ode*.
[3] Probably Lord Auchinleck's twelve splendidly bound quarto volumes containing
transcripts of the Auchinleck "charters and family papers" which Boswell refers to
below, 29 August 1780. In a letter to Robert Boswell, 21 May 1789, he calls this
collection "the Palladia of our Family." The volumes are now at Yale.
[4] The next three essays in *The Hypochondriack* were on death. At the end of the
second (December 1778), Boswell recommends Erasmus's book to his readers.
[5] Boswell's long quarrel with his father over the eventual disposition of the estate
of Auchinleck had been more or less settled in August 1776, with the signing of an
entail. Boswell had long held out for heirs male whatsoever of the body of Thomas Boswell, the founder. Lord Auchinleck's real preference was for heirs whatsoever of his
own body, but he appeared to yield so far as to offer an entail on heirs male of his

found it, not without some hesitation whether I ought not to take it into my own possession, as it was my title-deed.

After dinner it was fair, and I walked with James Bruce to the Broomhouse and there viewed the Water of Lugar in the greatest flood in the memory of man, and then walked through the Broomholm and down the bank to the old washing-green. I have put down a particular record of this flood on a paper apart.[6] I suggested to James Bruce that there should be an Auchinleck chronicle of remarkable things. He said that my father went through books like a moth, without getting any instruction from them, for he only scraped (writing on Tuesday 3 November) the leaves clean. There is however this remark to be made: that he is the reverse of a moth to them, as he preserves them by scraping off rusty spots, whereas a moth destroys them. So habitual has this scraping grown to him, that while I have been reading one *Caledonian Mercury*, I have observed him gravely scraping another, when it was to be made waste paper immediately after being read. This was like as if one should polish or paint a log of wood which is just to be thrown upon the fire to burn. I wrote to Sir John Pringle in the forenoon. At night played at whist. It was more satirical than just when I thought that one might say, "What a life is this! Talk without ideas, and card-playing without a stake!" Yet, except the peculiar satisfaction which I have in hearing my father's stories when nobody is by that can disturb my sympathetic delicacy, the saying was very well. It was indeed a soliloquy.

SUNDAY 1 NOVEMBER. (Writing on Tuesday 17 November.) It was a bad day, and we all stayed at home. I had the dining-room to myself in the forenoon, and was quite in the Auchinleck calm and solemn humour, and read the whole of Erasmus *De Praeparatione ad Mortem*, which I think

---

grandfather, with provision for inheritance by heirs general if that male line failed. The facts, as his marriage contract (now at Yale) shows, were that, though he could have made any disposition he pleased of the lands he himself had purchased, he had no power at all to entail the estate of Auchinleck he had received from his father either on heirs male whatsoever or on heirs general. That estate had come to him *already* entailed on heirs male of his grandfather. His disingenuousness in this matter was probably caused by reluctance to let Boswell know that his earlier threats to disinherit him (or at least to sell off the estate) had been pure bluff. The entail signed in 1776 brought Lord Auchinleck's own purchases into the entailed estate and also brought the list of heirs "called" up to date, but otherwise was in accord with the marriage contract of 1738. The marginal notation that confounded Boswell (actually a change in the wording of the contract made and initialled by the parties after it had been signed), made more explicit the rights to the succession of Lord Auchinleck's uncle and brothers. Why it should have disturbed Boswell so is not clear. The passage deleted in the original document is hard to decipher, and he may have misread it.

6 This paper has disappeared.

was first shown me in London in 1760 by either old or young Alexander, the painter. There was much unction in it, but also more weakness than I expected to find. But perhaps I considered as weakness that meek submission of reason to divine faith which religion requires, and from which I am too much estranged by being accustomed, as a practical lawyer, to continual close controversial reasoning. I regretted that there was no appearance of family religion today, not even reading of chapters. How different from what was the usage in my grandfather's time, or my mother's time!

MONDAY 2 NOVEMBER. Set out betimes on horseback; breakfasted at Milrig. Messieurs Hugh and Bruce Campbells and I rode to Riccarton to a meeting of the tutors of Treesbank in our co-tutor Bailie Richmond's house, where Major Dunlop met us. Mr. Macredie, being indisposed, could not attend. I was in a solid, comfortable frame and drank three glasses of wine, so as to shun singularity and yet be safe from intoxication. We wished much to purchase for our pupil the old Place of Cessnock from Mr. Fullarton of Rosemount; and in order to renew the negotiation, which the late Treesbanks had begun, Mr. Bruce Campbell and I had a chaise from Kilmarnock and drove briskly to Rosemount, where we arrived while a large company was sitting after dinner.[7] I drank some glasses of Madeira, and I found the large company put me into more agitation than I wished. The Earl of Dumfries was there. He was exceedingly attentive to me and pressed me much to give him a day at his house this week. But I told him I was afraid it would not be in my power. I was upon my guard, as I well knew that he and his Countess flattered themselves that they would get from me that road through our estate which my father had refused, and which in truth I was still more positive for refusing. While my father was not on visiting terms with the Earl I thought it not decent for me to visit him; and it was my resolution that if ever his Lordship and I should be neighbours, a stipulation never to mention the road should be a preliminary of our intercourse.[8] Mr. Bruce Campbell and I had a private conference with Mr. Fullarton, who repeated his promise of letting the Treesbanks family have the first offer, and took to considera-

---

[7] Boswell was tutor and curator to Treesbank's sons by his will. The scheme to buy the Place of Cessnock for George Campbell, heir male to Sir Hugh Campbell of Cessnock, was abandoned in December of this year. Hugh and Bruce Campbell were Boswell's second cousins. William Macredie of Perceton, another of the tutors appointed, was the father of Helen Macredie, Treesbank's first wife.

[8] Dumfries House is 1¼ miles west of Cumnock, and 2½ miles south-east of Auchinleck House. According to a document in the Boswell Papers at Yale, Lord Dumfries (Patrick Macdowall-Crichton, fifth Earl) in 1774 wanted to run a road almost due north from Dumfries House through the Auchinleck farm of Glenside to the Auchinleck Church road.

tion proposals which we made him for an immediate sale. We drove back to Riccarton and mounted our horses.

I went at night to Loudoun, and was received with the same frankness as usual. The old Countess, who on the 4th of September last had completed her ninety-eighth year, was as fresh in her mind as last year.[9] She made a very shrewd observation against the synod of Glasgow and Ayr, who, in their manifesto against the intended Act for repealing the penal statutes against popery,[1] set forth how adverse the disposition of their people is to it. "How then," said she, "is there such fear of popery increasing?" There was no company here. She sat till eleven struck.

TUESDAY 3 NOVEMBER. I must abbreviate. The Earl gave me a full account of all he knew of the war in Scotland in 1745–6.[2] Then we walked about two hours, and I went and surveyed the situation of the Old Castle of Loudoun. Mr. Hugh Campbell dined. I drank a little wine. Called at his brother in passing, and went to Bruntwood and drank tea and two glasses of wine, that I might renew with (writing on Monday 23 November) this laird the old friendship between our families.[3] He and his wife took my visit as a very kind compliment and told me all their distresses. He had sold off all the estate but eighty acres, and the price just paid the debts; and he and she (having no children alive) hoped to pass the rest of their days comfortably, when a bond of cautionry for Overton [4] to the Duke of Douglas for £300, with many years' interest, unexpectedly appeared. I promised to try to get DOUGLAS [5] to give an ease of this debt. After tea, wine was set down. I drank a glass to the prosperity of the family. He wanted me to drink more. I said I was a bad drinker, but that if it would do him good, I would drink both the bottles upon the table. He said very cordially, "It will do me good if you'll take another glass." I did so. I felt much satisfaction in thus renewing an old neighbourly connexion. I

[9] She was the widow of the previous Earl of Loudoun and mother of the Earl mentioned above, 23 September 1778. She seems actually to have been ninety-four. Boswell had taken Johnson to call on her in 1773.

[1] Already repealed in England and now proposed for repeal in Scotland (see below, 2 February 1779).

[2] Johnson in the previous year (19 September 1777) had proposed that Boswell write a history of it. Loudoun, as Colonel of the 54th Regiment of Loyal Highlanders (which he raised himself) and as Adjutant-General of the forces in Scotland, had probably seen as much of the war as anyone Boswell could have consulted.

[3] The laird of Bruntwood's name was Francis Moor.

[4] William Fullarton of Overton. Moor had signed a bond making himself liable for a debt of Fullarton's to the Duke of Douglas if legal methods of collecting the money from Fullarton failed. There is among the Boswell papers at Yale a letter from Moor to Boswell, 8 November 1778, expressing deep gratitude for Boswell's offer of assistance.

[5] Archibald Douglas of Douglas, hero of the famous Douglas Cause, whose claim to be heir to the Duke of Douglas Boswell had strongly supported in 1767.

had heart enough. But I regretted that I had neither wealth, interest, nor solid sense enough to help much to extricate the family to which ours had been obliged in need. Found at Auchinleck Mr. Shepherd, Minister at Muirkirk.

WEDNESDAY 4 NOVEMBER.[6] (Writing Monday 23 November.) Rode down to the Trabboch with ———— Currie, one of the tenants, as my guide. Liked the manner of this man better than that of most of the country people about us, he seemed to talk so frankly. From his state of affairs, which I believed honest, I computed that in twenty years he had not gained forty pounds. "But, Sir," said he, "I have brought up my family." Sandy Bruce and some men had gone down before me to Creochhill. I planted with my own hand several oaks and beeches, and left them to plant the rest. I made Hoodston ride with me to Barquharrie, where I paid my visit to Mr. George Reid and found him quite hearty.[7] He and I and Hoodston and the goodwife of Creochhill drank strong ale. I had engaged to be at the expense of enclosing a new grassyard there in place of the former one which I had filled with trees, and to pay rent for the former also as James Bruce should settle. I promised to the goodwife to pay for grass seed to the new one and to do as Mr. Reid should think right. Found Dr. Gillespie and John Webster at Auchinleck. They stayed all night. N.B. This page contains the history of the 5 November. The 4th will be found on the next.

WEDNESDAY 4 NOVEMBER. (Writing Sunday 29 November.) Planted a plane tree near the place where the old washing-house stood, to mark how far Lugar was out on the 31 October last. I carried this tree on my shoulder from the old wood to where I planted it. It was taken up from the Hern plantation. In the afternoon I planted three plane trees upon Stronis Acre, just by the house. Fingland dined.[8] I drank heartily both of porter and wine, so as to feel just the beginning of intoxication.

THURSDAY 5 NOVEMBER is recorded on the preceding page.

FRIDAY 6 NOVEMBER. After breakfast left Auchinleck in good, calm, cordial frame. My father had ordered the chaise from Mauchline to carry me to Kilmarnock, where I dined at Mr. William Brown's by appointment to meet with Sir Walter Montgomerie-Cuninghame on business.[9]

---

[6] Really 5 November. See Boswell's note at the end of the entry.

[7] Mr. Reid, the old Minister of Ochiltree, had been chaplain to James Boswell (Boswell's grandfather) and domestic tutor to Lord Auchinleck.

[8] James Chalmers of Fingland.

[9] Sir Walter Montgomerie-Cuninghame was the eldest son of Mrs. Boswell's late sister Elizabeth, owner of Lainshaw. Boswell, as Sir Walter's lawyer, had been trying to save something for Sir Walter from the wreck of the estate. See below, 5 February 1779, note 4.

Bruce Campbell also dined with us. I drank three glasses of wine. Called on Miss Todd and got from her some sermons and letters of worthy Dr. Cooper's.[1] But was disappointed in finding very few of his papers in comparison of what I expected had been preserved. I gave her two guineas. I planted three beeches in Stronis Acre in the morning. I drank tea at Mr. Brown's. His sister's Kilmarnock tone pleased me. It was a kind of rural music. Sir Walter accompanied me to Lady Crawford's.[2] Crookshanks, with whom I had passed many a pleasant hour at the late Lord Eglinton's in London, was there. Sir Walter and he went away after supper. Miss Hamilton, my Lady's cousin, was with her, which prevented me from being at my ease. Lady Mary was confined to her room with a swelled face.[3] I drank a very little wine.

SATURDAY 7 NOVEMBER. It was a wet, dull day. Captain and Mrs. Fergusson of Greenvale dined. I drank some claret. I sunk into gloom, I know not how. I was vexed, and thought meanly of myself. At night the Countess was in great grief for her amiable and accomplished Lady Eglinton.[4]

SUNDAY 8 NOVEMBER. Was still melancholy. But the day was pretty good. So I mounted Lady Mary's horse and had a servant to attend me, and set out to visit old Lady Eglinton.[5] When I got to Dreghorn I found that service was just begun in the church, so I ordered the horses to an inn, went to Mr. Macredie of Perceton's seat, and was agreeably surprised to find in a little, narrow, country kirk a most decent clergyman (Mr. Michael Todd), with a gown and band, and a distinct manly utterance. He lectured very well. My spirits instantaneously recovered. Our minds, like our stomachs, are restored to soundness sometimes by one thing, sometimes by another, we know not by what operation. It was dreary to me to see the old Countess of Eglinton sadly failed. Sir Walter met me at Auchans and accompanied me to Lady Crawford's, where he dined. I was

---

[1] David Cooper, parish minister at Auchinleck before Mr. Dun, was an M.D. of Leiden, but his career as a physician must have been brief, if indeed he ever practised at all.

[2] Jean Hamilton, Countess of Crawford, was Mrs. Boswell's intimate friend. She was separated from her husband, and lived at Bourtreehill.

[3] Lady Mary Lindsay, Lady Crawford's daughter.

[4] Her eldest daughter, wife of the eleventh Earl of Eglinton, who had died in January of this year, aged only twenty-one. Boswell had harboured fantasies of making her his second wife if he lost Mrs. Boswell.

[5] Susanna Kennedy, wife of the ninth Earl of Eglinton, and mother of the tenth and eleventh Earls. She lived at Auchans, and was at this time in her ninetieth year. "Her figure was majestic, her manners high-bred, her reading extensive, and her conversation elegant. She had been the admiration of the gay circles of life, and the patroness of poets" (*Journal of a Tour to the Hebrides*, 1 November 1773). She asked Boswell on this visit to "tell Mr. Johnson I love him exceedingly."

seized with a swimming in my head and dimness of sight on the road back. It continued long, and I tried to cure it by strong wine; but I was not well all the evening. Mr. Macredie came and sat awhile after dinner. I wrote a card to Lady Mary begging permission to visit her with her mother, which was granted. Life was no enjoyment to me this day except in Dreghorn Church.

MONDAY 9 NOVEMBER. (Writing Wednesday 2 December.) Was a good deal better. Had the Countess's coach to Eglinton, where I had not been since the year 1768. Was sensible of a great advance in the growth of the plantations, but was not affected with that degree of tender melancholy which I supposed I should feel on being here for the first time after the shocking death of my noble friend the late Earl, who first showed me the pleasures of elegant society,[6] and after the death of the amiable young Countess. I was just impressed with immediate ideas. I walked a good deal with the Earl and Colonel William Hunter. Before dinner the Earl showed Wanley's *Wonders,* which is his constant companion at inns; and indeed there are a few points where he and I are congenial. For we are both a little superstitious (he indeed is so only in smaller matters such as second sight), both have a regard for Highlanders, and both like curious books such as Wanley.[7] Major Hugh Montgomerie, Sir Walter, and several more dined. I was hurt that grace was not said, though the minister of the parish was there.[8] I found that the Earl would really be vexed if I did not drink with him; and as he has been always exceedingly obliging to me, I resolved to humour him as well as I could. Therefore after indulging myself in eating a variety of dishes dressed by his cook (Robert Woodside, an Irvine man, who had been for a considerable time in the Prince de Condé's kitchen at Paris, and performed admirably well), I drank small beer, strong beer, old hock, port, and claret till the Earl *dissolved* the company; and indeed I had fully enough of intoxication. But I retained my reason so well that I spoke little, being checked by the apprehension of ruffling the Earl's temper, so that I did not expose myself; and I had some

---

[6] Alexander Montgomerie, tenth Earl of Eglinton, was shot and killed (24 October 1769) on his own estate by a supposed poacher whose gun he was attempting to take away.

[7] *The Wonders of the Little World,* by Nathaniel Wanley, a seventeenth-century divine, is a collection of "prodigies of human nature," which shows (in the words of the *Dictionary of National Biography*) "omnivorous reading" and "indiscriminate credence." Robert Browning drew from it the subject matter of several poems, notably *The Pied Piper of Hamelin.* Boswell presented the Earl of Eglinton with a new edition of the book about 1785, in which he wrote "Principibus placuisse viris non ultima laus est" ("To have found favour with leaders of mankind is not the meanest of glories": Horace, *Epistles,* I. xvii. 35).

[8] Thomas Pollock, Minister of Kilwinning parish, 1770–1798.

degree of cordial enjoyment and animation by thinking of the family of Eglinton and my having married a Montgomerie. I went and drank tea with my old friend, Mrs. Reid the housekeeper, after which I was just able to walk safely to bed. It seems I was very sick, but I was not sensible of it.

TUESDAY 10 NOVEMBER. Awaked miserably ill. Had some coffee. A chaise from Kilmarnock came for me before nine, and I was glad to make my escape from this den of drunkenness. I grew better by air and the motion of driving. Called at Rowallan for the first time after Colonel Campbell's marriage with my friend, Miss MacLeod of Raasay. But they were gone to Loudoun. Breakfasted at King's Well, and took what I had often heard of but never tasted, but which came into my head upon my journey as what would do me good: some burnt brandy.[9] Was driven to Glasgow in a chaise from that city by Robert ———, who drove Miss Peggie Montgomerie and me to Portpatrick in 1769, a pleasing jaunt. Got to Glasgow about four. Dined heartily on cold roast beef and drank lemonade; was quite well. Drank tea with Dr. and Mrs. Marshall. Was quite at home at my inn, with calm, steady spirits. Supped on chicken broth (fried chicken);[1] had the best bedroom.

WEDNESDAY 11 NOVEMBER. (Writing from memory on Tuesday, 12 January 1779.) Was assured DOUGLAS was at Bothwell Castle. Drove there to breakfast. Found only Lady Lucy and his niece, Miss Stewart. Drove post in to Edinburgh; had a comfortable and happy meeting with my dear wife and children.

N.B. From this day till 1 January 1779 I have short notes, except of two days which have been somehow omitted. Breaks in my journal at large I find *must* happen. The winter passed upon the whole pretty well till the close of 1778. I had not much labour as a lawyer, but a competent crop of fees. I renewed my intercourse with Lord Advocate, and had him to dine at my house. I had Mr. Christian frequently with me. I once or twice drank more than was right, and strayed into three different strange countries.[2] I ended the year with Douglas at Bothwell Castle.[3]

9 Brandy in which some of the alcoholic content has been removed by burning.
1 Probably "friar's chicken," or chicken broth with eggs dropped in it.
2 The "short notes" record only social engagements, with desultory reference to professional concerns. The excursions "into three different strange countries" appear to be covered merely by four cryptic entries: "Writers' Court" (21 and 29 November) and "Walked to Portsburgh" (13 and 21 December).
3 The invitation to spend the New Year with Douglas at Bothwell Castle seems to have been a standing one after this year (see below, 2 January 1780; Review following 31 December 1780). Boswell perhaps solicited this first visit in order to intercede for the Laird of Bruntwood (see above, 3 November 1778).

FRIDAY 1 JANUARY. (Writing 12 January from short notes.) Walked with DOUGLAS to Woodhall.[4] It was a fine frost. The dinner was excellent, the wines admirable. I enjoyed highly the pleasures of the table, but both eat and drank too much. Shawfield gave me a curious challenge at game. He offered me five guineas to play at half-guinea brag [5] from the time when we rose from dinner till supper. I accepted, which I should not have done, as I have not nerves for that game. However, I was uncommonly lucky. Shawfield himself, Douglas, and I were the party. I had once twenty-five guineas, and I ended with my five augmented to about eleven. I had a rage for play and got a rubber after supper and lost. Drank only water at night, which did me good.

SATURDAY 2 JANUARY. Hard frost. Played whist with avidity and lost, but took from Woodhall £7.18.6. Drove post to Edinburgh. Comfortable to be at home again. Counted with pleasure the days that I had to be at home before setting out for London. Found them to be at least seventy. Poor Veronica had this day slipped upon the ice in the Grassmarket, fallen and hit her head against a stair, so that all around one of her eyes was bruised. She had said, "What will my papa say?" I was very affectionately concerned. It pleased me to find honest Effie sitting beside her and diverting her. π.[6]

SUNDAY 3 JANUARY. At home in the forenoon. Between sermons went to my father's; found him not well, with his old complaint.[7] His lady and I dined tête-à-tête disagreeably enough. To make some variety in my feelings, I drank too much bad port, came home inflamed, and after tea got into a shocking bad state of temper. As the only relief, got into bed about seven. Veronica prevailed with me to rise again before nine, by asking "to be allowed to help me on with my clothes, that she might learn

---

[4] The seat of Walter Campbell of Shawfield, on North Calder Water, about five miles north-east of Bothwell Church.

[5] Essentially identical with modern poker. The name comes from the "brag" implied in a player's challenging the other players to show cards equal in value to his own.

[6] One of Boswell's symbols for conjugal intercourse. The Greek character stands for the English word "pleasure."

[7] The "complaint" was a recurrent stoppage of the urethra requiring catheterization.

to do it when I was old." Grange was sent for. My good spirits returned. We supped agreeably, and drank a bottle of mountain.[7a] π.

[EDITORIAL NOTE: Short notes which have survived for the period from 12 to 31 January record (among other things) that Lord Auchinleck, whose complaint was so serious as to cause fears for his life, had recovered by 24 January; that Robert Dundas, the Lord President, meeting Boswell at his father's, shook hands with him for the first time in five years; and that Boswell, who found himself "in vigorous indelicate frame," heard Blair preach on holding the faith in unrighteousness and thought the sermon very applicable to himself. The notes are in general not only laconic but dry, though occasionally a single entry of such jottings takes on the immediacy and colour which inform the fully written journal. The entry for 30 January is one such: "Having risked yesterday, out between seven and eight to Portsburgh. Tedious to open. Man in closet. Wonderful presence of mind; *to it*. Man off. Going. But allured back: *twice*. Found I was known. Breakfast Lady Colville's. Calm, home. Sent card to Bishop Falconer to drink coffee. At five, with him.[8] Admirable, as in last age. Coffee and bottle port. How different from morning. Home quite good." The journal resumes with the first day of the month.]

MONDAY 1 FEBRUARY. Blanks in the record of my life have hitherto occurred too often. I have short notes or minutes from the last recorded day to this. But rather than wait for filling them up, or, more properly speaking, enlarging them in my book, I proceed from the first day of a month and of the spring. I lay long today, did little in the forenoon, went to the burial of the wife of Mr. Alexander Gray, Writer to the Signet, from her father a Mr. Stewart's house at Sciennes to the Greyfriars churchyard. I was perhaps somehow related to her, for I was one of the pallbearers, as was Hamilton of Wishaw, who is my relation.[9] I make it a kind of pious rule to go to every funeral to which I am invited, both as I wish to pay a proper respect to the dead, unless their characters have been bad, and as I would wish to have the funeral of my own near relations or of myself well attended. I did not feel the least symptom of melancholy or gloom today, so strong was my mind. How it was so, I cannot account. The Reverend Bishop Falconer, Mr. Brown, Librarian to the Faculty of

[7a] A form of Malaga, made from grapes grown on the mountains.
[8] William Falconer was Bishop of the see of Edinburgh in the Episcopal Church in Scotland. On this occasion he toasted Samuel Johnson.
[9] If Boswell was related to Mrs. Gray, it was presumably not through the Boswell line, but through his mother's family, the Erskines of Alva. Robert Hamilton of Wishaw (1731–1784) was the great-great-grandson of Boswell's great-grandfather, Sir Charles Erskine, Kt. "Single Speech" Hamilton, whom Boswell was glad to claim as a second cousin, was first cousin to Robert Hamilton's mother.

Advocates (who had been reader to Mr. Thomas Ruddiman, and talked much of him with the Bishop),[1] and Grange dined with us. It was quite a cordial and venerable day, as in the last age. They drank coffee and tea. I suppose the Bishop laid his hands on Veronica's and Effie's heads. I saw him do it to Sandy and Jamie, which pleased me. Grange supped with us. I was warmed with wine at dinner.

TUESDAY 2 FEBRUARY. (Writing Thursday the 4th.) Lord Monboddo, Maclaurin, Balmuto,[2] Hon. A. Gordon, and Mr. Dalzell, the advocate, dined with us. It was agreeable to think that two hundred and sixteen years ago there was an alliance between the family of Auchinleck and Mr. Dalzell's (afterwards Earl of Carnwath).[3] I drank above a bottle of claret, and was the better of it. Lord Monboddo, Mr. Gordon, and Mr. Christian drank tea. On my return home from a consultation at Mr. Rae's between nine and ten, I found Signora Marcucci, the Italian dancing-mistress who lives in our stair, had taken refuge with my wife, there being an outrageous mob against the papists.[4] It was strange that I heard nothing of it at Mr. Rae's, though just at the Cross. I got Grange and walked down

---

[1] Boswell had spoken to Johnson on 11 April 1773 of his scheme to write the life of Thomas Ruddiman, distinguished Scottish philologist and Librarian of the Advocates' Library.

[2] Claud Boswell, advocate, Lord Auchinleck's first cousin and brother-in-law. Lord Auchinleck's uncle, John Boswell, had so prospered in his profession of "writer" as to be able to purchase the ancient seat of the Boswells of Balmuto, to whom the Boswells of Auchinleck were a cadet branch. Claud Boswell was the last named heir male to be "called" in the Auchinleck entail. Though Lord Auchinleck's cousin, he was some two years younger than Boswell.

[3] Boswell's great-great-great-great-grandfather, John Boswell of Auchinleck, married Christian, daughter of Robert Dalzell of Dalzell and Elliok, in 1562. The Dalzells of Dalzell later became Earls of Carnwath in 1639, but the title had been forfeited in 1716 because of the overt Jacobitism of the fifth Earl. Boswell's friend Robert Dalzell, advocate, would otherwise himself have become Earl of Carnwath on the death of his father in 1787. Robert Dalzell's nephew was restored to the earldom in 1826.

[4] Parliament had recently passed a bill relaxing many of the penal laws enacted against Roman Catholics in England. The General Assembly of the Church of Scotland had in 1778 pronounced in favour of similar measures for Scots Roman Catholics, but popular fear of relief ran high in Edinburgh. "Copies of the following letter have been industriously dropped in several parts of this city; and we are informed that others, of the same bad tendency, have been handed about among journeymen of different denominations in town: 'Men and brethren, whoever shall find this letter will take as a warning to meet at Leith Wynd on Wednesday next in the evening, to pull down that pillar of popery lately erected there. A Protestant. ...P.S. Please to read this carefully, keep it clean, and drop it somewhere else'" (*Caledonian Mercury*, 1 February 1779). — On 19 April 1777, Boswell rode with Signora Marcucci to dine at Prestonfield. He "was enlivened to Italian pitch, though La Signora seemed so strict a religionist that I saw no prospect for gallantry" (Journal).

the High Street and found so many [4a] of the South Fencibles drawn up before the head of Blackfriars Wynd, in which Bishop Hay has his mass-house. But the mob had been for some hours employed in burning a house at the foot of Trunk [5] Close which formerly belonged to Lord Edgefield and had been lately purchased and fitted up as a Romish chapel. I went close to the scene of action and found so many both of the Town Guard and the Fencibles standing with their arms, which made me suppose that the people whom I heard knocking in the house in flames were extinguishing the fire. But to my astonishment I soon perceived that they were throwing in fuel, and the Lord Provost did not think it prudent to attack them. I was really shocked, and having called silence, I harangued to them a little very keenly; said I loved a mob, but was ashamed of them now, for what could the papists do worse than this? That if the bill should pass, let them march to London and hang Lord North, but as they were assured it was not to pass, why go on in this way? [6] A fellow who did not know me said, "You had better not speak so among the mob." I said, "I'm not afraid of the mob." One who knew me called out with a significant look and manner, "Mr. Boswell, you know we're in the right," and then was great huzzaing and no more could be said. It hurt me to see a large book, perhaps some venerable manuscript, come flaming out at one of the windows. One of the mob cried, "They" (i.e., the papists) "burnt us. We'll burn them." Another cried, "Think what they did to our worthy forefathers." It was striking to see what one has read of religious fury realized. I lost Grange in the crowd, and I went with Mr. John Pringle, the advocate, to the Calton Hill, where crowds were gathered, and there we saw the conflagration very fully. I came home about ten. Signora Marcucci and Grange supped with us.

I should have mentioned that I received a strange shock this morning. When I came to the Court I saw Mr. George Fergusson and several people around him looking surprised and concerned. I asked him what it meant. I shall not forget the affectionate appearance which he had when he said

[4a] A considerable number. This usage, frequent in Boswell's journal, can hardly have been peculiar to him, but we have not found it reported in any historical dictionary or other work dealing with the history of the English language.

[5] Boswell left a blank for this word, which has been supplied from an account of the riot printed in the *Scots Magazine*.

[6] Henry Dundas, Lord Advocate and Member for Edinburghshire, had announced that he would bring in a bill for Catholic relief in Scotland in the next session of Parliament. Scottish Protestants reacted furiously with resolutions and addresses. Even Catholics took alarm and wrote to Lord North asking that the bill be *not* presented. The Town Council of Edinburgh appointed a committee to consult with Dundas, who replied in terms indicating that he would no longer support relief. But the Protestant reaction had by that time got out of hand.

to me, "I am told your father's dead." I was stunned, and knew not what to think or do till Mr. Goodwillie was brought to me and told me that he was in a tavern last night when a card came in to Matthew Dickie: "Lord Auchinleck died this evening at eight o'clock." [7] I was then morally certain it was a brutal lie by way of a joke, as I must have heard of it. I sent immediately to Mr. Dickie and got the card, which was a palpable forgery, if that term can be properly applied in such a case. Yet I was not quite easy till Mr. Lawrie, whom I sent out to my father's to ask *if he was to be out today*, returned and brought me word that he was very well, and was to call his roll of causes at eleven. He accordingly came, looked very well, and gave as far as I could observe a cordial satisfaction to everybody. I got him by the hand with great affection, and was truly comforted after the alarm I had felt, which for a time made me quite giddy. I took no notice to him of the gross trick, and both Balmuto and Grange thought it best not to make any anxious inquiry to find out the wretch who had written the card. I this evening wrote to Dr. Johnson of Garrick's death,[8] and of my interviews with Bishop Falconer.

WEDNESDAY 3 FEBRUARY. (Writing Thursday the 4th.) The mob pillaged Bishop Hay's library in the forenoon with impunity. I went and sat awhile with my father before dinner. Commissioner Cochrane, Charles Preston, and John Webster dined with us.[9] I drank too much port, and was inflamed. Grange walked down with me with intention to go to Canongate-Kilwinning lodge, but there was no meeting, the mob was so violent again tonight.[10] A troop of the 11 Dragoons, commanded by my schoolfellow Captain Hart, were placed at the head of the Canongate to protect the corner shop possessed by Daniel Macdonald, grocer, a papist. The mob had broke his windows. I was quite keen to disperse them, and had it not been for worthy Grange I should probably have been hurt. He and I then went to Crosbie's, whom the mob had threatened, as he had drawn up the bill.[1] Twenty dragoons guarded his house for a while, and he had

---

[7] Matthew Dickie, formerly Boswell's clerk, had been practising as a writer (solicitor) since 1776.

[8] David Garrick, the great actor, had died on 20 January 1779. Boswell had known him since 1760 and had walked down the Strand arm-in-arm with him the previous spring (Journal, 24 April 1778).

[9] A gathering of relations. Basil Cochrane, Commissioner of Customs, was an uncle of Boswell's mother and brother to the late Earl of Dundonald. Boswell often consulted him in matters concerning his disputes with his father. Charles Preston, Cochrane's nephew, would succeed his father, Sir George, in the baronetcy later this year. Capt. John Webster was another cousin on his mother's side.

[10] Boswell, a Mason from the age of eighteen, had been Master of this lodge in 1773, 1774, and 1775.

[1] General studies of the riots do not attribute the authorship of the bill to Andrew

loaded guns and pistols in abundance, and friends about him. As we returned we saw the mob attacking the house of Bayll, the French cook upon the bridge. Grange and Miss Susie Dunlop supped with us.[2] Robert Boswell and Barlay sat awhile, they having been employed in getting some Catholics into the Castle for safety.[3]

THURSDAY 4 FEBRUARY. (Writing on Saturday the 6th.) I laboured well at law papers, though I was a little ill in the morning from having drank too much the day before.

FRIDAY 5 FEBRUARY. (Writing on Saturday the 6th.) Laboured well at a law paper in the forenoon. Dined with Mr. Gordon, Keeper of the Minute-Book. His brother (a Madeira-merchant), the Hon. A. Gordon, Grange, etc., were there. We drank plentifully both of Madeira and claret, and I was a good deal intoxicated. But our noisy merriment and cordiality were great. I had Answers to write for Sir Walter M.-C. to a complaint against him for cutting trees at Lainshaw, and it was necessary that paper should be done this night so as to be printed next forenoon.[4] It was wonderful how well I dictated seven pages, though there were some flashes of intoxication in it. My dear wife then made me bathe my feet in warm water and clear my stomach by drinking warm water, which made me pretty well, only that I talked grossly.

SATURDAY 6 FEBRUARY. (Writing Monday the 8th.) Was wonder-

Crosbie, the able and eccentric advocate who had been Boswell's partner as counsel for the defence in many criminal trials, but John Ramsay of Ochtertyre gives independent testimony to the fact: "Having drawn up the famous popish bill, [Crosbie] was set down as one of these victims of mob-justice. With his usual boldness and eccentricity, he prepared to give them a warm reception, by boiling kettles of pitch and tar and pouring them from the leads on the assailants" (*Scotland and Scotsmen in the Eighteenth Century*, 1888, i. 458 n. 1). Boswell's account, as certainly coming from an eye-witness, is probably more to be trusted than Ramsay's highly-coloured version.

[2] Susan Dunlop was the niece (and step-granddaughter) of Lady Wallace, the second wife of Sir Thomas Wallace, Bt. Her mother, Mrs. Frances Anna Dunlop of Dunlop, later became a favourite correspondent of Robert Burns.

[3] Barlay's name was Horatius Cannan.

[4] Mrs. Boswell's scapegrace nephew, Sir Walter Montgomerie-Cuninghame, laird of Lainshaw, had been left practically penniless by a settlement which his mother had made on her second husband. In the previous year, Boswell representing him as counsel, he had lost before the Court of Session a cause to have this settlement set aside, and the estate had been sequestrated on application of his creditors. Besides cutting trees, he had lately been removing furniture from Lainshaw House. On 12 January Boswell had warned him against cutting trees, telling him that a complaint against him might be made to the courts. On 28 January Boswell informed him that a Petition had indeed been given in against him, and asked him for a "full and candid account, that the best Answer we can may be made" (Register of Letters).

fully well, though not firm and steady. The paper which I had dictated last night required a good deal of correction. I dined at my father's. He appeared to be weary with failure. In the evening I was made happy with a very obliging lively letter from Lord Pembroke.[5] Drank tea at Dr. Young's. Signora Marcucci supped with us.

SUNDAY 7 FEBRUARY. (Writing on Monday the 8th.) Was at the New Church in the forenoon after breakfasting with Mr. Christian. Did not attend much to the young man who preached. Stayed at home in the afternoon to take care of Veronica, who insisted to go out to church. Went with Charles Preston and drank tea at my father's. In the evening Veronica said psalms and catechism, and Effie answered a few questions. Miss Cuninghame was threatened with consumptive complaints. I was somewhat drearily affected with thinking of her danger. I was not quite satisfied with the state of my own life at present. But was not very uneasy. π.

MONDAY 8 FEBRUARY. (Writing on Saturday the 13.) I dictated pretty well. Miss Susie Dunlop dined with us. π.

TUESDAY 9 FEBRUARY. (Writing on Saturday the 13.) This was the fast ordered by the King.[6] I did not think myself bound in conscience to keep it; and having a very long Memorial for Mackilston to write, I dictated busily all day.[7] My father was in church for the first time after his indisposition.

---

[5] "When do you visit the South again? My table is such as can only be tolerable to those who know and care as little for good living as I do and who are not married to hours: and whenever ye can take up with such discomfort, I shall always be happy to see you at it" (From Pembroke, 30 January 1779).

[6] To pray for a favourable outcome in "the just and necessary hostilities in which we are engaged with the French King, and the unnatural rebellion carrying on in some of our provinces and colonies in North America" (*Scots Magazine*, February 1779, xli. 105).

[7] No copy of this Memorial has been found, but it probably dealt with the cause of "the £1,000 bill abstracted from Old Mackilston" (Journal, 1 June 1778), in which we know Boswell was counsel. John Alexander of Mackilston died in September 1776, leaving his estate, except for certain legacies, to his grand-nephew, John Shaw, who was to assume the name of Alexander. A grand-niece, Mary Kerr, cousin to John Shaw, who had lived in John Alexander's house for several years before his death and had received a legacy of £30 in his will, was found to be possessed of a bill of Alexander's for £1,000 which she claimed to have had from him as a free gift. John Alexander-Shaw sued for its return, maintaining that she had obtained it fraudulently. The Lord Ordinary (Gardenstone), having heard Alexander-Shaw's Condescendence and having taken Mary Kerr's declaration in presence, awarded the bill to Alexander-Shaw without proof of the Condescendence (23 July 1777), adhered to his interlocutor (22 November 1777), and refused two more Representations without Answers. She reclaimed to the Lords, who on 28 January 1778 refused her Petition without Answers. A second Petition from her, however, was ordered to be answered. Boswell's printed Answers, 27 February 1778, of which a copy is preserved in the

WEDNESDAY 10 FEBRUARY. (Writing on Saturday the 13.) Sir Walter M.-C. arrived to dinner. In the evening we had a fine party at cards and supper: Miss Ord and Miss Nancy, Miss Susie Dunlop, Sir Henry Hay-Makdougall, Mr. Baron Norton, Mr. Nairne, Dr. and Mrs. Young, Mr. Christian, and Sir Walter. We had cheerfulness, elegance, and sobriety. My dear wife and I were both quite pleased. π.

THURSDAY 11 FEBRUARY. (Writing on Saturday the 13.) I dined at General Skene's with Balmuto and several more. Drank liberally. Sir Walter, Grange, and Mr. James Baillie supped with us.

FRIDAY 12 FEBRUARY. (Writing on Sunday the 14.) Sir Walter, Dr. Deans from Stewarton, and Matthew Dickie dined with us. Deans had not been in Edinburgh for above twenty years. It was comfortable to see him with my wife and her children. I drank rather too much cider and porter and port. Surgeon Wood and Apothecary Moncrieff drank tea with us. Sir Walter and I then settled some business at William Wilson's.[8] I was restless after I came home, and took Sir Walter with me a walk down to the Abbey. When we returned, Major Hugh Montgomerie was sitting with my wife and Miss Cuninghame, and as he had engaged to sup at Walker's and was to set out for London next morning, he pressed us to be of the party, to which we agreed. I was in stout spirits, and drank strong beer and wines very heartily, there being with us Glenlyon's brother (an old captain of Fraser's who had been much wounded at the taking of Quebec, one of the biggest men that I ever saw, and though the descendant of one of those who committed the massacre at Glencoe, a very worthy man),[9] Duntroon (another Campbell, captain in the Western Fencibles [1]), a brother of Nisbet of Greenholm's, Bruce Campbell, and a Mr. Charles MacNeil from Campbeltown, whom I did not like, as he affected not to have anything of a Highlander about him. Sir Walter and Hugh Montgomerie were gone about one. But I was by that time deep in intoxication

---

Signet Library, provide a full narrative of the action to that date. The Lords must have decided to hear the cause, for Boswell's journal of 1 June 1778, quoted above, shows him taking proof. The outcome of the cause has not yet been traced.

[8] Boswell and Sir Walter no doubt had a good deal of business to discuss with William Wilson, W.S., Sir Walter's solicitor and agent. See above, 5 February 1779 and n. 4.

[9] When Macdonald of Glencoe delayed signing the oath of allegiance to King William III, he and more than thirty members of his clan were massacred (February 1692–1693) by order of the Privy Council. Campbell of Glenlyon led the band of slayers. Boswell thought his drinking companion was that Campbell's grandson and representative, John Campbell of Glenlyon, but finding out later that he was his brother, Archibald Campbell, he made the necessary corrections, overlooking, however, one "Glenlyon" farther on in the entry.

[1] His Christian name was Neill.

and Highland enthusiasm, so that Glenlyon [2] and Duntroon and I were the warmest friends, sung *"Hatyin foam eri"* [3] again and again, shook hands, and made kindly professions, pouring down strong rum punch without souring. In short it was an extraordinary riot, and I did not get home till five in the morning.

SATURDAY 13 FEBRUARY. (Writing on Sunday the 14.) I awaked before nine very ill. Fell asleep again and did not awake till one. Was in (writing Tuesday 16 February) sad wretchedness and afraid I could not recover. My dear wife had been frightened and kept from rest all night. Lay till five. Rose giddy and dejected. Had two long papers upon my hands and a *Hypochondriack* to write for Tuesday's post. Had a short consultation, as if in a palsy.

SUNDAY 14 FEBRUARY. (Writing Tuesday the 16th.) Was little better. Stayed at home in the forenoon, and being quite miserable that I had not written to my dearest friend Temple for above three months, and wanting much the consolation of friendship, wrote to him. Went to the New Church with my wife in the afternoon and had some comfort in hearing Mr. Walker preach, but was woefully deficient in steady principles. Grange had gone to the country for a day or two. Paid a visit to my father, whom I had not visited since Sunday last. My two daughters and Sandy followed me, and though it came on a pretty heavy rain, they were sent away without the coach. Such cold and unfeeling treatment shocked me. I went home with them. I was feeble and sunk. My father was failed, and his appearance affected me gloomily. Yet I envied the steady, regular, prudent conduct he had maintained through life, and did not think with any pleasure of the superior warmth of enjoyment in various ways which had been my lot. I drank coffee and grew a little better at night. Was affectionate to my wife and children.

[EDITORIAL NOTE. For the days remaining till his departure for London, Boswell kept only brief notes, part of them dictated to his clerk, John Lawrie. He indulged in more expeditions to Portsburgh (19 February, 1 March), and had a remarkable dream that a bit of glass was caught in his throat: "coughed till I was stressed" (i.e., "till I strained myself, till I was fatigued"). Sir George Preston died on 2 March, and on 5 March Boswell went to Valleyfield. "Dreary coffining Sir George. It impressed mortality so strong. Lady Preston crying and feeble." Next day: "Decent

[2] See the last note but one.
[3] A Gaelic song, taking its title from the refrain *"Tha tighinn fodham éiridh,"* meaning "It comes upon me to arise"—i.e., for the Jacobite cause. Boswell's phonetics are English. He learned the song while touring the Hebrides with Johnson (*Journal,* 8 September 1773).

funeral. Was pretty firm. Visited Lady Dundonald at Culross. Gravel walk revived ideas of my mother, etc." It is a great pity that Boswell thus allowed Sir George Preston to pass from his life and journal in a sort of parenthesis, as he did Lady Preston who was to die eight months later. Both, as he had recently said (see above, 16 October 1778) had been like parents to him and his wife ever since their marriage.]

WEDNESDAY 10 MARCH. (Writing in London, 26 March.) My dear wife had everything in good order for my London journey, and gave me a comfortable dish of tea between five and six. We parted affectionately, and at six I got into the Newcastle diligence, Mr. Lawrie faithfully attending. I was more composed than ever before on such an occasion. A good, quiet, south-countryman went with me as far as Kelso, where we dined. I drank no wine. I was alone the afternoon. I read in *Le Sopha*, which Wilkes had lent me,[4] and in a Cornelius Nepos which I bought at Kelso. Lay at Wooler, where I only drank tea. My mind was calm. But I was distressed somewhat with anxiety about my father, who was not well when I left him. But Mr. Wood assured me there was no immediate danger; and I trusted that if there should be danger, I would hear in time to get down to him. Moreover, I considered with regret that I could do little good to him when present, as he was now so abstracted from his children by his second wife. I must own that I was very desirous not to be from home at the time of his funeral, as I had resolved it should be sumptous [5] for the honour of the family, as that makes a lasting impression. Our family has always had it.

THURSDAY 11 MARCH. (Writing in London, 2 April.) Got to Newcastle to dinner. Found my brother John remarkably well.[6] Mrs. Atkins, his landlady, whom I visited first, told me that he was odd and ill-tempered. But he went with me to my inn, where I dined, and he eat something and drank porter and wine really socially. I had drank only water yesterday, but was glad to take something better with John and indulge brotherly affection. He talked quite sensibly in every respect but of his confinement formerly. I sat a little both with Dr. Hall and Mr. Leighton. John drank coffee with me. Two sons of Stothart, the smith

---

[4] A "moral tale" by Crébillon. Wilkes had been a personal acquaintance of the author.

[5] See above, p. 21 n. 6.

[6] Lt. John Boswell, Boswell's younger brother, suffered from periodic attacks of insanity. After being for some time a patient in Dr. John Hall's St. Luke's House, a mental hospital in Newcastle, he had gone to board with Mrs. Aitken, widow of a dissenting clergyman who had once been Lord Auchinleck's tutor. Dr. Hall and James Leighton, surgeon in Newcastle, however, continued to keep an eye on him.

at Auchinleck, who follow that trade at Newcastle, came to us for a little. I went to bed to take a little sleep.

FRIDAY 12 MARCH. Got into the diligence about two with a disagreeable old sailor and his old wife, who went with me all the way to York, where I found the Assizes. Got myself clean and went to the concert and Assembly, which was elegant. Met several counsel whom I had seen at Carlisle last autumn. Waited on Judge Willes, who received me most courteously; made me eat some supper, though his was over, and drink some wine with him, nobody being there but the Marshal of Court. He was pleasant and sensible too, and I felt myself quite as I could wish: an agreeable Scotch gentleman creditably received by an English judge. I then called on Counsellor Macdonald and drank some negus with him and his lady. Returned a little to the Assembly. Had called twice on Dr. Burgh, the learned, ingenious, orthodox Irish gentleman to whom I had a letter from Mr. Cayley last May, when I was so sunk that I could not go to see him.[7] He was not at home. Went to bed cheerful. Let me be thankful to GOD for such good spirits.

[EDITORIAL NOTE. Boswell's later London journals (that of 1778, printed in *Boswell in Extremes*, is the best example) usually begin as finished narratives, fully and carefully written in bound notebooks, but soon collapse into hasty records of various degrees of fulness written on loose leaves of various sizes. The fully written journal this year breaks off with Boswell only halfway to London. The complication of engagement lists, notes, and fully written entries which begins with the day of his arrival there is described above in the section of our Introduction headed "Documentation," as are also our devices for establishing a readable text. All that the reader really needs to know for proceeding is that square brackets indicate editorial expansion of crabbed passages while angular brackets indicate defects in the manuscripts the restoration of which involves a considerable degree of conjecture. How it happens that some portions of this record are now published for the first time is also explained in the section on Documentation.]

MONDAY 15 MARCH. Arrived.

TUESDAY 16 MARCH. <Rose well, agit>ated yet steady. Called on Mr.

---

[7] William Burgh, layman and politician, had in 1774 attacked the Unitarian doctrines of Theophilus Lindsey in a work entitled *A Scriptural Confutation of Arguments against the One Godhead of the Father, Son, and Holy Ghost*, and had in consequence been rewarded with an Oxford degree of D.C.L. Though Irish by birth, Burgh had long lived in York. William Cayley was Rector of Thorpe, Godfrey Bosville's parish.

Robert Preston and talked with him about James Cuninghame.[8] Then walked to Bolt Court to wait on Dr. Johnson. Met Mr. Collet, his barber, who said he was not up yet.[9] Therefore I went first and sat a little with Mr. Jones, who told me he had been ill and had now given up being the conductor of the *London Chronicle*. I then found Mr. Strahan at home, and was pleased with his wealthy plumpness and good animal spirits and his wish to communicate to me all that he knew concerning Dr. Johnson. I next went to the Doctor's and found him sitting at breakfast, attended by Mrs. Desmoulins and Mr. Levett and a Mr. Tasker, a clergyman who had written *The Warlike Genius of Britain* and several other occasional poems. My revered friend embraced me with cordial complacency,[10] though (strange to tell) I found that he had been angry with me for writing with anxiety about him, after his being long silent. He certainly has not quick and delicate sensations of affection and its concomitant anxiety; and therefore suspects that professions made by others are not true, which I am sure mine are. He looked better than ever I saw him do, and I was in better health and spirits than I ever experienced, so all was gladness. After a few kind inquiries, he resumed the irksome business in which Tasker had engaged him, which was reading his poetry. Tasker had seen the Doctor at the performance of the *Carmen Seculare* set to modern music,[1] had made him a present of some of his poetical pamphlets, and thus had obtained an invitation to come and see him. The Doctor was now engaged in the perusal of a translation of the *Carmen Seculare* into English verse by this Tasker. After he had done, Tasker asked him bluntly if upon the whole it was a good translation? Dr. Johnson, who is truth itself, was sadly puzzled for a little what answer to make, <wishing> at least, I suppose, <not to condemn> as he certainly could not commend the performance. With great address he answered thus: "Sir, I do not say that it may not be made a very good translation," <or some

[8] Captain Robert Preston of the East India Company sea service (later Sir Robert Preston of Valleyfield), Boswell's first cousin once removed, was helping Boswell place another of the orphaned Cuninghames. Preston having arranged passage to India for the boy, Boswell somehow detached him from a private academy in Hampstead, the proprietor of which threatened to hold him for his dues, and advanced £100 for his outfit and passage with credit for another £100 at Madras. James had sailed on the *Ceres* on 8 March.

[9] "For the last twenty-four years of his life Mr. Matthew Collet officiated as [Johnson's] barber" (from a passage marked for deletion in Paper Apart "Varia" for the MS. of the *Life of Johnson*, p. 966).

[10] That is, complaisance. Johnson's *Dictionary* permits the spelling "complacency" for both meanings.

[1] In the *Life of Johnson* Boswell expands this to "the *Carmen Seculare* of Horace, which had this year been set to music and performed as a public entertainment in London for the joint benefit of Monsieur Philidor and Signor Baretti."

such> exquisite evasion. Nothing whatever in favour of the performance
was affirmed, and yet the poor fellow was not shocked. Tasker appeared
to me to be a foolish, scatter-brained creature. He was a lank, bony figure
with short black hair. He had an idiotical grin, showing his teeth while
he talked, and uttering in a squeaking tone while the Doctor read to himself his *Ode to the Warlike Genius of Britain*,[2] "Is that poetry, Sir? Is it
Pindar?" "Why, Sir," said the Doctor, "there is here a great deal of what
is called poetry." Tasker, while the Doctor read, gave me some abrupt
exclamations, such as, "My muse has not been long upon the town." And
(meaning his poem), "It trembles under the hand of the great critic." The
Doctor, in a tone of displeasure, said to him, "Why do you praise Anson?"[3]
<I knew> not the reason of his being <so annoyed> and did not trouble
him by asking. The Doctor proceeded, "Here is an error, Sir; you have
made Genius feminine." "Palpable, Sir," cried Tasker, "I know it. But
it was to pay a compliment to the Duchess of Devonshire, with which her
Grace was pleased. She is walking across Coxheath, in the militia uniform,
and I suppose her to be the Genius of Britain."[4] "Sir," <said the Doctor>
"you are giving a reason for it, but that will not make it right. You may
have a reason why two and two should not make four. But they will still
make four. <You may> as well make ———."[5] I interposed and said, "As
the Duchess is moving along in her military uniform, with hat and feather
and everything else, might not the gentleman, instead of making Genius
feminine, make the Duchess masculine?"

I got back to Dilly's at three and dined, Dr. Jefferies (a Civilian)[6] and
Mr. ———, a woollen manufacturer at Wilton (two violent Dissenters,
against any test),[7] being the company. Their untutored tumultous talk

---

[2] Some years after the publication of the *Life of Johnson* (which suppresses William
Tasker's name), Isaac D'Israeli met him at a watering-place in Devonshire and
recognized him at once from his resemblance to Boswell's description.

[3] Johnson probably said "Amherst"; at any rate it is he, not Anson, who is praised
in the poem. The third edition is dedicated to Amherst.

[4] In the eighth stanza of the *Ode*:

> Art thou Britannia's Genius? say!
> Or, in the softer features of thy face,
> Trace we the likeness of the Malbro' race?
> Hail! fair Devonia! hail!
> Thy powerful charms prevail.

[5] Boswell left a blank (apparently for several words) here, surely because he could
not recall the precise terms of Johnson's comparison and hoped to recover them later.
When he wrote the *Life of Johnson,* he gave up and omitted the sentence.

[6] That is, a practitioner of Civil Law, Professor at Gresham College.

[7] In effect, completely opposed to the principle that none but persons professing
the established religion should be eligible for public office in England. From the late
seventeenth century on, all persons filling any office civil or military had been obliged

disgusted me.[8] After tea, I marched to the other end of the town, intending to have called at General Paoli's [8a] to inform him of my arrival, that my room might be prepared, and at Sir John Pringle's, that I might not be long in town without waiting on him. But Lady Margaret Macdonald, on whom I called first, kept me so long that I had only time to get back to my habitation in the Poultry at a regular hour. I eat something light, read some of Dr. Johnson's *Prefaces to the Poets,*[9] and went cheerful to bed.

[EDITORIAL NOTE: Boswell turned up at Paoli's for breakfast on the 17th, and presumably moved into his house that day. In the next week he saw Johnson at least three times (on the 19th, 23rd, and 25th) and Burke at least twice; dined out almost every night (on the 19th at The Club), and renewed friendship with Bennet Langton, Thomas Barnard, General Oglethorpe, and Godfrey Bosville. The following journal entry for 26 March, recording only Johnsonian matter, was later revised by Boswell and used as printer's copy for the *Life of Johnson.* We now print it for the first time as Boswell originally wrote it.]

FRIDAY 26 MARCH. Dr. Johnson said he expected to be attacked when his *Lives of the Poets* came out. The worst thing you can do to a man is to be silent. An assault of a town is a bad thing, but starving it is still worse. An assault may be unsuccessful; you may have more men killed than you kill. But if you starve [the town] you are sure of a victory. I said an assault may only serve to show the strength of a town.

Talking of Sir Joshua having Macpherson with him, I said Sir Joshua was a very universal man, quite a man of the world.[1] JOHNSON. "Yes, Sir.

---

to take certain oaths devised to exclude Roman Catholics, and to receive the sacrament of the Lord's supper according to the rites of the Church of England.

[8] For the spelling "tumultous," see above, p. 21 n. 6.

[8a] The remainder of this paragraph is now printed for the first time.

[9] He was probably reading from printed but unpublished sheets furnished by Dilly, as he had in 1778. The first instalment (vols. 1–4) of the *Prefaces ... to the Works of the English Poets* (later titled *Lives of the English Poets*) was published in this spring but probably not so early as March. No advertisement earlier than the end of June has been reported. Johnson had sent the King a presentation set by 10 March, but says that the books were at that time not quite printed off. He had sent a presentation set to Mrs. Thrale by 9 April.

[1] As revised for the *Life of Johnson,* this passage reads, "Talking of a friend of ours associating with persons of very discordant principles and characters." Sir Joshua would indeed have found much in James Macpherson's principles and character that clashed with his own. Macpherson was widely reputed to be a literary impostor, and had certainly threatened Johnson with violence for saying so. Moreover, he was leader of the Government press which was defending the American war (Reynolds opposed it) and had attacked Reynolds's patron and intimate friend Admiral Keppel. (See below, p. 62 n. 5.) Reynolds, however, picked his guests not because he liked

But one may be so much a man of the world as to be nothing in the world. I remember a passage in Goldsmith's *Vicar of Wakefield* which he was afterwards fool enough to put out: 'I do not love a man who is zealous for nothing.' " BOSWELL. "That was a fine passage." JOHNSON. "Yes, Sir. There was another fine passage too which he put out. A young man anxious to distinguish himself said he started new propositions. 'But,' said he, 'I soon gave this over, for I found that generally what was new was false.' "

I said I did not like to sit with people of whom I had not a good opinion. Said he, "But you must not propagate [2] your delicacy too much, or you will be a tête-à-tête man all your life."

[EDITORIAL NOTE: The tiny scrap which remains of the notes for Saturday 27 March appears to show that Boswell saw Johnson on that day. The entries for 28, 29, 30 March are now first printed.]

SUNDAY 28 MARCH. A<t ten> Portuguese Chapel. <Calmly> devout. Found Lord Mountstuart.[3] He was easy. Walked with him to Langton's, where he had said he would not let me into his house, as I told everything. Saw I must guard against this. Langton and I walked to Tyburn and were *happy*, contrary to Pope's "never is." [4] He owned he had had all my enthusiasm about London and players. Saw Mrs. Montagu's <house> [and said it looked] like a billiard-player <aim>ing for a pocket into <the> Square.[5] Langton said Johnson had a sacred horror for religion. Dined Sir John Pringle agreeably with Colonel ———— [6]

them but because they were well known and could be of use to him in his profession. His appointment-book seems to indicate that he was painting a portrait of Macpherson at this time: appointments at painting hours on 16, 22, 26 March, and 2 April, and a second appointment, certainly for dinner, at five o'clock on 26 March, the very day Boswell is recording.

[2] That is, "cultivate." The reading of the *Life of Johnson* is "indulge."

[3] John Stuart, Lord Mountstuart, later fourth Earl and first Marquess of Bute, had been Boswell's travelling companion in Italy. His father, the third Earl of Bute, was Prime Minister, 1762–1763. Boswell had hopes of obtaining preferment through Mountstuart's influence.

[4] The words arbitrarily transcribed "contrary to" are represented in the manuscript by the symbol meaning "versus" or "against" which Boswell regularly employs in citing legal cases. "Pope's 'never is' " is explained by a previous passage of the journal: "Such glimpses of pure felicity are permitted, to cheer us in our way and give us a persuasion by experience that *man may* be blest. Pope [*An Essay on Man*, i. 96] says he 'never *is*, but (is) always *to be*, blest.' ... But this night I *was* fully happy in immediate sensation and hope" (Journal, 17 March 1778).

[5] Mrs. Montagu was building a great new house, designed by James ("Athenian") Stuart at No. 1 Upper Berkeley Street, in the north-west angle of Portman Square. She did not move into it till the end of 1781.

[6] An abbreviated name not yet deciphered. It looks like "Mart." Possibly Arthur George

<who told> me Mrs. Montagu's <mot on > Marchmont, " 'Polwarth *is* a slave' now not irony should Mr. Hugh not remain." [7] Quite easy in coach with Thrales, <felt> gay. Found Dr. Johnson <there> [8] with Miss Burney. Supped quite [9] . . .

MONDAY 29 MARCH. Had read Joel Collier and some of Warton's *Pope*.[1] At breakfast fine. [As to] marriage of daughters [I said they had] no rights but [must do] as we please. JOHNSON. "Nay, this [is] childish. Now you're [your] one-and-twenty self." Epigrams cherished. "Hermit hoar." [2] In coach, to town, quite happy. [Dr. Johnson] said [that when I became laird] I should save six hundred a year. JOHNSON. "Will you go some yards out of your way for me?" [3] BOSWELL. "Will go twenty miles." Douglas [interlocutors] affirmed, beautiful <speech>.[4] Dined with him.

Martin, captain in the Coldstream Guards, colonel in the Army, who died major-general in 1782.

[7] Hugh Hume-Campbell, third Earl of Marchmont, Pope's close friend and one of his executors, while still a commoner with the courtesy style of Lord Polwarth, had been a conspicuous member of the Opposition in the Commons. Pope's "Cobham's a coward, Polwarth is a slave" (*Epilogue to the Satires*, ii. 130) was indeed heavily ironical. The allusion here is obscure but perhaps points to a developing family quarrel involving Lord Marchmont, his son-in-law Sir John Paterson, and his grandson Hugh Scott, younger of Harden. Paterson was elected M.P. for Berwickshire on Marchmont's interest on 15 April 1779. Hugh Scott, who came of age at just that time, announced his intention to contest the seat at the coming general election of 1780. Mrs. Montagu presumably implied that Marchmont would be shown to have no will of his own if he tamely allowed his grandson to unseat a candidate he himself had backed. Marchmont in fact bitterly resented Scott's intervention, and when his only son, Lord Polwarth, died without issue in 1781, cut Scott off from succession to the Marchmont estates.

[8] At Streatham, the country home of the Thrales.

[9] About seven letters undeciphered.

[1] *Musical Travels through England*, "by Joel Collier, organist," 1774, was written to ridicule Dr. Charles Burney's *Travels* (1771, 1773); Boswell says that it also makes "a slight attempt to ridicule Johnson" (*Life of Johnson*, under the year 1756). "Joel Collier" was a pseudonym. Boswell says the author was John Bicknell, d. 1787; the *Dictionary of National Biography* identifies the author as a musician named George Veal.— Joseph Warton's *Essay on the Writings and Genius of Pope* had been published so far back as 1756; the second volume did not appear till 1782.

[2] At Ashbourne, 18 September 1777, Johnson had improvised a stanza ridiculing the "bad style of poetry" into which he considered Thomas Warton to have got; on 9 May 1778, in London, he added a second ludicrous stanza, but would not repeat it for Boswell to record. For the two stanzas, see *Life of Johnson*, 18 September 1777.

[3] Thrale's coach, coming from Streatham, has crossed London Bridge and has proceeded up Cheapside and Fleet Street. Johnson is asking Boswell if he will allow the coachman to turn off Fleet Street into Bolt Court instead of proceeding directly to General Paoli's house in South Audley Street, Westminster.

[4] The interlocutors of the Court of Session in Duke of Hamilton v. Archibald Douglas

of statesmen, etc." [6] He wished to travel; repeated Martial's fine epigram on Aetna, ómitted by Addison.[7] I said he should travel as [Joseph] did till [he] heard Herod was dead (till a change of Ministry). Said he, "Herod will outlive me." "No, no," said I, "you'll out-herod Herod." [8] He repeated some fine passages from Cowley: *To [the] Royal Society* and of the Thames.[9] Said Johnson had given too much of Dryden's antagonists. He said Fitzherbert was miserable—had scurvy.[1] "But," said I, "hanging [is] not [usually prescribed] for that." BURKE. "[A] *scurvy* cure." After supper we talked of religion. He thought Christianity a healing system, a sacrifice. Would rather commit ten thousand sins than trust to his own merits. That as to eternity of punishment, he respectfully waived it. But if pushed, would deny it. Yet he would apply to it the text, "With men impossible, but with God all things possible." [2] As to [what he would say to] a son [of his pursuit] of women, respect and delicacy would prevent speaking. Should think of [a] son's licentiousness in that as of one's own: with tenderness and regret. That [it was] dangerous to preach limitation of punishment. All papists wished to be in purgatory. [We spoke of] Ossian. [He said there were] no *belles-lettres* [written] in Scots. Blair's *Dissertation* enough to damn [any] reputation for it.[3] He said Johnson would never correct what one suggested. BOSWELL. "*I* once made him [correct a line in *The Vanity of Human Wishes*: 'Spreads from the strong contagion of the gown' to] '*Burns* from the strong,' etc." [4] BURKE. "That is better than at first." BOSWELL. "Yes, as if he caught fire from the gown <itself,> like Hercules's shirt."

---

[6] *Paradise Lost*, iv. 763–766:

      Here love his golden shafts employs . . .

      . . . .

      . . . not in the bought smile

      Of harlots.

[7] A nest of puzzles. Martial has no epigram on Aetna; he does have one (iv. 44) on Vesuvius, but Addison does quote that epigram (under Capri) in his *Remarks on Several Parts of Italy*. The most plausible explanation would perhaps be that Burke quoted an epigram then attributed to Martial but now considered spurious.

[8] *Hamlet*, III. ii. 15.

[9] The Cowley passage "of the Thames" is from the ninth stanza of *To the Royal Society*.

[1] William Fitzherbert, M.P., Johnson's friend, had hanged himself in 1772 because of pecuniary troubles.

[2] Matthew 19. 26.

[3] There were in Gaelic no writings of a purely literary kind. Hugh Blair's *Critical Dissertation on the Poems of Ossian* (1763) was enough to destroy whatever reputation Macpherson's "translations" might have gained.

[4] Line 138. Boswell objected to "spreads" because the next verse ended with "spread": "O'er Bodley's dome his future labours spread."

THURSDAY 1 APRIL. Breakfasted David Rae. Called Sir John Pringle. Then Dr. Johnson. [He commended the] old Duke of Devonshire's "dogged veracity." Elphinston, [he said, was very] fit for a travelling governor. His manner so bad [no danger of a young gentleman catching it.] Like a drunken helot.[5] JOHNSON. "If pleasure be intellectual, more can be had in London for the money, even by ladies. You cannot play tricks with [your] fortune in a small place. Here [a] lady [may have a] well-furnished apartment and dress, [and] no meat in [her] kitchen. [When I first came to town,] at [the] Pineapple in New Street, Covent Garden, [I] dined for eightpence. About twelve men [met there] many [of whom had] travelled; expected to see each other [every day, but] did not know each other's names."

Called Dr. Wilson and Langton a little. Dined home, meagre; [6] Cambiagi, Poggi.[7] Then Langton's to write journal. [But] only read and talked. Much pleased with *Government of [the] Tongue.*[8] Read out paper of *Rambler* on Holy Thursday. Cloudy a little. Said Johnson could not give real scenes of life so clean as Fielding; always [covered] with bulk of sentiment like earth, not clean lines as in *Covent Garden [Journal.]* Langton said, "With no husk or fibre." [9] Supped there.

FRIDAY 2 APRIL. Good Friday. Dr. Johnson. Spoke of [our] ridicule [of Langton]. Burrows [in] sermon [at St. Clement Danes said] we must all give account [of our deeds,] even evil-speaking. JOHNSON. "Sense of ridicule [is] given [us, and may be lawfully used]. *Government of [the] Tongue* [would have us] treat all men alike." Dilly's. Dr. Wilson's. Sir

---

[5] Elphinston's name is omitted in the *Life.* "The Spartans would force [the helots] to drink too much strong wine, and then introduce them into their public messes, to show the young men what a thing drunkenness was" (Plutarch's *Lycurgus*, xxviii, translation by Bernadotte Perrin, Loeb Classics).

[6] That is, *maigre*, on Lenten fare.

[7] Anthony Poggi, a Corsican, was a painter; Cambiagi is not certainly identified, but may have been Giovacchino Cambiagi (1740–c. 1801), a Florentine printer who published a four-volume history of Corsica, 1770–1772.

[8] 1674, by the author of *The Whole Duty of Man* (probably Richard Allestree). Boswell's copy in the Hyde Collection bears the following inscription: "James Boswell, London, 1779. Presented to me by my worthy friend Bennet Langton, Esq., of Langton, as a book by which I might be much improved, viz., by the government of the tongue. He gave me the book and hoped I would read that treatise, but said no more. I have expressed in words what I believe was his meaning. It was a delicate admonition."

[9] Boswell actually wrote "wt. not husk or fibre," but there can be little or no doubt as to what he intended. Langton is suggesting an improvement on his figure of unobscured clean lines.

J. Pringle's. [The] Club. Memorandum: Like Clack's wife, though she did not make me break Ten Commandment.[1]

SATURDAY 3 APRIL. Breakfast home. Dinner home, meagre. (Lord Lisburne [pictured] Burke [as formerly] knocking at door and playing tunes; is now pulling down <hou>se). Then coffee. Then [the] Park; with Mrs. Vaughan to Chelsea.[2] Found Dr. Webster. Then Dr. Johnson's a little. ———, Lord Southwell's natural son,[3] and Mrs. Williams [sitting] at oysters. Up to his room. [He] opposed Heberden's toleration, and said, "You are so far hurt by knowing even one man does not believe. Would he let me teach his children not to be Christians?"[4] Of Burke's good evening with me [he] said, "If a man be orthodox in religion, I do not much mind his politics," (or, "will not quarrel with him.") Was quite well. Dilly's comfortable.

SUNDAY 4 APRIL. Easter. Breakfast Chapter [Coffee-house.] Then St. Paul's. Webster <there. No>bly devout. At altar thanked GOD for uniting Auchinleck and St. Paul's—romantic seat of my ancestors and this grand cathedral— "in the imagination which Thou hast given me." Dined Dr. Johnson. Allen; formal. Remembering nothing the Doctor said but [that] he was passing by a fishmonger who was skinning an eel alive, and he was angry [because] it would not lie still. Mrs. Knowles reading Swedenborg. Then Exchange Coffee-house. Dilly's. Home.

MONDAY 5 APRIL. Dined Langton's; carried there in Lord Mountstuart's coach. Lord Winchilsea, etc. Very well. Lord Mountstuart got into a familiar manner with me. Said he'd do for me of his own accord. Walked a good way with him. Supped H. Baldwin's; Lockyer Davis, etc. Very merry:

> After you have eat enough,
> Will you taste a printer's puff?

[1] In other words, "Remember when you write to Temple to say that you like Claxton's wife, though she did not make you break the commandment not to covet the wife of one's neighbour." John Claxton, F.S.A., counsellor-at-law of Lincoln's Inn, a common friend of Temple and Boswell, had married since Boswell's last visit to London. Boswell did include the witticism in a letter to Temple which he wrote on 6 April.

[2] Not identified. She was perhaps a connexion of Lord Lisburne's (whose family name was Vaughan), and if so may well have reported to Boswell Lisburne's saying concerning Burke.

[3] Mauritius Lowe, a painter, natural son of Thomas Southwell, second Baron Southwell.

[4] William Heberden, M.D., was "the last of the learned physicians," according to Johnson, whom he attended during his life and in his last illness. His doctrine of universal toleration had been conveyed to Boswell in conversation.

MRS. BALDWIN: "And see if it be good stuff." Mansion-house Ball with C. Dilly. Great spirits.

[From the *Public Advertiser*, 8 April 1779. By Boswell]

To the Printer of the *Public Advertiser*

6 April 1779

SIR,—I am by birth a *North Briton*, as a *Scotchman* must now be called, but like a great many of my countrymen love much to come to London. And why not, Sir? as since the union of the two kingdoms, which deprived us of all national dignity and all the advantages of a vice-court and of a parliament in our own district, London is now the metropolis of the whole island, the grand emporium of everything valuable, the strong centre of attraction for all of us, His Majesty's British subjects, from the Land's End to Caithness. Full of high notions of this GREAT CITY and of its CHIEF MAGISTRATE, the LORD MAYOR, in the *abstract*, without respect of persons (as I am now old enough to know that the Mansion-house is successively inhabited by men of all characters, and that *there*, as at Baldock's mill,

> The grave and the gay, the clown and the beau,
> Without all distinction promiscuously go),[5]

I went last night to the ball at the Mansion-house, and having feasted my eyes and my ears for some time, I desired to have a little negus to recruit my animal spirits. But what was my astonishment, Sir, when the waiters told me I could not have it; it was all gone, they had no more wine. Several ladies and gentlemen, I found, were in the same state of disappointment that I was. Upon which, Sir, I asked an English friend if this could possibly be countenanced by the Lord Mayor. I was informed he was a Mr. Alderman Plumbe, but that his penuriousness was excessive.[6] I was determined however that he should not escape quite *impune*,[7] if he

---

[5] From the very popular ballad "The Maid of the Mill," said to have been written c. 1745 by the then curate of Baldock in Hertfordshire in praise of Mary Ireland, daughter of the miller and inn-keeper of Baldock. Most of our information concerning the piece comes from the *Memoirs* of Boswell's irresponsible acquaintance Percival Stockdale. The first stanza runs:

> Who has e'er been at Baldock must needs know the mill,
> With the sign of the Horse, at the foot of the hill;
> Where the grave and the gay, the clown and the beau,
> Without all distinction promiscuously go.

[6] Samuel Plumbe, Sheriff in 1776–1777, Mayor 1778–1779, Vice-President of the Honourable Artillery Company, President of St. Thomas's Hospital, had a general reputation for stinginess. His wife was Henry Thrale's sister.

[7] Without punishment.

had any *feeling*, and that I should be, if not a *thorn*, at least a *thistle* in his side. Accordingly, away I marched to find his *Lordship*; and pray, Sir, how d'ye think I found him occupied? Upon my honour (and I can bring fifty witnesses, with a city marshal at their head), I found him standing without his gown or chain, in a bag-wig and marone [8] coat, with his back leaning against the staircase, telling the company not to go upstairs, in order that he might get rid of them. Up I went, though, in the first place to the Egyptian Hall, to see what was doing; and *there* was a number of ladies and gentlemen standing up for a country dance; but when they called for music, they were told the music were discharged [9] by the Lord Mayor to play any more without fresh orders; and in a little time they moved off, amidst the hisses of the company, who I took it for granted would have instantly broke his lamps into shivers with a just indignation.

But to return to my negus, *his Lordship*, having come upstairs, stood despondent in one of the antechambers. I went to him, and with a low bow addressed him thus: "My Lord Mayor, I ask pardon for giving your Lordship this trouble, but I beg your Lordship would order me a glass of negus. I am afraid your Lordship is ill used by some of your servants. I asked for negus, and they told me there was none."

Now, Mr. Woodfall, upon the word of an honest man, which *you know* I am, I shall give you literally what passed, without the least exaggeration. His Lordship with awkward surprise and confusion said, "Sir, I *wish* you had asked for it sooner." I would not quit him. "My Lord," said I (putting the breasts of my coat in a buttoning attitude), "I have got a little cold; if you'll let me have a single glass, I'll be obliged to you. Here, Sir" (calling one of his silver-laced attendants who approached us), "if your Lordship will please give your orders to one of your servants—" "Sir," (replied THE LORD MAYOR of LONDON), "I have no command of the negus"—and slunk away.

Now, Sir, are not you Englishmen a set of pretty fellows? You talk with horror of an Edinburgh mob committing a few outrages, and you say not a word of a London mob the very week after breaking half the windows of

---

[8] Maroon. As an adjective denoting colour, this word was just coming into the English language. (The ultimate source is Italian *marrone*, "chestnut.") Boswell's use of it is interesting as antedating by twelve years the first occurrence noted in the *Oxford English Dictionary*.

[9] The presence of an off-print of this letter among the Boswell papers at Yale (type arranged in one long column on a narrow slip of paper, with blank verso) makes it likely that Boswell had a number of copies printed to give away. In the Yale copy he has written "forbid" opposite "discharged," probably as a gloss. "Discharge" in the sense of "forbid" was a Scotticism, but in this letter one thinks he would have tended to introduce Scotticisms, not to remove them.

your peaceable citizens. You talk of Scotch poverty, yet I will venture to say that at no public entertainment in the pettiest borough in Scotland would a gentleman have been refused a glass of negus. The Provost (or Mayor) of little Lord Galloway's little borough of Whithorn [1] would have lived on herrings and water for a week, rather than have his *toon* (*town*) so disgraced. At Edinburgh, *Walter Hamilton,* our worthy LORD PROVOST, would have ordered a DOUBLE BOTTLE, a SCOTCH PINT,[2] a BONUM MAGNUM of excellent CLARET (which by the way, Harry,[3] you would like very well to see) and would show that he "has the command" of a generous cellar. But in the *Mansion-house of the City of London* a glass of negus is not to be had after one o'clock in the morning; and the Lord Mayor, with all the authority of his office, has not the command of a little wine and water and sugar. So wretchedly inhospitable a house as your Mansion-house last night I never was in. Let Mr. *Wilkes,* if he can spare time from his new employment of *Defender of the Faith,* (as he is always encroaching on *royal prerogative,*) defend *English* liberality if he can.[4] Why, Sir, Whittington's cat must have starved had she been there. Though indeed I was not a *hungry* Scotchman; I wanted only a drop of *liquor*; and I went to the *fountain-head.* But, alas! it was quite *dry*; there was no *juice* in the *plum.* Yet this man, I am told, has amassed what you call a *plum* by *sweating* and *refining* gold.[5] A *sweat,* and a hearty one too, he ought to have. But to *refine* him will be no easy task. For my own part, all that I can say is, that be his wealth ever so great, this PLUMBE of yours is in my opinion at present not worth a FIG.

TANTALUS.

[1] "Lord Garlies [style of Lord Galloway before his succession] is a little man with a great flow of animal spirits. He has been indulged and even idolized by Lord Galloway, which has given him a petulant forwardness that cannot fail to disgust people of sense and delicacy. He is also got into the political tract [i.e. track, way], but as his parts are but inferior, he will probably never equal his father" (Journal, 25 September 1762).

[2] The old Scotch pint, still sometimes retained as a measure of wine, was equal to about three imperial pints (better than 3½ American pints).

[3] Henry Sampson Woodfall, printer of the *Public Advertiser,* to whom the letter is addressed.

[4] On 10 March Wilkes had supported in the House of Commons the bill for the relief of dissenting ministers and schoolmasters from such subscription to the Thirty-Nine Articles of religion as was required by the Act of Toleration.

[5] A "plum" was slang for the sum of £100,000. "Sweating," as applied to gold, designated any of at least three actions, one of them criminal. The one that Plumbe really may have been engaged in was a species of refining: the extraction of an easily fusible impurity in gold by heating and melting it out. Plumbe was a member of the Goldsmiths' Company (Prime Warden, 1769–1770).

TUESDAY 6 APRIL. Breakfast C. Dilly. Mickle came. Was weary of him. Wrote Temple. Posted to General's, and away to Streatham.[5a] "Would not be Burke," said she in opposition to me. JOHNSON. "No, you would gain nothing but breeches." She said well she would be Pascal.

Supped Lord Eglinton with Lord Glencairn and Captain Murray. Was on my guard with a neighbour. Heard that it was Captain <Hen>- derson who went home with me.[6] Sauntered an hour to Westminster. All quiet. [Saw] only old w—res. Different from death, which in general takes old and leaves young. But like fruit, where best are culled.

[EDITORIAL NOTE: Notes for Wednesday 7 April must once have existed, but they are now missing. The entry for that date from the first draft of the manuscript of the *Life of Johnson* is given in their stead.]

On Wednesday seventh April I dined with him at Sir Joshua Reynolds's. I have not marked what company was there. Johnson harangued upon the qualities of different liquors and spoke with great contempt of claret as so weak that "a man would be drowned by it before he was made drunk." He was persuaded to drink one glass of it, that he might judge not from recollection, which might be dim, but from immediate sensation. He shook his head, and said, "Poor stuff! No, Sir. Claret is the liquor for boys; port for men; but he who aspires to be a hero must drink brandy. In the first place, the flavour of brandy is most grateful to the palate, and then brandy will do soonest for a man what drinking *can* do for him. There are indeed few who are able to drink brandy. That is a power rather wished for than attained. Yet, as in all pleasure, hope is a considerable part, I know not but fruition comes too quick by brandy. Florence wine I think the worst. It is wine only to the eye; it is wine neither when you are drinking it nor after you have drunk it. It neither pleases the taste nor exhilarates the spirits." I put him in mind how jollily he and I used to drink wine together when we were first acquainted, and how I used to have a headache after sitting up with him. He did not like to have this recalled, or perhaps thought I boasted improperly; so would have a witty stroke at me: "Nay, Sir; it was not the *wine* that made your head ache but the *sense* that I put into it." BOSWELL. "What, Sir, will sense make the head ache?" JOHNSON. "Yes, Sir, when it is not used to it." No man who

[5a] See p. 60 n. 8.
[6] This name could perhaps also be read "Sanderson" or "Anderson." The *Army List* for 1779 shows a George Henderson, captain in the 13th Regiment of Foot, a Scots regiment. No account survives of Boswell's having gone home drunk from Lord Eglinton's, but nearly all the entry for 27 March is missing and other entries are defective. See below, 13 April 1779, fifth paragraph.

has a true relish of pleasantry could be offended at this, especially if Johnson in a long intimacy had given him repeated proofs that he valued him.

THURSDAY 8 APRIL. Many visits. Dined at Ramsay's. Dr. Johnson, Lord Graham, etc.[7] Dr. Johnson spoke much of Shakespeare's witches.[8] "A being of his own creation, [a mixture of] malignity and meanness, [with] no abilities; quite different from the Italian magician. King James in his *Demonology* says, 'Magicians command devils. Witches [are] their servants.' The Italian magicians elegant." RAMSAY. "Opera witches, not Drury Lane ones."

We talked of abilities not widely employed, such as in getting money, which he said he believed was not done without vigorous parts, though concentrated to a point. RAMSAY. "Like a strong horse in a mill. He pulls better."

Lord Graham, praising Loch Lomond, complained of [the] climate, and said he could not bear it. JOHNSON. "Nay, my Lord, don't talk so; you may bear it well enough. Your ancestors have borne it more years than I can tell."

Dr. Johnson was very polite to Lady Margaret Macdonald: "I have heard of the people taking <stones off the road,> [lest Lady Margaret's horse should stumble."]

Lord Graham commended Dr. Drummond at Naples; said he had high notions of liberty.[9] JOHNSON. "He's young, my Lord; all boys love liberty till experience convinces them they're not so fit to govern [them]-selves as they thought. We are all agreed as to our own liberty; [we would have] as much as we can get; but we are not as to [the liberty of] others. For, in proportion as we take, <others must gi>ve. I hardl<y wish> [that the] mob should have liberty [to govern us.] No man lately was at liberty not to have candles in his windows."[1] "The result," said

---

[7] Allan Ramsay, Principal Painter to His Majesty, was perhaps the most popular painter in London. In 1775 Boswell had intended to write the life of his father, the Scots poet of the same name. James Graham, styled Marquess of Graham, later became third Duke of Montrose. He was only twenty-three years old at this time.

[8] *Macbeth* had been played at Drury Lane the previous night.

[9] Alexander Monro Drummond, M.D. (d. 1782), the son of Johnson's friend William Drummond, a brilliant physician. He was at least in his late thirties at this time. Dr. Cullen described him as "the most learned, most ingenious, and most ornate physician ever bred at [Edinburgh] University" (Sylas Neville, *Diary 1767–1788*, 1950, p. 198). He had served as physician to Sir William Hamilton's first wife at Naples.

[1] It was normal practice to testify to one's satisfaction in the turn of public events by putting candles in one's windows. The mob frequently broke the windows of those who did not illuminate on occasions it considered joyous. Most recently (in February) Lord North's windows had been broken during the celebration of Keppel's acquittal.

Ramsay, "is [that] order [is] better than confusion." JOHNSON. ["The] result [is that] order cannot be had but by subordination."

Before d<inner> he maintained fidelity in a mistress more to be valued than in a wife, as more voluntary.[2]

FRIDAY 9 APRIL. <Lay> abed dreary for the first time. Heavy morning. Pascal did me some good.[3] Solander came and helped a little.[4] Sauntered about. Called Dr. Johnson's. Introduced to Tom Tyers, who said, "He goes on with his *Lives* farther than he intended. Like a chariot wheel, [he] catches fire as he runs." Pleased with him. Shaw came in and Nichols the printer, whom I followed and got promise of proofs.[5] Dined Sir J. Pringle's with General [Paoli], Ingenhousz, and Franchi; well. Evening *désoeuvré*.[6] Called Spottiswood a little, and Dr. Wilson. Not in. Then home. Capillaire and to bed. So-so day.

SATURDAY 10 APRIL. Breakfast Mrs. Mathew.[7] "Marriage" [she said] "must have [its] bass, tenor, treble; <i.e.> esteem, affection, passion." ... Sung that one song, "Like parrot, call the Doctor." Was quite fine at Mrs. Mathew's. MISS. "I hope, Sir, you don't think of me."

---

[2] This is perhaps the first allusion in the journal to James Hackman's murder of Martha Ray, Lord Sandwich's mistress (see below, following 10 April 1779).

[3] Johnson had given Boswell a copy of *Les Pensées* on 2 April to keep him from interrupting his own devotional reading.

[4] Daniel Charles Solander, the distinguished botanist who had accompanied Cook in his voyage around the world. As a Swede he would have found the international atmosphere of Paoli's house stimulating.

[5] "Thomas Tyers, son of Mr. Jonathan Tyers, the founder of that excellent place of public amusement, Vauxhall Gardens. . . . [He] was bred to the law; but having a handsome fortune, vivacity of temper, and eccentricity of mind, he could not confine himself to the regularity of practice. He therefore ran about the world with a pleasant carelessness, amusing everybody by his desultory conversation. He abounded in anecdote, but was not sufficiently attentive to accuracy. . . . [He] was exceedingly obliging to me, and . . . lived with Dr. Johnson in as easy a manner as almost any of his very numerous acquaintance" (*Life of Johnson*, 17 April 1778). John Nichols, printer of the *Lives of the Poets*, was a remarkably prolific historical and literary editor, and was author of *Literary Anecdotes of the Eighteenth Century*. William Shaw was author of *An Analysis of the Gaelic Language*, 1778, for which Johnson wrote the Proposals.

[6] Idle.

[7] Probably Henrietta Mathew, a prominent bluestocking, who conducted a salon which Mrs. Montagu, Mrs. Barbauld, and Mrs. Chapone attended; she and her husband were early patrons of Flaxman and Blake. It was formerly assumed that her salon was the setting for Blake's satirical *Island in the Moon*, but present-day scholars consider the satire to be much more general. It is not certainly known how Boswell made her acquaintance, but the journal suggests that it was through Paoli. She had a niece, Miss Lydia: "very agreeable; I *loved* her" (Journal, 15 April 1778).

Lady Margaret [Macdonald] a little. Said John Macpherson had a prosperous countenance.[8] Then A. Ramsay. Very lively. Talked of art and nature; if good-nature [were art. Agreed it was] the thing. Dined home in highest glee; resolved [to go to] play—*Gamester*. Message from Lord Eglinton for Bath.[9] Called and drank moselle [with] Macdonell [and] Small. Greig's pipes.[1] Too late [for] play. Cleared the way; satisfied on box. Drank porter with gallery-keepers. Supped Douglas's; friendly. Saw me into coach.

I had been [at] Dr. Johnson's; Paradise and Sastris. [Told] Mrs. Boscawen [she had] seen me before. SHE. "Yes, I owe [much] happiness <to you> and hope often." Pleased with this, <as I was> not fishing for a compliment. . . .

[From the *London Evening Post*, 8–10 April 1779.]

At six o'clock [7 April] Miss Ray quitted her house in order to go to the play. She was elegantly dressed that evening, and it was noticed that she looked unusually agreeable; it was also remarked that she was in an unusual flow of spirits and good humour. She took with her to the play Signora Galli, the celebrated Italian singer, who lived in the house and was kept by Miss Ray, leaving word that she should be at home to supper as soon as the play was over. At a quarter past six, Miss Ray and Signora Galli arrived at Covent Garden Theatre, and sat next to the King's stage box. She seemed the whole evening to be particularly well pleased, and at the conclusion, which was about half past eleven, as Miss Ray and Signora Galli were conducting to their coach by a nobleman, the fatal affair happened, and, as given in evidence before Sir John Fielding at five o'clock the next morning, was as follows: John Welsh, a watchman, deposed that he saw two ladies and a gentleman (Miss Ray, Signora Galli, and Mr. MacNamara) come out of Covent Garden Theatre at the conclusion of the play, the gentleman handing one of the ladies to the coach. That he also

---

[8] John Macpherson, friend and associate of James Macpherson, was elected to Parliament in this month. He later succeeded Warren Hastings as Governor-General in India.

[9] "Lord Eglinton was so good as to ask me to accompany him to Bath. But when his Lordship gave me the invitation, I was engaged to dinner for six successive days at different houses, some of the parties made on my account, so that I did not think I could with propriety break off" (To Lady Crawford, 28 May 1779).

[1] Both officers in Highland regiments serving in America: John Macdonell of Lochgarry, lieutenant-colonel commanding the 76th Foot, and John Small, major commanding the 2nd Battalion of the 84th Foot. Somebody played a Highland reel, probably on the bagpipes. Boswell later (22 February 1783) reports being in a company that included Macdonell which had gathered in a tavern at Edinburgh to hear "an excellent fiddler" play Highland tunes.

saw a gentleman in black (Mr. Hackman) cross the Piazza from Dennis's,[2] run towards the carriage, and take hold of one of the ladies' gowns (Miss Ray's), when the lady turning round, the gentleman in black put a large pistol close to her forehead and fired it off; that instantly he put another to his own head and discharged that, when both fell together; and that both pistols were *discharged* one immediately after the other. That the gentleman lay upon the ground beating himself about the head, endeavouring to kill himself and crying, "Oh! kill me, kill me! for God's sake, kill me!" That assistance came up, the gentleman was secured, the pistols wrenched out of his hands, and that the lady, who never spoke a word, was taken up and carried into the Shakespeare Tavern dead, and that the gentleman was also taken in there in a very bloody condition. . . .

Sir John Fielding was sent for from Brompton and arrived at the Shakespeare at three o'clock, where, after examining what evidence could be then found, [he] committed Mr. Hackman to Tothill Fields Bridewell. He lost a considerable quantity of blood by the blows he gave himself, and the ball struck him so forcibly as to knock him down. In his pocket was found a letter to his brother-in-law, of Craven Street, who married Mr. Hackman's sister. . . .

In his way to prison, he exclaimed, "What a change has a few hours made in me—had her friends done as I wished them to do, this would never have happened."

[EDITORIAL NOTE: The Rev. James Hackman was born in December 1752 and thus was only twenty-six when he attempted to end his brief and troubled existence at Covent Garden. He had begun life as an officer in the Army, having purchased a commission in the 68th Regiment of Foot at the age of nineteen. While he was upon recruiting service at Huntington in the winter of 1775, he was invited by the Earl of Sandwich to his house at Hinchingbrooke with another officer, a neighbour of the Earl's. There he met and fell desperately in love with Martha Ray, a young woman seven or eight years his senior, who had already been Lord Sandwich's mistress for more than a decade. She was the daughter of a stay-maker and had been apprenticed to a mantua-maker, but at sixteen was "removed into that higher sphere" by the Earl, educated in France, and brought up in "every accomplishment that could adorn a woman, par-

---

[2] A firm of fruit-merchants in James Street, on the northern side of Covent Garden. A firm styled Dennis and Cooper, Ltd., is carrying on business on a site identical with or very close to that which Dennis's occupied in 1779. In most accounts, Hackman is said to have waited in the Bedford Coffee-house, in the northeastern corner of the Great Piazza, close to the entrance of the theatre, until he saw the people beginning to come out. He must then have walked westward some way down the northern side of the Piazza, presumably to get a better view of the carriages as they drew up.

ticularly those of singing, and playing most exquisitely on the harpsi-chord" (*Public Advertiser* 9–10 April 1779). Her connexion with Lord Sandwich was open and notorious; she presided over his household, gave away the honours at the Admiralty, and bore him nine children, of whom five were living at the time of her death (one, at sixteen, was already a lieutenant in the Navy).[3] In spite of all this, Hackman offered marriage. At the end of 1776, hoping to make himself more acceptable, he threw up his commission and presented himself as a candidate for orders. He was ordained priest on 28 February 1779, and presented to the living of Wive-ton in Norfolk. He thereupon renewed his proposals to Miss Ray, but found her obdurate, apparently because she was not willing to leave her children. On 7 April he shot her and attempted to kill himself.

The letter in his pocket to Frederick Booth, an attorney, his cousin and brother-in-law, was a simple suicide note: "When this reaches you I shall be no more. . . . You well know where my affections were placed; my having by some means or other lost hers (an idea which I could not sup-port) has driven me to madness. The world will condemn me, but your good heart will pity me. . . . May Heaven protect my beloved woman and forgive this act, which alone could relieve me from a world of misery I have long endured. Oh, if it should ever be in your power to do her any act of friendship, remember your faithful friend J. Hackman." [4] This implied that his original intention had been only to kill himself, and that the murder of Miss Ray sprang from a momentary frenzy; but he carried two charged pistols (the cause of a great deal of public argument) and Sir John Fielding held that madness could not be offered as excuse, "as it appeared and can be proved that he was rational and sensible of his wick-edness at four in the morning, when I examined him, and has been so ever since." [5]

The affair naturally created an immense sensation, not merely because of Sandwich's political prominence (as First Lord of the Admiralty, he was a power in Lord North's unpopular administration and personally unpopular for his handling of the recent trial of Keppel), but because of its appeal as a *crime passionnel* and its overtones of the Young Werther. That Boswell should have failed to interest himself in so remarkable a criminal was not to be expected, but the affair of Hackman was soon to

[3] The second son, Basil Montagu, was the common friend of Wordsworth and Coleridge; his son Basil lived with Wordsworth and his sister at Racedown and Al-foxden, and was the hero of *An Anecdote for Fathers.* Wordsworth with a strange lack of taste gave the name of Martha Ray to the heroine of *The Thorn.*
[4] *Gentleman's Magazine,* April 1779, xlix. 213.
[5] Letter to Lord Sandwich, 10 April 1779 (George Martelli, *Jemmy Twitcher, A Life of the Fourth Earl of Sandwich,* 1962, p. 172).

bring him more public notoriety than even he could handle. His involvement begins in the following entry, when he calls twice upon Frederick Booth.]

SUNDAY 11 APRIL. Very ill. Ashamed to be seen by General. Up and out. Breakfast Douglas. Then Sir J. Pringle. Then Bavarian [Chapel]. Then walked [in] Park, and sat hour with Lord Loudoun. Told me of Stillingfleet's reproduction of moss. "Spirit," [he said,] "returns to [its] great source." [6] Called Booth. Then sauntered both into Tabernacle [7] and St. Giles, and Sardinian [Chapel for] vespers. Had come upon Mademoiselle Curtis, dentist.[8] Luck for adventures.

Dined Hoole's with Dr. Johnson and Mrs. Williams. The Doctor not fertile. We talked of going to Grand Cairo. He then run on with ostentatious geography: China, etc. Johnson not pleased with young Lucas for advertising his play [as] "kindly revised and recommended to the stage by that standard of literature, Dr. Samuel Johnson." [9] Yet he had revised, and [the] play had his red-ink markings on margin, and Lucas had a letter too which he showed. I asked, "You did not strike out much?" JOHNSON. "No, Sir." BOSWELL. "Then 'twas kindly revised." I said Macpherson had told Sheridan only half of [what] Dr. Johnson [said of him]; gave vinegar but not oil, so [a] bad salad.[1] Henderson and Ireland [called]. When [I] said

---

[6] Benjamin Stillingfleet, dilettante (in the old sense) and naturalist, is said by Boswell to have occasioned the term "bluestocking" by attending ladies' conversation parties (where his talk was much esteemed) in undress and wearing his every-day worsted stockings. (See below, p. 336 n. 9.) One of the earliest defenders and propagators of the Linnaean system in England, he certainly held that mosses, like flowering plants, propagated themselves sexually, but he could hardly have said very much more on the subject, for the reproductive organs of mosses were not discovered and described until shortly after his death. His *Miscellaneous Tracts* (mainly translations from Linnaeus and his disciples) have a great deal to say about the usefulness of mosses in the natural order; and like those writers he is eloquent in asserting Divine Providence in nature. Lord Loudoun, when Commander-in-Chief of the Forces in America, sent many foreign trees home to be planted at Loudoun Castle, and had probably made more than a cursory study of botany.

[7] Whitefield's Tabernacle, in Tottenham Court Road.

[8] There was a considerable influx of French dentists practising in London in this period, often in furnished rented rooms, and quite a number of them were women. This particular one has not been identified; it is not certain, in any event, that Boswell was consulting her about his teeth (information kindly supplied by Dr. J. Menzies Campbell).

[9] *The Earl of Somerset*, a tragedy, published this year in the same volume with *Poems to Her Majesty*. In the "Prefatory Address" Lucas wrote, "Dr. Samuel Johnson—to whom permit me thus publicly to express my gratitude for the peculiar kindness of his perusal, emendations, and good opinion of this work" (p. xxv).

[1] Johnson, on hearing that Thomas Sheridan had been granted a pension, remarked,

[I supposed] Davies's [account of Henderson] quite true, [he called him] "Psalmanazar the Second." <"Yes,"> said I, "and <his> wife Formosa?" [2]

Then <sat and> talked a little at coffee. Called Booth again. Then Sir J. Pringle's with Sir George Baker, who had from Walsingham [an] account of Hackman.[3] We talked well. Home and orgeat, easy and tranquil.

MONDAY 12 APRIL. Agreeably surprised with W[illiam] Brown's arrival, who gave me accounts of wife, etc.[4] Seward came after breakfast. I went with Brown to many places; quite alive. At Lord Loudoun's met laird of Fairlie. Dined General Oglethorpe's; Dr. Johnson and Langton and Paoli there. Talk of Commons and population, etc. Evening with Seward. Orgeat. . . .

TUESDAY 13 APRIL. (With Cleland.) [5] CLELAND. "Sterne's bawdy too plain. I reproved him, saying, 'It gives no sensations.' Said he: 'You have furnished me a vindication. It can do no harm.' 'But,' [I said,] 'if you had a pupil who wrote c—— on a wall, would not you flog him?' He never forgave me." FRASER.[6] "That was a hard knock to Sterne." BOSWELL. "A knock against the *wall*." I mentioned Burke with applause. CLELAND. "I don't like oratory so much dressed at the toilet of Flora. I am not satisfied with flowers: I must have fruit." BOSWELL. "But Burke is [an] orange tree; you have buds, flowers, and fruits all at once." (I told it [to] Burke that day. He said, "I wish I could get the fruit." BOSWELL. *"Bread* fruit.") Cleland said he had wrote his *Woman of Pleasure* to show the Hon. Charles Carmichael that <one> could <write> so <freely about a>

"What! have they given *him* a pension? Then it is time for me to give up mine." After a pause he added, "However, I am glad that Mr. Sheridan has a pension, for he is a very good man." Macpherson repeated to Sheridan the first part, but not the second, and it caused an "irreconcilable difference" (*Life of Johnson*, beginning of 1763).

2 Thomas Davies was the author of a laudatory biography (1777) of John Henderson, an actor known as the "Bath Roscius." Henderson is modestly asserting that Davies's praise is as wild as the lies of Psalmanazar. "Formosa" is both another allusion to Psalmanazar, who posed as a Formosan, and a pun on its meaning, "beautiful" ("That Davies hath a very pretty wife," Churchill, *The Rosciad,* l. 320).

3 The Hon. Robert Boyle-Walsingham, fifth son of the Earl of Shannon, was Sandwich's close friend, and had been sent by him to interview Hackman. He reported back to Sandwich that "the poor unhappy wretch is sensible of your goodness in forgiving him," but that he said "the greatest curse he could experience would be to live" (Martelli, p. 171).

4 William Brown was a solicitor in Kilmarnock.

5 Boswell had met John Cleland at Garrick's house in 1772 and called on him in April 1778. This is the most fully recorded conversation Boswell had with him.

6 Unidentified.

wom<an of the town without resorting to t>he <coarseness> of
[*L'École*] *des filles*, which had quite plain words.[7] What is strange, he
kept it five-and-twenty years, that is, the first part and half [the] second,
which was all wrote by the time he was twenty. The last was done when
he was older.[8] I said I wondered he kept it so long; that it did not burst
out.

He said the Count [Catuélan] (the French translator of Shakespeare)
said he had not only the finest situation of a house in London, but in
Europe. It was fine, romantic, and pleasant.[9]

He said Epicurus was now well defended as not being a sensualist;
that intellect and sense must unite in pleasure. I said, "Two horses in
post-chaise must draw equally." Talked to me of his father.[1] I said, "Why
should I not still have the pleasure of fine girls? But I'm [a] married man
and have four children." CLELAND. "I'd have you keep up your own
dignity: *nec lusisse pudet, sed non*, etc." [2] Said he understood the nerves
better than any <doctor> in Europe.

Said he had great respect for Johnson. CLELAND. <"What> makes

---

[7] A large defect in the manuscript makes the reconstruction of this sentence highly
conjectural. *L'École des filles* (Boswell left a blank for the first word of the title)
was written under a pseudonym by Michel Millot and first published at Paris in
1655.— Charles Carmichael, fifth and youngest son of the second Earl of Hyndford
and brother of John Carmichael, third Earl of Hyndford (Envoy or Ambassador
successively to Prussia, Russia, and Austria), died at Bombay in the service of the
East India Company at the age of twenty in 1732. Cleland, writing in 1749 to Lovell
Stanhope, a government adviser on criminal prosecutions, to implore dismissal of an
indictment for obscenity, indeed says that he worked up the first part of *Fanny Hill*
from a manuscript given him by young Carmichael. The second part he appears to
claim as entirely his own: "[It] had been promised, and would most surely have never
been proceeded to had I been in the least made sensible of the first having given any
offence; and indeed I now wonder it could so long escape the vigilance of the guardians
of the public manners, since nothing is truer than that more clergymen bought it in
proportion than any other distinction of men" (Public Record Office: photostat kindly
furnished by Prof. Lewis M. Knapp).

[8] There is a difficulty in the dates here which is not resolved by Boswell's statement in
the journal for 1 January 1793 that Cleland had told him that he kept the book
nine years before publishing it. But if we read "twenty" for "five-and-twenty," an
approximate reconciliation is possible. *Memoirs of a Woman of Pleasure* was published in 1748–1749. Cleland, who was born about 1710, could have finished "the first
part and half the second" by 1730 and the whole by 1740.

[9] Cleland lived in Petty France, Westminster, just south of St. James's Park. Milton
had lived there from 1652 to 1660.

[1] William Cleland was a friend of Pope's, and was thought to have been the original
of Will Honeycomb in the *Spectator*.

[2] *Sed non incidere ludum*: it's no shame to have frolicked, but it is a shame not to
have cut frolic short (Horace, *Epistles*, I. xiv. 36).

him so exquisite <is his sophi>str<y, for which he gi>ve<s> [such] <go>od reasons."

In the morning General Paoli said, "When a new subject is started, Johnson bends himself like a bow." He lectured me on thrice drinking too much. Said, "I'd be [felt to be] your enemy, but would always tell you"; a fine thought how one who tells real faults [felt to be an] enemy. Breakfast comfortably. General said he imagined *spirits* might work on minds predisposed to be affected, and thus [we had] witchcraft in one age and place and not in another. So ordeal [was] allowed by wise men. Innocent people, being confident, grasped [the hot iron] close, and, there being no air, were not burnt, as he had observed of velvet at Manchester held close on red-hot cylinder.

A little at Douglas's. A good while at Sir J. Pringle's. He said, "Vous êtes fait pour fanatisme et enthousiasme, mais pas pour raisonner sur la religion." boswell. "Comment donc faire?" pringle. "Suivre la religion de vos ancêtres." [3] We were well.

Sir Joshua; tried to get him to dine. He honestly owned [that he had been] up till four, and could not talk where something [was] expected.[4] I said, "You take sociality easily, [when it may be] had [by] only [coursing] in [the] field; you don't leap hedge <and> ditch to get at it. I <do not hesita>te . . ."

[Editorial Note: The bottom of the leaf has crumbled away. Two or three lines have been lost or survive in so fragmentary a state that they cannot be reconstructed. When the record begins again, Boswell and Burke are talking about Hackman. Boswell has perhaps said that he could imagine himself acting as Hackman did. Burke's reply may have begun, "If you believe that,]

. . . I must not keep company with you any more." boswell. (Taking his hand.) "But you must not use me worse than you have done." burke. " 'Tis like poor Dodswell, a friend of mine, who when Delany defended David's killing Uriah in battle, said, 'Delany shall not lie with my wife if I can help it.' " [5] I said he should not be hanged, [but] blown from mouth

---

[3] "You are made for fanaticism and enthusiasm, but not for reasoning on religion." "What shall I do, then?" "Follow the religion of your ancestors."

[4] Boswell seems to have tried to get Reynolds to absent himself from a good-sized dinner party at his own house (see below in this entry) in order to dine with him and the General; Reynolds countered by inviting Boswell to join *his* party. Reynolds's dinners were in fact something like a commons, and he did not always appear at them himself.

[5] Patrick Delany, a prominent Irish divine, did not overtly defend David's actions: he pronounced the seduction of Bathsheba a great crime and the murder of Uriah a

of cannon, like the grenadiers in the East Indies.[6] Natural to destroy what you cannot have." WILLIAM BURKE. "Tell Dr. Johnson that is what we are doing in America."

I mentioned [his saying of David Hume, "The] fellow [is a] Tory by chance." [7] "Yes," said Burke, "as he was an Epicurean, it must be by chance."

Dined home well. Cambiagi. Had walked in street with Langton, who was curious as to houses in St. Clement's churchyard. I, in returning, went in and got history from Mrs. Sarah Finch (seventy-seven), nine years there.[8]

Called at Booth's; walked a little with Duke of Argyll.

Had been asked to dine with Sir Joshua, with Burke and with Langton, whom I went [in] afternoon and found. Marquess of Lothian, Lord Portmore and son, Gen. Oglethorpe, Beauclerk, Mar<lay>. Quite lively. <Ca>ps like masquerade [at the] Pantheon. Camp of fifty women in Grosvenor Square. Mawhood no more sense than in brickbat. Bad champagne with King. Bad bread.[9] Oglethorpe harangued <on the> constitutional mode of redress; angry at our warm<th at colonies> when [we are]

---

greater, and he called David's supposed rationalizations of the murder "the accursed entanglements of sin." But by setting forth those rationalizations sympathetically and at great length, he somewhat deviously imparted a strong tone of defence to his severe judgments: "Uriah must die or Bathsheba must.... Honour would attend the fate of Uriah, infamy must attend that of Bathsheba. Uriah was a brave man and a faithful soldier. Could David ever bear to behold the brave man he had abused made privy to that abuse? Could that brave man bear to survive that abuse? Would not murder in this case be a kind mercy?" (*An Historical Account of the Life and Reign of David King of Israel*, 3rd edn., 1745, ii. 85, 320).

6 "I could wish that the royal prerogative could transmute the mode of punishment from that which is common to mean offenders to what would better suit the character of the sufferer" (Boswell's letter to the *St. James's Chronicle*, 15–17 April 1779). Execution at the cannon's mouth, considered less dishonourable than hanging, was practised in India (against the revolting Sepoys) as late as 1857. Hackman, it will be remembered, had formerly been an officer in the Army.

7 Johnson made the remark at Ostaig in Skye, 30 September 1773. Boswell rather cruelly repeated it to Hume in their last conversation, 7 July 1776.

8 Mrs. Finch sounds as though she might have been a recipient of parish bounty. If she was, the "houses" were no doubt the alms-houses which then stood on the east side of the churchyard. A survey of the parish made in 1732 says, "In the upper churchyard there are ... six alms-houses with six rooms, and twelve poor women in each house, who are allowed 2s. per week; and in the lower churchyard [the portion west of the church] are five rooms for poor women, each of whom has 2s. 6d. per week; they have also coals at Christmas if they can make interest to get them" (John Diprose, *Some Account of the Parish of St. Clement Danes*, 1868–1876, i. 43, 287).

9 Cues for after-dinner conversation, nowhere explained. Mawhood was a "tea-man's son" who quitted the Army and wrote comedies.

afraid of Spain and France; like man afraid <to figh>t [who] comes home and kicks his servant. Beauclerk, Langton, and I sat late. Talked till I was exhausted. A little too open and feverish. Stories of Dr. Johnson: Craster and the cat; "Mrs. Woffington wanting to play whore with me." [1]

WEDNESDAY 14 APRIL. Dined Sir John Dick's with General Paoli, two Langleys, etc., and Pleydel. Drank rather too hearty. Sat awhile with Allan Ramsay. Nothing to record.

(Give *this* gently).[2] In the India House Macpherson was got into a corner.[3] Dr. Douglas spoke to me in the highest terms of Dr. Johnson's *Prefaces to the Poets*. I catched the enthusiasm, and said, "I serve him on the knee: present him the golden cup." "But think," said Douglas, "of a man of seventy writing with so much fire!" "O wonderful man!" said I. Thus was Macpherson treated. (Next day.) Langton said we had kept roasting him: Douglas the great fire, I the clear tin plate throwing back the heat upon him—a very good image. I called him "Criterion Douglas." Langton said that was giving a nickname. "Well," said I, "Detector Douglas." Said Langton: "That is representing him as one of Sir J. Fielding's men." [4]

THURSDAY 15 APRIL. General Paoli came into my room before I was up, and cheered me with his cultivated gaiety. I called on Bishop Hay and sat a few minutes with him.[5] Then went to Langton's to breakfast by

---

[1] Boswell did not record these stories in the *Life of Johnson*, and they are probably now irrecoverable.

[2] A dated fragment which perhaps was intended for *Boswelliana*.

[3] The occasion which brought John Douglas, later Bishop of Carlisle and of Salisbury, Boswell, and Macpherson to India House was an uneventful annual meeting on the first Wednesday after Lady Day for the election of Directors, Chairman, and Deputy-Chairman ("the Chairs"). Lord North had threatened to take £1,400,000 from the Company's revenue for the budget or the national debt, and perhaps Boswell and his friends had gathered to see the effect of North's scare on the meeting. Friends of Company proprietors (that is, stockholders) were allowed to watch proceedings from a "strangers' bench" (in reality many benches); Douglas and Boswell had many friends among the proprietors and Macpherson was a proprietor himself through a nominee, and could enter in his own right (information kindly supplied by Dr. James N. M. Maclean).

[4] Douglas had attacked Hume's argument upon miracles, his book being entitled *The Criterion, or Miracles Examined*, 1754. He also had attacked Archibald Bower in several pamphlets, had exposed William Lauder's forgeries, and had taken part with Johnson in the detection of the Cock Lane Ghost (1763). "Detector" in the eighteenth century commonly meant "informer." Henry Fielding, the novelist and magistrate, had devised a plan for breaking up gangs of robbers by using informers, paid from a fund provided for the purpose. Sir John Fielding, his blind half-brother and successor as magistrate, continued the plan.

[5] The same whose "mass-house" had been burned in Edinburgh (see above, 2–3 February 1779). Boswell had met him soon after his own arrival in London, and

appointment. It was very agreeable, for we had a plenteous harvest of good conversation, and while we reaped with spirited emulation, did not cut one another with our sickles, as happens when the harvest is scanty or the reapers perverse. We then went, accompanied by his son (little George), to Hyde Park, saw the Marquess of Lothian's regiment of Horse Guards perform their exercise and evolutions, which were done with astonishing regularity and animation. I was quite delighted. The day was charming sunshine. Sir William Howe,[6] General Sloper, the Hanoverian General Freytag, and a number of remarkable men were upon the field. I relished all this highly, and expressed my satisfaction in lively terms. Langton paid me the compliment of saying that it was agreeable to see such a scene with me. For I was not, like many people, in a state of dull amazement or ill-humoured silence, but could talk of what pleased me. I observed how remarkable it was that such perfection of military discipline should be attained with good humour; not by fear, as in the King of Prussia's army, where you have just *l'homme machine*, but here the *machine* is *composée d'hommes*;[7] they are all fine fellows who act from inclination. An officer who stood by us observed that in this corps there are neither rewards nor punishments. The men all buy their places, and get no promotion but by purchase.

Langton asked me to call with him at Beauclerk's door to ask for his son, who was ill. I at first refused, "For," said I, "Beauclerk does not care himself about his son, and surely I do not care. I'll not affect it." "But," said worthy Langton, "should not one care? Should not one have kindly affection" (or some such expression), "and should not one do what is right even when there is no inclination?" This persuaded me; and as we walked along he mentioned that Dr. Henry More wrote one of his best books when he called himself off from what he had an inclination for at the

---

had accompanied him to the House of Commons on 18 March, when Lord North read a long petition from the Roman Catholics of Edinburgh and Glasgow for redress of wrongs suffered at the hands of the "misguided populace," and for the protection to which they felt they were entitled. The petition was referred to a committee. Hay wrote to Boswell on 16 April asking him "to write . . . to any of your acquaintances of the Town Council, as you saw and heard all that passed," to urge that they pay for the Roman Catholic losses in the riot. The Bishop wished the town to do this voluntarily, so as to avoid further animosity which might develop if Government stepped in.

[6] Sir William Howe had been Commander-in-Chief of the British forces in the Colonies from 10 October 1776 to 24 May 1778 and was engaged in a number of battles: Bunker Hill, Long Island, New York, White Plains, Fort Washington, Brandywine, Germantown, etc. Earlier this year he and his brother, Admiral Lord Howe, obtained a Committee of the whole House of Commons to inquire into their conduct of the war; the inquiry came to nothing.

[7] That is, "where you have just *man-machine*, but here a *machine made up of men*."

time, to what he was convinced it was right for him to undertake.[8] The influence of this excellent friend upon me is truly salutary to my mind. George was weary, and Langton carried him so far.[9] I observed that his tallness had the same *effect* when he walked with his son that Fitzherbert represented it to have when he walked with his father: "In walks Old Langton," said he, "with Young Langton like an umbrella over him." Langton said he was rather like the stick of an umbrella.

Beauclerk was just getting up, and sent us word he would be glad to see us. We sat above an hour while he breakfasted and talked very well indeed. He controverted Dr. Johnson's statement that a man cannot have pleasure in spending money who does not spend it fast; and he maintained that, supposing a <man> to know by calculation that from <his> living beyond his income his fortune will last him twenty years and no longer, it is better for him to make it last these twenty years, in which he can live agreeably enough, than to throw it all away in a short time, with whatever splendour. He maintained too in defence of Langton that if a man lives so that his son shall not have less than he has had, he is not to be blamed. "Langton," said he, "may exceed his present income, and so incur a debt. But if he lives, what is to fall into him will discharge that debt, so that his son will not have less than he now has; and if he dies, there will be a minority to recruit the family fortune. Everything," said he, "is comparative. Reduce the Duke of Bedford to £3,000 a year, which is in itself a very good fortune for a gentleman who has never had more, and you make him as completely miserable as I should be if reduced to £2<oo> a year. Great people have a certain established <rate of> expense which they cannot retrench. The Duchess of Marlborough is very great, and must have a great deal of show. She is very narrow, so as to be doing mean things every day; for example, she has a false back to a grate by which I suppose thirty shillings is saved, and she wants to save a great deal of money. She is very indolent and cannot take the trouble of managing her affairs, so must be continually cheated. These three circumstances make her very unhappy. They have a vast number of servants, and as they are every year wishing to retrench in order to save money, they once considered which of all their servants they could spare, and which do you think it was? Why, the confectioner—the servant whom they could do worst without except the cook. Every one of their servants has his own

---

[8] *Enchiridion Ethicum* (1667). "His mind being taken up at that time with some other studies that were marvellously pleasing to him, he was prevailed upon notwithstanding to lay them all aside, and immediately, through the force of these his own reflections, to set about it" (Richard Ward, *Life of ... Dr. Henry More*, 1710, p. 107).

[9] George was seven years old. "So far" (an expression often used by Boswell) means "a considerable distance." See above, 2 February 1779, n. 4ª.

particular business. The Duke has about thirty footmen. But there is a fellow whose particular business it is to light the lamps round the billiard table. The Duke and I were going to play one afternoon.[1] We desired to have the lamps lighted. A footman said he would go and call the lighter. The fellow neither offered to do it, nor did <he send the other to attend to> his business. <Finally I said> 'My Lord, we may stay <here forever in the> dark. Come, I'll light <one lamp while you> light the other.' It <is true in a> great house, where <many servants are> kept, that each <one must know his> own duty, otherwise <nothing would> ever be done, as no man would be answerable. Your cloth would never be laid. John would say, 'I thought Thomas would have done it'; and Thomas would say, 'I thought William would have done it.' " From this exact and lively picture I saw the difficulties of the art of using wealth.

We talked of Dr. Johnson's way of saying rough and severe things to people in company. Beauclerk said he wondered it had never happened that some violent man ——————.[2] He wished to see it to teach Johnson how to behave. "To be sure, a man would be a brute who did it. But it would do good." "O no," said I, "at his age." Beauclerk answered, "At his age he should be thinking of better things than to abuse people." Here was a more religious sentiment than I ever heard Beauclerk express. This was the most agreeable interview I ever had with Beauclerk. I told him next day that he was not only lively (or clever, or some such word) but good.

I walked to Langton's house with him, and he obligingly gave me some sayings of Dr. Johnson which I wrote down in his presence. I then hastened to Dilly's, where was a good dinner, the company: John Wilkes, Esq.; Old Sheridan; his eldest son, Charles (author of *An Account of the Late Revolution in Sweden*, whom therefore I call *Charles of Sweden*); Capell Lofft, Esq.; and Mr. Braithwaite of the Post-Office, clerk to the Postmaster General, a well-behaved man but modest and silent among *us*. Wilkes was late of coming. When he arrived, I said, "Now Sir, though I should *kill* <you, a>s a *Scotsman*, I must tell you that when Mr. Dilly asked *me* if you was coming, I did not answer like *Cain* when he had killed *Abel*, 'Am I my brother's keeper?' — 'Had *Cain* been *Scot*,' you remember. Here a *Scot* was not *Cain*."[3] "Ah," said he, "if all Scotsmen were . . ."

---

[1] The Duke of Marlborough was Beauclerk's brother-in-law.

[2] Boswell left a blank here which would have accommodated four or five words, presumably because he could not remember exactly what Beauclerk said and hoped to recollect it. The sense must have been something like "had not struck him."

[3] Boswell is quoting *The Rebel Scot*, by John Cleveland, lines 63–64:

> Had Cain been Scot, God would have changed his doom,
> Not forced him wander, but confined him home.

[EDITORIAL NOTE: At least a page of the journal is missing at this point. When the journal resumes, the subject of conversation has shifted. What follows to the end of the entry for this date is here published for the first time.]

... and in the *Dunciad*.

Sheridan said that Dr. Johnson said of Garrick's *Ode*,[4] "Sir, it is beneath criticism. It even bids defiance to parody." We talked of Sir John Dalrymple's strange ostentatious lie of having killed a seven-year-old sheep on purpose for Dr. Johnson.[5] I played a little with Wilkes's nonsense as to Scotland and ludicrously said, "You know killing a sheep is a serious matter in Scotland. You must send a trumpet round a whole parish to proclaim it and see who will take shares of it." "Nay," said Jack, "there are forty things to be done in Scotland previous to this. In the first place you must steal the sheep." "Bravo," cried I. "*She<er>* wit indeed upon my sheep sh<are> *shearing*. A pun," said I, "may be allowed now and then"; and I told how Dr. Johnson had admitted mine on comparing him to a turbot and saying he was not *fishing* for a compliment.[6] "Nay," said Sheridan, "he loved your fish so well that he was willing to take it with *pun sauce*."

Went to Coachmaker's Hall. Question whether cold apathy or extreme sensibility most conducive to happiness. ...[7] Home well to Dilly's after having been with Mr. Davenport, who obligingly promised [to] take [me] to trial.[8]

---

[4] Probably his *Ode upon Dedicating a Building and Erecting a Statue to Shakespeare at Stratford-upon-Avon*, 1769, which had been widely satirized in the months after it first appeared.

[5] At Sir John's house of Cranston, near Edinburgh, 20 November 1773, as Johnson was setting out for home after his tour of the Hebrides. Boswell suppressed his account of the matter when he published his *Journal of a Tour to the Hebrides* in 1785, but the printer's copy for the passage was recovered from Malahide in 1950 and was published in the Yale edition of the *Tour* in this series, 1961 (1963), pp. 450–451, facsimile at p. 392. Sir John had boasted of killing a seven-year-old sheep especially for Johnson, but never did so, though he went so far as to offer him a choice of foreleg (shoulder) or hind leg. "Accordingly none appeared, for which some foolish excuse was made."

[6] Johnson expressed "great contempt for this species of wit" (*Life of Johnson*, 30 April 1773, end), but Boswell in the *Life* records several of his own puns which Johnson accepted and some which Johnson made himself. The one recorded here, with Sheridan's comment, appears in the *Life* in a collection of undated "particulars" following 16 June 1784 ("Sir, you were a cod surrounded by smelts...").

[7] Coachmakers' Hall, in Noble Street, Foster Lane, was not far from the Dillys'. Boswell went there to attend some debating society like the "religious Robin Hood Society" he mentions in the *Life of Johnson*, 15 April 1781, as meeting in Coachmakers' Hall on Sunday evenings. We have omitted his minute of the nonsensical speech he made on this occasion.

[8] Thomas Davenport (later a serjeant-at-law and knighted), together with John

FRIDAY 16 APRIL.[9] Rose early at Dilly's; breakfast and away to Davenport. Found him quite comfortable and all well about him. But he maintained the shooting of Miss Ray to be unintentional. Was to go in Howarth's coach; full.[1] Took hackney. Saw Booth at door and shook hands. Davenport took me in to prompt. Good place at [counsel's] table. Lady Winifred. Miss Grace with [vial of] Paris vinegar [to smell,] which I said in her possession turned [into] essence of roses. Wilkes's note lively but unsuitable.[2] Affecting to see Hackman. Much pleased with Blackstone. Disgusted with Maseres's hum and ha.[3] Met Booth, *mains serrées*.[4]

Called Woodfall a little. A blackguard being was writing a well-expressed account of the trial. To Dilly's; wrote paragraphs and letter about it. Wrote to Temple. Then Baldwin, then Thomas, Silver Street, trying for *St. James's* [*Chronicle*].[5] Club. Quarrel between Johnson and Beauclerk.[6] Wine had no impression on me, I was so gloomy. Johnson, when I repeated Hackman's speech, [in which he confessed that he had done] wrong [and prayed for the] mercy of GOD, said with low-voiced piety, "I hope he shall find mercy." I was a man of consequence, as I could talk of it. Banks, Sir Joshua, Lord Althorp (new to me), Sir Charles [Bunbury], Steevens, Johnson, Beauclerk, and I the company. Talking of education, Dr. Johnson was for getting boy forward, because that is a *sure* good. Probable his sense in proportion to his learning. He was for engaging him first with English book of any kind, "Because," said he, "you've done a great deal when you've

---

Silvester, defended Hackman. Boswell had met him at Carlisle (see above, 22 August 1778).

[9] There are two entries for this date, one of them previously unpublished. The two have been conflated for this edition.

[1] Henry Howarth was one of the prosecutors for the Crown.

[2] Wilkes, apparently during the trial, sent Boswell a note which is now at Yale: "I always know where the greatest beauty in any place is when Mr. Boswell is there, for he contrives to be near her, but does not admire the first Grace more than Mr. Wilkes does." Mrs. Winifred Maxwell-Constable, grand-daughter and heir of line of the fifth Earl of Nithsdale, was generally accorded the style of "Lady Winifred," though the fifth Earl's honours had been forfeited in 1716. Her second son, William, b. 1760, married Clara Louisa, daughter of William Grace, who was probably our "Miss Grace." Lady Winifred was a friend of Burns, who wrote *Nithsdale's Welcome Hame* in her honour.

[3] The two judges: Sir William Blackstone of the famous *Commentaries*, Justice of the Common Pleas, and Francis Maseres, Cursitor Baron of the Exchequer and Deputy-Recorder of London.

[4] With clenched fists.

[5] Nathaniel Thomas was editor and part proprietor and Henry Baldwin publisher and principal proprietor of the *St. James's Chronicle*.

[6] The short note for 16 April reads, "Gave full account of the trial. Dispute about the two pistols. Johnson and Beauclerk (apart)." "Apart" probably means, "Record this separately." See Editorial Note, p. 89.

brought him to have entertainment from a book. He'll get to better books."
Called Thomas again about the letter concerning Mr. Hackman, quite
author<like>. Then Baldwin, <stopped at> Ashley's [Punch House];
very comfortable. Baldwin's next. He said I was like Bonnell Thornton, I
came in so very easily. Walked home.[7]

[From the *Public Advertiser*, 19 April 1779. By Boswell]

Mr. Booth, of Craven Street, brother-in-law to the unfortunate Mr.
Hackman, is as genteel and amiable [a] man as lives. The letter from Mr.
Hackman to him proves what might be expected from his feelings and
generosity. He was too much agitated to be present in court during Mr.
Hackman's trial, but remained without near to Newgate. Mr. Boswell,
who left the court as soon as sentence was pronounced, was the first person
who informed him of the fate of his relation and friend. Upon being told
that he was found guilty, and that, from the circumstances of the case, it
could not be otherwise, Mr. Booth eagerly asked how Mr. Hackman had
behaved. Mr. Boswell answered, "As well, Sir, as you or any of his friends
could wish: with decency, propriety, and in such a manner as to interest
every one present. He might have pleaded that he shot Miss Ray by accident, but he fairly told the truth: that in a moment of frenzy he did intend
it." "Well," said Mr. Booth, "I would rather have him found guilty with
truth and honour than escape by a mean evasion"—a sentiment truly
noble, bursting from a heart rent with anguish!

Dr. Johnson, the great moralist of the age, mentions in his *Rambler*
that Dr. Boerhaave never saw a criminal led to execution but he thought,
"Perhaps this man is, upon the whole, less guilty than I am." Let those
whose passions are keen and impetuous consider, with awful fear, the fate
of Mr. Hackman. How often have *they* infringed the laws of morality by
indulgence! *He*, upon one check, was suddenly hurried to commit a
dreadful act.

[From the *St. James's Chronicle*, 15–17 April 1779. By Boswell]

To the Printer of the *St. J. Chronicle*

Sir:—I am just come from attending the trial and condemnation of the
unfortunate Mr. Hackman who shot Miss Ray; and I must own that I
feel an unusual depression of spirits, joined with that *pause* which so
solemn a warning of the dreadful effects that the *passion of love* may
produce must give all of us who have lively sensations and warm tempers.
Mr. Hackman is a genteel young man, not five-and-twenty. He was several

---

[7] Dilly's, as the short note makes clear. Though Boswell slept more often at Paoli's, he
regarded Dilly's as equally a home.

years an officer in the Army, but having had his affections engaged by Miss Ray, he quitted that profession and took orders, having hopes that she would unite herself to him by marriage. Let not any one too rashly censure him for cherishing such a scheme. I allow that he was *dignus meliore flamma*, worthy of a more deserving flame; but she who could enchant for years, in the autumn of possession too, the First Lord of the A———ty, a nobleman so experienced in women, might surely fascinate in the blossom of courtship, a young officer whose amorous enthusiasm was at its highth. There is in love a certain delusion which makes a man think that the object of it is perfect, and that even the faults which he cannot but know she has had are purified and burnt away in the fire of his passion. Thus was Mr. Hackman lately situated; but whether from mere change, to which fancy is liable, or from considerations of prudence and interest, he found that Miss Ray no longer showed the same affection towards him as formerly. As his manners were uncommonly amiable, his mind and heart seem to have been uncommonly pure and virtuous, for he never once attempted to have a licentious connexion with Miss Ray. It may seem strange at first, but I can very well suppose that had he been less virtuous, he would not now have been so criminal. But his passion was not to be diverted with inferior gratifications. He loved Miss Ray with all his soul, and nothing could make him happy but having her all his own. Finding his hopes blasted, his life was miserable. He endeavoured to dissipate the gloom, but it overpowered him; and the consequences were told us today by himself in a decent and pathetic speech to Mr. Justice Blackstone, who presided at his trial. He was in great agitation, and I was afraid would have been incapable of utterance; but he collected himself, and read it with much pathos and energy from a paper which he held in his hand.

The audience were affected in the tenderest manner by this speech, and by a letter from the prisoner to his brother-in-law which he intended should be delivered after he had fallen by his own hands, and in which he prayed for blessings upon his mistress and entreated his brother-in-law, if ever it should happen that she should stand in need of his assistance, to give it for the sake of his departed friend. This letter proved that there was certainly no antecedent malice. But Sir William Blackstone very properly observed that to constitute the legal crime of murther it is sufficient if there be an intention at the time.[8] Accordingly Mr. Hackman was found guilty,

[8] "He said that the law did not require a long-formed scheme to kill a person to come within the crime of murder. If a man fired at A to kill him, but instead happened to kill B, the law held it to be murder, because it was in the commission of a felonious act: firing at A. If the prisoner had in his endeavour to dispatch himself, shot himself [*sic*], it for the like reason would have been murder. He was sorry to say that the prisoner's

and sentence of death was pronounced upon him for Monday next.

I could not but admire the candour and honourable regard to truth in Mr. Hackman, who acknowledged a design in a moment of frenzy, though he knew that death must be the inevitable consequence, when he might with much plausibility have said that the pistol which he meant to discharge at his own head, in Miss Ray's sight, took *by chance* a direction towards her head in the confusion in which he was, when she suddenly turned round to him. But he disdained falsehood or evasion.

His case is one of the most remarkable that has ever occurred in the history of human nature, but it is by no means unnatural. The principle of it is very philosophically explained and illustrated in *The Hypochondriack*, a periodical paper peculiarly adapted to the people of England, and which now comes out monthly in the *London Magazine*.[9] In the thirteenth number of that paper, published last October, is this passage:

To return to the passion of love with all its feverish anxiety, that being the principal subject which I wish to keep in view in this paper, it is to be observed that there is in it no mixture of disinterested kindness for the person who is the object of it. We have indeed many poetical instances of an affectation of this, where a rejected lover prays for blessings on his Delia, and hopes she shall be happy with a more deserving swain. But we may be certain that these are false expressions, for the natural sentiment in such a situation is hatred, and that of the bitterest kind. We do not feel for her who is the object of our amorous passion anything similar to the natural affection of a mother for her child, of which so fine a test is related in the Judgement of Solomon, where the true mother, with melting tenderness, entreated that her child should be delivered to a stranger who contended with her for the right to it, rather than it should be destroyed. On the contrary, the fondness for the object of our love is purely selfish, and nothing can be more natural and just than what Lucy in the *Beggar's Opera* says to her dear Captain Macheath, "I love thee so that I could sooner bear to see thee hanged than in the arms of another." The natural effect of disappointed love,

---

case bore much stronger against him. He had two pistols about him, which had the appearance of a double design. As to the plea of insanity, or frenzy of the moment, which the prisoner called it, it was not every start of passion, every tumultuous heat of the brain, which could be allowed as an excuse for the crime of murder. There must be a total deprivation of the senses, so that in no action of life he was capable of conducting himself. If the jury could suppose the prisoner at the time to be under that influence, they must acquit him; otherwise it was incumbent on them to find him guilty, regardless of the consequences." The jury found him guilty without retiring (*London Chronicle*, 15–17 April 1779, xlv. 366).

[9] Boswell was of course himself the author of *The Hypochondriack*.

however shocking it may appear, is to excite the most horrid resentment against its object, at least to make us prefer the destruction of our mistress to seeing her possessed by a rival. I say this is unrestrained nature; and wherever passion is stronger than principle, it bursts forth into horrid deeds. Not many years ago a young gentleman of very good family in Ireland was executed for the murther of a young lady with whom he was in love, whom he shot in the coach with her father, as she was on the road to be married to another. And so strong was the sense of untutored mankind in his behalf that the populace rose in a tumultuous manner to rescue him from justice, and the sentence of the law could not be fulfilled but by the aid of a large body of soldiers.

The use to be made of so striking an instance as that of Mr. Hackman is to make us watch the dawnings of violent passion and pray to God to enable us by His grace to restrain it. "Think ye that those on whom the Tower of Siloam fell were greater sinners than others? I tell you nay. But except ye repent ye shall all likewise perish." [1] These were the words of the Saviour of the world; and in humble allusion to them, I would say to all who are conscious that their passions are violent, "Think ye that this unfortunate gentleman's general character is, in the eye of Heaven or of generous men in their private feelings, worse than yours? No, it is not. And unless ye are upon your guard ye may all likewise be in his melancholy situation." While human justice is to be satisfied, let us consider that his crime was neither premeditated cruelty nor base greediness. He is therefore an object neither of abhorrence nor of contempt; and upon such an occasion I could wish that the royal prerogative could transmute the mode of punishment from that which is common to mean offenders to what would better suit the character of the sufferer. This, however, is but a slight consideration on which it does not become us to dwell while we should be employed on what is of infinitely greater importance. Let us unite our fervent prayers to the Throne of Heaven that this our brother may obtain forgiveness through Jesus Christ, and be admitted in another state of being to everlasting happiness. I am, Sir, yours, etc.

J. B.

[Editorial Note: Boswell included in neither of the journal entries for 16 April any detailed account of the quarrel between Johnson and Beauclerk over Hackman's intentions, but in the shorter of the two, as mentioned above (p. 85 n. 6), he indicated that he had already recorded it separately or (more probably) planned to make such a separate record soon. This "paper apart," which after revision served directly as printer's

[1] Luke 13. 4–5, paraphrased.

copy for the *Life of Johnson,* is now printed in the form in which Boswell originally wrote it.]

As the—I know not what word to use, whether *dispute, contest,* or *altercation*—between Johnson and Mr. Beauclerk at the Literary Club, 16 April 1779, has been much talked of and may be misrepresented, I think it right to write down exactly what passed.

We were talking of Hackman. Dr. Johnson argued, as Judge Blackstone had done, that his having two pistols with him was a proof that he meant to shoot two people. Mr. Beauclerk said no. For that whoever intended to kill himself took two pistols that he might be sure of doing it at once. Lord [Charles] Spencer's cook shot himself with one pistol, and lived ten days in great agony. Mr. Delmis, who loved buttered muffins but durst not eat them because they disagreed with his stomach, resolved to shoot himself; and then he eat three buttered muffins for breakfast before shooting himself, knowing he should not be troubled with indigestion. *He* had two charged pistols. One was found lying charged upon the table by him after he had shot himself with the other. "Well," said Dr. Johnson with an air of triumph. "You see here one pistol was sufficient." (With great deference to him, his conclusion was not just, because it only so happened that one *was* sufficient. Two *might* have been necessary.) Mr. Beauclerk replied smartly, "Because he was dead." And either then or a very little after, being in anger at Dr. Johnson's triumphant remark, said, "This is what you don't know, and I know." There was then a cessation of the dispute; and some minutes intervened, during which dinner and the glass went on cheerfully. When all at once, Dr. Johnson abruptly said, "Mr. Beauclerk, how come you to talk so petulantly to me as, 'This is what you don't know and I know'? One thing I know which you don't know: that you are very uncivil." Mr. Beauclerk said, "Because you began by being uncivil (which you always are)." The words in parenthesis were, I believe, not heard by Dr. Johnson. Here again there was a cessation of arms. Dr. Johnson told me that the reason why he waited some time at first without taking any notice of what Mr. Beauclerk said was because he was thinking whether he should be angry. But when he considered that there were present a young lord (Lord Althorp) and Sir Charles Bunbury, men of the world to whom he was little known, they might think they had a right to take such liberties as Beauclerk did, and therefore he would not let it pass. A little while after this, the conversation turned on the violence of Hackman's temper. Dr. Johnson then said, "It was his business to *command* his temper, as my friend Mr. Beauclerk should have done a little ago." "I should learn of you," said Mr. Beauclerk. Dr. Johnson answered, "You have given *me* opportunities enough of learning, when I have been

in your company. No man loves to be treated with contempt." Beauclerk (with a polite [2] inclination towards the Doctor) said, "You have known me twenty years and however I may have treated others, you may be sure I could never mean to treat *you* with contempt." "Sir," said the Doctor, "you have said more than was necessary." [3] Thus it ended; and Beauclerk's coach not having come for him till very late, Dr. Johnson, with Mr. Steevens, sat with him a long time [4] after the rest of the company were gone; and he and I dined at Beauclerk's on the Saturday se'nnight thereafter. There were present at the dispute Sir Joshua Reynolds, Banks, Lord Althorp, Steevens, Sir Charles Bunbury, and myself.

After all, as Gerard Hamilton said at Lord Pembroke's table, there was nothing in it to make a noise about or some such expression. I did not mark it. [5]

SATURDAY 17 APRIL. Breakfast. Called Robert Preston a little. Wrote long to Temple. Dined Langton's with Dr. Johnson, Blackburn, etc. Beauclerk came afternoon. Dr. Johnson was admirable. Said of Mallet's *Duke of Marlborough*, "He griped [6] for materials, and thought of it till he exhausted his mind. Sometimes happens [that] men entangle themselves in their own schemes. Fitzherbert had no more learning than what he could not help. To be contradicted in order to make you talk [is] mighty unpleasing. It makes you *shine*, but 'tis by being *ground*." I was anxious to see Mr. Hackman. Went to Newgate. Booth not there. Ashley's Punch House, very agreeable.

SUNDAY 18 APRIL. General Paoli prays for state or degree of my <sobriety>. [7] At St. Stephen's chapel, etc. [8] Very desirous to see Mr. Hackman.

---

[2] The draft has three trials for this word: "genteel," "polite," and "smiling." The *Life of Johnson* retained "polite."

[3] Boswell made two trials for this phrase: "was necessary" and "you needed to do." He settled on "was necessary."

[4] "A long time" is a later addition, though probably made in 1779. Boswell left a blank in the draft, hoping to learn the exact amount of time from Beauclerk or Steevens (George Steevens, who revised Johnson's edition of Shakespeare).

[5] That is, "I wrote no detailed account of it at the time." As has been pointed out above (p. 85 n. 6), he had at least decided to write such an account by the time he wrote the shorter journal entry for 16 April. The inclusion of a remark made by W. G. Hamilton "at Lord Pembroke's table" shows that the paper apart was not written till 28 April or later. See below, the entry for 20 April.

[6] The *Life of Johnson* has "groped."

[7] Paoli was so worried by Boswell's reckless drinking that he wrote him a letter warning and scolding him. See below, p. 346 and n. 8.

[8] Unexplained. Not a house of worship: St. Stephen's Chapel (the chapel of the old Royal Palace of Westminster) had long been used as the meeting-place of the House of Commons. Perhaps someone suggested that it would be the proper place for Paoli to

Left line for Booth. Found Lord Pembroke. Giardini came.[9] Giardini and his Lordship <all> proper, propriety itself. What a contrast to Hackman's situation![1] Pembroke said he himself had had two pistols when afraid of assassin. I said, "Natural to <shoo>t mistress." Said he, ["To shoot] Lord Sandwich natural." Said I, "Othello shoots his Desdemona. <Doubt if he de>served max<imum penalty.>" Said Lord Pembroke, "Had he shot Lord Sandwich, he might have said with Othello, 'I've done the state some service.' " [2] <Said> of Beauclerk, "This man presumes too much on his infirmities."

I told Burke of contest between Johnson and Beauclerk. Said he, "Between Fury and Malevolence." I. "The <bear and>—what is a small animal <that stands ground?"> BURKE. "A polecat." BOSWELL. "Is <that spirit>ed enough?" "O yes," said Burke. BOSWELL. "Palmer [3] wondered how I could help Johnson's <fury a>long." BURKE. "He'd [4] rather see <your e>xecut[ion] than none." "But," <said I, "he> recovers me." "Yes," said <Burke, "he ta>kes you to [the] Humane Society [afterwards.] He has it [5] in his breast."

Lord Loudoun a little. Dined Strahan with Dr. Johnson. He said little. Went to his house afterwards, and he talked well of Langton's exceeding [his] income, [and said his] excuse [that] of all spendthrifts. Went with him in coach to Mrs. Vesey's door; calm. . . . Anxious to see Mr. Hackman. . . . Cambiagi's, Chancellor's, etc.[6] . . . <C. Dilly n>ot home.

---

offer his intercessions in, because so much of Boswell's drinking was done in the company of Members of Parliament.

[9] Felice di Giardini, violinist and composer, at various times leader of the band and director of the Opera, was at this time playing first violin at the Pantheon concerts. Dr. Burney declared that among individual performers, only Garrick was more applauded than Giardini. Joseph Cradock had at one point approached Giardini for Miss Ray when she had considered going on the stage.

[1] Pembroke was a notorious rake, and Boswell implies that he and Giardini were birds of a feather.

[2] *Othello*, V. ii. 339.

[3] Dr. Richard Palmer, Rector of Scott Willoughby, Lincolnshire, and of St. Swithin's, London; prebendary of Canterbury; formerly chaplain to the House of Commons. It is not known when or how Boswell first met him, but they were on terms of easy acquaintance at least as early as 1769. On 23 March 1779 Boswell had taken him along when he went to call on Johnson, and on another day (probably 25 March) he had been one of a small dinner company that had included Johnson and Boswell.

[4] Johnson would.

[5] The Humane Society. The Humane Society had been founded in 1774 by Dr. William Hawes for the recovery of persons apparently dead, especially from drowning. Boswell was later elected a Steward of the Society.

[6] Unexplained. "Cambiagi's" appears after "Strahan's" in both of Boswell's engagement lists for this day, "Chancellor's, etc." in one of them. Boswell probably made

MONDAY 19 APRIL. C. Dilly came home. Tea fast. Away to Newgate. Mr. Akerman very obliging.[7] Into press-yard. Steevens there; disagreeable [when] unrestrained by Johnson. Hackman quite "My thoughts are fixed on Heaven." Horrid noise. Got along: Constable Webb; then tall Cludd. Saw [execution] quite well. Little affected in comparison of what might [have] been expected. Read Pascal. Talked with hangman if he heard what he said to clergymen. "No. I thought it a point of ill manners to listen on such occasions." [8] Told about fixing rope, etc. Away and drank white wine. [Then] beef [and] porter. Quite elevated. Afraid to meet people in street. In Parliament Street [met] sailors; one walking in kennel [9] with boots. Punch at Rummer.[1] Write this day apart. House of Lords a little; hot. Saw Mortimer.[2] Sat awhile in passage with Dr. Kippis. Told Wilkes of Lord Sandwich's being prayed for. WILKES. "Where?" BOSWELL. "In cart at Tyburn." WILKES. "Very proper place." Said I: "As founder." [3] Went to Mrs. Burke's [for] tea and managed well. Finished at Dr. Webster's with claret and Welsh rabbit. Claret h<urt>. Very ill. Ashamed that General <should see>. Vexed at news having my name [as] <riding in> coach with Mr. Hackman. Was sa<dly unea>sy.

[From *Lloyd's Evening Post*, 16–19 April 1779.]

A little after five this morning the Rev. Mr. Hackman got up, dressed himself, and was at private meditation till near seven, when Mr. Boswell

---

calls on both men after leaving Johnson. As stated above, Lord Thurlow was Chancellor at the time.

[7] Richard Akerman was Keeper of Newgate from 1754 until his death in 1792. This is Boswell's first mention of him in the journal, although he seems to have been acquainted with him for some time previously.

[8] Edward Dennis was hangman from 1771 until 1786. He had executed "Sixteen-String" Jack Rann, the Perreau brothers, and the Rev. William Dodd.

[9] Surface-drain of the street, the gutter.

[1] The famous tavern of this name at Waterside, Charing Cross, was destroyed by fire, 7 November 1750. Others adopted the name, but Boswell seems to be closer to the site in Charing Cross than to any of the other locations. Perhaps a temporary establishment had opened near where the old one had stood, to trade on its reputation.

[2] Obscure. Perhaps Hans Winthrop Mortimer (1734–1807), at this time M.P. for Shaftesbury. He was notable for having won in 1776 a judgement of £11,000 for bribery from Thomas Rumbold, rich Indian administrator who opposed him in the election of 1774. Rumbold, who in 1777 had gone back to India as Governor of Madras, had just been made a baronet (27 March 1779).

[3] Sandwich was linked with Tyburn by his common nickname of "Jemmy Twitcher," taken from the clever thief in *The Beggar's Opera* who "peached" Macheath. Sandwich had been closely associated with Wilkes in the notorious group known as the Monks of Medmenham Abbey, but when Wilkes's papers were seized by government agents, he helped collect evidence against him.

and two other gentlemen waited on him and accompanied him to the chapel, where prayers were read by the Ordinary of Newgate, after which he received the Sacrament. Between eight and nine he came down from chapel, and was haltered. When the sheriff's officer took the cord from the bag to perform his duty, Mr. Hackman said, "Oh! the sight of this shocks me more than the thought of its intended operation." He then shed a few tears, and took leave of [the] two gentlemen in a very affecting manner. He was then conducted to a mourning-coach, attended by Mr. Villette the Ordinary, Mr. Boswell, and Mr. Davenport the sheriff's officer, when the procession proceeded ... to Tyburn.... On his arrival at Tyburn, he got out of the coach, mounted the cart, and took an affectionate leave of Mr. Boswell and the Ordinary. After some time spent in prayer, he was tied up, and about ten minutes past eleven he was launched into Eternity. After hanging the usual time, his body was brought to Surgeons' Hall for dissection.[4]

TUESDAY 20 APRIL. Uneasy about my *name* [as] attending Hackman. Called Skeffington and Marlay in coach to settle [when we should] dine [at] Lord Pembroke's.[5] They were quite genteel. Dean talked of Dr. Johnson at Mrs. Vesey's, [how he had said of] Le Texier, "A buffoon. We'll make a party; I'll give the fellow sixpence."[6] Marlay said, "I was glad: these *bitches* who [praise Le Texier though they] don't understand." Talked of my *name* being in papers (in cart with Hackman) as a joke. I was vexed; [was for] going express or sending to Johnson [for advice.] Called Lord Pembroke. [He] declared he did not think it me; there were a hundred Boswells. This relieved me at once. "Well," said I, ["it shows the] importance of [a] man to himself. I'm not entitled to say *I* was meant." Settled [to] dine with him Wednesday. Then Burke's, and consulted him

[4] This account appeared in the evening of the day of Hackman's execution. Much the same account appeared in the *Public Advertiser* (20 April) and the *St. James's Chronicle* (17–20 April). The *London Chronicle* (17–20 April), with little other change, substituted "Mr. Porter" for "Mr. Boswell" throughout. The Rev. Moses Porter of Clapham was a close friend of Hackman's.

[5] Richard Marlay, Dean of Ferns (later Bishop of Clonfert and of Waterford) has already appeared in this journal as a guest at Sir Joshua Reynolds's on 13 April 1779. He was elected to The Club in 1777. Maj. William John Skeffington was an Irish friend of Marlay's.

[6] A.-A. Le Texier, a Frenchman who began life as a civil servant, gave very successful public readings of plays, adapting his voice and bearing to each character and even suggesting appropriate action. He read only French plays in French. Garrick had given him his protection when he came to England in 1775, but their friendship seems later to have deteriorated. Boswell did not include this remark of Johnson's in the *Life of Johnson*, and the reasons for Johnson's low opinion of Le Texier apparently remain unrecorded.

as friend. Said 'twould make it worse if I controverted. They would put in, "Mr. Boswell [was] not in coach. *But*, etc." BURKE. "Was not you in Newgate?" BOSWELL. "Yes." BURKE. "Was not you [at] Tyburn?" BOSWELL. "Yes." BURKE. "Why then, they only sent you in a coach. Besides, why be angry at [their] making you perform one of the most amiable Christian duties: [to] visit [those] in prison?" Saw him *study* Acts of Parliament. Then went to Baldwin's t<o get> *St. James's* [*Chronicle* to] tell mistake of name. Th<en to> Woodfall's and left a good paragraph in <tone of> waggery. *Lloyd's* the same. Din<ed home with> two Sherrys,[7] Dilly, Lecturer Walker,[8] <Ticke>ll, and Braithwaite. Curious day.... <Supped> [9] with General Oglethorpe.

[From the *Public Advertiser*, 21 April 1779. By Boswell]

It was not Mr. Boswell but the Rev. Dr. Porter of Clapham who so humanely attended the late unfortunate Mr. Hackman. Mr. Boswell had for a day that praise which is so justly allowed to generous tenderness; but he has taken care that it shall be enjoyed by the worthy person to whom it was due.[1]

WEDNESDAY 21 APRIL. Do not remember the forenoon. Dined Fullarton's. Earls of Glencairn and Balcarres,[2] Forth an Irish intelligencer (good countenance and bold talker), Currie an Irish gentleman and Burgh the same, Anstruther, Robertson, Wilkes and Tickell (meeting for first time), Janes the chaplain. Wilkes began instantly. Told Tickell, "Much obliged

---

[7] That is, the Sheridans, probably Thomas and Charles Francis, as on 15 April.

[8] "Lecturer" Adam Walker was a remarkable autodidact and popularizer of natural philosophy. He made up for lack of formal instruction by incessant study of borrowed books, and his lectures on astronomy in Manchester were followed by successful lecturing visits to most of the larger cities in Great Britain and Ireland, culminating in a lecture in the Haymarket in 1778, encouraged by Joseph Priestley. He continued to lecture in London and was engaged as lecturer to a number of public schools, including Eton, Westminster, and Winchester. His inventions besides the "coelestina," a harpsichord capable of producing continuous tones, and an "eidouranion" or transparent orrery, included wind and steam carriages, a system of domestic thermo-ventilation, irrigation machines, and the rotatory lights on the Scilly Isles. It was one of his lectures that first roused Shelley's interest in science.

[9] Three or four words are missing or so fragmentary as to be illegible. "Supped" is entirely conjectural.

[1] The paragraph was repeated in *Lloyd's Evening Post* (20–22 April); the *St. James's Chronicle* (17–20 April) had printed the erroneous paragraph on an inside page but had not printed (or was still printing) its last page when Boswell's correction arrived. The correction, reduced to one sentence, appears in the same issue as the story.

[2] Balcarres, who had fought gallantly at Ticonderoga (1777) but had been compelled to surrender under Burgoyne's convention, had returned to Great Britain under parole.

for your speech for me. If you'll make me another for next session, I'll be damned if I don't speak it." [3] Tickell was much pleased with him. They spoke of Pope. Wilkes said he [4] did not understand what Lord Bolingbroke gave him to versify. It was "A mighty maze of walks [without a plan."] Bolingbroke [told Pope], "You don't understand," [and Pope changed it to] "but not without [a plan."] [5] (I told what Lord Bathurst said.) Tickell thought "without a plan" very well: [meant] without a plan here. "Wait [the] great Teacher, [Death."] [6] Wilkes laughed at the *Essay* [and parodied it:]

> Why has not man a nose to smell a rat?
> The answer's plain: that man is not a cat.[7]

Tickell gave us some fine imitations of Burke, by Jack Townshend as he said. We talked of wit [which is] merely *jeu de mots.* 'Tis wit, yet cannot be translated; 'tis inferior to wit of sentiment.[8] Long argument about Garrick's character. Wilkes bitter. I said he should pay half a guinea when he mentioned either Scotland or religion. All went cheerful, and claret made no impression to hurt me at all. Tickell attacked Johnson's sentence about Cowley: ["An intellectual digestion that concocted the] pulp [of learning] and [refused the] husks." [9] "Say it as well," said I. Told him Dr. Johnson said *Anticipation* a mighty fine thing. TICKELL. "I shall digest the pulp." Tickell said [there was] only one *debater*—Fox—who overbears [his opponents.] Surely many [could be] gr<eat orato>rs if they would. Wilkes said Burke eloquent, but <had not the right> kind of eloquence; [his was] wild Irish eloquence. As Apelles's [painting of a] fine <woman had su>ch flesh [that some] said [she had] fed on roses, Burke's [art gives]

---

[3] Wilkes is alluding to Tickell's *Anticipation*, a pamphlet published a few days before the opening of Parliament in November 1778, in which Tickell forecast the debates satirically.
[4] Pope.
[5] *Essay on Man*, i. 6 indeed did originally read, "A mighty maze of walks without a plan," but was changed in later editions to "A mighty maze! but not without a plan."
[6] *Essay on Man*, i. 92.
[7] *Essay on Man*, i. 193–194:
> Why has not man a microscopic eye?
> For this plain reason, man is not a fly.
[8] The company (probably consciously) was echoing Addison's tests of false and true wit: "The only way...to try a piece of wit is to translate it into a different language" (*Spectator* 61; see also *Spectator* 62).
[9] "A memory admitting some things and rejecting others; an intellectual digestion that concocted the pulp of learning but refused the husks, had the appearance of an instinctive elegance, of a particular provision made by nature for literary politeness" (*Life of Cowley*, ¶ 5).

a fine woman, <but fed> on potatoes and whisky: beautiful, not sublime.¹ <It does not> shake you. Lord Chatham's *studied* eloquence Olympian. ... It was a very good day.... Wilkes, Tickell, Jones, Anstruther there afterwards at coffee.

[EDITORIAL NOTE: For 22 and 23 April we have only the record of Boswell's engagements for dinner and tea: "Thursday 22—Sir J. Dick's— Mrs. Bosville. Friday 23—Home."]

SATURDAY 24 APRIL. After eight hours' sleep, awaked gloomy and relaxed. *Knew* I was so, and *hoped* it would soon be better with me. Sent note to Lord Cassillis to wait on him. After breakfast Hoole called for a little.

Went to Lord Cassillis. Said we had been in an awkward situation, and it was time to put an end to it. Stated my zeal at his election, [and complained of] his neglect of me: never calling, though Lord Eglinton always did, not employing me as his lawyer against this very messenger-man.² He would not acknowledge the first. Said the last was wrong. But the lawsuit was begun the very day after his brother's burial. I said I was now going to ask of him what, if he granted [it] would settle all: £50 to [be given to a] worthy friend, no matter whether post, pension, or *riding*— Johnston in south. "Johnstons and Jardines," said he, "*ride* thieves aw." Said I: "Let him ride." ³ He said *upon his honour* he would do all he could, and he was to dine today with Sir Grey Cooper. I said if he got it, I was satisfied. Then we were very well, and I promised to dine with him one day.

Was very lame.⁴ Called on Lord Marchmont, Lord Mountstuart, Lord

¹ Wilkes is quoting Plutarch, but somewhat inaccurately. Euphranor said Parrhasius's Theseus had fed on roses, but his own Theseus on beef. "Beautiful, not sublime," is a gibe at Burke's early considerable publication, *A Philosophical Enquiry into the Origin of Our Ideas of the Sublime and Beautiful*, 1757.
² Alluding to the Parliamentary election of 1774 when Lord Cassillis, then David Kennedy, advocate, was the candidate as Member for Ayrshire of the "noble association" against Sir Adam Fergusson of Kilkerran, supported by the "independents." Boswell's energetic work in this campaign for the "noble association" and his rift with his father over it are detailed in *Boswell for the Defence*, pp. 201–203 (Heinemann ed., 211–212). Boswell professed to believe that Sir Adam was descended from a messenger-at-arms.
³ Boswell's "riding" bears the old Scots sense of getting goods by predatory incursion on horseback, in the old-fashioned method of the Border. Cassillis is quoting or adapting a "popular saying" which Walter Scott gives in the form "Elliots and Armstrongs
⁴ He was suffering from ingrown toe-nails, an affliction he had experienced during his Corsican tour but had been free from since 1766.
ride thieves all" (*Poetical Works*, 1833, i. 393).

Exeter, Lord G<raham, and sat> with General Oglethorpe and took down <notes of> his life.[5] It rained a good deal, which I suppose had occasioned my gloom. Home and wrote Oglethorpe's notes of life [hitherto] omitted, and letter to Sir Charles Preston. Took some soup, etc., with General Paoli. Oglethorpe called in coach and carried me to Beauclerk's. Lady Di not with us. Johnson, Sir Joshua, Langton, Jones, Steevens, Paradise, Dr. Higgins.[6] I mentioned Wilkes's attack on Garrick: [a man] with no friend. JOHNSON. "I believe he's right. Garrick so diffused [it was] ᾧ φιλοι, οὐ φίλος,[7] [he] had no man to whom he wished to unbosom himself. [He] saw people always ready to applaud him, and always for the same thing; so [he] saw life with great uniformity." I said he did not need a friend, as he got from everybody all he wanted.—"What is a friend? One who supports you and comforts you while others do not. 'Tis the cordial drop for [the] nauseous draught. But no occasion for it if draught not nauseous.[8] His cup all capillaire." JOHNSON. "Many men would not be content to live so (I hope I should not be content), but would wish to have a friend with whom to compare mind[s] and cherish private virtues." Somebody mentioned Lord Chesterfield as having no friend. JOHNSON. "There were more materials to make friendship in Garrick had he not been so diffused." BOSWELL. "Garrick was pure gold, only beat out to thin leaf; Lord Chesterfield, tinsel." JOHNSON. "Garrick was a very good man; the cheerfulest man of his age and a decent liver in a profession which is supposed to give indulgence to licentiousness. A man who gave away liberally money got by himself. He began the world with a great hunger for money; the son of a half-pay officer, bred in a family whose study was to make fourpence do as much as others made fourpence-halfpenny do. But when he had got money he was liberal." [I mentioned] Wilkes's attack on "eclipsed [the] gaiety of nations."[9] JOHNSON. "[I] could not have

---

[5] Boswell took further notes on 9 May 1779. Seven leaves of notes for this project survive in the Boswell Papers.

[6] William (later Sir William) Jones, the great Orientalist; Paradise, also much admired for his linguistic attainments, was Greek on his mother's side and was born in Salonika; Higgins, who is mentioned only twice by Boswell (both times as a guest of Beauclerk's), is thought to be Bryan Higgins, physician and chemist.

[7] "He had friends, but no friend." The saying is from Diogenes Laertius, Bk. V, ch. i, and is attributed to Aristotle.

[8] Boswell is quoting John Wilmot, Earl of Rochester:

> That cordial drop Heaven in our cup has thrown
> To make the nauseous drop of life go down...
> (*A Letter from Artemisia...to Chloe*, ll. 44–45).

[9] In his *Life of Edmund Smith*: "At this man's table I enjoyed many cheerful and instructive hours, with companions such as are not often found; with ... one who has gladdened life ... with David Garrick, whom I hoped to have gratified with this character

said more nor less, for 'tis truth; 'eclipsed,' not 'extinguished,' and his death did eclipse; 'twas like a storm." BOSWELL. "But why 'nation*s*'?" JOHNSON. "Why, exaggeration must be allowed. Besides, nation*s* [may be said] if we allow the Scotch to be a nation and to have gaiety, which they have not. *You* an exception; and let us candidly admit [that there is] one Scotchman who is cheerful" (here some Greek phrase). BEAUCLERK. "But he's a very unnatural Scotchman." BOSWELL. " 'Harmless pleasure' [seems] too elegant or weak." JOHNSON. "Nay, 'harmless' [is the] highest praise of pleasure. Pleasure a word of dubious import." BOSWELL. "True, Sir, *pleasure* a high word." Of Wilkes he said, "One may say of him as Boileau [said of a French wit], 'Il n'a de l'esprit que contre Dieu.' [1] I have been several times in company with him, but never perceived any strong power of wit. A general effect [by various means; he has] a cheerful countenance and a gay voice. Besides, 'tis his trade. It would be as wild for Wilkes to go into company without merriment as for [a] highwayman to take the road without his pistols."

Of drinking he said, "One who exposes himself has not yet the art of getting drunk. A sober man when drunk readily enough goes into other companies, undertakes anything. But he has not the art of inebriation. I used to slink home. <One> accustomed to self-examination will be conscious when he's drunk, though an habitual drunkard will not be conscious. Dr. James for twenty years [was] not sober. Yet in his pamphlet on fevers he appealed to Garrick and me for his vindication from [a] charge of drunkenness. [It was] not published till after his death, so [the appeal was] left out.[2] A. Millar, who got £60,000 by his trade, [was] so habitually drunk that Strahan for twenty years did not know it.

"Dr. Taylor the most ignorant man I ever knew, but sprightly. Ward the dullest. Taylor challenged me to talk Latin, ha! ha! I quoted some of Horace, which he took to be part of my own speech. He said a few words well enough." Beauclerk mentioned that Johnson said Taylor was an in-

---

of our common friend; but what are the hopes of man! I am disappointed by that stroke of death which has eclipsed the gaiety of nations, and impoverished the public stock of harmless pleasure" (Samuel Johnson, *Lives of the English Poets*, ed. G. B. Hill, 1905, ii. 21).

[1] "He is witty only against God." In the *Life of Johnson* Boswell reduces this saying to anonymity, presumably because he could not find it in the writings of Boileau.

[2] Robert James had prepared a long *Vindication of the Fever Powder*, including a vindication of his own character, to accompany his *Dissertation on Fevers*, first published in 1748. He died in 1776, by which time the death of some of his principal opponents had caused him to revise and shorten his manuscript. When the *Vindication* was finally published in the eighth edition of the *Dissertation* (1776), it had been divested by himself or others "of every personal reflection on individuals," and of the appeal to Johnson and Garrick.

stance how far impudence could carry ignorance. Beauclerk told several short stories very well. Paradise [said] not a word; Jones little more than to ascertain exactly what Johnson said of [Wilkes's] cheerful countenance and gay voice.

Dr. Johnson before dinner told me he was glad I was not in coach with Hackman, and that it was right to contradict it, as people thought (and *he* thought) I had put the paragraph in myself. After coffee Johnson and I were set down by Sir Joshua at his sister's. By the way Johnson said there was in Beauclerk a predominance over his company that one did not like. But he was a man who lived so much in the world that he had a short story for everything, was always ready to begin and never exhausted.

At Miss Reynolds's we had tea plentifully. He said in answer to Burke's <remark that> affection from children to parents is not so necessary as of parents to children, and that [there would be] no harm though children at [a] certain age should eat parents. "But, Sir, if this were known generally to be the case, parents would not have affection for children." "True," said I; "for it is in expectation of return [that parents are so attentive"] and I told story of Veronica's asking to help me on with [my] clothes [so that she would know how] in [my] old age.[3] Sir Joshua <said that it had been a> good day. JOHNSON. "No, Sir. There was nothing said . . ." [4]

SUNDAY 25 APRIL. My sore foot was troublesome. Portuguese Chapel. Saw Chamber-Counsellor Sheldon there.[5] Poli, etc., dined.[6] I took General's coach and called Allan Ramsay's a little. Then Chancellor's. Lord Advocate and Ilay Campbell with him.[7] He took me by the hand and pointed to me to sit down, but never said a word to me, but conversed with them. Lord Advocate addressed discourse to me and I *took* share of conversation. Then home and went with General Paoli and Gentili to Sir John Pringle's.

MONDAY 26 APRIL. Left foot swelled and inflamed so that I could

[3] See above, 3 January 1779.
[4] The last sentence was written in the margin, which has crumbled. Perhaps a dozen words are irrecoverable. The entries for the next two days are now printed for the first time.
[5] Robert Sheldon (1744–1830) was "chamber-counsellor" only because, as a Roman Catholic, he could not qualify for admission to the bar. He took the lead in establishing the Catholic Committee and acted as its secretary.
[6] Giuseppe Saverio Poli, Neapolitan physician and naturalist. He was elected to the Royal Society a few days later (6 May 1779).
[7] Ilay Campbell, the advocate in greatest practice at the Scots bar at this time, later succeeded Henry Dundas as Lord Advocate; he was made Lord President of the Court of Session in 1789 and created a baronet in 1808.

not stir without pain. Dr. Wilson was to breakfast at any rate. Consulted him. Seward came a little. Went to bed above clothes and was obliged to send apology to Allan Ramsay, where Dr. Johnson was. Begged the Doctor would call on me. Was quite apprehensive of gout or mortification. Dined in my room light.

Evening Dr. Johnson and Sir Joshua came. I said, "I'm vexed to be confined by so slight a thing. Would rather have something worth while to confine me." "No, Sir," said Dr. Johnson, "you would not. The confinement would be the same and the evil so much greater." Showed me clearly [that] my affectation of *sentiment*, by which I really had deceived myself into a belief of being in earnest, was foolish. I maintained afterwards to General Paoli that it was what every Frenchman would have said. "And every woman," added Seward. The very sound of Dr. Johnson's voice roused me from my dejection. I had been *so very low*.

[EDITORIAL NOTE: We have no certain information as to how Boswell spent Tuesday 27 April, but he presumably stayed in at General Paoli's and nursed his sore foot. On Wednesday 28 April, though still very lame, he was able to drive in the General's coach to dine at Lord Pembroke's with Dean Marlay and Major Skeffington, as previously arranged (see above, 20 April 1779). On Thursday 29 April he wrote to Johnson the letter that follows below. In the previous spring he had arranged for Lord Marchmont to call on Johnson on a given day and at a given hour to tell him what he knew about Pope, whose intimate friend he had been. Boswell had done this, however, without consulting Johnson; and Johnson, when informed of the arrangement, balked and said he would not be at home and did not care to know about Pope. Boswell has now put the whole matter in train again.]

London, Thursday 29 April 1779

DEAR SIR,—I have delivered your *Lives of the Poets* [8] to my Lord Marchmont, who told me he had called on you twice, though he left a card only once. He has obligingly fixed *Saturday next at twelve o'clock* for receiving you and me to hold a conference on Pope. I trust that you will be punctual to this appointment, for it would vex me exceedingly if it should fail on your part.

My foot is somewhat easier and I drive about town in General Paoli's coach. If you can have a carriage from Mr. Thrale's and will do me the

[8] See above, the note at the end of 16 March 1779. In the *Life of Johnson* Boswell says that Johnson made Marchmont "a present of those volumes of his *Lives of the Poets* which were at this time published," but he probably meant by that merely to remind the reader that what was published in 1779 was only a first instalment. The remaining six volumes, including the life of Pope, did not appear till 1781.

honour to come and fetch me tomorrow, I will go down with you and stay all night and we can come up together on Saturday morning in good time. I wish to be at Streatham again, and regret that I have been so little there this spring, owing to a multiplicity of engagements in this wonderful metropolis.

My wife has written to me a very wise letter mentioning that although my father is in no immediate danger, yet he is so much indisposed that she thinks I should not be absent. I have therefore resolved to set out on Tuesday next, being the first day after finishing another term at the Temple.[9] I entreat, then, that you may be so kind as to stay in town Saturday, Sunday, and Monday. On Saturday and Sunday it is hoped you will dine at General Paoli's, and Mr. Dilly begs you may dine with him on Monday. I have never been here without prevailing on you to give him one day. He has asked no company as yet for Monday.

You will receive this early tomorrow morning. I should be glad [if] you could find an opportunity to send me an answer. Send an express if it will not cost too much to me, at General Paoli's, South Audley Street. At any rate I shall depend on your being at General Paoli's between eleven and twelve on Saturday. Lord Marchmont lives fast by the General's.

Pray present my best compliments to our friends at Streatham. I am ever most faithfully yours.

[EDITORIAL NOTE: Boswell's proposed jaunt to Streatham was apparently not convenient for Johnson or the Thrales, for Boswell says in the *Life of Johnson* that on the appointed morning Johnson came to him from Streatham. The paragraph that follows was written on a blank leaf of his retained copy of the letter to Johnson printed above.]

Next [1] morning, not long after eleven, the Doctor came, dressed in his best suit and Parisian wig, and drank chocolade and tea at General Paoli's; after which we went to Lord Marchmont's, who said very politely, "I am not going to make an encomium upon myself by telling you the high respect I have for you, Sir." After the interview, when I told the Doctor how vexed I should have been, considering my Lord's civility, if he had not come, the Doctor said he would rather have given twenty pounds.

---

[9] Boswell, though he had not yet made up his mind to quit the Scots bar, was slowly acquiring the qualifications he would need if he were to be admitted an English barrister. Thomas Sheridan had caused him to be entered in the Inner Temple so far back as 1761, and in 1775 he had begun "keeping his terms" (dining in Commons on the last dining-day of a term).

[1] Reckoning not from the date the letter was written but from that on which it was received.

[EDITORIAL NOTE: It is probably safe to assume that the dinners appointed at Paoli's for Saturday and Sunday held. That for Monday 3 May certainly did: Boswell dined with Johnson at Dilly's, as planned. Next morning he left London with Charles Dilly, pausing overnight in his way north at Southill, the Dilly family residence in Bedfordshire, to take a kind farewell of Edward Dilly, publisher of his first important book and for eleven years his warm-hearted friend. Dilly, who died within the week, cried with affection at seeing him. Boswell missed the fly at Biggleswade, but overtook it at Buckden, and travelled on to Newcastle. "An agreeable young widow," he wrote to Temple, "nursed me and supported my lame foot on her knee. Am I not fortunate in having something about me that interests people at first sight in my favour?"

At Newcastle, where he lay over as usual to see his brother John ("surly though sensible"), he came unexpectedly on his old Roman acquaintance, Thomas Charles Bigge, and was easily persuaded to pay an overnight visit to Bigge's nearby seat of Benton Hall. He arrived home in Edinburgh in good spirits in the evening of 10 May, the children next morning vastly happy to see him. Mrs. Boswell, as it turned out, had been too anxious and his sacrifice of two weeks in London unnecessary, for his father had recovered enough to face the trip to the country, and was just leaving. "You shall never see me go to London again till you desire me," Boswell told him; immediately (and characteristically) scaling the promise down to, "that is to say, till you think there is a good reason for my going." The General Assembly sat down on the 20th. Boswell had the cause of the Donors at Dunfermline coming up there on the 26th, and had planned to leave immediately afterwards for Auchinleck, but was persuaded by a fee of five guineas to stay a day more and defend Peter Lumisden, tenant in Peel, who had been convicted of adultery by the synod of Perth and Stirling but had appealed to the General Assembly on grounds of inadmissible evidence.]

TUESDAY 25 MAY. Writing case for Lumisden. Commissioner [Cochrane] dined and drank tea and was really cordial.

WEDNESDAY 26 MAY. Cause of the Doners heard and won.[2] Late in Assembly. Dined with the Lord Commissioner, and said to McDowall and Kennedy, "It's as much as our life's worth not to drink plentifully after being so long in." Drank too much. Was ill.

[2] This important cause is explained at some length in *Boswell in Extremes*, p. 127, n. 2. The Donors, who had provided a meeting-house for the Rev. Thomas Gillespie of the Relief Church, had on Gillespie's death in 1774 petitioned to be admitted to communion with the Church of Scotland as a chapel of ease, and were strongly opposed by the ministers of Dunfermline. The cause had been before the Assembly in 1774, 1775, 1776, and 1778. Boswell was counsel for the Donors.

THURSDAY 27 MAY. In General Assembly getting time fixed for Lumisden; committee appointed at eight. Dined at the Golf House with the West Fencibles. Vastly jovial, but drank greatly too much. Capt. James Campbell came up with me. I was not able to speak. But at any rate, committee had resolved not to hear us. Home very ill.

FRIDAY 28 MAY. Awaked ill and vexed at excess. Thought it very wrong that I had not been able to speak. No tickets to be had in flies. So stayed another day. Lucky this, as the cause came on in the Assembly and I spoke a little; so won my fee.[3] Was assured by the committee that they would not have let me speak at any rate. But as I was conscious I was not able, it was a nice casuistical case whether I could take my fee. Harry Erskine said I should. For it was my *luck* that they would not let me speak. But as I spoke this forenoon in the Assembly, the thing was made clear. I had first seen the Highland mutineers pardoned on the Castle Hill, the West Fencibles being all drawn up.[4] Resolved after many dubious schemes to set out on horseback. Dined cheerfully with wife and children, and mounted at half past three. Riding was very uneasy to me. Stopped at Whitburn and drank fine beer and tea. Rode on to Holytown. All my bones sore. To bed directly.

SATURDAY 29 MAY. Sir John Whitefoord was up with me between six and seven and carried me in his chaise to Glasgow. I breakfasted alone. Then waited on the Duke of Gordon and the North Fencible officers, to see that regiment having brought me by Glasgow. Drank some tea with them and was asked by his Grace to dine, but said I was obliged to go on to Auchinleck. Saw eight companies of the regiment on the Green. Mounted before three, dined Waterside by Galston. Called at Milrig a minute. Heard father had been ill. Got to Auchinleck about nine. Father better and rather more kind. Dr. Gillespie and Mr. Stobie there.

SUNDAY 30 MAY. Lady Auchinleck, Dr. Gillespie, Mr. Stobie, and I went in the coach to church and heard Mr. Millar,[5] helper to Mr. Dun. Home after the forenoon service. Dr. Gillespie went to Logan, and re-

[3] The Assembly affirmed the sentence of the synod, which is to say that Boswell lost his cause.

[4] On 20 April a party of about fifty recruits for the 42nd and 71st Regiments of Highlanders mutinied at Leith and refused to embark because of a report that they were to be drafted into a Lowland regiment. In the fighting which followed, several men were killed; of twenty-five taken prisoner, three were tried at court-martial and condemned to death. This day the King's free pardon was read to them.

[5] Alexander Millar ("wee Millar") would a few years later win immortality of a sort by being included in Burns's *Holy Fair*. Burns said he gabbled orthodoxy because he wanted a manse, but in his heart believed it to be old wives' fables.

turned in the evening.[6] I went to the seat at the Waterside, and under the rock as usual worshipped GOD, saying part of the Church of England liturgy. Saw James Bruce a little.

MONDAY 31 MAY. Got on horseback early. Convoyed Dr. Gillespie to Ochiltree. Then viewed George Paton's dikes; not in good order. Home to breakfast. Walked out a little with father and the ladies. Fingland dined and drank tea; Logan and Hallglenmuir dined.[7] Dr. Gillespie returned at night.

TUESDAY 1 JUNE. Rode down with James Bruce and surveyed the Trabboch, particularly last winter's plantations. Called at Trabboch Mains and stood on Old Castle. Fine farm. Bruce Campbell was at dinner at Auchinleck.

WEDNESDAY 2 JUNE. Rode over to Bruce Campbell's to breakfast. He and I then looked at disputed road between Treesbank and Cairnhill; met Bruntwood. Returned in good time to dinner: Sir John Whitefoord, Logan, Old John Boswell, young Polquhairn.[8] Was uneasy lest my father should not entertain properly. But he was remarkably well. Told stories very humorously and gave us three bottles of claret. I was disturbed a little with what I drank. Engaged to dine with Sir John on Friday. Never felt my mind less subject to fretful sensibility.

THURSDAY 3 JUNE. Set off early to see poor Miss Cuninghame. Rode the young horse. He started with me on the road, and I was very near falling. Was seriously impressed by this. Breakfasted at Mitchell's inn, Kilmarnock, comfortably. Sent for Mr. Brown, who rode down with me to Doura. Saw Lord Glencairn's burial-place at Kilmaurs. Found Miss Cuninghame quite pale and emaciated and solitary. It was very affecting. But I put on cheerfulness. Brown was called up, and he and I drank some strong ale. Sir Walter was at Kilwinning at the papingo.[9] He was sent for, and came after dinner. Brown went home before it. Miss Cuninghame

---

[6] Lord Auchinleck's complaint having become chronic, Dr. Gillespie's daily attendance was now required. See below, 7 June 1779.

[7] Fingland's name was James Chalmers, Hallglenmuir's was Alexander Mitchell. Mitchell's mother was a Boswell, sister to John Boswell, "Old Knockroon." Hugh Logan, "the laird of Logan," had a reputation for humour and hospitality.

[8] The laird of Bruntwood, as noted above, 3 November 1778, was named Francis Moor; the laird of Polquhairn, Adam Craufurd Newall (or Newall Craufurd), d. 1790. We have not yet recovered the Christian name of his son. "Mr. Craufurd, son of Polquhairn," was one of the last guests Boswell entertained at Auchinleck (8 January 1795).

[9] The papingo or popinjay was a wooden bird or mark shot at, originally with bow and arrows, later by fire-arms, in an annual contest (see Scott's *Old Mortality*, chapters 2 and 3). Kilwinning was famous for its addiction to this amusement.

and I and Mrs. Rutherfurd sat at table. Poor girl! She said she sometimes thought it was better for her not to recover, as she had already suffered a great part, and she would have to suffer it all over again. She spoke really with resentment (just indeed) of Lady Auchinleck, and said she wished only she could live to see her obliged to quit Auchinleck, which, though she might have pride enough to conceal it from me, would vex or gall her (or some such word). She said *how* could she set herself up in the corner of the seat at church, and pretend to be religious, when nothing could be more wicked than to estrange a father from his children? She might well be said to make religion a cloak for maliciousness.[10] I drank temperately, and then had tea, and bid her farewell. Sir Walter convoyed me a little way. I got home in good time, and was so shocked with thinking of Lady Auchinleck's barbarous indifference that I was very silent. At night alone, I was tenderly sad for the amiable, distressed young creature, Miss Cuninghame.

FRIDAY 4 JUNE. My father proposed to me to go out with them in the coach. *She* was fretted when she heard of it. He said, "He" (i.e., I) "is going to Ballochmyle." She answered, "Let him *gang*." She talked of the day being hot for two horses in the coach, and that they had intended to go up by the kirk; and tried every way to shift. But I was calm and said, "I can go any way. I'm your man." So I *did* go as far as Brackenhill. There I came out. Surveyed John Jamie's former plantation —very poor—and the Clews Mount, which required thinning to let up the beeches, and got to Ballochmyle two hours before dinner. Walked with Sir John. Nobody at dinner but Gavin Hamilton.[1] I had not been in this house for ten years. Was easy and well. We drank four bottles of claret. Then tea. Miss Whitefoord and her governess with us. Home quietly. Logan joined me last night at the Haugh Mill, very drunk and very good-humoured. Said: "I would do anything to serve you. I court you. But you winna court me." I declare my heart softened towards him. But I would make no advance till I should meet him sober. There was only presumptive evidence of his having made Pollach vote for Sir Adam Fergusson contrary to his promise, and Hallglenmuir assured me Pollach said it was not so.[2] He was an honest man, and certainly knew.

SATURDAY 5 JUNE. Upon a hint from my father, walked round the

[10] 1 Peter 2. 16.

[1] The "Gau'n Hamilton" of Burns's "Holy Willie's Prayer," written to celebrate Hamilton's victory in 1785 in the presbytery of Ayr over the kirk session of Mauchline, which had censured him for his liberal views. Hamilton was Burns's immediate landlord of Mossgiel (from 1783).

[2] Hugh Mitchell of Pollach may have been Alexander Mitchell's brother. This is another reference to the Ayrshire election of 1774. See above, 24 April 1779.

Tenshillingside avenues. James Bruce was with me. It was quite comfortable talking of *the family* in different times. James suggested to me in
confidence that I might do well to prevent too many tacks [3] being granted at
present. I came home quite weary, thirsty, and hungry, and took some
oatcake and milk with most agreeable luxury. Mr. and Mrs. Dun and
———— dined. Mr. Dun had a little serious conversation with my father.
I got Mr. Dun out a little with me to Balingapebrae, and talked with
him in a friendly way. He said he had observed Lady Auchinleck keeping
at a distance from my father all who had a real regard for him. He applied
very well to my father's being *managed*, the text, "When thou wast young
thou girdedst thyself," [4] etc. He reported a ridiculous complaint of his
helper that I picked my nails in church.

SUNDAY 6 JUNE. I went to church in coach with Lady Auchinleck,
and had my servant with my horses following. Mr. Millar lectured on
the Prodigal Son. I stayed between sermons, and had Hallglenmuir and
Old John Boswell at bread and cheese and ale quite in the old style
of the family, and did very well. Then walked into Lord Dumfries's
park as formerly. Afternoon, Mr. Millar preached on "Stand fast in the
faith," [5] etc. Home and drank tea. Then liturgy at seat at Waterside.
Short calm walk with James Bruce, who owned *it were to be wished*
there were an *infallible* interpreter of the Scriptures.

MONDAY 7 JUNE. During this night for the first time since I left
Edinburgh, evacuation in sleep. Weakened by it a little and moisture of
rainy morning. My father was uneasy and impatient for Dr. Gillespie.
After breakfast he was pretty social with me, as he has been all this time,
when we were *allowed* to be together. I rode over and paid a visit to Mr.
Reid, quite fresh. Told me he was a year older than I imagined—eighty-
three.[6] Said my grandfather was of a melancholy and fretful temper from
his mother, his father being a most pleasing-tempered man. That Balmuto [7] would have said, "Are you in the pet? Keep it." (This my father
said was not true, for Balmuto always treated him with respect.) He said
both my grandfather and grandmother had a partiality for Uncle James.[8]
That he asked his father, "Whether do you like me or my sister best of all

[3] Leases. The tacks at Auchinleck were usually set for a period of nineteen years.
[4] John 21. 18.
[5] 1 Corinthians 16. 13.
[6] He lived to be ninety.
[7] John Boswell, brother of Boswell's grandfather, who purchased Balmuto. For Boswell's other relations discussed here, see the genealogical chart in *Boswell: The Ominous Years*, pp. 374–379.
[8] Dr. John Boswell's twin brother. He was a writer (solicitor), and had been dead for
twenty-five years.

your children?" (never mentioning Sanders [9] or John.) "You impudent rascal," said Auchinleck, "I like Sanders's little finger better than your whole buik." [1] This, said Mass [2] George, was not true. He said James asked what had been the names of the lairds of this family. "David, John, James," said his father. "O papa," said James, "it's a pity it should go out of the name." His father was angry at this. My grandfather made three wills, one on each of his sons. Mr. Reid was witness to all of them. James would not go to the funeral. Put on a *very* white coat, and came down to the opening of the papers, and insisted his was the real will. But Alexander's was the last. Upon his having a son named *David*, my grandfather settled on him 20,000 merks, which was at his own disposal.[3] My grandfather grew fresher in mind six weeks before he died. A few days before his death he for the first time said he had hopes (or good hopes) of eternal happiness. We drank small beer and strong beer very moderately. He said it was wonderful that people grip faster to the world as they grow older. He quoted Tillotson as saying that it is like two friends parting.

I was with my father in the library some time before dinner. I mentioned to him what Mr. Reid said of my grandfather's hopes, and I observed how anxious my grandfather had always been. "Ay," said my father, "he was timorous." During this stay at Auchinleck I several times tried to lead on my father to speak seriously of death. But he never said much, never spoke with any frankness. Once I said that a man who has done his duty need not be afraid. "Ay," said he, "but who has done his duty?" I observed that his great labour as a judge had certainly hurt his health. He said, "If I have hurt my health in doing my duty, I do not grudge it." (I think that was the phrase.) Sir Walter came and dined. I was dissatisfied with *his* unsteady conversation, and not pleased with my own want of force of mind. I dreaded being representative of the family of Auchinleck, lest it should be sadly lessened in my time. I received a letter from my dear wife, the first since I left her last, telling that she had been ill again with a spitting of blood and that she was very anxious for my return. This alarmed me much. I resolved to set out next day.

[9] That is, Alexander.

[1] Body, carcass.

[2] A customary mode of addressing, or referring to, Scottish ministers.

[3] Because his own eldest son, who died in infancy, had borne that name. In naming their children, the Boswells followed the custom usual in Scotland with established families: first son named for father's father, second son for mother's father, etc. Lord Auchinleck was named for his mother's father, Alexander Bruce, Earl of Kincardine. Old James's three wills concerned only his personal estate. Lord Auchinleck was not only heir of entail of the landed estate of Auchinleck but in fact had been laird from the time of his marriage (1738). Old James at that time had relinquished the title to him, receiving half the rents for the rest of his life.

My father said it was most proper. I talked to him by ourselves, and said I was sorry to leave him sooner than I intended. But I would come out and see him the end of some week during the Session. He said, "So you can," and seemed to take it kind. He was to go to Ayr to James Neill's house, and go and come between that and Auchinleck.[4] As I walked in the library with him, and found him clearer than for some years and really manly, it shocked me to think of his *death*. I felt sincere *affection* for him. Sir Walter went away. I walked some with him and James Bruce. Lady Auchinleck's bad conduct towards my dear wife hurt me more now that she was ill. I bid my father adieu cordially.

TUESDAY 8 JUNE. According to my strange custom of *clearing my affairs*, as it were, before a journey, I had sat up till one last night writing journal and other things; and I was called at five, so I was not quite well. James Bruce was with me betimes. I wished to impress on my mind that there was no great distance between Auchinleck and Edinburgh. Dr. Gillespie promised to write to me about my father every week. James Bruce walked with me half-way to the kirk, and we looked at trees and hedges. I felt myself taking a serious concern in them. I breakfasted at Mr. Dun's very comfortably. His helper was my guide to Hallglenmuir, where we dined; and though it came on a heavy rain and hail, I felt no dreariness even in a moorland house. We rode by Dalblair, which I surveyed with unskilful satisfaction at its extent and regret at its small rent.[5] Came to Douglas Mill, accompanied by Hallglenmuir and Mr. Millar, the helper, and passed the night very well without any riot or even levity, but was just as I wished to be.

WEDNESDAY 9 JUNE. Breakfasted with Mr. Thomson at Lanark, and found the young Campbells doing pretty well but too bashful and indifferent about me. Mr. Thomas Smith, clerk to Mr. Charles Brown, Writer to the Signet, rode with me to Edinburgh, and was a good-humoured, intelligent companion. Found my dear wife better. Miss Dick with her.[6] The children were quite overjoyed to see me again. Effie and Sandy actually cried. This was very fine. Auchinleck did seem not far off. π.

THURSDAY 10 JUNE. Rode out to Musselburgh to see the 7 Regiment of Dragoons reviewed, but was too late. Only saw them upon the field

---

[4] Dr. Gillespie's practice was in Ayr and as he could not travel to Auchinleck twice every day to perform the operation which Lord Auchinleck now required, Lord Auchinleck had arranged to spend each night in Ayr, coming home every morning.

[5] Boswell had bought Dalblair, a large moor farm east of the Auchinleck estate, in 1767, and the financial complications of the purchase were to haunt him for the rest of his life. The rents were still less than a fair rate of interest on the purchase price.

[6] Janet Dick, eldest daughter of Sir Alexander Dick.

after all was over. Miss Susie Dunlop dined with us. I had sat awhile in the forenoon with Sir William Forbes, who said he liked the mystics because they make every part of life religion, so as to be serving GOD in all the common affairs of life. I walked home with Miss Dunlop and sat awhile with her, and then drank tea with Sir William Forbes by appointment, but without much satisfaction, as we could have no intimate conversation, his lady and others being present.

FRIDAY 11 JUNE. Nothing done at all. Was plagued for an hour and a half by young Borthwick of Crookston, under pretence of preparing for a consultation about an English peerage in his family. Miss Macredie drank tea and supped with us.[7]

SATURDAY 12 JUNE. (Writing Tuesday the 15th.) The Session sat down. But there were only six lords present, so nothing could be done. It was indecent to see no quorum. Old Thomas Belsches said to me that if such a thing were to happen in Westminster Hall, the King would be addressed with a complaint. I was in good steady health and spirits. Sir Alexander Dick came in his chaise and carried me and Sandy out to dine with him. He was amiable and pleasing as ever as we drove along. But after dinner he seemed failed and took a nap. It hurt me to see his decline. It was agreeable to think that his daughter, Miss Dick, was staying with my wife at present. After tea Sir Alexander's coach carried me home, as it rained hard. Mr. and Miss Macredie and young Macredie supped with us. π.

SUNDAY 13 JUNE. Was at the New Church forenoon and afternoon. Called and sat awhile at Dr. Webster's between sermons. In the evening read with my wife some of *Morale chrétienne, par* Pictet.[8] Heard my daughters repeat psalms and catechism.

MONDAY 14 JUNE. (Writing Wednesday 16.) I had yesterday received a letter from my father, enclosing his excuse to Lord President for not coming to the Session. I had asked him to send it to me, as it was decent and proper for his son to deliver it, and as I knew that my waiting on the President, which I had not done for several years, would be agreeable to my father; and this was a good opportunity. I called this morning. But he was confined to bed with a flying gout, so I did not see him, but left the letter. In the evening, however, I wrote a few lines to him, mentioning that I had called and begging he would write to my father not to come in to this Summer Session. He sent me for answer that he was not able to write, but I should hear from him. This forenoon I was consulted by the Earl of Dundonald on a troublesome cause between him and Captain

---

[7] Jane Macredie was a sister of Campbell of Treesbank's first wife. Campbell of Treesbank was Lord Auchinleck's first cousin.

[8] A work of the late seventeenth century, by the Swiss theologian Benedict Pictet.

William Roberton.[9] His Lordship, Commissioner Cochrane, and Mr. Ramsay of the Excise dined and drank tea with us. A little wine and rum punch disturbed me. I was unable, at least quite unwilling, to labour. Miss Dick left us this morning.

TUESDAY 15 JUNE. Should have written and sent off *The Hypochrondriack* No. 21. But delayed it from mere aversion to any kind of application. There were judges enough in the Court today. Business in the Court of Session appeared to me more dull and inconsiderable than ever, except when my mind has been sick with low spirits, which was not the case now. I found a motto and wrote some notes for No. 21.[1] Lord Dundonald, Dr. Webster, and Mrs. Mingay supped with us.[2] I drank negus but was kept up till one, which gave me a headache. My wife and I drank tea with Mr. Claud Boswell and his sister, Miss Menie, who had come to town for two days to put his house in order.[3] I read in the Advocates' Library Aikin's *Essay on Natural History as Applicable to Poetry.* I read it all through and was pretty well pleased with it. Walked half round the Meadow with Lord Monboddo. Felt a deficiency of knowledge and of vigour of mind.

[9] The old Earl of Dundonald, Boswell's great-uncle, had died, aged eighty-seven, on 27 June 1778. His son and successor, Archibald Cochrane, a well-known projector and inventor, had in 1773 hired Capt. William Roberton, late of the Marines, to manage his coal and salt works at Kincardine, Culross, and Valleyfield. The cause concerned the interpretation of the agreement between the two as to Roberton's pay, conditions of working, and compensation for pay lost by leaving the service. Roberton claimed £2,000 sterling. On 15 July 1779 (the business Boswell was engaged in on the present day and on 25 June) the Lord Ordinary (Alva) awarded Roberton £979. Roberton reclaimed to the Inner House, but the Lords, after much further argument, sustained the interlocutor on 26 February 1780. The Decreet in the cause fills 334 pages. Eleven years later Roberton was still pursuing Dundonald's creditors in an attempt to get his money.

[1] "But as it would be foolish to bring a cloud of witnesses for the evidence of a plain and simple matter, it must be reckoned equally so to muster an host of authorities to back an opinion of no difficulty. The Dutch and German authors are remarkable for the multiplicity of their quotations, so that their pages are quite brown with *italics*; and I remember a ludicrous comparison which one day occurred to me, that a page of a German divine or lawyer was like a slice of rich plum pudding. It is quite a mosaic work, quite an inlaid table, and resembles a beggar's gown, in which there is no large piece of the same cloth, but an aggregate of various rags. Such writing is a proof of poverty of sentiment in an author himself; though on the other hand a proper mixture of apposite quotations gives a richness to composition" (*The Hypochondriack*, No. 21, "On Quotation").

[2] Dr. Alexander Webster's wife, Mary, now dead, was a sister of Boswell's mother. His daughter Ann married Captain Eyre Robert Mingay, of the 66th Regiment of Foot.

[3] Claud Boswell and his sister Marion were Boswell's first cousins once removed, Lord Auchinleck's first cousins, and brother and sister to Lady Auchinleck.

WEDNESDAY 16 JUNE. Was in a state of indifference. Read in the library (for No. 21 *On Quotation*) James Ist's first speech to his English Parliament and the Speaker's answer, penned, I am (writing Friday the 18th) persuaded, by the King himself.[4] Balbarton and Mackilston dined with us. Miss Dick returned at night. I drank tea at the Hon. A. Gordon's.

THURSDAY 17 JUNE. Was at the review of the West Fencibles on Leith links. Was much pleased and animated. But was put out of conceit with the drudgery of the profession of the law. Major Montgomerie and Captain Kennedy of that regiment went home with me before dinner and refreshed themselves with cider and Madeira and rum and water. I drank some cider and Madeira, which warmed my animal spirits and made me think for the time of good social intercourse as the most valuable employment of time. I began to [4a] my *Hypochondriack* No. 21 and laboured close at it all the afternoon, hoping to have it ready for the post. But could not accomplish it. So wrote to Mr. Dilly that it should come by next post. Wrote with a fluency of ideas and expression which surprised me. But was uneasy to feel myself much averse to labour as a lawyer, and at the same time uneasy that my practice seemed to be scanty this Session, only two consultations having come. I dwelt with comfort on the estate of Auchinleck. But I resolved to be assiduous this first session of my father's absence, as that was to be considered as a trying era for me, because people might imagine that I would not apply to business when he was not present. The Hon. Bute Lindsay, whom I had met at the review, supped with us. I felt myself disturbed between a wish to be hospitable and a kind of incapacity for it, from anxiety so as to be *cumbered*, and awkwardness.[5]

FRIDAY 18 JUNE. Lord President had sent me yesterday a letter to my father. I called on him again this morning. But he was gone to Arniston. Worthy Grange had returned last night. I sat awhile with him in the forenoon. He dined and drank tea with me, and we went and heard Wesley preach in the evening,[6] and afterwards were at the roll-calling of

[4] In his essay, JB quoted from both speeches and reaffirmed his opinion that James wrote the response of the Speaker. Sir Edward Foss, on the contrary, found the speech of the Speaker (Sir Edward Phelips) characteristic: "His address to the King is in his usual ponderous style, and he apparently vied with His Majesty which should most fatigue the audience" (*Biographia Juridica*, 1870, p. 573).

[4a] Scots for "began."

[5] That is, between an embarrassing degree of anxiety and awkwardness.

[6] Wesley was in Edinburgh from the 16th to the 20th. On one of these days Boswell called on him (although neither Boswell's nor Wesley's journal records this) in order to question him concerning a ghost-story which Wesley believed. "His state [statement] of the evidence as to the ghost did not satisfy me" (*Life of Johnson*, after 3 May 1779).

the West Fencibles with my wife and the children. Was uneasy that I could not consistently with my business upon hand ask a number of the officers to sup with me. Felt a kindly sort of pity for them, as if they did not know well where to spend the evening. This was foolish, I dare say, as they probably were most of them agreeably engaged, and perhaps pitied me as a dull drudge. Miss Dick went home today. I finished No. 21 and sent it off. But a long Memorial for Lord Dundonald hung over me. π.

SATURDAY 19 JUNE. (Writing Tuesday the 22.) Craigengillan's daughters and Miss Ellie Ritchie dined with us.[7] I drank tea at Grange's and conversed rationally on the value of land and such solid topics with him and Mr. Gordon, Keeper of the Minute-Book.[8] My wife and I played cards and supped at Mr. Sinclair of Freswick's. John Fordyce was there, the first time of my being in company with him since his bankruptcy. I took no manner of notice of him, as I have all along thought that his living in plenty while numbers have been reduced to indigence by him, is (without going deeper) such dishonesty that he ought not to receive any countenance. Besides, his manners are forward and assuming, and he is a fellow of low extraction. It was unpleasant to sit in his company. It kept me from being gay and convivial.

SUNDAY 20 JUNE. Heard Mr. Walker lecture and preach in the New Church in the forenoon. Dined with Lord Monboddo, to whose card of invitation I had answered that I seldom dined abroad on Sunday; but I considered him as a *sacerdos*,[9] by whose conversation my mind was improved. Maclaurin and Runciman, the painter, were his other guests. Maclaurin told my Lord that he liked his book better than anything he had read upon metaphysics.[1] But that the great defect in all the systems as to a future state (that of Mahomet excepted) was that they did not represent the next world as agreeable, so that we would much rather choose to remain in this. Monboddo said if a man had a proper taste for intellectual pleasure, which was the highest of any, he would think a

---

Johnson had written Boswell a letter of introduction to Wesley during his last visit to London.

[7] John McAdam of Craigengillan, small Ayrshire laird, warm friend of both Boswell and Burns, had grown rich and respected through shrewd management. He had two daughters.

[8] He kept the Minute-Book in the Court of Session from 1766 to 1800.

[9] A priest (Latin).

[1] The first volume of Monboddo's *Ancient Metaphysics* (written in defence of Greek philosophy) was published this year. James Burnett, a judge in the Court of Session with the title of Lord Monboddo, was an able lawyer remarkable for his pre-Darwinian evolutionary views, which turned up in his other major work, *Of the Origin and Progress of Language* (1773-1792) .

future state very agreeable. Maclaurin owned that his father had great satisfaction in mathematics.[2] "Well," said Monboddo, "if there is so much satisfaction in the contemplation of lines and figures, which is but an inferior species of intellectual enjoyment, how much more must there be in the contemplation of higher subjects, of GOD and providence and all his operations?" But to have this high relish, our minds must be cultivated and spiritualized. Monboddo would not allow a philosopher to indulge in women as a pleasure, but only as an evacuation; for he said that a man who used their embraces as a pleasure would soon have that enjoyment as a business, than which nothing could make one more despicable. We drank above a bottle apiece of claret, and I was sorry to give over drinking it. After tea Maclaurin persuaded me to accompany him to Bayll's, where we drank some more claret with Charles Boyd, Charles Hay, Mr. Wight the advocate, and Mr. Wright, lately pardoned for being out in 1745. Maclaurin had resolution enough to break up in good time. But I had drank too much, though not to intoxication. This comes of deviating from my decent rule of not dining abroad on Sunday. I had heard Veronica and Effie say the Lord's prayer and psalms in the forenoon. My mind was sound enough, and though I had no high felicity, I was not at all unhappy. But I had nothing elevated about me either of my present or future state, as I have had in warmer and younger days.

MONDAY 21 JUNE. (Writing Thursday 24.) My wife was seized again with a little spitting of blood. I did very little. Grange dined with us.

TUESDAY 22 JUNE. Dictated some. My wife had no more spitting of blood. Miss Susie Dunlop supped with us. π. I drank tea at Lady Colville's.

WEDNESDAY 23 JUNE. Attended with some satisfaction to the reasonings of the Lords upon causes before them. Miss Macredie dined and drank tea. Commissioner Cochrane and Mr. James Baillie drank tea. I again called at Lord President's. His servant said he was gone out a little. I left a card with my name, and resolved not to call again till he either called on me or made some advance. I was not in good humour at present, though not very bad either. I was dissatisfied at not making a better figure in life; at not having more business as a lawyer, nor any office under Government. I thought myself insignificant. This was not reasonable. But who is long content in this state of being?

THURSDAY 24 JUNE. (Writing Saturday the 26.) Attended to the de-

[2] His father was Colin Maclaurin (1698–1746), Professor of Mathematics at the University of Edinburgh, and one of the greatest mathematicians of the century. He made his most important contributions to geometry, but is most remembered now, ironically, for the "Maclaurin series," a theorem which is not properly his own discovery (information kindly supplied by Prof. W. Wistar Comfort).

cision of some causes by the Lords. Major Montgomerie and Grange supped with us. I was warm-hearted, but did not drink to excess.

FRIDAY 25 JUNE. Was happy at finishing a troublesome Memorial for Lord Dundonald. Drank tea at Mr. Samuel Mitchelson's, Junior, the Earl's agent, and talked of the cause. This week, and particularly this day, fees came in so well that I got up again in spirits as to my practice at the bar. Balmuto drank tea at my house, but it was over before I came home. However, he sat awhile after. Lady Forbes and her sister, Miss Hay, called. Sir William Forbes supped abroad. So I agreed with them to meet them at the roll-calling of the West Fencibles, if they would come and sup with my wife and me; and I would endeavour to have with them any of the officers they should point out who could come. Sir James Campbell, Sir William Cuninghame, and Captain Kennedy were engaged. But Duntroon and Lieutenant Hamilton of Barnes came. We passed the evening very cheerfully and parted early. My wife was the better of such a scene as this. And as the Fencible officers who are quartered in the Castle must be at home by eleven at night, I thought I might frequently bring some of them home with me after roll-calling to a moderate repast, which would be an enlivening and cordial meeting without the inconveniencies of rioting and late hours.

I was now in very good spirits. But what was I doing? I was engaged in no sort of study. I was not improving my mind. I had a fine letter this week from my friend Temple which humbled me. For it showed me that he continued constant to literature, so that *in himself* he was much my superior. But then as a social being I had the advantage of him.[3] I was doing pretty well as an advocate. I was bringing up my children. I had good hopes of obtaining some preferment by Lord Mountstuart's interest, and if I lived, I was to succeed to an estate of £1,500 a year. It however hurt me to be sensible that I was deficient in vigour of mind, was not enough a *man*. But then I could not tell but others, who appeared to me sufficiently manly, might feel as I did. Upon the whole, I had no just reason to complain. π.

SATURDAY 26 JUNE. (Writing Wednesday 30.) Sat awhile with Sir

---

[3] Boswell had written on 3 May 1779, "It would be sad indeed if I were disappointed of meeting you this year after so long a separation. You and I and worthy Johnston will walk in the King's Park and have all the good ideas we ever possessed agreeably revived." Temple replied, "I propose great pleasure to myself in conversing with you and worthy Johnston in the scenes you allude to and in recollecting the passages of our early and unexperienced years. Upon a comparison, I am apprehensive we shall find our notions of things and of happiness very different from what they were at that candid period. Literate amusement and conversation will no longer bound our wishes (at least yours)" (15 June 1779).

William Forbes. Grange dined with us. He and I walked to Leith, drank a bottle of porter, eat speldings [4] and bread, and walked up again.

SUNDAY 27 JUNE. Heard Dr. Blair in the forenoon and Mr. Walker in the afternoon. Dr. Webster dined with us between sermons. He drank to poor Miss Cuninghame in a mode truly remarkable, as perhaps the last time: "All happiness to her here and hereafter." We were both warmed a little with wine, though we drank but little. Mrs. Mingay also dined. I heard the children say the Lord's prayer, etc. I read a good part of Goldsmith's first volume of the *History of the Earth* with pleasing wonder.

MONDAY 28 JUNE. Sat awhile with Maclaurin and got instruction from him on the law concerning adjudications.[5] Dined early and hastily, that I might attend the judicial sale of Crawfordston, which I was informed would go cheap. Matthew Dickie engaged to be my cautioner [6] to the extent of £1,200. I have really a rage for buying land in the shire of Ayr, and I had a kind of curious inclination to purchase this small estate because my grandfather had written in old Crawfordston's chamber.[7] But it went £200 above my price. Mr. Campbell of Airies, who purchased at this sale the lands of Barnwell, and whom I therefore called *George Barnwell*,[8] Mr. Vans Hathorn and Mr. Thomas Baillie, writers, Sir William Cuninghame and Duntroon, Fencibles, supped with us. The quick rotation of the glass to let the Fencibles have a share before eleven, was continued some time after they went away, so that I drank too much. But I was hearty, and had a client and agents with me.

[4] Defined by Boswell in his *Journal of a Tour to the Hebrides* (18 August 1773) as, "Fish (generally whitings) salted and dried in a particular manner, being dipped in the sea and dried in the sun, and eaten by the Scots by way of relish."

[5] That is, a diligence, or process for transferring the estate of a debtor to a creditor, carried on as an ordinary action before the Court of Session. The Lords of Session could, by such a decreet, appropriate a person's lands, inheritances, or any heritable right to his creditor, called the "adjudger." Boswell probably needed instruction on the law in connexion with a Petition he was writing for the postponed creditors of Lainshaw (below, 6 July 1779).

[6] Surety. The property, in Tarbolton parish, Ayrshire, had belonged to Andrew and David Crawford of Crawfordston.

[7] When he had completed the course at the College of Glasgow, Boswell's grandfather was apprenticed to Robert Crawford of Crawfordston, Writer to the Signet. The indenture, dated 1690, is in the Boswell Papers. He was contracted for "the space of two years" upon the payment of £200 "Scots money," for an apprenticeship in the law. "During his said apprenticeship he shall not haunt, frequent, nor use carding, dicing, drinking, nor any idle nor vicious company." He apparently remained with Crawfordston until 1695, when he obtained his father's permission to go to Leiden to read Civil Law.

[8] The hero of George Lillo's famous bourgeois tragedy of the prodigal apprentice, *The London Merchant*, 1731.

TUESDAY 29 JUNE. (Writing Wednesday 7 July.) Nothing to remark during the day. Major Montgomerie and Mr. John Wauchope were with me at night considering the Ayrshire roll, the Major being to stand candidate.[9] I felt that I was no politician. They supped with me soberly. I dined this day at Prestonfield, Sandy with me. Sir W. Cuninghame and Major Brown there.

WEDNESDAY 30 JUNE. Nothing to remark.

THURSDAY 1 JULY. Walked out before dinner to the Pleasance. *æ.*[1] Lady Dundonald and her sons George and Andrew and Miss Macredie dined with us. The Countess drank tea. Major Brown, Grange, and Matthew Dickie and Mr. William Paterson, writer in Kilmarnock, supped with us. I was temperate.

FRIDAY 2 JULY. Dined Mr. Baron Gordon's; Lord Monboddo, Maclaurin, etc., there. Was hearty, but had not enough of conversation; drank too freely. Drank coffee and tea. Paid a visit at Old Lady Wallace's. Played at whist and brag and supped at Maclaurin's; Lady Wallace,[2] in full beauty and gaiety, and several more company there. Was quite gay. Drank too liberally. Sauntered on the street.

SATURDAY 3 JULY. Sir James Campbell (Lieut.-Colonel), Captains Earl of Glencairn, Craigends, and Dunure,[3] and Lieutenants Sir William Cuninghame and McDowall of the West Fencibles, Lord Monboddo, Mr. Crosbie, Lady Colville and Lady Anne Erskine and Miss Susie Dunlop dined with us. Major Montgomerie was engaged, so was the only one of the mess at Fortune's that was not with us. I was steady though jovial, and passed an excellent day, though without much other conversation than social dialogue; and although I drank freely, I was not drunk. In the evening my wife was in uncommon good humour, just as during courtship. It was very fine.

SUNDAY 4 JULY. Was somewhat uneasy with the excess of yesterday. Lay long and breakfasted in bed. Then Grange and I walked out to Prestonfield and found worthy Sir Alexander very well, and had a pleasing walk and social seat in the garden, we three alone, the sun shining warmly upon us. We dined with him. Had his chaise into town, and drank tea at my house, where we found Old Lady Wallace. In the evening I heard the children say psalms, etc., and read some of Goldsmith's *History of the Earth.*

---

[9] Hugh Montgomerie, later twelfth Earl of Eglinton, was elected to Parliament in 1780 but unseated on petition in 1781; he sat again 1784–1789 and 1796.

[1] Explained in the entry for 9 July.

[2] "Young Lady Wallace," Eglinton Dunlop, styled Lady Wallace. See above, 29 September 1778, and note.

[3] Alexander Cuninghame of Craigends and Thomas Kennedy of Dunure.

MONDAY 5 JULY. (Writing Monday the 12.) It was an exceeding wet day. Grange dined with us. I took a chair and went to the judicial sale of Lainshaw, which was to have come on this afternoon. It hurt me much that Lainshaw, where I had been so happy and which had been a very permanent idea in my mind, should be disconnected. There was but one offerer, and we got the sale adjourned till next day.

TUESDAY 6 JULY. I gave in a Petition to the Lords for the postponed creditors on Lainshaw, and had a warm debate at the bar with the counsel for Douglas, Heron, and Company, who wanted the sale to proceed. But I got it adjourned to Thursday the 15. This was a sort of reprieve.

WEDNESDAY 7 JULY. Grange dined with us. I wrote to several people: Craigengillan, Fairlie, etc., to see if they would bid for Lainshaw.[4] I had written last night on the subject to Lord Eglinton. Grange and Mr. James Baillie supped with us.

THURSDAY 8 JULY. I received a very kind letter from my father telling me he was better, and insisting I should not come west to see him during the Session as I had intended to do. I was really uneasy about Lainshaw. I was vexed that a low man such as Speirs at Glasgow should purchase a seat of the Montgomeries, my wife's family. But alas, has he not purchased Elderslie, the seat of Sir William Wallace?[5] It was, however, vexing that it should be sold cheap. Much did I wish to be able to purchase it. But in the present state of money and credit, I felt my own impotence, and saw distress and a gaol before me if I should venture on it. I was to dine with Major Montgomerie at the mess at Fortune's. I went up to him in the Castle before dinner; drank some excellent porter, which set me a-going. Walked down with him to the mess and drank so heartily there that I was quite intoxicated. It was a very hot day. I went to the roll-calling at night on the Castle Hill, and talked a great deal to many people. I did not recollect one word that I said. But Mr. Lawrie told me that Lord Dunmore[5a] and I took off our hats to one another and bowed very often. So we had been very complimentative. His Lordship had dined at the mess, but was sober. I asked him and Sir James Campbell and Sir John Paterson of Eccles to sup with me, and I went home to give notice. They all came, but by that time I was so ill that I was obliged to go to bed. My valuable spouse behaved admirably, had supper prepared, and pressed them to stay. But they did not.

[4] Boswell wrote to Lord Eglinton, John McAdam of Craigengillan, Alexander Fairlie of Fairlie, Chief Baron Montgomery of the Court of Exchequer, George Graham of Kinross and several others. Eglinton made no reply; the rest pleaded inability, citing as cause the depression of business brought on by the American war.

[5] Elderslie, traditional birthplace of Sir William Wallace, is in Renfrewshire. Alexander Speirs bought it and built a mansion there on the Clyde.

[5a] Well known to American historians as the last Royal Governor of Virginia.

FRIDAY 9 JULY. I awaked in sad distress and in great vexation at what had happened last night. I was very grateful to my wife and said she was worth a million. After being a little in the Court of Session, I waited on my three last night's guests. Sir James Campbell was ill and confined, but the other two very obligingly supped with me this night, as did Mr. Nairne and Miss Susie Dunlop. We were quite sober. Lord Dunmore did not drink one glass out. He talked very well. I had some enjoyment during this day (which was also very warm) in cooling my blood with lemonade. Grange and Balbarton dined with us. My father had desired me in his letter to wait on the Lord President and tell him he was better. As I had left my name at his house and had never heard from him, I did not choose to appear to court him; and therefore I just showed him the letter as he sat today in his chair in the Court of Session. I had been for several days uneasy on account of my being in the Pleasance on Thursday the 1st current. I was now safe. Estrangement had discovered my deviation. I was sorry for it. She was very good. π.

SATURDAY 10 JULY. It was very agreeable to be calm and easy after yesterday's fever. I spoke very well before the Lords for a *cessio bonorum* to young Carruthers of Hardriggs.[6] Grange and I walked slowly out to Prestonfield. It was a very warm day. We sat down in the garden and eat raw turnips. There was no company at dinner but Mr. Mercer, the wine-merchant, and Mr. Robert Gillespie. The worthy Knight was remarkably well. But had little conversation in comparison of what I have heard him have. I was indolent myself and satisfied with little. Grange and I walked in to tea and drank it agreeably with my wife. Painter Donaldson also was with us.[7] I went up to the Castle and sat awhile with Duntroon. He and Sir William Cuninghame and Grange and Captain Graham of the Scots Dutch,[8] Mrs. Dr. Grant, and Miss Grant supped with us cheerfully. I drank only cider, one glass of wine, and negus. I was existing easily, my sore toe excepted. But I was neither advancing in knowledge, nor rising in life, nor, in short, doing anything of which I could boast. Yet I was very well satisfied. Even my practice as a lawyer was very scanty. What a state of mind is this? Not a bad one. π.

---

[6] John Johnston borrowed the process of this cause, 8 July 1779, and never returned it, but one does not need the process in order to explain the point at issue. Christopher Carruthers, only son and heir of John Carruthers of Hardriggs, wished permission to make a total surrender of his whole property, on oath, in favour of his creditors, and so escape perpetual imprisonment for debt. Boswell had represented his father in 1768 in a dispute with the Duke of Queensberry over the use of common land. The Carrutherses were close neighbours of Johnston's.

[7] John Donaldson had painted miniatures of Boswell (1769) and of Mrs. Boswell (1775–1776), both untraced.

[8] A Scottish brigade in the service of Holland.

SUNDAY 11 JULY. (Writing Friday 16 July.) Commissioner Cochrane came and went to the New Church with me. We heard a Mr. Arthur preach. The Commissioner did not choose to go to church above once a day. He dined with us, and he and I sat quietly at home in the afternoon and drank cider and negus. He drank tea with us. In the evening I was troubled with a kind of nervous fretfulness and impatience, so that I could not hear the children say much. I read some of Goldsmith's *History of the Earth*.

MONDAY 12 JULY. Mr. Alexander Wood looked at my sore toe, which was very painful. He advised me to wait till it was better, and then he would cut the nail. Either yesterday or today my dearest wife found out from me that my visit to the Pleasance had been in the day and when sober, which hurt her. Little was done today. I dined and drank tea with Miss Sempill, and was introduced to her nephew, Lord Sempill's eldest son.

TUESDAY 13 JULY. Little done. My practice was sadly deficient, and my toe very troublesome. I acknowledged to my wife Widow ———.[1] She was justly hurt, and I was sadly uneasy. Begg of Dornal drank tea with us.

WEDNESDAY 14 JULY. I never passed a more insignificant summer than I am now doing. Balmuto, Grange, Barlay, Mr. William Macdonald, and Mr. Robert Boswell dined with us quietly and soberly. They drank punch and I drank negus. I just acquiesced in being free from hypochondria.

THURSDAY 15 JULY. I had tolerable practice this week, though but little money. The sale of Lainshaw came on before Lord Elliock. It sold for about £2,000 more than it would have done on the 5th, which was so much that I gained to the younger children by obtaining an adjournment. All my endeavours by writing to different people to try if they would bid for Lainshaw proved ineffectual. While the macer was calling out, "The lands and estate of Lainshaw," I felt as if I were stunned by some dismal, wonderful casualty. I was glad that Mr. Cuninghame, who had a gentleman's name, got it rather than Mr. Speirs.[2] My dearest wife was much affected. When I came out from the sale, I met her walking from a shop in the Parliament Close. Grange and I accompanied her home. She went into her own room a little and shed tears. I could almost have done the same. Grange drank tea with us. At eight o'clock he went with me to the Pantheon, to which I had been particularly invited this night, as it was

[1] Possibly "Steven." In the notes for journal for 19 February 1779, Boswell refers to the object of his attentions as "Stevena."

[2] William Cuninghame of Bridgehouse had made his fortune in the tobacco trade, just as Speirs had, but Cuninghame's had come at a single stroke. After British reverses in the American war he had sold one large stock of tobacco at a fantastic profit.

to be debated "Whether the British Legislature could alter the Articles of the Union?" I had no mind to go. But as they had made me an honorary member, I thought it would be uncivil to resist a pressing invitation. I was pretty well entertained. But what was strange, I was so bashful inwardly that I delayed to speak till I had only time to give a short flourish seconding a motion to adjourn the debate till this day sennight, that it might be maturely considered. Grange came home with me and we supped on cold meat and drank negus. My valuable spouse had recovered her cheerfulness, and we were comfortable. She was so very good as to be disposed in two nights' time to forgive what I feared would have remained long against me. I vowed fidelity, and it was my sincere resolution to devote my utmost attention to make her easy and as happy as possible, and now that her own family was quite extinguished, to make up to her for the want to the utmost of my power. It is amazing how callous one may grow as to what is wrong by the practice of it. I trust this night's resolutions will by GOD's grace make me act as a good husband and father of a family. My father's absence this summer, I suppose, lessened my practice. But it gradually habituated me to be without that respectable protection. π.

FRIDAY 16 JULY. (Writing Monday the 19th.) Lord Eglinton had arrived from London yesterday. I went and sat awhile with him this morning, and was cheered by former ideas of the Montgomeries. I never mentioned Lainshaw to him, as he had not answered my letter about the sale of it. I had again run myself to the last day, or last but one, for writing my *Hypochondriack*. I searched a long while in the Advocates' Library for a motto on *Imitation* or *Coincidence* in different writers, and thought I should never find one, which fretted me. At last I found one in Statius. I wrote pretty easily. But was not ready for the post.

SATURDAY 17 JULY. My toe was very uneasy; but what was worse, I for the first time since I last left London felt myself in low spirits. A *cessio bonorum* for young Hardriggs, in which Grange was agent and very anxious, came on. I spoke well enough. But the Lords were not in good humour, and delayed it till we should *condescend* more specially.[3] This disconcerted us a good deal. I should have dined at Prestonfield by invitation with Andrew Frazer and his lady and some more company. But was so sickly in mind that I could not bear the thoughts of cheerful company, and so contracted by disease that I grudged coach hire. So I sent an apology. I was vexed afterwards. Grange dined with us. I drank some cider and one glass of wine. During the state of dulness of feeling which my mind had experienced since I last returned to Scotland, I had, while I could bear it, made an experiment whether Dr. Johnson would write to me first. I began

[3] "Condescendence" in this sense is a specification of particulars; in other words, a fuller explanation.

to be uneasy and to think how much I should suffer if he should die during such an interval. This day as I sat at dinner I had the pleasure to receive a very kind letter from him, wondering at my silence, afraid that some ill was the occasion of it, and desirous to hear from me. I wrote by return of post, confessed the experiment, but said I should never again put him to any test.[4] I roused myself and wrote a very good additional Condescendence for young Hardriggs. Grange and Mr. James Baillie drank tea with us. π.

SUNDAY 18 JULY. I had resolved to try what rest would do for my sore toe; and as I had also a pretty heavy cold, I lay in bed all forenoon, drank tea and eat bread and butter and honey plentifully, and read *Rasselas* from beginning to end. I resolve to read it once every year. I rose before two and dined on soup maigre and bread and water. Lay all afternoon upon a sofa and read in Goldsmith's *History of the Earth, etc.*, and in Burke's *Sublime and Beautiful*, which it is strange to think I never read before. I fell into a slumber some part of the time, and awaked disturbed, thinking of death, of Lainshaw being sold, and of other dreary subjects. I was gloomy and dejected. I heard the children say little today. It lessened me sadly in my own estimation to be conscious of such a *break* in my existence. But I should conceal it.

MONDAY 19 JULY. (Writing Wednesday 21 July.) My spirits were very bad. I dictated a law paper with difficulty. Lord Eglinton called for a little before dinner. I was awkward and indifferent, and had no satisfaction in anything. My toe was painful, and I had an excoriation which alarmed me lest it might be a taint from my Pleasance adventure. But I hoped it might be only a little heat from the very warm weather. Grange dined with us. I finished today Burke's *Sublime and Beautiful*. Wrote to Dr. Johnson upon various topics.[5]

TUESDAY 20 JULY. Was still in worse spirits than yesterday. But dictated law very well. My dear wife insisted on my going in a coach with her and Veronica and Effie and Sandy to the sands of Leith to see part of one of the races. There was no sport.[6] But the variety of company

---

[4] Johnson wrote on 13 July, after making an anxious inquiry of Dilly. Both this letter and Boswell's reply appear in the *Life of Johnson* (13, 17 July 1779).

[5] Boswell summarizes the letter in the *Life of Johnson*, where he assigned it the date 22 July: "gave him an account of my last interview with my worthy friend, Mr. Edward Dilly . . . informed him that Lord Hailes . . . had sent me three instances of Prior's borrowing. . . . My letter was a pretty long one and contained a variety of particulars; but he, it should seem, had not attended to it, for his next to me was as follows: . . . 'Are you playing the same trick again, and trying who can keep silence longest?' " (*Life of Johnson*, 22 July, 9 September 1779).

[6] Possibly, "The race was not close enough to be interesting"; probably, "No race was

did me good insensibly. I was much obliged to her. She also persuaded me
to go to the Assembly at night, which did me more good. Before I went to
it, we had a visit from Lord Chief Baron.[7] I came home before twelve and
drank negus cheerfully.

WEDNESDAY 21 JULY. (Writing on Saturday 24 July.) This day I
insensibly recovered good spirits. Grange dined with us, and he and
I drank cider with relish. I dictated law well.

THURSDAY 22 JULY. I had in the course of this session resumed my
old seat in the *Laigh Parliament House*[8] and copied some more of the
Privy Council records. Nothing composes my mind more than that kind
of occupation. I associate it with being like my father, a laborious antiquarian. Miss Dick was with us at present. I went this evening to the
Pantheon, and in order to oblige the Society who had made me an honorary member and to get some reputation among people of various ranks
and professions who would spread it, I had studied the question, and I
spoke really well to show that such Articles of the Union as are not plainly
temporary, or when no reservations are made, cannot be altered by the
British Legislature, which *sits under those Articles.* The debate becoming
rather too grave and serious, I rose again and made a reply which produced
high entertainment and applause, expressing my anxiety lest the fair part
of the audience should go from the Pantheon with a decision which would
alarm them. For of what were we debating—Whether a *contract* is to be
kept? Whether Articles of *Union* are to be kept? I assimilated the Union
between England and Scotland—the stronger and the weaker country—
to a contract of marriage, and I mentioned (as I sometimes look into old
books) a curious pamphlet, published about the time of the Union, *On*

---

run during the time that we were there"; certainly not, "No race was run this day." On
20 July 1779 "His Majesty's purse of one hundred guineas was won by Duke Hamilton's Hercules 1, the Hon. Francis Charteris's Flora 2" (*Edinburgh Advertiser,* 16–20
July 1779, xxxii. 45). The long stretch of bare sand at Leith was the chief place for
horse-racing in Scotland. The City Purse was carried on a pole or halberd from the
Council Chambers to Leith by a town officer in livery, accompanied by a file of the
City Guard, a drummer, and a huge and constantly growing throng of citizens on
holiday. Long lines of tents and booths stretched along the shore, and the scene had
the general aspect of a carnival.
[7] James Montgomery, head of the Court of Exchequer, an appointment with a larger
stated salary than that of the Lord President of the Court of Session. On his retirement in 1801 he was created a baronet.
[8] The lower Parliament House, its basement storey. During the late summer and
autumn of 1772, Boswell had been making extracts from the records of the Privy
Council of Scotland "copying any curious passages.... I think I may make a good
publication of these abstracts" (Journal, 24 November 1775). He is here returning to
the project, but he never completed it.

the Marriage of Fergusia and Heptarchus.[9] I had great pleasure tonight in speaking, and the question carried by a great majority for my opinion.[1] Grange had supped before I got home, but he drank negus with me comfortably. I got a letter from James Bruce written this morning at Auchinleck, which brought it near in idea. It came by my father's maids.

FRIDAY 23 JULY. I dictated very easily. My wife and I dined at Lord Chief Baron's; Lord Eglinton, Lord Haddington, etc., there. It was half an hour after six before we sat down to table, the race was so late. My toe was painful. Mr. Wood told me today I had a corn which he would cut, and the thought of an *operation* frightened me. I also still feared some taint, so was not at ease. However, I took claret plentifully, though it was not of flavour to my relish. Sir Patrick Warrender (with those I have mentioned) and I sat till half an hour past twelve very socially, drinking slowly. I walked home. By the way from bad habit stopped a little with a girl on the street, but soon took myself and had no sort of connexion with her. Was not drunk, but took warm water and cleared my stomach.

SATURDAY 24 JULY. (Writing Monday 2 August.) Was exceedingly ill and obliged to lie all forenoon in bed. It vexed me that I had several causes to attend. But Mr. Lawrie got them well managed for me, and it is wonderful how the mind acquiesces in necessity. Was better after getting up and taking soup, and my wife and I walked out and saw my father, who had come in last night. I fairly told what had detained me. He was much better. Dr. Gillespie had come with him. In the morning I had received two letters from my brother David. He appeared to be more indifferent than I could wish.

SUNDAY 25 JULY. Was at New Church forenoon and afternoon. Heard the children say psalms and catechism. Drank tea at my father's.

MONDAY 26 JULY. Mr. and Mrs. Ramsay from Alloa dined with us. She drank tea.

TUESDAY 27 JULY. My father came to the Court and called two causes. I dined with him. Wished to have somebody to divert me at night. Matthew Dickie supped with me.

WEDNESDAY 28 JULY. Practice was very scanty and I was sadly discouraged. Commissioner Cochrane called on me in the morning and told me that my father was anxious to have Dr. Gillespie to attend him con-

[9] By the Rev. William Wright (d. 1724), Minister of Kilmarnock. Boswell had picked up a copy of this curious allegory in his last jaunt to London.

[1] "The adjourned [see above, 15 July 1779] debate . . . was resumed . . . before as numerous and respectable an audience as the former. The speakers on both sides displayed uncommon abilities in point of eloquence as well as argument; and . . . the question was sifted to the bottom and at last decided by a majority of 177 to 33" (*Caledonian Mercury,* 24 July 1779).

stantly and intended to settle upon him £200 a year during his own life and £50 a year after his death, during the Doctor's life; and the Commissioner said that he had said to my father that his son should be informed of all his transactions now; that my father answered, "Might he not dispose of his own money?" but added, "You may do as you please." The Commissioner therefore desired that I would meet him at my father's in the evening and tell my father that I approved of the plan. I suggested that I should now have an additional £100 a year from my father, as my family was increased. The Commissioner said it had occurred to himself. But that it should not be mentioned at present when my father was giving away £200 a year. I had some difficulty as to the propriety of this bargain with Gillespie, when it was first mentioned. But I considered that as my father had done a great deal for his family, he had a good right to make himself comfortable; that what he paid in his own time would probably not have been saved for me; and that £50 a year was not a heavy burthen upon me. I made no objection to the Commissioner, and agreed to meet him. Lady Wallace, Miss Susie Dunlop, and Miss Dick dined with us. I went to my father's after dinner, and when I had him alone, told him that I thought he was quite right to secure Dr. Gillespie. It shocked me when he pronounced the words, "He is to have £50 a year *after I'm dead.*" My father's death is to me a dreary idea. He seemed pleased with what I said as to his fixing Gillespie. But he showed himself still shrewd and sagacious, for he suggested that it should be inserted in the agreement with Gillespie that he should have his £200 a year only while he was able to officiate, as he might perhaps become incapable. I drank tea at my father's. His lady was as disagreeable as ever. But I was wonderfully guarded. I never thought I could have been so much so. It is, however, disagreeable to me to be obliged to practise any dissimulation. I dictated well for Lord Dundonald today. Andrew Frazer, Donaldson the painter, Grange, Balmuto, and Sir William Cuninghame supped with us. My spirits were bad. I just went decently through the evening. Was glad to see my old friend George Frazer's son, whom I had known from my youth. But the thoughts of death and the changeable nature of all things in this life sunk me.

THURSDAY 29 JULY. (Writing Tuesday the 3 August.) Did little. It was a very wet day.

FRIDAY 30 JULY. Did little. Went with Lady Colville and Lady Anne Erskine and dined at Sir Adolphus Oughton's very agreeably. My wife was invited too, but was confined with a swelled face. Came home mellow. Grange supped with us.

SATURDAY 31 JULY. Dined at my father's, my two daughters and Sandy with me. Nobody at table but himself and Lady Auchinleck and her sister and Robert Boswell. He seemed to be indifferent about the children. As there were no strangers there before whom I could be ashamed of the coldness to my children, I was pretty easy. Stayed to tea. This was a very poor week. I got but two guineas. I was vexed too at Grange's uneasiness that Christopher Carruthers's *cessio bonorum* was put off again, and that he did not think me keen enough about it. In the evening I read so much of a journal kept by the deceased Mr. Bogle of Hamilton Farm, which had been produced in a process of reduction of a bond for £5,000 obtained from him by fraud.[2] He had absolutely died of intemperance and dissolute conduct of every kind. Yet he had for some time kept a regular diary of his life and account of his expenses; and in that diary his acts of profligacy were recorded in plain terms, and his folly and vanity set down, while at the same time there were several reflections on his own insignificancy and on the unhappiness of life, which I excerpted.[3] Reading this journal made me uneasy to think of my own. It is preserving evidence against oneself; it is filling a mine which may be sprung by accident or intention. Were my journal to be discovered and made public in my own lifetime, how shocking would it be to me! And after my death, would it not hurt my children? I must not be so plain. I will write to Dr. Johnson on the subject.[4] Lieut.-Colonel Nisbet Balfour and his sister, Mrs. Boswall, supped with us.

[2] Bogle's uncle (William Bogle) had brought the action against John Yuil, to whom Bogle had granted the heritable bond. The uncle held that the bond should be reduced (i.e., annulled) because John Bogle was "in such a state of absolute incapacity as rendered him totally unfit for transacting business or understanding the importance of any deed. . . . That no value was given for the bond, nor no accounts instituted and settled at the time the bond was signed and that the whole transaction was unknown to Mr. Bogle's relations" (*Edinburgh Advertiser*, 20–23 July 1779). The bond was reduced 22 July 1779.

[3] The excerpts follow. Boswell identified them only as having been taken from "the journal of a dissipated, profligate young man, J.B. of H.F. near Glasgow": "The day after a debauch with women, 'Walked home in the morning, admired the industry of the people of London; from them saw how trifling myself was, and from having had the highest happiness saw how poor it was.—Dine with W. Adam; preserve my own agreeable way.—Had a long discourse with R.B. Jun., who thought in my way; said he would not live seven years over again.—Had fine thoughts on my own insignificancy compared to all the crowd about me, which made me happy and content.—Resolved to have a week of pleasure, instead of which, as always happens, it proved one of pain.—Found heat of urine for the first time and that I was clapped.—Rather melancholy but to have a good opinion of myself as the best way to make others do the same.—Went to Assembly; behaved like H. Dundas, which took vastly.—My prenticeship expired. Have been exceedingly happy all my prenticeship; but man was not born to be so happy always; we must take now and then a view of the dark side of things on purpose even to enjoy happiness.' "

[4] No correspondence on the subject appears to have survived.

SUNDAY 1 AUGUST. (Writing Friday the 6 August.) Heard ———— in the forenoon and Dr. Blair in the afternoon. Visited my father in the evening. Heard the children say psalms and catechism. Supped at Mrs. Thomas Boswall's, a farewell supper for Colonel Nisbet Balfour and some of his friends. Had no high social satisfaction nor did not intoxicate myself. I keep very strictly my resolution of observing the sanctity of Sunday. I refused to dine at Maclaurin's today with the Marquess of Graham. I thought I might sup abroad on so particular an occasion. Besides, the holy day is then over.

MONDAY 2 AUGUST. (Writing Wednesday 11 August.) It was a wet day. I wrote an additional Condescendence for young Hardriggs. Grange and I went and saw *Macbeth* acted. He supped with me.

TUESDAY 3 AUGUST. Dined at my father's.

WEDNESDAY 4 AUGUST. Was quite idly and socially inclined. Met the Hon. Alexander Gordon in the street, and agreed with him that he should dine with me or I with him according to the preference of who had the best dinner. His was found best. So I dined heartily with him and his lady and drank strong ale and port and old hock till I was somewhat intoxicated. I was cordial with him. I drank tea there too. Afterwards took Grange with me to the Castle and visited Duntroon (Mr. Gordon having gone to the play); and Duntroon, Grange, and Mr. John Moir, Writer to the Signet, supped with me.

THURSDAY 5 AUGUST. Balbarton dined with us. My wife and I drank tea at Lady Dunonald's, all the children with us. I supped at Lord Kames's with Mr. Nairne and Lady Wallace. Passed a very cheerful evening.

FRIDAY 6 AUGUST. Was applied to by the Honourable Andrew Erskine for a loan of £50 by a letter yesterday.[5] Wrote to him today that I was vexed I could not supply him, as my credit with the bank was almost exhausted. But I desired he would call on me in the Parliament House this forenoon. He did so, and talked in such a manner that I resolved to try what could be done. I spoke to my dear wife, who, with her usual generosity of disposition, was for my advancing the sum, as I had found honest James Baillie ready to let me have it in case I should want it before the first of February, on which day Erskine had engaged to repay it. Grange dined with us. In the evening I lent Erskine the money, telling him it was really a favour. I hope I shall one day be easy in my circumstances, for I have friendship in a high degree. I sauntered in the New

[5] Erskine, younger son of the fifth Earl of Kellie, had been Boswell's close friend since 1761. *Letters between the Honourable Andrew Erskine and James Boswell, Esq.* had been one of Boswell's earliest literary publications. Erskine had applied to Boswell for money on several occasions before this, and Boswell had usually sent it.

Town with Erskine. I said it was a misfortune to have too lively an imagination—to see the end of our pursuits—for that prevented us from being keen. Erskine said, "Seeing their end often prevents their beginning."

SATURDAY 7 AUGUST. Spoke pretty well in the Inner House on a short reduction on death-bed.[6] Grange and I walked out to Prestonfield and dined very comfortably; a Miss Trotter of Mortonhall, the Rev. Mr. Bennet, and Mr. Craig, the architect, there. Sir Alexander was remarkably well. I drank too much cider and currant wine and port, so as to be intoxicated to a certain degree. But I was sufficiently happy. Walked in to town after tea. Grange supped with us.

SUNDAY 8 AUGUST. (Writing Friday 13 August.) Surgeon Wood called, poor Effie having been ill. He was violent against my father's settlement on Dr. Gillespie, which he said Gillespie told him was £200 a year for five years certain, besides £50 a year for his life afterwards. This stunned me. But I resolved to keep myself quiet, and thought it might be set aside as an imposition upon an old man in a state of failure. I was so much disturbed by it that I did not go to church, but sat awhile with Grange and gave vent to my uneasiness. Was at the New Church in the afternoon and heard Mr. Grant, teacher in Watson's Hospital. Heard my daughters say psalms and catechism. Visited my father in the evening.

MONDAY 9 AUGUST. (Writing from notes on Tuesday 24 August.) My wife and I dined at my father's.

TUESDAY 10 AUGUST. Accounts came of poor Miss Cuninghame's death. My wife and I were engaged to dine at Lady Colville's. She could not go. I dined there myself, just the two ladies and I. Mr. Fairlie of Fairlie and Matthew Dickie supped with us. My wife bore the news of her niece's death pretty well. But it affected us both in a tender manner.

WEDNESDAY 11 AUGUST. This day the Summer Session rose. It vexed me that I had received not one half so much money in fees as I had done in other summer sessions of late years. Yet it was some comfort to me that my practice was apparently not less; nay, that I had written more than last Summer Session.

THURSDAY 12 AUGUST. (Writing from notes on Tuesday 24 August.) Was uneasy about the settlement on Dr. Gillespie. Called on Lord Advocate and talked to him confidentially of my father's failure, and of that settlement. His Lordship, though he and I have not been on good terms for years, was very obliging, seemed to think the settlement might be reduced on incapacity and imposition, but was of opinion that it could not affect me as heir of entail. I thought being thus confidential might pave

[6] That is, the setting aside of a deed or will made on death-bed. In Scots law such dispositions of property were at this time voidable. The particular cause has not been identified.

the way to Lord Advocate and me being better together. I began today to endeavour to recover the Greek language.

FRIDAY 13 AUGUST. I dined at Bayll's as Sir William Cuninghame's guest at the West Fencible mess. Was too warm-spirited and drank too much, so that I was a good deal intoxicated.

SATURDAY 14 AUGUST. Awaked very ill. Drank a deal of tea in bed, grew better, walked out to Prestonfield. Accompanied Lady Dick, Miss Dick, Mr. William Dick, and Captain and Mrs. Frazer to Moredun and dined with Mr. David Stewart Moncrieffe. My wife was asked, but could not go so soon after hearing of her niece's death. I had little relish of the garden or of anything but the dinner, wines, and fruits. I however did not drink much.

SUNDAY 15 AUGUST. (Writing from memory, Tuesday 24 August.) The Reverend Mr. Nicholls, Temple's friend, was now in Scotland with Lord Findlater, and had called on me. I visited him today between sermons in the hotel kept by Dunn. I was in such bad spirits that I could not relish him. I am not sure whether I was at the New Church twice or not. Heard the children say psalms, etc. Mr. Nairne supped with us.

MONDAY 16 AUGUST. Mr. Lawrie went to the country in the afternoon. Miss Susie Cuninghame, Mrs. Ballantine and three of her boarders (Craigengillan's daughters, and Miss Ellie Ritchie) dined and drank tea with us. I dictated today from notes kept by the clerk of the Pantheon my speeches in that Society on the Articles of the Union. I was very low today and had no pleasure in life nor could imagine none. It must be remembered that I was at my father's every day, generally awhile in the evening.

TUESDAY 17 AUGUST. Lord and Lady Macdonald, Captain and Mrs. Frazer, Mr. Maclaurin, and Mr. David Erskine supped with us. It was a dull party. We played at whist before supper. I lost ten shillings. I wrote No. 23 of *The Hypochondriack* yesterday and today.[7]

[7] "On Reserve," an essay which contains a great deal of introspective comment by Boswell. "If pride be the passion in which a man takes most delight, he cannot gratify it more effectually than by reserve.... Such is the weakness and imperfection of human nature that it will not bear to be too closely examined in any character; and therefore he who lays himself quite open will infallibly be lessened in the estimation of all around him.... An hypochondriac is sometimes so totally incapable of conversation, having a mind like an exhausted receiver, and organs of speech as if palsied, that when his ideas and his vivacity return, effusion is a pleasure to him, in which he can hardly resist an excess of indulgence. But, let him consider that by dissipating his spirits he is preparing himself for languor, dejection, and pain; and let him therefore provide against future attacks by saving his stores. Let him also consider that he runs a great risk of discovering circumstances which his enemies may afterwards employ against him, and which in his hours of gloomy sensibility it will be a torment to him to recollect."

WEDNESDAY 18 AUGUST. Mr. Nicholls breakfasted with us. His neatness and vivacity hurt me a little by contrast with myself. He and I and Maclaurin walked on the Calton Hill. Either yesterday or today my wife and I drank tea at Dr. Grant's.

THURSDAY 19 AUGUST. Mr. Nicholls breakfasted with us. Balbarton and I walked out and dined at my father's. My father had the first draught of a mug of porter, and took so hearty a one that I, who came next, took the rest. So we finished a mug between us. Captain Graham of the Dutch service was at tea when I came home. He and Grange supped with us. I drank negus.

FRIDAY 20 AUGUST. I dined at my father's. Dutch Captain Graham and Robert Boswell were there. I called after tea on old Mr. Scott, late of Hopsburn, and his grandson, Dr. Andrew Wilson's eldest son, who had come down from London to visit him. Mr. Scott had the house of Grange taken. He was not at home. But I was shown into a room to write a note to invite him and Mr. Wilson to dinner next day. I found this Grange a comfortable old mansion, like some family seat two hundred miles from Edinburgh.

SATURDAY 21 AUGUST. Mr. Scott, Mr. Wilson, Balbarton, Dr. Gillespie, and Miss Dick dined with us. My spirits grew good, I know not how.

SUNDAY 22 AUGUST. By appointment when in good spirits last night, worthy Grange and I walked out to Duddingston church and heard the apostolic Mr. William Bennet (as I call him), and saw the Earl of Abercorn sitting with stately decency in his loft. After which we walked into the manse and tasted Mr. Bennet's whisky, then accompanied Lady Dick to Prestonfield, and found the excellent Sir Alexander pleasingly well. It was a charming day, and he walked with us in the garden as amiable as ever. There was nobody at dinner but ourselves. We walked home quietly. My wife and Miss Dick had walked out to Prestonfield thinking to find us there. Effie made tea to us, Veronica being in the garden. I did not hear Veronica say anything divine tonight. Effie and Sandy did what they could. Grange supped with us.

MONDAY 23 AUGUST. The alarm of the French and Spanish fleets being in the Channel kept up an agitation.[8] I really felt little. My toe was

[8] "The combined fleets . . . were first discovered by the *Southampton* frigate . . . on Saturday, August 14. . . . On Sunday, the 15th . . . the combined fleets were seen off Falmouth, and were judged to amount to one hundred sail. . . . After parading in and out for three days, they disappeared on the 19th. . . . During the stay of so formidable an armament so near, the people on the coast were in the utmost confusion, many removing their persons and most valuable effects; but at the same time the most vigorous exertions were made to give them a warm reception if they

now very easy. I drank tea at Robert Boswell's. Did not see the Doctor.

TUESDAY 24 AUGUST. (Writing on Monday 6 September.) Miss Dick came to us again. She and Miss Jeanie Innes and Dr. Young supped. We had whist before supper.

WEDNESDAY 25 AUGUST. I dined at Commissioner Cochrane's. General Stewart was there. I drank a bottle of claret. Was heated. Called at a house in Portsburgh and had some porter. P.D.[9]

THURSDAY 26 AUGUST. Grange dined with us. I took a desire for rum punch, which I generally dislike, and drank heartily of it. He and I drank tea with M. Dupont and Miss Scott at their country-house near Broughton.

FRIDAY 27 AUGUST. Mr. Wallace, Sheriff of Ayrshire, dined with me (*mirabile dictu!*) for the first time.[1] Grange, Matthew Dickie, and Major Montgomerie also were with us. I was in a sad state of mind, being glad to exist in sensual comfort alone.

SATURDAY 28 AUGUST. Effie and I walked out and breakfasted with Lady Colville. I dined at Maclaurin's with Dr. Calvert, a Doctors' Commons lawyer, and others, and drank a large quantity. I was still uneasy since Wednesday. Lady Colville and Lady Anne Erskine came to my wife and me in the evening, played whist and supped. I was rather too mellow.

SUNDAY 29 AUGUST. My father was in his own seat in the New Church. But he looked to be much decayed. My wife and I were there too. I went out in the coach with him and the ladies and dined with him. Lady Auchinleck read aloud a sermon of Dr. Blair's after dinner. My wife and children came to tea. It was sad work. I heard the children say divine lessons at night. Dr. Webster and his daughter dined with my wife today.

MONDAY 30 AUGUST. Went with Maclaurin, Crosbie, and Sinclair of Freswick and saw the observatory.[2] Maclaurin pressed me so cordially to dine with him again that I accepted. We drank pretty freely. Then Fres-

---

had attempted to land" (*Scots Magazine*, August 1779, xli. 450). The fleet (which numbered sixty-six ships of the line) sailed up the Channel as far as Plymouth, but did not succeed in bringing on a general engagement with the British fleet under Admiral Hardy, which could muster hardly more than half its strength.

[9] This abbreviation or cipher does not appear again in the journal, but its general significance is clear from the entry for 28 August. Possibly Peggie Dundas (see *Boswell in Extremes*, 28 August, 2 September 1776; 5, 16 February 1777).

[1] Boswell may mean that Wallace regularly declined invitations or that this was the first time he had ever invited him. He had certainly known him from the time of his admission to the bar in 1766 and had probably known him even longer. Wallace (an Ayrshire man) had been appointed Professor of History at the University of Edinburgh in 1755, Keeper of the Advocates' Library in 1758, and Professor of Scots Law in 1765.

[2] A structure on Calton Hill which had been begun in 1776, but was not finished until 1792.

wick and Mr. W. Wallace and he and I played whist and supped and played again. I lost and was fretted inwardly. Grange dined with my wife.

TUESDAY 31 AUGUST. Matthew Dickie had been frequently asking me to make an appointment with him to dine at my father's. My father had said to me he would be very glad to see him when I said he talked of coming out; but as dinner had not been specified, I was uneasy this morning to think that I had engaged Matthew for today. So out I went, and mentioned before my father and Lady Auchinleck that he was talking of dining there today. Upon which she flew into a very violent passion and abused Matthew most terribly, alleging that it was he himself who had written, by way of wit, the false card on the 2 February last pretending to announce my father's death. I declared upon my honour I never suspected him, and I was surprised how she had heard of such a shocking thing. She in rage answered, "I hear much more than that," seeming to signify that she heard bad things of me. I was quite calm, and said it was hard to entertain such a suspicion against a poor man unless she could give a reason. She said my father had never heard of it before. He insisted to know what it was, and I told him. He acquitted poor Matthew of any suspicion; and with more spirit than I thought he now could show, insisted that I should bring him out to dinner. I did so; and my father was very cordial with him, and was really entertained by having an old Ayrshire acquaintance to talk to. He even snubbed the old sister before him.[3] Dr. Gillespie was not there today. Matthew went away, and I stayed and drank tea. Lady Auchinleck appeared as smooth to him as if he had been her intimate friend.

WEDNESDAY 1 SEPTEMBER. Dr. Webster sent to me that he was to dine at my father's today, and would be glad to meet me there. I went with my wife and the children to look at a country-house near Musselburgh, and then dined at my father's. I drank just as much as to give me a relish for more; so when I returned to town (after being passionate at home from hasty pride) I got Matthew Dickie to go with me to Dalrymple's tavern and drink punch. We first tried if we could find any of my acquaintance sitting at Walker's. But there were only some of the Town Council. Neither could I find anybody at the Cross. I was at this time conscious of what is the state of a man who has a craving for strong drink; and I dreaded being perhaps at some future period of my life a wretched sot. However, I persisted. At Dalrymple's I found Mr. Elliot, the bookseller, and Mr. Smiton, the bookbinder, just rising from their bowl. I ordered a fresh one. Messrs. Elliot and Dickie sat some time, but were

---

[3] Margaret Boswell, Lady Auchinleck's older sister, who lived with her.

obliged to leave me. Mr. Smiton sat steady, and I made our landlord Dalrymple join us and tell all his adventures as a cook. In short I did not rise till between eleven and twelve, indeed *about* midnight. I came home after this strange debauch and eat eggs and drank negus alone; and then, after having gone to bed with my dear wife, I started up in shocking gloomy intoxication and raved in solemn rage about my being miserable. It was a horrid night.

THURSDAY 2 SEPTEMBER. Was in deep melancholy. Life was quite black to me. Grange and Mr. Robert Syme, Junior, dined with us. I grew better after eating and drinking. Miss Dick, who had gone away yesterday or the day before, returned this evening.

FRIDAY 3 SEPTEMBER. I had heard yesterday of the arrival of Colonel Montagu Stuart.[4] I waited on him this forenoon and found him courteous enough. He had always been very civil to me; and as his lady is my wife's particular friend, at least old friend, and he Lord Mountstuart's brother, it was proper for me to show him what attention I could. He was engaged to dinner every day till Wednesday. I engaged him for that day. I then called at Robert Boswell's, and was carried in to see his father, who was now wonderfully restored to his senses.[5] He was reading aloud to one of his daughters some poetry (I know not what) when I entered his room. He was sitting in an easy chair with a tartan night-gown and white nightcap, and was so thin that he looked just like a spectre. I was struck with a kind (writing Tuesday 14 September) of confused trepidation on first seeing him. But except that he was a little fretful, and his saying that it was several years since he saw me, he was really pretty much in his former usual way. It was very comfortable to have him thus revived, as it were. I was Sir James Campbell's guest at the mess, and drank rather too much. But I was happy to see Colonel Stuart. Grange, who had drank freely somewhere, supped with us.

SATURDAY 4 SEPTEMBER. Was awhile with Colonel Stuart before dinner. Dined quietly at home, but was in low spirits. Miss Dick went home this morning. I supped at Middlemist's oyster-cellar [6] with Lord

---

[4] The Hon. Col. James Stuart, second son of the Earl of Bute, was heir to the estates of his mother, only daughter of Edward Wortley Montagu and the famous Lady Mary.

[5] Dr. Boswell had apparently been in such a state as not to receive any visitors (see above, 23 August 1779). Boswell seems not to have seen him since 24 May of this year.

[6] Oyster-cellars (dingy low-ceilinged restaurants lighted by tallow candles, serving raw oysters with punch or porter) had recently become popular in Edinburgh. "Most of [them] have a sort of long room where a small party may enjoy the exercise of a country dance to the music of a fiddle, harp, or bagpipe. But the equivocal character

Glencairn, Sir James Campbell, Major Montgomerie, Duntroon, etc., and got into excellent glee. Had resolution to quit them at one in the morning. Lord Glencairn, who was very much in liquor, went with me. He had made me many professions of regard, which from so honest a man were valuable. I supported him to the head of Writers' Court, where he lodged.

SUNDAY 5 SEPTEMBER. Went to the New Church, but finding nobody from my father's there, was uneasy about him, came out of church again, and went to him. Found him pretty well. In the afternoon was at the New Church with my wife and heard a north-country minister preach pretty well. In the evening we all were at Lady Dundonald's in a most comfortable way. Nobody there. Heard the children their sacred exercises. Grange supped with us.

MONDAY 6 SEPTEMBER. Nothing to mark down.

TUESDAY 7 SEPTEMBER. Dr. Young and Mr. John MacGowan played at whist and supped with us. I drank punch, and was calmly social.

WEDNESDAY 8 SEPTEMBER. Colonel Wortley Stuart, Lord Glencairn, General Skene, Major Montgomerie, Mr. Maclaurin, and Miss Clemie Elphinstone dined with us. Stuart seemed to be friendly. We drank heartily. He and I and Lord Glencairn sat a good while by ourselves. I was strong today. But after they were gone I grew very intoxicated.

THURSDAY 9 SEPTEMBER. (Writing Wednesday 15 September.) Awaked very, very ill. Had engaged to dine at Fortune's with Colonel Stuart and see him set out, as he was to go this day for Bute. He had sat up all night drinking and gone to bed in the morning. So he lay all day. However, as I grew better, and thought it a compliment to him, I dined at Fortune's with Lord Glencairn, Matthew Henderson, and Bailie Wordie; and the two former and I sat till Stuart came to us. It is wonderful what joy there is in excess. I stood it better today than yesterday. Stuart set out about twelve. I came home not drunk though I had above two bottles of claret.

FRIDAY 10 SEPTEMBER. Was very well in health, but in bad spirits. Grange dined with us. Mr. and Mrs. Mitchelson, Dr. Young, and Mr. William Wallace played whist and supped with us.

SATURDAY 11 SEPTEMBER. Was in exceeding bad spirits. Met Mr. Alexander Boswall, who had come to town for a little with General Smith. He and I and my wife and two daughters and Sandy were entertained by him with sweetmeats at Elder's. I went with him and visited

---

of these houses of resort prevents them from being visited by any of the fair sex who seek the praise of modesty, or pique themselves on propriety of conduct" (Hugo Arnot, *History of Edinburgh*, 1788, p. 354). Lucky Middlemist's cellar (celebrated by Robert Fergusson in "Caller Oysters") was in the Cowgate.

General Smith. I was quite listless and disconsolate all day, and could do nothing.

SUNDAY 12 SEPTEMBER. Heard young Walker in the New Church in the forenoon and Dr. Blair in the afternoon. Had no satisfaction. Was puzzled with a letter from Miss Sibthorpe [7] desiring information for her father and mother as to the education at Glasgow and the expense of it. Could not get a distinct account. Felt myself very impotent in business. Talked of it with Dr. Blair, whom I visited today between sermons. My wife and I and the three eldest children drank tea at my father's very disagreeably. My dejection of mind could ill bear his shockingly cold behaviour. In the evening the three children went through sacred exercises admirably. This was a real pleasure to me amidst my hypochondria.

MONDAY 13 SEPTEMBER. (Writing on Friday the 17 September.) Was quite restless and could do nothing. Grange dined with us. I received a letter from Dr. Johnson, angry with me for a long silence, when in truth he had made no return to a long letter of mine.[8] Was very callous from melancholy, but *felt* even an unmerited reproof from *him*.

TUESDAY 14 SEPTEMBER. Asked Adam Smith's opinion at the custom-house as to education at Glasgow. He preferred it to Edinburgh. He said, "We never meet, though we live now in the same town." "Very true," said I. "What can be the meaning of it?" "I don't know," said he in his awkward, mumbling manner. I fairly told him that I did not like his having praised David Hume so much. He went off to the board huffed, yet affecting to treat my censure as foolish. I did not care how he took it. Since his absurd eulogium on Hume and his ignorant, ungrateful attack on the English university education, I have had no desire to be much with him.[9] Yet I do not forget that he was very civil to me at Glasgow. I went out with Commissioner Cochrane and dined with him. No company there. Drank very little. Came to my father's to tea. The Countess of Sutherland and her grandmother there.

WEDNESDAY 15 SEPTEMBER. (Writing Saturday 18 September.) Dined out at the Coates with Mr. Ilay Campbell, who had taken the

[7] Boswell's second cousin, daughter of Robert Sibthorpe of County Down. Her grandfather, General Cochrane, was Boswell's great-uncle. Her parents were planning to send a son, Stephen James, to a university (see below, 28 September 1780).

[8] See above, 17 July 1779.

[9] Smith, who had been appointed Commissioner of Customs in 1777, had declared in a letter to William Strahan which Strahan had affixed to Hume's *Autobiography*, 1777, that he had always considered Hume "as approaching as nearly to the idea of a perfectly wise and virtuous man as perhaps the nature of human frailty will permit." His attack on English university education (he had himself studied at Oxford as well as at Glasgow) occurs in *The Wealth of Nations*, Bk. V, ch. 1: "Of the Expense of the Institutions for the Education of Youth."

house there as summer quarters. Had no satisfaction in existence; did not drink too much.

THURSDAY 16 SEPTEMBER. Some French ships had come up the Firth of Forth, as far as Inchkeith almost, last night. This gave an alarm which animated me a little.[1] Surgeon Wood and Grange dined with us, and the latter walked with me in the Meadow. I had called in the forenoon at Dr. Gillespie's and seen his wife and him. My father and Lady Auchinleck came in their coach and took them out an airing; more than was ever done for my wife. I drank tea at my father's. He was very dull. The Commissioner was there. I was not happy.

FRIDAY 17 SEPTEMBER. Walked up to the Castle and saw the West Fencibles alive for action, should they have an opportunity, and cannon put upon carriages to be taken to Leith; in short, the appearance of war. But I was quite indifferent about everything. Nothing gave me any satisfaction at present but eating and drinking and lying in bed. Commissioner Cochrane and Miss Dick dined with us.

SATURDAY 18 SEPTEMBER. (Writing on Friday the 24 September.) Though in sad low spirits, got the 24 number of the *Hypochondriack* finished; and what was a curious experiment, except the first page, I read none of it over before sending it off, that I might be agreeably surprised with it in print.[2] Maclaurin called on me in the afternoon and he and I drove in a hackney-coach to Leith and Newhaven and saw the batteries which were erected to guard the coast. It was a dreary damp afternoon; I was sunk and dejected, and viewed the batteries as I have done potato beds at Auchinleck.

SUNDAY 19 SEPTEMBER. Heard Dr. Blair in the forenoon and Mr. Walker in the afternoon. Drank tea at my father's. Heard the children say sacred lessons agreeably. They were particularly fond of the Creed. Was somewhat better. Grange supped with us.

MONDAY 20 SEPTEMBER. Had for some time inclined to give warning to my servant, James Clark (writing Sunday the 26), as he did not give sufficient attendance. But was so weak-nerved that I could not bring myself to do it till this morning, and then I did it very awkwardly. The poor fellow received his warning, though sudden, with much steadiness; yet I could not help pitying him. I was in great pain all day about it. For warning a servant from a good place is in my apprehension a distressing thing to him; so that there really should, as I think, be very good cause

[1] This was John Paul Jones's squadron of French vessels sailing under the American flag. He had intended to burn the shipping at Leith, but bad weather prevented him from approaching the shore. The great fight between the *Serapis* and the *Bonhomme Richard* occurred just a week later.

[2] It is on censure.

for it. This however is not the common opinion; and, as Grange observed, I probably suffered more upon this occasion than James did. I was for engaging no other servant till he got a place, and if he got none, was for keeping him.[3] This was not the firmness of a master of a family. Grange supped with us.

TUESDAY 21 SEPTEMBER. Had a hogshead of Malaga bottled. Grange dined with us, and he and I drank a bottle of my old Malaga and a bottle of cider. When at dinner, I received a message from Colonel Stuart that he would be glad to see me at Fortune's as soon as I could come. This was kind. Therefore I resolved to go. Went about five. What I had already taken had intoxicated me to a certain degree. I drank a good quantity of claret with him, Matthew Henderson, etc.; and growing uneasy, took to strong gin punch, which soon quite knocked me up, and I was brought home in a chair, I know not how. The Colonel in a very friendly manner asked me to go up with him, see his regiment at Leeds in Yorkshire, and then go on to London: "and," said he, "you have a very good excuse to your father: that you are going to see my brother before he goes abroad,[4] which I think you should, and the journey up shall not cost you a farthing." I agreed to go. I also engaged to go with him next day to Kirkcaldy to visit Mr. Oswald, and to dine with him at Sir A. Oughton's on Friday, and General Skene's on Saturday.

WEDNESDAY 22 SEPTEMBER. Awaked excessively ill. Sent to Colonel Stuart that I could not go with him to Fife. Lay in bed till between five and six. Told my wife of the Colonel's proposal to carry me up. She readily agreed, thinking it might be for my advantage, in getting me the Colonel's interest joined to his brother's. Only she trusted that I would not drink hard. Grange supped with us.

THURSDAY 23 SEPTEMBER. Called on Commissioner Cochrane and talked with him of Colonel Stuart's proposal to me. He approved much of my accepting it, and said my father would be much in the wrong if he did not approve of it. I went to my father's and with some hesitation mentioned it. To my agreeable surprise he did not oppose it. Worthy Grange was much for it. So that I had many opinions to confirm my own. Mr. Robert Boswell, his wife and sisters dined with us, and the ladies drank tea. Grange supped with us.

FRIDAY 24 SEPTEMBER. Was in somewhat an awkward state of uneasiness lest Colonel Stuart's proposal might have been only the momentary sally of a drinking fit, and that (writing Sunday 19 December) I might appear ridiculous for having thought him in earnest. He returned this day

[3] Clark had been with Boswell since some time in May 1778. Boswell kept him eight months longer.
[4] Lord Mountstuart had been appointed Envoy to the Court of Sardinia.

between two and three. I saw him for a few minutes at his hotel, and we talked of our journey as a fixed thing. He went to dine at Sir Adolphus Oughton's. I dined with Mr. Alexander Boswall and General Joseph Smith at their hotel. Robert Boswell made a fourth man. Colonel Stuart was to sup with me this night. Mr. Boswall gave me this advice: that if I would drink much, I should keep to one liquor. His talk was too rapid. My wife, who has more discernment than I have, undertook to find out from Colonel Stuart if he really wished I should go with him. He came early tonight; and I left them awhile together. Maclaurin was my only other guest; and though at first I was a little uneasy that I had not more company, it was better as it was. For Maclaurin was very good company till two; and then the Colonel and I had an admirable cordial seat by ourselves till about seven. We drank a good deal of my own importation claret (by means of Wight), which he liked much. We drank slow, and were both merry and rational. It pleased me very much to hear him declare that he loved his wife now as much as he had ever done. I never before drank for hours without a toast.[5] But he convinced me that it was very easy and pleasant. I was much taken with his manly good sense and knowledge of the world. My jaunt with him was now clearly fixed. I was not at all drunk.

SATURDAY 25 SEPTEMBER. I rose quite well in the forenoon. Walked out to Sir Alexander Dick's and surprised them with my sudden London journey, and asked their commands for Willy,[6] whom I promised to see. They took my visit kind, as I meant it. I dined at General Skene's with Colonel Stuart, Sir James Campbell, Major Montgomerie, etc. Was in excellent spirits and drank freely, but came off in good time, so that I was not drunk.

SUNDAY 26 SEPTEMBER. Was at the New Church in the forenoon. My father was in the seat. I went out to his house in the coach with him and Lady Auchinleck. By the road he talked a little of my setting out with Colonel Stuart next day, and seemed pretty indifferent. His being so was in my opinion a sign of his being failed. For had he been quite himself, he would have been violent against it. I then called on Maclaurin and told him I was to set out next day. He said I would drink

---

[5] A French gentleman (François de la Rochefoucauld), observing in 1784 the curious customs of the natives across the Channel, explained the necessity of toasts: "After . . . mere thirst has become inadequate reason for drinking, a fresh stimulus is applied by the drinking of 'toasts,' that is to say, the host begins by giving the name of a lady; he drinks to her health and everyone is obliged to do likewise. . . . If more drinking is required, fresh toasts are always ready to hand; politics can supply plenty" (*A Frenchman in England*, ed. Jean Marchand, trans. S. C. Roberts, 1933, p. 31).

[6] Sir Alexander's son and heir, now an ensign in the 1st Regiment of Foot Guards.

half a hogshead of claret before I returned. I dined comfortably at home; heard Dr. Blair in the New Church in the afternoon, and my wife and I (and some of the children, I think) drank tea at my father's. I did not take leave of him tonight, as I expected I should be out to wait on him next day before setting out.

[EDITORIAL NOTE: Boswell kept a separate "Journal of My Jaunt with the Honourable Colonel James Stuart" which he himself in a letter to Johnson (7 November 1779) described as "truly a log-book of felicity." One would very much like to read a journal of Boswell's so characterized by Boswell himself, but it is unfortunately and unaccountably missing— the only major journal of his now unaccounted for. Is it possible that he put it with the papers he prized most—Johnson's letters to him and his to Johnson—and that, like those papers, it got lost because he took such special pains to preserve it? He was at Leeds on 30 September and in London by 4 October, remaining there till the 18th. Late on the 18th he reached Lichfield, and late on the 19th pushed on to Chester. At Chester he must have stayed two weeks or a little more. On 6 November he reached Carlisle, and on the 9th was back in Edinburgh. The first draft of the *Life of Johnson*, which here follows in lieu of the missing journal, is probably a pretty thorough report of his meetings with Johnson in autumn 1779—the only "second crop in one year" [7] he ever had from Johnson during the entire period of their acquaintance—but is by no means an adequate substitute for the missing journal, especially for the portion dealing with Chester. It does, however, print for the first time some bits of Johnson's conversation later deleted from the draft, and provides in full the original text for a notorious passage which Boswell printed but cancelled before publication.]

On Monday 4 October I was with him before he was up. He sent for me to his bedside, expressed a satisfaction at this incidental meeting with as much vivacity as if he had been in the gaiety of youth. He called briskly, "Frank, go and get coffee and let us breakfast in splendour." I had at this time several good interviews with him which it is unnecessary to distinguish particularly. I consulted him as to the appointment of guardians to my children. "Sir," said he, "do not appoint a number of guardians. When they are many, they trust one to another and the business is neglected. I would advise you to choose one; let him be a man of respectable character who for his own credit will do what is right; let him be a rich man, so that he may be under no temptation to take advantage; and let him be a man of business who is used to conduct affairs with

[7] *Life of Johnson*, immediately preceding 4 October 1779.

ability and expertness, to whom therefore the execution of the trust will be easy." [8]

On Sunday 10 October we dined together at Mr. Strahan's. He said, "A man had better have ten thousand pounds at the end of ten years passed in England than twenty thousand pounds at the end of ten years passed in India, because you must compute what you *give* for money; and a man who has lived ten years in India has given up ten years of social comfort and all those advantages which arise from living in England." He told us that the ingenious Mr. Brown, distinguished by the name of *Capability Brown*,[9] told him that he was once at the seat of a great man [1] who had returned from India with great wealth, and that he showed him at the door of his bedchamber a large chest which he said was once full of gold; upon which Brown observed, "I am glad you can bear it so near your bedchamber."

We talked of the state of the poor in London. JOHNSON. "Saunders Welch, the Justice, who was once High Constable of St. Giles's and had great occasion to know the state of the poor, told me that I underrated the number when I computed that twenty a week (that is, above a thousand a year) died of hunger—not absolutely of immediate hunger, but of the wasting and diseases which are the consequence of hunger. This happens only in so large a place as London, where people are not known. What we are told about the great sums got by begging is not true. The trade is overstocked. And you may depend upon it, there are many of them who cannot get work. A particular kind of manufacture fails. Those who have been used to work at it can for some time work at nothing else. You meet a man begging; you charge him with idleness. He says, 'I am willing to labour. Will you give me work?' 'I cannot.' 'Why then, you have no right to charge me with idleness.' "

We left Mr. Strahan's at seven, as he had said he intended to go to evening prayers. As we walked along, he complained of a little gout in his toe, and said, "I shan't go to prayers tonight. I shall go tomorrow. When-

[8] The following January Boswell appointed his wife and Sir William Forbes to be co-curators and co-tutors (see below, 6 January 1780). Upon the death of his wife he substituted Thomas David Boswell's name for hers by a codicil.

[9] Lancelot Brown was head gardener at Stowe and afterwards at Hampton Court and Windsor. His nickname came from his habit of saying that grounds which he was asked to lay out had "capabilities." For a gardener, he led a heady social life: he shared the private hours of the King and sat down at "the tables of all the House of Lords" (*Correspondence of William Pitt, Earl of Chatham*, ed. W. S. Taylor and J. H. Pringle, 1840, iv. 430 n. 1). Mrs. Montagu considered him "a great poet" of gardens, and called his works "sweet pastorals and gentle elegiacs" (Reginald Blunt, *Mrs. Montagu, "Queen of the Blues,"* 1923, ii. 123).

[1] In revising Boswell abandoned caution and named Lord Clive.

ever I miss church on a Sunday, I resolve to go another day. But I do not always do it." This was a fair exhibition of that vibration between pious resolutions and indolence which many of us have too often experienced.

I went home with him and we had a long quiet conversation.

I showed him a letter from Dr. Hugh Blair mentioning that Lord Bathurst told him that Pope's *Essay on Man* was written in prose by Lord Bolingbroke and that Lord Bathurst added that he himself had read it in that state.[2] JOHNSON. "Pope may have had from Bolingbroke the philosophic stamina of his *Essay*; and admitting this to be true Lord Bathurst was no liar; but the thing is not true in the latitude that Blair seems to imagine; we are sure that the poetical imagery which makes a great part of the poem was Pope's own. It is amazing, Sir, what deviations there are from precise truth in the account which is given of almost anything. I told Mrs. ———,[3] 'You have so little regard to truth that you never tax your memory with the exact thing'; now what is the use of the memory to truth if one is careless of exactitude? Lord Hailes's *Annals of Scotland* are very exact, but they contain mere dry circumstances. They are to be considered as a dictionary. You know such things are there and may be looked at when you please. When you have read them, you close the book, and find you have nothing in your head. Robertson paints; but the misfortune is you are sure he does not know the people whom he paints, so you cannot suppose a likeness.[4] Characters should never be given by an historian unless he knew the people whom he describes or copies from those who knew them." BOSWELL. "Why do people play this trick which I observe now when I look at your grate, putting the shovel against it to make the fire burn?" JOHNSON. "They play the trick, but it does not make the fire burn. *There* is better (setting the poker perpendicularly up at right angles with the grate). In times of superstition they thought that as it made a cross with the bars, it would drive away the witch." BOSWELL. "By associating with you, Sir, I am always getting an accession of wisdom. But perhaps a man, after knowing his own character, the natural strength of his mind, should not be too wise." JOHNSON. "Yes, Sir; be as wise as you can. 'Aliis laetus, sapiens sibi':[5]

[2] Boswell had written to Blair on 20 September, asking him to send what he remembered of this account of Lord Bathurst for Johnson's use in writing the life of Pope. In the *Life of Johnson* Boswell prints Blair's reply in full at this point.

[3] The revision names Mrs. Thrale.

[4] William Robertson, whose history of Scotland had appeared in 1759, was a much more widely read historian than Hailes.

[5] "Gay with others, wise when alone." This maxim remains untraced. Boswell later charged Johnson with inventing it himself, and Johnson did not deny it. See below, his letter to Johnson, 22 October 1779.

Well pleased to see the dolphins play,
[I mind my compass and my way.] [6]

You may be wise in your study in the morning, and gay at a tavern in the afternoon. Every man is to take care of his own wisdom and his own virtue, without minding too much what others think.

"Dodsley first mentioned to me the scheme of an English dictionary, but I had long thought of it." BOSWELL. "You did not know what you was undertaking." JOHNSON. "Yes, Sir. I knew very well what I was undertaking, and very well how to do it, and have done it very well." BOSWELL. "An excellent climax! And it *has* availed you. In your Preface you say: 'What would it avail me in this gloom of solitude?' [7] You have been agreeably mistaken. You have had more happy days since that time than you ever had before."

I mentioned to him a dispute between a friend of mine and his lady concerning conjugal infidelity, which my friend maintained was by no means so bad in the husband as in the wife.[8] JOHNSON. "Your friend is right, Sir. Between a man and his Maker it is a different question; but between a man and his wife a husband's infidelity is nothing. They are connected by children, by fortune, by serious considerations of community. Wise married women don't mind it. They detest a mistress but don't mind a whore. My wife told me I might lie with as many women as I pleased provided I loved her alone." BOSWELL. "She was not in earnest." JOHNSON. "But she was. Consider, Sir, how gross it is in a wife to complain of her husband's going to other women. It is that she has not enough of ———." [9] BOSWELL. "And was Mrs. Johnson then so liberal? To be sure, there is a great difference between the offence of infidelity in a man and his wife." JOHNSON. "The difference is boundless." BOSWELL. "Yes, boundless as property and honours." JOHNSON. "The man imposes no bastards upon his wife." [1] BOSWELL. "But Sir, my friend's lady argued that

---

[6] From Matthew Green's *The Spleen, a Poem*, in Dodsley's *Collection*, 5th edn. 1758, i. 45, ll. 926–927. Not being sure of more than line 926, Boswell made a marginal note to himself, "Take it from *The Spleen*." He later wrote a marginal direction to the printer to "leave room for three lines." Only line 927 was afterwards added.

[7] In the Preface to the *Dictionary* (last paragraph).

[8] "A friend of mine and his lady" were actually Boswell himself and a married woman not his wife whom he does not name and whom no one has ventured to identify by conjecture. He recorded the conversation in his journal under date of Good Friday (5 April) 1776, but says in the next entry that it really occurred on 6 April.

[9] Boswell at least momentarily regretted this bowdlerization, and wrote "tail" lightly above the dash. His final version read, "It is that she has not enough of what she would be ashamed to avow."

[1] After writing the whole of this paragraph, Boswell got a feeling that at this point he had repeated something he had entered earlier. "See if this not on a Good Friday,"

a wife might take care that her infidelity should not be worse than that of her husband, which, said she, it would not be if she never went astray but when she was with child by her husband." JOHNSON. "Sir, from what you tell me of this lady, I think she is very fit for a bawdy-house." BOSWELL. "Suppose a woman to be of such a constitution that she does not like it. She has no right to complain that her husband goes elsewhere." JOHNSON. "If she refuses it, she has no right to complain." BOSWELL. "Then as oft as a man's wife refuses, he may mark it down in his pocket-book and do as he pleases with a safe conscience." JOHNSON. "Nay, Sir, you must consider: to whore is wrong in a single man, and one cannot have more liberty by being married." [2]

He was this evening violent against the Roman Catholics; said, "In everything in which they differ from us they are wrong." He was even against the invocation of saints. In short, he was in the humour of opposition.

On Tuesday the twelfth October I dined with him at Mr. Ramsay's with Lord Newhaven and some more company of whom I have no memorandum except of a beautiful Miss Graham, a relation of his Lordship's who asked Dr. Johnson to hob or nob with her.[3] He was flattered by such pleasing attention, but politely told her that he never drank wine; but if she would drink a glass of water, he was much at her service. She accepted. "Oho, Sir," said Lord Newhaven, "you are caught." JOHNSON. "Nay, I do not see *how* I'm *caught.* But if I'm caught, I don't want to get out again. If I'm caught, I hope to be kept." Then when the two

---

he wrote in the margin. With this lead he turned up in his journal his conversation with the unnamed lady (see the last note but one) and in the manuscript of the *Life of Johnson* his discussion of it with Johnson on Easter Sunday, 7 April 1776. On comparison, it appeared that the two conversations undoubtedly took off from the same text, but that the only portion of the present conversation that really repeated the other was the two sentences that follow at the point of the text to which this note is appended: "BOSWELL. 'But, Sir, my friend's lady . . .'" to ". . . fit for a bawdy-house." He first decided to let the passage stand here ("Mem. to take this out of former" he wrote in the margin), but on second thought wisely reversed himself, deleted it here, and let it stand under 7 April 1776.

[2] This paragraph, minus the repeated sentences and with some revision that did not much refine its bluntness, was printed in the first edition, but cancelled before publication. On 10 February 1791, Boswell wrote to Malone, "I wonder how you and I admitted this to the public eye, for Windham, etc., were struck with its *indelicacy,* and it might hurt the book much. It is however mighty good stuff." In the cancel he adumbrated most of what had originally been printed, but omitted Mrs. Johnson's liberality and the detail of the pocket-book.

[3] Helen Mary Graham next year married Sir Henry Watkin Dashwood, Bt. She later became Lady of the Bedchamber and governess to the Royal Princesses through the influence of Lord Newhaven, who was her mother's brother.

glasses of water were brought, smiling placidly to the young lady, "Madam, we'll reciprocate."

Lord Newhaven and he kept up an argument for some time concerning the Middlesex election.[4] He said, "Parliament is bound by law as a man is bound where there's nobody to tie the knot. As it is clear that the House of Commons may expel and expel again and again, why not allow of the power to incapacitate for that Parliament, rather than have a perpetual contest kept up between Parliament and people?" Lord Newhaven took the opposite side, but said, "I speak with great deference to you, Dr. Johnson. I speak to be instructed." This had its full effect upon Johnson. He bowed his head to a complimenting nobleman [5] and called out, "My Lord, my Lord, I do not desire all this ceremony; let us tell our minds to one another quietly." After the debate was over, he said, "I have got lights on the subject today which I had not before." This was a great deal from him, especially as he had written a pamphlet upon it.

He observed, "The House of Commons was originally not a privilege of the people, but a check for the Crown on the House of Peers. I remember Henry VIII wanted them to do something. They hesitated in the morning, but did it in the afternoon. He told them, ' 'Tis well you did, or half your heads should have been upon Temple Bar'; but the House of Commons is now no longer under the power of the Crown and therefore must be bribed."

All that I have preserved of his conversation at this time [6] is only that he said, "I have no delight in talking of public affairs."

I told him that when I objected to keeping company with a notorious infidel, a celebrated friend of ours [7] said to me, "I do not think that men who live laxly in the world as you and I do have a right to assume such an authority. Dr. Johnson may, who is uniformly strict. It is not very consistent to shun an infidel today and drink too freely tomorrow." JOHNSON. "Nay, Sir, this is sad reasoning. Because a man cannot be right in all things, is he to be right in nothing? Because a man sometimes gets drunk, is he therefore to steal? This doctrine would very soon bring a man to the gallows." After all, however, it is a difficult question how far sincere

---

[4] The notorious election of 1768–1769, at which Wilkes (who was in prison) was four times elected to the House of Commons and as often declared by the House to be incapable of election. Johnson in 1770 had published *The False Alarm* to justify the action of the Ministry and the majority in the House of Commons.

[5] Paoli made an exquisite remark on this: "Lord Newhaven and Johnson, who held down his head to have the full pail of flattery poured on" (Journal, 7 May 1781, 2nd entry).

[6] This was made much clearer in the revision: "What I have preserved of his conversation during the remainder of my stay in London at this time ..."

[7] Probably Gibbon ("notorious infidel") and Burke ("celebrated friend").

Christians should associate with the avowed enemies of religion, for, in the first place, every man's mind may be more or less "corrupted by evil communications"; [8] secondly, the world may very naturally suppose that they are not really in earnest in religion who can easily bear its opponents; and, thirdly, if the profane find themselves quite well received by the pious, one of the checks upon an open declaration of their infidelity and one of the probable chances of obliging them seriously to reflect, which their being shunned would do, is removed.

He, I know not why, showed upon all occasions a reluctance to go to Ireland, where I proposed to him that we should make a tour. JOHNSON. "It is the last place where I should wish to travel." BOSWELL. "Dublin, Sir?" JOHNSON. "Only a worse capital." BOSWELL. "Is not the Giant's Causeway worth seeing?" JOHNSON. "Worth seeing, yes; but not worth going to see."

Of an acquaintance of ours whose manners and everything about him, though expensive, were coarse, he said, "Sir, you see vulgar prosperity." [9]

A foreign minister of no very high talents who had been in his company for some time quite overlooked, happened luckily to mention that he had read some of his *Rambler* in Italian and admired it much. This pleased him greatly. He observed it had been translated *Il genio errante*—though I have been told it was rendered more ludicrously *Il vagabondo*; and finding that this minister gave such a proof of his taste, he was all attention to him, and on the first remark which he made, however simple, exclaimed, "The Ambassador says well.—His Excellency observes—" and then he expanded and enriched the little that had been said in so strong a manner that it appeared something of consequence. This was exceedingly entertaining to the company who were present, and many a time afterwards it furnished a pleasant topic of merriment.

I left London on Monday eighteenth October and accompanied Colonel Stuart to Chester, where his regiment was to lie for some time.

[Boswell to Johnson] [10]

Chester, 22 October 1779.

MY DEAR SIR,—It was not till one o'clock on Monday morning that Colonel Stuart and I left London, for we chose to bid a cordial adieu to Lord Mountstuart, who was to set out on that day on his embassy to Turin. We drove on excellently and reached Lichfield in good time

[8] 1 Corinthians 15. 33; St. Paul is thought to have been quoting Menander.

[9] None of Boswell's editors has yet ventured a guess as to the identity of this "acquaintance of ours."

[10] *Life of Johnson,* 22 October 1779. None of the originals of Boswell's letters to Johnson that appear in the *Life* have been recovered.

enough that night. The Colonel had heard so preferable a character of the George that he would not put up at the Three Crowns, so that I did not see our host, Wilkins. We found at the George as good accommodation as we could wish to have, and I fully enjoyed the comfortable thought that *I was in Lichfield again*. Next morning it rained very hard; and as I had much to do in a little time, I ordered a post-chaise, and between eight and nine sallied forth to make a round of visits. I first went to Mr. Greene, hoping to have had him to accompany me to all my other friends, but he was engaged to attend the Bishop of Sodor and Man, who was then lying at Lichfield very ill of the gout.[1] Having taken a hasty glance at the additions to Greene's museum, from which it was not easy to break away,[2] I next went to the Friary, where I at first occasioned some tumult in the ladies, who were not prepared to receive *company* so early; but my *name*, which has by wonderful felicity come to be so closely associated with yours, soon made all easy; and Mrs. Cobb and Miss Adey reassumed their seats at the breakfast-table, which they had quitted with some precipitation. They received me with the kindness of an old acquaintance; and after we had joined in a cordial chorus to *your* praise, Mrs. Cobb gave *me* the high satisfaction of hearing that you said, "Boswell is a man who I believe never left a house without leaving a wish for his return." And she afterwards added that she bid you tell me that if ever I came to Lichfield, she hoped I would take a bed at the Friary. From thence I drove to Peter Garrick's, where I also found a very flattering welcome. He appeared to me to enjoy his usual cheerfulness; and he very kindly asked me to come when I could and pass a week with him. From Mr. Garrick's, I went to the Palace to wait on Mr. Seward. I was first entertained by his lady and daughter, he himself being in bed with a cold, according to his valetudinary custom.[3] But he desired to see me; and I found him dressed in his black gown, with a white flannel night-gown above it; so that he looked like a Dominican friar. He was good-humoured and polite; and under his roof too my reception was very pleasing. I then proceeded to Stow Hill, and first paid my respects to Mrs. Gastrell, whose conversation I was not willing to quit. But my sand-glass was now beginning to run low, as I could not trespass too long on the Colonel's kindness, who obligingly waited for me; so I

[1] Dr. Richard Richmond.

[2] "This afternoon I saw with Dr. Johnson the museum of Mr. Greene, an apothecary, a wonderful collection to be made by a man like him in a country town. He had his curiosities neatly arranged, with their names printed at his own little press, and he had at the top of the first flat of his staircase a board with the contributors marked in gold letters. He had also a printed catalogue, which I bought at the bookseller's. He was a bustling, good-humoured little man" (Journal, 23 March 1776).

[3] The Rev. Thomas Seward, Canon Residentiary of Lichfield, lived in the Bishop's Palace. His daughter was Anna Seward, poetess, "the Swan of Lichfield."

hastened to Mrs. Aston's, whom I found much better than I feared I should; and there I met a brother-in-law of these ladies, who talked much of you, and very well too, as it appeared to me.[4] It then only remained to visit Mrs. Lucy Porter, which I did, I really believe, with sincere satisfaction on both sides.[5] I am sure I was glad to see her again, and, as I take her to be very honest, I trust she was glad to see me again; for she expressed herself so that I could not doubt of her being in earnest. What a great keystone of kindness, my dear Sir, were you that morning! for we were all held together by our common attachment to you. I cannot say that I ever passed two hours with more self-complacency than I did those two at Lichfield. Let me not entertain any suspicion that this is idle vanity. Will not you confirm me in my persuasion that he who finds himself so regarded has just reason to be happy?

We got to Chester about midnight on Tuesday; and here again I am in a state of much enjoyment. Colonel Stuart and his officers treat me with all the civility I could wish, and I play my part admirably. "Laetus aliis, sapiens sibi," the classical sentence which you, I imagine, invented the other day, is exemplified in my present existence.[6] The Bishop, to whom I had the honour to be known several years ago, shows me much attention, and I am edified by his conversation.[7] I must not omit to tell you that his Lordship admires very highly your *Prefaces to the Poets*. I am daily obtaining an extension of agreeable acquaintance, so that I am kept in animated variety; and the study of the place itself, by the assistance of books, and of the Bishop, is sufficient occupation. Chester pleases my fancy more than any town I ever saw. But I will not enter upon it at all in this letter.

How long I shall stay here I cannot yet say. I told a very pleasing young lady, niece to one of the prebendaries, at whose house I saw her, "I have come to Chester, Madam, I cannot tell how; and far less can I tell how I am to get away from it."[8] Do not think me too juvenile. I beg it of you, my dear Sir, to favour me with a letter while I am here, and add to the happiness of a happy friend who is ever, with affectionate veneration, most sincerely yours,

JAMES BOSWELL.

[4] Probably William Prujean, who married Sophia Aston, sister to Mrs. Jane Gastrell and to Elizabeth Aston, a spinster of seventy-one whom Boswell styles "Mrs."
[5] "Mrs." Lucy Porter, a spinster of sixty-four, was Johnson's stepdaughter, though only six years younger than he.
[6] See above, p. 141 n. 5.
[7] Dr. Beilby Porteus was at this time Bishop of Chester. In 1787 he became Bishop of London.
[8] Boswell himself identified this young lady by a note in the *Life of Johnson* as "Miss Letitia Barnston."

If you do not write directly, so as to catch me here, I shall be disappointed. Two lines from you will keep my lamp burning bright.

[Extract, Boswell to Langton]

23 December 1779

. . . I was a forthnight at *Headquarters* at Chester, where I declare I passed my time more happily than I ever did in any place—I know not if I should even except London—for the same portion of time. The general hospitality of the people, the curiosity of the town itself and the beauty of its environs, and the animation of a military society gave me the most cheerful spirits. . . .

On Monday 27 September there begins a separate journal of my jaunt with the Honourable Colonel James Stuart, of which I have pretty full notes.[9]

I have also notes of journal, after my return from that jaunt, till Saturday the 18 December inclusive, on which day the Session rose for the Christmas vacation.[1] No period of my life has been more sound and cheerful than this. The stock of fine spirits which I laid in upon the jaunt kept me in all this former part of the Session quite as I could wish. I wrote twice the number of pages of law papers that I did in the same space last winter. I went through business with ability and ease. I had not the least hypochondria. I relished life much. I was several times out at dinners and suppers, and had several companies with me; and I was very little intoxicated at any time. I was one week confined to the house with a cold, which was very general this winter in Edinburgh, but it did not sink my spirits. I had been troubled for some time with a scurvy on my thighs and legs, for which I drank a decoction of guaiac [2] and sassafras. My left great toe troubled me a good deal. Mr. Wood cut out the nail which fretted the flesh, and made me apply vitriol to burn and dry the fungous substance, but it was not yet well when the Session broke up. On Monday 6 December I began to rise early, and ever since that day got up with ease. I was only once with a coarse Dulcinea, who was perfectly safe. I however must own that amongst many good circumstances of this period of my life, I omitted to write to many eminent friends in England, which was so much loss to my elegant improvement. Young Arniston [3] seemed to take much to me, which was agreeable, as there had been a friendship between

[9] This journal has not been recovered. See above, the Editorial Note following 26 September 1779.

[1] Except for the death of Lady Preston on 7 November (which he does not mention), the period for which we omit notes is well covered by this review.

[2] Guaiacum, a resin used medicinally for gout, rheumatism, and skin diseases.

[3] Robert Dundas, son of the Lord President.

his grandfather and mine and my father and his father; in short, an hereditary kindness, which, though interrupted by his father's bad conduct to our family at last Ayrshire election, was not to be lost.[4] He supped with me very cheerfully one night. My wife was in as good health this winter as I ever saw her, till a week before the Session broke up, she also was seized with the cold, and had a pretty severe cough. As she was with child, I was afraid she might be much the worse of coughing. My brother John was in Edinburgh all this period, but never would call upon me, having an unhappy prejudice against me.[5] Yet when I called on him he was civil enough. My children had all what we thought the chin-cough [6] in a mild degree. My father was seized (18 November) with the cold, and it rose to a high fever, his pulse being at ninety-five. He had at the same time an obstinate cough, and his bladder was in a bad state. He was for several days really in danger, and Dr. Gillespie said to me that he feared it would stand hard with him this winter. I was out every day calling on him for some time, but saw him little. However, I found that his illness made him more kindly. One night he said to me, "I am much obliged to you for this visit." He grew better, and though much shaken, was pretty well again before the Session broke up. I must record a curious dialogue which I witnessed between him and John Stobie when he was lying in bed one forenoon, better, but weak. "Come awa', John. Are aw the Lords of Session living yet?" "Ay, my Lord. But mony a ane's wishing them dead. Ony body that has a post has folk to wish them dead." "Wha are expectants now?" "Plenty of expectants, my Lord." My father was not in the least discomposed by this odd suggestion. He had been remarkably well the few days of this Session that he attended the House. The study shown by his lady to prevent my being with him alone was offensive. I was a little uneasy to think that I had neglected to get him to sign an addition to the entail of Auchinleck allowing of liferent leases to any tenant and of nine hundred and ninety-nine years' leases in our village. But it would have been indelicate to have troubled him with it while really ill. I did not see

---

[4] "He behaved in a most ungentlemanly manner to me, in privately persuading my father to make votes in Ayrshire against the nobility whose cause I had warmly espoused, and [had] done a most unfriendly thing to my father in leading him to do the very thing which he had for a course of years condemned" (Journal, 6 August 1774. For a full explanation of the Lord President's "bad conduct," see *Boswell for the Defence* for that date).

[5] John had come back to Edinburgh during Boswell's absence, and had taken lodgings there. Boswell had unfortunately removed some old gloves and shirts from John's effects stored in his house, and had used them himself because he thought they "would spoil by lying" (Journal, 7 September 1776). He had repeatedly offered to pay John for them, but John preferred to retain his grievance.

[6] Whooping cough.

my uncle the Doctor during this period. I regret this. But lameness and bad weather were against going to the New Town. Having been for so many weeks the intimate companion of Colonel Stuart, I had insensibly become so far assimilated to him as to have high manly notions; for mental qualities are communicated by contagion as certainly as material qualities. I cannot analyse the effects of my last autumn jaunt, but I felt them very animating. Indeed, I have a wonderful enthusiastic fondness for military scenes. My wife however observed that my temper was grown more violent since being with Colonel Stuart. I perceived this to be true. But I did not think it a disadvantage to me. I read but little in this period, but what I did read was better digested by my mind than usual. I read Blumenbachius *On the Unity of Mankind,* and *Anecdotes of Bowyer,* the learned printer.[7] I did not study Greek as I intended. I put it off.

SUNDAY 19 DECEMBER. (Writing on Monday the 20th.) It was a very wet day. So I stayed at home and made the children say divine lessons. In the afternoon I read one of Mr. Carr's sermons aloud, and my wife another. At night after we were in bed, Veronica spoke out from her little bed and said, "I do not believe there is a GOD." "Preserve me," said I, "my dear, what do you mean?" She answered, "I have *thinket* it many a time, but did not like to speak of it." I was confounded and uneasy, and tried her with the simple argument that without GOD there would not be all the things we see. "It is He who makes the sun shine." Said she: "It shines only on good days." Said I: "GOD made you." Said she: "My mother bore me." It was a strange and alarming thing to her mother and me to hear our little angel talk thus. But I thought it better just to let the subject drop insensibly tonight. I asked her if she had said her prayers tonight. She said yes, and asked me to put her in mind to say them in the morning. I prayed to GOD to prevent such thoughts from entering into her mind. π.

MONDAY 20 DECEMBER. (Writing Tuesday the 21.) By talking calmly with Veronica, I discovered what had made her think there was not a GOD. She told me, she "did not like to die." I suppose as she has been told that GOD takes us to himself when we die, she had fancied that if there were no GOD, there would be no death; so "her wish was father to the thought"—"I wot through ignorance."[8] I impressed upon her that we must die at any rate; and how terrible would it be if we had not a

---

[7] The first book, by Johann Friedrich Blumenbach, Professor of Medicine at Göttingen, had been lent to Boswell by John Law, Archdeacon of Carlisle. The first edition of John Nichols's *Anecdotes Biographical and Literary of Mr. William Bowyer* (which was the basis of his *Literary Anecdotes*) was not published until 1782, but in 1778 twenty copies of "a slight sketch" of it were printed and sent to Bowyer's friends. The copy Boswell read may have been sent to him by Sir John Pringle.

[8] 2 *Henry IV,* IV. v. 93; Acts 3. 17 ("I wot that through ignorance ye did it").

Father in Heaven to take care of us. I looked into Cambrai's [9] *Education of a Daughter,* hoping to have found some simple argument for the being of GOD in that piece of instruction. But it is taken for granted. I was somewhat fretful today from finding myself without fixed occupation; and my toe seeming not to heal. But my mind had a firm bottom. Captain Bosville called in the forenoon and took leave, as he was to set out for London next day.

TUESDAY 21 DECEMBER. (Writing on Wednesday the 22.) I had not been at my father's for several days. The weather had been very bad and my toe uneasy. I sent out a note to his lady last night to know how they were, hoping to dine there today; and that if she was to be in town with the chariot, it would be charity to carry me out. She was in town and sent it for me, and I called at her mother's and found her there. And then she and I drove out. My father was remarkably well. But with his health his harshness was returned. I had thought it would be proper for me to go to Auchinleck for some days this vacation and see how things were going on. But when I spoke of it to him, he said, "Ye hae nae skill." I afterwards said, "So you don't think it would be of use that I should go west this vacation? If that is the case, I shall not go, for it would cost me some trouble and some bank notes." Said he: "Ye had as good keep them in your pouch." I therefore laid aside thoughts of going. Claud, Robert Boswell, and Stobie were at dinner. It was a disagreeable scene. After dinner my father, recollecting no doubt my aversion to the Lord President and the too good cause of it, drank his health, "—and may all that don't like him be despised and contemned." This was really shocking. Yet his memory was wretchedly bad as to other things. He asked me if I ever visited Old Erskine's wife (who died several years ago), and if they had "ony bairns." [1] After Claud and Robert were gone, I was a little with Mr. Stobie privately, and I suggested to him that tacks should not be set on the estate of Auchinleck at present, for if I was to get an entailed estate and tacks on it, I would have no power. The little wretch answered, "Sae muckle the better. It 'ill keep ye frae playing the fool." As Grange well observed, he ought to have been kicked; and nothing but

---

[9] That is, Fénelon's; he was Archbishop of Cambrai.

[1] This was indeed what Johnson would have called a "morbid oblivion" (*Journal of a Tour to the Hebrides,* 19 August 1773, end). James Erskine, advocate and Knight Marshal of Scotland, was third cousin to Lord Auchinleck's first wife, Boswell's mother, an Erskine of the Alva line. He had married his first cousin, Frances Erskine, and was nephew and ultimately heir male, as she was daughter and ultimately heir of line, of the Earl of Mar who had been attainted for his part in the Jacobite rising of 1715. She had been dead for more than three years, and they had two sons, both of whom Boswell had been counsel for before committees of the House of Commons. See below, 27 December 1779.

hearing me treated as I am, daily and hourly, at my father's could have made him dare to be so impertinent. I must have patience in my present state. Dr. Gillespie drank tea there. I had a chair to take me home.

WEDNESDAY 22 DECEMBER. (Writing Thursday the 23). Wrote several letters to friends in London. Kept the house all day to let my toe heal if it would. Grange dined. Drank strong ale and cider and eat pickles, all which produced an uneasiness in my stomach. Took a good deal of pains this and former days to settle a dispute between Mr. James Craig, baker, Deacon Convener of the Trades of Edinburgh, and William Watson, poulterer. Mr. Craig was much satisfied. Watson was unreasonable. Time must finally adjust it.[2] Grange drank tea. It was very cold.

THURSDAY 23 DECEMBER. (Writing Friday the 24th.) Attended the funeral of the Earl of Caithness. His Lordship had died here above three weeks or a month ago. But the corpse had been kept till instructions should come from his family in Caithness where to inter him. It was fixed to be in Roslyn Chapel. I was solemnly pleased with this funeral. I thought of the grandmother of Thomas Boswell, the first laird of Auchinleck, having been a daughter of the family of Caithness.[3] I went and came with Mr. Gilbert Mason in his post-chaise. I was the only man who kept off his hat in the venerable chapel, so rare is pious reverence in Scotland.[4] Bailie Macqueen came up to me in the street after I returned, to consult me about something. I took him home with me to dinner. Grange joined us after dinner. My wife and I supped and played whist at Dr. Young's; Sir William and Lady Forbes, Sir Philip and Lady Ainslie, etc., etc., there. A very cheerful evening.

FRIDAY 24 DECEMBER. (Writing Saturday the 25th.) Did little. Time just glided on. Dined at Mr. Solicitor Murray's with Major Flint of the 25th Foot, commanding four companies of it in the Castle, Mr. George Wallace, and several more. A motley company. Was happy to meet worthy Flint after an interval of about four years, and felt myself pleased with military ideas when I looked at his regimentals and heard him talk of his regiment. I eat and drank too much for my scurvy and sore toe. But could not resist salmon, goose, or brandy. Drank claret moderately. Would have sat longer. But could not bear a forward priggish fool,

[2] We have found nothing further concerning this business. If settled by Boswell, it was obviously an arbitration, settled out of court, but his Decreet could have been registered in the Register House.

[3] Lady Margaret Sinclair, daughter of William Sinclair, Earl of Orkney and Caithness, was the mother, not the grandmother, of Thomas Boswell. Boswell wrongly believed William Boswell of Lochgelly, son of David Boswell of Balmuto and Lady Margaret, to be Thomas's father. Actually he was his older brother.

[4] The weather was very cold (see below, 25 December) and the chapel, which had been desecrated in 1688, was unglazed and open to the weather.

Stewart Macarthur,[5] and would not warm in his company. Was at a consultation at Mr. Rae's. Felt his superiority as a knowing lawyer. Uneasy a little from excess, at night I was in danger of peevishness. But escaped it. The Hon. Major Erskine, who had just come over from Dublin, sat with me part of the forenoon, as did Major Montgomerie. My wife was exceedingly good to me tonight, and said, "Will you ever say again that I don't love you?" I answered that I never would.

SATURDAY 25 DECEMBER. (Writing on Sunday the 26th.) Lay longer in bed than usual. The forenoon slipped away, I knew not how, so that I did not get out to see my father as I intended. Grange dined with us comfortably, as he always does on Christmas Day; and he and I and my two daughters went to the English Chapel in the afternoon. Effie was there for the first time, I having made a rule to begin to take each child to it in the sixth year of its age. It was very cold, and the congregation was thin. I had not such warmth of devotion as I have sometimes experienced. Yet I was very well. The children were impressed with good thoughts of Christ. The town was illuminated on account of the news of a victory in Georgia over Count d'Estaing and the Americans.[6] It gave me no pleasure, for I considered that it would only encourage a longer continuance of the ruinous war. Grange and Signora Marcucci drank tea with us. While we were at it, my brother John came in. He had called before this. He was silent and sulky, and soon asked me to go into another room with him. I did so. But found he only wanted to shun the company. He sat a short while. I engaged him to dine with us on Tuesday. It was painful to find him so unsocial. Though he took no notice of the children, Veronica gave a pleasing and curious proof of natural affection. She had never seen him before that she could recollect. But she said, "I like him." Signora Marcucci supped with us. I was easy and really as I could wish to be. π.

SUNDAY 26 DECEMBER. (Writing on Monday the 27th.) Heard Dr. Blair lecture and preach in the forenoon. He preached on "All is vanity," [7]

---

[5] Archibald Macarthur Stewart, advocate, was notorious for such eccentricities as dressing in white and keeping a litter of pigs in his bedroom.

[6] On 9 October the British troops in Savannah had repulsed a combined attack by a French fleet and expeditionary force under Admiral Charles Hector, Comte d'Estaing, and an American army under General Benjamin Lincoln. The news reached London on 20 December, and a *London Gazette Extraordinary* of the day published the dispatches. This *Gazette* arrived in Edinburgh at 9:30 p.m. on 24 December. The *Caledonian Mercury* printed it in full the next evening, saying that on 20 December the guns of the Tower of London "were fired . . . the first time these some years for *good news.*" The *Mercury* continues, "And this evening, for the same reason, a general illumination took place throughout this city and suburbs."

[7] Ecclesiastes 1. 1.

but smoothed it over prettily. He said no man who would calculate fairly would find that he had more hours of unhappiness than of happiness or ease. In short, he tried to *modify* the general infelicity of life too much. I shook my head as he preached. I sat awhile with Mr. David Erskine between sermons. I dined at my father's with him and his lady. He was in pretty good health, but not in the least cordial. I was obliged to be constantly upon my guard while the *noverca* [7a] lay in wait to catch at every word. I read aloud after dinner at her desire one of Fordyce's *Sermons to Young Women.* I was quite disgusted with the affected, theatrical style. I left out many superfluous words in many sentences. Yet they were still florid.[8] My father very judiciously said they were not for Sunday. I then read in Duncan's commentary on the first chapter of the Hebrews, the learned cast and correct language of which pleased me much. Indeed the chapter itself is noble. I stayed to tea. Dr. Gillespie came in after it. I walked both out and back again; and my toe was sore and inflamed and mysterious, so that I was really uneasy about it. I had mentioned our having half a seat in the New Church along with my father while I was at his house today. *She* opposed it in so shameless a manner, showing that she would not have *any* connexion between him and my family, that I was quite fretted and vexed. I was in a sad frame after I came home. For although, as Grange observed t'other day, my father's life was now not desirable even by his friends (and I added he now lived only for his second wife), I had still such an affection for him as affected me tenderly. Yet I suffered much. My daughters said divine lessons. π.

MONDAY 27 DECEMBER. (Writing on Tuesday the 28th.) Mr. Lawrie went this day to the country, which made me put off several letters till he should return to copy them, I having some time ago sworn him to secrecy upon the Bible. Old Erskine, who had drank tea with my wife on Friday and missed me, had sent me a card desiring to see me this forenoon. I had accepted of being one of his trustees, being mindful of his kindness to me when I was raw and fiery and on bad terms with my father.[9] I walked down

[7a] Latin for stepmother, quoting Virgil's *iniusta noverca* (*Eclogues*, iii. 33). Boswell first calls her this in 1777.

[8] A single sentence from James Fordyce's third sermon, "On Female Reserve," will justify Boswell's strictures: "But for those wicked—I turn from them to you, ye pretty helpless creatures, who have lost—it may be, happily—merciful Heaven! must I say, happily lost your parents? or whose parents yet alive, but lost to themselves and their offspring, have in the blindness of indulgence or the barbarity of neglect abandoned you to your own untutored conduct."

[9] "Old Erskine's" style of Mar was merely one of courtesy. The Mar estates had been forfeited in 1716, but two friends of the family, James Erskine, Lord Grange ("Old Erskine's" father) and David Erskine, Lord Dun, had bought back part of them and had put them under an entail by which they descended successively to "Old Erskine's"

to him to his present habitation, Lord Napier's house in the Abbey Close, and breakfasted with him. He was in bed, and complained of a sprained *ankle*, but probably this was to save his *heels* from being laid fast. For his creditors were pressing, and his house was in the Sanctuary.[1] He talked very plausibly. I then went to Mr. John Syme's, and was shown his very accurate books of all the lands in the Stewartry of Kirkcudbright: their extent, valuation, proprietors, etc., with alphabetical indexes of lands and persons. They pleased me much. I had not seen Lady Colville since my last English expedition. I had made my peace by means of my wife and an epistle; and this day Major Erskine carried me out in the coach and I dined with her. No company there. Just she and Lady Anne, the Major, and Andrew.[2] Their sneering and censoriousness, and their narrow preference of Edinburgh to London for happy living, disgusted me. But I kept my temper well, and drank more than a bottle of claret. I was firm in my own opinion as to England, which I have now tried sufficiently and find it more and more confirmed. My dear wife had some good soup for me at night. My toe was very sore, and Wood allowed me to put a poultice to it.

TUESDAY 28 DECEMBER. (Writing on Wednesday the 29th.) I must remark a curious incident. I dreamt that I saw the cause of my toe being so painful: viz., a piece of the nail sticking in the flesh. When I took off the poultice this morning, I observed a piece of nail appearing through the ball of my toe. Dr. Gillespie called. He desired to see it. He said it should be pulled out with a forceps. I took hold of it with my finger and thumb, and out it came. I was then at once easy, except that the wounded flesh smarted a little. Wood called, and I showed him how I was relieved. I had now only to let the wound heal. My brother John dined with us. He was silent and sour at dinner. But grew better after it, and he and I drank port negus really comfortably. The children paid him great attention, and he seemed kindly somewhat to them. But was strangely shy to my wife. Did not even drink to her. She was angry with him, which vexed me; for she should have considered it was disease. He drank tea with us. My wife was again exceedingly good to me tonight.

---

wife and his eldest son. (See above, p. 151 n. 1.) "Old Erskine" having been declared by a Decreet Arbitral, 9 November 1779, to have an interest in two earlier family trust dispositions and, being deeply in debt, was putting himself under trustees for the behoof of his creditors. The Trust Deed was signed on 20 January 1780 and registered on 19 February 1782. The trustees, headed by the Earl of Buchan, were mainly Erskines or Erskine descendants. Boswell was an Erskine, and he and "Old Erskine" were fourth cousins through common descent from John Erskine, Earl of Mar (1562–1634).
[1] Holyrood Abbey and its vicinity had for centuries been a sanctuary for debtors.
[2] The Hon. Andrew Erskine, Lady Anne Erskine, and Major Archibald Erskine (later Earl of Kellie) lived with their widowed sister, Lady Colville.

WEDNESDAY 29 DECEMBER. (Writing on Thursday the 30th.) My toe was pretty easy. I idled away the forenoon, I know not how. I felt myself somewhat languid and uneasy for want of stated occupation. I dined at Dr. Gillespie's and stayed tea. Captain Lawrence Campbell of the 71st, who had escaped after the taking of Stony Point,[3] and the Rev. Mr. Fitzsimmons of the English Chapel were there. I insensibly drank rather too much of different liquors, but guarded my tongue. Grange supped with us comfortably.

THURSDAY 30 DECEMBER. (Writing on Friday the 31st.) Again idled away the forenoon. Called at the custom-house and talked a little with Commissioner Cochrane about my father's giving me another £100 a year, which the Commissioner had proposed. He seemed to think I would get it. I then visited my father. He had on his wig for the first time and looked greatly better. I had been a little with my brother in his room this forenoon, and found him quite social. Robert Boswell, his wife and sisters, Dr. Grant, his wife and eldest daughter, Dr. Gillespie, and Grange dined with us, and all but Grange drank tea. Dr. Grant and I went to the playhouse and saw the first part of *Henry IV* and a harlequin dialogue entertainment called *The Touchstone of Truth*.[4] Wilkinson's Falstaff did not please me. He spoke too fast.

FRIDAY 31 DECEMBER. Yesterday and today laboured *invita Minerva* [5] at a New Year's Day address for the *Caledonian Mercury*; and though it was but short, got it done only at night, and sent it careless whether it should be inserted or not. My wife and I dined at Prestonfield. It was hard frost. My toe was uneasy. I was fretful.

[3] A fort on the Hudson which had been captured by the British, was captured in turn by Gen. Anthony Wayne in July of 1779.
[4] By Charles Dibdin.
[5] "Doggedly, without inspiration," a phrase from Horace (*Ars Poetica,* 385).

1780

SATURDAY 1 JANUARY. As usual at the beginning of a new year, I made up a state of my affairs, and found with uneasiness that I was really in a disagreeable situation, having debts which I was obliged to pay, while my funds could not be commanded for some time, as I had advanced a good deal for my wife's nephews, whose patrimonies could not be touched but by a circuit at law. Upon the whole, I had as much as I owed, reckoning my books and furniture; and I had spent £100 less than last year. Worthy Grange sat with me while I made my calculations, and comforted me. I had said the day before yesterday that I would dine at my father's today. My wife was *invited* this morning for the first time this winter. There was nobody but my father and Lady Auchinleck and my wife and I at dinner. Miss Boswell came to tea. My father was quite callous. It was very galling. I began tonight again to write ten lines each day, hoping to do one full year.[6]

SUNDAY 2 JANUARY. When I do not mention the date of my writing, it is always on the day recorded. I intended to have gone to Bothwell Castle on Monday. But as my toe was still sore, I resolved to nurse it, and stay in the house one whole week to give it ease and let it heal. And as the weather was very cold, I thought it would be more agreeable to visit Mr. Douglas in the spring vacation. Found my *Mercury* address inserted. Liked it.[7] I lay in bed till the afternoon, and read in Sir David Hamilton's

---

[6] Boswell was attempting to revive an exercise in self-discipline which he had practised for considerable periods of time while he was on the Continent. A similar resolve on New Year's Day 1779 had been kept for three days; this year he seems to have persevered to 17 January (see the entry for that day) but only the verses for 1–12 January have survived. He starts this series optimistically enough:

> Perhaps at lucky random I may strike
> A brilliant thought which Johnson's self might like. . . .

[7] Boswell wrote the address in the character of the publisher of the *Caledonian Mercury*. He defends the newspaper's policy of even-handed reporting: "It has . . . been his study . . . to pay a proper deference to the several opinions which have prevailed even on this side of the Tweed. While one of the most learned and respectable societies in Scotland refused to subscribe supplies or testify their approbation, it would ill have become the publisher of a newspaper, however clear in his own opinion, to treat all opposition to the measures of Government as factious and unwise. In one article he cannot doubt that all will agree; for all, surely, are averse to the encroaching dominion

Private Christian's Witness for Christianity. I was pleased with the mystical piety of his mind, but could not acquiesce in all his instances of particular experience of Providence in the course of his life; for example, that when he was successful in practice and began to be elated, there was a change for the worse, and when he humbled himself, there was a successful turn. I cannot think that GOD would make his patients thus dependent upon their physician's spiritual workings. That would be like the doctrine of those who hold the effect of the holy sacrament to depend on the priest who administrates it. It appeared to me that worthy Sir David was, without knowing it, of too much importance in his own imagination, under the deception of humility as being entirely influenced by the operations of the Divinity. I doubted [7a] that he might be mistaken in thinking that changes upon his patients happened precisely at the same times with changes in his mind. He does not mention *patients*, as he wished not to be known; but when one is informed that a physician wrote the book, it is plain patients are meant. Abating the objections which occurred to me, and a weakness at times observed by my wife, the book is full of religious unction and amiable practice. Nor would I take upon me to deny that he may sometimes have had answers to his prayers by extraordinary effects. I no doubt read his book with much partiality from having heard all my life of his excellent character and great friendship for my grandfather.[8] The style is not good, being all long, long sentences and often incorrect. The children said divine lessons very well. I talked to them of the fall of man, the curse of death, and the restoration by Christ. Sandy was very angry with Adam, and said he should have been put in the guard. I was in a dull, easy frame. I wondered to find death and immortality affect me very little. I was however very well, upon the whole. But it is amazing in what diversity of states a thinking man will perceive

---

of France. He means that all will rejoice at the quarrel between the American Army and the French General who insolently summoned the garrison of Savannah to surrender to His Most Christian Majesty, but was repulsed in a manner very ill-suited to his confident bravado" (*Caledonian Mercury*, 1 January 1780). The first newspaper reports probably misjudged Admiral d'Estaing's protocol. At the date of his first summons (16 September) he had not yet made junction with General Lincoln, but he explained in a second letter that as soon as the junction was effected the demand would be made jointly by the Americans and the French.

7a Rather thought, suspected.

8 Sir David Hamilton (Old James Boswell's uncle on his mother's side) may have conferred solid benefits on his nephew, but he certainly did not give him much of his time. Having encouraged the young man to go to Leiden to study, Hamilton let his obsequious and anxious requests for advice go unanswered, finally informing him through a third party that he was much too busy to answer letters. So far as the documents at Yale show, his benefactions consisted solely of a number of pious letters sent to Old James and his wife later on.

himself to exist, and how unlike the impressions of the very same objects will be at various periods. This evening I have no ardent desire for anything, nor have I on the other hand any lively fear. My wife, to whom I read but a little of Sir David Hamilton's book, thought very meanly of him. Since I wrote what is on the other side of this leaf, I have seen more of his weakness, such as his disapprobation of forms and love of long graces. Commissioner Cochrane told me that Dr. ———, who was very angry that he was knighted for his eminence as a man-midwife, made these lines upon it:

> "Rise, Sir David," said the Queen: [9]
> "The first c—t knight that e'er was seen."

MONDAY 3 JANUARY. Had dreamt again of my toe, and that a piece of nail was deep in it. Felt it very uneasy when I rose after breakfasting in bed. Resolved to have Mr. Wood to cut it effectually. Sent a note to him to come this forenoon or tomorrow forenoon, so as to have daylight. He did not come today. I had a strange *desire* to *taste* of *pain*, as one will *long* for what is bitter. I sat with my nightcap on all day, and did nothing but bring up so far my Register of Letters sent and received, of which I had only loose notes from April last. Grange drank tea with us. My mind, though listless, was not unquiet. I had indeed neither elevation nor gaiety. But I was content with mere tranquillity. I was fretful only when the children made noise. π.

TUESDAY 4 JANUARY. Breakfasted in bed. After I got up, continued my Register of Letters. Mr. Wood came. Would not cut my toe, but said he would separate the flesh from the nail by stuffing in lint, and would dress it every day, and cure it, be it what it would. I had no appetite for pain today. My brother John called for a little. He was in a strange humour, and talked of returning to Dr. Hall's St. Luke's House. I asked him to dine, but he would not. Grange dined and drank tea. I wrote to Temple.[1]

WEDNESDAY 5 JANUARY. Mr. Lawrie had returned last night, so that I had him to pay accounts and do many things for me. His services are very convenient. Perhaps they accustom me to be too helpless. I brought up my Register of Letters to the end of this year. Dr. Gillespie sat awhile

---

[9] Anne. He was her physician.

[1] Boswell had not written for some time, so he had to bring Temple up to date on his visit to Chester, his studies, his ingrown toe-nail. "My mind is at present in a state of tranquillity, or rather good insensibility. I have neither elevation nor gaiety; but I am easy." He closes with a reminder of Temple's debt (of £45) which he must ask for because of the financial pressures brought on by his help to his wife's nephews (To Temple, 4 January 1780). See below, p. 171 n. 6.

with me. Grange drank tea. My brother John came and drank a dish of coffee. He was grievously sulky. I was very passionate at night.

THURSDAY 6 JANUARY. (Writing on Friday the 7th.) My passion on Wednesday night was occasioned by a very trifling cause, which is not worth mentioning. Yet it was shockingly violent, and was directed against my dear wife, who, though now in good health, was with child, and required tender treatment. I was much vexed with myself both last night and this morning. Yet I was this morning in an obstinate fit, and would take no breakfast till my wife came and solicited me after hers was over, though I had a headache. I insisted with her that she ought in duty as a wife to be ever attentive, ever ready to soothe my temper and be complaisant. She said very sensibly that she had been educated without that timorous restraint in which I had been kept, and that it was much easier for me not to insist on subjection than on her to submit to it. But she was certainly wrong in contradicting my favourite notions and partialities. In particular, she was much to blame in endeavouring to counteract the principle of *family* which has prevailed in the family of Auchinleck from generation to generation. She said, and perhaps with some truth, that our pride and high estimation of ourselves as if German princes (my phrase) was ridiculous in the eyes of other people, who looked upon us not only as no better than any other gentleman's family, but as a stiff and inhospitable family. But as I have great enjoyment in our fancied dignity, and cannot be persuaded but that we do appear of more consequence in the country than others, from a certain reserve which has always been maintained, and am also of opinion that this pride makes us act in a nobler manner, I wish to encourage it; and my wife therefore should at least not oppose it. My son Sandy seems to imbibe it as I could desire. I catechize him thus: "What is your first duty?" "My duty to GOD." "What is your second duty?" "My duty to the family of Auchinleck." "Who was the first laird of Auchinleck?" "Thomas Boswell." "From whom did he get the estate?" "From his king." "Who was his king?" "King James the IV of Scotland." "What became of Thomas Boswell?" "He was killed at Flodden Field fighting with his king against the English, for Scotland and England were then two kingdoms." "Who was Thomas Boswell's son?" "David." "What became of him?" "He fought for his sovereign, Queen Mary, at the Battle of Langside, lived a worthy gentleman, and died at Auchinleck." [2] He seems much pleased with this genealogical instruction.

---

[2] It was not David, the second laird, but David's son John, the third laird, who fought at Langside (1568). David did not even fight for Queen Mary: he followed his stepfather, Cuninghame of Caprington, to the Battle of the Butts (1544), fighting in the English interest against his brother-in-law, the Earl of Arran, Governor of the Kingdom in the infancy of Queen Mary. Boswell's enthusiasm for Scots history and the genealogy

I shall go on with it and habituate him to think with sacred reverence and attachment of his ancestors and to hope to aggrandize the family.

My father, I should have mentioned before this, when well recovered, appeared very well satisfied not only that the power of long building leases but also that of liferent leases should be added to the entail, and he ordered Stobie to call on Mr. David Erskine and get these additions made.[3] His agreeing to the last was a sign of failure, for he was formerly against it, as giving more power to the heir in possession, though indeed it is a wise and beneficial power. I sent a note about the alterations to Mr. David Erskine, and must now see them made out and put into the Register. It occurred to me on reading over the entail lately that the clause which was at my desire inserted giving power to the last heir male called to choose any of the descendants of Thomas Boswell, was truly giving it to that heir's daughter or nearest heir female in prejudice of an heir female descending from my father, unless that heir should have an enthusiasm like mine for male succession. I considered that if such a power were to take place soon—for instance, if Claud were to be last heir male while Veronica is alive—it would be very hard that his daughter should cut her out. I wished to guard against this. But I was afraid to touch upon the clause for fear my father should insist to have it annulled altogether. I considered that I might perhaps save such a fund as to purchase myself a power of settling our estate on heirs male forever, by so far altering the entail, and fixing that any heir who should call that alteration in question should forfeit all right to my fund. I felt already some uneasiness at the thought of being fettered by an entail. Yet it does no more than prevent me from selling or loading my estate with debt, which I would be very sorry to do. It is well worth mentioning that yesterday when I talked of being despotic in a county if I were rich, Grange said that I could act only from the information of others were I in the great situation that I figured, and would be just "a tyrannical tool to oppress worthy people."

My brother John dined with us. But was sour and sneering while my wife sat. I recollected having some years ago injured him by turning him away abruptly when he called, I suppose to dine with me, on a day when I had a good deal of company; and it was agreeable to think that I now made up for it by attention to him. My large Consultation Book had been neglected by me for about nine years. As it is a very accurate and well-written register of my practice, it would have been a pity not to carry it on. I therefore resolved to transcribe into it two pages of the leaves which

---

of the family of Auchinleck was genuine but was based on very little accurate information.

[3] David Erskine, Writer to the Signet, originally framed the entail. For a general note on the entail, see below, 7 January 1780.

I have kept, every day, which I calculated would bring it up to this Session in thirty days. I did my task today.[4] In the night between the 3d and 4th current, I thought with sudden anxiety of my having as yet neglected to make a nomination of tutors and curators to my children, which was all I could at present leave them. I next evening wrote it, appointing *one* friend in whom I had full confidence, as suggested to me by Dr. Johnson in autumn last.[5] That friend was Sir William Forbes, banker, whom when I mentioned to Dr. Johnson, he said he was just thinking of. And with him I joined my dear wife, of whose disinterested affection I have had so many proofs. This was the first deed that I ever wrote *in contemplation* (to use our law phrase) of my death; and what is strange, I felt a sort of tremor while I wrote. I must write to Sir William and beg he will accept of the trust. I hope he will not refuse.[6] Mr. Wood dressed my toe tonight. There was a little matter issued from the flesh, and he said he was not sure but there might be some nail under it. Veronica had this winter played on the harpsichord so wonderfully well by the ear that we got a music-master for her, Mr. Cooper. He began to teach her on Monday 3d current.[7] She now read pretty well, and was fond of reading.

[4] Boswell's Consultation Book (now in the National Library of Scotland) is carried only to the end of the Summer Session (11 August) 1772. The loose leaves continuing the record are not known to exist.

[5] See above, 4 October 1779.

[6] "I, James Boswell ... considering the uncertainty of life, and having at present nothing else to settle upon my children but the probability of kind attention, good education, and prudent management of what fortunes they may have by leaving them under the best guardians whom after much consideration I can choose, do therefore ... nominate and appoint my dear wife ... and my excellent friend Sir William Forbes ... to be their tutors and curators. It is my wish that all my children may be partly educated in England, and any of my sons who have a disposition for learning may be kept some years at the University of Oxford; and I hope they will be brought up with an attachment to Auchinleck the seat of their ancestors, of which they are heirs by entail" (from the copy in the register of the Registry Office, Edinburgh, dated 4 January 1780). Boswell added a codicil a few days later (8 January 1780), declaring that the tutors and curators should not be liable for omissions, but only for their actual intromissions; and a further codicil, 12 October 1791, appointing Thomas David Boswell to fill the place of his wife, now deceased, as guardian. (Legal guardians of girls under twelve and of boys under fourteen were styled "tutors"; legal guardians of children beyond those ages but under twenty-one were styled "curators.")

[7] The *Ten Lines* for 4 January 1780 (Veronica was not yet seven years old):

> Sure, I may tune a sweet poetic lay
> While I can hear my eldest daughter play
> Upon the harpsichord with so much ease
> That some fine spirit seems to touch the keys.
> How pleasing is it thus to be amus'd;
> Henceforth my lot shall never be accus'd
> Of being bad as long as Heav'n allows

FRIDAY 7 JANUARY. During this recess or vacation I have ceased to rise early, and have had great enjoyment of lying in bed. This day passed quietly on. My brother John came in the afternoon and drank tea. Was in the same humour as he appeared these two last times. He also called and sat a little in the forenoon. I was in a good deal of uneasiness today, from looking at a copy of the wretched deed which my father prevailed with me to copy over and sign, under melancholy fear of his selling the estate, soon after I came of age.[8] I dreaded that perhaps he might leave me under trustees. Yet I thought that the entail put an end to all settlements of the estate before it, and any made after it would be set aside on incapacity. I pleased myself too with imagining that, in the worst event, I might by Lord Mountstuart's interest obtain relief by an Act of Parliament. The state of my debts too gave me uneasiness, as I had risked too much to support my wife's nephews, but upon honour unasked by her.[9] π. (Part of this page written after twelve, night.)

SATURDAY 8 JANUARY. I this morning beat Sandy for telling a lie. I must beat him very severely if I catch him again in falsehood.[1] I do not recollect having had any other valuable principle impressed upon me by my father except a strict regard to truth, which he impressed upon my mind by a hearty beating at an early age, when I lied, and then talking of

---

> Veronica to bless my grateful vows,
> Sent morn and ev'ning earnest to the throne
> Of the immortal King who reigns alone.

[8] The "copy of the wretched deed," executed 7 March 1762, is among the Boswell papers at Yale. In it Boswell waived the claim he had under the entail in his mother's contract of marriage to unrestricted succession to the estate of Auchinleck, and consented, in case he succeeded, to be put under trustees of his father's choosing, he to receive one half of the free rents and to be allowed to reside in Auchinleck House if he chose to do so. Lord Auchinleck, having concluded that Boswell was a hopeless wastrel, had extorted this extreme concession by threatening to sell the estate. He could have sold the lands he had purchased himself (no inconsiderable property), but, as we have seen above (31 October 1778), his threat to sell any of the lands he had received from his father exceeded his powers.

[9] Boswell reflects upon some of these troubles in the *Ten Lines* for 8 January 1780:

> Long have I struggled with a load of debt,
> Weak to contract and foolish to forget.
> Three hundred pounds a year my father gives,
> But who genteelly on three hundred lives?
> 'Tis true the bar, of which I don't complain,
> Brings me sometimes a very handsome gain,
> But though my wife is moderate indeed,
> As yet our income always we exceed.
> A thousand pounds I owed my father paid,
> I trust again to have his powerful aid.

[1] The only instance we know of in which Boswell beat any of his children.

the *dishonour* of lying. I recollect distinctly having truth and honour thus indelibly inculcated upon me by him one evening in our house, fourth storey of Blair's Land, Parliament Close. Mr. Wood dressed my toe this forenoon. It was a little more painful, but he said it was doing well. I trusted to him, having defied him to cure it, by way of piquing him as a chirurgeon. I idled away much time today in clearing the drawer of my writing-table, etc., and did not write letters as I intended. My brother John drank tea with us. He was quite sensible, but very cross. I pitied him and was angry at the same time. Grange also drank tea.

SUNDAY 9 JANUARY. (Writing on Monday the 10th.) Had taken physic the night before; so was in a state of *"valetudinarian indulgence"* (to use an expression of Dr. Johnson's in conversation with me).[2] Balmuto visited me between sermons, and Mr. James Donaldson, bookseller and printer, drank tea with us. I kept the house all day, and heard the children say divine lessons. I told them in the evening so much about *black angels* or *devils* seizing bad people when they die and dragging them down to hell, a *dark* place (for I had not yet said anything of *fire* to them, and perhaps never will), that they were all three suddenly seized with such terror that they cried and roared out and ran to me for protection (they and I being in the drawing-room), and alarmed their mother, who came upstairs in a fright, and she and Bell Bruce took them downstairs. This vexed me. Yet without mixing early some *fear* in the mind, I apprehend religion will not be lasting. Besides, however mildly we may interpret the divine law, there *is* reason for *some* fear. I this day finished the reading of Sir David Hamilton's book. He recommends such confidence in *experience upon the soul* without *argumentative conviction* as I am afraid might be dangerous. For if one's soul, for instance, should glow with licentious love, there will be an *irrational experience* that "this must be right." Yet Sir David's system is, it must be owned, somewhat similar to the *axiomatic* and *common-sense* doctrines of Reid, Oswald, and Beattie.[3] Mr. Donaldson sent me some *Critical Reviews,* which entertained me a good deal at night, sitting by the fire in my wife's bedroom, where for some time past we have supped comfortably. All last week I did not taste any fermented liquor, nor shall I till I find some call upon me. My wife read to me tonight the *Critical Review* on Dr. Johnson's *Prefaces to the Poets* (No. 1st of that critique) and considerable extracts. I was happy at this, for I regret that one of such good sense reads so little.

[2] *Journal*, 16 September 1777; Johnson's dicta are somewhat expurgated in the *Life of Johnson.*

[3] The names of Thomas Reid, James Beattie, and James Oswald, all Scots philosophers, had been linked by Joseph Priestley's attack on them (1774) in the *Examination of . . . Reid's Inquiry, . . . Beattie's Essay, and . . . Oswald's Appeal.*

MONDAY 10 JANUARY. (Writing on Wednesday the 12th.) Mr. Wood, who had not called yesterday, dressed my toe today. It was more painful. Mr. Johnston of Carnsalloch sat awhile with me. In the afternoon, while Grange was with me, my brother John came in, and was so sulky that I grew rather too warm and spoke strongly to him of his behaviour. He drank tea in the drawing-room and then came and sat in the room by me, in obstinate perverse silence, till about eight, and then went away. I was hurt by having such an object before me. My wife observed that he was so disagreeable that one suffered less for him than if he were dejected; and that his shocking manner would make one shun the least appearance of insanity, for that it excited disgust. This was a good memento to me, who sometimes have fancied something dignified and amiable in madness.[4] I idled away this day and did none of my Consultation Book.

TUESDAY 11 JANUARY. (Writing on Wednesday the 12th.) The Session sat down again. I went to the Court in a chair. After a long quiet confinement, the bustle of the Court seemed harsh, and it was unpleasant to perceive how little one cared for another. I should have mentioned that I yesterday did what I had long meditated but had been restrained by magnifying the scheme too much. Biography is my favourite study; and amongst other lives I had wished much to write that of *Mr. Alexander Lockhart—Lord Covington.* I had put down a few notes from what conversations I had held with him occasionally.[5] But I thought the best method was to try if a man of his distinguished abilities would himself furnish me with materials. Yesterday I took resolution and wrote out a series of queries, and addressed a letter to him begging that he would favour me by answering them. I had the packet delivered to him today just as he was leaving the House, that he might read it calmly, and that some time might intervene between that and my seeing him. My mind was less firm today than for some time past, and I felt a kind of timid

[4] From the *Ten Lines* for this day:

>   ... By me sits
> My brother John, disturb'd with dreary fits
> Of sullen madness; sometimes on the ground
> His eyes are fix'd; sometimes they stare around;
> Sometimes with childish laughter he seems pleas'd,
> As if his mind were for a moment eas'd;
> Then on a sudden shakes his hands and head
> And discontent is o'er his visage spread.

[5] These notes are not known to have survived. John Ramsay of Ochtertyre says that Boswell "hovered like a vulture above the dying judge, in quest of anecdotes" (*Scotland and Scotsmen*, i. 138 n. 1)—a description more vivid than accurate. Boswell's last notation of having recorded materials for Covington's life occurs on 20 July 1782, some four months before the old judge's death.

uneasiness lest Lord Covington should think that I took too much liberty with him, and should disregard my request, and perhaps be offended.

I found Dr. Gillespie when I came home. Mr. Wood came and dressed my toe while he was with me; and today they both saw a corner of the nail in the flesh, pretty deep; but Mr. Wood could not get at it to cut it out till the fungous flesh at the side was more separated from the nail. I heard today that Lord Eglinton had come to town on Sunday; and before my toe was dressed, he came and paid us a visit. I had a desire to dine with him at Fortune's today just to enjoy social eating and drinking. But as he had engaged to sup with me next day, my wife wisely persuaded me to dine at home, especially as I had company tonight at supper.

My brother John came in the afternoon, and was still more sulky and perverse than on any day this winter. I told him in plain terms that I could not admit him to my house if he behaved in such a manner. He did not mind me, but went to tea, and sat all the time with his hat on, and frowned horribly. He then followed me into the dining-room and placed himself on the opposite side of the fire to me; and when I spoke to him and he did not choose to answer, made a noise as if going to spit. He showed a good deal of shrewdness and even a sort of wit amidst his gloomy, horrid ill-nature; for, as he had railed against me for having used some linen of his, the value of which I was always ready to pay him, when he abused Scotland compared with England, and I asked him why then he had come to Scotland, he said, "Don't you know? What do you hold in your hand?" "A paper," said I. "Of what is it made?" said he. "Of rags," said I. "And of what are rags made?" said he. "Of linen," said I. I had perceived his drift. He now thought he had hit me full. Upon which, "What is a man's face made of?" said he. "Of skin and bone," said I. "Of *brass*," said he. A little after, when I wanted to talk with him, he called out, "I've given you the parole: *brass*." Once he called me a scoundrel; and as he held a staff in his hand, and even lifted the tongs, I was in some apprehension of his doing violence. It was a sad trial. As company were to sup with me, I had to leave him, saying I was going down to Mr. Johnston's, and I really did go. He still sat. But upon my wife's coming into the room and sitting down, or appearing to stay, he went off; and then she came to Mr. Johnston's and informed me. I was much affected by him tonight, and thought of writing to his father, or going out to him in a chair next day, that he might have proper measures taken to prevent him from harassing my family and exposing himself and his relations.[6] Grange well observed

[6] From the *Ten Lines* for this day:
> This night more sad and hideous he appears,
> Frowning so angrily as serious fears
> Ev'n in a brother's bosom to excite,

that my father and Lady Auchinleck should have the weight of so disagreeable a business, for that, as I was not allowed to interfere in other things, I should *not* in *this*. He and Carnsalloch and Conchie supped with us.[7] For ten days I had drank no fermented liquor. Tonight I drank small beer and Madeira and water. I felt my mind feeble, and company rather a trouble to me. I was idle today, though I should have written some law. I did nothing to my Consultation Book. There was a pretty deep snow and very hard frost. π.

WEDNESDAY 12 JANUARY. (Writing on Friday the 14th.) After a night's sleep since venturing to address Lord Covington for memoirs of his life, I was still uneasy till I should know how he would receive my application. This day at ten, while the Lords were going to the bench and his Lordship was passing through to take his seat in the Outer House, I met him, and having said, "My Lord, did you get a letter from me?", he answered in a very courteous manner, "Yes; and I'll give you an answer. But—" here he shook his hand as if he had said, "But I'm so old I cannot answer distinctly enough." I was very happy and said, "Your Lordship's very good. I hope you're very well." "Far from it," said he mildly.

I was a short while in court; and then went to Dunn's Hotel and waited upon Lord Eglinton, with whom I sat more than an hour, somebody or other being with him all the time till he was just going out, when I sounded him if he would lend me any money, but found he would not. He said it was foolish in him to pay his brother's debts. I said no. For he could have done nothing that would have given him more satisfaction and been more to his honour. He said it was foolish except as to his own satisfaction. For if he had bought land with the money, would he not have had more influence in the county than by paying these debts? This was a shrewd remark. I am never very happy in his company, for he has no high opinion of me; and as we are not of congenial tempers, I am under restraint. Balbarton came and dined with us. We had also worthy Grange; and we three drank warm port negus moderately and comfortably. Balbarton said he had seen eighty New Year's Days. My brother John called. Was told I was not in. But he walked upstairs. Hearing voices in the dining-room, he went away and did not return this night, which was

---

For who can tell but he like Cain may smite?
I'm sure he has not to complain of wrongs,
Yet once I saw him sternly grasp the tongs.
Although fell broodings seem to work his brain,
I wish to think him harmless in the main.

[7] If "Conchie" is a territorial designation like Carnsalloch (Peter Johnston), we have been unable to locate the property or discover the appropriate family name. Perhaps it was a nickname for Alexander or Allan Maconochie, of which name Conchie is a variant (G. F. Black, *The Surnames of Scotland*, 1946, p. 166).

lucky. Lord Eglinton, Lord Glencairn, Colonel Macdonell, and Mr. John Wauchope supped with us. Mr. Wood promised to come, but did not, nor did he call today. I very foolishly drank first Madeira, and then two bottles of port, Lord Glencairn and I taking that liquor; and after his Lordship and Wauchope were gone, I joined Lord Eglinton and Colonel Macdonell in strong rum punch, so that altogether I was quite destroyed.[8]

THURSDAY 13 JANUARY. (Writing on Friday the 14th.) The inflammation and sickness from riot, and the violent frost had given me a terrible headache. I got up about nine, but was obliged to go to bed again. I lay all day in great pain till the evening. My brother John drank tea with my wife, and was shockingly sulky. I rose at nine and was sadly vexed. Mr. Wood did not call today.

FRIDAY 14 JANUARY. (Writing on Saturday the 15th.) I rose pretty well. It was the most intense frost that I ever felt.[9] But I went to the Parliament House, though I really suffered severe pain from the cold. My brother John being in a state either of great insanity or terrible perverseness, I was quite at a loss what should be done with him. My spirits were sadly sunk. Worthy Grange joined me in opinion that my father and his lady should take the direction of so disagreeable an affair. I walked out to my father's and sat a little while with him by ourselves, and found him in good calm temper. When his lady came into the room, I mentioned my dilemma as to poor John. She treated my concern with abominable unfeeling ill-nature, as if I had only an affectation of humanity, and said she had borne more from John than I had, or would have done; but that I felt much more for myself than for my neighbours; and that it was very easy for me to keep him out of my house if I chose to do it, by speaking to him in a determined manner that I would send to him when it was convenient for me. I told her she was fit to be captain of a man-of-war. My father sat by quite unconcerned. I was hurt at her in-

---

[8] The *Ten Lines* for this day:

> If I don't write my lines before I sup
> And with my guests partake a hearty cup,
> Without prophetic spirit one might lay
> A handsome bet without much risk to pay
> That I should not compose a single line,
> Whether my drink be negus or pure wine.
> For this same night I have two noble peers
> Who sober mortals would affect with fears
> To grace my table, and when such I see,
> My heart grows warm, and I indulge in glee.

[9] On this day at 9 a.m. the temperature in Edinburgh was 5° F.; in Glasgow the same morning the thermometer dropped to 14° below zero F. According to the *Scots Magazine* (January 1780, xlii. 54) this was "much greater [cold] than any ever observed in Britain."

fernal harshness, but governed my temper. Dr. Boswell's two daughters dined there today, as I did. When I was going away, my father showed a little extraordinary kindness, for he said to me, "Now that you can walk, let us see you often." When I came home, I found that my brother John had called and tried to get into the dining-room, but, as my wife and I had concerted, the door was bolted. Mr. Wood called when I was out. I dictated law pretty well, but was by no means in a state of enjoyment. Only at night I loved my wife warmly, though I was affected with thinking of the deplorable situation I and my children would be in if she should die, which a pretty severe cough which she now had made me fear. π.

SATURDAY 15 JANUARY. (Writing on Sunday the 16th.) It was painfully cold. I was a little while in the Parliament House, and in very bad spirits. I had a return of hypochondria in that way as to see nothing worth while. Sat a little with worthy Grange. Then went home and wrote *The Hypochondriack* No. 28, having only two or three notes beforehand.[1] Wrote wonderfully well, considering my state of mind. Dined at Fortune's at the annual meeting of Mundell's scholars, a very thin company and nothing joyous in it.[2] Slipped away quietly about seven, very sober; revised Mr. Lawrie's copy of my *Hypochondriack* and wrote to Mr. Dilly calmly, having drank some green tea. Also studied part of a long cause on which I had a Memorial to write. Was somewhat uneasy that my practice since this year began was very scanty. Was much affected with reading tonight in the *London Chronicle* that the celebrated Captain Cook was killed.[3] Mr. Wood did not call today. My brother John called this afternoon again, but the dining-room door was again bolted. So he went away.

SUNDAY 16 JANUARY. For some nights past (at least for two), I have had dreams of which I have had a recollection when I awaked, which is rare with me. But my dreams were not very significant. Last night I

---

[1] "It is no doubt one of the most difficult tasks in the world to convey to an author a candid disapprobation of his works, or even to correct them in any degree without offending him. Whatever he may affect...there will in most cases be found such a secret regard in any author's breast for anything he has written that he will be uneasy if anyone else does not view it in the same light. His parental affection will make him tender even of the slightest expressions, and he will not easily forgive the salutary touches of criticism" ("On Criticism," *The Hypochondriack*, No. 28, January 1780).

[2] The former pupils at James Mundell's private academy, which Boswell attended from 1745 or 1746 through 1748 or 1749. The anniversary meeting was usually held on this, the third Saturday in January. Members of the club were addressed by nicknames they had as "schule laddies" and any deviation was punishable by fine.

[3] Cook was clubbed to death in Hawaii by natives, 14 February 1779. Boswell had dined with him at Sir John Pringle's, 2 April 1776.

dreamt that my brother David was come home, and that I saw him and said to him that I was told he was grown a great black man, but it was not so; and that he was very much the same as when he went away. He did not seem to be pleased with this. He was fatter than when he left us. I regretted in my own mind that there was little happiness upon our meeting again. This is the first time that I have seen him since he went abroad, as far as I remember. I shall be anxious till we hear from him whether the Court of Spain will give him leave to remain in that country, or if he is to come home immediately, which I hope will be the case.[4] This morning there was a thaw, but the damp was very cold. I went to the New Church in the forenoon. Lord Stonefield's chaplain preached, but did not fix my attention. My spirits were better. I went out in the chariot with Lady Auchinleck and dined at my father's. She read one of Mr. Robert Walker's sermons in the afternoon. I stayed tea. My father was quite assimilated to an old woman by living constantly with two. It was a very wet evening. I came home in a chair. Mr. Wood dressed my toe. The children said divine lessons.

MONDAY 17 JANUARY. (Writing on Saturday the 22.) I had set apart this day for writing a dull paper. But Lord Eglinton called and asked me so cordially to dine along with him at Leith, just he and I and Colonel Macdonell and Willie Haggart, that I could not refuse. So I went down with him in a hackney-coach to Lawson's, where Mr. Haggart only joined us; and we three took a good Scots dinner, and drank bumpers till near twelve o'clock at night. Our conversation was not lively but cordial. I should have been comfortable had not the Earl been quite despotic in making me drink hard. He sang *"Row me owr the lea-rig, my ain kind dearieo"* [5] with so much taste that I could almost pay a headache to hear it again. He and I drove up in a post-chaise. I came out at the north end of the New Bridge and walked home. I was excessively sick and in violent uneasiness, though not so much intoxicated as I have been on some occasions. I this day omitted my ten lines, which broke a year's series.

TUESDAY 18 JANUARY. (Writing on Saturday the 22.) Awaked in terrible distress. Thought I would lie all day. But upon my wife's suggesting that being frequently out of the House would hurt my practice, I resolved to show myself in court if it were but for a few minutes. So I went about eleven, when I was surprisingly better. I took a hackney-coach and went to Leith with my wife and daughters and Sandy, and saw a part of the West Fencibles that had come over from Fife. We met

[4] Spain had declared war against England in June of the previous year.
[5] Row = roll; lea-rig = the unploughed ridge between two cultivated fields. The song is now known in the purified revision of Robert Fergusson, "Will ye gang o'er the lea-rig?"

with Lord Eglinton, who was just setting out for London. We eat raw oysters at Mrs. Thomson's. I was quite feeble and dejected. By the way home we found Grange walking, and as it snowed, carried him home, and he dined with us. Mr. Wood was not with me either yesterday or today.

WEDNESDAY 19 JANUARY. (Writing on Saturday the 22.) Was a good deal better. The frost was very keen. Dictated tolerably. Mr. Wood dressed my toe. He said I was the worse for Monday's riot.

THURSDAY 20 JANUARY. (Writing on Saturday the 22.) Was now pretty well, but my spirits were still shattered. Was uneasy at my practice being diminished. Mr. Lawrie was of opinion with me that my father's absence from the House did me hurt. I never before this winter felt real uneasiness from embarrassed circumstances. For I knew not how to raise £200. I had written both to Temple and Dilly on the subject; and I trusted most to English friends.[6] Sir William Forbes and Mr. Hunter, with whom I sat awhile this forenoon, said they could let me have a little money only for a few months. I called on my father today and found him placidly insensible. My brother John came and dined with us today, without invitation, though he would not come the two preceding days when invited. He was sulky. I was weakly humane enough to ask him to tea. He came and was very disagreeable. I dictated well. Mr. Wood did not call today.

FRIDAY 21 JANUARY. (Writing on Monday the 24.) My wife and I dined at Balmuto's. I just kept myself quiet in a coarse company. I mean where conversation was Scottishly rough. I did not drink much, but when I came home was not inclined to do any business; and luckily I had none that required immediate dispatch. I found a letter from Lord Covington, in very obliging terms, but waiving particular answers to my queries. This was a disappointment to me. But I thought I would get answers from him in conversation. I eat a couple of eggs, drank tea, and went to bed. Lay long awake. π.

---

[6] He wrote to Temple on 4 January 1780: "My wife's nephews stood so much in need of my assistance that I have advanced between seven and eight hundred pounds for them, which I have borrowed at £5 per cent. A demand is now made upon me which I *must* answer early in February; and I must by no means inform my father. May I beg of you, my dearest friend, to remit me £200, for which I will send you my bill? Pray do it if you possibly can, for I am sadly put to it. At any rate I trust that you will remit me what you owe me, as I am obliged to collect all that I can scrape together." (Boswell deleted this last sentence before sending the letter, but not so thoroughly that it cannot be read.) Temple replied that he could not at present remit anything: "Have you so soon forgot my application to you on my sister's account, and how incapable I was so very lately of answering a demand upon me by so near a relation?" (From Temple, 1 February 1780).

SATURDAY 22 JANUARY. (Writing on Monday the 24.) The cold was really painful. At a meeting of the Faculty of Advocates I spoke with spirit for our behaving liberally to the good town of Edinburgh in agreeing to pay our share of the contribution to repair the damages of the Roman Catholics. Mr. Andrew Balfour was against our paying, and asked where was the difference between this and subscribing to the Edinburgh Regiment, which was treated with contempt by a majority? I answered warmly that every man would speak from his own feelings. But I saw a great difference between subscribing to a regiment raised to *commit* injuries upon our fellow-subjects, and contributing to *repair* injuries which had been committed. I sent a note of this to the *Caledonian Mercury*, but did not mention *who* had made the answer.[7] I walked out to my father's, who had catched a fresh cold. Lord Advocate called on him for a little to talk about his Justiciary gown. I did not join them till they were done with it; and then I convoyed Lord Advocate to the gate into the Meadow from my father's field. He told me that the King had given it in command to Lord Stormont [8] to lay before him the pretensions of the several candidates for being judges, being resolved to prefer those who will be most for the advantage of this part of the country. He and I talked quite easily. I dined at my father's. He was in a bad frame, talking of the evil of contracting debt, and recalling my bad management. I got home about four o'clock. Mr. James Baillie drank tea with us, and in a very friendly manner engaged to supply me with money for some time. I dictated well and finished a long Petition. But I had no vivid enjoyment of life.

SUNDAY 23 JANUARY. (Writing on Tuesday the 25.) The frost was so intense, and my body so susceptible of cold by not getting any exercise taken by reason of my sore toe, that after being dressed to go to church, I resolved to stay at home.[9] The children said divine lessons in the most agreeable manner. Indeed I find them quiet and good on Sunday much more than on other days. Little Jamie was now a fine child as ever I saw. On Thursday last he first began to speak by uttering one word, *here*, which he continues to cry briskly. Mr. Wood called between sermons and began to cut the nail out of my toe. But it was so painful with the cold that I could not bear it, and he desisted very humanely. Dr.

[7] The Faculty (13 January 1778) had declined to subscribe to the Regiment, ostensibly on the ground that they were not a corporation of the city of Edinburgh—actually because a considerable number of the members opposed the American war. Boswell's "spirit" seems to have carried the day on this occasion: they unanimously resolved to pay their proportion of the levy. Boswell's note appears in the *Caledonian Mercury* for 25 January 1780.

[8] Lord Justice General (titular Head of the High Court of Justiciary). He was also Secretary of State for the northern department.

[9] The temperature was 15° F. at 7 a.m.

Webster dined with us. I was so cold in the afternoon that I went to bed before seven, just for warmth and quiet repose. Read some of *Ancient Metaphysics.*[1]

MONDAY 24 JANUARY. (Writing on Friday the 28th.) Was busy dictating law papers. Grange and Mr. Lawrence Hill dined with us. Mr. Wood did not call. I received tonight a most friendly letter from Mr. C. Dilly agreeing to lend me £200 for two years. This was truly pleasing.

TUESDAY 25 JANUARY. (Writing on Friday the 28th.) Lady Dowager Colville had called on me on Saturday and asked me to dine with her today with Lords Glencairn and Balcarres. But I kept to my engagement with Lord Monboddo, who had Sir David Carnegie, a very pretty young man, his mother and sisters, Mr. Baron Gordon, etc., to dine with him. I was in a state of *indifference,* so that I really cared for nothing. I drank rather too much claret, as I always do at Monboddo's. I went at eight to Lord Kames's, where I had not been all this winter, which hurt my feelings, as he has really been at all times exceedingly obliging to me. I found Mrs. Drummond by herself and in very good humour. She and I talked cheerfully.[2] My Lord came home between eight and nine from dining at Lord Braxfield's. He had taken so much wine as to be visibly intoxicated a little. He shook hands with me in the most cordial manner, and both he and his lady readily accepted of my apology of indisposition that I had been so long of seeing them. He said that he would not live long. I forget his exact words. But that was the meaning. She said to him he was very well. He answered keenly that he knew or felt that he would not live long. He fell asleep on a chair. Before this Mr. David Hume, advocate, had come in. Though I was offended by his publishing his uncle's posthumous poison,[3] I liked the sedateness of his manner. Lord Kames was waked when supper was on the table, and he recovered wonderfully. But we had no interesting conversation. I resolved to see him oftener. Worthy Grange said to me this forenoon, when I acknowledged to him Lord Kames's kindness to me, that I should not allow myself to speak, or if possible even to think, ill of him.

WEDNESDAY 26 JANUARY. (Writing on Saturday the 29.) Was much better in mind. Saw things with steadiness. Dictated well. In the evening

[1] Lord Monboddo's new book; see above, 20 June 1779. Boswell is preparing for a dinner with Monboddo on Tuesday.

[2] Henry Home, Lord Kames, Lord of Session and of Justiciary, a prolific writer on diverse subjects. He left a well-earned reputation for judicial severity and a partly legendary reputation for judicial indecorum. He was at this time eighty-three years old. His wife bore the style of Drummond because she owned the estate of Blair Drummond in her own right.

[3] Hume's *Dialogues Concerning Natural Religion,* which were published by his nephew in 1779, following instructions left by the author.

Sir Walter Montgomerie-Cuninghame came to town and supped with us. There was something about him which revived his uncle Lainshaw [4] in my imagination. But I was displeased with his want of solid qualities.

THURSDAY 27 JANUARY. (Writing on Saturday the 29.) Sir Walter and Mr. Andrew Blane dined with us. Before dinner Mr. Wood came, and I felt myself resolved to bear the pain, so he cut a good deal of the nail of my great toe out of the flesh. The operation hurt me much. But as soon as it was over I perceived that I was much relieved, for I felt only the pain of a green wound instead of the pain of my toe irritated by the nail in it. Grange drank tea with us. At eight o'clock I had a party which I had long projected—a social meeting in the public house under the pillars in the Parliament Close, where Dr. Pitcairne used to take his bottle every evening. It was called the *graping* office, from groping in the dark. It was lately advertised ignorantly by the name of the *Grapewine* Office. Grange had engaged for us the very room where the Doctor sat. It was underground from the pillars, very low-roofed, and had no window.[5] The party was Grange, Mr. James Baillie, Mr. John Graeme, and myself. Sir Walter was admitted as an additional man. We had oysters and minced pies, and drank whisky punch and were heartily merry. I did not drink too much. Miss Preston, who was come to town for a while, called in the forenoon. π.

FRIDAY 28 JANUARY. (Writing on Monday the 31.) Miss Susie Dunlop, Sir Walter, Grange, and Mr. Daniel dined with us. My wife was ill with a cold which made her dull of hearing and alarmed her. I had a load of papers lying on my table, and felt a dread of the labour of dictating which hung over me. But I could evade it for a while, so was pretty easy in the mean time. All the company except Grange drank tea.

SATURDAY 29 JANUARY. (Writing on Monday the 31.) It is unpleasing to observe how imperfect a picture of my life this journal presents. Yet I have certainly much more of *myself* thus preserved than most people have. I was hurt by a furious decision of the Lords this forenoon against a client of mine, Grigor Grant, a sheriff officer in Edinburgh, proceeding as I thought upon the narrow ground of what they *supposed* he knew, though there was no *legal document* of it.[6] The weather was now much milder. My toe was very easy. At one o'clock there was a meeting of several of Sir Walter Montgomerie-Cuninghame's creditors in the Exchange Coffee-house. But it was found that he could not give a state of his affairs sufficiently distinct as yet. He resolved to go home and return

[4] Mrs. Boswell's brother, James Montgomerie of Lainshaw (d. 1766).
[5] Archibald Pitcairne (1652–1713), Edinburgh physician, poet, Jacobite, and wit, addressed the goddess "Greppa" in more than one of his Latin poems.
[6] This cause has not yet been traced.

with an accurate state. He and I dined with his agent, Mr. Andrew Blane, and also drank tea. Mr. Blane's sister and Miss Grissie Wallace made the rest of the company. I know not when I have been more comfortable than I was here. We had a good dinner neatly served up in a clean new house in St. David's Street, New Town, and I had full liberty to drink negus as I chose, without being asked to take more than I liked. Sir Walter followed me home, as I took a chair. He complained with some justice that I treated him as if he were still a boy. I should guard against this, which I find so disagreeable in my father. I went down to Grange and brought up him and Mr. James Loch to supper. *π*.

SUNDAY 30 JANUARY. (Writing on Monday the 31.) Awaked placid and cheerful. The change from hard frost to milder weather was benignant to me. I was dressed in good time and walked out with intention to go to the New Church. But in the street it occurred to me that I would not go and join with Presbyterians on the 30th of January.[7] So I returned and sat awhile with worthy Grange, and then came home and found Sir Walter. Mr. Wood called and took a part of our dinner. He had not called since Thursday. As my toe was easy, he would not open it down yet. The children said less of their divine lessons than usual today. After dinner, I was in a guzzling humour and eat a great deal of roasted cheese;[8] and Sir Walter and I drank each two bottles of strong beer. He set off between four and five on his way home. I was very drowsy, and consoled myself with the intention of going snug to bed after tea. But Sir Charles Preston came to tea; and as my wife saw that he meant to stay supper, she asked him and he agreed. This was right in her, but it was very hard on me. I could hardly talk at all. I suffered as one must do with company in the country. After he went away I unloaded my stomach.

MONDAY 31 JANUARY. (Writing on Tuesday 1 February.) Rose much better than I could have expected to be. Dictated a good deal with pretty good ease. My wife kept her room with the cold and deafness. Lady Auchinleck called on her. Sandy insisted to go out and dine with his grandfather, whom he had not seen for a long time. Lady Auchinleck carried him out in the chariot with her. I was in very reasonable spirits today. My brother John, whom I had asked to dine but who sent me word that he could not wait on me, had desired Mr. Lawrie to see if I could be at leisure at seven to settle accounts with him. I was at leisure; and he came and was as clear-headed as a man could be. He was even cheerful in his appearance, but I found that he had a pleasure in keeping up his charge that I had not accounted fairly for his effects; so we came to no settle-

---

[7] The anniversary of King Charles's execution, then a fast in the Church of England.

[8] Boswell first wrote "toasted," and then changed it, the reverse of what one would have expected. "Roasted cheese" is a Scotticism.

ment. I regretted tonight his unhappy disease, as he was so well that I could look on him as a comfortable brother till he came upon the accounting. Andrew Erskine called before dinner and paid me £50 which he owed me, with interest. It is strange how he and I, who once were so much together, live now quite apart. I told him I had not felt poverty till this winter. But that it was nothing in comparison with what he and I had felt (meaning hypochondria). He said it was next to that. I agreed. Poor fellow, he has not such a prospect as I have of relief from poverty. But then he has no wife or children. I read last week *Elements of Beauty, etc.*, just published by Mr. John Donaldson, the painter, of which he had sent me a present. There were fine assemblages of words in his performance, but I could not discern much solid or distinct meaning. It vexes me to think how little I read.

TUESDAY 1 FEBRUARY. (Writing on Wednesday the 2.) Was in very good spirits. My practice was brisker, which enlivened me. Between two and three there was a meeting of Mr. Erskine of Mar's trustees: the Earl of Buchan, his brother Mr. Henry Erskine, Lord Gardenstone, myself, and Mr. Lawrence Inglis. We met in Bain's Tavern, President's Stairs, and had soup, accepted of the trust deed, and appointed an accurate state of Mr. Erskine's debts, funds, and claims to be prepared. There was a manliness and a fashion about Erskine amidst his embarrassed affairs that, though I knew he at that moment might be apprehended for debt, I could not but hold him in consideration. My having looked upon him in my early years as a grand English-bred man ("*Old Erskine*") no doubt aided my imagination in respecting him.[9] I dictated well today, and in short had a comfortable existence. π.

WEDNESDAY 2 FEBRUARY. (Writing on Friday the 4.) Was in excellent spirits, so as to feel myself pleasant even in the Court of Session. Came home soon from the House. My two daughters and Sandy walked out with me to my father's, where I had not been since Saturday sennight, nor my daughters all this winter. We were received well enough. My father was in good temper, but seemed to be much failed today. His lady, I found, was set upon making him buy a house in the New Town. I thought it most prudent not to interfere, though it vexed me to observe her selfish views. Mr. Robert Boswell was there also at dinner. I brought the children home early. Dictated well.

THURSDAY 3 FEBRUARY. (Writing on Friday the 4.) This was a fast by Proclamation. As I was now dubious whether the Americans were not in the right to insist on independence, I did not go to church. I sat in all the forenoon. I had resolved to employ it in making notes of a dull proof

---

[9] "Old Erskine" (see above, 27 December 1779) had studied at Oxford.

for drawing a Memorial which I had delayed too long. But I thought I would look into my journal in London in 1762, that I might console myself in Edinburgh by being reminded that I had been as weary and melancholy in London as here. And I was so engaged by my own life that I read on all the time that I had appropriated to the Memorial. This was wrong. I was sickened in mind by reviewing my own sickly weakness. Yet I thought that it was not fair to judge of London now to me by what it was when I had a narrow acquaintance in it. For *now* how delightful is it to me! And I can scarcely imagine that it would not continue to be so were I constantly there. Dr. Webster called and sat some time with me, and I was waited on by Mr. William Tait, son to Mr. Alexander Tait, who was to be examined next day on the Scots Law.[1] Mr. Wood called, as I had sent for him. But as my toe was quite easy, he would not open it down yet. Miss Susie Dunlop dined with my wife. I dined with Mr. Erskine of Mar at his house in the Abbey Court, Lord Napier's. I knew that he was liable to be apprehended for debt, and I wondered to observe his high spirits. Lord Gardenstone and Dr. Heron were the rest of the company till Harry Erskine, who could not get in time to dinner, joined us. We drank very moderately. There was not much good conversation. Harry Erskine and I drank tea after the rest were gone. I liked to be with my Erskine kindred. After I came home, I went and sat awhile with Grange. I could do nothing, not even write my journal. I could not help a gloomy imagination of this day like an old Edinburgh Sunday.

FRIDAY 4 FEBRUARY. (Writing on Wednesday the 9.) Balbarton and Grange dined with us. I was comfortably well. In the forenoon I visited Old Lady Wallace, and Lord Kames, who was confined with a cold. He asked me to sup with him both tonight and Sunday. I declined the first but promised for the last.

SATURDAY 5 FEBRUARY. (Writing on Wednesday the 9.) After the Court, Grange went with me for a little into Signora Marcucci's school and saw Veronica dance a minuet very well. Then he and I walked out to Sir Alexander Dick's, as I was resolved that the first long walk I took with my whole toe should be to Prestonfield. Sir Alexander was remarkably well. Mr. John Macpherson and Mr. Robert Gillespie and Mr. Andrew Bennet were at dinner. After they were gone the worthy Baronet grew exceedingly cordial and social, called for a bottle of his best claret and a toasted biscuit, and was quite lively and classical. Mr. Gillespie returned and we had another bottle, the conversation then taking a more rustic turn. We were excellently happy. We drank coffee and tea, and had his

[1] Boswell was one of the Examinators. He served as Public Examiner in 1767 and 1768; as Private Examiner in Civil Law, 1770 and 1775; and as Private Examiner in Scots Law, 1772, 1780, and 1783.

chariot to town. He said the only inconvenience he felt from old age was that he could not go about and see his friends so much as he would wish to do. Grange was supremely pleased. I was a little heated and fretful after I came home, having taken rather too much wine.

SUNDAY 6 FEBRUARY. (Writing on Friday the 11.) Was at the New Church in the forenoon. Grange dined with us, and in the afternoon I read to my wife and him and the children two of Mr. Carr's sermons. The children said divine lessons well. I went and paid a short visit to M. Dupont. In the evening Veronica and I sat a good while on the settee in the drawing-room by ourselves. I was dotingly fond of her, and talked with earnest, anxious, tender apprehension of her death; how it would distress me, but that I must submit to GOD's will and hope to meet her in Heaven. She was quite enchanting. I prayed extempore while we knelt together. I supped at Lord Kames's by particular invitation; three Miss Baillies of Jerviswood, Lords Braxfield and Kennet, Young Mar, etc., there.[2] There was no relish tonight either instructive or lively. π.

MONDAY 7 FEBRUARY. (Writing on Friday the 11.) Dictated pretty well. Dined at my father's; Commissioner Cochrane, Dr. Gillespie, Stobie, and my brother John there. Sat awhile with David Erskine talking of additions to the entail of Auchinleck. Young Mar, Miss Preston, and Surgeon Wood supped with us.

TUESDAY 8 FEBRUARY. (Writing on Friday the 11.) Grange dined with us, and he and I drank cider joyfully to the success of our trial for expenses in the cause, Brown against Smith, as to which a long Representation by me was appointed to be answered.[3] At night my wife was very good to me.

WEDNESDAY 9 FEBRUARY. (Writing on Tuesday the 15th.) Nothing to record but that I was busy.

THURSDAY 10 FEBRUARY. (Writing on Tuesday the 15th.) Dined at my father's, Robert Boswell there. Called on Dr. Blair and sat awhile with him. Drank tea with Mr. Nairne and saw him firmly persuaded that living quietly and out of the bustle of life was the most agreeable way. Sat a little with the Hon. A. Gordon, who was indisposed.

FRIDAY 11 FEBRUARY. (Writing on Tuesday the 15th.) Sir Charles

---

[2] "Young Mar" was "Old Mar's" eldest son.
[3] The cause was a dispute over boundaries. John Brown, merchant of Glasgow and owner of Lanfine in Ayrshire, complained that William Smith, who owned a small property across the river Irvine from Lanfine, had caused the currents of the Irvine to change course and encroach on his land. Boswell represented Smith. The cause had come before Lord Kennet as Lord Ordinary nearly two years before (Journal, 24 February 1778).

and Miss Preston, Miss Semple, Mr. Wellwood, Dr. Blair, and Surgeon Wood dined with us, and all but Wood drank tea. It was a creditable day. But there was no vivid conversation. So I was not gratified. London has made my taste too high. Was a little intoxicated.

SATURDAY 12 FEBRUARY. (Writing on Tuesday the 15th.) That unhappy being, James Gilkie, had a question before the Lords as to his being admitted a procurator. I had drawn a very conciliating paper for him, which really had a good effect. The cause was delayed. But the Court seemed to be humane towards him.[4] I was engaged to dine at Craighouse with Lord Covington. Grange and Mr. Lawrie walked with me to the avenue foot. Mr. Murray of Broughton and Charles Boyd and I were all the company. It was a very good day, upon the whole. Mr. Murray carried me to town in a chaise which he had. I went to the Hon. A. Gordon's, not intending to stay; but got to whist and brag, and grew keen (as I always do) in an uneasy manner. Lost only three and sixpence, yet was vexed, so ill does gaming agree with my temper. I supped there. Mr. Walter Scott, Writer to the Signet, played at *that*,[5] and Lord Haddo came in after supper. I was feeble-spirited and indifferent, and felt myself like a child, or a sick old man. When I came home I was vexed that my wife had been uneasy from uncertainty where I was. I found a letter lying for me from my brother David that he was preparing to return to Britain. It gave me most comfortable joy. It was quite romantic to think of seeing him again. My wife was very good to me.

SUNDAY 13 FEBRUARY. (Writing on Tuesday the 15th.) Heard Dr. Blair in the forenoon and Mr. Walker in the afternoon. Called for a little at my father's between sermons. David's return was full in my mind, and cheered me affectionately. It was strange to observe how cold his father was. I said to him that it was very comfortable that David was coming home. That when David set out he had said, "Poor man, I'll never see him again." But it had turned out more agreeably. He said nothing, I think. Miss Susie Dunlop dined with us. Lord Macdonald and Mr. James Baillie drank tea with us. After which the children said divine lessons, and I prayed extempore with my two daughters kneeling by me.

---

[4] James Gilkie, whom John Maclaurin described as a parody of James Boswell, was the litigious and unpredictable "writer" who had engaged Boswell in an interesting cause of police brutality resulting in homicide, 1777–1778, and had had the cause finally thrown out of court because he had signed the list of witnesses issued with the Criminal Letters (Indictment), though he was not a procurator recognized by the Court of Session.

[5] Boswell's italics. It is not clear just what he means, but a satiric reference to Mr. Scott's strictness is probably intended. He was the novelist's father.

They were pleasingly affected. I went to Lord Kames's and got more materials for his life.[6] Young Mar supped with him, which he took very kindly. I drank to my shaking hands with him at a hundred.

MONDAY 14 FEBRUARY. (Writing on Wednesday the 16.) Washed my feet for the first time this winter, my toe being now well. Was in a fretful frame, there being some scurvy breaking out again slightly upon my legs and thighs. Grange accompanied me to Leith, that I might introduce John Boswell, my kinsman David's second son, to Captain Napier, who was to place him on board of a tender.[7] Grange walked on the pier till I talked with David, who did not seem to relish putting his son into a tender. I promised to talk with Captain Napier to have his intentions explained. But he was not at the rendezvous. Grange and I eat some raw oysters and drank a little brandy. This loaded my stomach and I was uneasy. Mr. Robert Syme, Junior, and Matthew Dickie dined with us. I drank rather too much negus, and was not well. Lady Lucy Douglas's death shocked me.[8]

TUESDAY 15 FEBRUARY. (Writing on Wednesday the 16.) Was not at all right. The Court of Session disgusted me in the forenoon, and in the afternoon I grew so low-spirited and languid and fretful that I could do nothing, but sat moping by my fire. I should have written *The Hypochondriack* No. 29. But had not a single thought. I was not ashamed of showing my wretched disease before Grange and Mr. Lawrie. I once thought of getting into bed and being quiescent at once. But was persuaded to sit up and have Grange to eat a bit of supper and drink some negus with us, which relieved me a little. How sad is it that I am subject to such dreary fits, which absolutely deprive me, while they last, not only of happiness but even of the very imagination of happiness! It hurt me that I made my valuable wife uneasy, especially when she was with child.

WEDNESDAY 16 FEBRUARY. (Writing on Thursday the 17.) Rose a good deal better. Began my *Hypochondriack* No. 29[9] and wrote with

[6] Boswell began collecting materials and notes for a life of Kames on 19 February 1775: "I spoke to Lord Kames to give me notes of his life. He said he would if I would write it before his death. But like Cicero he would ask to have it done in a flattering manner." Boswell finally put together a considerable collection of notes, documents, and materials, but the project was never completed. His materials (paraphrased) finally furnished matter for six foot-notes by Alexander Tytler, Lord Woodhouselee, in the second edition (1814) of his life of Kames.

[7] The following year Boswell tried to get this boy a commission in the marines, but was apparently thwarted by Sandwich's reluctance to accept any candidate for a commission younger than sixteen. David Boswell was the dancing-master at Leith, so despised by Lord Auchinleck.

[8] Wife of Douglas of Douglas, she was only twenty-eight and left four children.

[9] Few of the essays show clearer connexion with the state of mind recorded in the

tolerable ease. I had on Tuesday forenoon sat awhile with Sir William Forbes at the counting-house, but was so languid that it was a pain to me to keep up conversation even with him. He advised me not to think of settling in London, and argued very justly that I should correct the error of my imagination which made me look upon Edinburgh as so narrow and inconsiderable. But still, as Sir John Pringle said to me, I was born for England; and I am so much happier in London—nay, anywhere in England—than in Edinburgh that it is hard I should be confined to this place. However, I must prudently wait till I see if my circumstances shall ever be such as to enable me to live in London. I went out and dined at my father's. Just he and his lady and I at table. He was in a dull, cold humour and seemed quite indifferent about me. This was very hard. But I could not help it.

THURSDAY 17 FEBRUARY. (Writing on Saturday the 19.) Finished my *Hypochondriack* No. 29 with satisfaction, and dictated easily in law too. Mr. Daniel drank tea with us. π.

FRIDAY 18 FEBRUARY. (Writing on Saturday the 19.) Had not much relish of life, neither was I very uneasy. Balmuto and his sister Miss Menie, Mr. Nairne, Mr. George Wallace, Mr. David Erskine, and Mr. John Hunter dined with us. I was steady and rational in appearance. But though I did not drink much more than a bottle of wine, I was disturbed by it. My wife was at Signora Marcucci's Public[1] with my daughters,

---

journal at the time of their composition: "I once happened to overhear a conversation between two grenadiers of the 56th Regiment of Foot, one of whom expressed his aversion to the fatigues, severities, and dangers of a campaign, while the other talked with heroic ardour of encountering them, concluding his speech in these words, 'Let me be the man who is envied, not he who is pitied.' I regret that I did not take down the name of this gallant soldier who uttered a truly noble sentiment with a native dignity of manner. . . .—Amongst men who, as dependent beings, eager for happiness in a world where happiness is rarely to be found, must ever be influenced by views of self-interest immediate or more remote, it may be affirmed that pity would not exist were it not from the consideration that they may stand in need of it in their turn. For what thinking man is not convinced that he is liable to variety of evil; and that the kind commiseration of others if delicately shown will soothe and alleviate his wretchedness. . . .—These considerations, which experience proves to be just, should make us very cautious of complaining to people indiscriminately. An hypochondriac is very apt to do this. A sickly man goes about to everyone who pretends to skill in physic, or who he thinks has been ill like himself, hoping to obtain a cure or a palliative. So a hypochondriac whose mind is sickly and who suspects that others are not well, his distemper having in common with the jaundice an imaginary transference or communication of itself, is perpetually trying to obtain hints for relief, and while his spirits are sunk in despondency, lays open all his weakness" (*The Hypochondriack*, No. 29, February 1780).

[1] Signora Marcucci's "Public" was an exhibition of dancing by her pupils to which their parents were invited. The word in this sense has hitherto been recorded only as

who she told me danced well; and indeed I regretted that I did not go and see them. I walked in the street some time to sober myself. Was disgusted with seeing the coarse Edinburgh whores, so much more refined am I now. Then Hon. A. Gordon met me in the street. I went to his house and eat oysters and cold beef and drank small beer with him. When I came home, was sick and threw up.

SATURDAY 19 FEBRUARY. (Writing on Monday the 21.) Was in languid spirits from having drank rather too much yesterday. Felt the practice of the law a burthen. Hesitated between labouring hard all day on law papers or taking a walk to rouse me. Preferred the latter. Took Veronica with me to Lady Colville's. Frost had returned, and the cold was intense. Veronica behaved exceedingly well. I insensibly agreed to dine with her Ladyship, though at first resolved against it. So took Veronica home, and went out again. Dined well, nobody there but Lady Anne, the Major, and Mr. Andrew. Came to town in the coach with the Miss Elphinstones. Mr. James Baillie, who had drank tea with my wife last night, drank tea with us again tonight. My spirits were so sunk that I was just going to steal into bed. My wife wisely prevented me. I studied Lord Eglinton's political causes.

SUNDAY 20 FEBRUARY. (Writing on Monday the 21.) What an insipid and often what an uneasy life do I lead in Scotland! The cold was very severe today; but, being more hardened, I felt it less than I did some weeks ago. I heard a Mr. Henderson lecture twice on the Good Samaritan in the forenoon, or rather was present without hearing; and I heard with pretty good attention a fine discourse by Dr. Blair on the house of mourning in the afternoon. My wife and Phemie were with me. Miss Semple, Miss Preston, and Mr. Macredie dined with us between sermons. I drank tea at my father's, who was failed but not at all morose today. But his lady was very disagreeable. When I came home I found Sir Charles Preston had drank tea with my wife. The children said less of their divine lessons than usual. I went by special invitation and supped at Lord Kames's; Sir John Stewart and his lady, etc., there. I was cold and unhappy and got very little for my life of him.

MONDAY 21 FEBRUARY. (Writing on Wednesday the 23.) Dictated well, though my spirits were dull. Miss Susie Dunlop dined with us. Between eight and nine went to Fortune's on a consultation on Lord Eglinton's political causes, which were to come on before the Lords on Wednesday. Mr. Wight, the laird of Fairlie, and Messieurs John Wauchope and

---

an Americanism (earliest example 1823 in M. M. Mathews, ed., *A Dictionary of Americanisms on Historical Principles*, 1951), but Boswell's casual use of it in 1780 shows that it must have come to America from England or Scotland.

George Cumming, the joint agents, made the company. After business was over, we supped, and drank claret till about three in the morning. I was riotously inclined and thought that a hearty dose of wine might produce a change upon my spirits for the better. When I got home, I was shockingly rude (as I was informed, for I soon was insensible).

TUESDAY 22 FEBRUARY. (Writing on Wednesday the 23.) Rose very ill. But went to the Parliament House and appeared in eight causes, that I might do my duty and afterwards get to bed. In one of the causes there was an oath to be read by me. With much difficulty I made it out, for my eyes wavered grievously. I took care not to get into conversation with anybody; and as the crowd was offensive to me, I went between causes and walked in the space where the shops are. Much did I long for this difficult warfare being over. At last it *was* over, and home I went. The cold was intense and my sickness and headache severe. I got into bed and fell asleep. Awaked before three, still in pain. But soup and small beer and toasted bake [2] did me good. My dearest wife's kindness when I did not deserve it was very great. I rose about six. Worthy Grange drank tea with us. I was shattered. Yet I declared that the state in which I now was seemed to be ease compared with my hypochondriac uneasiness for some time past. I eat a comfortable supper. π.

WEDNESDAY 23 FEBRUARY. (Writing on Friday the 25.) Was somewhat better. The Court of Session was so much engaged with trying one Reid, accused of forgery, that for a good part of the Session for some time past most of the lawyers have had nothing to do in the Inner House. This day however the Lords determined a parcel of Ayrshire votes, after which I went to my father's and sat awhile with him, negatively well. Walked half round the Meadow. Worthy Grange dined with us. I drank tea at the Dowager Lady Wallace's. Miss Susie Dunlop was elegantly dressed and went to the play. The old lady and I sat some time after she was gone, and I was the better of matter-of-fact conversation. Miss Dick came to us at night.

THURSDAY 24 FEBRUARY. (Writing on Friday the 25.) Either yesterday or today, sitting by Mr. John Swinton at the bar, I told him that I must make a bargain with him as Dr. Pitcairne did with his friend: that he should come back and tell him what the other world was. [3] And he should

---

[2] Scots for biscuit.

[3] Pitcairne alludes to this in his poem "Ad Robertum Lindesium." David Irving, in his *Memoirs of George Buchanan,* prints the following note on the poem, as a comment which he believes Pitcairne himself communicated to a friend: "Robert Lindsay, grandchild, or great-grandchild, to Sir David Lindsay of the Mount, Lyon King at Arms, etc., being an intimate condisciple with Archibald Pitcairne, they bargained, anno 1671, that whoever died first should give account of his condition if possible. It happened

tell me what it was to be a Lord of Session after he was on the bench, which he would be among the first.[4] I said I was afraid it was a dull life. He said he was afraid so too. But then he added that one never tires sitting reading or writing in one's study, and he supposed it might be like that: a kind of negative enjoyment. I had visited Craigengillan and his lady on Monday forenoon. I called at my father's this forenoon, but they were out an airing in the carriage. At two there was a meeting of Old Erskine's trustees at Mr. Inglis's on Heriot's Bridge. I attended bodily. But my mind was quite feeble. I thought everybody had more force of mind than I had. I could have cried from weak, painful dejection. Miss Dick dined with us. Lady Craigengillan, the laird of Fairlie, Grange, and Matthew Dickie supped with us. I drank negus; and cheerful, easy chat relieved me agreeably.

FRIDAY 25 FEBRUARY. (Writing on Monday the 28.) Lady Colville, her sister and brothers, and Miss Dick dined with us. I was very comfortable, but without animated gaiety. My wife's cough continued to trouble her. This forenoon it rained. In the afternoon came snow and very hard frost.

SATURDAY 26 FEBRUARY. (Writing on Monday the 28.) Called at my father's. Commissioner Cochrane came. It was dull and unpleasing. The frost was intense. But as I now walked enough, it did not penetrate me as before. I dined at Mr. Baron Gordon's; Lord Monboddo, Crosbie, etc., there. I was in excellent spirits. But there was little good conversation. London and Dr. Johnson have made me unhappy in ordinary company. But it was much to be easy, in place of saying within myself as I did some days ago, *"I exist in misery,"* so weary and fretful was I. Lord Monboddo and I stayed tea. Both he and the Baron were violent against Lord Kames. They both said they knew him to be a worthless scoundrel. Monboddo said he was malevolent against people, not only for censuring his writings, but for not admiring him. He said he was excessively dull as well as wrongheaded, and that he was suitably employed only when he compiled the *Dictionary of Decisions*, which just required drudgery. The Baron said he was avaricious and envious, and would cut your throat if he could do it safely. I was somewhat confounded to hear him attacked in terms so very

---

that Lindsay died about the end of 1675, when Archibald Pitcairne was at Paris; and the very night of his death, A.P. dreamed that he was at Edinburgh, when Lindsay attacked him thus: 'Archie,' said he, 'perhaps ye heard I'm dead?' 'No, Robin.' 'Ay, but they bury my body in the Grey Friars. I'm alive though in a place whereof the pleasures cannot be expressed in Scotch, Greek, or Latin.'...Since which time, A. Pitcairne never slept a night without dreaming that Lindsay told him he was alive" (1817, pp. 423–424).

[4] Swinton's promotion was, as a matter of fact, the next but one. He succeeded Lord Covington in 1782.

strong. I said he had always been very good to me. When I got home, I found that though I had taken care to be quite sober, I was in a restless state which was still more uneasy than my general drowsiness at night, for I could not have the immediate relief of sleep. I went to bed without supper. But for the first time these many nights, tossed in a wakeful state for perhaps an hour.

SUNDAY 27 FEBRUARY. (Writing on Thursday the 2 of March.) π. Instead of going to church in the forenoon, walked to the Abbey, somewhat solemn, and then called on Lady Dundonald, whom I found hearing her son Andrew translate some of the Latin New Testament into English. I took him home with me to dinner, Miss Semple and Dr. Webster with us. Heard a Shetland minister preach in the New Church in the afternoon. Went out to my father's and drank tea. He was not in good humour. Came home also to tea. Sir Charles Preston and Mr. James Baillie there. After Baillie went away, the children said divine lessons well. Worthy Sir Charles sat by, and was quite easy. He and Grange supped with us. I was in placid fine spirits.

MONDAY 28 FEBRUARY. (Writing on Thursday the 2 March.) Did nothing but settle two bills which I owed Grange, by paying him out of my cash account with the bank and money lodged with Sir William Forbes and Company. Drank tea with him and eat milk bakes and honey comfortably. Miss Preston supped with us. π.

TUESDAY 29 FEBRUARY. (Writing on Thursday the 2 of March.) To please good Sir Charles Preston, a company of us dined with him at the tavern kept by *Jack*, who was once his servant. His two uncles,[5] Dr. Webster, and young Robertson Barclay, were brought by him, and the Hon. A. Gordon and Mr. James Baillie by me. We drank heartily of claret, and were so well that we agreed to meet in the same place again next Wednesday. I came home and went to bed without supper.

WEDNESDAY 1 MARCH. (Writing on Sunday the 5th.) The Hon. Alexander Gordon and I dined at Lady Colville's; Mr. Erskine of Cardross and his lady, etc., there. We drank liberally of good claret; then went to coffee and tea and played at whist. I never grow better at the game, yet play and bet very foolishly. I lost about two pounds, which vexed me in my present state of want of money; and Lady Anne Erskine observed justly that I should not play, because I then appeared inferior to others. I shall scarcely ever do it, as I have not attention enough. Gordon and I stayed supper, and as it was a wet night, had my Lady's coach to town. Yesterday I was uneasy to think of Lord Covington's disappointment by Lord Braxfield's getting my father's Justiciary gown, which, by the influence of the

---

[5] Col. Robert Preston and Commissioner Cochrane.

Dundases and his own prejudice against Lord Covington, he would not resign unless Lord Braxfield should get it, though Lord Covington had Lord Mansfield's promise. I admired the spirit with which Lord Covington bore his disappointment. He was as attentive and acute upon the bench as ever. I had spoken to Lord Advocate for him, pressing the hardship of disappointing him. My Lord gave me a very solid answer: that it would be wrong to give the gown resigned by one old man to a man still older, especially as Lord Kames, a very old man, had one of them. He added he would agree to Lord Covington's getting it if Lord Kames were out of the way. He said the Chancellor [6] was firm against giving it to Lord Covington, which he said would be a job.[7] But Lord Stormont desired Lord Advocate to think of some mark of the royal favour to Lord Covington. I still could not help thinking, or at least feeling, that Lord Covington might have been gratified with being a Justiciary Lord, which I suppose the narrowness of his views makes him look upon to be as great a dignity as it appeared to me when a boy at school.

THURSDAY 2 MARCH. (Writing on Thursday the 9th.) Dined at my father's, Robert Boswell there. Drank tea at Horatius Cannan's, my first visit to him and his young wife.

FRIDAY 3 MARCH. (Writing on Thursday the 9th.) Miss Dick and Grange dined with us. I sent a note at night to Maclaurin sincerely sympathizing with him on the death of one of his sons and anxious to hear how his wife was. I got an answer from him that she was dead.[8] Burke in his *Sublime and Beautiful* says we have some pleasure from the distress of others.[9] There was an agitation in my mind tonight which was better than melancholy. Yet I felt for Maclaurin and his children, thinking of my own situation, should such an event happen in my family. My wife was much affected. π.

SATURDAY 4 MARCH. (Writing on Friday the 10th.) Dined at Lady Colville's; Lord Elphinstone's family, Kingcausie and Lady Mary there.[1]

[6] Lord Thurlow.

[7] "Transaction in which duty is sacrificed to private advantage" (*Concise Oxford Dictionary*).

[8] Maclaurin's son, about five years old, was seized with whooping cough, which was succeeded by fever. His wife, lying in at the time, survived her son only seven hours.

[9] "I am convinced we have a degree of delight, and that no small one, in the real misfortunes and pains of others; for let the affection be what it will in appearance, if it does not make us shun such objects, if on the contrary it induces us to approach them, if it makes us dwell upon them, in this case I conceive we must have a delight or pleasure of some species or other in contemplating objects of this kind" (Section xiv).

[1] James Irvine of Kingcausie; Claud Boswell married his grand-daughter and heiress. "Lady Mary" was Irvine's second wife, Mary Forbes, daughter of the Earl of Granard.

Was not joyous, but well enough. Being a little intoxicated, I called at Portsburgh in my way home with a gross appetite. But luckily had not an opportunity. Drank a little whisky. Horatius Cannan and his young wife, Mr. James Baillie, and Mr. Robert Syme, Junior, supped with us. Was easy and cheerful, but rather vulgar.

SUNDAY 5 MARCH. (Writing on Friday the 10th.) Heard Mr. Walker in the forenoon and Dr. Blair in the afternoon. Was at Mrs. Maclaurin's burial between sermons. It did not shock me so much as I supposed it would do. My apprehension of my dear wife's death was not so lively as it has been sometimes. Called on Lord Braxfield by appointment at five and walked out with him to my father's and drank tea. Lord Braxfield announced to him his pension of £200 a year being fixed, to begin just where his salary ended. He affected indifference about it, which I did not like, and he was in bad humour with me. After I came home my children said divine lessons very agreeably. π.

MONDAY 6 MARCH. (Writing on Monday the 13th.) Breakfasted at Lady Colville's with Major Erskine, setting out for Ireland the next day. Dined at Horatius Cannan's; Craigengillan and Mrs. McAdam and several others there. Busy at night dictating a Petition.

TUESDAY 7 MARCH. (Writing on Monday the 13th.) Called on Maclaurin before dinner. He appeared to be wonderfully easy. In the evening my wife and I were at Signora Marcucci's ball and saw our daughters dance very well. I could not quite divest myself of a strange dejected bashfulness. Sandy was with us for a little.

WEDNESDAY 8 MARCH. (Writing on Monday the 13th.) Dined at Jack's tavern with the same company that met there last Tuesday. Only the Hon. A. Gordon was ill and could not come, and Robert Syme, Junior, was brought by me. We were more moderate than before, as I was engaged to attend my wife at *The Duenna* and *Fortunatus*,[2] bespoke by the Faculty of Advocates. I was as fond of her this evening as ever. I did not relish the play much, being uneasy with wine.

THURSDAY 9 MARCH. (Writing on Monday the 13th.) Clerk Matthew, Mr. Stobie, Balbarton, Messieurs Spalding-Gordon, Vans Hathorn, and Thomas Baillie dined with us. It was a burthen to me to entertain them, I was so languid. Yet the good animal spirits of most of them did me some good. I drank negus. An engagement for Dr. and Mrs. Young to play whist and sup with us tonight had quite escaped my memory. Luckily we were at home, for they came, and my wife had a neat supper with her usual cleverness, and the evening went on easily.

FRIDAY 10 MARCH. (Writing on Monday the 13th.) Craigengillan and

---

[2] Sheridan's comic opera and Henry Woodward's farce.

Mrs. McAdam, Commissioner Cochrane, and Grange dined with us. I had been shut up for two hours in the Court of Session attending as counsel for Macredie, a Stranraer merchant accused of fraudulent bankruptcy, whom the Lords were examining. My spirits were bad. I drank some rum punch today, which never agrees with me. Grange and I walked down to the Canongate, and strolled looking at some curious old houses on the south side which had once been the lodgings of people of rank. This amused us, and we returned to tea. I was not in a happy state. π.

SATURDAY 11 MARCH. (Writing on Monday the 13th.) Was somewhat uneasy that my fees this Session amounted to less than they had formerly done. Apprehended a failure of my practice now that my father did not attend the Court, and thought I should be unhappy for want of business. Yet I was sensible that a great deal of the coarse labour of law in Scotland would hurt my mind; and I should have considered that one of my fortune should be satisfied with little practice. I however dreaded insignificance, while at the same time I had all this year as yet been so averse to the business of the Court of Session that I had no keenness for it, as I once had, and wished always to have anything I had to do decently over. I saw no opportunity for ambition in this narrow sphere. What practice I had, I had with the dignity of a gentleman; not having used the artifices which many advocates have done, and not debasing myself by familiarity with vulgar agents. Fain would I have indulged gay, animating hopes of exerting myself in London. But I felt indolence and gloom too heavy upon me, and I was conscious that I could not persist in uniform application. Then I considered that the expense of living in London would impoverish me, and that I might perhaps in my hypochondriac discontent wish for the *home* of Edinburgh. I was sick-minded today. The Session rose, which was rather dispiriting to me, as I was not to go to London and would mould in inactivity.

I dined at my father's. Lady Auchinleck had a headache and did not dine with us. But she with venom talked to me of people being quick to see others failed, which was not a sign of a good disposition. She plainly meant my being sensible of my father's failure, which it is possible she does not perceive clearly, and wishes not to see, as her consequence depends on his life. I kept my temper. My father was very ungracious. I came home today quite sunk, as I often do from my father's, which is really sad. I was engaged to sup tonight with Mr. John Swinton. But having had a hint in the morning from Mr. Ilay Campbell, who was to be there, that they were to have a dance, and when I came to the door having heard a fiddle and the noise of dancing, I considered that such merriment was very unsuitable to my present gloomy, fretful state of mind, and that it was probably a hearty meeting of people all intimate with one another, while I was not intimate with any of them. I therefore returned home, and sent a card that something had happened which prevented me from being there. Had it been a company where I would have been missed, my benevolence would have made me go, though disagreeable. But with some of my friend Colonel Stuart's judicious firmness, I avoided what I disliked. I passed the evening quietly with my wife.

SUNDAY 12 MARCH. (Writing on Thursday the 16th.) Having gone to bed last night ruminating on my melancholy, I awaked this morning with this text full in my mind: "Howbeit this kind goeth not out but by prayer and fasting." [3] This seemed to be a supernatural suggestion that piety alone could relieve me from the evil spirit. I was much impressed with it, and my devotion was fervent today. Heard Dr. Blair in the forenoon and I think Mr. Walker in the afternoon. Was a little at my father's between sermons. Dined at Lord Monboddo's with Mr. David Rae, Lady Duffus and one of her grand-daughters, a Miss Sinclair, and Mrs. Hamilton and some of her boarders. The invitation was to see the rising generation of females. We were very cheerful. But my Lord and I drank too much claret. I stayed tea. Walked home a good deal inflamed; met an old acquaintance in the street, and was in danger of being licentious with her, so soon had wine overpowered my morning seriousness, which was indeed "like the morning cloud." [4] However, I got off. Sir Charles Preston and Grange supped with us. Sandy said no divine lesson today, and Veronica and Phemie said but little. I must never dine abroad on Sunday. My wife was hurt by my being again on the confines of low debauchery. I was very uneasy.

MONDAY 13 MARCH. (Writing on Thursday the 16th.) It was quite a tempest. Old Erskine breakfasted with me. My wife did not appear. While his straitened circumstances were humiliating, his spirit and anecdotes amused me. Grange had received an express that his mother was just dying, and the man who came had heard she was dead; so he was to go south next day. She was very old and had not been a kind mother to him, so he was not grieved. He dined with us today. I was not at all right. Yet I wrote letters wonderfully well. I called a little on Craigengillan at night, to see him, as he was to go west next day.

TUESDAY 14 MARCH. (Writing on Thursday the 16th.) Was relaxed and gloomy. Paid a visit to Colonel Mure Campbell and his lady,[5] whom I had not seen since her marriage. Grange set out today. I bid him adieu

[3] Matthew 12. 21.

[4] Hosea 6. 4, paraphrased.

[5] The former Flora MacLeod, daughter of John MacLeod of Raasay.

cordially. Wrote letters well.[6] Was at Marcucci's Public and saw my daughters dance. Supped at Old Lady Wallace's; Colonel Mure Campbell, Captain Campbell of Ardkinglass, Miss Clemie Elphinstone, and Miss Katie Muir there. Had called before supper at Mr. Wellwood's to visit Sir Charles Preston, who was ill with a rheumatism. Sat a little there. Grew easy and cheerful tonight, I knew not how. The company at Lady Wallace's was as agreeable as any that I have been in for some time. I drank very moderately. π. Read yesterday and today Langhorne's *Effusions of Friendship and Fancy.*

WEDNESDAY 15 MARCH. (Writing on Wednesday the 22.) Was a little at my father's. Colonel Mure Campbell, two Miss MacLeods of Raasay, and Mr. Wallace, our sheriff, supped with us. Mrs. Mure Campbell was ill and could not come. The evening went on very well.

THURSDAY 16 MARCH. (Writing on Wednesday the 22.) Had sat up till two last night, though without drinking to excess. Was at the New Church forenoon and afternoon, as it was the Fast Day before the Sacrament. Called at my father's a little between sermons. Miss Semple dined with us. My wife and I drank tea at Mrs. Boswell's of Balmuto; Miss Menie only there. My mind was somewhat sounder at present. Yesterday and today wrote *The Hypochondriack* No. 30. Wondered how I could write so well.[7]

---

[6] Boswell seems to be using these letters as a way out of his melancholia and his disappointment at not going to London. (To John Wilkes): "I am afraid I shall not be in London this spring. . . . I have now two sons and two daughters; and some of them are beginning to cost me pretty handsomely. But as they are a multiplication of myself, I consider that I am dancing and playing on the harpsichord, and cheerfully amused in their little persons. If Lord Mountstuart would but get me an office which would enable me to live in London except when at Auchinleck, I should be happy indeed. I have no doubt of seeing you at Auchinleck and hearing you acknowledge that it abounds in classical scenes." (To Pembroke): "It is not a little hard upon me to want what I enjoy so much. Will your Lordship be charitable enough to send me a little of your interesting politics and your agreeable gaiety? For in this country we are, I think, very unconcerned about the public and very dull in private. How is our friend Beauclerk and how does Lady Di like Bloomsbury? Charles Fox's duel was a lively incident. But were not he and his antagonist rather far from each other when they fired? I remember a *bon mot* of Dempster's when it was said that the late Lord Lyttelton and Lord Marchmont had almost fought a duel about the authenticity of *Fingal.* Somebody said he should have liked to see them fight. 'That you could not have seen,' said Dempster. 'They would have stood at such a distance that no one man could have seen them.' "

[7] "It was not till next day that it was finished."—BOSWELL. The essay is the first of four on the subject of drinking: "I do fairly acknowledge that I love drinking; that I have a constitutional inclination to indulge in fermented liquors, and that if it were not

FRIDAY 17 MARCH. (Writing on Wednesday the 22.) Attended Lords Gardenstone and Stonefield at the visitation of some disputed property near the Calton. Mr. Harrower at Torryburn, who takes the trouble to pay my nurse's shilling a week which I allow her,[8] dined with us. The conversation of a man of good plain sense in his comfortable rank of life pleased me, and I have always agreeable ideas presented to my mind when I see people from that part of the country where my dear mother was born. My wife and I drank tea, played cards, and supped at Dr. Monro's. Our two daughters were there at tea, music, and dancing. It was a very good scene. But I wearied a little, and saw how the fondness of parents may trouble other people with the performances of their children. After supper Mr. Bannatyne MacLeod, the advocate, gave us an account of poor Mac- Leod of Muiravonside, who is troubled with alternate fits of high and low spirits. I questioned him closely, and he said that when Muiravonside is low he lies most part of his time in bed; that he talks as sensibly as at other times, but says he is *bedeviled*; that he knows exerting himself would cure him, but he cannot do it. I was struck with the representation of his case, dreaded that I might be just as he is, saw *hypochondria* in a despic- able light, and was very uneasy. Affecting quite an easy curiosity, I asked Dr. Monro what could be the cause of it. He said I must learn that in the other world. For physicians themselves were subject to it, and could not tell. At present the stagnation of my spirits for want of objects to rouse them is, I suppose, my malady. I was excellent company tonight.

SATURDAY 18 MARCH. (Writing on Thursday the 23). Was at the New Church, and got myself into a very composed frame.

SUNDAY 19 MARCH. (Writing on Thursday the 23.) Was at the New Church during the whole service, forenoon and afternoon. Received the Holy Sacrament as a memorial of Christ's death and a public evidence of my faith. But was offended by the irreverent form of the Presbyterians. My father was there in the forenoon, and communicated. He looked very old

---

for the restraints of reason and religion, I am afraid I should be as constant a votary of Bacchus as any man." He suggests that it is allowable to try drunkenness "by way of a desperate remedy" as a cure for hypochondria.

[8] Boswell no doubt means his wet-nurse, the woman who suckled him as an infant. We have not turned up her name in the Boswell papers, but this reference and a letter from Lady Preston to Boswell, 16 October 1766, make it likely that she lived at Torry- burn, which is only two and a half miles from Culross and about half that distance from Valleyfield House. The letter shows that Boswell had been providing his weekly subsidy from the time that he was admitted to the bar, that is, from the time that he began earning money of his own. Lady Preston had charge of initiating it (she found the nurse in considerable want, indeed lacking "some necessary parts of clothing"), and probably continued to administer it to her death in 1779.

and very unkindly. Miss Semple and Dr. Gillespie dined with us between sermons. The children said divine lessons in the evening. But some bad fit had seized Veronica, for she said to me in a kind of plaintive, upbraiding tone, "I am not to go up to Heaven. I am just to rot." I quieted her, but was hurt to think of the darkness which covers our hopes of futurity unless when Christian faith bears us up.

MONDAY 20 MARCH. (Writing on Tuesday the 23.) Was at the New Church, after which my wife and I and my daughters and Sandy drank tea at my father's, dully and ungraciously. My father grew very uneasy with his old and now constant complaint.

TUESDAY 21 MARCH. (Writing on Thursday the 23.) My mind was now in a better state, though at intervals I was exceedingly gloomy. I this day dictated a law paper with more vigour than I have done of late. In the forenoon I visited my father and found him pretty well again. Sandy was with me. π.

WEDNESDAY 22 MARCH. (Writing on Friday the 31.) Walked out to Sir Alexander Dick's and dined and drank tea. Had Sandy with me. There was no company there. Conversation flagged a little.

THURSDAY 23 MARCH. (Writing on Friday the 31.) Called at Dr. Webster's in the morning and saw John, who was now in town, and Sandy, returned from an East India voyage. Was at a consultation at Mr. Ilay Campbell's, and found myself pretty clear. Called a little at my father's in the evening. Dr. Webster and his sons John and Sandy, Captain Mingay, and Mr. Robert Syme, Junior, supped with us. I was cheerful, yet sober.

FRIDAY 24 MARCH. (Writing on Friday the 31.) Had fixed to go this day with the Solicitor [9] to pay a visit to our worthy friend Douglas after the death of Lady Lucy. I got up easily a little after six, was at the Solicitor's at seven, and had some breakfast; and then he and I set out in a post-chaise, our servants riding behind. Our conversation was on literary and sensible topics. We took a second breakfast at Livingstone, and got to Bothwell Castle in good time. We met Mr. Douglas riding out with his nephew, Mr. George Stewart. He turned with us, and we walked till dinner. The Solicitor thought it best to take no notice at all of Lady Lucy's death, and I agreed with him. There was a visible sadness about Mr. Douglas, though he bore his distress with manly composure. Captain Roberton of Earnock and a Captain Stewart, married to Earnock's niece, dined with us. Miss Stewart of Grandtully was here. We did very well at dinner, and I drank freely but not excessively. In the evening the Solicitor played at backgammon with Mr. Douglas and afterwards at

[9] Alexander Murray.

brag with me. I lost about three pounds, and so unfit am I for gaming that this loss vexed me. I alwise [10] remember Dr. Johnson's remark that there is more suffered by losing at play than enjoyed by gaining, so that it is upon the whole an evil. I was tenderly affected when the three little boys came into the room after dinner. I felt myself uneasy at being alone tonight, and was long of falling asleep. I was uneasy to think that I had not kept this day, being Good Friday. I had not adverted to its being that sacred anniversary when I fixed on it for going to Mr. Douglas's. I just by chance heard somebody mentioning it in the street the day before. I regretted living in a Presbyterian country. However, I thought that I was not indulging in merriment. I was at the house of mourning.

SATURDAY 25 MARCH. (Writing on Monday the 3 of April.) We all rode out as far as Woodhall. Shawfield was hunting the fox. We paid a visit to his lady, and returned to dinner. In the evening arrived Mr. Randolph. I won back all that I had lost the night before except six shillings. Mr. Douglas tried to play at whist. But broke off and made his nephew take his hand. I was in rather too high spirits and drank too much, though not to be drunk.

SUNDAY 26 MARCH. Awaked ill. Had some soup in bed, rose, walked out, and recovered very well. Mr. George Stewart and I went to Bothwell Church. The other gentlemen walked. I tried today to read some of *Evelina*, a novel by Miss Burney, but it did not engage me. Even *La Nouvelle Héloïse* seemed flat. Want of appetite for mental food is a sad thing. The day went on comfortably enough. I read upon this jaunt Burke's *Speech on Public Economy*, and both wondered and was delighted.[1] The Solicitor and I had fixed to set out next morning. Mr. Douglas said at night, "Much obliged to you for this kind visit." I told him I would be there again. He said, "That's right."

MONDAY 27 MARCH. The Solicitor and I had a good breakfast early, and then set out. We descanted on the hardship of living in the country when one is not used to it. At Whitburn I had cold mutton and a bottle of excellent beer, and was cheered by the refreshment. The Solicitor could not partake. We drove to his country-house at Murrayfield, where I agreed

[10] Properly, "in every way," but by this time in Scotland practically interchangeable with "always."

[1] Boswell had written to Burke on 2 March from Edinburgh ("this cold, unimportant place") to congratulate him upon this speech: "Your allusion to the birth of Pallas, previous to your *Speech upon Public Economy*, appears now to be more applicable to the then great future subject than your modesty seemed to allow, as it has proved truly *capital*." He asked that Dilly be permitted to join Dodsley in its publication, and that Burke send him a copy of the speech in franks as soon as it was printed. He is probably now reading this requested copy, although there is no other reference to the speech in any correspondence or in the Register of Letters.

to set him down. But finding Mrs. Murray at dinner, I agreed to stay, so dismissed the chaise and sent my servant home before me. We dined quietly and drank a bottle of claret apiece, and the Solicitor walked with me very near to the town. It was agreeable to be thus social with the son of an old friend of my father's. I was welcomed by my dear wife and children, and happy to be at home again. π.

TUESDAY 28 MARCH. (Writing from notes on Friday 7 April.) Called at my father's a little. Was in bad spirits. Mr. Daniel called in the evening. I could not be at all social, and did not ask him to sup. I was ashamed of myself.

WEDNESDAY 29 MARCH. (Writing from notes on Friday 7 April.) Breakfasted at Lady Colville's. She was ill and could not rise. So Lady Anne entertained me. I dined and drank tea at my father's, Dr. Gillespie there. He and I took a walk after dinner, and he said my father would be the better of going to Auchinleck and seeing his trees and improvements. I told the Doctor I was glad to hear him talk so, for that people had said he would keep my father in Edinburgh for the convenience of his own practice. I thought I would observe the Doctor's conduct as to this, and treat him accordingly.

THURSDAY 30 MARCH. (Writing from notes on Friday 7 April.) Dictated a law paper. Met at Mr. H. Erskine's with him and Lord Alva about Old Erskine's affairs. Was nervous and not well.

FRIDAY 31 MARCH. (Writing from notes on Friday 7 April.) I think I called at my father's. I also called on Old Erskine and on Lady Dundonald, who asked me to dine with her, which I did. John and Alexander Webster were there. Old Erskine came in after dinner. We all stayed tea. My spirits were very flat.

SATURDAY 1 APRIL. (Writing from notes on Friday 7 April.) Miss Preston had drank tea with us one day of this week, and my wife and I engaged to drink tea this day at old Lady Leven's, where Miss Preston was. We went accordingly. I had not been in her Ladyship's company for about four-and-twenty years, not since I had seen her drinking tea with my dear mother. Though now in her eightieth year, she was entire in her mind and quite cheerful. Dr. Andrew Hunter, the Professor of Divinity, was there. I was, I know not by what means, in good spirits. The old Countess told me that when Dr. Hugh Blair was a probationer, she heard him preach and was struck with him; and upon going home told her Lord, who was confined to the house, that she had heard a young man of superior abilities, and though their own parish had been supplied the year before, my Lord might get him another settlement. My Lord wished to hear him. She applied to one of his acquaintance, and got him to preach in the family. My Lord was so much pleased with him that he got him a presentation to Collessie, the next parish to his own. I called at Old Lady Wallace's a little. My wife and I played whist and supped at Sir William Forbes's. I continued to be in good spirits. Sir William, Ilay Campbell, Nairne, and I sat up drinking claret till near two in the morning.

SUNDAY 2 APRIL. (Writing from notes on Saturday 8 April.) Awaked very ill, and lay till five in the afternoon. I had not drunk to great excess. But I suppose sitting late, and the cold air, and perhaps some dish that disagreed with me, had produced a sickness and headache. I was well in the evening, and heard the children say divine lessons. Little Jamie had for some time forgotten to cry *here*, but cried *Ma*, and *a* (for *ay*).[2] π.

MONDAY 3 APRIL. (Writing from notes on Saturday 8 April.) Called at Mr. H. Erskine's a little, and had him to explain Old Erskine's affairs, which he did in a very clear manner, so that I understood them. He then brought out a manuscript volume of his own poems and read one to me, a translation from one of the Greek minor poets, in very pretty verse.[3] I was still under the cloud which has hung on my mind, though with intermissions, for some time. I called a little on John Webster. While in bed yesterday, I thought with concern how I had both a brother and an uncle in the same town with me whom I had not seen for a long time. My affection warmed, and I resolved to see them. Their being both victims to our family disorder, while it was a melancholy consideration, was also a tender one. I called on my brother John a little in the evening. But he was very silent and sour, and refused to sup with me along with John and Alexander Webster. They and Captain Mingay and Mr. James Donaldson supped. I drank negus and was calm.

TUESDAY 4 APRIL. (Writing from notes on Saturday the 8th.) Called on my father a little in the forenoon; as I returned, met Robert Boswell and went home with him. Saw my poor uncle, whom I had not seen since 3 September last. He was now very weak, and his legs were shrunk so that he could not walk. He was in bed, and was quite emaciated, and spoke indistinctly. But what he said was sensible enough, though his memory was

---

[2] Parentheses added by editors, who assume that *ay* means "yes." But Boswell could perhaps have meant, "cried *Ma* and *a* continually."

[3] This volume, now in the National Library of Scotland, contains a number of poems which have never been published. Imitations of the minor Greeks include "Idyllium of Moschus on the Death of Bion"; "Anacreon, Ode 53"; and "Epigrams from Posidippus and Metrodorus, for and against Life." Some idea of the quality of the verse can be derived from one couplet of "Epigram from the Latin, To a Brother and Sister Blind; the One of the Right Eye, the Other of the Left":

Sweet, lovely pair, each of an eye bereft
Alcon the right, fair Leonil the left

(information kindly supplied by A. S. Bell, Assistant Keeper, National Library of Scotland).

decayed. I do not think I should have known him had I seen him without being told who it was. He seemed very glad to see me, held my hand, and brought my face down to salute me. He spoke with relish of old hock; and I told him I was lucky enough to have seven bottles of it, very good, and I would send him first two, and if he liked it, he should have the whole. He expressed his usual impatience for it. So I went home and sent him two bottles; and Robert told me that he took three or four bumpers of it, and next morning when he awaked, the first thing he said was to let him have some negus of it. I dined at Mr. George Wallace's; Sir James Grant, the Craigs of Riccarton, Rev. Dr. Dick, etc., there. It was a good day, though without conversation as at the *prandia deum* [4] to which I am used in London. I drank excellent claret, not to excess. Stayed tea.

WEDNESDAY 5 APRIL. (Writing from notes on the 8th.) Hallglenmuir and Old John Boswell called on me. Hallglenmuir brought me very discouraging accounts of the setting of Dalblair, in so much that he was for my lowering the rent eight or ten pounds. I walked with them to Leith and called at Mr. David Boswell's, and engaged him and his son James, now a midshipman, to dine with me today. My wife never would agree to my having poor David at dinner, because of his being a dancing-master; but I lately prevailed with her upon his son's coming home a midshipman. I was flat in spirits and embarrassed with all things, but by reason I exerted myself very decently. I waited on Admiral Sir John Lockhart-Ross, to whom James Boswell had offered himself and been engaged for his ship, and I recommended the young man to him. I had a good clannish dinner: Balbarton, John Boswell, David Boswell, James Boswell, Robert Boswell, myself, and my two sons; making eight Boswells (seven at table, as Sandy sat), and my two daughters nine, and my wife and Hallglenmuir, both Boswells' bairns.[5] I got into a most comfortable frame. We had abundance of solid dishes, and we drank heartily. Robert left us early. But we drank three bottles port, one Mataró, and about one and a half rum in punch. I drank punch, and what was a *curiosa felicitas,*[6] I was not disturbed by it in any way, either in mind or body, so well can cordiality preserve a man. Balbarton stayed tea. I went out a little to my father's in the evening; found him at cards with his women (as Dr. Johnson said) [7] and his physician.

---

[4] Feasts of the gods.

[5] Margaret Boswell's mother (Veronica) was Lord Auchinleck's sister. Alexander Mitchell of Hallglenmuir was a grandson of David Boswell of Craigston and consequently a first cousin of the dancing-master.

[6] An extraordinary blessing. Boswell is adapting to his own experience Petronius's fine characterization (*Satyricon,* 29.1) of the style of Horace. In Petronius the words mean something more like "studied felicity."

[7] This may be an obscure allusion to something which passed during Johnson's visit

Drinking did not at all appear upon me. I sat about an hour. This week I have been dutiful to relations.

THURSDAY 6 APRIL. (Writing from notes on Tuesday the 11th.) Hall-glenmuir breakfasted with us, after which he and I walked out to my father's and sat a little. We met my brother John in the Meadow, and although he had not seen Hallglenmuir for many years, he recollected him, but was not frank at all. Hallglenmuir came home with me, and I wrote letters to my tenants of Dalblair, offering them their possessions with deduction of £8 upon the whole each year for four years. I was engaged to dine at Commissioner Cochrane's. Dr. Gillespie and I walked out. Dr. Webster was the only other guest. We had a good rational day. I was in excellent spirits. Dr. Webster and I had the Commissioner's chaise into town. By the way, Webster and I talked of my not having visited the Lord President for several years. I explained the President's bad behaviour in taking advantage of my father's failure, to make him act so foolishly in the Ayrshire election. But that as this was politics, I forgave him now, and would go out with him to Arniston and see his Lordship. But I doubted whether it would be best to talk over what was past. Webster with his ad-mirable good sense and experience of mankind was clear that there should not be a word said. But I should just go see him, and drinking a glass of wine would be understood as putting an end to all differences; and he added the President would be very happy to see me. So it was agreed.

FRIDAY 7 APRIL. (Writing on Tuesday the 11th.) I read some in a curious book of discourses by ΔΙΩΝ, an author whom Maclaurin lent me. I could not read the Greek with any ease, so read mostly the Latin trans-lation. I read three of the discourses: one to prove that the *Iliad* was all a fiction, one upon slaves, and one upon custom.[8] I had read part of the book before today. I wrote a good deal of this journal and part of a letter to Temple. I was very well. Yet gross desire hurried me to a coarse paramour. I did not however risk with her. π.

SATURDAY 8 APRIL. (Writing on Tuesday the 11th.) Wrote more to Temple. Read some of the second volume of the *Biographia Britannica.* My agreeable ideas and wishes for distinction and relishes of life revived. I dined at my father's, Robert Boswell there. Lady Auchinleck was con-fined to her room. My father was somewhat more kindly than usual. When I went away, he said, "Good-night, my dear Jamie." I went home with Robert and drank tea. His father was very low tonight and could not see

---

at Auchinleck—a visit scantily reported in the *Tour to the Hebrides* (2–8 November 1773).

[8] Dio Chrysostom, Greek rhetorician and philosopher of the first century. Boswell probably read Nos. 11, 10, and 76 of *Orationes*, which in some editions were published in Greek and Latin in parallel columns.

me. He soon lost his fondness for the old hock. As I sat at home at night, I got a card from Hallglenmuir and Old John Boswell to come an hour to them at Dalrymple's. Hallglenmuir had been at Dunfermline getting some money due to him, and was to go west next day. I thought he had some interesting matter to communicate. But I found him and Mr. Boswell and David Boswell at Leith and the schoolmaster of Leith, just met to be merry. So I took a glass or two of punch, and left them. How thoughtless is Hallglenmuir in his perplexed affairs!

SUNDAY 9 APRIL. (Writing on Thursday the 13th.) Heard a Mr. Jones, Lady Glenorchy's chaplain, lecture and preach with neat English vivacity in the New Church in the forenoon, and Dr. Webster preach in his own church in the afternoon. The children said divine lessons. I was at my father's a little in the evening.

MONDAY 10 APRIL. (Writing on Thursday the 13th.) Dined at Dr. Gillespie's with Commissioner Cochrane, Dr. Webster, and John. Was in sound spirits, but drank so as to be intoxicated a good deal, so that I ranged an hour in the street and dallied with ten strumpets. I had however caution enough left not to run a risk with them. Told my valuable spouse when I came home. She was good-humoured and gave me excellent beef soup, which lubricated me and made me well.

TUESDAY 11 APRIL. (Writing on Saturday the 15th.) Called on Dr. Webster a little. Was very well. Visited my father in the evening. Sir W. and Lady Forbes, her father Dr. Hay and his son John (both for the first time), Mr. Ilay Campbell and Mrs. Campbell (for the first time), Dr. and Mrs. Young, Mrs. Glen-Gordon (for the first time), and Major Hugh Montgomerie supped with us. We had cards before supper and were very cheerful; and though the gentlemen sat till two in the morning, we did not drink to excess.

WEDNESDAY 12 APRIL. (Writing on Monday the 17.) Breakfasted with Lady Colville. Lady Anne was ill and did not appear. I always feel a kind of constraint in the company of the ladies of Kellie, knowing their satirical turn and having been with them in my early life while I was awkward and timid. But we have all along been on a good footing, and what is rare, they have been as well with me since my marriage as before, and have kept up a good intercourse with my wife. It was, I recollect, a remark of one of themselves many years ago that a man's female friends before marriage are seldom his friends when he has changed his state. I began today to amuse myself with reading the Register of Baptisms for the City of Edinburgh, beginning with the year 1700, and taking notes of all the persons now alive whom I knew. Miss Susie Dunlop and Mr. Robert Syme, Junior, dined with us. I drank a very little wine. Miss Dunlop and my wife and I played at *vingt-et-un*. Why should I be vexed that I am not superior to the generality of men, who really do not pass their time more rationally than I did this day? After a long silence, I received a letter today from Dr. Johnson. He mentioned Topham Beauclerk's death, which some time ago affected me a good deal; for the death of one so fashionable and spirited and knowing and witty as he was damped my spirits. Dr. Johnson rebuked me in this letter for complaining of my melancholy, and charged me for the future not to talk of it, and then it would not trouble me. His advice may perhaps be good. I shall try to follow it.[9] π.

THURSDAY 13 APRIL. Read in the Register of Baptisms. Dined at Mr. David Erskine's; his brother Cardross and several more there for a whist party. Mr. Graham of Airth, whom I had never seen before, was there. I was entertained with his extraordinary vivacity, variety of ideas, and volubility of talk. I drank about a bottle of claret, and then, being engaged to play whist at Mrs. Glen-Gordon's, slipped away. My wife went with me. There was a cheerful company of five ladies and five gentlemen, and a genteel supper. It was a very pleasant evening.

FRIDAY 14 APRIL. (Writing on Monday the 17.) Was awhile in the Advocates' Library looking for a motto for a *Hypochondriack*. Found one in Aulus Gellius. Read a little in the Register of Baptisms. Dined at my father's, Dr. and Mrs. Gillespie there. Lady Auchinleck confined to her room.

SATURDAY 15 APRIL. (Writing on Monday the 17.) My dear wife has for some months been troubled with a cough, sometimes better, sometimes worse. This morning she had a severe fit, so that she spit some blood. This frightened her and made me uneasy. But I hoped that the blood came only from her throat. Sandy has had a deafness from a cold for more than a month. Mr. Wood says it will go off. All this winter from a weakness in his eyes he has squinted at times. I have often washed his eyes with cold water. He grows fast and is stout-made, like a true son of Auchinleck. I set myself to write *The Hypochondriack* No. 31, and found that a chapter in Aulus Gellius with a translation into English saved me almost all the

---

[9] "You are always complaining of melancholy, and I conclude from those complaints that you are fond of it. No man talks of that which he is desirous to conceal, and every man desires to conceal that of which he is ashamed. Do not pretend to deny it; *manifestum habemus furem* ["we have the undeniable thief"—a legal maxim]; make it an invariable and obligatory law to yourself never to mention your own mental diseases; if you are never to speak of them, you will think on them but little, and if you think little of them, they will molest you rarely. When you talk of them, it is plain that you want either praise or pity; for praise there is no room, and pity will do you no good; therefore, from this hour speak no more, think no more, about them" (From Johnson, 8 April). This was essentially the same advice Boswell had given his readers in *The Hypochondriack*, No. 29.

labour of composition at this time.[1] Mr. James Baillie drank tea with us. Commissioner Cochrane had called in the morning. I went at night to the play (to *The Beggar's Opera*), to have London ideas revived and to meet Miss Susie Dunlop, who had asked me to be there. Finding that she was in a box with a very disagreeable woman, I did not go near her, but sat in the pit. I was rather callous to the songs, which used to affect me in a lively manner, and came away when two acts were done. Played whist and supped at Maclaurin's. There was singing too. It hurt me to see all appearance of regret for a wife so lately dead effaced. Yet (writing on Wednesday the 19 April) is it not good sense to get free of grief as soon as one can? However, there is something in doing so which shocks my feelings.

I should have mentioned that last night I had a very lively dream that I was at Constantinople. That it was the season of a great religious ceremony, and that I was admitted into a mosque, where I saw a company of Turks sitting round a table with the cloth laid and plates and other preparations for a repast. I remember a good deal of gilding upon what appeared to be china-ware on the table. I suppose my dreaming imagination has given a Turkish cast to the Christian sacrament of the Lord's Supper. I remember I was very devout in this dream, and it left a pleasing impression on my mind. I have long thought that Mahomet had a divine commission, and so, I am pretty certain, Sir John Pringle once owned to me he thought.

SUNDAY 16 APRIL. (Writing on Thursday the 20.) Was too late for church. The children said divine lessons. Dr. Webster, Miss Dunmore, and Miss Mackye from Glasgow dined with us. Heard Mr. Walker in the afternoon. Drank tea at my father's.

MONDAY 17 APRIL. (Writing on Thursday the 20.) Sat awhile reading in the Register of Baptisms. It was a coldish, damp day. Did little. Miss Susie Dunlop drank tea with us.

TUESDAY 18 APRIL. (Writing on Thursday the 20.) Dictated well a good deal of law paper. Went out with Commissioner Cochrane and dined at my father's. Poor Hallglenmuir was in much distress, as the Douglas and Heron Bank threatened to bring his estate to sale to get pay-

[1] An anecdote of a "man from the Island of Crete" who drunkenly held that Plato praised drunkenness. Gellius sets the record straight from Plato's *Laws*, concluding (in Boswell's lively, if headlong, translation), "He thought therefore that we should engage with pleasures as if in a field of battle, and among the rest with the pleasure of drinking: that we may be safe from them, not by flight or absence, but, by vigour and constant presence of mind and a moderate use of what is agreeable, may maintain temperance and continence; and that our souls being once warmed and comforted, we may get rid of any latent, cold sadness, or torpid timidity."

ment of £1,000 for which they had a preferable security on his estate. To get the sale delayed (writing on Friday the 21 April) was a matter of great consequence to him, and this could not be done unless some friend would advance the £1,000, come in place of the Ayr bank, and have patience. I had mentioned to Commissioner Cochrane that I wished my father would do it, and the Commissioner seemed to acquiesce, and be inclined to forward the scheme. But when I proposed it today in his presence, he sat quite silent, while my father refused strongly to interfere. He treated my humane application with contempt, saying, "They flatter *him*." [2] I was obliged to desist. Sandy came after dinner. I played whist with my father and his lady and the Commissioner. My two daughters came to tea. My father's indifference about all of them was sad. In the evening I continued to dictate as I could wish to do.

WEDNESDAY 19 APRIL. (Writing on Friday 21 April.) Finished my law paper quite to my satisfaction. Dined with Commissioner Cochrane at Commissioner Lockhart's, a hearty good dinner. No other company there but a Miss Christie and Mr. Ross, Secretary of the Post-Office. I drank porter and port and Madeira and a bottle of claret, and wished for more. I stayed tea. After which, having still a desire for more social drinking, I went to the Cross and sent a caddie to find out where Dr. Webster was. He was at Mr. Samuel Mitchelson, Junior's. I called there and found them tête-à-tête upon Lord Dundonald's affairs. They however drank one bottle of claret with me. And then I drank tea with Mrs. Mitchelson and talked a great deal of nonsense which vexed me afterwards. I then wandered an hour in the streets and followed girls, but happily did not go with any of them or run any kind of risk. It was however very disagreeable to think that I had from intoxication (writing on Saturday the 22) been so foolish as to debase myself by intruding at Mitchelson's, and so gross as to follow after low Edinburgh whores. I had been cutting my great toenails this week and had hurt the flesh, and by walking a good deal today they were both inflamed. The toe which troubled me before was much swelled and very painful. I put a poultice to it and went to bed. My dear wife had soup ready for me, which I took comfortably amidst my contrition.

THURSDAY 20 APRIL. (Writing on Saturday the 22.) Was in great pain and much dispirited. Lay in bed all forenoon. Read ten of Dr. Blair's second volume of sermons. Did not relish them so much as I expected to do. Found too much uniformity of flourish and not enough of philosophy. Misses Dunmore, Mackye, two McAdams of Craigengillan, and Kitty

[2] The "him" is probably Boswell: "People like Hallglenmuir can wheedle *him*, but they can't *me*."

Douglas, sister to the Duchess of Douglas's heir,[3] dined and drank tea with us. I roused myself from indolence, and was the better of young and cheerful company. After dinner I read one of Dr. Ogden's *Sermons on the Articles of the Christian Faith*, which I had got from London lately, that I might compare his manner of preaching with Blair's, and I found it much superior. Blair in his sermon on GOD's unchangeableness showed his opinion that prayer *doth not avail* with our Heavenly Father, and that man is indeed fatally carried on. Such a system is dreary and dispiriting, and I am convinced is not true. I read the rest of Blair's second volume this night.

FRIDAY 21 APRIL. (Writing on Saturday the 22.) Had cried much in my sleep, having dreamt that Veronica was shot dead. Mr. Wood, for whom I had sent yesterday, called this morning and said my toe looked worse than he had ever seen it; but all that could be done was giving it rest and poulticing it till the swelling was gone. I read some of Palmer on Human Liberty against Priestley for Necessity, and was refreshed by it. This I did after dinner. But in the forenoon I was wretchedly relaxed, and humbled to find that I could be reduced to low spirits in so short a time by so slight a complaint. Major Montgomerie sat awhile with me. Lady Auchinleck paid us a visit. I talked to her of Hallglenmuir and wished she would persuade my father to lend him the £1,000. She said he had it not, and if he were to begin to embarrass himself by borrowing money to lend to other people, he would get into the same confusion which was so ruinous to other people. That he had let a farm of £36 a year to Hallglenmuir for which he did not expect to get rent, which was pretty well. That it would be impossible to extricate Hallglenmuir, and it was better to bring his circumstances to a crisis, and afterwards, if one could afford it, give his family £50 a year. She talked with so much rational sense and showed such strength of mind that I could not but be pleased with her. I was convinced.[4] I tried to dictate a *Letter to Lord Braxfield on His Promotion To Be a Lord of Justiciary,* which I had meditated for some time and wished to publish before he began his first circuit.[5] But I had no

[3] Archibald Douglas, son of the Duchess's brother James. Katherine Douglas later succeeded him in the property.

[4] This is the first favourable comment that Boswell makes upon Lady Auchinleck in his journal. He later came to think quite highly of her.

[5] A "characteristical" pamphlet in which Boswell recommends that the circuit criminal courts actually be conducted "in the most solemn, exact, and regular way," as enjoined by the statute. Lord Auchinleck, whom Braxfield was succeeding, had built up a reputation for dignity and probity perhaps not equalled by any of his colleagues, and Boswell may well have feared that the appointment of Braxfield would increase the abuses with which he charges the Bench. It appears from the entry for 29 April that he has Lord Kames in mind as an example of judicial indecorum. Boswell did not

vigour of mind at all. So let it alone. Mr. Bruce Campbell and Mr. Robert Boswell drank tea with us. I was cheered by them. Before they went away, Lieutenant David Cuninghame arrived from Doura on his way to return from his brother's to join his regiment. We asked him to take a bed with us, which he accepted. He drank tea, went out awhile, returned and supped, and was quite at home. But his want of sense displeased us.

SATURDAY 22 APRIL. (Writing on Thursday the 27.) Wrote a good deal of my *Letter to Lord Braxfield*, and was as animated as I could wish to be. David Cuninghame dined at Robert Boswell's. He and Major Montgomerie supped with us. Was sober.

SUNDAY 23 APRIL. (Writing on Friday the 28.) My toe was a good deal better. But I kept the house all day, and read one of Dr. Ogden's sermons and heard the children say divine lessons. Veronica read some aloud in my large quarto Oxford prayer-book with cuts, bound in red morocco and gilt. She and Phemie and Sandy are taught to have a reverence for this book. They repeat the Creed along with me, and then kiss the prayer-book. Lady Wallace and Miss Susie Dunlop drank tea with us, and they and David Cuninghame, who had dined, and Mr. Nairne supped with us. I did some more of the *Letter to Lord Braxfield*. It was solemn writing. Phemie said today, "Christ is just like GOD." Said Veronica: "He's a part of GOD." Very well. π.

MONDAY 24 APRIL. (Writing on Friday the 28.) Was awaked with a card from Dr. Webster that Lord President had fixed this day for us to dine with him at Arniston; that we must not disappoint him, and that the Doctor would call on me with a post-chaise at half past eleven. I was somewhat muddy from having drank strong port negus overnight, but I shook off indolence and prepared myself for a scene which I had for a considerable time wished to realize. I prayed to GOD to bless a reconciliation this day with an old friend of our family. Luckily my toe had healed so much as to be very easy. I dressed myself in my Chester coat and waistcoat, and got into as good a frame as I could wish. At twelve Dr. Webster was (writing on Monday 1 May) at the head of our court, and away we drove most comfortably. It was a pleasing, clear, mild day, and my mind was gentle. As this was a scene of some importance, I shall be at pains to write it down minutely and well.

I had not been at Arniston for seven years. I observed a change to the better whenever [6] we approached it. We got there about half an hour after two. I entered the threshold with some agitation, wish-

---

meet his own deadline: the Circuit Court sat down on 27 April and the pamphlet was published on 8 May.

[6] As soon as: a Scotticism.

ing that the first meeting between the President and me were over. He was out an airing. Dr. Webster and I sat for some time in the old dining-room by ourselves, looking into Arnot's *History of Edinburgh.* Then came Mr. Goldie, the Minister of Temple, who did not say much. Then came Sheriff Cockburn, and then old Sheriff Dundas, who was staying at Arniston. Dempster once observed to me with approbation that the Arniston family all stick together and support one another. At length entered the President, swaggering in a suit of light grey cloth with mother-of-pearl buttons. He took me by the hand and asked me how all was at home, and the awkwardness was nothing like what I apprehended. Then came his amiable son, who had been out with him, and he and I met very agreeably. The President went and put on clean linen, and then returned to us. He talked away with his usual flow of animal spirits; arraigned the judgement of the Court of Session finding themselves not competent to review a sentence of the justices and commissioners adjudging a man to be a recruit. "And why?" said he. "Because Sir Michael Malcolm, one of the justices, was Kennet's friend (Kennet acknowledged to me afterwards he believed they were in the wrong); and because the man came from the Mearns,[7] where Monboddo was connected." In this last reason he was mistaken. For Monboddo had no connexion with the parties. It proved to me that he is in the habit of abusing Monboddo for partiality, as Monboddo does him; nay, that he does not spare better friends among his brethren when they differ from his opinion even in his absence. He took out of his pocket-book the copy of a letter from Mr. Dunning to Sir Adam Fergusson assuring him that a review of such adjudications as recruits was never doubted of in England.

We waited dinner till past four o'clock for Sir Archibald Hope, who then came from the hunting. At dinner the President sat at the head of his table, I on his right hand, and Dr. Webster on his left. The dinner as usual was substantially good. I eat heartily as his Lordship did; and he soon called for a glass of white wine and had Dr. Webster and me to join him. Many a hearty hob and nob there was. I was cheerful but guarded. My wife cautioned me not to drink. For she said that would spoil all. However, the claret was admirable; and as the grave yet pleasing satisfaction of reconciliation so engaged my mind that wine did not affect me quickly, I drank freely of it but not to excess. The President drank port and water, only tasting the claret to be sensible that it was good. He addressed a great deal of his discourse to me, and from time to time as he chuckled, shook hands with me. He repeated a lively thought of mine in a paper for Sir Alexander Dick about Lord Abercorn's

[7] Kincardineshire.

horse being in quest of prescription in Duddingston Loch, a thought which must have been told him, for my paper was never before the Inner House.[8] He told how, when Charles Erskine said in the General Assembly that he was a Presbyterian, but according to law, my grandfather said, "Moderator, I was a Presbyterian when it was against law"; [9] applauded my grandfather's spirit, and cried, "Eh, Old James!" But his address was complete in one instance. He cried, "Come, I'll fill a bumper to my worthy old friend, Affleck. Here's to him, honest man. Long may he keep you, James, from being laird." A bumper went round. Here was a compliment paid to my father, to *the present* representative of our family, after having done honour to *the past*. But that *the future* might, as he supposed, be pleased with the prospect of succession and see that his Lordship would be equally friendly with him, he jogged me and whispered, "It won't do long." He said to me, "I shall be happy to see you here whenever you are at leisure." There was much merriment, and everybody seemed pleased. I was lucky enough, without forwardness but from the neglect of everyone else, to beg leave that his right-hand neighbour might be allowed an extraordinary toast: a bumper to Mrs. Dundas. She was at London and Miss Dundas, her daughter, with her. After he had said, "I'll give you but one bottle more," and in that bottle we had drank to the roof-tree of Arniston, he cried, "Come, I'll have one other bottle more to all your roof-trees"; and we had it. Dr. Webster told me we had two bottles each. I was gladdened, not intoxicated. When going away, the

[8] There had been a dispute of long standing between Sir Alexander and Lord Abercorn over Duddingston Loch, which was bounded partly by Prestonfield, Sir Alexander's property, and partly by Duddingston, which belonged to Lord Abercorn. Various charters granted the loch to Sir Alexander, with the reservation that Lord Abercorn had the right of pasturing and watering his horses and cattle on the shore adjacent to his own property. On 16 November 1769 Sir Alexander petitioned the Court of Session to have definite boundaries set for the loch, a right which Lord Abercorn challenged on the ground that Sir Alexander had a right only to the water itself, and that the boundaries must be allowed to fluctuate. Judgement was pronounced in favour of Sir Alexander. In a letter to him, written in London, 3 October 1769, Boswell promises to send "Answers to Lord Abercorn," presumably the document in question. No copy of it has been found. He may have suggested in it that one of Lord Abercorn's horses, a persistent trespasser, was attempting to establish ownership of the loch by unchallenged occupation for certain periods of time.

[9] Episcopacy was re-established in Scotland in 1661. Since Boswell's grandfather was born in 1676 or even a little earlier, he must have had vivid memories of "the Killing Time"—the years at the end of the reign of Charles II when John Graham of Claverhouse and his dragoons were shooting Covenanters on sight in Ayrshire. Richard Cameron, the Covenanting leader, was killed in Auchinleck parish, and probably on the Boswell estate, in 1680. James II granted complete toleration to all his subjects in 1687, but the Presbyterian Church of Scotland was not established by law till 1690.

President shook hands with me and said, "My dear James, nobody wishes you better than I do." And Dr. Webster told me he said to him, "I'm very happy with this meeting."

Thus was a reconciliation at length brought about between the President of the Court of Session, the hereditary friend of our family, and me. It was sincere on my part. For I had forgiven him for some time. What a blessed precept is that of our SAVIOUR to forgive those who have injured us! I have omitted to mention that after dinner he told how he and Sir Lawrence Dundas had been on bad terms for years; how he had resolved there should be an end of it, and had gone to Sir Lawrence at Buxton, saying there had been misunderstandings, and they should now be forgotten; and so all went on well. This was a very good instance of his having done as I was now doing, supposing Sir Lawrence to have been in fault. Dr. Webster and I chatted quietly in the chaise, and got to town about ten. I insisted (writing on Tuesday 2 May) that he should come home with me. He stipulated that he should have first a dish of tea, and that we should drink only one *chopin* [1] bottle of claret after supper. We had tea and then prayers, and then excellent soup and some good dishes. I had no chopin bottles of claret out of the cellar, so set down a Scotch pint. He was resolute, and made one half of it be bottled, and we drank only the other half. I felt myself a little uneasy at the *stomach*. But my *heart* was happy. I thought myself obliged to Dr. Webster's friendly interposition on this occasion. I should have liked to have seen the cards or letters which passed between him and the President about it, as his memory is not accurate; but he had burnt the President's. He told me he had written to the President that Mr. Boswell wished to wait on his Lordship and draw a veil over misunderstandings, and he and I would dine at Arniston any day he pleased next week except Wednesday; that the President had answered he would be exceedingly happy to see us, but that nothing must be mentioned either of past or future. I doubt he did not report it right. However, the President certainly behaved very well in the matter. David Cuninghame had been ill today, and scarcely dined. He supped at Mr. Daniel's and did not come home till after we were in bed.

TUESDAY 25 APRIL. (Writing on Wednesday the 3 of May.) Rose in good health and spirits. Was one of the jury on the service of John Francis Erskine, Esq., [2] as heir of entail in the estate of Alloa, etc. There was a hearty dinner at Walker's. Dr. Webster and I were next one another. It was a joyous afternoon. Old Mar and Mr. William Wemyss, Writer to the

[1] A Scots liquid measure equal to a Scots half-pint, or about an English quart.
[2] "Young Mar."

Signet, and I had some supper at a side-table.[3] Dr. Webster and Mr. David Erskine took none. We five were left sitting long after everybody else. I was strong this afternoon, and imagined that the claret did not make an impression on me. But I grew intoxicated all at once, and was obliged to go home.

WEDNESDAY 26 APRIL. (Writing on Wednesday 3 May.) Had been very ill in the night-time. Continued to be so forenoon, as I recollect. But I have no distinct remembrance of this day. Miss Mackye and Miss Dunmore played at *vingt-et-un* and supped with us. I drank tea at my father's. But could not get him by himself to mention my having been at Arniston. Commissioner Cochrane came and brought us letters from my brother David come to Paris. Joyful news.

THURSDAY 27 APRIL. (Writing on Wednesday 3 May.) I have no distinct recollection of this day. I finished my *Letter to Lord Braxfield* either yesterday or today, and read it to Mr. Nairne, who was much pleased with it in general, but suggested some judicious hints which made me leave out parts of it. Mr. David Erskine, seeing me from his window this afternoon, would have me to come in, and he and I and another gentleman drank two bottles of claret. I was in excellent spirits. I said to Nairne that if I had a pamphlet to write every day, I should be happy. David Cuninghame had dined with us. I drank tea with him at Old Lady Wallace's. I had been at my father's today and told him of my having been at Arniston, which pleased him much.

FRIDAY 28 APRIL. (Writing on Friday 5 May.) My wife and I and David Cuninghame dined at my father's; Dr. Gillespie and Mrs. Gillespie there. After tea my wife and I had the chariot to town, as it rained. David Cuninghame and Mr. Daniel supped with us. I was very cheerful. My *Letter to Lord Braxfield* went to the press today. I employed Mr. Adam Neill to print it, as I might be suspected for the author had Mr. Donaldson been the printer.

SATURDAY 29 APRIL. (Writing on Friday 5 May.) Worthy Grange had returned last night. He breakfasted with us today. I got twenty-four pages of my *Letter to Lord Braxfield* in print, and was much pleased with the spirit and expression, as was Grange. I had felt a little uneasiness from thinking that it would perhaps give pain to Lord Kames, whose improprieties and parsimony on the circuits it pointed out keenly; [4] and this

---

[3] As explained above (27 December 1779), "Old Mar" was John Francis Erskine's father, but the entailed estate to which John Francis Erskine succeeded had been held by his mother, daughter of the forfeited Earl of Mar. John Francis Erskine was later (1824) restored to the earldom of Mar.

[4] "Far from the Bench of the High Court of Justiciary be the vulgar familiar phrase; but farther still be that 'foolish jesting' which is so incompatible with the solemn busi-

morning I had a letter from good Mr. William Nairne suggesting the same humane scruple. Grange however thought that Lord Kames would not feel the censure; and I thought that if he should, he deserved it. So I resolved to go on. My wife and I, our daughters, and Sandy and David Cuninghame dined and drank tea at Prestonfield. A beautiful day. Worthy Sir Alexander called himself and took us all in his coach, except David Cuninghame, who rode. He and Grange and Mr. James Baillie supped with us.

SUNDAY 30 APRIL. (Writing on Friday 5 May.) Was at the New Church in the forenoon and heard a Mr. Macaulay (I think), a preacher.[5] Dr. Webster dined with us, and I gave him the half of the pint bottle of claret which we left on Monday night. It rained hard in the afternoon, so I stayed at home. Read one of Ogden's sermons, and heard the children say divine lessons very agreeably. My mind was full of my *Letter to Lord Braxfield*, the whole of which I had now in print. D. Cuninghame dined and supped out. π.

MONDAY 1 MAY. (Writing on Friday the fifth.) Mr. Neill, the printer, had suggested that if my *Letter to Lord Braxfield* was not entered in Stationers' Hall, it would be reprinted in newspapers. So I determined not to publish till that was done. I thought first of sending nine copies by the fly.[6] But I thought it safest to send them by post under Mr. Strahan's cover, which I did this night. Poor little Jamie was taken ill yesterday afternoon with a severe vomiting and purging during his teething, and continued to be ill all this day. His mother and I were in great uneasiness about him. David Cuninghame and Miss Susie Dunlop dined with us. I drank tea at my father's. David Cuninghame supped at Dr. Young's. As he was to set out early next morning in the fly, I sat up and drank a little port with him, and bid him farewell.

TUESDAY 2 MAY. (Writing on Friday the fifth.) I intended to have dined at my father's. But Commissioner Cochrane came and insisted I should go out with him in his chaise and dine with him. I did so. My

---

ness of the court, and would be so offensive in any of its judges.... The public purse for the expense of the circuits will afford no excuse for a scanty penurious appearance. The Lords of Justiciary should not contract their travelling equipage into that of a couple of private gentlemen on a jaunt of pleasure, but should remember that it is the train of a court, composed of different members" (*Letter to Lord Braxfield*, p. 25). Kames is not mentioned by name.

[5] That is, one licensed to preach, but not the settled minister of a parish.

[6] Under the Copyright Act of 1709, nine copies of the book were to be deposited on its registration in Stationers' Hall, these copies to be delivered on demand to the libraries of the British Museum, the Faculty of Advocates, Sion College, and the universities of Oxford, Cambridge, Edinburgh, Glasgow, St. Andrews, and Aberdeen.

strong spirits kept me quite firm. Yet I began to tire of this tête-à-tête. Last night (I think) my father made me such a family speech as he has not done since his second marriage. He said, "You know all my study (or scheme) is to leave a good estate to you." He talked of the necessity of good management, and when I told him that I was now convinced of that and acted accordingly, he said, "I wish you could get your wife to think in that way." I saw that means had been used to prejudice him against her. And I assured him upon my honour that nobody was more economical than she was. I spoke strongly to him on this head. For it vexed me to find that he entertained a suspicion against her which she so little deserved. In the evening John Webster sent that if I was at home, he would eat an egg with me. I received him. But I was not delighted (as Dr. Johnson says) with his uncultivated style of conversation. Yesterday and today I wrote several letters with good spirit. I sent Dr. Johnson my *Letter to Lord Braxfield*, to show him my mind was not languid; and I begged he would review it for my private satisfaction. Mr. James Norris, Lady Dick's nephew, now a bold seaman, and little John Dick drank tea with us.

WEDNESDAY 3 MAY. (Writing on Saturday the 6th.) Little Jamie was pretty well again this morning, thank GOD. I had worthy Grange to accompany me to the Quakers' Meeting in Peebles Wynd, that I might revive agreeable mild religious impressions which I had here in company with my dear mother, I believe twenty years ago. Two women from London preached, and one man from Newcastle preached and prayed. But none of them had a pleasing manner. Sandy and I dined at my father's. Nobody there. My father was very dull.

THURSDAY 4 MAY. (Writing on Saturday the 6th.) Was still in most excellent spirits. Breakfasted with Lady Colville and read her some notes of Dr. Johnson's conversation in Edinburgh. Walked with her in the garden. Lady Anne was ill. Grange and I walked out and dined at Prestonfield. A charming forenoon. Mr. Butler, Lady Dick's brother, whom Sir Alexander (after the famous Admiral Smith) calls "Tom of ten thousand," was there.[7] We drank about a bottle of port apiece, and were hearty. Had the coach to town. Miss Mackye and Miss Dunmore played *vingt-et-un* and supped with us. Veronica could now play *vingt-et-un*.

FRIDAY 5 MAY. (Writing on Tuesday the 9th.) Drank tea at my father's. He was dull. Messieurs Maclaurin, David Erskine, Charles Brown,

[7] Thomas Smith, at that time a lieutenant, had in December 1728 compelled a French captain at Plymouth to haul down his pennant in passing the British colours. He was dismissed from the Navy for exceeding his instructions, but was almost immediately restored. Popular report greatly exaggerated the incident and gave Smith more fame than he deserved.

Mr. and Mrs. Mitchelson, and Miss Cuninghame of Bonnington supped with us. We had whist and brag before supper. I lost a little, but it did not disturb me. I was in a good firm frame. We (the men) sat till three in the morning drinking claret. I was not a bit the worse for it.

SATURDAY 6 MAY. (Writing on Tuesday the 9th.) Little Jamie pronounced *papa* on Wednesday last, and continues to do it. My toe is never well yet, but pretty easy. This morning my son Sandy was made very happy with the present of a little Shetland sheltie from Mrs. Mitchelson, which she got from Mr. Honeyman of Graemsay. He rode on it today, forenoon and afternoon. Lieutenant Butler, Lady Dick's brother, and more of my friends from Prestonfield, Messrs. Daniel and Stokes, my last travelling-companions from Carlisle, and worthy Grange dined and drank tea, except Gillespie and Norris. All was hearty and well.

SUNDAY 7 MAY. (Writing on Tuesday the 16.) Was at the New Church in the forenoon. My father was there. I do not remember the name of the minister who preached. My wife was not well and stayed at home. It rained so in the afternoon I stayed at home. The children said divine lessons agreeably.

MONDAY 8 MAY. (Writing on Tuesday the 16.) My *Letter to Lord Braxfield* was published. I kept out of the way. Went with the children to Lauriston,[8] where they all three rode on Sandy's sheltie. Sandy himself rode boldly. My daughters and I were invited by the Reverend Dr. Bell into his garden, which was very pleasant. We then walked to Lady Colville's, where they were happy. Balbarton, Grange, and Mr. Lawrie dined with us. I am from this day to mark Mr. Lawrie's dining or supping with us, because he is no longer like one of my family since having a wife and house of his own. My wife and I played cards and supped at Mr. S. Mitchelson's, Junior, with Mr. David Erskine, etc. Mr. Charles Brown had read part of the *Letter to Lord Braxfield,* and quoted parts of it. The company agreed that the author was in the right. I was not charged with it.

TUESDAY 9 MAY. (Writing on Tuesday the 16.) Yesterday the weather was delightful. It was (writing on Wednesday 17 May) also so today. Sandy rode all the way to Prestonfield, James Clark, my servant, leading his sheltie and walking by him. I walked all the way, happy to see him so; and Grange went almost to the avenue to give us a convoy. Sir Alexander and I had a pleasing walk in the garden, and he obligingly asked me to send the sheltie to run on his grass. I accepted of the kind offer. The Rev. Mr. Bennet, whom I met today for the first time since his return from London and Bath, and Robert Gillespie dined. Butler and Norris also were still with the Knight. I drank just enough to warm me. It rained hard

---

[8] A district to the south of Portsburgh and the Grassmarket, containing open fields.

in the afternoon and Sandy and I had the chaise to town, and the sheltie was left.

WEDNESDAY 10 MAY. (Writing on Wednesday the 17). Two men were to be hanged in the Grassmarket today: Dalgleish for robbery, Donaldson for shop-breaking. I felt a strange inclination to go and see the execution as usual. But I resolved to avoid it, as it always makes me gloomy for some time after. I therefore went out and dined at my father's. Dr. Webster happened to be there. We did not get wine enough. So I settled to sup with him, which I did. But he had no claret, so we did not indulge liberally.

THURSDAY 11 MAY. (Writing on Wednesday the 17.) I had gone last night to the Justiciary Office by way of looking the record for the authenticity of a trial at Glasgow mentioned in my *Letter to Lord Braxfield.* I knew it to be authentic, as Mr. Nairne was my authority, but I wished to see the particulars and hear what the clerks said of the pamphlet. I was mentioned as one of the authors or persons supposed to be the writer. I denied it, as a man is entitled to do, as to deny his being at home, because denying is the only mode of concealing what a man has a right to conceal. Mr. Crosbie, Mr. Hugo Arnot, and the Hon. Henry Erskine were also mentioned. The author was allowed to be well-informed. I asked if Gilbert Stuart could have done it. Mr. Norris said, "Give him (G. Stuart) the materials, he could write it." I asked if he was much acquainted with any of the Clerks of Justiciary. This forenoon I called on Crosbie and introduced the *Letter*. I was surprised to find he had not seen it, but he said he heard it was very severe. I paid a visit to the Miss Ords, and then to Young Lady Wallace, whose indelicate effrontery made her beauty affect me little. I had first of all paid a visit with my wife to Lady Maxwell of Pollok at Walker's Hotel. Was engaged to dine with Lady Colville. Had a good family dinner, no company there; walked in the garden and stayed to tea.

FRIDAY 12 MAY. (Writing on Wednesday the 17.) Called on Sir William Forbes at his counting-house. Had a little social tête-à-tête with him. He spoke of the *Letter to Lord Braxfield*, and asked me if I was not the author. I denied it even to him, though I scrupled a little, considering my confidential regard for him. But I wished to be concealed, at least for some time, as much as possible. He seemed to like the *Letter* much. Mr. Daniel gave a dinner today at Princes Street Coffee-house to Grange and me and Messieurs Butler and Norris, M. Derosey,[8a] a Swede, and a Mr. Cooke. We

---

[8a] Gideon Herman de Rogier (1738–1814), physician (M.D. in this year from Uppsala). He had come to England in 1777 as tutor to two young Swedes, who spent some time in London, Oxford, and Edinburgh. At Edinburgh Rogier himself studied medicine and botany in Edinburgh University. His family was of French-Huguenot extraction,

were exceedingly jovial. Lady Maxwell of Pollok, her brother-in-law Mr. Cathcart, and Mr. David Steuart, her husband's cousin, and Grange supped with us. I was heated with my drinking at dinner, but conducted myself very well. Only played too keenly at brag. Lost a little, which always vexes me more or less. Did not drink to excess after supper. This was an entertainment truly of duty, from respect to the Pollok family and particularly Mrs. Montgomerie of Lainshaw.[9] David Steuart praised the *Letter to Lord Braxfield* very much. Grange was afraid I would discover myself, I was so warm. He, Mr. Nairne, Mr. Lawrie, and Mr. Neill, the printer, only knew it in Scotland.

SATURDAY 13 MAY. (Writing on Thursday the 18.) Was very ill when I awaked. But considered that I had done no great harm, and my intoxication was partly owing to duty. Got up to dinner, and then took my daughters and Sandy to drink tea at my father's. They were but little encouraged. Was much hurt that it was not in my power to let Hallglenmuir have a loan from me of twenty guineas.

SUNDAY 14 MAY. (Writing on Thursday the 18.) Called on Mr. Wallace, Sheriff of Ayrshire, and heard an account of the Precognition against Matthew Hay, whose trial was to come on at Ayr soon and was an interesting question.[1] My wife and I were at the New Church in the forenoon and heard Mr. Finlayson, a minister from Shetland, who preached very well. My father was there. Dr. Webster dined with us. I was at the New Church in the afternoon and heard Mr. Walker. My wife took my daughters and Sandy to a low seat, as they are not welcome to my father's seat. They said divine lessons well in the evening. My wife and I and they walked out and paid a visit to Lady Colville. It was a sweet evening.

MONDAY 15 MAY. (Writing on Monday the 22.) Received a card that my affectionate uncle, Dr. Boswell, died this morning. Though he had been almost dead for more than a year, I was struck with the actual event. Though Death over him "his dart shook but delayed to strike," [2] the *stroke* was affecting when it really happened. One day before this, I had walked along the New Bridge with Principal Robertson, who told me he had read the *Letter to Lord Braxfield*, and that it would

---

and the name retained its original French pronunciation. Boswell, who had a good ear, seems very far off here, but the fact is that English spelling has no unambiguous way of indicating the sound of French *gi.*

[9] Mrs. Montgomerie of Lainshaw, widow of Mrs. Boswell's brother, James Montgomerie of Lainshaw, was Lady Maxwell's sister-in-law.

[1] See below, 8 and 9 September 1780.

[2] *Paradise Lost,* xi. 491–493:

And over them triumphant Death his dart
Shook, but delayed to strike, though oft invoked
With vows, as their chief good, and final hope.

do good, for it would show the judges they are not above censure. He thought it must be written by a man of business, well acquainted with the Court. I mentioned Gilbert Stuart. He said it had not the *bounce* of his style. I suppose Robertson has felt it like a boxer's head thump the pit of his stomach.[3] "It is a plain style," said he. "But very well written," said I. He agreed. I then met Crosbie, and wondered to find he had not yet seen it. But from what he had heard of it he said, "I take it to be written by one of the old Clerks of Justiciary." Robert Auld was then mentioned, either by him or me. Grange dined with us; and then I went and called on Mr. Robert Boswell, whom I found in submissive tranquillity. Mr. George Wallace had in a very friendly manner offered me a loan of fifty pounds. He had called some time ago (I know not if I have marked it) to put me in mind of it, and to ask when I would have it. I said at Whitsunday. I called on him this forenoon, before I heard of the Doctor's death. But he had first called on me. I sent to him to beg he would drink tea with me. He came with the money in his pocket, and I gave him my bill. His conversation, full both of facts in common life and learning, did me good. In the forenoon I had been at Sir W. F. & Co.'s counting-house, where was Dr. Blair. Hunter, I thought to induce me to own it, said the *Letter to Lord Braxfield* was well spoken of. I said nothing; for Sir William Forbes had before that again asked me if I was the author, and I had again denied it. I went in the evening to the Meadow with intention to visit my father. But it was too late. Mr. George Wallace accompanied me. We met Harry Erskine, who asked me if I had seen the *Letter to Lord Braxfield.* I told him I had, and asked him his opinion of it. He said, "Very well." "Very well!" said I. "It is capital." I had before this denied it to George Wallace. He asked Harry *who* was the author? He said he did not know. I looked him steadily in the face and said, "Do you *really* not know?" He denied again, but looked embarrassed, and said, "I know Lord Kames will believe I wrote it, and I must go and assure him I did not; for some of the things mentioned in it happened when I was with him." "Oho!" said I. Said he: "John Swinton's penetration has found out that Lord Hailes wrote it." "Well," said I, "do you know, I was going to mention Lord Hailes. It is very like him. There is a seriousness and an anxiety about the dignity of the Court which he has." "Yes," said Harry, "and he has not the faults pointed out in it." Said I: "The only passage

[3] Stuart, a brilliant but violent and dissipated man, had been in 1779 an unsuccessful candidate for the Professorship of Public Law in the University of Edinburgh. He believed his failure to have been due to Robertson, whom he went out of his way to attack in his *Observations concerning the Public Law and the Constitutional History of Scotland*, 1779 ("an author of elegant talents, and of great industry, but who is nowhere profound," p. 175).

not like him is that where the independency of juries is asserted.[4] But he may have written that to disguise himself." Said George: "Lord Hailes *can* write in a lively style." "Do you know," said I, "Mr. Erskine, they say that it is written by Robert Auld and seasoned by you"; and when we parted I said, "Good-night; Auld and Erskine, Beaumont and Fletcher." I had some scruple as to all this disguise. Yet I thought it allowable, and it was very entertaining.

TUESDAY 16 MAY. (Writing on Tuesday the 23.) Called at my father's in the forenoon. He did not seem to be much affected with his brother's death. I wrote a good deal of *The Hypochondriack* No. 32,[5] but could not be ready for the post. Grange and Mr. Lawrie dined with us.

WEDNESDAY 17 MAY. (Writing on Tuesday the 23.) My father and Lady Auchinleck paid us a short visit in the forenoon and heard Veronica play on the harpsichord. They had called some forenoons ago when my wife and children were out. Though my father was not at all cordial, I was glad to see him again under my roof. He did not take much notice of Veronica. I went out and dined with him today. Mr. Stobie, who was in town in his way to Auchinleck, was there. My father was little moved with his brother's death. Indeed it was a circumstance rather to be wished. Yet natural affection, and its being so near a *memento mori* to himself, might, I should have thought, have made it more affecting to him. I thought at dinner how different it would have been had his brother *Johnnie* died when they were both boys at Auchinleck. ————.[6]

THURSDAY 18 MAY. (Writing on Tuesday the 23.) I should have mention that James Clark, my servant whom I kept on at last Martinmas from

[4] "But is there not, my Lord, too often an intention discovered by the Bench, to direct and control the jury? While points of law or form are agitated in the course of a trial, it is the part of the judges to give full light and instruction to the jury. But ought the judges to discover to the jury the opinion which they have formed as to the fact? And after the jury have returned a verdict upon their great oath, have the judges any right to censure that verdict because the jury have not entertained the same notions of the nature of evidence in general, or of the evidence upon that trial in particular, that the judges have done? . . . All encroachments of one department of administration upon another, whether in the state or in courts of judicature, should be steadily resisted" (*Letter to Lord Braxfield*, pp. 16–18).

[5] Yet another on drinking: "Writing upon drinking is in one respect, I think, like drinking itself: one goes on imperceptibly, without knowing where to stop; and as one calls for the other bottle to his friends, I press the other paper upon my readers. Happy should I be could I flatter myself that this paper will be received with as hearty a satisfaction as is generally felt upon the opening of an additional bottle" (*The Hypochondriack*, No. 32).

[6] This dash at the end of an entry, which now begins to appear occasionally in the MS., is clearly a private symbol, probably of the same nature as the asterisk, π, and V, which Boswell had previously employed.

humanity, behaved still worse by being quite idle, so that I could keep him no longer. He took a public house, so that on Tuesday he left me, with a good ...

[EDITORIAL NOTE: Two pages, containing the rest of the entry for 18, all of 19, and the beginning of 20 May, have been removed at this point. The fragmentary sentence with which the entry for 20 May now begins may be completed in some such form as, "George Wallace and I went to Prestonfield."]

[SATURDAY 20 MAY.] ... Sandy accompanying us. He was happy to ride his sheltie. Lady Elizabeth Lindsay, a fine little creature, was there. We were social after dinner; Robert Gillespie, Samuel Mitchelson, Junior, there, as Captain Butler and little Norris were to set out on Monday. Mitchelson carried Sandy and me to town in his chaise, and sent it home with us. I have always found him very obliging, so that I regret the petulance of his manner and there being no cordiality between him and me. He commended the *Letter to Lord Braxfield* after dinner, and said, "I hear it was written by Mr. James Boswell." "He denies it," said George Wallace, and told how Harry Erskine had been embarrassed when charged with it. Old Erskine of Mar had been with me in the forenoon and talked of it, though he had not seen it. He controverted the doctrine which he was told was in it as to the independency of juries. He and Grange and Mr. George Wallace supped with us. We were exceedingly cheerful. Mar told a great many stories. Grange doubted of their perfect authenticity.

SUNDAY 21 MAY. (Writing on Thursday the 25.) I had long intended to go to the Glassite Meeting-house and hear Robert Boswell preach.[7] I chose this day, as I fancied there might perhaps be something of a funeral sermon on Dr. Boswell. Grange went with me. Mr. Lawrie showed us to the gallery. He sat in view. Grange and I were concealed. It is, I believe, more than twenty years since I was in this meeting-house, when my mind was tender and sore with religious terrors. I was pleased to find that they were not in the slightest degree renewed today. We were disappointed, for Robert did not preach. A man whom I did not know and John Young, a writer, preached. The latter harangued with a clear, strong voice and a fluency of words. But he uttered strange doctrine. He in explicit terms asserted predestination and election, and inculcated that his hearers should not only not imagine that anything they could do to distinguish

[7] Earlier in the journal Boswell had described the doctrines of the Glassite sect and argued them with Robert Boswell (10 April 1777). They are succinctly formulated in the inscription on the tombstone of Robert Sandeman (uncle to Robert Boswell's wife): "The bare death of Jesus Christ, without a thought or deed on the part of a man, is sufficient to present the chief of sinners spotless before God."

them from the most profligate had the least influence in obtaining their salvation, but if they had even a wish to be better, that they might recommend themselves to GOD, they were departing from the Christian faith. What a wretched system is this which makes us absolute machines, and destroys the connexion between morality and religion, taking away from us the hopes and fears of a future state, where we are to be judged according to our conduct in this life, under the benign influence of the propitiation offered up by Jesus Christ. The Glassites indeed require morality as an *evidence* of faith. But if a man is persuaded that it is to have no *effect*, he will act foolishly if he does not gratify every passion so far as he can do it with safety. I thought that such *teaching* as I heard today should not be allowed. The only circumstance in this meeting not of a piece with their dreary creed was very fine singing in parts. It reminded me of a choir of monks or nuns. I could not but reflect with some uneasiness on the state of uncertainty which all men of all religions must be in as to their happiness after death; since, whether it depends on *election* or on *pious merit*, we cannot *know* with *confidence* that *we* are of the blessed number. I comfort myself with the notion that in progress of time there will be universal felicity. Grange dined with us between sermons, and he went to the New Church and heard Dr. Blair preach beautifully and rationally. My wife and Sandy and I were in my father's seat. He had not been in church today. Miss McAdam of Craigengillan and Miss Ellie Ritchie and Grange drank tea with us. The children said divine lessons in presence of Grange. He and I walked down to the Abbey of Holyrood House, and in the garden near it, which was once Dr. Alston's botanical garden. I was in excellent health and spirits. ———.

MONDAY 22 MAY. (Writing on Thursday the 25.) Dr. Gillespie and his brother George, surgeon to the Fourth or King's Own, Commissioner Cochrane, and Robert Syme, Junior, dined with us. I communicated to Syme my being the author of the *Letter to Lord Braxfield*, in order to employ him in advertising a meeting of jurymen on the 1 of August next, to take it under their serious consideration and assert their rights and privileges. This advertisement I thought would promote the sale much, and perhaps a meeting might really be held. Letters (post-paid) addressed *To the Secretary of the Jury Association at Edinburgh* were to have due attention paid them. Clerk Matthew was to be told to deliver any that should come, to Mr. Syme; and I thought there was a chance of good amusement.[8] The Commissioner did not stay tea. After tea Dr. Gillespie

---

[8] "There was, however, no meeting, nor any letter sent, yet it was thought to be serious, and quickened the sale of the *Letter*. Robert Syme, Junior, and I wrote against and for the meeting in the *Mercury*."—BOSWELL. Three letters, the first and third signed "Lelius" (by Boswell) and the second "An Enemy to Faction" (Syme) appeared 8, 17,

and I walked out to my father's. I sat awhile. But he said little tonight, and when both his women and Doctor are present, I am very guarded. The Doctor tonight hinted to me, as he had done (writing 26 May) once before, that he wished my father would give up Auchinleck to me altogether. I protested against it, and declared upon my honour I never would go to it upon these terms. I was aware of his interested views, and I disliked the taking possession of another man's place in his own time. Dr. Gillespie spoke much in favour of Lady Auchinleck's great care of my father. I was prudent.

TUESDAY 23 MAY. (Writing on Monday the 29.) Dined at my father's, Commissioner Cochrane there. My wife and I played cards and supped at Dr. Young's. I was in perfect good spirits.

WEDNESDAY 24 MAY. (Writing on Monday the 29.) Robert Syme, Junior, dined with us. I drank some brandy and port, and was restless. Walked out to Portsburgh and drank some whisky, and indulged with a coarse but safe companion. Felt myself debased, and was cured.[9] Called on Grange, who had been drinking after dinner and was in joyous spirits. Went with him to a tavern in the Old Post House Stairs, and supped and was merry with John Graeme, James Baillie, George Kirkpatrick, and Johnston, a wine-merchant.

[EDITORIAL NOTE: Two pages, containing the entries for 25–27 May, have been removed.]

SUNDAY 28 MAY. (Writing on Tuesday the 30.) Grange and I made another trial to hear Robert Boswell in the Glassite Meeting-house. But he was gone to preach at Leith. We however stayed and heard one sermon by the same man who preached last Sunday, before John Young. We were better pleased with his mild, serious manner, though his *Antinomian* doctrine was the same. I received this morning a letter from my brother David, which I opened and read in the Glassite Meeting-house. It announced his arrival in London. It was comfortable to think he was again in Britain, and no sea between us. Grange and I walked round the Calton Hill. Miss Susie Dunlop dined with us. I stayed at home in the afternoon and read all Dr. Ogden's sermons on the Christian articles. I called at

---

and 26 July in the *Caledonian Mercury*. Boswell resorts to mystification in the first, where he assumes that the *Letter to Lord Braxfield* is "a piece of *English manufacture out of Scotch materials*," but turns to direct puffery in the third: "Your correspondent asks, what are the privileges of jurymen? I refer him to the *Letter to Lord Braxfield*, where they are well defined, and of which every juryman, upon every trial, should have a copy in his pocket as a *talisman* to guard him against usurpation."

[9] This passage, from the comma in the preceding sentence, has been inked out by Boswell.

my father's in the evening. I had the day before received a letter from Hallglenmuir dated *on board* at Greenock, going abroad on account of his debt. I was hurt to think of a good obliging parish laird being thus removed.[1] Sir James Colquhoun, Dr. and Mrs. Grant, Rev. Messieurs Donald Macqueen and Thomas Smith, and Grange were with us at night. We had *prayers*, as our phrase is: that is, a prayer by Mr. Smith, and then a Sunday's supper.

MONDAY 29 MAY. (Writing on Friday 9 June.) Lord Loudoun had arrived from London yesterday to hold consultations on the ruinous state of his affairs.[2] I had alwise [2a] been obligingly treated by him, and was very desirous to show my gratitude in his distress. I called for his Lordship last night, and having missed him, wrote a note begging the honour of his company at supper this evening. He agreed to come. I had an application today to appear as counsel for certain feuars in the Gorbals [3] of Glasgow against the Rev. Mr. Anderson, their minister, a General Assembly cause. My difficulty was that he was John Stobie's brother-in-law. My wife wisely suggested I should consult my father. So I went to him, he having this day come to his house in Adams's Square. As Anderson had not employed me, he was, according to his old sagacity, for my taking the other side; so I agreed. Lord Loudoun and Mr. John Hunter supped with us. My Lord kept up an appearance of cheerfulness wonderfully well. I showed him the greatest respect. We were sober.

TUESDAY 30 MAY. (Writing on Friday 9 June.) Pleaded in the General Assembly for the people of Biggar against the patron very well.[4] Did not

---

[1] Hallglenmuir described his action as being "entirely with a view to serve my personal creditors," as he hoped to delay the sale of his land until "things take a turn and land can be sold at its value; in that case they will be paid every shilling." Boswell endorsed the letter, "Dated at Greenock, on board and under sail. That he is gone abroad on account of his debt. Hoping I will do what I can for my absent friend, that he may return and end his days in his native country." And, added at a later date, "N.B. he died abroad."

[2] The Loudoun papers in the Huntington Library contain masses of documents dealing with Loudoun's efforts to straighten out his affairs, which had apparently been pretty much left in the hands of his mother, who died on 5 or 6 April 1779 in her ninety-fifth year. (See above, 2 November 1778.) He put his estate under trustees for the benefit of his creditors, and died in 1782. Sorn Castle, the dower-house in which Boswell had paid his last visit to the old Countess, was sold in that same year.

[2a] See above, 24 March 1780 n. 10.

[3] The Gorbals is an ecclesiastical district of Glasgow (see below, 3 June 1780).

[4] A typical case of the struggle of the "Moderate" party in the Church to uphold lay patronage and of the "Popular" party to resist it (see above, 19 September 1778). Lady Elphinstone, the patroness, had presented Robert Pearson, a probationer, to the church at Biggar. In order for the settlement to be legal, the people, through the elders and heads of families, had to subscribe to a "call," which in this case they

get out till seven. Came home; could not dine, but drank tea and eat bread and butter. Was happy with my dear wife. Supped at Lord Traquair's; Commissioner Clerk,[5] etc., there. Played a rubber at whist. Had resolved never again to play deeper than a shilling a game. Won a trifle. Was gay and satisfied.

WEDNESDAY 31 MAY. (Writing on Friday 9 June.) Dined at Mr. John Hunter's with Lord Loudoun. We were cheerful and drank a good deal. I got home in safety however.

THURSDAY 1 JUNE. (Writing on Friday the 9.) The day passed on, waiting at home in case a cause should be heard.

FRIDAY 2 JUNE. (Writing Friday the 9.) Made an admirable appearance for the people of Fenwick against the patron, the cause for which I waited at home yesterday. John Home told me afterwards it was the best he had ever heard (or seen) at that bar.[6] I dined after it with the Lord Commissioner [7] after seven. Was warmed with wine. Dr. Andrew Hunter carried me to sup at his house, the first time I had been in it. His lady was ill and could not appear. Her sister, the Hon. Miss Napier, was at table, and there were several ministers; psalms and prayers and formal conversation. I was much upon my good behaviour.

SATURDAY 3 JUNE. (Writing on Sunday the 11th.) Pleaded the cause of the feuars of Gorbals against the Rev. Mr. Anderson. Was mild and decent. It turned out a wicked cause on the part of my clients. But *the fact* was concealed from me.[8] I came out and dined cordially with my dear wife, and returned and heard the decision in favour of Mr. Anderson.

---

quietly declined to do. Later the patroness was able to secure the "concurrence" of some of the non-resident land-holders of the parish and of several heads of families. By a close vote (85 to 77) the Assembly upheld the settlement. Henry Erskine was counsel for the patroness.

[5] George (later Sir George) Clerk, Commissioner of Customs.

[6] The same sort of case as that of the people of Biggar, with the same result. The tutors of the young Earl of Glasgow, patron of Fenwick, presented Archibald Reid, a probationer. Not a single person in the parish came to hear his trial sermons, and no one signed the call except the patron's factor. Mr. Reid, when soberly informed by the parish that they were completely unwilling to have him as minister, replied that he should not cease to pray "in spite of all the devices of the devil and his emissaries" that their hearts would be turned to him. Moreover, he shocked the parishioners by alluding to "the great Shepherd and Bishop of souls, who was *not called*, but despised and rejected by the people" (*Scots Magazine*, May 1780, xlii, 276–278). The settlement was upheld, 85 to 67.

[7] George Ramsay, eighth Earl of Dalhousie, was Lord High Commissioner to the General Assembly of the Church of Scotland, 1777–1782.

[8] Mr. Anderson was accused of adultery with one Helen Simpson. The defence maintained that the prosecutors had bribed her with money and drink to sign a paper declaring Anderson to be the father of her children, and that, among the witnesses for

SUNDAY 4 JUNE. (Writing on Sunday the 11th.) Waited on the Lord Commissioner, being earnest to sit in my father's seat in the New Church the last day of its existence, as this week the church was to be demolished in the inside in order to be put into a new form.[9] I fulfilled my purpose, and just seated myself at the foot of it, next to Maclaurin. I meditated curiously on my remembering this seat almost as far back as my memory reaches—of my pious mother sitting at the head of it—of my dreary terrors of hell in it—of my having an *impression* of its being so connected with the other world as to be as permanent. Yet now it was to be removed, and not a vestige of it to be left. A multitude of ideas went through my mind. But my spirits were so gay and my mind so sound that I had no uneasiness, and even wondered that there should ever be such a thing. Maclaurin joined in singing psalms. Religion seemed light and easy and universal. A Dr. Cramond at Yarrow, who had been minister of a dissenting congregation in England and was like an Englishman, preached agreeably enough. I dined with the Lord Commissioner, who has all along shown me an attention which I felt with pleasing gratitude, at least in proportion to the favour. I was for the first time in company with General Mackay, with whom I had a good deal of conversation: upon the merit of his regiment, the Scotch Fusiliers; the advantage of having a good chaplain to attend a regiment; and the pleasure of drinking a little brandy. We agreed very well. I went home after dinner. Miss Susie Dunlop and the Hon. Patrick Boyle drank tea with us, after which he and I paid a visit to my father. In the evening the children said divine lessons.

MONDAY 5 JUNE. (Writing on Monday the 12.) Dined quietly at home. Before dinner shook hands with the Rev. Mr. Anderson at the Cross and assured him that if I had known how bad a cause my clients had against him, I would not have appeared in it. He was satisfied with my candour. Attended the magistrates and drank the King's health.[1] Called on

---

the prosecution, one had been transported for life after a capital conviction and had returned illegally, one was a common prostitute, and one (Helen Simpson's mother) had been heard to declare that if swearing a lie would hang the defender, she would do it. The Assembly dismissed the whole process and "seemed unanimous in expressing in strong terms their disapprobation of the prosecution" (*Scots Magazine*, May 1780, xlii. 278–279).

[9] Johnson had visited this church on Monday, 16 August 1773, and had found it "shamefully dirty" (*Journal of a Tour to the Hebrides*). The New (or High) Church occupied what was once the choir of St. Giles's. In the reconstruction a gallery blocking the east window was to be removed, and the pews, which had been of all shapes and sizes, were to be regularized.

[1] In observance of his birthday, 4 June. "The magistrates gave an elegant collation in the Parliament House to several noblemen and gentlemen, and drank the healths of the King, Queen, Royal Family, Sir George Brydges Rodney [news of whose victory

my father. Heard Sir John Pringle was come. Waited on him. He seemed to be somewhat failed. It was *comfortable* to see him in Edinburgh. But he did not impress me with equal *greatness* as when in Pall Mall. The Rev. Dr. Andrew Hunter, Dr. Findlay at Glasgow, Messrs. James Thomson, Andrew Mitchell, Moody at Perth, and Professor Anderson at Glasgow supped with us. We had prayers before supper. All was decent and well.

[EDITORIAL NOTE: Six pages, containing the entries for 6–11 and the beginning of 12 June, have here been removed. As the journal resumes, Boswell is awaiting the arrival of his brother David.]

[MONDAY 12 JUNE.] . . . today. So would not be from home. About seven in the evening (writing Tuesday the 20) they told me that a gentleman in a chaise at the head of the court wanted to know if I was at home. I said yes, being persuaded it was he. In a little he appeared walking from the eastmost entry in a light grey frock. There was a *little* of the air of John. I received him in the drawing-room. He embraced me with warm agitation and said, "You see me the same affectionate brother as ever"; and he shed some tears. My wife soon came to us, and she was agitated as he was. I was duller. The children came, and he was curiously happy to see them and they him. After a few minutes of desultory conversation, we went to our father's. When we entered the dining-room, he ran to his father, embraced him, much agitated and with tears, and kissed his hand; and then saluted Lady Auchinleck respectfully. He talked with great composure and accuracy, but I thought with formality and what appeared to me affectation. At first I thought his countenance such that I should not have known him. Twelve years and eight months must no doubt make a considerable alteration on a face from nineteen to about thirty-two. But by degrees his likeness appeared again to me. He said he should not have known me. Miss Boswell and Dr. Gillespie came in, and we stayed supper. Our father was placid, and more cheerful than ordinary. We left him a little after ten and walked home. Sat awhile with my wife, and then he went to bed in my little north room. On his arrival we told him that my father's people, not having room for him, had a lodging ready, for which my father was to pay; and we asked him whether he would have that or accept of our small room. He said, "I'll do anything that's agreeable. I want to see you all live in harmony together." At our father's he said, "I think it is more natural for me to live either with my father or my

---

over the French fleet had just been received], etc., during which the City Guard, who were drawn up in the Parliament Square, fired volleys of small arms" (*Edinburgh Advertiser*, 6 June 1780, xxxiii. 358).

brother, and if you please" (to Lady A.) "I will take the room which my brother offers me." She seemed not quite fond of this. But it was so settled. I felt myself under some restraint with him, his manners were so mild and grave and correct, contrasted with the familiarity of Edinburgh.

TUESDAY 13 JUNE. (Writing on Tuesday the 20.) David was polite and orderly at breakfast. The Session sat down today. I was in the House for a little, and had the satisfaction to see my father again on the bench and looking really well. I soon came home. Robert Boswell visited David. Then David and I visited Dr. Webster, Commissioner Cochrane at the custom-house, who did not know David at first, and Robert Boswell's family. We called at Sir W. Forbes and Company's counting-house, where he saw Messrs. Garioch and Hay, who had been in it when he was there. But Sir William was not in, and Mr. Hunter was in the country. We also called at Sir John Pringle's, who was not at home. We dined at my father's; my wife, Balbarton, Balmuto, and Robert Boswell there. My father had asked me to be landlord. For he dined from home, for the first time I believe for a year past, except the day when he removed to his present house, when he dined at Commissioner Cochrane's. He could not refuse a select party at Sir John Pringle's. Balbarton was much pleased with David. After dinner David and I walked to Sir Alexander Dick's, who was ill with an asthmatic complaint and could not attend at Sir John Pringle's to make the fourth survivor of an old club. He was very courteous to David, who was pleased again with Prestonfield, and said it made one like Edinburgh. We walked to town. I left him, I think, at his father's, and went to Sir John Pringle's a little. Then came home and found the Hon. Alexander Gordon sitting with my wife and David. I insisted on his supping, which he did. But David was disgusted at his manner, and showed it with some heat.

[EDITORIAL NOTE: Four pages, containing the entries for 14–17, and perhaps part of that for 13 June, have been removed at this point. The entry for the 15th must have contained some mention of the birth of Elizabeth, Boswell's last child.]

SUNDAY 18 JUNE. (Writing on Friday the 23.) David and I went to the English Chapel in the forenoon. I was happy in a considerable degree. Then called on Lord Monboddo (not at home), then on Lord Kames, whom we found wonderfully well. I was not uneasy to think of the keen reflections pointed at his conduct in my *Letter to Lord Braxfield*, for I thought he deserved them. We saw his lady a little. Then David and I dined calmly at home, Veronica, Phemie, and Sandy with us. All the three, after we had drank tea at my wife's bedside, went with us to our father's (having first said divine lessons in presence of their uncle), and from thence we all went to Broughton and visited M. Dupont and Miss Scott, who rejoiced to see David again. He and I next paid a visit to Sir John Pringle, and then supped at home. Till this day David's manner, which seemed affected, had hurt me somewhat, and I was shocked to a certain degree to find him, as I thought, grown strange. But tonight we sat up and talked with a confidential freedom which pleased me.

MONDAY 19 JUNE. From this day till the 13 September inclusive, I have notes for a part of the time and a journal sufficiently full for the rest, written upon octavo double leaves put up and titled by themselves. In a general view, my mind was rather sickly while I remained at Edinburgh. But I acquired much more tranquillity at Auchinleck, where my brother David and I were from Wednesday the 16 August to Wednesday the 13 September.

[EDITORIAL NOTE: Boswell, as usual after his wife's confinement, goes roving, with the usual acknowledgement and the usual unhappy result ("14 JULY.... In a wild desperation, for last time, Pleasance. 15 JULY.... I came home to tea and had an affecting conversation with wife, having confessed wandering.... 17 JULY.... Mr. Wood called evening").[2] On 28 and 29 June he dictated a law paper he thought well of, and was happy when it drew applause (1 JULY).[3] On 27 July he read for the first time Donald MacNicol's abusive *Remarks on Dr. Samuel Johnson's Journey to the Hebrides* (1779), and the next day consulted Maclaurin as to whether the work was actionable.[4] (His reference to the book in the *Life of Johnson* shows that he believed the real author to be Macpherson.) Maclaurin probably advised against prosecution. In any case, Johnson, on reading MacNicol, merely made the "pleasant observation" that the fellow must be a blockhead to bring out an attack that cost five shillings. "No, Sir, if they had wit, they should have kept pelting me with pamphlets" (*Life of Johnson*, just preceding 18 February 1775).]

SUNDAY 30 JULY. Took salts. Read part of Dr. Clark to renew belief of Supreme Being. Sir J. Pringle and Mr. Nairne sat awhile between sermons. Read a good deal of my London journal in 1762 and 3, and was humbled by my weakness. David and Miss Tait dined. Read Dr. Blair's

---

[2] Encounters of this kind almost certainly explain the mutilation of the journal above, 25 May, 6 and 13 June.

[3] Duff and Mercer v. Justices of the Peace. See below, 29 November 1781.

[4] As an attack on Johnson, not on himself. For example, "I will be bold to affirm, that no man has ever yet seen Dr. Johnson in the act of *feeding*, or beheld the inside of his *cell* in *Fleet Street*, but would think the *feasts of Eskimeaux* or the *cottages of Hottentots* injured by a comparison" (*Remarks*, p. 78).

sermon on GOD's unchangeableness. Took after it as a cure one of Ogden's on prayer.[5] Then children said divine lessons. Grange with me at night.

MONDAY 31 JULY. Rather better. David and I dined at our father's with Sir John Pringle. I was calm, but envied every man not sickly. Took half a glass of wine in water.

TUESDAY 1 AUGUST. Miss Dick and Grange dined. Miss Dick stayed tea. There was no meeting of jurymen.[6] I walked at night to Sir John Pringle's and back again. I was well with him. But the walk made me a little uneasy. David supped out.

WEDNESDAY 2 AUGUST. David dined at Dr. Gillespie's. I went with him at night to father's. I then called on John a little. Had affectionate concern about him. But found him not at all inclined to be well with me. He would not agree to dine with me.

THURSDAY 3 AUGUST. Had headache. Dined with David at Mac-laurin's. Sir John Pringle, Lord Monboddo, etc., there. Was quite feeble in spirit. Heard conversation on happiness. Monboddo alone spoke with relish of old age and prospect of futurity. Sir John said the prospect was faint. Was so ill in the evening that I could not sup at the Hon. A. Gordon's with David. Was obliged to go to bed. Mr. Wood came and made me take sack whey.[6a] Got a sweat.

FRIDAY 4 AUGUST. Better. Nobody but David with us at dinner. Mr. Lawrie went to the country for a day or two. Grange joyous with extract, Brown against Smith.[7] Drank tea.

SATURDAY 5 AUGUST. Sat a little with Sir J. Pringle in the forenoon. My father, Lady Auchinleck, and Miss Boswell dined. Dull. But it was decent and a compliment to us. They went away at four. Then Grange, David, and I went and saw Watson's Hospital for the first time.[8] I was fatigued. Sir John Pringle came and sat in the evening till near ten. My spirits were better. He pleased me by reviving London ideas, and by impressing me (while I considered him) that a man should do what he finds agreeable, without too much consideration or attention to what others think.

[5] Blair held the "subjective" theory of prayer, Ogden maintained its real efficacy. Boswell had discussed these theories (and some practical applications) in his journal during the Hebridean tour, 20 August, 3, 19 October 1773.

[6] See above, 22 May 1780.

[6a] Made by combining two parts of skim milk with one part of sack.

[7] "Joyous" because his ability to get an "extract" meant that a final settlement of the cause had been reached, and that execution of the judgement was ordered.

[8] Watson's Hospital was founded in 1723 (though construction of the building was not begun until 1738) as a home and school for the sons of "decayed" merchants. The building which Boswell visited stood on the site of the present Royal Infirmary. George Watson's College (a boys' day-school in Colinton Road) and George Watson's Ladies' College (George Square) perpetuate the endowment.

SUNDAY 6 AUGUST. Commissioner Cochrane came in the morning and he and I went to the Tron Church. Dr. Drysdale lectured. I was pretty easy. Mr. Wood had called and told me I was doing as well as could be wished. Walked on Castle Hill with Commissioner Cochrane and Sir J. Pringle. The Commissioner and Dr. Webster dined with us. Commissioner and I sat *in* the afternoon.[9] He drank tea. I just felt with him as twenty years ago, but firmer. The children said divine lessons. Lady Colville called between sermons. Daniel at night to take leave.

MONDAY 7 AUGUST. My wife and brother David and the three children and I dined at my father's. David, Sandy, and I drank tea at Mr. Alexander Donaldson's. Tolerably well.

TUESDAY 8 AUGUST. Called on Mr. Wood in the morning. Mr. Lawrie returned this forenoon. My brother David and I dined at Mr. George Wallace's. Home to tea. Dictated well enough. Drank at dinner only the third of a glass of Malaga. Sir John Pringle there. Conversation pretty good.

WEDNESDAY 9 AUGUST. Dictated well. David dined at Mr. John Hunter's. He and I drank tea at Lady Colville's. I called on my father, and he was confidential with me about John. I respected his calm solid sense, though I could not but regret his feeling so little. We were well together for a little by ourselves, he having called me into his room with him. I said I hoped he was now pleased with me. He said "*Yes,*" but not with warmth. I said if he would tell me anything, it should be done. He said the great point was to be frugal and sober. I spoke of how much he had done. He said he had been lucky in having a good wife— two good wives, he might say. I said he was better now than he had been five years ago. He repeated, "Threescore and ten years do sum up," down to "*remove.*" [1] I wished to hear him talk on religion, but saw no fair opening. When we returned to the drawing-room, I proposed to Lady Auchinleck to take Sandy with them. She said she had care enough without him, and said (I think) she had no wish to live but to take care of my father, and in a whimpering tone talked of his being the worse of being at Auchinleck. She said that perhaps, being overjoyed at my brother's return, I might think it was to be a merry meeting at Auchinleck. But it was quite different. My father went there to be quiet and retired. That company disturbed him, especially at night; and why have people who wanted to drink and be merry and would go away and say he was useless? It was hard, when people were willing to give up the world, that they could not be allowed to live in their own way. She said she was glad she had spoken

---

[9] By emphasizing *in*, Boswell means that they stayed at home and did not go back to church for the second sermon.

[1] That is, he repeated Psalm 90. 10 in the Scots metrical paraphrase.

to me. I said, "Well then, I give you my word of honour I shall not invite anybody. If you will be so kind as mention anything, it shall be done." I wanted to know if my father's bonds to my children did not leave them independent of me. She said she had never read them. But she should look them out. But I would not, she said, have my father to write them over again now. She was for people making settlements when in good health, but not to be troubled when indisposed. I said it was proper to alter what was wrong in settlements. She said she never had been so anxious. In short she talked absurdly. I kept my temper finely, and I was really disposed for peace. I was in good spirits tonight. David supped at Mr. Maconochie's.

THURSDAY 10 AUGUST. David went and breakfasted at our father's. Then Sandy and I went and saw them set out. Dictated well today. Grange dined. David and I tea with him. Lady Colville and Lady Anne tea here. Was at Sir J. Pringle's with Maclaurin at night.

FRIDAY 11 AUGUST. Had my table clear, and was pleased that I had written more than double and received more than one half more fees than last Summer Session. David set out for Glasgow. Went with Sir A. Dick in his coach and dined. Grange met me. He and I walked in.

SATURDAY 12 AUGUST. Mr. Wood called on me for a little. Sir John Pringle called, and insisted on my staying a day to dine with him on Monday and make up a party of sons of his old friends. I agreed. Was a little in Justiciary Court at trial of David Reid, a forger.[2] Met with Mr. Ilay Campbell on a Submission where he thought an eldest son, to whom a tenement in Edinburgh was disponed by his father, failing himself, was not obliged to serve heir.[3] The Court of Session had determined the point differently. I wished to consult Lord Braxfield. Mr. Campbell said Lord B. would determine him. My Lord was so good as to go to Mr. Campbell's

---

[2] See above, 23 February 1780. Reid (whose crime was forging or counterfeiting the guinea-note of the bank of Scotland) was found guilty and hanged on 13 September. "He acknowledged the justness of his sentence, and his sincere regret for having behaved very indecently to the judges when sentence was pronounced" (*Scots Magazine*, October 1780, xlii. 554).

[3] The father's disposition was probably an entail or tailzie, naming a series of disponees in succession. The problem may have been whether his eldest son, who might have a title to succeed independently of the entail (e.g. under a conveyance by his grandfather), was nevertheless bound to serve as heir of entail to his father, and so subject his ownership, which might otherwise be absolute, to the fetters of the entail. Boswell's reputation as a lawyer cannot have been so contemptible as has been assumed if he was chosen to serve as arbiter along with Ilay Campbell, the greatest writing lawyer of the Scots bar, later Lord Advocate and Lord President of the Court of Session. And the journal records at least one earlier cause in which he and Campbell were paired as arbiters (3 January, 14 August 1776).

with me when he came out of Court, and was clear against his opinion. But struck out a new point quite clear which had not occurred either to parties or to us Arbiters. My wife and I dined alone today.

SUNDAY 13 AUGUST. Was at New English Chapel forenoon and afternoon. Very well. Went with Sir W. Forbes and drank tea. Looked at Dr. Price on Providence, etc.[4] Was comfortable. At night the children said divine lessons. Rev. Mr. Donald Macqueen and Grange supped.

MONDAY 14 AUGUST. Mr. Wood called and gave me directions about my health while in the country. My wife and I dined at Sir John Pringle's, a company of his old friends' sons: Solicitor, George Wallace, Maclaurin, Dr. Young, myself. He talked of religion. Maclaurin said he was *bona fide*,[5] and started his doubts. Sir John appeared to me to have very *small* Christianity, as was said of Shakespeare's Latin. Yet he believed *immortality* to be revealed. He seemed more happy than usual with this company. Maclaurin had read the most part of Luke in Greek the day before. Declared he spoke *bona fide*. I had my *Hypochondriack* No. 36 to write.[6] Went home and wrote some pages of it. Was hurried as usual before a journey. Went to bed about twelve.

TUESDAY 15 AUGUST. Got up about six. Finished No. 36 and was pleased. Mr. Lawrie attended faithfully. My valuable spouse had breakfast ready in good time. I was foolishly agitated with hurry about trifles. Grange came. My dearest wife and he and Mr. Lawrie went with me to the fly at the Corn Market. I was most grateful to her. Mr. Ross, the Under-Clerk of Session, and Mr. Robertson, a mercantile man of Glasgow, were my companions. Ross left us at Linlithgow, where we breakfasted. Were very conversable; I calm, and learning circumstances about trade. A gentlewoman came in at Falkirk. Got to Glasgow quiet, and not

---

[4] Richard Price, *Dissertation on Providence*, 1767.

[5] That is, he assured the company that he was sincere in his religious doubts.

[6] Actually No. 35, on the unwise imitation of the faults of famous men. "This delusive propenstiy to imitate the vices of eminent men makes it a question of some difficulty in biography whether their faults should be recorded. We have indeed the high example of Holy Writ, where we find the errors and crimes even of saints and martyrs fairly and freely related. But we ought not to assimilate ordinary human compositions to what carries a reverential awe. And notwithstanding that, it is to be feared that there have been too many instances of people offending under the mistaken sanction of Scriptural history. At the same time, truth is sacred, and real characters should be known. I am therefore of opinion that a biographer should tell even the imperfections and faults of those whose lives he writes, provided he takes a conscientious care not to blend them with the general lustre of excellence, but to distinguish and separate them, and impress upon his readers a just sense of the evil, so that they may regret its being found in such men, and be anxiously disposed to avoid what hurts even the most exalted characters, but would utterly sink men of ordinary merit" (*The Hypochondriack*, August 1780).

jumbled in my ideas. Drank tea. Then my brother David came in. Again pleased with his accuracy and rational way of thinking. We walked on Green, supped, and to bed early.

WEDNESDAY 16 AUGUST. Breakfasted Pollok cheerful with Lady Maxwell and Mrs. Montgomerie. Did not see Sir James. Comfortable on journey. Drove on to Auchinleck. David said on road when I said he was not now low-spirited, so as to be indifferent about life, "I deceive myself better than you do." This was a remark which, if made by some celebrated Frenchman, would have had fame: "Je me trompe mieux que vous." He owned the folly and emptiness of all things in the world when one *thought*. We were comforted and elated by seeing the seat of our ancestors. *Indifferent*, however, was our reception. We walked with James Bruce to the Old House and Garden. It was truly a feast to my mind to see all the scenes of my youth, and David here again after so long an absence. Was not much troubled with my illness.[7]

THURSDAY 17 AUGUST. Dr. Gillespie went to Barskimming. We walked with James Bruce and stood on Old Castle, where David ratified his promise to stand by it with heart, purse, and sword.

[EDITORIAL NOTE: Boswell refers to a ceremony enacted in October 1767 and memorialized in the document which follows. Of it Geoffrey Scott has said, "The romantically staged scene on the crumbling walls, the seal of investiture, the chaplains drawn from their pulpits at Auchinleck and Tundergarth and 'appointed for the occasion,' and the entire family of Bruces—mostly juvenile gardeners—proclaiming with one voice at a suitable moment selected by Boswell their fealty to his ancient line— all this appears more like the device of a boy of fifteen than a man of twenty-seven. It is an excellent example of that failure to grow up which accounts for so much of Boswell's artistic success and worldly failure. The central figure of this remarkable rite, David Boswell, was in every way his brother's opposite in character and temperament; slow, plodding, shy, conventional, and entirely unimaginative, he probably executed the role here assigned to him with quite inadequate gusto. One sees him, awaiting his cue, with eyes patiently fixed upon the Master of Ceremonies" (*Private Papers of James Boswell from Malahide Castle*, ed. Geoffrey Scott and F. A. Pottle, 1928–1934, i. 160–161).]

[David Boswell's Family Oath]

I, David Boswell, youngest son of the Right Honourable Alexander Boswell, Lord of Session and Justiciary, present representative of the

---

[7] Boswell inked out this sentence.

family of Auchinleck, do by these presents declare that, according to the usage of the family when any branch of it is sent forth into the world, I have stood upon the Old Castle of Auchinleck and have there solemnly promised to stand by these old walls with heart, purse, and sword, that is to say, that in whatever part of the globe my fortune should place me, I should always be faithful to the ancient family of Auchinleck, and give a reasonable obedience to the representative thereof. In consequence of which I was invested with a ring according to the usage of the family. All this was done upon the nineteenth day of October in the year of our Lord one thousand seven hundred and sixty-seven years, in presence of James Boswell, Esquire, my eldest brother and heir of the family; the Reverend Mr. John Dun, Minister at Auchinleck, and the Reverend Mr. Joseph Fergusson, Minister at Tundergarth, chaplains appointed for the occasion; I departing for Valencia in Spain, there to settle as a merchant. Also in presence of Mr. James Bruce, overseer at Auchinleck, and Alexander, John, Andrew, and James Bruces, his sons, all present having with one voice wished the continuance and prosperity of the ancient family of Auchinleck, and that the family of Bruce might ever flourish there. In testimony of which I now subscribe these presents, and seal them with the seal of my investiture, they being written by the said James Boswell, Esquire, and subscribed on the twenty-seventh day of the said month and in the said year of our Lord. Amen.

DAVID BOSWELL.

JAMES BOSWELL, Witness.
JOHN DUN, Witness.
JOSEPH FERGUSSON, Witness.   (*Seal*)
JAS. BRUCE, Witness.

[EDITORIAL NOTE: David's literalism comes through very clearly in the formal note of ratification he later added to the document.] [8]

After an absence of near thirteen years, I, the said David Boswell, being now returned from Valencia in Spain, where, on account of the prejudices of the inhabitants of that country against Old Testament names, I assumed the name of Thomas in honour of the first laird of our family, and being about to settle as a merchant in the city of London, have again stood upon the Old Castle of Auchinleck and, possessed of a decent fortune, have heartily ratified the preceding obligation; and in order that posterity may not be mistaken, it is proper to observe that the custom of the family therein mentioned must be understood not as an old custom but as com-

---

[8] The formal ratification is dated 11 September, presumably because Mr. Dun had come to breakfast at Auchinleck House that day and was available as a witness.

mencing with my going forth into the world, and to be continued in time to come. . . .

T. D. BOSWELL.

JAMES BOSWELL, Witness.
JOHN DUN, Witness.
JAS. BRUCE, Witness.

[THURSDAY, 17 AUGUST *continued*] Fingland dined. I drank half a glass of strong beer. We walked with him to Broomholm. Father was out in chariot.

FRIDAY 18 AUGUST. Had a headache. Father kept his bed some hours with cold and sore throat. Dr. Gillespie went to Ayr. I read Plutarch's life of Alexander the Great, and was animated with *ancient lore*. Yet thought much less of Alexander than I had done from half memory. Headache well at night.

SATURDAY 19 AUGUST. David and I breakfasted at Fingland's, James Bruce having walked with us half-way. I was quite well in mind. Walked about the holm and viewed the conflux of the Waters of Lugar and Ayr. Had as much satisfaction as in my early days. Thought I could live in the country. In the afternoon David and I and James Bruce walked to Craig-head Mount and saw the oak which David planted, and lay in comfortable calmness on the grass. Our father was in bad humour today. At night David sat a little in my room and had a dispute with me in favour of the *noverca*,[9] till he grew passionate and run off. I was displeased with him. Father's hoarseness continued, and he had a hiccup.

SUNDAY 20 AUGUST. It rained. Lady A., David, and I went in the chariot to church. Mr. Dun lectured on 23 Psalm. David's appearance in the loft with red coat, buff vest and broad gold lace, and buff breeches, was quite the completion of my fancy as to what he would be on his return from Spain. I was very sound. We came home after the forenoon's service. It rained very much in the evening. My father seemed failed. David read a sermon by a Mr. Hume, Minister at Greenlaw. I wrote some short letters. David had appeared to me yesterday very intelligent and firm. I saw that much of my unhappiness was *mouldy imagination*. I ought therefore to keep my mind clear by *realities* and activity. I went up this evening to David's room; found him reading Bourdaloue's sermons. He made an apology for his last night's heat. I freely excused him. He sat awhile in my room after supper, and we were comfortable. I was easier now than I have been at Auchinleck for several years. I walked a little out this evening, but soon returned. I was tenderly uneasy about my brother John. I wrote to him.

[9] See above, 26 December 1779, n. 7a.

MONDAY 21 AUGUST. David and I walked to the Old House and sat a little in James Bruce's. It rained at times today. David rode out along with the chariot in which my father and Lady A. went out an airing. I looked at various books in the library, and was listless and giddy-headed with variety of ideas. Thought myself a weak man. Dr. Gillespie dined at Sorn. I tasted strong beer today, just half a glass. Was disappointed at not having a letter from my dear wife, but not distressed with anxiety, as I thought she would have written if there had been any illness. Afternoon played whist. Evening found my father shrewd in law and smart upon my want of recollection.

TUESDAY 22 AUGUST. Major Montgomerie and Captain Fergusson of Auchinsoul paid a short visit after breakfast. I was a little awkward. Craigdarroch came and I settled with him for his rent up to Whitsunday 1779, except £14 for which he gave me his bill.[1] Mr. Dun arrived, and was very glad to meet my brother David again. He and I had a good deal of comfortable conversation about my dear mother, and about my father. I was glad to find that the hint I had given Mr. Dun last winter to write to him had produced a good pious letter. Mr. Dun told me in confidence that he heard my father had left £500 to Bruce Campbell. I mentioned it to my brother David. But neither of us supposed that it could be true. Bruce Campbell and his three eldest sons[2] dined here today, as did Mr. Dun and Craigdarroch. Early in the afternoon David and I and Mr. Dun went to the Mill of Auchinleck to the burial of George Samson, the miller, my father's foster-brother, aged seventy-five. We were carried into the house by ourselves. His brother, David Samson, and James Bruce were with us. His three sons came in for a little. John Samson in Ochiltree served the burial bread and wine, etc. I drank a little small beer and half a glass of white wine. David and I carried, along with the sons, for a little bit from the house. Then we mounted our horses. It was a very decent funeral. Perfect sobriety; sixteen horsemen and about two hundred people on foot. It was agreeable to see such a number of the tenants upon the estate well clothed. David seemed quite a son of the family. I told him that I was glad a funeral had happened while he was here, though I would not have wished one to die on purpose. We carried again when we came near to the churchyard, and assisted in letting the coffin down into the grave. James Samson, the eldest son, said the Samsons had been in the Mill of Auchinleck before the Boswells got the estate. This he could not

[1] Andrew Howatson of Craigdarroch was one of Boswell's tenants in Dalblair. Boswell was attempting to collect whatever he could of Dalblair's back rents.

[2] Hugh, James (probably), and Bruce. The name of the second son (who was born in 1774 and must have died young) is not recorded, but Scots custom warrants the inference that he was named for his mother's father.

know. They may however have been there from a very early period. (I have since found in the volume of extracts entitled *Boswell of Auchinleck*, "Donald McAlexander in the Mill.") [3] My brother and I drank tea at Mr. Dun's very cordially, and then rode home slowly. I was not the worse for this day's exercise. I played at whist with my father, etc. He checked me for calling out, "I deal, upon honour," and said, "Be composed." I did not like this at the time. But became sensible of the good effect of habitual composure; though indeed what is nature with him is restraint with me. I read at present hardly anything, and am shamefully indolent. But I am attending quietly upon my father.

WEDNESDAY 23 AUGUST. It was a damp day. Played whist both forenoon and night. Began to bring up journal of my tour with Dr. Johnson. [4] Walked out a little in the forenoon, and to the Old Garden with James Bruce, and pulled and eat gooseberries in the afternoon. Was happy seeing David show him his diamond ring and other valuables, and exact book of the commerce of Spain, etc. And to *really* find David an improved man returned home. At night the Doctor disputed for working on Sunday in harvest when it was a good day in midst of bad weather. The ladies opposed him. Their narrow positiveness in all their opinions strikes me with wonder. Though I despise them when I think, yet there is an immediate effect of a kind of authority in positiveness. My father sat snug without entering on the argument. I uncautiously mentioned this, and said Sir John Pringle was very desirous to know what his religion was. The ladies, I saw, were offended. They said it was very plain. I stopped short. But most certain it is, I have never been able to get him to talk with any frankness on religion, and Dr. Gillespie said that he said nothing on the subject last winter when very ill.

THURSDAY 24 AUGUST. My father had been uneasy with his complaint at six in the morning, and had continued so till eight not to disturb Dr. Gillespie. Then he was relieved. It was the Fast Day before the Sacrament in the parish. Lady A. and I went to church in the chariot; David and the Doctor rode. I said I wished I had brought out Sandy notwithstanding she was not for it. She said it would have been very impertinent. And she talked of the heavy charge she had already (meaning my father), and that she did perhaps more than was her duty. I abhorred her. Saw her *pride* in *keeping* him like a child, and her unfeeling selfishness in keeping his grandson at a distance. But I was silent. Mr. Chapman,

---

[3] See below, 29 August 1780.

[4] Boswell had kept only scanty rough notes for the last part of the tour (after 22 October to 5 November 1773). He here returns to the expansion of these notes. He had begun to expand them in 1779, but had then written only a single page. He was to continue this work at intervals through 1781 and 1782. See also above, 4 May 1780.

Mr. Reid's helper, lectured. The Doctor dined at Dumfries House. We came home between sermons. David and I walked to the natural bridge, Barnsdale, and along the burn to Gulzie Mailing after dinner in good rational spirits; and after tea went out on the roof of the house and enjoyed the prospect. I then wrote to Dr. Johnson easily.[5] Was anxious that I had not yet heard from my dear wife, and wrote to her. But after I had sealed my letter, Thomas Edmondson brought me one from her *later* dated than one she had written by the post, but which I had not yet received. They were all well. I was comforted and rejoiced.

FRIDAY 25 AUGUST. Walked after breakfast with David to Townhead and saw the woman that kept him, Effie Rule.[6] She was cordially glad. I was not pleased with his inanimate appearance. But it is his *manner*, I suppose from long habits of living in restraint among the Spaniards. We went into my Mount.[7] Then home, and met my father, etc., walking. Some country people talked with me on affairs. I was uneasy to feel myself so ignorant as not to be firm in my opinion. In the afternoon walked to Old Garden. Talked with John Hood and George Henry, tenants in Trabboch. Had another letter from my dear wife, which cheered me much. Was so well that I began to think that perhaps I was in a mistake as to the gloominess of human life, and that it was intended to be a very good state of existence. Read while in this frame Dr. Wallace's *Prospect* of more happiness than misery, in answer to Maupertuis.[8] But was not satisfied with his reasoning. Had a headache at night.

SATURDAY 26 AUGUST. Walked with David and the Doctor to the Old House. Went to enclosure with David. Then to sacred ground of St. Vincent's Chapel, and both of us sung "Sancte Vincenti, ora pro nobis." I know not if David was serious. I was. It is curious that St. Vincent is the tutelar saint of Valencia. Miss Boswell and I went to church in chariot; David and the Doctor rode. Mr. Gillies of Kilmaurs,[9] whom I now saw

---

[5] "My brother David and I find the long-indulged fancy of our comfortable meeting again at Auchinleck so well realized that it in some degree confirms the pleasing hope of *O praeclarum diem*! ["O glorious day!" (Cicero, *De Senectute*, last chapter)] in a future state.... The riots in London were certainly horrible; but you give me no account of your own situation during the barbarous anarchy. A description of it by DR. JOHNSON would be a great painting; you might write another *London, a Poem*" (To Johnson, 24 August 1780). Boswell is referring to the Gordon Riots, June 1780, following the Act of Parliament for relieving the Roman Catholics from some of their disabilities. Casualties ran into the hundreds.

[6] That is, took care of him as a child.

[7] "Mount James"; see above, 29 October 1778.

[8] One of several "prospects" covered in Robert Wallace's *Various Prospects of Mankind, Nature, and Providence* (1761).

[9] Mr. Dun's son-in-law.

for the first time, preached very well on the Sacrament from the words of the Corinthians, but his sermon was an hour and ten minutes. Mr. Young of New Cumnock preached on Isaiah, "If the Lord had not saved a remnant," etc. I did not attend much, but read in David's account of Spain. We sat in the chamber. The sermons, etc., were in the churchyard.[1] I was not in the least affected with gloom. But was weary. It was the space of *five hours* (all but five minutes) from our setting out till our return; so that the service must have lasted about four hours. In the evening, retired to my closet and seriously meditated and prayed and thought of my dear mother and prepared for commemorating the death of Christ. David came into my room at night and told me he had this evening been cold in spirit and cared for nobody, which vexed him. Yet he was active and not disposed to lie down in indolence. I saw in him a degree of our family melancholy.

SUNDAY 27 AUGUST. Rode slow to church. My father went in the chaise with the ladies, and looked really well before the congregation, but did not officiate as an elder as I have seen him do. I communicated, as did David for the first time. I was calmly religious, yet had shadows of doubt occasionally. But one may doubt of almost anything for a transient fit. My father and the ladies went home about two. David and I and Dr. Gillespie remained. I went to the chamber and heard Mr. Gillies from the tent on "We are bought with a price," [2] etc., and was pleased that he maintained the doctrine of Christ's atonement. We had him to eat cold chicken with us between sermons. In the afternoon, Mr. Robertson of Kirkconnel preached above an hour. I read some in Bourdaloue's *Sermon pour le jour de St. Louis*, which I had of my brother's, to counteract

---

[1] Because of the numbers attending, the sermons before the Sacrament were preached in the churchyard. The preachers had the protection of a covered pulpit, but the common people sat in the open air. Boswell and the others from Auchinleck House sat in a chamber in the Boswell "aisle," a lateral wing to the church built to cover the stairs going down to the burial-vault of Auchinleck, which is under the floor of the church. This chamber, in which the kirk session sometimes held its meetings, and in which the laird or his factor might collect the rents, had a fire-place, and was presumably furnished with arm-chairs like a small parlour. By leaving the outside door (possibly also a window) open, those within could hear the preacher haranguing in the "tent." The Boswell "aisle" was replaced in the nineteenth century by the handsome structure now called "the Boswell Mausoleum," actually a tomb for Sir James Boswell and his family. The reader will hardly need to be told that Boswell's record of this day and the two following provides a laird's-eye view of an occasion exactly parallel to Burns's *Holy Fair*, which is believed to commemorate the Mauchline Sacrament of 1785. One of the preachers ("wee Millar") figures in both accounts, and the final preacher at Auchinleck was Burns's own parish minister, William Auld.

[2] 1 Corinthians 6. 20 and 7. 23.

the dreariness of Presbyterianism. Poor David looked piteous this evening. His Spanish air was gone, and he was reduced to his original clay. It was near seven when service ended. I came home quite stupefied and fatigued. I desired to have some sack whey [3] brought to my room when I should be in bed. My father, who has no indulgence, spoke so harshly against this trifle that some regret which I had been tenderly fostering that my wife and children were not here was dashed off, and I comforted myself with the free happiness which I enjoyed in my own house. The sack whey however did me good.

MONDAY 28 AUGUST. I had meditated to stay at home today, not thinking it any duty to encourage so much unnecessary weary attendance.[4] But as my father was to go, I changed my mind, and rode slowly. Mr. Millar, Mr. Dun's helper, prayed above forty minutes and preached about an hour, and Mr. Auld preached an hour and ten minutes. The service lasted four hours. Indecent truly. How the people like it I cannot conceive—for it is to please them that the clergy labour so long. David's earnest attention to please the *noverca* did not please me. We got home about four o'clock. I was in pretty good spirits.

TUESDAY 29 AUGUST. Got the keys from my father, and showed David some of the charters and family papers in the elegant volumes.[5] Then looked by myself at several papers. David said it was a pity I was not active and laborious in all respects, as I really had great activity in some things. I liked to observe the firmness of his mind, though more contracted than mine. Went to the Broomholm to gather pebbles.[6] Got few. Saw for the first time a salmon stuck.[7] It was done by Sandy Bruce opposite to an ash tree which I made him mark with an S. Logan, Bruce Campbell, and Mr. James Wilson Junior, and his son dined. Evening whist. Fine day. I had kept *my* countenance well and led Logan to tell a story in a strange manner as he always does. *Noverca* said, "Few could have had such barbarity and duplicity." Sat up late writing.

[3] See above, 3 August 1780, n. 6a.
[4] The journal from this point through the first three sentences of the entry for 31 August is now printed for the first time. The fragment of the manuscript was recovered in Edinburgh in May 1963 by Mr. E. D. Buchanan from among the papers of Messrs. Howden and Molleson, Chartered Accountants, who had attended to various matters concerning the Auchinleck estate early in this century. It may have been detached from the rest of the journal because of its mention of Boswell's claim on Sir Adam Fergusson for £50, for which see the fifth note following.
[5] See above, 30 October 1778, n. 3.
[6] "Scotch pebbles": agates or other gems found in streams such as the Lugar Water, which Boswell was searching.
[7] Speared.

WEDNESDAY 30 AUGUST. Wettish day. Knockroon dined. Settled balance of rent due to me by Robert Chisholm and took his bill for it.[8] Was provoked to see his cunning. I had last night written Case for Sir Adam Fergusson as to the £100 which he had promised for the Corsicans in 1768 and had never yet paid, but evaded it so that Mr. Crosbie and I had paid out that sum for cannon over and above a great deal more.[9] I had my brother David to revise the scroll this forenoon and had satisfaction in being at last roused and doing it neatly, wondering however that I had delayed it so long. I thought that perhaps on the eve of an election he would pay rather than be exposed. I desired to have an answer; and having made a fair copy, I showed it to my father. While he read it, I stood by with that sort of awe which I felt in my earliest years while he was considering anything. He said it was all madness to engage in such a scheme, and that Sir Adam might pay or not as he pleased. I found it made little impression on him. I gave it sealed and addressed to Sir Adam to Knockroon to put into the post-office at Ayr. Either last night or this night finding my father alone in the library, I made a trial of his disposition towards my children, saying, "I must have them out here some time." He said, "For what?" or used some expression not encouraging. I directly said, "Would not you like to see them here?" I'm not sure whether he coldly said, "Some time," but I am certain he said, "What the plague would you bring bairns of their age?" I was shocked and changed the conversation. How strange and how lamentable is this want of affection! Yet let me consider that an old man may not like to be disturbed by children.

THURSDAY 31 AUGUST. Set out between six and seven, on horseback, my brother David accompanying me. Breakfasted at Mr. Bruce Campbell's. Then he went with us to Riccarton where a meeting of the tutors

[8] Chisholm was the other tenant in Dalblair.

[9] Boswell's "Case" reminds Sir Adam that in the summer of 1768, while he and Sir Adam were driving together in a post-chaise to Arniston, he had stated an intention of raising a contribution for the Corsicans, and Sir Adam had said that he would give a hundred pounds. Shortly after, on learning that the Carron Company would supply armament for the purpose at a bargain rate, Boswell and Andrew Crosbie had bound themselves jointly to pay £700 for a shipment of cannon and shot, little supposing they would have any difficulty in raising the required subscriptions. The stores were duly delivered at Leghorn at a total charge of something over £740. When Sir Adam was approached for his contribution, he declined to pay it on the ground that he had not promised anything for cannon. Boswell and Crosbie found themselves out of pocket £128. 13s. each, over and above the £50 which each had intended to contribute. Boswell admitted that the matter should have been brought to a head sooner, and was in every way temperate and conciliatory, but he was undoubtedly choosing as embarrassing a time to present his claim as could have been devised. Sir Adam, who had represented Ayrshire since 1774, was standing for re-election.

of Treesbank was fixed to be this day. We found Major Dunlop [1] there. We walked over to Kilmarnock. Met Sir Adam Fergusson on the street; shook hands with him and was polite but reserved, and said nothing of having written to him. His brother George [2] was there too. Talked a little with Mr. William Brown, whom I found less uneasy than I expected about the debt due to him by Alexander Cuninghame. Saw the great shoe warehouse of Wilsons and Company. Sat a little at Mr. Wilson's, and was introduced to his third wife. He and Mr. W. Brown dined with us at Riccarton, after Major Dunlop, Bruce Campbell, Bailie Richmond, and I had settled as to the education, etc., of our pupils. [3] I was calm but pleasant. I drank a glass of white wine and half a glass of port. Felt an inclination to drink, and was uneasy at the thought. Stopped short. Was displeased with my brother David, who, when Major Dunlop with a hearty air called to him to fill a bumper to a toast, answered with some heat, "Sir, I never choose to drink more than is agreeable to me." His rigid uncompliance has the advantage of my easiness in keeping him free from intoxication, but on the other hand he cannot be agreeable to most people. I felt really painfully upon this occasion. He might have declined the bumper with complaisant good-humour. Got home before supper.

FRIDAY 1 SEPTEMBER. A wettish day. Walked only down to James Bruce's in the forenoon. Felt there a fit of raving as when in my younger days. Got from him a parcel of my letters to him at the most foolish time of my life; viz., when I was from twenty-one to twenty-three. Was sunk by viewing myself with contempt, though then a *genius* in my own eyes. Burnt all but one or two of the best. [4] Was consoled to think that I was now so much more solid. Had a cloud of hypochondria today. Played whist at night, as I have done I believe every night except last night. My father seems to be amused by it, and plays it very well. Received an agreeable letter from my dear wife, which cheered me.

SATURDAY 2 SEPTEMBER. It was a fine morning. My brother David rode with me to Cumnock, where we breakfasted with Old Mr. John Boswell and his wife and daughters, and I was consulted on the settlements of Knockroon and Underwood, as to which I promised to make out notes. We then visited the widow of my good friend Dr. Daniel Johnston,

[1] John Dunlop was second cousin once removed to the Campbell boys' mother, his grandfather being a brother to her great-grandmother.

[2] Also an advocate, later (1799) advanced to the bench as Lord Hermand. He was helping Sir Adam in his electioneering and had also come for the trial of Matthew Hay (below, 8 September 1780), in which he was counsel.

[3] The Campbell boys, George James and David. "Pupils" indicates that both boys were under fourteen.

[4] No letters from Boswell to Bruce of this early period are now known to survive.

as to whose affairs I also promised to give my opinion in writing. We then rode to Knockroon and looked at it, and agreed that it should never belong to any other person than a branch of this family. Having engaged to dine with Mr. Dun, we arrived at the manse in good time, and he walked with us. Lord Dumfries's coach passed through the field above the glebe. We made our bows. The Countess, Lady Pen, Miss Crauford, Sir Hew Dalrymple, and young Lady Elizabeth were in it.[5] I was a little awkward, not having seen the Countess for years, and the families not being upon visiting terms on account of a misunderstanding about a road from Lord Dumfries's gateway.[6] I was resolved they never should have it. I was politely cautious. She said, "It is an age since we met. Shall we not see you?" I answered, bowing, "I am obliged to go with—This is my brother, Lady Dumfries"; and so I broke off gently. Mr. Dun, David, and I walked to Lord Dumfries's bridge, and I felt old ideas of grandeur which I had in the last Earl's time. As carriages passed with company going to the Earl's, I felt a satisfaction in thinking of the calm life at Auchinleck, free from the noise of rattling wheels and the disturbance of company, like the "beatus ille qui procul negotiis." [7] David, with all his firmness and accuracy, owned that he could not form a plan of living as one wishes to do, at the same time keeping what is called a hospitable house in the country, that is, having much company. I resolved to live in a very retired way. We looked at the gateway and access to and from it, as David and I had done in the morning, and David and I were quite satisfied there was no hardship upon the Earl. The two John Boswells met us; and they and Mr. Millar, Mr. Dun's assistant, and his daughters and son [8] were at dinner. Mrs. Dun was ill and did not appear till tea. It was as comfortable in *Auchinleck Manse* as ever I remember it. Life was a good thing. We passed our time agreeably. That, as David says, is enough. For what else shall we do in Heaven? But there must be no checks

---

[5] "Lady Pen" was Lord Dumfries's aunt, Lady Penelope Crichton Dalrymple, and Lady Elizabeth Penelope Crichton was his only surviving child. She became Countess of Dumfries in her own right, and was later married to Viscount Mountstuart, eldest son of Boswell's old friend Lord Mountstuart.

[6] See above, 2 November 1778.

[7] From Horace (*Epodes*, ii. 1); it continues:
> ut prisca gens mortalium,
> paterna rura bobus exercet suis
> solutus omni faenore

["Happy the man who, far away from business cares, like the pristine race of mortals, works his ancestral acres with his steers, from all money-lending free," translated by C. E. Bennett, Loeb Library].

[8] Mr. Dun's son (b. 1772) was named Alexander Boswell for Lord Auchinleck.

of conscience, so that there may be *"perfect peace."* [9] I just tasted brandy and drank half a glass of port. We had Mr. Halbert, the schoolmaster and session-clerk, ordered to attend with all his registers, which he did. Marriages and burials (or rather deaths) had been much neglected in our parish record. As in some cases such evidence might be important and was always matter of rational curiosity, I put him on a regular plan, which he promised to follow; I being to pay threepence for each death provided he missed none. He is paid by legal right for baptisms and marriages. Mr. Dun and Mr. Millar promised to keep him to the plan. When we got home we found Lord Braxfield, his lady, and daughter.[1] My father was animated, and sat at the foot of his table like what he used to be.[2]

SUNDAY 3 SEPTEMBER. Rode to church with Lord Braxfield, his coach and my father's chariot driving after us. My father looked well in church. Mr. Dun lectured on Romans 8. 33, etc., on election, upon which he talked strange, superficial things. To soften the revolting doctrine, he said that there would many be saved whose names were not written in the decree of election. In short he ventured to *suppose* a little. I am sorry I did not afterwards ask such a strong-headed man as Lord Braxfield his opinion on this inexplicable subject. I was clear at the time for no decrees, but full free-will, though I could not understand how beings endowed with it could be created. But neither could I understand beings created with the power of motion and not mere machines. I was quite easy upon the subject. Mr. Dun said a thing that I never heard before: that it is a notion in the country that it requires fifteen witnesses to prove perjury. He told them two would prove any crime, and he gave very good moral precepts to make election sure. Lord Braxfield was well pleased with him. My Lord and I rode home by Brackenhill. After dinner we all walked about the Old House. I drank one glass of wine today.

MONDAY 4 SEPTEMBER. Lord Braxfield and I walked down to the bank above the Broomholm. I asked him how he had attained to so great a knowledge of law. He gave me a full account of his studies,[3] which

[9] Isaiah 26. 3.

[1] Braxfield and Kames, the judges for the Southern Circuit, were appointed to sit down at Ayr on 6 September.

[2] In his proper place as master of the household. In eighteenth-century Scotland the mistress of the house presided at table and served the various dishes.

[3] "He said he had a good foundation of Civil Law. He did not attend a Scotch Law professor. He put on the gown before candidates for being advocates were being examined on that law. He read Mackenzie's *Institutions* with Bayne's notes. He thought well (now) of Bayne, though Lord Kames speaks of him with contempt. 'But,' said Lord Braxfield, 'Kames thinks nothing of any law book but [his own] *Principles of*

I have written down. We had James Bruce to join us, and we walked along to the seat at the old washing-green, where we met my father, etc., who walked so far with us. Lord Braxfield and I and James Bruce walked round by the hill, Gulzie Mailing, and natural bridge. I was in excellent sound spirits. Lord Kames and his lady and son came to dinner. I walked with Mr. Drummond [4] to the Old Garden. Was a little too lively, but soon checked my vivacity. I drank one glass of Madeira and one of claret. Was somewhat uneasy even by taking so much, and felt that company disturbed the calmness of Auchinleck. Lord Kames raved and Lord Braxfield roared—both bawdy. Got a kind letter from Dr. Johnson. All the company went away after dinner.

TUESDAY 5 SEPTEMBER. Fine day as yesterday. David and I and James Bruce rode to the Trabboch and viewed some of it well. Saw the plantation on Tarelgin march growing well, as also the trees which I planted at Creochhill. Consulted as to a plantation on the march between Hoodston and Chipperlaigan. John Hood seemed willing to agree to what I pleased. David and I dined and drank tea at Sundrum. Nobody there but a Dr. McIntyre, a surgeon in Carrick. I drank one glass of wine. I was calm but stayed too late, so that David was offended and had some reason, as it was dark most of the way home. I was vexed to find myself so dilatory. Got home safe.

WEDNESDAY 6 SEPTEMBER. Every morning James Bruce comes into my room before I am up, which does me good. A fine day. Made Sandy

---

Equity.' Now, he said, he would read Erskine. He turned up all the Acts of Parliament referred to, and he read also Sir George Mackenzie's *Observations* on them, in which he found very little. He read Craig *De Feudis*, but did not find so much in him as he expected. He read Lord Stair's *Institutions* three times. He said there was sometimes a perplexity in his style. But that made him think more attentively, and he found the meaning always solid. I said this was a good remark; for really the reading of a smooth modern style was like swallowing an eel: it passes through one without having time to be turned 'in sucum et sanguinem' [into vigour and blood: Cicero, *Epistolae ad Atticum*, 4. 16. 10]. He read Bankton's book [*An Institute of the Laws of Scotland*, 1751–1753, by Andrew Macdowall, Lord Bankton] when it came out, and he read Erskine's *Institute* in manuscript. But he said he had learnt law chiefly by *thinking*. The rudiments, to be sure, must be had from books, but he had acquired his knowledge by considering points by himself. He regretted as I did that the Civil Law was gone into disuse so much, as it was from thence that the great principles of reason and sound sense were to be drawn; and he said that it was true, what I observed, that it was the glory of our law to proceed on principles and be more of a system than the law in England. As to decisions, he said one should not learn law by reading them, but after studying a point should then see what the decisions have been upon it" (Paper Apart, Auchinleck, 4 September 1780, now first printed).

[4] Lord Kames's son, George Home, had added the name of Drummond, as heir to his mother's estate of Blair Drummond.

Bruce show me how he collects the cess.[5] Had first Thomas Edmondson and then James Bruce with me looking for pebbles; but though I looked pretty diligently from the old washing-green to the Broomholm with a very little interruption, did not get one. Gathered some nuts for my children. Was as happy at Auchinleck as in my earliest days. Hoped to see my wife and children happy here. In the evening had too warm an altercation with David concerning the *noverca*; said it was not generous in him to be indifferent when he saw me used so. He was hurt a little, but defended himself *rationally*. I resolved to be more guarded. He said I should associate with strong-headed people, and that he had found out that those who philosophized and did not mind real life were laughed at, however ingenious. This passed either yesterday or today. Dr. Gillespie's brother George came today after dinner.

THURSDAY 7 SEPTEMBER. David put me in mind of a good saying of my Professor Trotz at Utrecht of philosophical, low-spirited, miserable men: "In patria mea, stultos illos arboribus ligant, fustibusque quamplurimis dorsa eorum cedunt." [6] He and I and James Bruce went and saw David Aird and Hugh dig around the tree planted by him in 1767 on Craighead Mount, and put dung in the ground. It measured this day in highth ———, and round the stem ———. James Bruce said it would grow twice as much the next thirteen years as it had done the last. I was quite serene and comfortable this forenoon, and happy with a thought which never occurred to me before: that I might pass all the rest of my life in independent tranquillity at this place and have no reproach either from my own mind or the world as if I were acting improperly. For I would be at *Auchinleck*, which comprehends so many romantic, pious, and worthy ideas in my imagination—at the seat of my family—at home. This was quite a new way of thinking. I indulged the novelty with curious pleasure. I have from my earliest years been so habituated by my father to suppose it necessary to be of some profession, and to view a country gentleman who lives constantly upon his estate as an idle man, that it is not easy for me to think otherwise. But I am sensible that it is better—nay, necessary—for me to have more occupation, at least for some years; and it is consolatory to consider that I have always the respectable resource of Auchinleck. David and I rode over to Barskimming. Lord Justice Clerk received us with great kindness, walked with us, and sailed with us in his boat.[7] I was glad when he mentioned to me a circumstance which I have heard from my father: that Lord Justice Clerk's grandfather

[5] Land-tax.
[6] "In my country, they tie fools of that kind to trees, and beat their backs liberally with a cudgel"—that is, such people are insane.
[7] Barskimming is on the River Ayr.

left my grandfather sole tutor to all his children. We were much pleased with the beauties both of nature and art at Barskimming. Mr. Morthland, the advocate, came and dined also. No other company there. Mrs. Miller very agreeable. I drank one glass strong ale and one claret. Rode quietly home in gentle spirits. Played whist.

FRIDAY 8 SEPTEMBER. Wettish day. Mr. George Gillespie, who had been here all yesterday, stayed also this day. Somewhat agitated with thinking that the trial of Matthew Hay for poisoning was going on.[8] Had written both to A. Walker and Knockroon for news, and heard from both that the trial was not near a conclusion. In the forenoon a card was brought to me which the servant said had come by a gentleman who was alighted. It was from Sir Adam Fergusson, telling me that my *Case* was received; that there had not been a moment of leisure to answer it, but it should not be neglected. I was surprised in a little to find Sir Adam in the house. The Parliament being dissolved, he was exerting himself as a candidate; and he had sent in this card, I suppose, to keep me from pushing my claim at present. I knew not what his intention could be. But I

---

[8] See above, 14 May 1780. Matthew Hay, tenant farmer in Holms of Dundonald, was accused of having entered the house of a tenant of his, William Wilson, and of having put arsenic into a pot of sowens cooking over the fire, his motive being to kill Wilson's daughter and so conceal the fact that she was with child by him. The whole family of five having eaten of the sowens, Wilson and his wife died and the other members of the family were very ill. Boswell's absenting himself from a trial which gave him such concern calls for an explanation which is not forthcoming. One wonders, however, if the case of Bell the schoolmaster three years earlier does not provide it. Bell had asked Boswell to defend him; Boswell instead joined the prosecution and suffered great uneasiness in consequence (Journal, 29 November–2 December 1777). It is not improbable that he had declined to defend Hay, for Hay was an old client of his. In the first year of his practice at the bar (Spring Circuit at Ayr, 1767), he had undertaken to defend Hay on a charge of armed assault on the Surveyor of Customs at Ayr, and had secured from the Lord Advocate grudging agreement not to prosecute, plus a personal letter of reproof which more than hinted that he had been privy to the spiriting away of a material witness. Hay appears to have been a reckless and dangerous man who could learn nothing from his encounters with the law. Seven years after the fracas of 1767, he was convicted and sentenced to a small fine in damages for assault and battery on a man and his wife who said they were merely going about their lawful affairs along the highway when attacked. In a subsequent appeal by them to the Court of Session for an increase in damages, Andrew Crosbie, not Boswell, appeared as Hay's counsel. Boswell had perhaps then made up his mind to have no more to do with Hay, but his inquiry into the details of the Precognition against Hay (above, 14 May 1780) suggests that he had again been asked to be counsel. The counsel at the trial actually were Andrew Crosbie, George Fergusson, and Lord Maitland. (Maitland, better known as the Jacobin Earl of Lauderdale who fought a bloodless duel with Benedict Arnold in 1791, had been admitted to the Faculty of Advocates the previous summer.)

was easy with him, and he went away after dinner without a word said on the subject. It might have been galling to me to observe him carrying my father keenly upon his side, against Major Montgomerie, for whom I wished.[9] But I was happily indifferent, I know not how. I felt the pleasure of calmness.

SATURDAY 9 SEPTEMBER. Had James Bruce to walk with me by Stevenston to the Mill. Looked at *slaps*[1] in the fences and noted them down. Was in comfortable *family frame* hearing James speak of my grandfather. David had gone to see Auchincruive,[2] and had taken Sandy Bruce with him. It was not an unpleasing contrasted agitation to think of Hay's trial at Ayr, not far from us, while James and I were walking serenely here. Rested a little in miller's. Looked for pebbles. Got only one and some bits. Walked down the water-side to Loganston and viewed the bank lately fortified. James went home, and I looked for pebbles all the way to the end of the Langholm. Then went up by the Broomhouse. Rain came on. It did not sink my spirits. David returned after dinner and had some by himself. I witnessed his planting a beech in Stronis Acre, —— high, —— round. Played whist. In the evening Hugh Hair, one of the workmen, brought me from Ochiltree the news that Hay was condemned. I was more affected than I could have supposed. Was rendered faint and dismal.[3] Walked down to James Bruce's and told

[9] For many years political control of Ayrshire had been divided among the earls of Cassillis, Eglinton, and Loudoun. In 1774 Sir Adam Fergusson gathered a "democratical" coalition, nominally of landed gentlemen, but actually containing also the earls of Dumfries and Glencairn, and defeated the "aristocratic" candidate, David Kennedy. In 1780 the Cassillis, Eglinton, and Loudoun forces combined again, this time to support Hugh Montgomerie, eldest son of Eglinton's heir male and Eglinton's ultimate successor to the title, against Fergusson and his adherents. In October 1780 Montgomerie was elected, 65 votes to 55, but enough of his votes were successfully challenged, first in the Court of Session and then in a Select Committee of the House of Commons, for Fergusson to be declared the winner in April 1781.

[1] Gaps, breaches.

[2] "Auchincru" in the manuscript; a common eighteenth-century variant.

[3] An old story, first published by Lockhart in his *Memoirs of Scott* (1837, iii. 341–342) had its origin in this trial, though Lockhart had nearly all the circumstances wrong. According to him, Braxfield had often played chess with the accused ("a gentleman of good fortune" named Donald, whose crime was forgery), and after pronouncing sentence of death, made the atrocious remark, "There's checkmate to you, Donald!" Lord Cockburn, in *Memorials of His Time* (1856), asserted the essential historicity of the remark, though he connected it with Hay's trial and made Kames, not Braxfield, the speaker. According to him, Kames said, "There's checkmate to you, Matthew!" when the jury returned its verdict of guilty. Cockburn is not lightly to be dismissed, for he cites Lord Hermand as his authority, and Hermand was the George Fergusson who served as Hay's counsel. Nevertheless we think, as William Roughead did, that the most probable version is the one given by J. H. Burton in his *Narratives from Criminal*

him. Was obliged to take a little peppermint-water. Felt myself as weak as in my youngest days. Made James walk in the dusk with me almost to the house. Talked religiously with timorous dejection. Dr. Gillespie, who had gone to Ayr with his brother, brought us pretty full accounts of Hay's firm behaviour. I was shocked with the harsh satisfaction of the ladies on hearing the sad account. My father said to me, "Strange! have you been in James Bruce's all this time?" I ought to be on my guard not to lessen my dignity too much by indulging kindliness. Yet my father has too little. He is oak. I am finer but softer wood. I must mention his unwillingness to allow me to have any sway at all. I was before dinner today observing something as to the fences of the farms, in which I was certainly in the right. Miss Boswell upon this said something. He cried, "There she's following a *gowk*." [4] This was shocking. It made me resolve not to interfere. I was very gloomy tonight. I read some of Doddridge's *Sermons on the Evidence of Christianity*, which did me good. I had a fire in my room, and read more of Doddridge after I was in bed. I luckily fell asleep without suffering much from my imagination.

SUNDAY 10 SEPTEMBER. Rose in better spirits. David, Dr. Gillespie, and I walked to Ochiltree, where we were informed there was no sermon, but I maintained that we were not to hold it to be so till we were there, so as that decent appearances might be preserved. We asked different people in the village and were *assured* there was no sermon, so, as I had planned, we walked on to Barquharrie. I had all my old ideas of Ochiltree as fresh as ever. One should in youth stock his mind with agreeable ideas, which, though they should die away for a time, will revive again. We found Mr. George Reid quite hearty. He set before us a dram, white wine, strong ale, and bread. I drank a glass of ale. I then asked him to pray. He said he would sing a psalm and read also. He sung the 43 Psalm, all but the last verse, to the French tune; and he read the 16 Psalm in prose, and in the old-fashioned way read the title, "Michtam [5] of David." Then he prayed

---

Trials in Scotland (1852, ii. 64–65); he says he had it "from the son of a person who was officially present at the trial." According to him, Kames did make the remark, but he made it, not to Hay, but to Hay's counsel (presumably Crosbie), and at the conclusion of the testimony of the chemical experts. Joseph Black, the great Edinburgh chemist, and "Mr. Russell, surgeon" both reported that they had found arsenic in the barrel in which the supply of "sowen seeds were a-steeping." The contemporary account of the trial in the *Scots Magazine* (October 1780, xlii. 553–554) says that the judges patiently heard a protestation of innocence from Hay and that Kames at the end addressed him with due solemnity. Hay was hanged at Ayr on 13 October, asserting his innocence to the last.

[4] A cuckoo; letting herself be made a fool of.

[5] A word of uncertain meaning which occurs in the heading of several of the Psalms, including the sixteenth.

very well. The servants were in the room. It was truly comfortable and it was even wonderful to see my father's governor at the age of eighty-five, all but some days, quite entire in mind. I had a peculiar pleasing recollection of having been here in Mrs. Reid's time with my valuable spouse, then Miss Peggie Montgomerie, and having been *joked* with her, as the phrase is. Mr. Reid said my grandfather, even at his best, was subject to fits of melancholy. That he had taken most of his mother and Balmuto of his father. Balmuto used to say to him in a morning, "Well, are you in the pet?" "Yes, John." "Hawd you wi't." [6] Lady Barquharrie [7] used to tell what a cheerful man their father was, and that it would have done you good to hear him laugh. He said my grandfather liked his son James best, and so did Lady Betty. James was the best scholar when he was young, and was a man of strong parts. He said my father had done little in learning when he came to him. His father used to keep him standing two hours in a morning at his lesson; and Mr. Lawrence Dundas treated him very harshly, so that he by these means was averse to his book. [8] He associated much with two idle, worthless Irish lads called Carletons, and was much at the billiard-table. Mr. Reid was informed of this by old Margaret Kerr, and insisted to have my father's promise that he would no longer keep company with the Carletons; and as he was obstinate at first, he beat him heartily till he made him promise; and the very next week they were extruded the college. He said that upon the birth of my brother David, who was named for my grandfather's father, my grandfather was so well pleased that he gave up to my father 20,000 merks which he had upon the estate. He said my grandfather at times in his old age at Auchinleck took strange fancies; thought all his sons wished him dead, and told Mrs. Reid that Mr. Reid must carry his head to the grave. He said my grandfather at that time was some days better in his mind, some days worse. The late John Miller of Glenlee, who had a high regard for my grandfather, said to Mr. Reid, "I esteem you for paying attention to the ruins of a truly great man." Being with Mr. George Reid was really

---

[6] "Have you got the sulks?—Hang on to 'em." Boswell forgets that he had already recorded most of the material of this conversation (see above, 7 June 1779).

[7] Margaret Boswell, daughter of David Boswell of Auchinleck and sister of Boswell's grandfather, James Boswell. She married Capt. Hugh Campbell of Barquharrie. Bruce Campbell was her grandson.

[8] Lord Auchinleck's memoirs, now among the Boswell papers at Yale, detail his troubles with Dundas (the story is told in both the third and the first person): "At twelve he was taken to Edinburgh and ... was put to the College to the Humanity [Latin] Class then taught by Mr. Lawrence Dundas; this was a great loss, for he was not then ready for the College, and Mr. Dundas, though an able Latin scholar, had not a taking method with the students. I stayed two years in his class but cannot say I profited much. However, by my worthy father's assistance, I still learned some."

like conversing with one of the dead, at least it was so in respect to this world. I sent for Andrew Strahorn to meet me. I had lately a Memorial from him in which he said he was ninety-six. But I did not think him so old. He said he was a man in Mar's best year (i.e., 1715), and was a month at Glasgow in the militia. I asked, "Who commanded you?" "*Basil,*" said he. That was Commissioner Cochrane. I gave him charitably my best advice as to what he wished to have it. He was smart still, though he had lost an eye. I desired James Bruce to search the Ochiltree register for his age. He was born in a farm in that parish called "Back of the hill." We went in and saw the House of Ochiltree. Its ruinous rooms affected me with melancholy not unpleasing.[9] In the afternoon I read to the company a sermon of Doddridge's on the evidence of Christianity. The gloom of Hay's condemnation was gone.

MONDAY 11 SEPTEMBER.[1] Wet day. Mr. Dun came to breakfast. He and I had some good conversation, but his eager attention to worldly interest displeased me. In the library a curious mistake happened. Dr. Gillespie and I talked of *Sir John* being an Arian and having written a good deal upon divinity. We meant Sir John Pringle. Mr. Dun imagined all the time it was Sir John Whitefoord, and was not undeceived till he happened to tell he had a letter from Sir John in answer to one which he wrote to him on the death of his son. We said Sir John never had a son, and thus the explanation happened. Lord Justice Clerk and his lady dined and drank tea, and were very good company. I had a conversation of some length with my brother David in my room. He talked *rationally* of my *flights*, but was in the extreme opposite to imagination and gay frankness. I however now think him a good deal more agreeable than I did at Edinburgh, though his cool, attentive conduct to the *noverca*, and insensibility to her sour, resentful behaviour to a brother who had been all along warmly kind and generous to him, could not but give me uneasiness. I have had satisfaction in contemplating him at this time at Auchinleck as *constantly* neat and accurate, of which I have no idea from my own experience, but the reverse. Little circumstances present him to my mind in the most lively manner, as I believe is the case with everything. I mark then my sitting in his room with him, he intense upon some calculation, I reading his Spanish almanac or calendar and having foreign ideas. It is impossible to record fully one's *life* if all sensations are to be minutely described. I had today an excellent letter from my worthy friend Grange

[9] It was later restored and made habitable, and was occupied by the widow of Boswell's son, Alexander.

[1] It was on this day that David wrote and signed the ratification of the oath he had taken on the Old Castle (see above, 17 August 1780).

of Saturday's date, with good accounts of my family. I was really happy. In the evening had some conversation with my father in the library. I put it to him, and he could not find fault.

TUESDAY 12 SEPTEMBER. Both yesterday and today, was better in the morning than usual. Sir Walter M.-C. came to breakfast. I took him a long walk by the Old House and to the Broomholm. Found one pebble. He dined and drank tea. Dr. Gillespie dined at Barskimming. Sir Walter went home at night. His connexion with my dear wife made me like to see him, and he talked very sensibly today. David and I had a walk on the gravel before the house. He had told me lately that though he had not much affection, he felt it for my children. I again saw him with esteem as rational and accurate, but regretted his narrowness of mind and want of genial, open, cordial sociality, of which I have not traced a symptom. But I study character too closely. Mr. Dun told me yesterday that he and Mrs. Boswell of Knockroon, from what they had heard, thought I had much of my grandfather. But he in a friendly manner cautioned me to take care that my kindliness might not lead me to promise more than I could perform, and appear not to keep my promises. David said today that Dr. Johnson *bewildered* me; for he did not inculcate upon me the absolute propriety of settling in Scotland, where I could be of consequence. The *noverca* was very sour and untoward tonight. As I said to Mr. Dun, I took this as a *trial* and was patient. Dernconner told me yesterday that she made a cat's foot of my father, and that my father had quite a different liberty here in *his* father's time from what I now had. But let me consider how many free, agreeable years I have enjoyed in my *own house* with my wife and family instead of living in *misera servitus*, as we must have done with my father, and put that into the opposite scale to the evil of the *noverca*. After supper I talked too much to Dr. Gillespie. Quoted some of Dr. Johnson's sayings to him, which he was not capable of relishing with respectful admiration. Was sensible that my vivacity is not yet enough under regulation. *Why* wish to entertain everybody? I was in excellent spirits, being to set out next day.

WEDNESDAY 13 SEPTEMBER. During this stay at Auchinleck I have liked the country remarkably well. I have read Doddridge's *Sermons on the Evidence of Christianity*, which will be ever good supports to my faith, some of Steele's *Englishman*, parts of the *Dictionary of Arts and Sciences* printed for Owen. Got up pretty well today. Breakfasted with my father, etc., comfortably. Then David and I set out in a Cumnock chaise. The day was wettish. But we had satisfaction in looking upon the family estate as we drove along. Called for a little at Logan, where I had not been for eight or nine years, and had not been in the house since my marriage. Having found that there was not a clear proof of his having been a rogue at the last election,[2] and that he had been very obliging to Sundrum's sons, though their father had treated him harshly, I resolved to visit him again, and to begin while David was in the country. We stopped at Douglas Castle, where there was nobody but servants, and went through the house. Its magnitude struck me with great thought, and diminished Auchinleck. Whenever I grow too proud at home I must come to Douglas Castle for a little. We dined at Douglas Mill. I drank one glass of wine. Was dreary for a little space. Had dull dejection with moorland gloom, as in my youth. Recovered in the chaise. Little Vantage at night. David and I had disputed too warmly upon the road in the forenoon. I said he would be on a larger scale when he had been a winter in London; and I said his behaviour to the *noverca* was *butler-like*. He seemed hurt. I asked his forgiveness for hasty expressions. At night his precision and self-conceit fretted me. He said we should not travel together. I said I would not travel with him for five guineas a day.

THURSDAY 14 SEPTEMBER. (Writing on Friday the 29.) David and I got to my house to breakfast. Had the comfort and joy to find my wife and children all well. Little Jamie was now walking finely. He had lost his word *papa*, and could only cry *Bell*.[3] Jeanie Campbell from Liverpool and her brothers from Lanark were all in my house. I was happy to have worthy Treesbanks's children about me. My wife and I visited Colonel Mure Campbell and Lady Raasay, etc., at Mr. Hope's house in the Meadow. I was much pleased to hear that my wife had been remarkably kind to these worthy people in their distress, and had gone herself to Kirkliston for a nurse to the Colonel's little daughter, and had even lent our little Betty's nurse, which had been the mean of preserving its life.[4] I saw the infant and thought it might be Countess of Loudoun.[5] Called on several people. Grange dined with us. My spirits were excellent.

FRIDAY 15 SEPTEMBER. (Writing on Friday the 29.) Colonel Mure Campbell, Lady Raasay, Miss Jeanie MacLeod, Mrs. Vernon, and the Rev. Dr. Erskine dined with us. It was a dinner of comfort to the Colonel and his connexions. My brother David was at Commissioner Cochrane's. Dr. Erskine made a very good remark: that a mimic or one accustomed to observe imperfections is never a good public speaker, for he has a timidity from the apprehension of appearing ridiculous himself. They

[2] See above, 4 June 1779.

[3] For Bell Bruce, the nanny.

[4] Mrs. Mure Campbell had died on 2 September, shortly after giving birth to a daughter.

[5] In 1786 upon the death of her father (who in 1782 had become Earl of Loudoun), Flora Mure Campbell did succeed as Countess of Loudoun.

all drank tea. I managed very well, so as to drink but one glass in the time of dinner and one after, and yet to be fully social. If I can once get free of a notion that my company is dissatisfied when I do not drink with them, I shall do well. Dr. Erskine had baptized the Colonel's little daughter and had visited the family with pious goodness.

SATURDAY 16 SEPTEMBER. (Writing on Friday the 29.) David and I had an agreeable walk to Belleville, where we paid a visit to Lady Dundonald. I had all my old ideas at this place, where I have enjoyed much happiness, as fresh today as ever. David dined with his old master, Hunter-Blair.[6] Mr. Fraser, one of the masters of the High School, drank tea with us and examined the young Campbells excellently well, to settle what classes they should enter.

SUNDAY 17 SEPTEMBER. (Writing on Monday the 2 October.) Heard and joined devoutly in the first division of the forenoon service in the Old English Chapel, as I felt that I could not be easy without being at public worship. Was in the gallery concealed, and came off quietly, Grange and David waiting for me at Grange's. We walked out to Sir Alexander Dick's. Mr. Charles Hay walked out with us, and waited till David had bid adieu to the worthy Baronet, and then accompanied him to Edinburgh, David being to dine with Bailie David Steuart. I was in perfect serenity, and saw everything in a comfortable light. Worthy Grange was also quite happy, and we walked in the garden and eat fruit joyously. I drank one glass of currant wine. A heavy rain came on. We had the coach to town. My children and the three Campbells said divine lessons. I was pleased to have them all about me. My health was almost fully restored. At least I had little uneasiness, and my mind was unclouded.

MONDAY 18 SEPTEMBER. (Writing on Sunday the 8 October.) Commissioner Cochrane, Balbarton, Dr. Webster, and Mr. Wellwood dined with us to bid adieu to David, who was to set out next morning for London. Dr. Webster and Mrs. Mingay supped with us. We had prayers. I was quite well.

TUESDAY 19 SEPTEMBER. (Writing on Sunday 8 October.) Rose early and saw David into the Berwick fly. His sense and accuracy and sobriety made me esteem him. But his rigid uncomplying manners, except by force of studied complaisance, and his want of generosity in every respect (a strong instance of which was his not feeling with the least indignation what I, his kind brother, am obliged to suffer from the incessant ill-will of a *noverca* who governs my father as if he were a child), made me not love him. I went with George Campbell and breakfasted at his master

---

[6] The merchant under whom he had served his apprenticeship. Hunter-Blair and Sir William Forbes were partners.

Mr. Fraser's, where was Mr. French, David's master.[7] But David, being a little indisposed, could not be with us. I was soundly happy conversing with these schoolmasters. I walked with them to the school, and was present at Mr. Fraser's opening his class with a decent prayer, after which I heard him examine some of the boys on a passage of Caesar.[8] I was much pleased with his perfect investigation of the elements of the Latin and with his instruction in the sense, particularly the geography. David had grown better and gone to Mr. French's class, but I did not see him. I felt much satisfaction in my present superiority of understanding, while my vivacity recalled the state of a school-boy, and I thought I would yet advance in literature. I dined at Maclaurin's, and was introduced to Sir Lawrence Dundas. He said he hoped he and I would be better acquainted, and was very courteous.

WEDNESDAY 20 SEPTEMBER. (Writing on Sunday 8 October.) Dined at Commissioner Cochrane's; young Craigengillan and Mr. Logan, his tutor, there. Went to Lady Colville's and found her and Lady Anne and Mr. Andrew sitting after dinner. I was in excellent spirits. After the ladies (writing on Monday 9 October) had left us, he and I had some excellent conversation upon hypochondria. He said I was right in not struggling against it while it is strong. A man should just follow his inclination at the time. He said when one is in good spirits, everything, even the most indifferent, gives him pleasure. But we agreed that there was an essential difference between him and me. For he never had at any time the least anxiety as to a future state, as he was persuaded that it was in vain to think of it, as nothing could be known. He thought it might be; and that virtue and vice might be rewarded and punished. He said he had given over poetry, being convinced that he never could be better than a minor poet, and of these he had observed a succession all forgotten. I however think that to have moderate fame even for a short period is desirable. It is a pleasure. It is so much enjoyment. I had a good deal of satisfaction in conversing with him this afternoon. But I felt my advantage in believing a benignant revelation of immortality. We drank tea with the ladies. He walked with me to town.

My interview yesterday at Maclaurin's with Sir Lawrence Dundas gave me a good deal of satisfaction. It was adding a new distinguished

---

[7] James French was a brother-in-law of John Witherspoon, president of New Jersey College (later Princeton), a signer of the Declaration of Independence. "David" here is David Campbell, the younger of the Treesbank boys.

[8] Neither Boswell nor Sir Walter Scott (so far as we are aware) ever stated that they were in each other's company, but it is impossible to believe that they were not. If Scott (a boy of nine) was not absent from school this day, this was one of the occasions, for he was a member of Luke Fraser's class from 1778 to 1782.

ALEXANDER BOSWELL, LORD AUCHINLECK (1707–1782) in the gown of a
Lord of Justiciary, portrait by an unknown artist, now in the Center for
British Art and British Studies at Yale University. The head is copied
from a half-length portrait by Allan Ramsay showing Lord Auchinleck
in the gown of a Lord of Session.

MARTHA RAY (1742–1779), mistress of the fourth Earl of Sandwich; murdered by James Hackman in the Piazza of Covent
Garden, 7 April 1779. A magazine print; the portrait copied
from a painting by Nathaniel Dance. The scene below depicts
the assassination.

ROBERT MACQUEEN, LORD BRAXFIELD (1722–1799), painting by Sir Henry
Raeburn, about 1790, which now hangs in the Advocates' Library, Edinburgh. Lord Braxfield succeeded Lord Auchinleck on the Justiciary bench
in 1780, and it was on this occasion that Boswell wrote his anonymous
Letter to Lord Braxfield.

THE HONOURABLE TOPHAM BEAUCLERK (1739–1780), great-grandson of
Charles II and Nell Gwyn and one of the original members of The Club.
From a water-colour drawing, probably by G. P. Harding, inscribed in
an unknown hand: "Topham Beauclerk, from the original painted at
Padua by Brompton." The "original" is the painting by Richard
Brompton, "Edward Duke of York with his Friends..." now in the
Royal Collection.

A NOTE, by Samuel Johnson, to Sir Joshua Reynolds, who was presiding at The Club the night of 4 April 1781, excusing himself because Henry Thrale had died that morning. On the back is written, in George Steevens's hand: "Note to The Club, on Mr. Thrale's death."

CHARLOTTE ANN BURNEY (1761–1838), younger daughter of Dr. Charles Burney, the musician. An oval miniature by Charles Jagger, showing her as Mrs. Broome, 1798 or later, present whereabouts unknown, here reproduced from a photograph in the National Portrait Gallery. Her description of a dinner party at which she met Boswell, 7 April 1781, is printed for the first time in this volume.

SIR JOHN PRINGLE, BT. (1707–1782), the eminent physician and President of the Royal Society, who was a lifelong friend of Boswell and his father. His death, in January 1782, is recorded in this volume. The portrait, a half-length oval by Thomas Gainsborough, showing him wearing a brown coat and powdered wig, is now in the possession of W. R. Rees Davies, Q.C., M.P., London.

AN EXCELLENT NEW

WAR SONG.

THE WORDS ADAPTED

To Mr MUSCHET's Quick March

FOR THE

EDINBURGH DEFENSIVE BAND.

COLONEL CROSBIE takes the field,
   To France and Spain he will not yield,
But still maintain his high command
At the head of the noble DEFENSIVE BAND.
  Hark! what a glorious volley
  At the word of command of Major JOLLY! (a)
    On Heriot's Green,
    Now with wonder are seen,
The bravest Warriors in all the land!

  WITH stately air, and spirit gay,
    Behold them drawn up in battle array;
Such Champions never appear'd before,
Not in the most famous days of yore.
  How grand they look in their Blue and Yellow!
  Ev'ry man in the ranks is a capital fellow:
    With a lustre they shine
    Above all in the line;
Great Britain can't boast of another such Corps.

   THEY laugh at a broadside from daring PAUL JONES,
    For LAUDER (b) will set all their broken bones,
And GEORGE REID (c), who's their Printer, will give them their fill
Of th' infallible Tinctures and Balsams of HILL.
  WOODS, (d) on the Stage, will bring forth their great actions,
  And GIBSON (e) adjust their Accompts ev'n to fractions;
    Lofty SMITH (f) hold the Right,
    And all Stations BAIN WHYTE (g),
And JACK (h) furnish Liquors while Heroes can swill.

   To die, or to conquer, determin'd they seem;
    NEILSON (i) has ready their Widows Scheme;
And TOUCH (k) to their memory will drink a full bowl,
(All the Kirk (l) does for any departed soul.)
  To proudest perfection there's nothing a wanting,
  And in Painting's rich glow
    All the world must acknowledge their Music's enchanting:
    NAISMITH's (m) Canvas shall show
Their immortal atchievements from pole to pole!

(a) An eminent Master Tailor.
(b) Surgeon to the Corps, and a Member of the Royal College of Surgeons at Edinburgh.
(c) Who sells all Sir JOHN HILL's medicines, as appears by frequent advertisements in the
    CALEDONIAN MERCURY.
(d) The ingenious Actor and Poet.
(e) Secretary to the Band, and Writer in Edinburgh.
(f) An eminent Extracter, and the tallest man in the Corps.
(g) Agent, or Solicitor, before the Court of Session, First Clerk to Mr M'Laurin, Advocate;
    and the Gentleman who, in this City, first planned, and set on foot the embodying of a
    Band, so much to the Honour of Scotland.
(h) An eminent Vintner, and one of the Band of Music.
(i) Clerk to the Rev. Dr WEBSTER, first Projector, Framer, and Promoter, of the Ministers Wi-
    dows Fund.
(k) The Rev. Mr TOUCH, Chaplain to the Corps, and Minister of the West Kirk Chapel of Ease.
(l) The Kirk does not allow of prayers for the dead, and has not even a Burial Service.
(m) Who has already given various Specimens of his Talents, particularly in the elegant deco-
    rations in the High Church of Edinburgh.

An Excellent New War Song. Written by Boswell, printed by George Reid as a broadside, 7 1/16 × 17 3/8 inches, and sold at the Parliament House, Edinburgh, on 16 July 1782. The copy of this broadside at Yale is the only one so far reported.

character to my collection. He appeared to me not a cunning, shrewd man of the world, as I had imagined, but a comely, jovial Scotch gentleman of good address but not bright parts.[9] Lady Wallace was there, and entertained us exceedingly. I told her today that she was happy in saying a multiplicity of good things and none that were bad. There was nothing in flashing away sometimes well, often ill. She had fired above forty shot without missing. I had paid her a visit some days ago and also this forenoon; was amused and charmed with her, without being feverishly amorous. Several of the Town Council dined at Maclaurin's. We drank success to him.[1] I resolved not to be warm in the Town politics. I played at whist tonight and lost a little without fretting. Went home at nine. Had drank at dinner four glasses, and felt that quantity heat me. Wrote yesterday the *Hypochondriack* No. 36, I think all of it.[2] Sir Lawrence said, "I am old and lame and cannot visit my friends, but I shall be very glad to see you at my house." I waited on him this morning, and was well received by him, his lady, and son. I liked him much.

[9] Sir Lawrence, M.P. for Edinburgh, was a remote connexion of the Arniston family, but not on good terms with them. Boss of the Edinburgh political machine, he was in danger of losing his seat in Parliament because in the previous spring he had supported Dunning's resolution that the influence of the Crown ought to be diminished. At this moment he was engaged in a complicated struggle to delay the election of City Member until the succession of the new magistrates and Town Council, who could be counted on to return him. The existing city government (which was controlled by the Arniston Dundases) had a majority against him. His opponent was young William Miller, with whom Boswell had nearly fought a duel in 1774.

[1] Maclaurin may have been managing Sir Lawrence's politics. The present paragraph is a tangle of events of the 19th and the 20th.

[2] "*The Hypochondriack* . . . has lately returned from having passed some time in the country, where in a sound and placid state of mind he relished a rural life, and, divested of prejudice . . . considered the subject with a good deal of attention, and was convinced that there are better enjoyments in the country than he had before supposed.—There is a feeling of dignity and consequence in being master of land above anything else. It is the natural dominion of man over the earth, granted him by his Almighty Creator, and no artificial dominion is felt like it. What is the first minister of state in London, personally, when compared with a duke, or an earl, a knight, or a squire, the lord of a manor and a proprietor of extensive domains in the country? And the comparison will hold, in different gradations, between the power of men in offices which have been framed in political society and that influence which rises immediately and certainly out of the right to land.—He who is master of land sees all around him obedient to his will. Not only can he totally change the face of inanimate nature, but can command the animals of each species, and even the human race itself, to multiply or to diminish, to continue or to migrate, according to his pleasure. Limited as he is by our government and our laws, he is yet very essentially the arbiter of happiness and unhappiness over a district" (*The Hypochondriack*, No. 36, corrected from Boswell's revised set of the papers in the Boswell papers at Yale).

I even felt for him as a man ungratefully used in his old age. I visited today at Dunn's Hotel the Rev. Mr. Nicholls.

THURSDAY 21 SEPTEMBER. (Writing on Tuesday 10 October.) Went with Commissioner Cochrane and visited Sir. L. and Lady Dundas. The Rev. Mr. Nicholls and Grange dined with us. My spirits were so excellent at present that I was a full match for Nicholls in vivacity, so that I relished him better than when he was last here. After tea I went with him to his lodgings and heard him read his journal of his travels in Scotland. His landscape was very well done. But it wanted figures.[3] I again in my journals have little else but character, not having as yet attended much to inanimate objects. We read a little of *J.-J. Rousseau jugé par lui-même*, a new publication which we thought genuine. I was roused by his eloquence, but saw with a sound look that he was mad.[4] I stayed with Nicholls and supped. I eat apple pie and drank water, and had a deal of animated talk.

FRIDAY 22 SEPTEMBER. (Writing on Tuesday 10 October.) Dined at Commissioner Cochrane's; young Craigengillan and his governor, Dr. Adams, Rector of the High School, etc., there. I drank only water, and was quite as I could wish to be. Found my association of ideas in my boyish days as to the High School dissolved. Saw it as a good place for education.[5] What a world of chimeras had I when young! It is impossible to give a notion of this to others. Both Berkeley and Hume have a good deal of truth in their systems. Their fault is excess, by which, while they augment the dominion of perceptions, they annihilate the substance and power both of body and mind.

SATURDAY 23 SEPTEMBER. (Writing on Tuesday 10 October.) Carried Nicholls to visit Lady Wallace, after which we visited Maclaurin. I was as lively as when in London. Commissioner Cochrane, his son Willie,[6] young Craigengillan and his governor, the young Campbells, and the laird of Logan dined with us. I went in the evening to a concert for the benefit

[3] Norton Nicholls, close friend of Temple and the poet Gray, had last visited Boswell in Edinburgh in 1774. The journal of his travels in Scotland was never published and is not known to exist.

[4] Properly, *Rousseau jugé de Jean-Jacques,* of which the first dialogue had recently been published at Lichfield from a manuscript given by Rousseau to Sir Brooke Boothby.

[5] Boswell had not attended the High School although William Steven's history of the school represents him as a student there. The James Boswell in the High School lists was no doubt his first cousin, Dr. John Boswell's eldest son.

[6] Commissioner Cochrane's will in the Scottish Record Office shows that he had two natural children living in 1787, William and Elizabeth. There is nothing surprising in this, but it is most surprising that Boswell's journal should not previously have mentioned so near a relation (his mother's first cousin), and that he should never have mentioned him again. Elizabeth is not mentioned at all.

of H. Reinagle, and enjoyed it much. Nicholls and Maclaurin supped with us. We laughed a great deal, but Nicholls gave a ridiculous, profane account of his ordination, which offended me much. I could not check him before Maclaurin, who would have taken his part, and he would have grown worse. I was quite disgusted, and bore him only as my friend Temple's friend, in the common loose acceptation.

SUNDAY 24 SEPTEMBER. (Writing on Tuesday 10 October.) Stayed at home in the forenoon. Called on Nicholls to have talked to him of his indecent behaviour last night, but did not find him. Dined calm at home, and went in the afternoon with my wife to the Tolbooth Kirk and heard Dr. Webster preach. In the evening the children said divine lessons well. Major Montgomerie, with whom I had been yesterday and heard such a state of the votes in Ayrshire that his success was morally certain,[7] and young Auchinsoul, his aide-de-camp as I call him, supped with us. I drank water. Yet we were as cordial as if I had inflamed myself with wine or punch to the utmost.

MONDAY 25 SEPTEMBER. (Writing on Tuesday 10 October.) Nicholls was to set out this morning. I sent to see if he was gone, that I might have called if he was not. He was just stepping into the chaise. Perhaps it was as well I did not see him. I might have been too warm and have exasperated him. I shall write to Temple about him; and I believe shall have no more to say to him. For a profane clergyman is contemptible as a fool and detestable as a cheat.[8] I called on Major Montgomerie and went with him to Colonel Mure Campbell's. I then called on Harry Erskine, to whom I was at present equal in spirits. We walked out and met Lord Glencairn, the first time of my seeing him since his affairs were known

---

[7] See above, 8 September 1780.

[8] "Nicholls was some days here.... His foppery is unbecoming in a clergyman. But I was really much offended with him one night when he supped with me. Maclaurin, who I fear is an infidel, was the only other person in company. Nicholls gave a ludicrous account of his ordination. Said he applied to the Archbishop of York (Drummond), who asked him what books he had read on divinity. 'Why, truly, my Lord,' said he, 'I must tell you frankly—none at all, though I have read other books enough.' 'O very well,' said the Archbishop, 'I'll give you a letter to one who will examine you properly.' Accordingly he got a letter to a clergyman in London, who examined him—and to cut short this disagreeable story, Nicholls said that he did not well understand what was meant when desired to write on the necessity of a Mediator—that he wrote some strange stuff as fast as he would do a card to a lady; and that he had never read the Greek New Testament. He made a very profane farce of the whole. Maclaurin laughed exceedingly. I could only be grave. For if I had argued on the impropriety of the story, the matter would have been made worse while they were two to one.... I shall never receive him again into my house" (To Temple, 3–4 September, 3 November 1780). He met Nicholls again by chance at a club in London in 1789, and they "were civil to each other" (To Temple, 31 March 1789).

to be in disorder.[9] We all three took half a round of the Meadow. I was more particularly attentive than ever to show respect to the Earl. In the afternoon Mr. Shepherd, the Minister of Muirkirk, called on me. I had him and Grange to sup. His pedantic forwardness disgusted me, though I thought him a good man in essentials. We had prayers. My excellent spirits made me, like Charity, bear all things, hope all things.[1]

TUESDAY 26 SEPTEMBER. (Writing on Tuesday 10 October.) I had Mr. James Cummyng to dine with me, and was amused and interested with genealogy and antiquities of various kinds. He stayed till pretty late in the evening. This was a little feast. I should have mentioned some days ago a scene equal to any one in Sterne. I went to one McGrigor, a lapidary in the Potterrow, to get some pebbles cut.[2] The poor industrious lad had a room which served for kitchen and bed-chamber, and a closet off it which served for working in. He had a wife and a young child. His wife was busy washing plates in the room; and that the child might be kept without wearying, he had it set down on a board at a little distance from his wheel, the quick motion and noise of which amused it as well as if it had been dandled and sung to by its mother. A better picture of industry and contrivance in miniature cannot be imagined.

WEDNESDAY 27 SEPTEMBER. (Writing on Thursday 12 October.) I recollect nothing that passed. Yes, my wife and I dined and drank tea at Dr. Grant's, and old Lady Grant and I had much talk.

THURSDAY 28 SEPTEMBER. (Writing on Thursday 12 October.) Dined at Sir Lawrence Dundas's. Lady Wallace was there, as were Commissioner Cochrane and Dr. Webster, who had never seen her before. Even the Commissioner was amused, though a little afraid. Webster was delighted. Maclaurin was there too. The dinner was excellent, the dessert of fruits elegantly luxurious. I drank a few glasses of wine. I was good company. I liked Sir Lawrence more and more. There was a kindliness and even a simplicity in his manner that put me in mind of Lord Strichen. He talked a great deal of his *adventures*, as I may call them, with the Duke of Cumberland's army in 1745–6. I thought I might get materials from him for my intended history of that period.[3] We went to coffee and tea,

[9] He sold Kilmaurs in 1786.

[1] 1 Corinthians 13. 7.

[2] Grange had advised him a few days before to have the Boswell crest (the hawk on the title-page of this book) cut on one of the pebbles he had found at Auchinleck. "Said he, 'Let him perch on his native stone' " (*Boswelliana*, 22 September 1780).

[3] Sir Lawrence's war-time "adventures" (meaning presumably exciting or hazardous travels about Scotland with the Government forces) appear not to have been recorded, but there is plenty of information about his business dealings with the Army. Younger son of an impoverished branch of the Dundas family (his father kept a drapery-shop in the Luckenbooths), he set up as a merchant contractor. During the

so many of us. I felt some of that cloudy dreariness which has so often come upon me. I suppose I had loaded my stomach too much, and dress and good behaviour cramped me somewhat. On coming home I got a card from young Mr. Sibthorpe, with a letter from his father. The young man was arrived at Macfarlane's inn, and weary after his journey. So I wrote back I would wait on him in the morning and conduct him to my house to breakfast. Dr. Webster and Grange supped with us. We had prayers. I grew clear again.

FRIDAY 29 SEPTEMBER. (Writing on Saturday 14 October.) Called on young Mr. Sibthorpe and brought him and Mr. Irwin, scholar of Trinity College, Dublin, with me to breakfast. Dr. Webster came by appointment. It was agreeable to have an Irish cousin, a grandson of General Cochrane's, with us.[4] But as Mr. Irwin, who had been his tutor, had no instructions as to settling him, I was anxious; and though I had written to his father on Thursday stating the different schemes, I wrote again tonight. I had yesterday talked again on the subject with Adam Smith at the custom-house, and had agreed to breakfast with him today. Sibthorpe's arrival made me break this engagement, but I went to Smith before breakfast and made my apology. As he had been very obliging to me when at Glasgow, I thought it not right to keep altogether at a distance from him, though I disapproved of his praise of David Hume and attack upon Oxford.[4a] I walked about with Mess. Sibthorpe and Irwin in the forenoon. They dined with me along with old Lady Grant, etc., and they stayed the evening and supped.

'45, the recommendation of a friend who was aide-de-camp to the Duke of Cumberland brought him contracts for supplying Cumberland's army in Scotland and later in Flanders. At the time of his death in 1781, his personal fortune was reported as £900,000.—Johnson had suggested to Boswell during their Ashbourne jaunt that he might write the history of the '45 ("if you were not an idle dog": Journal, 19 September 1777), and Boswell had gone so far as to compose a title: *History of the Civil War in Great Britain in 1745 and 1746.* He says in the *Life of Johnson* (19 September 1777) that he abandoned the project on hearing that John Home was engaged on an account of "that interesting warfare." Home's book was not published till 1802.

[4] Boswell was General Cochrane's grand-nephew; he and Sibthorpe were second cousins. Boswell was helping to place him in a university (see above, 12 September 1779). In 1787 Sibthorpe consulted Boswell about his supposed claim to the Kincardine peerage, through his descent from General Cochrane's mother, Lady Mary Bruce, wife of William Cochrane of Ochiltree and elder daughter of the second earl. Boswell then corresponded with Robert Boswell, the Lyon-Depute, about the matter, but nothing ever came of it.

[4a] Boswell, returning to the practice of his earlier years, had written memoranda for 24 September and for this day. The present one (the original is written in Italian) reads, "Breakfast Adam Smith. Think of old times and his letters with some gratitude. but remain firm to religion."

SATURDAY 30 SEPTEMBER. (Writing on Saturday 14 October.) Mr. Irwin went off for Ireland. Dr. Webster, Mr. Sibthorpe, and I went to Valleyfield, the Doctor and I having intended to go this day. We could not get a chaise at the North Ferry, so were rowed up to Newmill by four boys. I called them the cat crew, for I said they were fit only to row cats in the first place, as being light, and next that if the boat overset, they could swim. I was in charming spirits, and conceived a design to write Dr. Webster's life.[5] The boys did finely. We got to Valleyfield to dinner, and were happy.

SUNDAY 1 OCTOBER. (Writing on Saturday the 14.) I perceive I must contract my journalizing. We went to Culross Church. I never was sounder or more cheerful in my life. Mr. McAlpine preached first. Then Dr. Webster mounted his original pulpit and preached short and eloquent on Revelation, Chap. ———. Mr. Sibthorpe and I paid a visit to Lord and Lady Dundonald. Returned to Valleyfield to dinner. The Rev. Mr. Rolland came in the evening. Dr. Webster said a prayer. I was just as I could wish.

MONDAY 2 OCTOBER. (Writing on Saturday 14.) I was Dr. Webster's amanuensis for a Memorial on Lord Dundonald's affairs.[6] The Rev. Dr. Cooper of the English Chapel at Edinburgh came.[7] We had Mrs. Agnes Preston, Dr. and Colonel Preston as part of the family at this time. Young Dundas of Blair, a curious being, dined. The day passed excellently. To mark all my ideas and reflections would fill a book. I breakfasted today with Mr. Stobie, and I saw the house in which Sir George Bruce of Carnock [8] lived.

TUESDAY 3 OCTOBER. (Writing on Saturday the 14.) Colonel Preston, Mr. Sibthorpe, and I walked to the Forest of Culross and viewed part of it as a specimen of what was to be Lord Dundonald's great fund of credit. I was as fond of Culross, and had my mind as serenely filled with such sentiments and affections as my dear mother gave me, as at the best periods of my youngest life. We met Dr. Webster at Lord Dundonald's, where we dined. I visited Mrs. Jean Erskine and Mr. Rolland. The Earl was very violent in argument after dinner.

WEDNESDAY 4 OCTOBER. (Writing on Saturday the 14.) Sauntered

---

[5] Boswell was considering this scheme as late as 1784, but, like his many biographical projects other than the *Life of Johnson*, it came to nothing.

[6] Lord Dundonald was more or less impoverished throughout his life. His estate was loaded with debt when he succeeded to it, and his unentailed estates were eaten up by the expense of his scientific pursuits (see above, 17 October 1778, n. 6).

[7] Myles Cooper, president of King's College (now Columbia University), New York, from 1763 to 1775, when he was forced to flee as a loyalist.

[8] Boswell's great-great-great-grandfather.

about till a headache, which distressed me in the morning, went off. Felt myself quite complacent in every view yesterday. At night sat awhile with Dr. Webster in his room, which was close to mine, and as we were neighbours, proposed he should pray; which he did, and I felt myself comforted. The same good practice was followed tonight.

THURSDAY 5 OCTOBER. (Writing on Saturday 14.) We set out after breakfast. This short stay at Valleyfield was most agreeable. I read some of Miss Burney's *Evelina*, and wondered at her talents. But I was much edified by *Letters of Certain Jews to Voltaire*,[9] of which I read the first volume. I resolved to read the other volume. I never drank above four glasses of wine any day. I had boiled milk and dry toast for supper, and really enjoyed peace and joy. I was a little concerned for Lord Dundonald's impending bankruptcy, but not much cast down, as Culross was not an estate of *his* family. I made witty verses on Dr. Webster's project of raising money by selling shares of the Culross Forest. I again wrote to Dr. Johnson to meet me at York. The only uneasiness I felt was in hearing from Stobie that my father had vested his executry in trustees for the payment of any debts he might owe, in the first place, and after that, to be conveyed to me. This was a kind of distrust of me, though it has been often done to make entails absolutely secure against any debt of the entailer's. He assured me my father had left no legacies, but only annuities of £60 to my brother John and £10 each to Dr. Boswell's daughters. I was still more uneasy at being told that Lady Auchinleck had locality lands for her jointure,[1] because that would keep me totally from all power over a part

[9] Philip Le Fanu's translation of *Lettres de quelques Juifs portugais, allemands, et polonais à M. de Voltaire*, by the Abbé Antoine Guénée. As a reward for this attack upon Voltaire, the Abbé was given a canonry in the cathedral of Amiens.

[1] Though Boswell now first hears of this disposition, it had been made four years before. In his contract of marriage, 25 November 1769, Lord Auchinleck had bound himself and his heirs to pay £200 on his death to Lady Auchinleck for mournings and the furniture for a house; also to provide her with a jointure for life of £150 a year, he reserving the option of making this either an annuity or a locality over lands. On 8 August 1776, the day after he and Boswell signed the entail, being "resolved to augment her said liferent and make it more suitable to my estate and to enable her to live more comfortably and in the station of my widow after my death," he had bound himself, his heirs and successors to "infeft and seise" her in liferent in a series of named farms within the estate of Auchinleck the rents of which amounted to a good deal more than £150. (In 1795 these rents were worth £500.) The provision of £200 for mournings and furniture was changed by this and a later disposition to £50 for mournings, all the furnishings of the house in St. Andrew's Square, the coach, the two best carriage-horses, and their harness. She had liferent of the house apparently from the time of its purchase. (Bond of Liferent and Disposition, Lord Auchinleck to Mrs. Elizabeth Boswell, his Spouse, 8 August 1776; Disposition, Lord Auchinleck to Mrs. Elizabeth Boswell, his Spouse, 24 March 1779; Trust Disposition, etc., by Lord

of the estate during her life. Stobie said like a little dog that it was better a stepmother should have no dependence at all upon the heir. He said Lady Auchinleck might have had what she pleased from my father, but nobody was less greedy than she was. Everything he had settled was of his own accord. He was for buying a house in Edinburgh and leaving it to her, and she would not hear of it. I said it would be better to give her a sum of money than the furniture in my father's house at Edinburgh; and I mentioned the report in the shire of Ayr that she had carried large trunks and boxes full of things from Auchinleck to Edinburgh. Stobie averred it was not true. I said she had taken great care of my father, and should be not only comfortably but liberally provided. What a deal of vexation has this second marriage of my father's occasioned to me, perhaps in some degree without reason on my part. Worthy Grange suggested that I might soon put an end to the trustees by putting money into their hands sufficient to discharge my father's debts. We got to Edinburgh in good time to dinner. Dr. Webster went to Lady Dundonald's. I was happy again with my wife and children. We shook hands with Major George Preston as we drove through the New Town. My wife and I invited Mr. Sibthorpe to stay in our house till settled with a professor.

FRIDAY 6 OCTOBER. (Writing on Sunday the 15.) Mr. Sibthorpe appeared both to my wife and me to be a most amiable young man; just seventeen, very little, somewhat dull of hearing, quiet, modest, of good principles, and of decent good sense. We had already an affection for him as if he had been our own child. He seemed happy living with us. He and I visited Lady Dundonald this forenoon and afterwards Commissioner Cochrane. Baron Maule was with him. He and I had a good deal of lively conversation while the Commissioner and Sibthorpe sat silent by us. As I expressed myself somewhat warmly on my friend Major Montgomerie's side, the Commissioner admonished me with a kind of heat which I did not like at the time. He said, "You are cutting your own throat. It will be told to your father that you speak at the Cross against his side, and he will be offended." Perhaps the old, cool, prudent Commissioner was right. Yet it is hard not to have the liberty of speaking when I have not a vote as I ought to have. My father has not treated me as a man should be treated, but has looked on me as a mere dependant on him. This has, I dare say, prevented me from making a greater figure in the world than I do. Though it may be it has secured me from splendid ruin. Lady Dundonald and her sons George and Andrew, and Balbarton dined and drank tea with us. The Countess was much pleased with Balbarton, and invited

Auchinleck, 1 March 1782; all three registered in the Books of Council and Session, 7 September 1782.)

him to come and see her. He stayed the evening, played whist and supped. It was truly cheering to see one past fourscore enjoying life. All gloom appeared fictitious.

SATURDAY 7 OCTOBER. (Writing on Sunday the 15.) My wife and three eldest children and Mr. Sibthorpe and I dined at Sir Alexander Dick's. I was in choice spirits, in so much that I was entertained even with Anthony Barclay.[2] Sir Alexander was all life. I had visited Lady Colville in the forenoon.

SUNDAY 8 OCTOBER. (Writing on Sunday the 15.) Mr. Sibthorpe and I were at the New English Chapel forenoon and afternoon, in Lady Colville's seat. I enjoyed devotion delightfully. I had on Friday written to Professor Robison, fairly and frankly stipulating that if my young friend Mr. Sibthorpe should be put under his care, he should hear nothing that might incline him to infidelity. I had a very satisfactory answer today, having sent my letter only yesterday. I replied, and as he was confined by a cold, called on him in the forenoon and was much pleased with him. The correspondence between us as to the young gentleman's being preserved from infidelity is worth preserving. Adam Smith had given me reason to fear the deistical influence of Scotch professors. Dr. Webster and Mrs. Mingay supped with us. Dr. Webster prayed.

MONDAY 9 OCTOBER. (Writing on Monday the 16.) Mr. Sibthorpe and I dined at Commissioner Cochrane's. It was a very wet day. He carried us out in his chaise, and sent it in with us again. I was so sound at present that I was content in any society. Mr. Sibthorpe was quite easy in our family, and not in the least troublesome. He generally goes up every evening to Dr. Grant's to a card party.

TUESDAY 10 OCTOBER. (Writing on Monday the 16.) This day alone I left Mr. Sibthorpe and dined with Mr. Hunter-Blair, where were Sir Lawrence and Lady Dundas, Maclaurin, Mr. Watts from New York, and Captain Kennedy, heir male of the Earl of Cassillis, who was married to Watts's daughter, etc.[3] Kennedy and I took to one another sympathetically.

---

[2] Boswell probably means no more than that he ordinarily found Barclay dull. Barclay was a Writer to the Signet, and in 1773 gave his residence as James's Court, on the fifth floor of the entry in which Boswell lived. The Boswell Papers preserve an unrevealing note from him to Sir Alexander Dick.

[3] Captain Archibald Kennedy of the Navy, later eleventh Earl of Cassillis, son of the Receiver General and Collector of Customs of New York, inherited from his father an estate near Hoboken, and from his first wife (a Schuyler) further large property, so that in 1765 he was said to own more houses in New York than any other man. Stationed at Boston when the famous stamps arrived, he declined to receive them on his vessel for safe custody, and for this supposed act of sympathy with the insurgents was removed from his command. After this he was very careful not to arouse further suspicion in the British authorities, so that the patriots of the Continental Army regarded him as a

There was a long drink of claret. I tired of the noise, though I drank a few glasses and sung with jovial humour. Between nine and ten as I passed by Lady Wallace's, I saw her at the window, and having beckoned her, she threw up the sash. I asked if she was in; she said yes. So I paid her a visit, heard her read several pieces of poetry of her own composition, made fine speeches to her, and also talked to her freely as to her conduct, as she was going to Bath. Her indelicacy disgusted me. I was not in such good spirits tonight as for some time past, being jaded.

WEDNESDAY 11 OCTOBER. (Writing on Monday the 16.) My fore-noons pass very idly. I have been only once copying the Privy Council Records, and indeed have read scarcely anything. Mr. Sibthorpe and I dined and drank tea at Mr. Wellwood's; Mr. Erskine of Cardross and Lady Christian there. I was in excellent spirits.

THURSDAY 12 OCTOBER. (Writing on Monday the 16.) One of these days I had a walk in the High Street with Andrew Erskine, who was then in bad spirits. I stipulated that we should say nothing of the Ayrshire election, but talk of ourselves and our own feelings. He said that bad spirits distressed one more than any real evil; and as an instance he mentioned that Miss Clemie Elphinstone had found the pain of a broken leg and the apprehension of lameness much easier than the uneasy weariness and discontent of hypochondria. I told Erskine I was to write Dr. Johnson's life in scenes.[4] He approved. This forenoon I visited Colonel Mure Campbell, and was much pleased with his conversation. He told me that when drinking with Lord Kellie and Shaw-Stewart, when they attacked religion, he said, "The great principle, the existence of a Supreme Being, is clear from all around us. And as to Christianity, I know that at present you can turn everything into ridicule. But, if you please, I will talk to you upon it tomorrow forenoon." I was happy to find the future Earl of Loudoun so good a man. He had two good expressions: he said Baillie, the Sheriff of Linlithgow, who moved or made a speech against the late opposition to Ministry, was a "*sub*reptile"; and that being too lenient to offenders was "criminal humanity." I said it was cruelty to the body

---

loyalist and confiscated half his property. His town house (No. 1 Broadway on the Battery) was appropriated for General Washington. John Watts also had suffered confiscation and proscription.

4 That is, was to build his book around his dramatic recordings of Johnson's conversation. It must be remembered that this method, which now seems so obvious, was highly original and daring. Such intimate treatment of a biographical subject was a violation of an unwritten law of biographical dignity. In his account of Paoli, Boswell had digested the chronological entries of his journal into one continuous narrative, and this is his first recorded intimation that he did not intend to do the same for Johnson.

politic not to cure, though severely, or cut off a diseased—a cancerous—part, as to which the phrase is to *extirpate*. We talked with vivacity of the Ayrshire election. I said, "Both the candidates will be *tools* of the Ministry. Instead of a coarse iron tool, let [us have] one of *steel—grey steel*," alluding to the first Seton, Earl of Eglinton, who was so called.[5] We walked a long time in the Meadow, after having talked two hours in the house. I mentioned to the Colonel my intention of offering myself a candidate at our next election, and that I had spoke of it to Lord Loudoun, who seemed to approve. The Colonel said he durst say Lord Loudoun would be very well pleased I should be the man. I said I did not desire any answer from the Colonel now. But I hoped he would keep in mind what I had proposed, and I mentioned Thomas Boswell of Auchinleck having been married to a daughter of the family of Loudoun.[6] Mr. Sibthorpe and I dined at Sir Lawrence Dundas's, whom I had visited again yesterday forenoon and found alone and talked with cordially of the President's conduct to my father at the last election, adding, "He is a hollow dog." Sir Lawrence said, "Do you think I don't know him?" The dinner today was as good as when I dined here before. Sir John Whitefoord, Maclaurin, etc., were there. We drank coffee and tea. Sir John and I grew a little warm upon my relating Colonel Campbell's conversation and mine on both the candidates for Ayrshire being Ministerial tools, and in his fretfulness maintained that Sir Adam Fergusson was not uniformly Ministerial, and said he would be at Colonel Campbell for this. After he went away, Sir Lawrence said Sir Adam was as hackney a Ministerial Member as ever went from Scotland. I played whist and lost, but was in fine spirits. Mr. Sibthorpe and I stayed supper quite easily. I eat an egg and drank water.

FRIDAY 13 OCTOBER. (Writing on Monday the 16.) Having been uneasy lest Sir John Whitefoord might give an erroneous account to Colonel Mure Campbell of what passed at Sir Lawrence's yesterday, I resolved to see the Colonel first this morning. So out I walked; but being too early for him, I called at Harry Erskine's, where came Old Erskine, whom I was really glad to meet again. My mind was so sound and clear, I fully relished ancient family—high spirit—vivacity, etc., etc. I breakfasted with Colonel

---

[5] Alexander Montgomerie (born Seton), sixth Earl of Eglinton (1588–1661). According to tradition, he was so called because King James challenged his right to the title and Eglinton hinted at a duel with the reigning favourite, Lord Somerset. The King withdrew his objections, and the incident, together with Eglinton's general readiness to use his sword, earned him the nickname.

[6] Thomas Boswell (d. 1513), the first laird of Auchinleck, married Annabella, daughter of George Campbell of Loudoun, Sheriff of Ayrshire. Lord Loudoun and the Colonel were also descended from George Campbell.

Mure Campbell, having first taken him out and put him on his guard in case Sir John Whitefoord should come and talk with him of what I had told. I was somewhat hurt to think that I was yet so apt to repeat what passed in conversation, though I am much cured of the bad habit. The Colonel took it so easily, I was made easy. I felt a slight fear of a duel ensuing, as I had heard of one at the Kirkcudbright election. I thought I could go on with it pretty well. Lady Raasay and Miss MacLeod breakfasted with us. The Colonel is one of those who animate and call forth my faculties. We were very happy this morning. I found that, as Captain James Erskine said I was a Tory with Whig principles, the Colonel was a Whig with Tory principles. So we did not differ in effect. Nay, though a professed Presbyterian, he had no objection to some livings of £500 a year to encourage merit, nor to a form of prayer, nor to a crucifix. Grange dined with us today and was introduced to Mr. Sibthorpe. I called a little on Maclaurin this forenoon.[7]

SATURDAY 14 OCTOBER. (Writing on Monday the 16.) Mr. Walton from Barbados, who was come to Edinburgh to study physic, brought me a letter of recommendation from Mr. Dilly. He had with him his companion in the same line, a Mr. Waller from Portsmouth. I asked them both to dine with us today, which they did, along with young Craigengillan and his governor, whom I visited yesterday, and the young Campbells. Miss Macredie drank tea with us.

SUNDAY 15 OCTOBER. (Writing on Monday the 16.) Commissioner Cochrane came in the morning and went with Mr. Sibthorpe and me to the New English Chapel. It was curious and pleasing to see him there. It gave me the agreeable view that in time "all may be saved and come to the knowledge of the truth." [8] As yet indeed he knew but little of religion. He dined with us, sat the afternoon, and drank tea. It was perhaps wrong to stay from worship on his account. But as I am not quite regular in town, it may be pardoned. The children said divine lessons agreeably at night. Mr. and Mrs. Erskine of Alloa and Dr. Webster supped with us. The Doctor prayed.

MONDAY 16 OCTOBER. (Writing on Saturday the 21.) It is strange that I should have omitted to mention on the 13 the news of Lord Cornwallis's victory over the Americans at Camden having arrived. That Dr. Webster sent me the letter he had from his son, the Colonel, and that Mr. Sibthorpe, Grange, and I supped with him that night and drank to

---

[7] Boswell here gives a forward reference to the entry for 16 October.
[8] "Who will have all men to be saved, and to come unto the knowledge of the truth" (1 Timothy 2. 4).

my gallant cousin, etc.[9] This day went on very well, while I was agitated with the fate of the Ayrshire election. Lords Eglinton and Kellie paid us a visit before dinner. I had by desire visited Lord Buchan this forenoon and heard him read a speech intended for the peers' election.

TUESDAY 17 OCTOBER. (Writing on Saturday the 21.) Visited the Earls of Eglinton, Cassillis, and Dunmore. Was in high spirits. Was introduced to Lady Dunmore and the two young ladies, beautiful young creatures with Parisian vivacity, air, and ease.[1] Went with Mr. Sibthorpe to the election of the peers.[2] Stayed a very short while. Sir Charles Preston, Major Preston, Mr. Wellwood, and the Rev. Dr. Cooper dined with us. I was disgusted by Cooper's coarse manners and unlettered conversation. This day at intervals of leisure I wrote No. 37 of the *Hypochondriack*.[3] I went with Mr. Sibthorpe to the Assembly. Was wonderfully easy and gay.

WEDNESDAY 18 OCTOBER. (Writing on Saturday the 21.) Visited the Earl of Loudoun. No news as yet of the Ayrshire election. Was anxious to uneasiness. Lords Eglinton and Kellie had gone this morning to the Hunters' meeting at Kelso.[4] I was much pleased to see Lord Kellie improved after an absence of about six years. He was more sedate and well-behaved, and not like Mount Vesuvius, as my uncle, the Doctor, described him formerly. I met Harry Erskine and went with him to Maclaurin's for a little, and got some difficulties in law cleared. Prevailed on Maclaurin to join Sir Charles Preston, Dr. Webster, and so many more of us at a dinner at Jack's. We were hearty. I drank very little, as I now constantly do, not six glasses at any time, but was excellent company. Maclaurin, Major George Preston, and I played at heads or tails for shillings, Dr. Webster exclaiming, "Dreadful! Gaming in miniature!" I had breakfasted today with Ulbster and revised some of his letters on the Scotch language addressed to me.[5] Maclaurin and I went from Jack's to Sir Lawrence Dundas's. Went into the drawing-room quite easy and sat with Lady Dundas and her company till the gentlemen came from the dining-

[9] James Webster commanded Cornwallis's right and began the attack. Cornwallis's victory over General Gates occurred on 16 August 1780.

[1] They had recently been in Paris. More interesting is their having before that lived some years in New York and Williamsburg. See above, 8 July 1779, n. 5a.

[2] Fourteen peers were re-elected, and the Duke of Atholl and the Earl of Glencairn were elected in place of the Earl of Bute and the Earl of Breadalbane.

[3] A second essay on life in the country.

[4] The Society of Hunters was a fashionable racing-club of Edinburgh.

[5] Sir John Sinclair of Ulbster's *Observations on the Scottish Dialect* was published in 1782. If, as Boswell implies, he at first contemplated printing it in the form of letters, he changed his mind. It is possible that Boswell had communicated to Sinclair the material which he had gathered for the Scots Dictionary which he had projected in 1764.

room. Lady Dundas had called on my wife yesterday, and my wife on her today, so that an acquaintance was forming. Sir Lawrence very kindly said he had a quarrel with me (or a phrase to that purpose) because I had not dined with him on Monday when Lord Kellie proposed it to me. I said I did not think I could take that liberty. He spoke so warmly in the affirmative that I said, "Well, I shall never do so again." "Then," said he, "I forgive you." I played whist and won. It was quite comfortable tonight. We stayed supper. Lord Cassillis, Lord and Lady Dalhousie, etc., were of the party. The Ayrshire election was still a mystery. Sir Lawrence was a warm friend to the Montgomerie interest. A rumour went that Lord Advocate was gone to Ayr, and as there was yet no accounts, something extraordinary was apprehended. I suggested that he might be gone to persuade my father to bring forth seven or eight votes of which he had renunciations, but which might be revived by redelivering the renunciations, which were not yet made effectual by registration.[6] I was grievously worked by this possibility. Sir Lawrence said he had been engaged in politics since the year 1747, and had named beforehand the Lords of Session on each question he had. This charge of partiality, which is very general and that too amongst our most sensible observers (for David Erskine told me a few days ago that, tell him the county and he would tell the votes of all—or perhaps he said *most*—of the judges in political questions), shocked me and made me dread being a Lord of Session. Yet I found Sir Lawrence erroneous in chronology; for he said he had stated an election cause of his to my father, who was to judge of it, in 1747, whereas my father did not come to the bench till 1754. As Maclaurin and I walked home, he said he wished Major Montgomerie success, for he liked him, and he hated George Fergusson [7] and "would crack him like a louse." He maintained that a man who was not vindictive had no warmth of friendship. He "would not ride the water on him." [8] For his part he never forgave. "Curse your enemies," said he with keenness. I said to him

[6] In 1774 the Lord President had persuaded Lord Auchinleck to make ten fictitious votes in favour of Fergusson. They did not "mature" in time for that election, but apparently Lord Auchinleck prudently got renunciations from all the nominal voters thus enfranchised and held on to them without registering them, in case they should be needed in the next election. If needed, they could have been redelivered to these nominal voters, since they would have "matured" by then. Boswell here reduces the ten votes of 1774 to seven or eight, perhaps because there had been deaths among the fictitious voters, perhaps because some of them were showing scruples. He says in his journal for 27 January 1775 that at that time four of the ten were resolved not to take the oath.

[7] See above, 31 August 1780, n. 2.

[8] Would not trust him in an emergency; literally, would not ford a river on his back.

he was encouraging a diabolical principle. I hope it was the spleen of the moment. I went home resolved to be distrustful of so unchristian a being.

THURSDAY 19 OCTOBER. (Writing on Monday the 30th.) Called on Lord Loudoun pretty early. He had no final account of the Ayrshire election, but that the previous votes were ten of majority on Major Montgomerie's side. After leaving him I got a letter from Sundrum with the joyful news, franked *Hu. Montgomerie.* I run to Lord Loudoun and wished him joy. Then to Sir Lawrence Dundas, then to Lord Cassillis, who was rather *cool.* He did not much rejoice that the family of Eglinton had succeeded. I was in capital spirits. Grange rejoiced with me. I dined at Dr. Blair's at North Merchiston; Commissioners Cochrane and Smith and Mr. Morehead there. It was a very tolerable party. In the evening Mr. Sibthorpe and I walked to the New Town in a storm of wind and rain and supped at Mr. Wellwood's with Sir Charles Preston, etc. I was cheerful, and more calm than I could have supposed after the Ayrshire victory. But there was danger from a petition.

FRIDAY 20 OCTOBER. (Writing on Monday the 30.) I recollect nothing but that Grange supped with us.

SATURDAY 21 OCTOBER. (Writing on Monday the 30.) Maclaurin and I went in his chaise to Craighouse and took up Lord Covington, and then we drove to Arniston, where we arrived between three and four. Nobody at home. The butler said he could only give us a bit of bread and a glass of wine; but when we seemed inclined to take it, he said he could not give us a fire. This was cold indeed. So we turned and jogged on to Melville, where we had intended to dine next day. Lord Advocate had Lord Glencairn and Sir William Murray sitting with him after dinner. We had some good things at a table by ourselves and excellent champagne. Then we joined and drank claret. I was allowed to be moderate. I felt myself quite comfortable here. I was satisfied that my prejudices against Lord Advocate were imaginary. Lord Glencairn went away. The rest of us went to tea and coffee with Lady Augusta Murray and old Lady Arniston, and played whist. I drank only water at night. I had a warm bedchamber, and was quite as I could wish.

SUNDAY 22 OCTOBER. (Writing on Monday the 30.) Breakfast was as good a meal as ever I saw it. Lady Arniston was wonderfully well. Lord Covington went away after breakfast. Lord Advocate expressed his wonder that I had never before been at Melville; and though it had rained a good deal and the ground was wet, he very obligingly walked with me over the best part of his place, which I found to be truly a treasure so near Edinburgh. The River of Esk and well-planted banks and well-dressed fields formed a goodly scene. He seemed to me the frankest and best-humoured politician that could be. I joked with him on the strange forgetfulness as to my father's votes. Told him I was trembling for some days for fear they should be recollected, and that he would have set them a-going. He said he certainly would if he had thought of them, and laughed with me. Maclaurin walked with us and led him to speak of the differences between Sir Lawrence Dundas and him till he really made me view his conduct with no violent disapprobation. I was quite easy with him, and felt with some pleasure the old connexions of my father with both his father, and grandfather by the mother's side.[9] I asked him if he never went to church; he said he generally did, and if we had not been with him, would have been there today. I was a little uneasy at my not being today at any place of worship. He said Sir Alexander Dick was the happiest man alive. This was a proof that he could think with some just delicacy of sentiment. Many people waited on him today. Several stayed and dined. I should have been very happy had not the assuming villain John Fordyce been there.[1] I wondered how Lord Advocate could receive him. I took no manner of notice of him, but was pleasant without looking towards him. I should have mentioned that there are at Melville five remaining trees which tradition says were planted by David Rizzio.[2] I saw four of them. Maclaurin and I returned to town at night. He was better tonight than when I last mentioned him. Dr. Webster and Grange supped with us. My spirits were fine.

MONDAY 23 OCTOBER. (Writing on Friday 3 November.) I dined by the Earl of Glencairn's invitation with the Countess, his mother, at the Coates. I wished to pay him all attention now that his affairs were embarrassed. Harry Erskine was there. We were well enough. I drank more claret than I have done for some months. I stayed tea and heard Lady Betty Cunningham play wonderfully well on the pianoforte. There was a circumstance which was unlucky. I did not recollect having once been in company with the Countess at the late Earl's, though she recollected having talked with me of Paoli. This was, I fear, a sad forgetfulness of a proud woman. I played a rubber at whist, lost a shilling, and walked home before supper.

[9] Sir William Gordon, Bt., of Invergordon. Lord Auchinleck's connexion with him is not apparent, but it may have been commercial. Sir William was a banker.
[1] Boswell has crossed out Fordyce's name. He had earlier felt that Fordyce had "good parts and a good heart" (Journal, 6 November 1762), but for some time he had been "disgusted" (Journal, 18 March 1778) by the spectacle of Fordyce, a bankrupt, living in luxury while his creditors were unpaid.
[2] The Italian musician who became a favourite of Mary, Queen of Scots. According to tradition, Melville Castle had been his residence.

TUESDAY 24 OCTOBER. (Writing on Friday 3 November.) I breakfasted at Lady Colville's. Sandy went with me. I supped at Sir Lawrence Dundas's. I played a rubber at whist and won sixpence. Sir Lawrence did not come from Lord Lauderdale's till it was near supper-time.

WEDNESDAY 25 OCTOBER. (Writing on Friday 3 November.) I dined at Prestonfield. Sandy walked out with me and home again, and I saw him ride on his sheltie. There was no company at the worthy Knight's today.

THURSDAY 26 OCTOBER. (Writing on Friday 3 November.) I breakfasted with Lord Eglinton, who was returned from the Hunters' Meeting at Kelso. He was not as warm as I was in his joy on Major Montgomerie's success; at least he was not so much so in appearance. I walked with him to Leith. He there joined Sir John Whitefoord, Andrew Erskine, and the bankrupt John Fordyce. I had at breakfast expressed my indigation at the countenance shown to that fellow; and when I saw that Lord Eglinton chose his company, I walked off. I called and sat a little at Broughton with old M. Dupont, who was ill with the gout. His spirits were French today, though Miss Scott told me that he was very apprehensive when ill. I dined at Lady Colville's with the Earls of Eglinton, Kellie, Matthew Henderson, etc. There is nothing to be recorded but that there was a good deal of animal spirits and much drinking. I was obliged to drink about two bottles. I walked home and was pretty well.

FRIDAY 27 OCTOBER. (Writing on Friday 3 November.) Got up with a very slight headache, but was somewhat uneasy to think that any company whatever could make me exceed in wine and depart from my general plan of sobriety. However, I thought that at times a little indulgence was not wrong. I was displeased that my drinking so much yesterday was from a kind of compulsion. Mr. Evory, a student of physic recommended to us by Miss Macbride, Mr. Robert Syme, Junior, and Mr. Lawrence Hill dined with us. I supped at Sir Lawrence Dundas's. Nobody at table but he and Lady Dundas and her niece, Miss Bruce. How curious is it that I am so easy in the house of a man whom I have known so short while, and to whom I was in keen opposition six years ago.

SATURDAY 28 OCTOBER. (Writing on Friday 3 November.) Our little daughter Betty was under inoculation and had many smallpox. My wife's anxiety made it difficult for me to persuade her to dine abroad. But by entreaty I prevailed with her to dine today at Sir Lawrence Dundas's. Mr. Sibthorpe was with us. She was well dressed and looked as well, perhaps better, than ever she did in her life, and she was quite easy. I was vain of her and very happy. Dr. Webster and Surgeon Wood were there. I sat by Mrs. General Scott, who expressed an inclination that our acquaintance should be renewed. It was a luxurious dinner. I enjoyed it much, and drank hock and claret with pleasure, but not to excess. My wife went away after tea. I played whist, lost a little money, and stayed supper.

SUNDAY 29 OCTOBER. (Writing on Friday 3 November.) Went with my wife to the Tolbooth Church in the forenoon and heard Dr. Webster, who dined with us. Went with her again in the afternoon and heard Mr. Kemp. Mr. Sibthorpe and our three eldest children were there too. In the evening the children said divine lessons very agreeably. I hoped to live better from this day, being now forty years of age.

MONDAY 30 OCTOBER. (Writing on Friday 3 November.) I dined at Lady Dundonald's; Mr. Sibthorpe, Dr. Webster, and Commissioner Cochrane there. It was very comfortable. Mr. Sibthorpe and I stayed tea. In the evening I toyed with a young lady, which had an effect that I have not experienced for some time but in a dream.[3] Mr. Sibthorpe went to lodgings tonight.

TUESDAY 31 OCTOBER. (Writing on Friday 3 November.) Sir Lawrence and Lady Dundas and Miss Bruce, the Lord Provost (on whom I called yesterday), Dr. Webster, Commissioner Cochrane, Mr. Hunter-Blair, Mr. Maclaurin, Surgeon Wood, and Mr. Sibthorpe dined with us. Veronica sat at table. Phemie and Sandy dined at Dr. Grant's and came to us after dinner. It was as good a party of the kind as could be. My wife had an excellent plain dinner, and my wines were very good. The conversation was mostly on Sir Lawrence's political contests. I drank too much, so as to be in some degree intoxicated. I was struck with a degree of wonder, while I actually saw at my table the *great . . .*

[EDITORIAL NOTE: Six pages of the manuscript, containing the entries for 1 to 6 November, have been removed at this point, and other large mutilations follow. Usually in cases of this kind enough hints survive to make the reason for the censorship only too clear, but this time, though the clues appear to be abundant, we have found great difficulty in reconciling them. Each piece of evidence will be discussed as it occurs.]

[TUESDAY 7 NOVEMBER.] . . . was quite well satisfied with myself tonight. Maclaurin said to me lately that a man might be very happy without being of consequence if he did not consider being of consequence as essential to him. I may come to think in that cool way as Maclaurin does. But at present I would rather be Burke than Lord Hopetoun.[4]

[3] Boswell inked out the greater part of this sentence. (Strictly speaking, we should perhaps say merely that the passage has been carefully deleted in the same ink as that of the original writing, and with a similar pen.)

[4] John Hope, second Earl of Hopetoun, owned the mines at Leadhills and was enormously rich.

WEDNESDAY 8 NOVEMBER. (Writing on Friday the 10.) Went out with Commissioner Cochrane in his chaise and dined with him. Lord Gardenstone was there. He entertained us with lists of the ages of eighteen kings, eighteen philosophers, and eighteen poets. The philosophers were by much the longest lived. The kings the shortest. Dr. Gillespie walked in with me and I sat some time at my father's, where I was pretty well received.

THURSDAY 9 NOVEMBER. (Writing on Friday the 17.) The New Kirk was opened in its new form, this being the Fast Day. I was there forenoon and afternoon, and was pleased to find the old association of gloomy ideas with its former appearance dissolved.

FRIDAY 10 NOVEMBER. (Writing on Friday the 17.) I remember nothing particular except that I indulged . . . at night with my dear wife.[5]

SATURDAY 11 NOVEMBER. (Writing on Friday the 17.) Was at the New Church, this being the preparation day before the Sacrament. Drank tea at my father's.

SUNDAY 12 NOVEMBER. (Writing on Friday the 17.) Received the Sacrament in the New Church. Was in a good calm frame. Regretted that we had not the decency of the Church of England established in this country. Miss Semple and Mr. Sibthorpe dined, drank tea, and supped with us. My daughters said divine lessons.

MONDAY 13 NOVEMBER. (Writing on Friday the 17.) I was at the New Church and heard a most excellent sermon by Sir Harry Moncreiff on "He that provideth not for his own household," [6] etc. He inculcated the duties of good economy on the one hand and kindly connexion with our kindred on the other. My father was in church. I thought the second branch of the discourse might touch him. I played whist and supped at Mr. Alexander Mackenzie's with Freswick [7] and his lady.

TUESDAY 14 NOVEMBER. (Writing on Friday the 17.) This was the first day of the Winter Session. I visited my father first. Then went to Lord President's, where most of the judges and Lord Advocate were. He received . . .

[EDITORIAL NOTE: Two pages of the manuscript have been torn out and removed. Nothing on either side of the gap hints at a cause for censorship.]

---

[5] Boswell inked out this sentence and the crucial word after "indulged" has not been read with any certainty. That the reference was sexual is a reasonable but not inevitable conclusion. Perhaps the indulgence was of the sort recorded at the end of the entry for 30 October 1780.

[6] 1 Timothy 5. 8.

[7] William Sinclair of Freswick.

FRIDAY 17 NOVEMBER. When I do not mention the day on which I write, it is to be understood that I write of the date. I was very unwilling to rise this morning, but was obliged to be in the Court of Session. Last night the street was covered with snow. This morning there was a thaw and all was black and wet. My spirits were low as upon many former occasions. I had a poor opinion of myself. I however was not deeply miserable. I had begun *The Hypochondriack* No. 38 yesterday, but had done very little to it. This afternoon I finished it very well.[8] This gave me some satisfaction. I also wrote to worthy Langton.[9] How insignificant is my life at present! How little do I read! I am making no considerable figure in any way, and I am now forty years of age. But let me not despond. I am a man better known in the world than most of my countrymen. I am very well at the bar for my standing. I lead a regular, sober life.[1] I have a variety of knowledge and excellent talents for conversation. I have a good wife and promising children. Sandy, upon being told some days ago that the Devil was once an angel in Heaven and thrown down for disobedience, asked me, "Who was Devil before him?" I said there was none. But I thought the existence of an evil principle a curious investigation. Mr. Sibthorpe continues to be with us generally at every meal but breakfast.

SATURDAY 18 NOVEMBER. (Writing on Monday the 20.) My father had been seized with a cold on Thursday, which confined him to the house, after having walked home that day very imprudently. I did not miss him in court yesterday. This forenoon I did, and called on him. He was asleep. So I did not see him. I sat awhile with Lady Auchinleck. I called on

---

[8] A third essay on country life.

[9] "Your account of the honours paid to our respected friend Dr. Johnson in the circle of eminent persons at Mrs. Vesey's gave me great pleasure. Let me, my dear Sir, repeat my request to you to put down for me in writing at your leisure whatever sayings of his you remember; and I believe you remember many. Some you have already done me the favour to dictate while I wrote, and they are in sure preservation. I join with you in admiration of his *Prefaces to the Poets* which we have seen, and in longing for those that are to come.... Lord Monboddo was I understand very well received in many companies in London. He returned to us very fond of the metropolis but preserving his absurd prejudice against Dr. Johnson. There is I fear no cure for him. He has lately had an accident in his family which would have disconcerted the philosophy of most men. His oldest daughter has married his clerk. But he does not seem to mind it" (To Langton, 17 November 1780). The daughter's name was Helen Burnett, her husband's, Kirkpatrick Williamson.

[1] If Boswell had allowed himself to engage in further "wandering" (see above, Editorial Note following 19 June 1780) at any time since October 31, it does not seem as though he would have declared here that he was leading a *regular* life. Whatever the latitude of his conscience as to the morality of such acts, he never ceased to consider and to report them as irregular.

Mrs. Drummond and on Baron Maule. Found neither of them. I had for a day or two had a cold myself. It grew worse today; and I took too much balsam of cappivi [2] at night, which loaded my stomach so that I was so ill that I could not call again at my father's. On Tuesday last there was a meeting at the Earl of Buchan's for the purpose of forming an Antiquarian Society in Scotland. I had a card from his Lordship inviting me to it. But as I think him a silly, affected being, I did not go; and I was pleased next day when I heard a ridiculous account of the meeting from Wight and Crosbie, who were there; as also that he proposed a house should be purchased for the Society. So there was expense for folly. [3] I wrote next day a card to him evading the Society. [4] I sat today three hours reading the Register of Baptisms and making notes from it of people whom I knew. [5]

SUNDAY 19 NOVEMBER. (Writing on Monday the 20.) Awaked with a severe headache. Was ill all day. Had not even any satisfaction in lying in bed, which usually is so agreeable to me. Phemie was very kindly to me. Veronica and she said short divine lessons in the evening, when I was a little easier. I was so sunk today that I had scarcely any thought.

[2] Properly spelled *copaiba*, a resinous juice obtained from various South American trees and shrubs. It was considered a specific for gonorrhea, but was recommended for many other maladies, including bronchitis, which was almost certainly what Boswell was taking it for on this occasion. If he had been taking it for gonorrhea, it would have been more appropriate for a continuing urethral catarrh from his infection of the previous July than for an acute infection acquired within the last four days.

[3] As a result of this meeting the Society of Antiquaries of Scotland was indeed founded on 18 December 1780, though the grant of a royal charter was opposed by the Faculty of Advocates and the Curators of the Advocates' Library. Boswell's opinion of Buchan was widely held: Lockhart in his *Life of Scott* calls him a "bustling ... meddlesome coxcomb ... silliest and vainest of busy-bodies," and justifies the adjectives with a delightful account of Buchan's premature plans for Scott's funeral during Scott's illness of 1819: "'I had long considered it as a satisfactory circumstance that he and I were destined to rest together in the same place of sepulture. The principal thing, however, was ... to show him a plan which I had prepared for the procession—and, in a word, to assure him that I took upon myself the whole conduct of the ceremonial at Dryburgh.' ... It had been settled, *inter alia*, that the said Earl was to pronounce an eulogium over the grave, after the fashion of the French Academicians in Père-Lachaise" (2nd edn., 1839, vi. 92).

[4] "My Lord, I had the honour of your Lordship's note; and though I do not find myself qualified for the proposed Society, I return your Lordship thanks for the compliment paid me" (To the Earl of Buchan, on the verso of Buchan's note of 6 November 1780).

[5] "Looking into the Register of Baptisms kept in this city, it was an agreeable circumstance to me to find that you was one of the witnesses of mine. I have no sacramental right to so much *orthodoxy* as I possess, for Dr. Robert Wallace baptized me, and you may be considered as a sponsor" (To Sir John Pringle, 28 November 1780).

MONDAY 20 NOVEMBER. (Writing on Tuesday the 21.) Was a little better. But stayed at home all day.[6] Dictated a Petition very well. There was a poor appearance of practice for me this Session, which hurt me somewhat; yet I was sensible that I could not go through a great deal of that coarse labour. So that it was unreasonable to repine. It was a dreary day of snow and cold.

TUESDAY 21 NOVEMBER. Continued to be rather better. It was hard frost. I went to the Court of Session. Had no relish of it. Was vexed to think that I was now forty and had no office from Government. Called on my father and sat with him a little. He was still loaded with the cold, and he was dull and without any kindliness. I was sadly hurt. Lady Auchinleck was confined to bed with a severe cold. I dictated pretty well in the afternoon. At night Mr. Muir, an agent, brought me a poor-looking Highland client with an involved series of claims to plead. I found out that Mr. George Fergusson had been his lawyer before. So I refused his fee, and, after thanking Mr. Muir, desired they might go to Mr. Fergusson. Perhaps I was wrong. But aversion to study perplexity, and uneasiness at seeing the wretched anxiety of the man, prevailed. Professor Robison came and I introduced Mr. Sibthorpe to him, and they went together to his house. In the forenoon I sat above two hours making extracts from the Register of Baptisms. That kind of research amused me. But I was humbled to think how little I read, and what inconsiderable objects occupied my mind. I am depressed by the state of dependence in which I am kept by my father, and by being actually in straitened circumstances. I felt with some warmth Lord Mountstuart's neglect of my interest.

[EDITORIAL NOTE: Six pages, containing the entries from 22 November to 1 December, have been torn out and removed at this point. Nothing on either side of the gap accounts for their suppression.]

SATURDAY 2 DECEMBER. (Writing on Monday the 4.) Was still in very bad spirits, but just resolved to bear my distress. Thought I had no *spirit*, no manly firmness. Went with Mr. Nairne and called on Lord Kames, who, though confined with a cold, was clear and lively. I wondered while he talked, and thought my dreary despondency foolish, since here was a man past eighty-four quite cheerful. We visited Mrs. Drummond also. I walked awhile in the New Town with Mr. George Wallace, who has a never-failing fund of conversation. Then walked on the Castle Hill with Grange, and groaned from low spirits. He and Mr. Lawrie and the three Campbells dined with us. Miss Susie Wellwood drank tea. At night π.[7]

[6] The Court of Session did not sit on Mondays.

[7] Boswell generally uses this symbol to record nuptial intercourse, but it perhaps has a qualified meaning here and at the end of the entry for 5 December, where it occurs

SUNDAY 3 DECEMBER. (Writing on Monday the 4.) Heard Dr. Webster in the forenoon, and after visiting the laird of Fairlie, who was in town, dined with *His Holiness.*[8] Heard Mr. Kemp in the afternoon. Was quite dull and dreary. Phemie, Sandy, and I drank tea at my father's. Veronica had a bad cold these two days. The children said divine lessons at night. Phemie and Sandy said theirs at their grandfather's, who was more kindly to them than usual. While quite sunk, and in the state of everything seeming "stale, flat, and unprofitable," [9] I tried to read some of Dr. Johnson's *Preface* to Milton, and was at once animated and ennobled. But it shocked me to think that Dr. Johnson must die. I hoped to meet him in immortality.

MONDAY 4 DECEMBER. (Writing on Tuesday the 12.) Breakfasted with Lady Colville. Only herself and her nieces [1] appeared. I was in sad low spirits. Called on Lord Alva, whom I had not visited for some years. His chattering and minute insignificance disgusted me. Dined at my father's. Drank tea at Mr. Macredie of Perceton's.

TUESDAY 5 DECEMBER. (Writing on Tuesday the 12.) Was still in sad low spirits. While in the Court of Session was uneasy and restless. Was vexed on account of a charge of fraudulent intention against Matthew Dickie, who had charged fees to me which had not been paid and had at first alleged to me they *were* paid, or counterbalanced by claims on me, and afterwards said that he *meant* to pay them if allowed. In my honest indignation against what I suspected to be dishonest, I had suspected him strongly, and had communicated my suspicion to Mr. Blane, the agent on the other side, who was his inveterate foe. Blane had accused him before Lord Hailes. I was apprehensive that poor Matthew, whom I had known from my earliest years, might be severely punished. I tried to soften Blane, but in vain. Mr. Alexander Tait also tried. I talked of the matter with Mr. Ilay Campbell, who was an old acquaintance of Matthew's. He said his *age* should protect him, but the bad practice should be checked; and he promised to try what he could do to put an end to the accusation. I am dwelling too long on this. But in my fretted, sore state of mind, it hurt me exceedingly. I was vexed to be the evidence against a *poor body* whom I looked upon as a kind of diminutive Falstaff, a droll knave but without

---

again. See above, the entries for 30 October and 10 November 1780, and below, the end of the entry for 28 December 1780. If the symbol is read in its usual sense, it pretty certainly acquits Boswell of having risked infection within the last nine days.

[8] Dr. Webster. The style had been invented by Boswell's cousin, Patrick Preston (Journal, 6 January 1777).

[9] *Hamlet*, I. ii. 133.

[1] Jean, Catherine, and Elizabeth Anstruther, daughters of Sir Robert Anstruther and Lady Colville's deceased sister, Lady Janet Erskine.

ill nature. The laird of Fairlie, Grange, and Miss Mary Currie dined with us. Fairlie's sound sense and practical knowledge did me some good. I tried what drinking a good deal of punch would do. It consoled me for the time. My wife was cheerful with Fairlie. π.

WEDNESDAY 6 DECEMBER. (Writing on Tuesday the 12.) Was still uneasy in mind. The Lords determined some of the Ayrshire votes,[2] and showed such a partiality as really sickened me. I appointed to meet Maclaurin this evening at Lady Dundas's to play at whist and sup. But when I went, I found she was gone to the country. I went to Lord Kames's and supped. Nobody there but just Mrs. Drummond and he and I. I said I came to get a supply of good spirits; and indeed his animation had a very happy effect on me for the time. I supped with appetite and drank near a bottle of sherry. He would not rise till past twelve.

THURSDAY 7 DECEMBER. (Writing on Tuesday the 12.) Was still uneasy in mind. Dictated pretty well. But concern about Matthew Dickie's danger hurt me. My dear wife suggested that it was very possible I had blamed him without good reason, and imputed to dishonesty what was only forgetfulness and confusion. This suggestion relieved me much. I sent for Sandy Walker, his clerk, to worthy Grange's, where we talked of this and drank some strong ale. It was after supper. How much obliged am I to my valuable spouse upon many, many occasions!

FRIDAY 8 DECEMBER. (Writing on Wednesday the 13.) I dined at the Lord President's. Lord Monboddo was there, I believe the first time for many years. I was not at all in spirits, and the President's uncultivated manners displeased me. I took care not to drink much wine. I called a little at my father's, and then went to a consultation on Lord Eglinton's politics.[3]

SATURDAY 9 DECEMBER. (Writing on Wednesday the 13.) Was somewhat better. My wife and I and our three eldest children dined at my father's. The two Campbells were with us. It was pretty comfortable. Sandy went through the family catechism, which I really thought gave satisfaction to his grandfather. I played whist and supped at Maclaurin's; Lord Maitland, David Erskine, and Cullen there. Cullen was so entertaining with his mimicry that (except D. Erskine, who went at two) we sat till four.

SUNDAY 10 DECEMBER. (Writing on Saturday the 16.) Awaked with a severe headache. Lay all forenoon. Had drank but about a bottle and a half, but was hurt by sitting up. Major Montgomerie, who had called the

[2] See the foot-note following this.

[3] That is, questions involving the validity of votes controlled by Lord Eglinton in the Ayrshire election. Sir Adam Fergusson had immediately petitioned for a judicial investigation, as Boswell had feared he would (see above, 19 October 1780).

day before, came and sat awhile by my bedside when I was better. I liked to see him as Member for Ayrshire, and hoped he would keep his seat. I would not have risen all day had I not been engaged to dine with Lord Monboddo for the first time since the misfortune of his daughter's marrying his clerk.[4] I went; and as I walked downstreet felt myself in better spirits than for some time past. There was too numerous and mixed a company at Lord Monboddo's. But I enjoyed life pretty well. I met here Mr. Dalzel, our Greek professor. Somebody mentioned Othello's speech in the Venetian Senate. Lord Monboddo himself repeated,

> That I have ta'en away this old man's daughter, etc.

His firm philosophy struck me. I drank moderately, stayed tea, and came home in a pretty good frame.

MONDAY 11 DECEMBER. (Writing on Saturday the 16.) Was not as I should be, but dictated pretty well.

TUESDAY 12 DECEMBER. (Writing on Saturday the 16.) Called on Major Montgomerie. Had him and Sir William Augustus Cunynghame to sup with me. My wife was very cheerful. I was dull, but did wonderfully well. Drank gin punch with the Major, and was somewhat warmed.

WEDNESDAY 13 DECEMBER. (Writing on Saturday the 16.) Was not at all well. Business was a burthen to me. I was fretted by it. I dined at my father's; just he and his lady and I at table. Was quite sunk at night. Worthy Grange tried to console me. I got a sudden invitation to sup at Dr. James Hunter's with Major Montgomerie, and after declining was so pressed that I went. This was a wonderful transition. I did better than I could have imagined. But was inwardly dark and cold.

THURSDAY 14 DECEMBER. (Writing on Saturday the 16.) Was still in wretched spirits. Dined with Lady Dundonald on a sudden invitation, to talk of her writing to Lord Eglinton to join in aiding her son by subscribing for a share of his Forest. There was no company there. I was insensibly cheered a little by her agreeable manners, her being so much in earnest in the business of life, and the recollection of the old Earl. In the evening I dictated pretty well, but had no satisfaction. I asked Mr. Blane by a note to call on me this evening, as I was hopeful I might prevail with him to desist from prosecuting Matthew Dickie. He came, though I had not spoken to him for a week, being angry at his *obstinate justice*, to say the best of it. But we came to no agreement. He seemed to require too much from Matthew. In the mean time, Lord Hailes had refused to report the accusation to the Lords, which was favourable. I was too anxious about the creature.

4 See above, 17 November 1780, n. 9.

FRIDAY 15 DECEMBER. (Writing on Sunday the 17.) Got up in sad hypochondria. Had several law papers and a *Hypochondriack* to be written without delay. Was quite in despair. Could not see any good purpose in human life. Thought . . .

[EDITORIAL NOTE: Eighteen pages, containing the entries from 16 to 26 December, have been removed from the journal at this point. Boswell finally managed to write No. 39 of *The Hypochondriack*: on hypochondria. It is one of the best essays in the series, and perhaps comes closest to being a personal testament. For many of the essays Boswell adopted a rather stiff, aloof, and pedantic literary persona, but in this essay the persona is almost indistinguishable from the Boswell of the journals of this period.]

The Hypochondriack No. 39

"In the multitude of my thoughts within me thy comforts delight my soul"—Psalms [94. 19].

The Hypochondriac is himself at this moment in a state of very dismal depression, so that he cannot be supposed capable of instructing or entertaining his readers. But after keeping them company as a periodical essayist for three years, he considers them as his friends, and trusts that they will make a kindly allowance for him. He is encouraged by the compliments which an unknown reader at the London Coffee-house has been pleased to pay him in this magazine for last month.[5] He may hope that there are many such readers.

Instead of giving this month an essay published formerly, of which I have a few that after a proper revision I intend to adopt into this series, I have a mind to try what I can write in so wretched a frame of mind; as there may perhaps be some of my unhappy brethren just as ill as myself, to whom it may be soothing to know that I now write at all.

While endeavouring to think of a subject, that passage in the Psalms which I have prefixed as a motto to this paper presented itself to my mind: "In the multitude of my thoughts within me thy comforts delight my soul."

Language cannot better express uneasy perturbation of spirits than the Psalmist has here done. There is in the idea of multitude disorder,

[5] "From the first appearance . . . I have been a constant admirer of that valuable and entertaining periodical paper; and am firmly persuaded it has greatly increased the number of your readers" (*London Magazine*, November 1780, xlix. 512). The writer (signed "Sobrietas") includes with his letter "an original letter exposing some of the bad consequences that arise from intoxication," to add to Boswell's comments on drunkenness as a vice in the third essay on drinking (No. 32).

fluctuation, and tumult; and whoever has experienced what I now suffer must feel his situation justly and strongly described.

Let me select some of those thoughts, the multitude of which confounds and overwhelms the mind of a hypochondriac.

His opinion of himself is low and desponding. His temporary dejection makes his faculties seem quite feeble. He imagines that everybody thinks meanly of him. His fancy roves over the variety of characters whom he knows in the world, and except some very bad ones indeed, they appear all better than his own. He envies the condition of numbers, whom, when in a sound state of mind, he sees to be far inferior to him. He regrets his having ever attempted distinction and excellence in any way, because the effect of his former exertions now serves only to make his insignificance more vexing to him. Nor has he any prospect of more agreeable days when he looks forward. There is a cloud as far as he can perceive, and he supposes it will be charged with thicker vapour the longer it continues.

He is distracted between indolence and shame. Every kind of labour is irksome to him. Yet he has not resolution to cease from his accustomed tasks. Though he reasons within himself that contempt is nothing, the habitual current of his feelings obliges him to shun being despised. He acts therefore like a slave, not animated by inclination but goaded by fear.

Everything appears to him quite indifferent. He repeats from *Hamlet*,

> How weary, stale, flat, and unprofitable,
> To me seem all the uses of this world.

He begins actually to believe the strange theory that nothing exists without the mind, because he is sensible, as he imagines, of a total change in all the objects of his contemplation. What formerly had engaging qualities has them no more. The world is one undistinguished wild.

His distempered fancy darts sudden livid, glaring views athwart time and space. He cannot fix his attention upon any one thing, but has transient ideas of a thousand things; as one sees objects in the short intervals when the wind blows aside flame and smoke.

An extreme degree of irritability makes him liable to be hurt by everything that approaches him in any respect. He is perpetually upon the fret; and though he is sensible that this renders him unmanly and pitiful, he cannot help showing it; and his consciousness that it is observed exasperates him so that there is great danger of his being harsh in his behaviour to all around him.

He is either so weakly timid as to be afraid of everything in which there is a possibility of danger, or he starts into the extremes of rashness and desperation. He ruminates upon all the evils that can happen to man, and wonders that he has ever had a moment's tranquillity, as he never was nor ever can be secure. The more he thinks, the more miserable he grows; and he may adopt the frantic exclamation in one of Dr. Young's tragedies:

> Auletes, seize me, force me to my chamber,
> There chain me down, and guard me from myself.[6]

Though his reason be entire enough, and he knows that his mind is sick, his gloomy imagination is so powerful that he cannot disentangle himself from its influence; and he is in effect persuaded that its hideous representations of life are true. In all other distresses there is the relief of hope. But it is the peculiar woe of melancholy that hope hides itself in the dark cloud.

Could the hypochondriac see anything great or good or agreeable in the situation of others, he might by sympathy partake of their enjoyment. But his corrosive imagination destroys to his own view all that he contemplates. All that is illustrious in public life, all that is amiable and endearing in society, all that is elegant in science and in arts, affect him just with the same indifference and even contempt as the pursuits of children affect rational men. His fancied elevation and extent of thought prove his bane; for he is deprived of the aid which his mind might have from sound and firm understandings, as he admits of none such. Even his humanity towards the distressed is apt to be made of no avail. For as he cannot have even the idea of happiness, it appears to him immaterial whether they be relieved or not. Finding that his reason is not able to cope with his gloomy imagination, he doubts [6a] that he may have been under a delusion when it was cheerful; so that he does not even wish to be happy as formerly, since he cannot wish for what he apprehends is fallacious.

In the multitude of such thoughts as these, when the hypochondriac is sunk in helpless and hopeless wretchedness if he has recourse only to his fellow creatures and to objects upon earth, how blessed is the relief which he may have from the divine comforts of religion, from the comforts of GOD, the Father of Spirits, the Creator and Governor of the Universe, whose mercy is over all his other works, and who graciously hears the prayers of the afflicted!

In order to have these comforts, which not only relieve but "delight the soul," the hypochondriac must take care to have the principles of our holy religion firmly established in his mind when it is sound and clear, and by the habitual exercise of piety to strengthen it, so as that the flame

[6] *Busiris,* Act III.
[6a] See above, 2 January 1780, n. 7a.

may live even in the damp and foul vapour of melancholy. Dreadful beyond description is the state of the hypochondriac who is bewildered in universal scepticism. But when the mind is sick and distressed and has need of religion, that is not the time to acquire it. The understanding is then wavering, and the temper capricious; and the best arguments may be ineffectual.

By religion the hypochondriac will have his mind fixed upon one invariable object of veneration, will have his troubled thoughts calmed by the consideration that he is here in a state of trial, that to contribute his part in carrying on the plan of Providence in this state of existence is his duty, and that his sufferings, however severe, will be found beneficial to him in the other world, as having prepared him for the felicity of the saints above, which by some mysterious constitution, to be afterwards explained, requires in human beings a course of tribulation. And in the mean time he may have celestial emanations imparted to him.

While writing this paper, I have by some gracious influence been insensibly relieved from the distress under which I laboured when I began it. May the same happy change be experienced by any of my readers in the like affliction, is my sincere prayer.

WEDNESDAY 27 DECEMBER. (Writing on Saturday the 30.) Dined and drank tea at Mr. David Erskine's with Lord Braxfield, the Solicitor, Harry Erskine, Maclaurin, and several more. I had been near an hour with Maclaurin last night in a dejected, uneasy state. His conversation can afford no relief to one in such a state. He said he would go mad if he were to study metaphysics, that his head turned when he thought of a Supreme Being, and that he imagined we were machines moved by motives. Such was his meaning. I have put his fatality into concise expression. I continued to be gloomy and had no relish of society. I sat by and saw whist played, and I betted against the Solicitor. Lord Braxfield, exultingly pleased that the Solicitor and Maclaurin, against whom he played, were losing, called out that Maclaurin, whom he had named "Captain," played like a colonel. I in the same humour called out, "And I'm sure his partner plays like a colonel." [7] The Solicitor, who was fretted by losing, lost his temper and said he would not be insulted. I grew warm and asked him what he meant. He said, "I shall let you know afterwards." Maclaurin and I were to play cards and sup at Cullen's. When the Solicitor went away, I said I would go to Cullen's and we should send for Maclaurin. I wished

[7] The jest is obscure and Murray's being piqued by it is equally hard to explain. Maclaurin may perhaps have been Captain in the Edinburgh Defensive Band, but he is not mentioned as such in Boswell's *Excellent New War Song* (see below, 16 July 1782).

to give the Solicitor an opportunity of explaining himself. When we got into the street, he said I had behaved to him in a way that no gentleman could put up with, and he desired to have satisfaction. "With all my heart," said I. "Then," said he, "what day is this?" "Wednesday," said I. "On Friday morning," said he, "at five o'clock in the King's Park." "Very well," said I. "Name your second," said he. "I shall," said I, "good-night"; and went and rung at Cullen's door. I had no fear; and what was curious, I was speculating all the time whether this could be a piece of fatalism, though there was a feeling of liberty. Cullen's servant luckily was long in coming; and in that space I thought that I should pass the evening disagreeably with such a duel hanging over me. I was conscious the Solicitor had no just cause of offence, and perhaps was not in earnest. So I took a sudden resolution, and run after him and overtook him. I asked him if he was in earnest. He said yes. But we got into conversation, and he said if I did not mean any offence, he was satisfied. I said, "How could I possibly mean it?" and I would refer it to the company. He said if I would tell them or tell Maclaurin that I meant none, that was enough. I said I would if he would go back with me, but he declined this. In short, there was to be no more of it. I then went to Cullen's, and he and I had a very good chat by ourselves for half an hour. Then came Counsellor Charles Dundas and his friend Counsellor Steele, an Englishman, and we played whist. Lord Maitland came, and then we played brag. Maclaurin came and sat by. I lost, but did not grudge it. We had a very good comfortable supper. It was the first time of my being at Cullen's. I was pleased to see all his furniture new, and his table well served, and an air of orderly ease. I drank some glasses of wine, and Maclaurin having mentioned the difference between the Solicitor and me, I related what had passed, which entertained the company much. Maclaurin told me that he and all the company thought the Solicitor in the wrong, which comforted me. Our conversation was neither brilliant nor learned, but did very well at the time. I was in better spirits than I had been for many days. I saw the intercourse of social life with some degree of satisfaction, though life be uncertain and indeed, to an expanding imagination, very short. We sat rather too late, which hurts me now.

THURSDAY 28 DECEMBER. (Writing on Saturday the 30.) Yesterday forenoon Commissioner Cochrane called on me for a little. This morning I sent a note to the Solicitor that all the company thought him in the wrong; that I was surprised and uneasy he had supposed what I was sure I did not mean. That a misunderstanding between him and me must not be made up by halves, and that I hoped he would call this forenoon and shake hands cordially with his old friend. He wrote to me that he would see me before dinner. He came and owned he was sorry, and we were quite reconciled. Thus a sad quarrel between two men whose fathers were friends, and who had all along lived on good terms, was prevented. I read this forenoon Hayley's *Epistles on History* and his notes with pleasure.[8] Mr. Baron Gordon, on whom I had called and sat awhile not long ago, called and sat awhile with me one day this week. Worthy Grange dined with us today. I relished my victuals and a little mountain and was even happy. He and I went and drank tea and sat near three hours with Miss Scott and M. Dupont. The old minister's orthodoxy seemed narrow, but his piety and worth were valuable. At night when in bed with my dear wife, I was wonderfully free from gloom, and trusting to Mr. Wood's opinion that I had no infection, I prevailed with her to allow me to enjoy her.[9]

FRIDAY 29 DECEMBER. (Writing on Tuesday 2 January 1781.) Grange dined with us. I was much better today. Lady Colville paid us a visit in the evening. I breakfasted today by appointment with Lady Dundonald, having sent Sandy yesterday to tell I was coming. He accompanied me. I felt the *local* effect of Belleville calming my mind. She showed me accurate states of the affairs of the Dundonald family, both in her husband's time and since his death. My attention was fixed, and I had pleasure in the immediate reading. She also showed me a number of letters from Mr. Rhodes, formerly a Commissioner of Excise here, of whose genius I had heard much. But I was disappointed; for though there was a neatness and a vivacity in his manner, there was not real wit. I thought his letters in general trifling; and his being willing to pass under the diminutive name of *Rhody* made me think slightingly of him.[1] But he was, I have been told, a pleasant companion, and must have been an excellent correspon-

[8] William Hayley, *An Essay on History, in Three Epistles to Edward Gibbon*, 1780.

[9] Boswell later inked out the significant words of this sentence. "Mr. Wood's opinion that I had no infection" cannot mean that Wood declared him cured of a gonorrheal infection acquired within the last two weeks: the time is too short for that. It probably means that, having risked an infection on or soon after 15 December, he had gone to Wood, and that Wood, finding no symptoms after an interval of ten days or so, had told him he could stop worrying. If so, it seems odd that the entries for 27 and 28 December should contain no certain hint of this particular worry or of relief from it. The passage, after all, is ambiguous. It could mean that Wood was only now declaring him free of the infection he had acquired in the previous July (above, p. 223), and that the nuptial rites here recorded were the first Boswell had celebrated in more than five months. If that interpretation is preferred, a special meaning must obviously be given to the Greek characters in the entries for 2 and 5 December.

[1] Boswell hated to be called "Jamie" and was probably not too fond of "Bozzy," though he seems never to have voiced his displeasure to Johnson.

dent for ladies. I was a little at my father's this afternoon. At night enjoyed.[2]

SATURDAY 30 DECEMBER. (Writing on Tuesday 2 January 1781.) My son Sandy is really a fine boy. I should keep a register of his progress. I put him to Mr. Stalker's reading-school last autumn, but he did not like it, and as I think six an early age enough, I did not force him. But he is honest and kind, and has quite the air and manner of a gentleman. On Christmas a glass of the chair in which Phemie and he came from chapel was broke. Mr. Johnston was positive the chairmen were wrong in alleging that any of the children had broke it, and my wife scolded them for attempting imposition. When Sandy saw the poor chairmen in danger of losing the price of the glass, he gently told his mother that he had broke it. There was in this confession both honesty and humanity. His mother praised him warmly and paid the glass cheerfully. Last time that he and I breakfasted at Lady Colville's, as we walked down the Bow, he was going to attack a boy who happened to jostle him. I said, was he not afraid, as the boy was much bigger than him? "What's the matter," said he, "when I'm stronger than him?" A spirited thought, to think one's self stronger than superior appearance. Courage is one of the most valuable qualities that can be possessed. I feel sad uneasiness from timidity. Talking of the fall of man and that it occasioned death, Sandy said one day some months ago with real indignation that "Adam should be put in the Guard." If Sandy turns out an eminent man, or is ever the representative of the family of Auchinleck, these anecdotes will be valuable to him.[3] He is now quite easy with me. He is very fond of his brother Jamie, and treats him with tender care. My wife and Veronica, Phemie and Sandy and I went to Prestonfield today in Sir Alexander Dick's coach, dined and drank tea comfortably. Sir Alexander was quite well. He said to me, "*C'est la grâce de Dieu.* I wonder at myself." At night enjoyed.

SUNDAY 31 DECEMBER. (Writing on Thursday 4 January 1781.) Stayed at home in the forenoon. Sat awhile with Grange. Was at the New Kirk in the afternoon and heard Mr. Walker. The children said divine lessons. I went awhile to my father's. I supped at Sir William Forbes's, and was in good spirits. Came home between eleven and twelve, that I might enjoy again this year, and did it.

[2] Boswell inked out this sentence.

[3] Boswell later began a section of Boswelliana headed "My son Alexander," but recorded only three anecdotes.

1781

Review of about seven weeks of my life, during which I neglected to keep my journal, except from the 5 to the 10 January, inclusive, of which I made short notes on a separate piece of paper while at Bothwell Castle.

(Writing 17 February.) I went to Bothwell Castle in very good spirits. But unluckily, I believe the very day after my arrival there, I read in Lord Monboddo's *Ancient Metaphysics* that there *could be no such thing as contingency*, and that every action of man was absolutely fixed and comprehended in a series of causes and effects from all eternity; so that there was an universal Necessity. I then looked into Lord Kames's *Sketches*, where, though he retracts his foolish notion as to there being an intended delusive feeling of Liberty, he maintains the necessity of human resolutions and actions in the most positive manner. I was shocked by such a notion and sunk into dreadful melancholy, so that I went out to the wood and groaned. I had with me Volusenus [4] *De Animi Tranquillitate*, passages of which were a comfort to me, and I read some of Montesquieu's *Persian Letters*, one of which is in favour of human liberty and fairly denies the universal prescience of GOD, which indeed is incompatible with liberty. But still the arguments for Necessity were heavy upon me. I saw a dreary nature of things, an unconscious, uncontrollable power by which all things are driven on, and I could not get rid of the irresistible influence of motives.[5] The Marquess of Graham came to us the evening after my arrival. (Writing 20 February.) Captain Roberton of Earnock, Captain Stewart, son of Blairhall, and Hamilton, son of Aikinhead, as also Mr. Alexander Maconochie, made chiefly up our company, . . .

[EDITORIAL NOTE: Eight pages, containing the remainder of the "Review," have been removed.]

[4] Florence Wilson or Wolson, a Scotsman, who published the work at Lyons in 1543. Boswell owned a copy, and quotes from it more than once in *The Hypochondriack*.
[5] Boswell, continuing to worry about "Liberty and Necessity," sometime in February wrote on the subject to Johnson, who replied vigorously: "I hoped you had got rid of all this hypocrisy of misery. What have you to do with Liberty and Necessity? Or what more than to hold your tongue about it? Do not doubt but I shall be most heartily glad to see you here again, for I love every part about you but your affectation of distress" (*Life of Johnson*, 14 March 1781).

FRIDAY 16 FEBRUARY. (Writing on Sunday the 25.) Mr. Hunter-Blair paid me a bet of a rump and a dozen,[6] laid above ten years ago, that I should be first married to a widow. I named the company. We dined at Fortune's, nine in number nine: [7] he and I, Colonel Mure Campbell, Hon. A. Gordon, Sir W. Forbes, Mr. David Erskine, Grange, Maclaurin, Surgeon Wood. It was a most jovial day.

SATURDAY 17 FEBRUARY. (Writing on Sunday the 25.) I was ill after my indulgence, but went and did what I had to do in the Court of Session. Grange and Mr. Sibthorpe and Don Martino, an unfortunate Spaniard who was at the dancing-school with my daughters, dined with us.

SUNDAY 18 FEBRUARY. (Writing on Sunday the 25.) Was at the New Church all day. Dined at my father's. Sir Charles Preston and Grange and Colonel Mure Campbell supped with us. The Colonel had just come in a friendly way without invitation. We were very comfortable. We drank the last bottle of my old Madeira. The children said divine lessons very agreeably.

MONDAY 19 FEBRUARY. (Writing on Sunday the 25.) I dictated a great deal, and was in a vigorous frame of mind. I had shunned the society of the Duchess of Gordon. But Maclaurin had insisted I should play cards and sup with her this night at his house. I did so, and found her very good company.[8] She asked us all to sup with her next Saturday. There were no other men but Lord Monboddo and Captain Edgar. My wife and I dined at Hunter-Blair's. I was sober enough, lost only a pound, and drank freely at night. Monboddo and I drank a bottle with Maclaurin between one and two when the rest were gone, and we were pleasant.

TUESDAY 20 FEBRUARY. (Writing on Sunday the 25.) Was troubled somewhat with a cold. The Hon. Captain Hamilton of Bourtreehill and his brother, Captain Bute,[8a] dined with us. I drank port negus and was quiet. My wife was alarmed by spitting some blood.

WEDNESDAY 21 FEBRUARY. (Writing on Sunday the 25.) Dictated well. Went to the play of *Henry IV, First Part*, and saw all the High School in the Theatre. It was a fine scene of boyish amusement and

[6] A rump of beef and a dozen of claret.

[7] Boswell probably means "nine persons in room No. 9"; or perhaps the words are a tag from a song, and should be punctuated "nine in number, nine."

[8] The Duchess was Lady Wallace's sister. Boswell may have shunned her merely because of her coarseness and eccentricity. He records her saying to the King (who had asked her how she liked London), "It's frizzle-frizzling aw the morning and knock-knocking aw the neght" (all morning dressing the hair and all evening bustling about). Boswell adds, "This was natural enough for Jeanie Maxwell" (Journal, 19 March 1772).

[8a] Lindsay, younger son of the Earl of Crawford. His older brother Robert had assumed the name Hamilton as heir to his mother's estate of Bourtreehill.

tumult. The profits of the play went to pay for the new school. So all the masters and all the boys were there. My wife kept her bed all day.

THURSDAY 22 FEBRUARY. (Writing on Sunday the 25.) This was a General Fast by Proclamation.[9] Lady Dowager Colville came to my seat and heard Dr. Blair. I then drove awhile about in her coach with her. She told me she knew by my face whether I was well or ill. I was at present excellently well. Liberty and Necessity was quite a *distant* speculation, which did not affect me. I walked round the Meadow with Mr. David Erskine and got some useful instruction from him as to our Ayrshire political cases. I dined at my father's. He was in very bad humour; and though I had engaged to be counsel on Lord Eglinton's side with his consent and approbation, he seemed to be quite angry at my zeal. I regretted inwardly that he had so little knowledge of or value for his son. I could not help it.

FRIDAY 23 FEBRUARY. (Writing on Sunday the 25.) Was in keen agitation about our Ayrshire election. Had seen in the newspapers that three counsel on each side were admitted before the Committee on the Orkney election. Mentioned this to Mr. Cumming, who said, "Then there will be Lee and Wight and you." [1] He told me that even if Crosbie had gone to London, I was to have been preferred. This was very agreeable. It gave me a good reason to state to my father for my going to London. I dined (for the first time, having been ill when asked last year) at the Earl of Moray's. The dinner and wines were admirable. He had a capital French cook bred in the Prince of Condé's kitchen. I enjoyed the feast much. General Lockhart was there, and had been advised by his physician to drink wine freely. So I saw him in a new and much more jovial style. We drank liberally. Then the Earl and Countess carried me in their chaise to Sir Philip Ainslie's, where we played cards and supped. I had rather too much wine, so did not relish Sir Philip's elegance so highly as last time.

SATURDAY 24 FEBRUARY. (Writing on Wednesday 7 March.) Was very ill in the morning, but attended the Court. Mr. and Mrs. Hunter-Blair, Balmuto and Miss Menie, and some more company dined with us.

[9] "To pray for a divine blessing on His Majesty's arms by sea and land."
[1] Since 1770, controverted elections had been tried before a select committee of the House of Commons (selected by lot, subject to one nomination by either side), rather than before a Committee of the whole House, as previously. Up to this time Boswell seems to have assumed that only *two* counsel on each side would be admitted, and that under that limitation he would not be one of those chosen to present the case. The counsel who actually appeared before the Committee were Thomas Erskine (not John Lee), Boswell, and probably Alexander Wight. Archibald Macdonald (like Erskine an English barrister) and John Maclaurin seem also to have been counsel.

I drank moderately and was comfortable. I had engaged to sup with the Duchess of Gordon. But my wife was so much fatigued with last night's watching that I could not keep her awake another night, and I myself was sorely weary; so I sent an excuse that I was indisposed. My wife's spitting of blood had gone off.

SUNDAY 25 FEBRUARY. (Writing on 7 March.) Was at New Church all day; some time at father's. The children said divine lessons. Sir Charles Preston and Grange and Colonel Mure Campbell (who came in a friendly way without invitation) supped with us cordially.

MONDAY 26 FEBRUARY. (Writing on 7 March.) Dictated busily.

TUESDAY 27 FEBRUARY. (Writing on 7 March.) Was busy with the Ayrshire election business. I was now kept quite in a fever with it, I was so keen. The agitation kept off all melancholy.

WEDNESDAY 28 FEBRUARY. (Writing on 7 March.) Clerk Matthew, Messrs. Robert Syme, Lawrence Hill, and several more dined with us. I was in a convivial frame and drank rather too much port. Supped at my father's. After he went to bed, was rather too warm on the Ayrshire election with the ladies. Dr. Gillespie was there.

THURSDAY 1 MARCH. (Writing on Wednesday the 7.) Dined at Lady Colville's; Hon. A. Gordon and his Countess and Lord Justice Clerk there. Andrew [2] was very good company. My spirits were just as I could wish. In the evening after a consultation at Mr. Rae's, went home with Mr. John Wauchope and had a very merry conference, he and I and his partner Cumming, on our Ayrshire politics. Mrs. Wauchope sung and played to us, and we drank *plotty*.[3]

FRIDAY 2 MARCH. (Writing on Wednesday the 7.) My wife and I dined at Balmuto's. Lord Monboddo and Mr. Maclaurin were there. I drank moderately, and went home soon and dictated well.

SATURDAY 3 MARCH. (Writing on Wednesday the 7.) It is amazing how the warmth of my anxiety for Major Montgomerie's election cleared my mind of all gloomy vapours. Harry Erskine gave me some good hints upon it today. He walked to Leith with me, and came and took a share of my family dinner. At night I was in an excellent social frame. Called on Maclaurin; asked if he was busy. Found he (writing on the 8) was not. Told him I was come to eat cold meat and drink one bottle of wine with him. We talked over several questions in the Ayrshire politics, supped and drank a bottle apiece of good claret. We were quite social and comfortable. I only regretted that he had not religion. He said, however, it

---

[2] Andrew Erskine, Lady Colville's brother.
[3] A hot drink, composed of wine or spirits with hot water and spices.

was a great happiness to believe in immortality, and as Sir John Pringle, who was once an infidel, was now a believer, so might he.

SUNDAY 4 MARCH. (Writing on Saturday the 10.) Heard Dr. Blair in the forenoon. Stayed at home in the afternoon. The children said divine lessons. Colonel Mure Campbell supped with us most comfortably.

MONDAY 5 MARCH. (Writing on Saturday the 10.) I had devoted all this week to Major Montgomerie's election business, and resolved not to dine or sup abroad but at my father's. I dined there today. I laboured excellently.

TUESDAY 6 MARCH. (Writing on Saturday the 10.) We had a great many of our political cases decided this day. I was very warm. I avowed it. I said, "Major Montgomerie is my friend, my social friend. I love him as a brother. I only wish your Lordships knew him as well as I do." The President somehow or other got into an absurd passion today, and said there was much said of independency. There was not an independent gentleman in Ayrshire. I fired and called out, "No, my Lord?" "No," said he, "nor yourself neither." I replied warmly, "I beg your Lordship's pardon," and I think I added, "Not so!"—and then said, "I crave the protection of the Court." Some of the Lords shook their heads to make me quiet, and some about me also composed me; and so it rested. I dictated excellently today.

WEDNESDAY 7 MARCH. (Writing on Saturday the 10.) We had another series of political cases. The President was much calmer today. I was very angry at what he had said, and wrote a determined letter to him, which I showed to my friend Sandy Gordon.[4] He advised me not to send it, but he would carry it to Lord Braxfield and let *him* talk to the President. Grange dined with us today. I dictated with vigour.

THURSDAY 8 MARCH. (Writing on Saturday the 10.) Was in excellent spirits. Mr. Wauchope insisted that I should dine at his house with the laird of Fairlie and Colonel Craufurd of Craufurdland. As this was just a company who would talk only of the Ayrshire election, I agreed; and we were hearty and talked well of it. I then dictated as I could wish to do.

---

[4] "Your Lordship yesterday asserted from the chair that there was not an independent gentleman in Ayrshire. . . . I will not entertain an imagination that your Lordship meant to attack the spirit of the gentlemen of Ayrshire. For as one of their number, though not a freeholder, I would say that such a reflection is impertinent and false. Your Lordship, the head of civil justice in Scotland, certainly cannot wish to hurt and offend the gentlemen of Ayrshire, unprovoked. What suddenly burst from your Lordship yesterday has that effect on such of them as have yet heard of it; and it undoubtedly will have a still stronger effect if nothing shall be said by way of apology or explanation" (signed draft, To the Lord President, 7 March 1781).

Before dinner my father and I signed an alteration of the family entail, giving larger powers in letting leases.[5]

FRIDAY 9 MARCH. (Writing on Saturday the 10.) Called in the morning on Sandy Gordon, who told me Lord Braxfield had been with the President and would himself tell me what passed. Accordingly, I went to the robing-room, and Lord Braxfield told me the President desired him to say to me that he did not mean to say anything against the gentlemen of Ayrshire or any one of them; that he only meant to say they were not independent of party. This was pretty well. The President came up and we shook hands, but he said nothing. I dictated well. Sandy Gordon and Painter Donaldson drank tea with us.

SATURDAY 10 MARCH. (Writing on Sunday the 11.) I was not yet satisfied with the President's conduct. Sandy Gordon thought he should say something in public. I resolved to wait on his Lordship this morning. I called about nine. He was not got up. I went to Maclaurin's and talked to him, and he also thought the President should say something in public. I went again before ten, and was shown into his own study, where he was at breakfast by himself. He asked me if I would have some tea. I said I had breakfasted. His clerk was present. I said to him I wanted to speak a single word to Lord President. He left the room. I then in a calm tone told his Lordship that what he had said of the gentlemen of Ayrshire had hurt them. He seemed a little fluttered, and said he had said something to somebody of it (trying to evade it), and that he certainly did not mean to offend the gentlemen of Ayrshire or any one of their number, which I might tell them from him. "I am very well convinced of it," said I, "and I am sure I should be the last man in the world to lay hold of expressions hastily uttered in heat. But, my Lord, you said in public that there was not an independent gentleman in Ayrshire. Should not your Lordship take an opportunity of mentioning publicly that you did not mean what has been supposed? I think it would become your dignity." He shrugged his shoulders at first, and did not seem to like a public declaration. But seeing me firm he said, "If I can find an opportunity easily of bringing it in, I will do it. I meant no more than what I said of Roxburghshire, and will say of every county where there is a contested election: that both parties go on doing everything they can, and that none of the gentlemen vote sometimes one way, sometimes another. But I certainly did not mean any reflection against (writing on Tuesday the 13) the gentlemen of Ayrshire or any one of them. There is not," said he, "a more honourable man than Mr. Montgomerie of Coilsfield or than Mr. Hamilton of Sundrum." This was very well. He then said, "Will you tell me, James,

---

[5] See above, 27 October 1778, n. 5.

how does it stand? For I really don't know." "Why, my Lord," said I, "I'll tell you in general that if your Lordships' opinions hold good, we are sure of the election." "Ay?" said he. "Why," said I, "they have but two of majority against us in the Court of Session; and, my Lord, all the votes we have got there are gold tried in the fire.[6] They have passed the ordeal. For the Court was much against us." "James," said he, "it is true." He added, "I declare to GOD that in these political questions I have been at the utmost pains to keep my mind free from bias to one side or another." "My Lord," said I, "we give you credit for it." "Now," said he, "you'll perhaps be angry if I give you an advice." "By no means," said I. "I have often been obliged to your Lordship for good advice." "Then," said he, "keep your temper before the Committee. You have done very well in this business. Only you have now and then been heated." "My Lord," said I, "your Lordship certainly does not dislike a man for having a little heat of temper. I am obliged to you for your advice, and shall be upon my guard." He said, "I am sorry I shall not see you before you set out. You will come to me when you return?" "I certainly shall, my Lord." "You will perhaps be a little crestfallen then." "I hope not, my Lord." I really liked him this morning.

Mrs. Dundas desired to see me. I drank a dish of tea with her tête-à-tête, and was gay. Then went to the Court. The President took an excellent opportunity of making an apology. Talked of heat on both sides, and said, "By the by, I am sorry an expression of mine has been misunderstood. I did say there was not an independent man in this county. I will say so of every county where there is a warm contested election. But I certainly meant no disrespect to the gentlemen of the county or any one of them. I certainly did not mean that Lord Justice Clerk is not independent, or that Lord Auchinleck is not independent, or that Mr. Montgomerie of Coilsfield or Mr. Hamilton of Sundrum are not independent. I mention these gentlemen because I have a special regard for them." Somebody at the bar invidiously said, "A palinode!"[7] I warmly bore down any such reflections, and said, "Very well. Very handsome. 'Un gentilhomme est toujours gentilhomme.'" Thus this affair was settled in the most agreeable manner. I was much obliged to my friend Sandy Gordon for keeping me in the lines of prudence as well as spirit. I dictated, or rather corrected, the notes of the Lords' opinions. I had pushed on a case to a hearing in presence, and fixed one of Sir Adam's votes not to be reckoned before the

[6] The count as originally returned was sixty-five votes for Montgomerie and fifty-five for Sir Adam Fergusson. The Court of Session had thrown out enough of Montgomerie's votes to give Fergusson a majority of two.

[7] Originally, an ode or song in which the author retracted something said in a former poem; in Scots Law, a judicial recantation.

Committee. In short, I was active and animated and full of hope. How very different from the dreary metaphysical wretch that I had been! I supped at my father's.

SUNDAY 11 MARCH. (Writing on Tuesday the 13.) Heard Mr. Walker in the forenoon. Felt as when in a church in London. Grange and I and Sandy walked out and dined at Prestonfield. In the evening the children said divine lessons. I was damped a little by a letter from Wight which Wauchope read to me today, saying that the Committee would lay great weight on the decisions of the Court of Session. I was really uneasy. I supped at Old Lady Wallace's, where was Colonel Mure Campbell, and I was quite gay and entertaining. When I came home, being a little flustered, I took a proud pet because my wife, who had not been well and was half asleep, was not in unison with my joyousness; and for the first time I angrily went to bed in another room. She rose and asked me to come to her. I sulkily would not. This was a very bad effect of intoxication.

MONDAY 12 MARCH. (Writing on Tuesday the 13.) Was agitated with the prospect of London. Had a good consultation at Mr. Wauchope's. Announced to my father (what I believe he knew well enough before) that I was to set out next day, being engaged as counsel. He affected surprise, and said *I* was an *independent man* who did not consult him as to my going. *She* said, "At a certain time of life a son is independent of parental authority." "No," said he; "I never was independent of *my* father's authority." She wickedly said, "I am of your opinion. But that is just as people think." I said, "A man at a certain age is entitled to judge for himself. A man is a fool or a physician at forty." [8] I dined at my father's; Commissioner Cochrane, Balbarton, Mr. Stobie, and Dr. Gillespie there. In the evening my wife and I were at Marcucci's ball, and had the pleasure of seeing Veronica and Phemie dance very well. I was quite pleasant and happy.

On Tuesday 13 March I set out for London, and returned on Saturday 9 June. I have a separate journal of that period.

TUESDAY 13 MARCH. Busy going about in forenoon. Was not light-headed. Took leave of father; cold but not so ill as I supposed he might. Grange dined with us. Adieu calm to wife and children. At six went to Cameron's; Wauchope, Cumming, Anderson, Lieutenant Cameron all there. Glass of white wine and set off. Grange went with me as far as Liberton. Supped Bank House. Travelled all night. Was quite firm, having a settled steady purpose. Of what consequence is it for man to have his mind thus filled! 'Tis like a trunk well packed. None of his ideas or sentiments are hurt by being shaken and rubbed, as in loose, vacant mind.

---

[8] A Scottish proverb, based on a saying attributed to the Emperor Tiberius.

At Hawick was joined by Scott of Gala. We knew each other by sight and character, and conversed well. We breakfasted at Langholm and took whisky in our last cup of tea, and parted. I was alone all the rest of the way to Carlisle.

WEDNESDAY 14 MARCH. Got to Carlisle between two and three. Shaved and shifted. Was recollected by my landlord, Beck, who, being an old singing man in the Cathedral, accompanied me to prayers. The organist was ill or absent. So there was no music, and the congregation was very small. Yet I was excellently devout. I returned to the inn and dined well, and set out between four and five in the coach for London. Supped at Brough, but was not allowed time to sleep.

THURSDAY 15 MARCH. Was alone till I got to Ripon, where I dined. There I was joined by a Yorkshire leather-dresser, Mr. Gilbertson, silversmith at Ripon (a brisk little man), and by a boy returning from Ripon school to his father in London. We went on very well. Supped at Leeds. But still no sleep.

FRIDAY 16 MARCH. Went on well. Supped at Wansford. But found sleep still eluded us. The people at every inn lied in persuading us that we were to go to bed at certain places, but when we reached them, we were told the coach had come in later than usual, and there was not time. Thus were we tantalized. I however slept a good deal in the coach. But I felt this irregularity so uneasy to me that I resolved never again to take the Carlisle stage-vehicles.

SATURDAY 17 MARCH. Stopped at Biggleswade. Walked about. Mr. Gibson, the old vicar who has had the living since the year 1740, civilly joined me, and we went and saw his church. Then arrived Mr. Dilly's chaise, with a letter from Mr. Charles that he was at Southill [9] and would have met me with the chaise, but was lame. Drove quite happy to Southill. Was most cordially received. The weather was charming. Mr. Macaulay, a young Scotsman just in orders as a parson, was with us.[10] I was hearty and temperate.

SUNDAY 18 MARCH. Squire Dilly and I walked out and viewed rich fields and saw Lord Torrington's summer-house and Lord Ongley's summer-house. Met Mr. Smith, the parish minister, and paid him a visit. Went to church, where I was comfortably devout. Dined hearty. Mr. Smith

[9] "Squire" John Dilly's seat in the eastern part of Bedfordshire.
[10] "Mr. Macaulay" was probably Aulay Macaulay, uncle of Lord Macaulay, who in this year became curate of Claybrooke, Leicestershire. If he was, it seems odd that Boswell did not mention that he was the nephew of the Rev. Kenneth Macaulay of Cawdor who was host to him and Johnson on their tour of the Hebrides, and eldest son of the Rev. John Macaulay of Inverary, whom they met at Inverary, and whom he described in his journal as an acquaintance (25 October 1773).

came and drank a glass with us; and he, Mrs. Smith, and Miss Smith drank tea and supped with us. I liked him well. He was sedate and well informed, and brightened into cheerfulness. I was quite at home here.

MONDAY 19 MARCH. Mr. Charles and I set out about six o'clock in his brother's chaise; breakfasted at Welwyn, took post-chaise there, drove to Barnet, changed again, and on to London. I never approached it so agreeably. I was not light-headed. I was not in a flutter. My mind was *fixed* by thinking of the Ayrshire election. After safely *landing* at my old quarters in the Poultry,[1] I sallied forth and called on my brother David in Great Distaff Lane, Friday Street. Our meeting was a little awkward, as he and I had written letters in no cordial style about my settlement on him, which he had given up.[2] Called on Major Montgomerie after not finding Mr. Spottiswoode. He was not at home. But I met him in the Park. Went to the House of Commons. Saw John Wilkes, gay as ever. Heard a good debate on the report of the Berwickshire Committee. Went home with Mr. Spottiswoode and dined; Rev. Mr. Johnston at Leith with him. Called on Dr. Johnson. Not at home.

TUESDAY 20 MARCH. Called Dr. Johnson. Not at home. Breakfasted with Mr. Burke, and was in admirable spirits. Then went to Spottiswoode's and by engagement dictated some of the election brief. Dined Mr. Dilly's; Old Mr. Sheridan, Mr. Braithwaite, Dr. Mayo, and my brother there. Was quite well. At eight had a consultation at Macdonald's. Home in good time.

WEDNESDAY 21 MARCH. I should have mentioned yesterday that as I was walking in Fleet Street home to dinner, I unexpectedly met Dr. Johnson. I said, "This is strange, for us to meet in this way." He carried me into Falcon Court and asked me kindly after my family. I was hurried, as it was late. He said, "I love you better than ever I did." He engaged to be at home the afternoon of this day. I went to General Paoli's and breakfasted. Found my room occupied by a Mr. Saul, who was to leave it by and by. The General offered to put up a bed in another room for me. I insisted rather to remain at Mr. Dilly's till my room should be vacant. I found a card of invitation to dine today at Mr. Thrale's, now in Grosvenor

---

[1] Charles Dilly's town house and shop.

[2] These letters have not been recovered and the failure in cordiality remains unexplained. In 1775, after requesting and receiving from David a "genteel settlement" on Mrs. Boswell and the children in case he and not Boswell should succeed to Auchinleck, Boswell had settled £1,500 on David should it turn out that he got no more from his father than he had already received. At the time of making this settlement Boswell had not been happy because David had *asked* for it ("I should have spontaneously done as much for him"), and had had fears that he might later repent of his generosity (Journal, 17, 27 October 1775). See also below, 21 March 1781.

Square.[3] I sat awhile with Lord Eglinton, whom I found to be much in earnest about the election. I sat also awhile with Sir John Pringle, I think today. He told me Colley Cibber said there were "good pickings in old age." I finished what remained of the brief. Dined at Mr. Thrale's, whom I found not at all well. He introduced to me Mr. Crutchley, who he said was his best friend.[4] I was hearty here; but Dr. Johnson, finding that I was not at General Paoli's, supposed I did not get the card to dine; and so polite and attentive was he that he went home, as he had engaged to be there. I went to Sir Lawrence Dundas's and was cordially received; his son (our nominee),[5] John Ross Mackye, etc., with him. Drank tea with the ladies. Then repaired to Dr. Johnson's; found him and Mrs. Williams. We went up into his room. He thought I did right in closing with my brother's offer about my settlement on him, for though he was in a mistake, it proceeded from greediness and putting no confidence in me. Yesterday he said he was to go out in the morning. "Early?" said I. "Why," said he, "a London morning does not go with [6] the sun." He spoke with contempt of Government for suffering the horrid riots last summer. Said: "King Charles the Second, no, nor King William, would not have suffered the capital to be burnt while they had their guards." [7] I stated Cameron and Roebuck's cases to him. He was clear for us.[8] He gave me a deal of

[3] Thrale was very ill. Craving the stimulus of London gaiety, he had removed from Southwark on 30 January to a furnished house in Grosvenor Square, and was there eating and drinking himself to death.

[4] Thrale believed Jeremiah Crutchley to be his illegitimate son, and named him one of his executors.

[5] For the Committee to hear the Ayrshire election cause. A list of forty-nine members of the House was compiled by lot, and this list was submitted to the counsel and agents for both sides, who struck from it all but thirteen names. To these were added the name of the Lord Advocate, nominated by Fergusson's counsel, and that of Thomas Dundas, nominated by Montgomerie's counsel.

[6] The manuscript has the alternative "by"; "with" is the reading of the *Life of Johnson.*

[7] The "Gordon Riots" (2–9 June 1780), so called from Lord George Gordon, who led a mob to the Houses of Parliament to present a petition for the repeal of the Roman Catholic Relief Act of 1778. The result was a dreadful riot continuing over several days. Roman Catholic chapels and houses of Roman Catholics were destroyed, Newgate was set on fire and all the other prisons broken open, and the Bank of England was attacked. Order was finally restored by the military, who killed or wounded over four hundred persons. Twenty-one were later hanged for taking part in the riots. In order to understand the situation, one must remember that the country was prosecuting an unsuccessful war.

[8] Cameron and Roebuck were presumably two of the Ayrshire electors whose votes were in question. See below, 1 April 1781, the discussion of the vote of Gordon of Culvennan.

the original *copy* of his *Lives of the Poets* which he had kept for me. I carried them home.[9]

THURSDAY 22 MARCH. Breakfasted (I think) with Captain Preston; Mr. and Mrs. Foulis there. Dined at Mr. Thrale's; Dr. Johnson, Dr. and Miss Burney, etc., there. Dr. Burney and I drank to our acquaintance, now *come of age*, as somebody said, it being now exactly twenty-one years since I first met him at the late Lord Eglinton's. I got nothing to record of Dr. Johnson today. I had been with worthy Langton before dinner, and I drank tea with him. Mr. Charles Dilly went to Tunbridge yesterday. I was quite at home in his house. I supped at the British Coffee-house with Major Montgomerie, etc.

FRIDAY 23 MARCH. This day was the ballot for the Committee to try the Ayrshire election. I think I breakfasted with Major Montgomerie. If not, I was with him yesterday and with Captain Preston today. I was a good deal agitated while the ballot went on. Wight, Maclaurin, Spottiswoode, Jolly his clerk, and I dined at Spring Garden Coffee-house, a dinner on the election. Had a consultation at Erskine's in the evening.[10] Mr. C. Dilly returned today.

SATURDAY 24 MARCH. This morning my brother David breakfasted with us, and was in very good humour. At eleven our Committee met. I was a little fluttered, but spoke well. I suffered sad torment while the Committee was locked up, and I dreaded that they might find the judgements of the Court of Session conclusive. But I was relieved from this fear. I dined at General Paoli's. Then went to Mr. Thrale's and found Mr. Seward there. Then called on General Oglethorpe. He seemed much older and visibly failing or decayed. But perhaps I was mistaken.[1] I supped at Spottiswoode's with Mr. John Irving. Drank too much port.

SUNDAY 25 MARCH. Had a headache from drinking so much last night. Had written a part of No. 42 of the *Hypochondriack*.[2] Was to finish the rest of it today. Breakfasted at home. Then went to the Roman Catholic Chapel in Moorfields; heard mass and a Lent exhortation, and was the better. Called Mr. Forbes's and had a very agreeable interview with him and his wife. Then came home and finished No. 42 of the

---

[9] Boswell used this copy for the lists of "various readings" in the *Lives of the Poets* which he gives in the *Life of Johnson* at the beginning of 1781.

[10] Thomas Erskine, barrister, later (1806) Lord Chancellor and Baron Erskine of Restormel. A younger brother of the Earl of Buchan and Henry Erskine, advocate, he was a distant cousin of Boswell's. He, instead of John Lee (see above, 23 February 1781), had been appointed English counsel to speak before the Committee. See below, p. 345 n. 3.

[1] He lived more than four years longer.

[2] The second of three essays on marriage.

Hypochondriack. Then went to Sir John Pringle's to dinner; my brother David, Mr. T. Payne, the bookseller, and Dr. Saunders there. Was very well indeed. Then went for a little to Sir Lawrence Dundas's and got a private conference with Erskine, who gave me good hopes for Major Montgomerie. Returned to Sir John Pringle's; Dr. Kippis and Dr. Towers there. They laughed at Priestley's fatality. Things went on as one could wish.

MONDAY 26 MARCH. The Committee met at ten o'clock. I spoke with ease and fluency, and was well heard. But we lost a point which we thought ourselves sure of gaining. I was cast down. I dined at Mr. Thrale's; nobody there. I drank tea at Mr. Spottiswoode's, and could hardly keep up my spirits. I went to Mr. Thrale's in the evening and supped; Dr. Johnson and Mr. Crutchley there. I said to the Doctor he might have been kinder to Gray.[3] He very justly said he could not be kind. He was entrusted with so much truth. He was to tell what he thought; and if people differed from him, they were to tell him so. I should have mentioned that Seward told me a good pun of Dr. Johnson's without intending it. Of Monboddo he said, "This man of Greece (grease) who oils himself every day." [4] He said Mrs. Montagu had dropped him, and that there were people whom one would like very well to drop but would not wish to be dropped by.

TUESDAY 27 MARCH. I spoke very well in the Committee, merely in the argumentative way. Lost another point which we should have gained. Began to be a little habituated to such misfortunes and to bear them more easily. Langton attended today. He and I tried to take Dr. Johnson with us to The Club. He sent us down word that he was not to go, and was dressing. This, Langton said, was being deficient in the charities of human nature, for he might have come to us. The Doctor told me afterwards he feared being teased to go. Langton and I went. It was a very numerous meeting; fourteen in all. Mr. Burke was there, and had his joke just as he liked. He said the Dean of *Ferns* sounded like a barren title. I said Dr. *Heath* should have it. Dr. Johnson afterwards said, "Dr. *Moss* should be his curate." [5] I drank a good deal of wine. Sir Joshua Reynolds, Steevens,

---

[3] In his *Prefaces to the Poets.* Boswell must have seen the life of Gray in manuscript, proof, or an advance copy. It was not published until May 1781.

[4] Monboddo, in imitation of the ancients, anointed himself at night before going to bed.

[5] Richard Marlay, later Bishop of Clonfert and still later of Waterford, a member of The Club, was at this time Dean of Ferns. "Dr. Moss" and "Dr. Heath" were Charles Moss, D.D., Bishop of Bath and Wells, and the Reverend Benjamin Heath, Head Master of Harrow School. He did not become D.D. until 1783, but Boswell might easily have been unaware of the fact.

and I drank two bottles after everybody else was gone. I was somewhat intoxicated, but not much. Repaired to Dilly's and slept well.

WEDNESDAY 28 MARCH. Erskine spoke on our side in the Committee today, inimitably. I really trusted that we could not possibly lose the question. The honest Major and I walked about in sad anxiety while the Committee were locked up, and when they determined against us, we were grievously hurt.[6] I dined at General Paoli's, and recovered my spirits. Met there Baron Grothaus, a Hanoverian, who had been in Corsica. My spirits rose, and I was very gay.

After coffee went to Mr. Thrale's. Found Mrs. and Miss Thrale, Dr. Johnson, and Mr. Crutchley sitting at tea. I had some, and was comfortable. The Doctor was offended at the Bishop of St. Asaph's coming to our club.[7] He said, "A bishop has nothing to do at a tippling house. There is nothing immoral in it. Neither would it be immoral in a bishop to whip a top in this square. But I hope the boys would fall upon him and apply the whip to him. There are gradations. There is morality, decency, propriety." "Two of which," said Mr. Crutchley, "are violated by the Bishop." "A bishop," said the Doctor, "should not go to a house where he may meet a man leading out a whore." (Perhaps he said wench.) I said, "I did not know our tavern admitted women." "Depend on it, Sir," said the Doctor, "any tavern will admit a well-dressed man and a well-dressed woman. They will not perhaps admit a woman whom they see every night walking by their door as a street-walker. But, Sir" (and these were, I think, his very words), "a well-dressed man may lead in a well-dressed woman to any tavern in London. Taverns sell meat and drink, and will sell it to anybody who can eat and can drink. You may as well say that a mercer will not sell silks to a woman of the town."

He found fault with the Bishop of Chester for going to routs, at least for staying long at them. "He may go to them," said he, "and receive attentive respect while it is paid him. But when that ceases, he is then to retire." "Poh!" said Mrs. Thrale. "The Bishop of Chester is never minded at a rout." "Why then," said I, "when a bishop

---

[6] The Committee found the judgement of the Court of Session not conclusive, and itself judged the qualifications of each voter, without regarding the Court of Session's decision. But it eventually found enough disputed votes in Sir Adam Fergusson's favour to give him a majority, and pronounced him elected. This explains Boswell's encouragement at its earlier decisions and his eventual disappointment in the outcome.

[7] In November 1780 Jonathan Shipley, Bishop of St. Asaph, was elected to The Club, and Beilby Porteus, Bishop of Chester (see above, p. 147 n. 7) and later of London, was blackballed.

is in a state where he is nobody, it is improper." Said Dr. Johnson: "Mr. Boswell has said it as correctly as could be."

He and I were left alone. I tried in vain to bring him upon Liberty and Necessity. He shunned it, with a general averment for Liberty. We saw Mr. Thrale for a little. The Doctor and I then set out in a hackney-coach. He went home. I came out at Newman Street and supped agreeably with Mr. Charles Boswell from Jamaica, his wife, and brother.[8] I should have mentioned that Mr. Thrale told me on my last coming to London that I might now see Dr. Johnson drink wine again; for that though he would not at dinner, he drank some at night. He would even drink a bottle. This change from "severe to gay" (to reverse the light and shade of Pope)[9] delighted me. On Monday evening I saw him swallow some port greedily.

At our club on Tuesday Sir Joseph Banks, whom we call our Chancellor of the Exchequer, opened the budget; that is to say, he is our treasurer and gave us a state of our affairs. We buy our own wine and pay the master (or rather mistress, the man being dead) 1/6 for each bottle of claret we drink, and 1/– for each bottle of port. Taxes are levied annually for this wine. We had all the matter done today in parliamentary form. We had two guineas apiece to pay for the current year. But there was a question as to arrears. The first defaulter was Charles Fox: unanimously ordered that he should pay. Then *I* was read out. Upon which Mr. Burke, who sat next me, said, "By all means let him pay. If we can get anything out of Scotland, let us have it. We get a little land tax" (he had said before). "But by the Customs and Excise we some years literally don't get a shilling. Besides," said he, "the Scotch were so violent for taxing their brethren in America that they should certainly be taxed themselves. The Club will consider of this. For I know no other reason why Mr. Boswell should pay for last year when he was not in London." It carried that I should not pay, because I held no place under Government, which Dunning, upon my telling him what had passed, said was the case with very few of my countrymen. Then Lord Charlemont was read out. "Ah," said Burke, "the Irish *won't let* you tax them." My Lord, who is one of the Volunteer officers, said he had come in his regimentals on purpose to defend himself. He was excused. So was the Dean of Ferns, being Irish. So was the Bishop of Killaloe, for he had formerly (when Dean of Derry) sent The Club a hogshead of claret to make up for his deficiency. It was hinted that the Dean of Ferns should do the same; and it was observed that the way to get a bishopric was to send a hogshead of claret to our

---

[8] Sgt. John Boswell ("Old Knockroon").
[9] "From grave to gay, from lively to severe" (*Essay on Man*, iv. 380).

club. Dr. Johnson was excused because of his not drinking wine; and my account of his swallowing it greedily was considered by Burke as representing him rather under a kind of disease, a *rage*, as the French say; and that till he could drink as an honest fellow he was not to be reckoned among the taxed. Sir Robert [1] Chambers was going to be excused. "What!" said Burke, "a man who is in the very centre of wealth, and absent to get money? No." It was agreed he should be taxed. Somebody suggested that he might commute his arrears by sending a hogshead of wine. I moved that it should be a hogshead of Madeira that had been in the East Indies; and it being ordered that this should be intimated to him, it was afterwards suggested that a hogshead was not a Madeira measure, but a pipe. I moved that the word "hogshead" be erased and instead thereof be inserted the word "pipe." Dr. Adam Smith came last; and Burke and I were clear that a Commissioner of the Customs, who holds a lucrative place and was absent only because he is a tax-gatherer, should be taxed; which was ordered. Dr. Johnson did not relish a repetition from me of this pleasantry. He said, "I am glad I was not there." Yet it was very well, I thought. Gibbon alone stickled for Smith, because he is a brother infidel. He is a disagreeable dog, this Gibbon. Mrs. Thrale said, "He squeaks like Punch. I imagine he'll squeak [2] indeed before he dies, as he had a religious education." "Yes," said I ludicrously, "he is an infidel puppet: *le marionet infidel*."

There was not a bad *jeu d'esprit* of mine at The Club. Before dinner Banks called me "Mr. Crosbie." Said I: "He takes one Scotch lawyer for another. If it had been any other animals, he would have known the difference better." This was a pleasant allusion to his skill as a naturalist, and took off the awkwardness of the mistake. We talked of Dr. Johnson. I said that he could make himself very agreeable to a lady when he chose it. Sir Joshua agreed. Gibbon controverted. Dean Marlay said a lady might be vain when she could turn a wolf-dog into a lap-dog. Steevens told several anecdotes of Dr. Johnson. But I will have them in writing from him, that they may be correctly recorded.[3] Steevens has a very full mind and very animated powers of communication. He has the character of being very malignant. He will, it is said, write in the newspapers against people with whom he is living intimately. Said Dr. Johnson: "No, Sir, he is not malignant. He is mischievous. He only means to vex them." But surely there is evil in this, though the distinction by the

---

[1] Boswell left a blank for the first name.

[2] Confess, recant (American "squeal").

[3] See the *Life of Johnson* immediately before 22 June 1784 for a series of anecdotes which Boswell did obtain from Steevens. It may or may not include the ones Steevens told this evening.

Doctor be well put. I said he was a man of good principles but bad practice; for he defends religion, yet he carried off a man's wife. The Doctor said I was right.[4] I was quite happy the evening I spent at Mr. Charles Boswell's, whom I had not seen since autumn 1769. His lady was very agreeable. I was glad they were married now. I had warmly recommended it.[5] My spirits were gay and I indulged them; and seeing John Boswell, compared my then gaiety with my dreariness in Scotland. I *must* allow my temper an easy play.

THURSDAY 29 MARCH. The Committee went on sadly against us. I began now to grow callous. I think I dined today at Mr. Thrale's.

FRIDAY 30 MARCH. It was "Tu ne cede malis, sed contra audentior ito" [6] with me in the Committee. I really spoke well. Dined at Sir Joshua Reynolds's, an excellent day; Dr. Johnson, Lord Charlemont, Langton, Eliot of Port Eliot (whom I saw today for the first time), Mr. Burke, Dean Marlay, and a worthy Irish gentleman, Sir Annesley Stewart, there. I was in delightful spirits. Burke was playful. "Will you have any of the sounds of the cod?" "No, I thank you." "You're all for sense?" "Oh, I did not think the *sound* had been an echo to the sense." [7] The definition of a good manor: "Est modus in rebus (a modus in the tithes), certi denique fines (and certain fines)." [8] I said man was a distilling animal. Dr. Johnson

[4] It must be kept constantly in mind that a good two thirds of this entry (everything from "I should have mentioned" on p. 297), though dated Wednesday 28 March, is a huge addendum not only to that day but also to the two preceding. The report of the conversation at The Club on Tuesday 27 March was already remarkably convoluted, part of it being presented directly under the proper date, part as reported the next day to Johnson and Mrs. Thrale. In the addendum, Boswell employs both modes, and here has passed suddenly and without notice from the first to the second. By mention of Steevens's anecdotes he and Johnson are led into a discussion of Steevens's character, repeating to some extent what he had recorded in his journal (and later put into the *Life of Johnson*) under date of 13 April 1778. His charge here that Steevens had "carried off a man's wife" is, however, not in that entry and appears not to be reported anywhere else.

[5] "The evening" which Boswell mentions so remotely was *this* evening: see above, p. 297. At the time of his former visit the couple were living together but were not married. Boswell thought she had a "decency of behaviour very different from that of a kept mistress," and felt that it was "out of character for a son of Auchinleck to be living in a licentious style" (Journal, 15–16 September 1769).

[6] "Do not give in to misfortune, but march all the more boldly against it" (Virgil, *Aeneid*, vi. 95).

[7] Pope, *Essay on Criticism*, l. 365 ("The sound must seem an echo of the sense"). The sound of the cod is its swimming or air bladder. It was formerly cooked and a piece included with each serving of the fish.

[8] Horace, *Satires*, I. i. 106; the proper translation is "There is a measure of things; there are, in short, fixed limits." In the punning sense employed by Burke, a modus was a moderate fixed sum paid instead of a tithe; and a certain (as opposed to an un-

mentioned some author who says that monkeys will kill a sheep and roast it and eat it, which he thought a lie. I said cookery was a proof of reason. BURKE. "If it be cooking eggs, for there is reason in roasting of eggs." He was merely sportive today, unless when he talked a little Opposition politics to Lord Charlemont.

Mr. Eliot told us of a liquor the Cornish fishermen drink, which they call "mahogany": two parts gin, one part treacle, well beat together. Dr. Johnson observed it must be modern, as mahogany [is] modern in this country. I said it was similar to Atholl porridge: whisky and honey. "That's better," said Dr. Johnson. I mentioned Dr. Johnson's scale of liquors: brandy for gods, etc.[9] Burke said he loved to be a boy, to have the careless gaiety of boyish days; so would drink claret. "So would I," said Dr. Johnson, "if it would do that for me. But it does not. It neither makes boys men nor men boys. You'll be drowned by it before it has any effect upon you."

We talked a good deal of Walter Harte, who had travelled with Mr. Eliot. He said Harte's book did very well in German. Indeed it was not English.[1] But he had been at great pains. He had been with him on the spots, the fields of battle. Langton spoke with rapture of Gustavus Adolphus. Dr. Johnson said Harte was excessively vain. "He gave copies in MS. of his book to be revised by Lord Chesterfield and Lord Granville. Now how absurd was it to think that two such noblemen would revise so big a MS. Poor man, he left London the day of the publication of his book, to be out of the way of the great praise he was to receive; and he was ashamed to return when he found how ill his book was received. It was unlucky in coming out the same day with Robertson's *History of Scotland*. His *Husbandry* is good." "Better," said I, "than his heroic history; he turned his sword into a ploughshare." A new wig which I wore today, made by *Nerot* (whom I called the *old lion*, in allusion to *Nero* in the Tower, of famous memory),[2] introduced the subject of wigs. I said nothing was a greater proof of the association of ideas than Hogarth's print of wigs, where you see all char-

---

certain) fine was a fixed payment made to the lord of the manor on the admission of each new tenant.

[9] Rather "for heroes." See above, 7 April 1779.

[1] Harte had also been tutor to Philip Stanhope, Lord Chesterfield's natural son, to whom the *Letters* were written. Of the style of Harte's *History of Gustavus Adolphus*, Lord Chesterfield wrote: "It is a bad style of a new and singular kind: it is full of Latinisms, Gallicisms, Germanisms, and all *isms* but Anglicisms; in some places pompous, in others vulgar and low" (*Letters of . . . Chesterfield*, ed. Bonamy Dobrée, 1932, v. 2348).

[2] The Tower had lodged the royal menagerie from an early period. Horace Walpole mentions Nero the lion in a letter of 1763 to Henry Seymour Conway.

acters exhibited merely by wigs, with which they have no natural or real connexion.

I ventured to mention a ludicrous story in the newspapers: that Dr. Johnson was learning to dance of Vestris.[3] Lord Charlemont, in order to bring him out, asked the Doctor gravely if it was true. The Doctor answered, "How can your Lordship ask so simple a question?" But afterwards, whether from unwillingness to be deceived or appear so, or from real good humour, he kept up the joke and said, "Nay, but if anybody were to answer the paragraph and contradict it, I'd have a reply, and would say that he who contradicted it was no friend either to Vestris or me. For why should not Dr. Johnson add to his other powers a little corporeal agility? Socrates learnt to dance at an advanced age, and Cato learnt Greek at an advanced age. Then it might proceed to say that this Johnson, not content with dancing on the ground, might dance on the rope; and then there might be the elephant dancing on the rope. Lord Grimston wrote a play, *Love in a Hollow Tree*. He found out it was a very bad one, and therefore wished to buy up all the copies and burn 'em. The Duchess of Marlborough had kept one, and when Lord Grimston was against her at an election, she had an edition printed, and prefixed to it as a frontispiece an elephant dancing on a rope, to show that Lord Grimston's writing comedy was as awkward as an elephant dancing on a rope." He carried it on thus with much pleasantry. What became of me next I do not recollect. Only I think I supped at Sir Lawrence Dundas's, and went to Dilly's at night, where I indeed am quite at home.

SATURDAY 31 MARCH. Had a keen battle in the Committee. Dudley Long, one of the members, was invited at my wish to dine today at Mr. Thrale's. I had mentioned it to him yesterday or before. Today he took

---

[3] "It astonished many people that the great luminary of English literature, Doctor Johnson, could so far descend from his philosophic consequence as to visit the opera-house and speak praisingly of the *King of Capers*. However, says a correspondent, the secret has at length got abroad. The Doctor wanted a few *lessons* but did not choose to be at the expense. This being hinted to the elder Vestris, he sent a very polite letter offering his services, at the same time observing that the honour of being the *master* of the greatest *scholar* in the universe would be considered as an ample recompense for his *labour* and attention. The philosopher, it seems, accepted the proposal; and our correspondent assures us that the Doctor has improved so rapidly in the *minuet de la cour* that it is thought he will be done out of hand in less than a fortnight. The Doctor's first appearance in public, it is said, will be before their Majesties at St. James's, and that he is to be honoured with the fair hand of her Grace of Devonshire; such is the rumour of the day" (*Morning Post*, 21 March 1781). Gaetano Apollino Baldassare Vestris (1729–1808) became the leading dancer of the Paris opera and retired from the stage in 1781. This was one of his several visits to England. This "ludicrous story in the newspapers" has not previously been located.

me into his chariot with him. It broke down at Charing Cross. I told him afterwards I would stand or fall with him. My ease in getting my counsellor's wig, gown, and band put on at Nerot's Hotel in King Street, St. James's, and then getting on again my wig like hair well dressed, is admirable. General Paoli said to me, "You live easily." It is very true. I get through life lightly.

We had at dinner Dr. Delap and Mr. Selwyn, late banker at Paris, and Dr. Johnson and Langton. I mentioned Strahan's sleeping on the Committee and saying he had made up his mind on a case. "If," said Dr. Johnson, "he is such a rogue as to make up his mind on a case without hearing it, he should not be such a fool as to tell it." "I think," said Long, "the Doctor has pretty plainly set him down as both rogue and fool." Long was remarkably genteel, and softly and sweetly gay; "A man without effort," Mrs. Thrale said, using Dr. Johnson's expression as to Beauclerk. He said several lively things. But from "dilatory notation" [4] I have lost them, and they were not uttered loud enough to reach Dr. Johnson. Seward was also here at dinner. Poor Mr. Thrale was very lethargic. However, we knew we were welcome and drank by him, and the claret being excellent, there was a constant supply of generous spirits. Long took little. His flame was not so violent as mine. Did not exhaust the wine so fast. We went upstairs to coffee and tea. There was a rout here tonight, and a great deal of good company. Dr. Johnson did not do much. He and I and Langton sat on a settee and talked, I forget of what. Mr. Ramsay, the painter, was of the party, and by a very lively mind in a very decrepit body gave a convincing proof that the *mind* or *soul* or *spirit* is distinct from *material substance*. Dr. Solander was here. Mrs. Thrale said he was the best man in the world for a rout. For you might put him into any room filled with any company, and he at once was one of them. Then carry him into another room, and he instantly is one of the company *there*. I said, "Throw him where you will, he swims." I met here tonight Miss Owen, a Welsh lady of £10,000 fortune whom I regarded at Bath, where she was with Mrs. Thrale. We were glad to meet again. She had not been in London for a long time. But I really fell in love with Miss Sophy Streatfield,[5] a beautiful young lady of family and some fortune, exceedingly accomplished and even a Greek scholar. I had

---

[4] A phrase used by Johnson in his *Journey to the Western Islands of Scotland* (ed. Mary Lascelles, 1971, p. 147).

[5] Boswell, whose ear and memory for names were remarkably good, had trouble with this one, spelling it on this occasion Stretford and later (7 May 1785) Stetfield. Miss Streatfield had the faculty of being able to shed tears on request, and of attracting married men. Thrale had displayed such amorousness toward her as to make his wife jealous.

some conversation with her and Miss Burney (*Evelina*) about Dr. Johnson. Miss Streatfield, though she respected him highly, said she was afraid of him. Miss Burney said she was much pleased to see him and me together, the constant attention with which I followed him. I supped (I think) at Sir Lawrence Dundas's.

I then went to Lord Eglinton's. Found Major Montgomerie and a Mr. George Barker, an English gentleman, with him. They were drinking punch. He asked me what I'd drink. "A bottle of claret if you please, my Lord." I had it and relished it. He looked his watch. I was bold and triumphant, feeling that *my* spirits beat down the wine. "My Lord," said I, "I see you wish to go to bed." "I do," said he. "Well," said I. "But if you'll sit half an hour till I drink another bottle of claret, I'll be obliged to you." "Well," said he, "I will sit up." I asked Barker, and he cheerfully agreed. I took the second bottle also with great relish. It was now about two in the morning. I had intended to go to General Paoli's tonight. But did not like to *enter* at such an irregular hour. So went to the City to Mr. Dilly's. (This is the history of *Sunday night*. I shall mention Saturday when recording Sunday. On Sunday however I went with an invalid [and] two horse grenadiers and [sat] two hours and drank brandy and water.) [6]

SUNDAY 1 APRIL. On Saturday night after leaving Mr. Thrale's, I went to Lord Eglinton's, where I found Major Montgomerie and Shaw-Stewart. The Earl was a little *dry*, and would not humour Stewart and me enough. When we left him and got into a hackney-coach, Stewart begged we might drink a little more punch together. I agreed, and went with him to the British Coffee-house. It was locked up. I rapped furiously. A fat, steady Englishman with a bushy wig and brown clothes took a fixed stand in the street to watch us. I asked him what he wanted. He answered the street was as free to him as to me. I went up to him and, laying my hand on his shoulder, said, "Friend, we mean no harm. We only want some punch." "Off hands, Sir," said he. "Damn you," said Stewart to me, "let the gentleman alone." Growing impatient, I asked for Stewart's cane, and broke every pane of glass above the door, three in number. The noise awaked the house, and Stewart having called in his name for one, the door was opened. The fat fellow followed, and we perceived him standing in the middle of the coffee-room. "You see now, Sir," said I, "that we meant no harm." Still he was steady and unmoved. "Will you drink with us?" said I. "Will you have brandy? or what will you have?" With a consummate neglect of us, he just pronounced the word *no*, and said, "I'll

---

[6] Boswell even in his fully written journals does sometimes through inadvertence omit words crucial to the sense: See below, 1 April 1781, n. 2. This sentence in any case is a cramped interlinear afterthought.

have a drop of water." Then called, "Here, waiter, I'll be obliged to you for a glass of water." He got it, drank it, and walked off without saying a word. This was quite a true-born Englishman; an honest, steady, sulky man who took care that a house should not be robbed in the night. It was lucky he did not beat me black and blue for challenging him. Stewart and I had a bowl of punch made. But I could take but very little of it. I walked to Dilly's. It was very cold and dreary in the Strand. But I made out my march.

This morning I had some sickly feverishness, but not a great deal. Ross, our Edinburgh patentee, breakfasted with Mr. Dilly and me and asked my aid in getting Sir Lawrence Dundas to approve of a renewal of his patent. I was truly cordial towards him.[7] I was to meet Wight at Spottiswoode's at eleven. But as I wish to be at mass every Sunday, I went first to the Bavarian Chapel, and in the crowd below was devout. Got to Spottiswoode's about twelve. They excused me, as I had been the night before with Lord Eglinton. We talked of the vote of Gordon of Culvennan, on which the election now turned; and all the charters, etc., being laid before me, I had a room to myself and wrote out a clear, strong state of the case. I had no scruple at doing this on Sunday when time was so short.

I then went to Mr. Thrale's, where I had a kindly general invitation to dinner and supper. I said I had a silver ticket. "A gold ticket," said worthy Thrale. Dr. Johnson and I were a little while together alone. He dictated to me a good argument upon the effect of a deed being registrated.[8] "This," said he, "you must enlarge in speaking to the Committee. You must not argue in a popular assembly as if you were arguing in the schools. Close reasoning will not fix their attention. You must say the same thing over and over again in different words. If you say it but once, they may miss it while not attending. It is unjust, Sir, to censure lawyers for multiplying words. It is necessary."

We had at dinner Sir Philip Jennings-Clerke and Mr. Perkins, clerk to Mr. Thrale, who has a salary of £500 a year. Sir Philip looked to me like an ancient Welsh gentleman. He was plump and jolly, his hair white and well dressed with a goodly bag to it, and he wore a black velvet coat, a rich embroidered vest, and extraordinary rich lace ruffles. Mrs. Thrale said

---

[7] Ross held the patent of the Theatre Royal in Edinburgh, and apparently had to renew it at seven-year intervals. According to J. C. Dibdin, the season of 1780–1781 had "turned out very badly, and on one of the last nights Ross went clandestinely to the doors, took away the whole receipts of the house and himself directly afterwards to London" (*Annals of the Edinburgh Stage*, 1888, p. 180).

[8] Boswell prints it in the *Life of Johnson*, following 21 March 1781.

they were quite old-fashioned. Dr. Johnson attacked the Opposition, and said he was sorry Sir Philip continued so long with them. "But," said he (laughing), "when Sir Philip comes to the years of discretion he'll leave them." (Sir Philip, I suppose, was about sixty.) "Ay," said I, "when Sir Philip is as old as his ruffles. They are respectable ruffles. They look like an ancient family. They are Tory ruffles. They are quite the Cocoa-Tree.[9] It is said that lace ruffles are dipped in coffee to give them a dark colour. Sir Philip's have been dipped in chocolade."[1] "Ah, Sir," said the Doctor, "ancient ruffles and modern principles do not agree." "I shall not forget these ruffles," said I. "No," said Mrs. Thrale, "you'll have 'em at your fingers' ends." Sir Philip however defended the Opposition as to the American war ably and with temper, and I joined him. He then said that the majority of the nation was against Administration. Said Dr. Johnson: "I am against Administration. But it is for having too little of what Opposition thinks they have too much. Were I Minister, if any man wagged his finger against me, he should be turned out. For that which it is in the power of Government to give at pleasure to one or to another, should be given to the supporters of Government; and if you will not oppose at the expense of losing your place, your opposition will not be honest. You will feel no serious grievance; and the present Opposition is only a contest to get what others have. Sir Robert Walpole acted as I would do. As to the American war, the *sense* of the nation is with Administration. The majority of those who can understand is with it. The majority of those who can only hear is against it. And as those who can only hear are more numerous than those who can understand, and the opposition is always loudest, a majority of the rabble will be for opposition."

Mrs. Thrale and he [2] talked of Dudley Long. She praised him much. "Nay," said the Doctor, "my dear lady, don't talk so. Mr. *Long's* character is very *short*. It is nothing. He fills a chair. He is a man of a genteel appearance, and that is all. I know nobody who blasts by praise as you do. For whenever there is exaggerated praise, everybody is set against a character. They are roused to attack it. Now there is Pepys. You praised that man with such disproportion that I was incited to lessen him perhaps more than he deserves. His blood is upon your head. So now, Mr. Long. And by the same principle, your malice defeats itself. For your censure is too violent. No, as Roger Ascham says, 'You are

[9] Alluding to the famous Tory chocolate-house and club of that name.
[1] Boswell always gives this word the spelling (and no doubt the pronunciation) which he had learned in Holland in 1763–1764.
[2] Omitted inadvertently. "I" is also possible.

neither a friend nor a ——— foe.' Or to give you Dr. Young, ———." [3] "Come," said she, "you must not attack my favourite poet." Said somebody: "This is the character of my mistress." "And of my mistress's poet," said the Doctor. "And yet" (with a pleasing pause and leering smile), "she is the first woman in the world. Could she but restrain that wicked tongue of hers, she would be the only woman in the world. Could she but command that little whirligig—" "Well," said I, "now that you have finished the portrait, you have done very well. The first sitting was a very unfavourable likeness." (Said she: "That was the *dead colour*.") "But when you have given the last touches—the grace and the glowing colours —it is a fine picture." I might have added, "And you'll put my mistress in a good *frame*."

She told us of little Selwyn, the banker, an insignificant-looking being in a mixed spring velvet who dined here yesterday and never said a word. It seems he is so miserable that he was impelled to complain even to Seward, whom he hates and who he knows despises him. He accosted Seward in the street and owned he was a most unhappy man, for he could not talk. "I am invited to conversations. But I have no conversation." I told with success the ludicrous story of Roberton of Bedlay, who, when a woman who let lodgings told him, "They are just a guinea a week, you furnishing coal and candle," earnestly objected, "But I tell you, woman, I have no coal or candle." Selwyn, it seems, is a worthy, obliging man, and has been able to acquire a fortune of £4,000 a year. Dr. Johnson observed that man commonly could not be successful in different ways. "This man," said he, "has spent the time in getting £4,000 a year when he might have learnt to talk; and now he cannot talk." Said Perkins: "If he had got his £4,000 a year as a mountebank, he might have learnt to talk at the same time that he was getting his fortune." A droll remark enough; and as it came from the confidential clerk of the brewhouse, was smartly and eagerly applauded by Mrs. Thrale.

Mr. Seward and Sir John Lade and Mr. Harry Smith, a relation of Mr. Thrale's, came in. Sir John was a mere fashionable nonentity in company. Being only a centaur, he seemed but half, and scarcely half, an animal in company. *He* fills a saddle. [4] Long's only filling a chair was brought over

---

[3] "Also for manners and life, quick wits commonly be ... neither fast to friend, nor fearful to foe" (The *Scholemaster*, near the beginning). Johnson had written a life of Ascham. Boswell omitted both literary allusions in the *Life of Johnson*.

[4] Sir John Lade, a famous foxhunter, was Thrale's nephew. He later married Laetitia Darby, or Smith, who had been under the protection of the Duke of York and was reputed before that to have been the mistress of "Sixteen-string Jack" Rann, the highwayman. Upon Sir John's coming of age the preceding August, Johnson had written his satiric "Short Song of Congratulation," one of the finest specimens of his lyric gift.

again. (I wish I had said, "He may fill the chair of a committee.") Mrs. Thrale said to the Doctor, "Sir, it is because he is quiet and does not exert himself with force. You'll be saying the same of Mr. Smith, who sits so quiet there." This was ill-bred, and she was deservedly flogged. "Nay, Madam," said the Doctor, "what right have you to talk so to me? Both Mr. Smith and I have reason to take it ill. *You* may talk so of Mr. Smith. But why do you make *me* do it? Have *I* said anything against Mr. Smith? You have *set* Mr. Smith that I might shoot him. But I have not shot him."

Seward said (I imagine with some intentional petulance) that when he was at Edinburgh [5] he had seen three volumes in folio of Dr. Johnson's sayings collected by me. "Nay," said I, "I must put you right, as I am very exact in authenticity. You could not see folio volumes of his sayings, for I have none. You may have seen octavos and quartos. Now," said I, "this is inattention which one should guard against." "Sir," said the Doctor, "it is a want of concern about veracity. He does not know that he saw any volumes. If he had seen 'em, he could have remembered their size." The Doctor did not make sufficient allowance for inaccuracy of memory. But, no doubt, carelessness as to the exactness of circumstances is very dangerous, for one may gradually recede from the fact till all is fiction.

I went away for a little and called at General Oglethorpe's and Lady Margaret Macdonald's, but found neither of them at home. Returned to Thrale's and had cold meat and some wine, but I recollect no conversation. Then called at Lord Eglinton's; found his Lordship and Major Montgomerie and a Mr. Barker, an English gentleman, drinking punch.[6] I was asked if I would drink wine. "If you please, my Lord." "What?" "A bottle of claret." I had it, and my conversation was so gay and yet so placid, as the apprehension of losing our election hung upon me and calmed me, that the Earl was pleased though I drank a different liquor. He dislikes nonconformity in drinking. Wine had no power over me tonight, my animal spirits were so strong and so dilated with the election. I gloried in my strength *vis-à-vis d'un héros bacchique.* "I see," said I, "my Lord" (as he looked his watch) "you are inclined to go to bed. If your Lordship could sit half an hour till I drink another bottle of this excellent wine, I would take it very kind." Barker cheerfully agreed to sit, and the Earl agreed. I think the Major was not well, and went away. Barker was a good-humoured Whig. I had a brush with him however as a Tory, and the Earl did not dislike my ancient spirit. I thought his Lordship's delicacy and point of honour towards another peer too refined,

[5] In July 1777.
[6] The same meeting as that recorded under 31 March, here given its proper date.

when he would not agree to my bringing before the Committee the illegal and unconstitutional bargain between Lord Glencairn and Lord North, by which, on condition of being made one of the sixteen peers, the Earl gave ten votes; that is, just voted by ten mouths for Sir Adam Fergusson.[7] I should have mentioned that this evening Dr. Johnson said, "Mr. Boswell never was in anybody's company who did not wish to see him again."

[EDITORIAL NOTE: There are no entries for 2 and 3 April, but beginning with 4 April the record is continued, with a few gaps and many duplications, and in a bewildering variety of styles. For full description of the documents and of the method followed in making a text, see above, p. xxv, under "Documentation." The note for 4 April says only "Call of The Club." We enlarge this by a bit from the first draft of the manuscript of the *Life of Johnson* which comes at the end of the entry for 1 April.]

Mr. Thrale appeared very lethargic today, but was not thought to be in immediate danger, but on Wednesday the fourth he expired. Johnson was in the house and thus feelingly mentions the event: "I felt almost the last flutter of his pulse and looked for the last time upon the face that for fifteen years had never been turned upon me but with respect or benignity." Upon that day there was a call of the LITERARY CLUB, but Johnson excused his absence. . . .[8]

[EDITORIAL NOTE: The note for 5 April reads, "Saw Mr. Thrale and Lady Margaret. At Dr. Johnson's, Sir J. Hawkins there. House of Lords. Dined home." If the reference to Thrale is not misdated, it can only mean that Boswell saw him in his coffin. "Lady Margaret" was no doubt Lady Margaret Macdonald, whom Boswell had missed on 1 April. We enlarge the note for 6 April ("Queen's Arms with Dr. Johnson, etc.") by the first draft of the manuscript of the *Life of Johnson*.]

On Friday sixth April [Johnson] carried me to dine at a club which at his desire had been lately formed at the Queen's Arms in St. Paul's

---

[7] According to theory, the peers of Scotland met and freely elected sixteen of their number to sit in the House of Lords. Actually, the Prime Minister sent down a list of the peers whom Government wished elected, and these were usually chosen. It was against this practice that Lord Buchan had protested in his "speech" (see above, 16 October 1780; he was not allowed to deliver it, and published it as a pamphlet). In the election of 1780 the Duke of Atholl and the Earl of Glencairn had been elected to fill vacancies. According to Boswell, this was just a job: Glencairn to be put on the Government's list of representative peers if he would agree to deliver the ten votes he controlled for the ministerial candidate in the House of Commons.

[8] By a note which is reproduced among the illustrations following p. 250.

Churchyard. He told Mr. Hoole that he wished to have a *City Club*, and asked him to collect one. "But," said he, "don't let them be *patriots*."[9] The company today were very sensible well-behaved men.

SATURDAY 7 APRIL. Hoole's with Dr. Johnson, etc. Lord Advocate was our *sworn* enemy.[1] Highland laird: " 'Tis referred to my oath."[2] Plum-Pudding Club: Dr. Johnson puts the reasons into it.[3] [Governor Bourchier said] distinctions by birth in India dead weights on merit. Man *cannot* raise himself and family. Merit does not get all it may get. Orme said absurd to have those permanent distinctions. The Doctor showed a *principle* in it. "They think different races of men to be preserved as different races of dogs: mastiff, spaniel, cur. The Brahmins think themselves the mastiff of mankind. So in metals, gold. The others never *can* be gold." BOSWELL. "Grindall cuts nabobs for stone and finds diamonds in their bladders."[4] SEWARD. "You think this is a brilliant thought; right to give it to Grind-all to polish. I don't think much of it; 'tis only for a table after dinner." I said afterwards, " 'Tis *wine*, not a fine *water*." Supped Sir Lawrence's.

[EDITORIAL NOTE: Another account of this dinner exists; it is much fuller and more entertaining than Boswell's, and depicts *him* as the most interesting of the guests. Made by Fanny Burney's younger and prettier sister, Charlotte Ann, it is now we believe published for the first time from a fragmentary diary of hers in the British Library (Egerton MSS. 3700 B). Charlotte was twenty years old in this year, a lively girl devoted to puns, repartee, and laughter, in every way equipped to relish Boswell's social gaiety and to make a more vivid and credible record of it than exists anywhere else.]

On Saturday last[5] I dined, drank tea, and supped at my new friends', the Hooles. At dinner there were no females but Mrs. Hoole, Mrs. Wil-

---

[9] "A factious disturber of the Government" (Johnson's second definition of "patriot" in the fourth edition of his *Dictionary*, 1773).

[1] Henry Dundas, the Lord Advocate, was a nominee of Sir Adam Fergusson's party in the Committee which was trying the Ayrshire election. See above, 21 March 1781, n. 5.

[2] Another jest developing out of the mention of being put under oath. Sir Allan Maclean, when sworn, withdrew his testimony in a famous case at law: "A man will *say* what he will not *swear*" (*Journal of a Tour to the Hebrides*, 10 November 1773).

[3] We have been unable to find that there actually was a club of this name. Boswell or some other punster says that The Club or the anonymous new club at the Queen's Arms might well be named "The Plum-Pudding Club" because of the raisins (reasons) that Johnson puts into it. The word raisin was commonly pronounced *reez'n* in 1781; Webster defended that pronunciation as late as 1828.

[4] Grindall is identified in Boswell's entry for 8 April 1781, below.

[5] 7 April 1781. Miss Burney, as her date-line shows, was writing on Tuesday 10 April.

liams, and me. Of gentlemen, there were Mr. Boughton-Rouse,[6] who did me the honour to make a point of sitting by me—but I can't get acquainted with him. He is civil to me, too, but there is an *horteur* [7] in his manner that *knocks me up.* He is a young, handsome, dark, fierce-looking man, and they say he knows almost every language that can be named. By all accounts his head is quite a *Babel!* But he has no "convivial hilarity" [8] about him, and *those* are the characters to my taste, people that make an *ado.* It was droll enough they all got my name so pat. They all called me by my name at full length. Somehow everybody almost catches my name. I'm glad it is not an ugly name; I'm glad I've not *got a bad name.*

Mr. Boughton-Rouse sat at one side of me and Governor Bourchier on the other, a prosing governor enough.[9] Opposite to me sat Dr. Johnson, in deep mourning and much out of spirits for the death of his friend Mr. Thrale, who died of a stroke of apoplexy last Wednesday morning. Next to Dr. Johnson sat Mr. or Captain (I know not which) Orme, who everybody admired but me.[1] I thought him a *serious clout* [2] and not agreeable, and he said *"this here,"* too. Next to Mr. Boughton-Rouse sat a *bony Scote,*[3] and next to him sat Mr. Hoole and his son, and next to him

---

[6] John Hoole was writer and compiler of India correspondence at the India House, and his guests of this day reflect his professional connexion. Charles William Boughton-Rouse, later a baronet, had gone to India as a "writer" in the Bengal civil service and had held various judicial and administrative offices there. He was about thirty-six years old and was M.P. for Evesham.

[7] *Sic.* Miss Burney and her correspondents may have used this spelling as a joke on somebody's bad pronunciation of French.

[8] Marked as a quotation by Miss Burney. It sounds like Johnson but we have not been able to attribute it certainly to him.

[9] Charles Bourchier had been Governor of Madras, 1767–1770, and had built a sumptuous mansion in Shenley, Herts. Miss Burney's pun implies that she found him as dull as a domestic tutor.

[1] Robert Orme is well known to history as the favourite aide-de-camp of General Braddock, at whose side he was on 5 July 1755 near Fort Duquesne when Braddock received his fatal wound; he was wounded himself, and it was he who wrote the official account of the action. Boswell's statement in the *Life of Johnson* (7 April 1781) that he "had been long in the East Indies" answers the question which historians have asked as to what became of him after 1756. He had resigned his commission (captaincy in the Army, lieutenancy in the Coldstream Guards) then, and twenty-five years later would commonly have been styled "Mr."

[2] A dialect word from the same root as "clod" (of earth), and having the same sense. The readings "dont" and "dout" are also possible, but harder to gloss convincingly. "Clod" is confirmed by Miss Burney's attribution to Orme of the rustic "this here."

[3] Miss Burney is mocking the pronunciation of some Scot of her acquaintance, probably, Professor Joyce Hemlow thinks, Isabella Lumisden, wife of the engraver Robert Strange. (Boswell found Mrs. Strange's broad Scots trying.) In early Scots, *bonny* was

the flower of the flock, Mr. Boswell, the famous Mr. Boswell, who is a sweet creature. I admire and like him beyond measure. He is a fine, lively, sensible, unaffected, honest, manly, good-humoured character. I never saw him before. He idolizes Dr. Johnson, and struts about, and puts himself into such ridiculous postures that he is as good as a comedy. He seems between forty and fifty, a good-looking man enough. N.B. He has a wife in Scotland, so there is no *scandal* in being in raptures about him.

He made a *bon mot* upon me that procured him great applause during dinner. They were speaking of the Indian women burning themselves upon the death of their husbands, and in the midst of it, Mr. Boswell called out from the bottom of the table, "Miss Burney, and what do *you* think of this burning scheme?" "Oh," one of 'em cried, "she had much rather *live*, I dare say!" "Ay," replied Mr. Boswell, "then, Miss Burney, you would not like to be a *flaming beauty* in India, I fancy."

They were speaking of the German *eaters*.[4] "Sir," cried Mr. Boswell, "they are wolves, they are absolutely wolves!"

Dr. Johnson said that he had been told (by somebody that the tone of his voice said he depended upon) that "poison might be extracted out of bread." "Then perhaps," says Mr. Boughton-Rouse, "Dr. Cadogan, when he said bread was the most unwholesome food in the world, might tell us that he meant on account of the poison." [5]

---

always spelled *bony,* indicating a long vowel; *The Oxford English Dictionary* (1888) observed that the pronunciation *bōnie* is often heard in Scotland. The Mediaeval Latin form of *Scot* was *Scōtus,* not *Scŏttus,* and this no doubt affected some strains of the vernacular.

[4] Presumably, "the eating habits of the German people"; possibly a reference to some particular gastronomic athletes, alleged to be German, who gave public exhibitions of gluttony. In his tour of Germany Boswell remarked on the heartiness at table of the Germans, but did not charge them with extraordinary voracity.

[5] Boswell reported this saying of Johnson's too, not in his journal notes but in a note apparently intended for the collection he called "Boswelliana." Like Miss Burney he failed to catch the name of Johnson's authority: "Dr. ——— told Dr. Johnson he could extract a strong poison from bread. 'That,' said I, 'would be hard on the staff of life—taking man's staff to break his head.'" Bread at this time seems to have been under indictment both as being dangerously adulterated and as being unwholesome even when made of certified ingredients. As far back as 1757 the charge of adulteration had been pressed in a furious anonymous pamphlet entitled *Poison Detected: or Frightful Truths . . . in a Treatise on Bread*; it had more recently been repeated in Smollett's *Humphry Clinker,* 1771 (letter of Matthew Bramble, London, 8 June). In the summer of 1778 there had been a great deal of complaint in the newspapers of the badness of the bread being issued to the encampments at Warley Common and Coxheath. Topham Beauclerk wrote facetiously to Bennet Langton that Dr. Fordyce had gone to both camps "in order to poison the troops with bread" (C. N. Fifer, ed., *The Correspondence of James Boswell with Certain Members of The Club,* 1976, p. 85).

Miss Mudge came in to tea. During dinner they were talking of the Indian notions of their castes in life, that whatever caste they are born into they are to remain, and so all the tribe of successors. So Mr. Boswell came and placed himself between Miss Mudge and me at the tea-table and called to the gentlemen who had been talking of the Indian castes, "Gentlemen, I like *my cast* very well now."

Mr. Boswell said he had an engagement at General Paoli's, and turned to Miss Mudge and me and cried *he was sorry for it*; at which I shook my head at Dr. Johnson, as much as to say he must wish to stay to be in his company; at which Mr. Boswell put himself in one of his ridiculous postures and cried, "Nay, shake not your gory looks *that* way!" [6]

They say Mr. Boswell has such a passion for seeing *executions* that he never misses one if he can help it; and he *seemed* as if he had all their terms by heart,[7] for just after he had been complaining of being obliged to go, the maid came and told him the *coach was at the door;* he turned to his friend and cried, "Here, the sheriff's officers are at the door!"

He is a charming creature. He told me he would call here, but I am afraid he won't.

SUNDAY 8 APRIL. Had chocolade at home. Then adored in the Portuguese Chapel. Called on Major Montgomerie in Warwick Street, Golden Square, and drank some tea. Went to Captain Preston's.[8] Mr. Grindall, the great surgeon of the London Hospital and much employed by the East India people, came with his chariot. I said he cut nabobs for the stone and found diamonds. He was a fine, frank, sensible, jolly Englishman. We got into his chariot and were at once acquainted, for I showed him that I was a liberal anti-ministerial Scotsman. It was a delightful day, and the excellent roads pleased and filled me with a degree of wonder. Preston rode. Captain Clarke and ———, Mr. Foulis's clerk, walked to Hackney toll-bar, near which Grindall mounted his horse, which his servant had waiting for him, and Clarke and ——— got into the chaise with me. Old Foulis received us in his blunt, hearty way. He had Jervoise Clark Jervoise sitting with him on a morning visit. I said I was sure he was on the right side in Parliament when I found him with Mr. Foulis. Said Foulis: "Some of the other side come too. But they get it." "Ay," said I, "you tie them to the halberds. You give them a flogging." We sauntered through the garden, greenhouse, and hothouse, and anon were

---

[6] *Macbeth*, III. iv. 50–51, intentionally altered.

[7] He knew all the ceremonial of executions at first hand.

[8] Boswell is starting on a jaunt to Woodford to visit Charles Foulis, director of the Sun Fire Office and owner of extensive properties in the East Indies. Robert Preston was Foulis's heir.

called to dinner. I asked for cider and had it, the weather was so summer. The company relished it much. Had a plentiful good dinner, admirable malt liquor of different sorts, old port, and bonum magnums of claret till we had full enough. Our talk was tumultous,[9] careless, and joyous. Old Charles Foulis sat like Jove in his chair. There was a complacency in every countenance in company, and I was quite happy. Foulis is violent against the present Ministry. He would hang up four without trial just to be doing, just to clear the way: Lords Mansfield, North, Sandwich, Loughborough; [1] and then he would consider what is next to be done. He had his rallying pleasantry upon Preston as joining a little with Lord Sandwich as an elder brother of Trinity Hospital.[2] "Here's this Elder Brother," said he, "a pretty fellow indeed, who drinks the health of Palli*see*r, damn him.[3] However, Bob is right. Let him go on with them a little till he is well established, and then let him tell them a piece of his mind." John Wilkes was one of my toasts. Grindall and I grew warm friends, shaking hands cordially. "Sir," said he, "you shall dine with John before you leave London." Only Preston and I stayed all night. We had plenty of coffee and tea, and Mrs. Foulis's civility and good humour charmed me. Then the card-table was set, and we played two rubbers at whist, hugging ourselves that we were out of the reach of Presbyterian prejudices. Preston and I were partners, and neither lost nor won. We had rich rum punch at intervals, and had also some more cider. Then was a comfortable bit of supper, and a little drop of punch after it, with wine if one chose it; and then in good time to bed. I had an elegant spacious

[9] See above, p. 21 n. 6.

[1] The Earl of Mansfield was Lord Chief Justice of the Court of King's Bench; Lord North was Prime Minister; Lord Sandwich was First Lord of the Admiralty, and Lord Loughborough was Chief Justice of the Court of Common Pleas. Loughborough had been a prominent member of Lord North's administration as Solicitor-General.

[2] Properly Trinity House, of which Trinity Hospital (or College) was an adjunct. Trinity House is the hall of a corporation ("The Guild, Fraternity, or Brotherhood of the Most Glorious and Undivided Trinity, and of St. Clement") which since the reign of Henry VIII has had charge "of lighthouses and sea-marks, the securing of a body of skilled and efficient pilots for the Navy and mercantile service, and the general management of nautical matters not immediately connected with the Admiralty" (H. B. Wheatley and Peter Cunningham, *London Past and Present*, iii. 408). Any master or mate skilled in navigation could be admitted as a "Younger Brother"; Preston had just this year been elected an "Elder Brother" or officer. Lord Sandwich was Master. Sir Winston Churchill frequently wore the uniform of an Elder Brother of Trinity House.

[3] Vice-Admiral Sir Hugh Palliser (the name was properly stressed on the first syllable). See above, p. 62 n. 5. According to Horace Walpole, Lord Sandwich, Palliser's chief in the Admiralty, tried to restore him to favour by proposing a toast to him at a dinner of Trinity House. John Courtenay refused to drink it; Preston apparently did not.

chamber. Preston attended with the assiduity on board a ship to guard against fire; saw me into my nest, and took away the candle. What a hearty day! How totally different was I from the weary and desponding hypochondriac which I sometimes am.

MONDAY 9 APRIL. Before eight Preston was in my room. "James, get up. I have got a place in the coach for you." I was alert, jumped up, and my heels beat on the floor responsive to his call. I was in an agreeable feverishness from yesterday's generous living. Tom, Mr. Foulis's black boy, attended me well and put on my wig. I got a basin of tea. The coach came to the door, which hurried me. I took the basin of tea in my hand as I walked to the coach door, that it might cool in the air. Drank it off, and then throwing three shillings into the basin, called, "Here, Tom, take you the grounds." A smart, lively young gentleman of Woodford, who had something of Wilkes's manner, was in the coach. We talked away. We took in a plump servant-maid, whom I kissed and was gay with, and by degrees the coach was quite full. I joked on everything we saw. There was *"Eve's* Manufactory." That, I supposed, must be aprons. All jokes do in a hackney-coach. There came on a pretty smart rain. A well-looked, stately woman who sat on the coach-box begged as a favour we would make room for her in the coach. I told her all the seats were filled. But if she chose to sit on my knee, and the company had no objection, she was heartily welcome. This being agreed, in she came, and I had a very desirable armful. She was a widow with three children. She had suckled the son of Mr. ———, brewer in Winchester Street, and continued in his service. But having had ill health, went to a friend's at Woodford for country air, was going up to her master's for a single day and night, and then to return to Woodford. I grew very fond of her, cherished her in the coach, and when she went from us, kissed her repeatedly and warmly, and wished to be better acquainted with her. Such incidents are marrow to my bones. Observing many *boxes* [4] on the road today, I said they should all be rented by poets, for it would require a great deal of imagination to suppose them country-houses. Preston got to town before me on horseback. I breakfasted with him heartily. My brother came, and we talked of Bruce Boswell's bargain to have an East India ship, which Preston thought not advisable in the present state of things. [5] I regretted that it was not in my power to assist him with money, and I was sorry for his unskilfulness in the way of the world. He came to me in the evening at Mr. Dilly's and talked with anxiety of his situation. I expressed my friendly wishes, but at the same time took notice of

[4] Small country-houses.
[5] Bruce Boswell was the second living son of Dr. John Boswell, hence Boswell's first cousin.

his ignorance of life. He had written me a letter begging my aid, and informing me that he had to lay down £4,000 on the spot next morning at ten o'clock. I told him this was a letter to be written to Rumbold.[6] But it was really strange that a man who had been twenty years at sea should write such a letter to *me*, who could not raise 4,000 pence. (General Paoli said, "Don't lend him fourpence. He will not do good.")

After being dressed, I went with Mr. Dilly and a number of his friends to Old Mr. Sheridan's introductory lecture on elocution at the Standard Tavern, Cornhill, where I said he erected the standard of eloquence, to which we repaired. The Rev. Dr. Towers was one of our number. We were first shown into a small room where Sheridan was with the apparatus of an orator: a decanter with water, a large glass, and a bottle of capillaire to clear and smooth and mellow his voice. Then we were ushered into the great room, where a company of about fifty gentlemen and twenty ladies was assembled. He read his lecture very well, though he complained he was ill, and the room was by much too large for his voice. I was very well pleased to have the system which I had formerly heard now revived; [7] and it was very just when moderated by an understanding less enthusiastic on the subject than Old Sheridan's. He also read Dryden's *Alexander's Feast* very well, only now and then his voice took its high tones and cracked.[8] Lady Craven [9] sat directly opposite to him. I said she could give him as good as he brought, and, if she chose it, they might keep it up; might play at shuttlecock together. She was attended by Mr. Corry, Member for Newry, a genteel young Irishman whom I called her Cory-

---

[6] Sir Thomas Rumbold, Bt., formerly Governor of Madras, had recently been dismissed from the service of the East India Company. At this time, his name was a synonym for fabulous wealth.

[7] In the summer of 1761 in Edinburgh Boswell heard Sheridan's lectures upon the English language, and "was often in his company" (*Life of Johnson*, beginning of 1763; see also F. A. Pottle, *James Boswell, the Earlier Years*, 1966, pp. 64–65).

[8] "One of [R. B. Sheridan's] sisters now and then visited Harrow, and well do I remember that . . . she triumphantly repeated Dryden's *Ode upon St. Cecilia's Day*, according to the instruction given to her by her father. Take a sample:

> *None* but the brave,
> None but the *brave*,
> None *but* the brave deserve the fair"

(Dr. Parr to Thomas Moore in Thomas Moore's *Memoirs of R. B. Sheridan*, 1827, i. 11). This account is confirmed by Thomas Sheridan's *Lectures on the Art of Reading*, where the *Ode* is printed with directions for pauses and emphasis (information kindly supplied by Dr. Donald H. Alden).

[9] The daughter of the fourth Earl of Berkeley, writer of plays, amateur of private theatricals, and Horace Walpole's correspondent, whom he much esteemed for her beauty and frankness. She was separated from Lord Craven in 1780, and in 1791 married the Margrave of Anspach, whose mistress she had become.

don. He knew me again, as did Henderson the player and young Beaufoy the Quaker, whose father is the immense vinegar-merchant.[1] I said he was fit to be contractor to Hannibal. Dr. Johnson told me of an epitaph in Clapham churchyard on a vinegar-merchant, "qui sicut alter Hannibal, ad famam et opes aceto viam sibi patefecit." [2]

I went a little to Change. Then came home to Mr. Dilly's, and he and I and the Rev. Mr. Davis of Islington drove in a hackney-coach, through a great part of the city which I never saw before, to Wellclose Square, where we and my brother, and Mr. Braithwaite of the Post-Office and Captain Boyd, a Kilmarnock man in the Canada trade, all dined with the Rev. Dr. Mayo, who gives a dinner to some of his friends every Monday, and dines abroad all the other days of the week. His maid and one of his daughters served us. We had a hearty plain dinner and port and white wine—nay, a bottle of claret. It was curious to think that this was an independent teacher. I was in a high flow of spirits. But though there was conversation enough for the time, there was nothing to carry away. I only recollect one saying of my own. Talking of my religion . . .[3]

THURSDAY 10 APRIL. Sat awhile Dr. Johnson's. Went with him in Sir Joshua's coach, and then Sir Joshua to Bishop of St. Asaph's door. Home dinner.

WEDNESDAY 11 APRIL. H. Baldwin, hearty. Supped with Sir Thomas Blackett at Charles Boswell's, who told me he'd die at Braehead.

THURSDAY 12 APRIL. Dinah; after, Townley's busts, etc.[4] To Sir Joshua's and wrote. Coach went for Dr. Johnson. All three to Bishop of Chester's. Very well. Berenger there. Home with Sir Joshua. [I said,] "Let us diffuse." Song made.

[EDITORIAL NOTE: The "song" can only have been the *Ode by Dr. Samuel Johnson to Mrs. Thrale upon Their Supposed Approaching Nuptials* which Boswell published anonymously in 1788 [5] and excerpted among imitations of Johnson's style in the *Life of Johnson*, calling it "a poem not without characteristical merit" ("specimens of various sorts of

---

[1] Mark Beaufoy. The business still existed in 1958 at 87, South Lambeth Road, as "Beaufoy, Grimble & Co., Ltd., Vinegar Brewers."

[2] "Who, like a second Hannibal, cleared his way to fame and riches by vinegar," an allusion to Livy, Bk. 21, ch. 27. Livy says that Hannibal made a roadway over the Alps for his army by heating the rocks and pouring vinegar on them.

[3] The entry breaks off at the bottom of a page. Rough notes add only that Boswell "supped Lord Eglinton."

[4] Dinah is unexplained, but see below, 30 April 1781, n. 4. Charles Townley was a collector of Roman sculpture. His collection was later purchased by the British Museum.

[5] *Sic.* It was deliberately misdated 1784.

imitations of Johnson's style," following November 1784). A manuscript of the *Ode* in his hand among the Boswell papers is written on the verso of a wrapper addressed to Sir Joshua, and so presumably dates from this very evening. That Boswell should have written such a piece at the moment when he did write it—only eight days after Thrale's death and the day after his burial—will to most right-minded people seem in the worst possible taste and explicable only as a prime example of Boswell's ability to entertain incompatibles simultaneously. By all means, so long as the bad taste is not assumed to imply a bad heart. If Boswell's *Ode* sprang from malice, it was only the sunny malice of a faun which Meredith saw lurking in the smile of the Comic Spirit. It is true that Boswell indulged in a lifelong practice of publishing scurrilous and spiteful newspaper squibs on persons who had somehow displeased him, but that is not what is in question here. Practice of the anonymous lampoon was very common in the eighteenth century, and was by no means confined to blackguards. Boswell's son Alexander, a very masculine and honourable person, lost his life in a duel which had been provoked by just such tactics. Boswell was at least impartial, for he published anonymous scurrilities on himself as well as on other people. But there was no question of animosity in the present case. He was not angry with Johnson or Mrs. Thrale, and he had liked and to a considerable degree had respected Thrale. He did not have a prurient mind and he actively disliked bawdy conversation and most bawdy writing. ("You too like the thing almost as well as I do," Wilkes had written to him on 22 June 1765, "but you dislike the talk and laugh about it, of which I am perhaps too fond.") The excepted area was words for music: it is most significant that what Boswell composed on 12 April 1781 was a song. British and Irish folksong, as everyone knows who has looked into the background of the lyrics of Gay, Ramsay, Burns, and Moore, combined exquisite airs with very dirty—or at least very earthy—words. Boswell was a good singer, he loved to sing to gentlemen after dinner, and the songs of his own composing were likely to be indelicate. The intention was wit or *double entendre*, what he himself called ludicrous fancy. He had always considered some of Johnson's whale-talk funny ("I say the *woman* was *fundamentally* sensible"),[6] and, without slacking for a moment his sense of love and admiration of the Rambler, could imagine the risibility inherent in the Rambler's idiom if applied to love-making. The externalizing of such fancies, he felt, did no harm if the results did not get reported to the persons concerned; and he really seems to have felt no more sense of treachery in developing them than he would have if Johnson and Mrs.

---

[6] See below, 20 April 1781.

Thrale had been characters of his own invention. He was by no means the only one among Johnson's close friends who made Johnson matter for comedy in ways which they would have been most unwilling for Johnson to know about. Garrick convulsed The Club with imitations of Johnson's tumultuous fondness for Tetty, Reynolds wrote dialogues satirizing Johnson's tendency to choose his side in an argument by sheer whim and to silence his opponent by interruption. Nobody among Johnson's close friends seems to have scolded Boswell for writing the *Ode* or even to have disapproved of it. It was composed, stanza by stanza, at Reynolds's, one suspects with Reynolds's encouragement and applause. Boswell "gave" (probably recited) it two nights later at Reynolds's to a company consisting (besides Reynolds) of Edward Craggs Eliot, his wife, daughter, two sons, and a tutor. Boswell admitted that he was "too much intoxicated," but if there had been any strong evidence of shock, he would have remembered it and would have recorded it.

We are glad none the less to report that this particular *jeu d'esprit* landed him first and last in a good deal of anxiety. A letter of condolence which he wrote to Mrs. Thrale on 26 April ("Mr. Boswell . . . hopes she will believe he feels all he ought to do, though his gaiety of fancy is not to be subdued") almost certainly combines an apprehension that she has learned about the *Ode* with a determination not to go too far in apology. (He was mistaken. She apparently knew nothing about the piece till she read the stanzas quoted in the *Life of Johnson*, and then did not suspect him of writing it). He showed (or sang) the *Ode* to Wilkes, and Wilkes teased him by threatening to tell Johnson about it when he and Johnson dined for the second time at Dilly's.[7] Boswell had already experienced Johnson's anger for merely proposing to write a poem in which Johnson's name was to be coupled with Mrs. Thrale's—"Sir, if you have any sense of decency or delicacy, you won't do that"[8]—and he continued to worry after Wilkes failed to make good his threat. On 6 November 1781 he wrote to T. D. Boswell, "anxious lest my epithalamium in an hour of pleasantry has been maliciously told to Dr. Johnson and he offended, being very irritable. Begging him in confidence to call on the Doctor and sound him about me and let me know what passes. But to give no hint of my fear."[9]

The text of the manuscript follows. Stanzas within brackets, later additions, are taken from the printed version. The order of stanzas is

[7] See below, 8 May 1781. Boswell does not record Wilkes's teasing in the journal, but mentions it in a letter to Wilkes, 14 February 1783.

[8] Journal, 31 August 1773.

[9] Register of Letters.

also that of the printed version. The manuscript has two stanzas (6 and 10) which are not in the printed version; the order of its stanzas as compared to the present text is 2, 3, 13, 1, 6, 7, 8, 14, 10, 11, 12.]

EPITHALAMIUM ON DR. J. AND MRS. T.[1]

1

If e'er my fingers touch'd the lyre
In satire fierce or pleasure gay,
Shall not my Thralia's smiles inspire?
Shall Sam refuse the sportive lay?

2

My dearest darling, view your slave,
Behold him as your very Scrub,[2]
Ready to write as author grave,
Or govern well the brewing tub.

3

To rich felicity thus rais'd
My bosom glows with amorous fire;
Porter no longer shall be prais'd;
'Tis I myself am Thrale's entire.[3]

[1] The manuscript has been folded twice and docketed. On one of the blank spaces left on the outside after folding appears the following in Boswell's hand: "Nos sane nuptiarum vota non aspernanter accipimus. Epist. Siricii Papae in Baron. Annal." ("We certainly do not hold marriage vows in contempt," a sentence from a letter of Pope St. Siricius, quoted in the *Annales Ecclesiastici* of Caesar Baronius.) This is the motto of *The Hypochondriack* No. 43 (on marriage), which would have been published about 1 May 1781. It probably had nothing to do with the *Ode*, but was jotted down here because Boswell at the time had no other piece of paper handy. He would hardly have furnished evidence of his authorship of the *Ode* by giving it the same motto as a *Hypochondriack*, a series he did not sign but acknowledged. When he printed the *Ode* in 1788, he gave it a motto from Horace: "Tauri ruentis/ in venerem tolerare pondus: To bear in copulation the weight of a ramping bull" (*Odes*, II. v. 3–4).

[2] Lady Bountiful's man-of-all-work in George Farquhar's *Beaux' Stratagem*. He drives the coach on Monday, ploughs on Tuesday, follows the hounds on Wednesday, duns the tenants on Thursday, goes to market on Friday, draws warrants on Saturday, and serves as butler on Sunday (III. iii).

[3] Johnson's wife, a widow twenty years older than he, who had died in 1752 after a marriage of nearly seventeen years, had been a Mrs. Porter. "Thrale's entire," a favourite malt liquor of Thrale's brewery, was still sold before World War II under that name by his successors, Messrs. Barclay and Perkins, but has since been discontinued. The pun however is a double one. An "entire" (short for "entire horse") is a stallion.

4

[Piozzi once alarm'd my fears,
Till beauteous Mary's tragic fate
And Rizzio's tale dissolv'd in tears
My mistress, ere it was too late.

5

Indignant thought to English pride!
That any eye should ever see
Johnson one moment set aside
For Tweedledum and Tweedledee.] [3a]

6

Desmoulins now may go her ways,
And poor blind Williams sing alone;
Levett exhaust his lungs in praise;
And Frank his master's fortunes own.

7

Congratulating crowds shall come
Our new-born happiness to hail,
Whether at ball, at rout, at drum;
Yet human spite we must bewail.

8

For though they come in pleasing guise,
And cry, "The wise deserve the fair!" [3b]
They look askance with envious eyes,
As the fiend looked at the first pair.

9

[Ascetic now thy lover lives,
Nor dares to touch, nor dares to kiss;
Yet prurient fancy sometimes gives
A prelibation of our bliss.]

10

From thee my mistress I obtain
A manumission from the power
Of lonely gloom, of fretful pain,
Transported to the Blissful Bower.

[3a] For the like of Piozzi. "Tweedledum and Tweedledee," now an expression denoting general insignificance, was in its origin directed specifically at musical performers. "To tweedle," an accepted technical term, meant to produce a high-pitched musical note.

[3b] Dryden, *Alexander's Feast*, ll. 13–15, altered. See above, 9 April 1781, n. 8.

11

Charming cognation! With delight
In the keen aphrodisian spasm,
Shall we reciprocate all night,
While wit and learning leave no chasm? [4]

12

Nor only are our limbs entwin'd,
And lip in rapture glued to lip;
Lock'd in embraces of the mind
Imagination's sweets we sip.

13

Five daughters by your former spouse
Shall match with nobles of the land;
The fruit of our more fervent vows
A pillar of the state shall stand! [5]

14

Greater than Atlas was of yore,
A higher power to me is given;
The earth he on his shoulders bore,
I with my arms encircle Heaven!

FRIDAY 13 APRIL. Good Friday. Solemn with Dr. Johnson. His old friend [Edwards]. BOSWELL. "You meet only at church." EDWARDS. "Best place except Heaven; [hope we shall] meet there, too." [6] Dr. Johnson told me that there was very little communication between Edwards and him after their unexpected renewal of acquaintance. "But," said he (smiling), "he met me once and said, 'I am told you have written a very pretty book

---

[4] The printed version improves on this, though it was a pity to lose "charming cognation" (affinity or connexion):

> Convuls'd in love's tumultuous throes,
> We feel the aphrodisian spasm;
> Tir'd nature must at last repose,
> Then wit and wisdom fill the chasm.

[5] "Pillar of the state" echoes Dryden's *Mac Flecknoe*, l. 109, where the phrase is applied to Shadwell, the Ascanius to Flecknoe's Aeneas.

[6] On Good Friday (17 April) 1778, as Johnson and Boswell were coming away from the service at St. Clement Danes, Johnson was accosted by Oliver Edwards, a college companion whom he had not seen for almost fifty years. Edwards went with them to Johnson's house and stayed for a leisurely conversation. The scene is perhaps the most charming in the entire *Life of Johnson*. What follows in the text from this point till further notice is taken from the first draft of the manuscript.

called *The Rambler.*' I was unwilling that he should leave the world in total darkness, and sent him a set."

Mr. Berenger visited him today and was very pleasing.[7] We talked of an evening society at a house in town of which we were members, but of which Johnson said, "It will never do, Sir. There is nothing served about there, neither tea nor coffee, nor lemonade, nor anything whatever; and depend upon it, Sir, a man does not like to go to a place from whence he comes out exactly as he went in." I endeavoured for argument's sake to maintain that men of learning and talents might have very good intellectual society without any little gratifications of the senses. Berenger joined with Johnson and said that without these any meeting would be dull and dry. He would therefore have all the slight refreshments; nay, it would not be amiss to have some cold meat and a bottle of wine upon a sideboard. "Sir," said Johnson to me, "Mr. Berenger knows the world. Everybody loves to have good things furnished to them without any trouble. I told Mrs. Thrale that as she did not choose to have card-tables, she should have a profusion of the best sweetmeats, and she would be sure to have company enough come to her."[8] Coffee. Then tea. [Went to] Langton and made him read Holy Week *Rambler.*[9]

I have preserved his [Johnson's] ingenious defence of his dining with two bishops in Passion Week, a laxity at the time when he wrote his solemn *Rambler* upon that awful week I am convinced he would not have done. It appeared to me that by being much more in company and indulging himself more in luxurious living, he had contracted a keener relish of pleasure, and was consequently less rigorous in his religious rites. This he would not acknowledge, but he reasoned as follows: "Why, Sir, a bishop's calling company together in this week is, to use the vulgar phrase, not *the thing.* But you must consider laxity is a bad thing but precision is also a [1] bad thing, and your general character may be more hurt by precision than by dining with a bishop in Holy Week. There may be a handle for reflection: 'He refused to dine with a bishop in Holy Week, but was three Sundays out of church.' " "Very true," said I. "But

---

[7] Berenger was Gentleman of the Horse and first equerry to George III; he wrote two books on horsemanship. Mrs. Thrale reports that Johnson "once named Mr. Berenger as the standard of true elegance," though someone objected that he "too much resembled the gentlemen in Congreve's comedies" (*Johnsonian Miscellanies,* ed. G. B. Hill, 1897, i. 254).

[8] The few remaining words of this paragraph are taken from the journal notes.

[9] *Rambler,* No. 7. The text now returns to the first draft of the manuscript of the *Life of Johnson,* 12 April 1781.

[1] What follows from this point is from a stray leaf of expanded fully-written journal. Although the conversation probably took place on the 12th (under which date it is entered in the *Life of Johnson*), Boswell seems to have recorded it for the 13th.

suppose a man to be uniformly good, would it not be better to refuse dining with a bishop, and so not to encourage [a bad example] by his countenance?" There I had him. But he got off by force of sophistry: "Why, Sir, you are to consider whether you might not do more harm by lessening the influence of a bishop's character by refusing him than by going to him." His argument was evasion. For either the thing is wrong or not. If not, don't disapprove of it. If wrong, don't countenance it. But his love of great company and good dinners predominates. I believe he would have refused when he was writing the solemn *Rambler*. I supped at Sir Lawrence Dundas's very pleasantly.

SATURDAY 14 APRIL. Wrote a good deal at home. Dinner Sir Joshua's; Lord Charlemont, Lord Grantham, Colman, Malone (1st),[2] Charles Greville, Sir W. Chambers. I defended the Inquisition in absence of Dr. Johnson. "Twiss a gross counterfeit; not even quicksilver upon him."[3] I stayed evening with Mr. Eliot, and now [met] his lady, Miss Eliot, two sons, and tutor. Gave Dr. Johnson's epithalamium. Had "mahogany": fish, tin, and copper.[4] Called him "Old Oporto."[5] Thought of getting a seat in Parliament. Too much intoxicated.

SUNDAY 15 APRIL. Breakfast Chapter Coffee-house. Then St. Paul's. Mr. Winstanley preached. Solemn service. Highly devout. Dr. W. Scott there. He walked with me to Dilly's till I ordered bed at night. Then called Dr. Johnson; not returned. Then King's Bench Walk. I was animated to come to English bar.[6] Then parted a little. Alderton's Coffee-house. Soup. Then Dr. Johnson's, well. Scott came. Arguing whether Addison wrote *Spectator* when drinking. He said Blackstone composed his *Commentaries* drinking bottle of port. Said Johnson: "What composition is there in Blackstone's *Commentaries*? Only taking from other books and putting into his." "Pardon me," said Scott, "judgement, and on great points, eloquence."

I had told Doctor that in a company where I was it was wished to know his authority for the shocking story of Addison's sending execution

---

[2] Boswell here records his first meeting with Edmond Malone, who was to become his great friend and adviser.

[3] Richard Twiss, writer on travel. Who made this hard judgement is not clear. Johnson praised his books, but Boswell had heard unfavourable accounts of his "absurd forwardness" (Journal, 24 March 1776).

[4] For "mahogany," see above, 30 March 1781. "Fish, tin, and copper" (three staple products of Cornwall) was a favourite Cornish toast, probably proposed on this occasion in the Cornish drink.

[5] Eliot's seat was at Port Eliot. Port wine was originally called Oporto from the city in Portugal (Portuguese, "the port").

[6] By "Dr. W. Scott," the great ecclesiastical lawyer, better known by his later title of Lord Stowell.

into Steele's house.[7] "Sir," said he, "it is generally known; it is known to all acquainted with the literary history of that period. It is as well known as that he wrote *Cato*." I was silent. But I have asked many people: Sir Joshua, Steevens, Malone, Lord Charlemont, and others, and none of them had heard it.

We talked of the Oxford education compared with the Scotch. Dr. Johnson defended it nobly, and showed that now, when all could read and books were so numerous, lectures were unnecessary. "If your attention fails and you miss a part of the lecture, 'tis lost. You cannot go back as you can do on a book." Scott agreed. "Yet," said I, "you read lectures." [8] He smiled. "You laughed at them for coming," said I. He owned it. Scott in some degree checked my ardour for the English bar by telling me that when a man sets himself seriously to it, he must give up a great deal of what makes London so agreeable; must go little into company; devote his time to business; be ready to receive attorneys. But then he comes into company with a consequence. "Ay," said I, "and he gets wealth, which does so much." Scott and I agreed that it was possible Mrs. Thrale might marry Dr. Johnson, and we both wished it much. He saw clearly the Doctor's propensity to love *the vain world* in various ways.[9]

Scott went away. We had dinner; Allen, the printer, like a little frog blowing himself up to be like the stately ox.[1] Gave me the proverb, "Stuff a cold and starve a fever." When dinner announced, "Hardly any accounts that could come from Rodney would be better news than this to you and me." [2] Mrs. Williams peevish; Mrs. Desmoulins answering her and making signs; Mrs. Hall, John Wesley's sister, very like him and preaching at table

[7] "Execution" for non-payment of debt. Johnson had included this anecdote in his *Life of Addison*.

[8] Scott was Camden Professor of Ancient History at Oxford, 1773–1785.

[9] Mrs. Thrale's biographer, James L. Clifford, in quoting this passage asserts that "Mrs. Thrale never even remotely considered such a marriage. . . . She reverenced Johnson as a father and confidant, but as a lover—the idea was absurd!" (*Hester Lynch Piozzi*, 1968, p. 200). "*The vain world*" is probably an allusion to the "vain pomp and glory of the world," in the Order for Baptism of *The Book of Common Prayer*.

[1] Edmund Allen was the landlord of Johnson's house in Bolt Court. Boswell found him highly amusing: "Though he was of a very diminutive size, he used, even in Johnson's presence, to imitate the stately periods and slow and solemn utterance of the great man" (*Life of Johnson*, 10 April 1778).

[2] About a month before this time, dispatches had arrived from Admiral Rodney (in command of the fleet in the West Indies) announcing that he had captured the Dutch islands of St. Eustatius, St. Martin, and Saba early in February. No more dispatches reached England until April 23.

in his manner; old Macbean, now a poor brother of the Chartreux.[3] Soup, hashed veal's head, bacon-ham, fowls, broccoli, roast lamb, asparagus, pudding, porter, one bottle port. When done, I asked Doctor if he'd give us any more wine. "I have no more wine. But you may have *poonch*." Mrs. Desmoulins made it. Produced today for first time his silver salvers which he had bought fourteen years ago. Little conversation. Only complained that he never could get John Wesley to talk long enough.

I mentioned the Religious Robin Hood, and that tonight the subject was to be, "And many bodies of the saints which slept arose," etc.[4] Mrs. Hall said it was a very curious subject, and she'd like to hear it discussed. The Doctor angrily said, "One would not go to such a place to hear it. One would not be seen in such a place—to give countenance to such a meeting." I thought, however, quietly that I'd go tonight, as the question was awful and interesting. Mrs. Hall agreed with the Doctor. But said, "I should like to hear *you* discuss it." He was reluctant. We talked of the resurrection. She maintained the same body. "Nay," said the Doctor. "We see it is not to be same. For the illustration of grain sown is used, and we know grain that grows is not same with what is sown. You would not have one rise with a consumptive body. It is enough that there is such sameness as to distinguish." She said she was curious to know if what was put into the earth at burial ever did spring up again. The Doctor left it in obscurity.

He said if apparitions were disbelieved, it was against the existence of the soul between death and the last day. He said the question simply was whether departed spirits ever had the power of making themselves perceptible to us. He said, "A man who should see an apparition could only be convinced himself. His authority would not convince another, and his conviction, if rational, must be founded on being told something which cannot be known but by supernatural means."

He mentioned a thing which I never heard before was common; that is, *being called*. My clerk Brown assured me that he heard his brother, who went to America, call him from a wood near Kilmarnock one evening; at least his brother's voice called *"Cobie"* from the wood as he was walking home along the highroad, and the next ships brought accounts of his death. Macbean asserted calling being well known. Dr. Johnson said that one day at Oxford when turning the key of his chamber, he heard his mother distinctly call, *"Sam."* She was then at Lichfield. But nothing ensued.

[3] Alexander Macbean had formerly been Johnson's amanuensis. He had been admitted to Charterhouse Hospital on Johnson's application only four days before this dinner.
[4] Matthew 27. 52. "Religious Society, for Theological Enquiry, will be held every Sunday evening, from half past seven o'clock till nine, at Coachmakers Hall, ... Cheapside. ... Admittance ... 6d." (*Daily Advertiser*, 14 April 1781).

Mrs. Hall and Mrs. Williams were both speaking at once in answer to something that he had said. He grew angry and called out, "Nay, when you both speak at *woonce*, it is intolerable" (or some such word). Then taking himself and softening, he said, "This one may say though you are ladies." The term *ladies* applied to the two old animals was truly ludicrous. He brightened into gay humour, and addressed them in the words of the *Beggar's Opera*:

"But two at a time there's no mortal can bear."

"What, Sir," said I, "are you going to turn Captain Macheath?" There was as much pleasantry in this as I ever saw. And the contrast between Macheath, Polly, and Lucy, and Dr. Samuel Johnson, blind, peevish Mrs. Williams, and ancient, lean, preaching Mrs. Hall was exquisite.

The Doctor left us. Mr. Macbean and I *chiefly* had two little bowls of punch. I then slipped away. As I got the door shut, the Doctor, whether lounging in garden or lurking in corner, knew I was gone, opened the door, and roared after me, "Mr. Boswell! Mr. Boswell!" I had turned the corner of Allen's house and was stealing off, pretending not to hear. But as I took a check of conscience in practising any artifice with my revered friend, I came back. He asked me where I was going. I told him to St. Dunstan's to hear Romaine for the first time. We had talked of him at dinner. I said I'd come back. I went, and was most agreeably entertained. There was something in his look pleasing and short-sightedly lively, like the look of my dear Mrs. Stuart. His text was in the first chapter of the Revelations: "I am he that was dead," etc. There was nothing gloomy in his manner, though the Methodistical system is so, and a robust fellow in a green coat and black wig groaned and sighed often at the ends of sentences, I suppose from habitual sadness contracted by hearing other preachers of that class. I could not but feel wonder and some degree of contempt for the man. Romaine seemed to call his audience to Heaven as a bird-catcher does with a whistle. His manner was quite cheerful. It was as if he had been singing, "Will you go to Flanders, my Molly O?" [5]

"Will you go to Heaven, my hearers O?"

When I returned to Dr. Johnson's, he was gone to church. I called on old John Rivington (not at home), and then I went to Alexander Donaldson's and eat a biscuit and drank a glass of white wine. Then I repaired to Coachmakers' Hall, where the solemn text was discoursed of really with decency and some intelligence, not one of seven (the first of whom was concluding as I came in and the other six I heard out) having thrown

[5] The old words to the air *Gramachree*, now usually associated with Moore's "The harp that once through Tara's halls."

out any irreligion or even levity. They did not however illustrate much. They differed in opinion as to apparitions being seen in later ages. But I thought the opinion *for* was best supported, and Mr. Addison in the *Spectator* was brought as an authority. There was a pretty good number of men and some ladies. The men were none of them to appearance of the mere vulgar. I wearied, however, and then went to Mr. Forbes's, where I found my brother sitting with him and Mrs. Forbes. Miss Douglas, her sister, a very genteel woman whom I had never seen, and my acquaintance Miss Bell Waugh of Carlisle came in. It was good easy conversation. Miss Waugh went away. We had a comfortable family supper. One warm dish and plenty of cold meat, and for my cold an excellent bishop [6] was made. My cousin, Bruce Boswell, also supped. I told Mrs. Forbes I was glad to come here when indisposed, as she was my nearest female relation in London.[7] I liked this night exceedingly well. Went home to Dilly's; he out of town.

[EDITORIAL NOTE: There is a gap of three days in the journal, and no conversations for those days are reported in the *Life of Johnson*. The journal resumes with notes for a conversation at Mrs. Garrick's on 20 April, which Boswell in the *Life* recalls as "one of the happiest days that I remember to have enjoyed in the whole course of my life."]

FRIDAY 20 APRIL. JOHNSON. "Mudge's sermons good, but nothing practical.[8] He grasps more sense than he can hold. He takes more corn than he can make into meal. He opens a wide prospect, but it is so distant it is indistinct. Blair, though the dog is a Scotsman and a Presbyterian and everything he should not be—I praised his sermons. Such was my candour." Mrs. Boscawen said, "Such his great merit to get the better of all this." JOHNSON. "Why, my candour and his merit together." Before dinner Hollis was talked of.[9] Mrs. Carter said he talked uncharitably of people.

[6] One of Johnson's favourite drinks before he became a water drinker. "Bishop: a cant word for a mixture of wine, oranges, and sugar" (Johnson's *Dictionary*).

[7] Mrs. Forbes's exact relation to Boswell is not established, but she was probably the daughter of James Douglas, brother of Sir John Douglas of Kelhead (d. 1778). This James Douglas was a physician of Carlisle, which would account for the presence of Miss Bell Waugh. Boswell's mother and James Douglas's mother were half-sisters.

[8] Reynolds, according to the *Life of Johnson*, had just praised Mudge's sermons. Johnson had written an obituary character of Zachariah Mudge, which Boswell inserted in the *Life* just before the entry for 30 March 1781.

[9] Thomas Hollis was a wealthy gentleman of republican principles. Boswell reports in 1764 that all the principal libraries he had visited abroad contained gifts of books of British republican writings, bound in red morocco and stamped in gilt with symbols of liberty, sent by a certain unknown whimsical Englishman. This was Hollis. He also sent a group of his books to Harvard College, and one of the pre-Revolutionary buildings there is named for him.

Dr. Johnson with great sophistry said, "Who is the worse for being talked of uncharitably? Hollis a dull, poor creature as ever lived." He said he believed Hollis would not have *done* harm to a man of opposite principles. "Once at the Society of Arts when an advertisement was to be drawn up, he pointed me out as a man who could do it best. This was kindness to me. I slipped away." Mrs. Carter doubted he was an atheist. "I don't know that," said the Doctor, smiling. "He might perhaps have become one if he had had time to ripen. He might have exuberated into an atheist."

Dr. Burney said he was once observing Garrick looked old. "Why, Sir," said Dr. Johnson, "no man's face has had more wear and tear." Mrs. Garrick looked very well. Talked of her husband with complacency. Said death was now the most agreeable idea to her. Elegant dinner; variety of fine garden things from Hampton. MRS. GARRICK. "There's all sorts of wines and Lichfield ale." I expressed much satisfaction at this. Sir Joshua, Burney, and I had a glass of it, and drank Dr. Johnson's health. JOHNSON. "Gentlemen, I wish you all as well as you do me." Miss More was chaplain and sat at foot of table.[1] She said, "I have very little in me of that which makes a critic." We had champagne, etc. Claret. Then another bottle in ice after Mrs. Garrick had gone up to Bishop Killaloe and other afternoon company, and were comfortable. I had said to Mrs. Boscawen at table, "I believe this is about as much as can be made of life." I was really happy. My gay ideas of London in youth were realized and consolidated. I did my part pleasingly.

Up to tea and coffee; Ramsay, Chamberlayne, Mrs. Reynolds,[1a] etc., there. Somebody said the life of a mere literary man could not be very entertaining. Dr. Johnson contradicted this, and said as a literary life it could. "But," said I, "better also that he has some active variety: that he goes to Jamaica, or—he goes to the Hebrides." Went off well. He said Campbell married a printer's devil.[2] SIR JOSHUA. "Why, I thought that a creature with a black face and in rags." JOHNSON. "Yes, Sir. But I suppose he had her face washed and put clean clothes on her. And she did not disgrace him. The woman had a *bottom* of good sense." We tittered and laughed. He perceived it and cried, "Where's the merriment?" Then, I believe wilfully, choosing a still more ludicrous word, and looking awful to show his

---

[1] Hannah More, perhaps now best known for her edifying children's books, was a great friend of both Johnson and Horace Walpole, one of the few who bridged that gulf.

[1a] Frances Reynolds was a spinster. In the eighteenth century the style of "Mrs." was frequently accorded to unmarried ladies.

[2] Dr. John Campbell, whom Boswell had met in 1769. Boswell suppresses the name in the *Life of Johnson*, substituting "a very respectable author."

power of restraint over us, he added, "I say the woman was *fundamentally sensible*"—as if he had said, "Hear this and laugh if you dare." We were all close.

Mr. Chamberlayne was a very communicative literary man. He told us that a poor woman brought Clarke's Caesar to Beauclerk and asked five guineas. That though this appeared high price, gave it to her. Then went to Elmsley, who told him great rarity; would give fifteen guineas for it. Beauclerk sent her the other ten. This book sold at his auction for forty-three guineas.[3] We had lemonade and orgeat. I was not at all intoxicated, but gaily serene. Dr. Johnson and I walked away together. Stopping by rails of Adelphi and looking on Thames, I said with tenderness I thought of two friends we had lost who lived here: Garrick and Beauclerk. "Ay," said he, "and two such friends as cannot be supplied." I walked with him to Temple Bar, and then wished him good-night and came home, I think quietly.

[EDITORIAL NOTE: Although there are now no entries in the journal for 21–23 April, the *Life of Johnson*, in an undated collection following 8 May 1781, preserves an account of an evening which the journal entry of 29 April enables us to identify as 22 April. Though in a "paper apart" from the main manuscript of the *Life*, it appears to have formed a portion of Boswell's first draft.]

SUNDAY 22 APRIL. Another evening Johnson's kind indulgence towards me had a pretty difficult trial. I had dined at the Duke of Montrose's with a very agreeable party, and his Grace according to his usual custom had circulated the bottle very freely. Lord Graham and I went together to Miss Monckton's,[4] where I certainly was in extraordinary spirits and above all fear or awe. In the midst of a great number of persons of the first rank, amongst whom I recollect a noble lady of the most stately decorum, I placed myself next to Johnson, and imagining myself

[3] Just the day before, as lot 2279 of the sale of Beauclerk's library. The facts seem to be that Beauclerk, having found that the booksellers priced a clean, well-bound large-paper copy of the book at twenty guineas, offered "Mrs. H." seventeen guineas for hers, as it had to be cleaned and rebound.

[4] Later Countess of Cork and Orrery, a vivacious bluestocking nearly forty years younger than Johnson. In the *Life of Johnson*, Boswell led into the present paragraph by an account of the "bluestocking clubs" and Johnson's occasional attendance at them. As a "singular instance" of the ease with which Johnson could talk with Miss Monckton, Boswell relates the following: "One evening . . . she insisted that Sterne's writings were very pathetic. Johnson bluntly denied it. 'I am sure,' said she, 'they have affected *me*.' 'Why,' said Johnson (smiling and rolling himself about), 'that is because, dearest, you're a dunce.' When she afterwards mentioned this to him, he said, with equal truth and politeness, 'Madam, if I had thought so, I certainly should not have said it'."

now fully his match, talked to him in a loud and boisterous manner, desirous to show the company how I could contend with Ajax. I particularly remember pressing him upon the importance of the pleasures of the imagination, and as an illustration of my argument asking him, "What, Sir, supposing I were to fancy that the (naming the loveliest duchess in His Majesty's dominions) [5] were in love with me, should I not be very happy?" My friend, with much address, evaded my interrogatories and kept me as quiet as possible, but it may easily be conceived how he must have felt. [6]

[EDITORIAL NOTE: There is no entry for Monday 23 April.]

TUESDAY 24 APRIL. Breakfasted Sir Joshua. Read "Verses to Miss Monckton." Was gay and happy.

WEDNESDAY 25 APRIL. Mr. Lumisden [7] breakfasted with us and I forget who more. Got into Richmond coach. Charming day. Mrs. March, wife of Mr. March, pocket-book seller on Ludgate Hill, and her son, a fine boy like my little James, with me. I was really good. Arrived happy; agreeable reception. [8] Chatted well. Then in garden; beauteous Sally at window. Tea. Evening sung "Ah, me" by Goldsmith. [9] She was delighted. Elegant room.

THURSDAY 26 APRIL. Breakfasted pleasingly. Then [she went] to her toilet [1] and I wrote journal. Then I called Sally and had *some* liberty.

---

[5] The Duchess of Devonshire.

[6] In the *Life of Johnson* Boswell prints as a foot-note here five silly stanzas which he wrote next day to Miss Monckton apologizing for his behaviour. "The lady was generously forgiving, returned me an obliging answer, and thus I obtained an *Act of Oblivion*, and took care never to offend again."

[7] Andrew Lumisden (brother to Mrs. Strange, mentioned above, p. 310 n. 3) was secretary to the Old Pretender when Boswell first met him in Rome in 1765; they had renewed their acquaintance in Edinburgh in 1773.

[8] He had come down to visit Colonel Stuart and his wife. (Stuart had left his regiment in the West Indies some months before because of ill health, and had been under treatment at Bath.) "Yesterday I came down to this paradise to our amiable friend, Mrs. Stuart. I thought her husband had been to return from Bath today. But it seems he is grown worse, and is to stay longer at Bath. So she and I and her daughters make the party. I have had a cold and been hoarse this forthnight, not having time to take care of it. I hope I shall now get rid of it. I have also a sprain in one leg which requires rest, and I have set apart three days for this calm retreat" (To his wife, 26 April 1781).

[9] "Ah me! When shall I marry me?," a song intended for *She Stoops to Conquer*, but not used. If Goldsmith had not given Boswell a manuscript copy of it in 1773, it would have been lost.

[1] Where Boswell followed her and procured a lock of her hair, now with the Boswell papers. He endorsed the wrapper: "Honourable Mrs. Stuart's. Cut 26 April 1781 by myself at her toilet. Richmond Hill."

Was placid and gay. Made out "Verses on Bishop of Killaloe." [2] Day
passed charmingly. Called Lady Di; in London. Left note if [I might]
breakfast next morning. Card came evening to come at 11. Mrs. White
with us.

FRIDAY 27 APRIL. Up gay. Breakfasted pleasingly. Fine to see her
with the children, hearing one French and t'other harpsichord. Walked
to Cambridge's; nobody at home. Returned; sorry for being so long absent. Quite tender friendship. Had been at Lady Di's; second breakfast
with her. All . . .[3]

SATURDAY 28 APRIL. Breakfasted fine. Sweet with Sally. Lady Di
not up. Took gentle leave. [Rode with] ladies' maids from Lady Pembroke's, Mrs. Thomson. Dull dinner with Sir Thomas Blackett. Hastened
to Academy. Had been too conscientious to go Dr. Johnson and Dr.
Beattie.[4] Newton by me at first.[5] All well. Lord Townshend, seeing
Francklin, "I shall frighten away this reverend gentleman." FRANCKLIN.
"No, I'm here as an artist." [6] LORD TOWNSHEND. "I love to drink under the
auspices of a clergyman." DUKE OF HAMILTON. "In vino veritas." [7] SIR
JOSHUA. "Very well." LORD TOWNSHEND. "Opposition in England once consisted of three: Old Vyner and Young Vyner (Young Vyner now grown

[2] The verses (fourteen four-line stanzas) are mildly amusing, but because of topical
allusions require more annotation than would be appropriate for the present volume.
The last stanza runs:

> Versed in divine and human lore
> (All else is but vain glory),
> He is (I cannot praise him more)
> A Christian and a Tory.

The full text may be seen in C. N. Fifer, ed., *The Correspondence of James Boswell
with Certain Members of The Club*, 1976, pp. 414–416.

[3] A leaf is probably missing at this point.

[4] Having accepted an invitation to dine with Sir Thomas Blackett, he was too conscientious to beg off and go with Johnson and Beattie to the annual Exhibition Dinner of the Royal Academy, to which he had subsequently been invited. But after
dining with Blackett (brother-in-law of his "chief," Godfrey Bosville), he joined the
company at Somerset House. (The *Daily Advertiser* for 30 April prints the list of
those invited to the Academy dinner, "Mr. ——— Boswell" being the last name but
one.)

[5] Francis Milner Newton, portrait-painter, was Secretary of the Royal Academy, as
Boswell himself explains later on in the entry.

[6] Thomas Francklin, D.D., Professor of Greek at Cambridge, miscellaneous writer,
translator of Sophocles and Lucian, was Chaplain to the Royal Academy and succeeded Goldsmith as its Professor of Ancient History.

[7] A Latin proverbial expression usually taken to mean "Truth [comes out] in wine,"
that is, men in liquor reveal their true thoughts. The Duke of Hamilton suggests
translating it as an allegory of Townshend's last remark: "A clergyman in a group
of drinking companions is Truth among revellers."

Old Vyner), and George Townshend, your humble servant. My brother Charles, who was a much better Latin scholar, said, 'You've mistaken the saying "in *vino* veritas" and have it "in *Vyner* veritas." ' " [8] SIR JOSHUA. "You don't know Duke of Hamilton. My Lord Duke, Mr. Boswell." DUKE. "Very happy to see Mr. Boswell." By and by, DUKE. "Mr. Boswell, I believe this is the first time I have had the pleasure of seeing you. I hope it shall not be last." [9] LORD TOWNSHEND. "King, tipsy's [1] 'quicquid delirant [reges].' " I. "Rather, 'regis ad exemplum.' " DUKE. (To Lord Townshend.) "Or rather, 'de te fabula narratur.' " [2] Lord Townshend said he was going to draw caricature of Vestris. He drew best when he had a bottle of claret. [3] Sandby said, "I think the paper may now be laid before his Lordship." I. [referring to the] double bottles, "*These* you have from us—the Scotch pints." [4] By and by a general toast, "The Beggar's Benison." Banks, next [to] Sir Joshua, said, "The two Presidents [5] have laid their heads together for a toast, and produced 'The Beggar's Benison.' " "You are obliged to us for that," said I, and told the story of Queen Mary's father, who did as Lord Townshend would do.

---

[8] George Townshend, after 1764 Viscount Townshend, Lieutenant-General in the Army (he was at Dettingen and Culloden, and became chief in command at Quebec after the death of Wolfe), had been a highly controversial Viceroy of Ireland from 1767 to 1772. Boswell had met him at Dublin in May 1769 and later spoke of "the congeniality of their dispositions" ("Memoirs of James Boswell, Esq.," *European Magazine*, June 1791, reprinted in F. A. Pottle, *The Literary Career of James Boswell, Esq.*, 1929 and later, p. xxxvii). His anecdote of the Opposition of three was based on fact, though somewhat exaggerated. On 14 June 1758, in the House of Commons, he, the two Vyners (father and son), and two other Members had formed the entire minority against the bill to increase the judges' salaries.

[9] A possibly ticklish situation. Nobody had ever ventured to present Boswell to the Duke of Hamilton (at this time in his twenty-fifth year) because nobody could be sure how the Duke would react. His mother, eight years before, had still been so resentful of Boswell's extravagant support of the defendant in the great Douglas Cause that she had treated him with angry rudeness when her second husband, the Duke of Argyll, had brought him to her tea-table. The Duke of Hamilton's frank and cordial response seems to have been quite sincere, but Boswell's journal records no further meetings between the two.

[1] As Boswell explains later on in the entry, the Duke of Hamilton had just told of seeing the King tipsy at a ball.

[2] The two peers and Boswell are showing off their store of Latin tags more or less appositely. The people suffer for the folly of their kings (Horace, *Epistles*, I. ii. 14); the manners of the whole country are formed after the King's example (proverbial); change the name and the story fits you (Horace, *Satires*, I. i. 69–70).

[3] Townshend was a brilliant and original political caricaturist.

[4] See above, p. 68 n. 2.

[5] Sir Joseph Banks was President of the Royal Society.

"You're much mistaken, Sir," said Lord Townshend, "for poor as my purse is, my p—k is worse." 6

He had called Sir Joshua, "Will you give us one cool bottle of claret?" They were taking away the former. "No," said Lord Townshend, "Let us first take the widow." 7 Duke of Hamilton gave an account of the last ball at Queen's Palace, and said he never had such hard work; danced from————till six in morning except hour and half at supper. Pitied Princess Royal; commanded to dance with her. She grew ill and was obliged to retire.8 "Now, a ball is such a treat to her. And the King was tipsy." "What!" said Lord Townshend. "If Lord Shelburne had said this, I should have thought it Opposition. But from the Duke of Hamilton—" "No, really," said the Duke, "it was true. When I came home, I said to the Duchess, 'The King tonight drank a glass more than usual; at least I thought so.' ("Very guarded," said somebody. Indeed it was expressed with courtly correctness.) But next morning the first man I met who had been there said to me, 'Did not you think the King tipsy?' I then was convinced I was right." I asked if the King had drank much. "I suppose five glasses," said the Duke.

I said, "Your Grace was very good to my nephew, Sir Walter Montgomerie." His Grace regretted him, and said, "He loses himself"; but he praised very much his brother in the Hamilton regiment and said all the officers spoke well of him and loved him. I told how I was in advance for him, but the Duke did not seem to attend to it; nor to my having two doses of Hamilton blood by two marriages in our family.9 When Loutherbourgh, etc., etc.,

6 The story as we have seen it reported in print was that James V of Scotland, once journeying to the East Neuk of Fife disguised as a bagpiper, came to a brook which he could not cross conveniently because it was in spate. A stout beggar-girl carried him through the water on her back, and when he tipped her more generously than she expected, gave him her "benison" (blessing): "May your prick and your purse never fail you." In Boswell's version, the King seems to have tried to get by with amorous offers rather than coin.

7 He must mean "what remains in the bottle," though we do not find that sense of "widow" recorded in any of the dictionaries. In present-day usage a "widow" is a bottle of champagne, so called from the famous firm Veuve Cliquot, but the firm seems not to have existed with that name until 1806. In any case, if Boswell is writing as accurately as he usually does, "the former" should mean "the bottle of claret on the table."

8 Charlotte Augusta Matilda, never a beauty, and at this point apparently somewhat sensitive to the Court's efforts to prove her one.

9 Lady Janet Hamilton, natural daughter of the first Earl of Arran, married David Boswell, second laird of Auchinleck, in February 1531–1532; by his legitimate heir Arran was also progenitor of the Marquesses and Dukes of Hamilton. Anna Hamilton, daughter of James Hamilton of Dalzell, married David Boswell, sixth laird of Auchin-

were named, I said to the Duke 'twas fine to sit in such a company, where all [were] eminent. 'Twas like being in Heaven: [would ask,] "Who's that?" [and be told] "Gabriel," etc. The claret was not good. The Duke said he should have stayed longer if it had. He was fond [1] to make Rheinhold sing, and indeed he sung admirably. I came in quietly after dinner and sat down by Mr. Newton, the Secretary, who was very polite. Then Banks came near me. Then I got up; went to Dr. Johnson and Dr. Beattie. Little said. The Doctor looked ill. He and Lord Townshend were once tête-à-tête a little. I said, "What an explosion [might have occurred!]" [2] BURKE. "Always happy to meet you. My Lord Carmarthen, allow me to introduce my friend, Mr. Boswell." Just saw his Lordship. (Gen. Paoli said he was hurt; his horns were too heavy for his head. "Or rather, I should say that after being too heavy for his head, their roots are grown down to his heart.") [3] The Bishop of Chester was kind, and hoped I heard he had called. The Bishop of St. Asaph cordial. We talked of town and country; I for first, he for second.

Lord Sheffield was with us a little at first. Lord Townshend had some witticism about Coventry. Said Lord Sheffield: "Whether is it worse to be sent *to* Coventry or *from* Coventry?" [4] This, I suppose, was doing his best, and he walked off. I proposed drinking down the room: i.e., all the ladies whose pictures were in the exhibition to be toasted. Lord Townshend gave Duchess of Cumberland. Sir Joshua very properly objected to it. He was right; for in King's own Academy should not give one not received at Court. [5] Besides not right [to] toast lady of blood royal. Some-

---

leck, in 1666. The Dalzell Hamiltons descended from James Hamilton of Cadzow, grandfather of the first Earl of Arran.

[1] Eager.

[2] We have not discovered why Boswell thought this conjunction potentially explosive.

[3] Lord Carmarthen had married Amelia Darcy, later Baroness Conyers in her own right. He divorced her in May 1779, after she had eloped with John Byron (father by a second marriage of Lord Byron the poet).

[4] "To send a person *to* Coventry" in ordinary parlance means to refuse to associate with him; "to send a person *from* Coventry" is the normal way of saying that Coventry has elected him its Member of Parliament. Sheffield had recently been seated for Coventry on petition and a second poll after the corporation through influence had secured the return of his opponent.

[5] George III was infuriated when he learned that his brother, the Duke of Cumberland, had in 1771 clandestinely married Anne Horton, a widow, daughter of an Irish peer; and matters were not helped when in 1772 another brother, the Duke of Gloucester, revealed the fact that he had been married to the Dowager Countess Waldegrave for more than five years. The result was the Royal Marriage Act (1772) which required the permission of the Sovereign or Parliament for legally valid marriage of members of the royal family.

body said (I think Duke Hamilton), "I'll give Queen." Supped at Burke's, excellently happy.

SUNDAY 29 APRIL. Got up well. Breakfasted well. Then adored in Portuguese Chapel. Then visited Graham of Fintray at Duke of Atholl's. Then Mr. Constable.[6] Then home; Mrs. Bach and Miss Farren with General.[7] I was enchanted with Miss F., and said how unlucky I was to dine abroad last Sunday. "I was with old blind man.[8] But you, General, had young blind boy with wings." Then left card, Duke Hamilton's. Then took up General at Grosvenor Gate. Away to Kensington Garden. Lord Eglinton joined us. I was quite *étourdi* with the beautiful variety. Met Mrs. Ward. Walked with her; "Have you good eyes for use? I know what they are for ornament. Can you find out General for me?" Met Dempster, vastly happy. Lord Kellie joined us. Told story of Foote's French servant, angry at magpie: "Sacré Dieu, que ce bougre parle anglais!"

Had met Lord Graham. Came up with him as he was lighting. He opened door of chariot and took down step. Went in a little. Duke asked [me] to stay. I agreed, and sent note to General. Mr. Crosbie very agreeable there. He and I took to each other much. Read Killaloe verses. Was quite happy. Drank liberally but not too much. Home; dressed. Miss Monckton's, very pleasing and well. Lady Craven courteous; [said] sorry not at home [when I called.] "You must come either very early or very late." BOSWELL. "I cannot move my settee." She drew her chair near. Lady Mary Lowther talked easily with me, first time in her company. Fine music and singing. Sir W. Howe, Lady Buckingham. Coterie with Burkes, senior and junior, Lady Payne, Sheridan, Mrs. Crewe, who talked of my state last Sunday. I said I had got Act of Oblivion—better than pardon. Fine night.

Went to Burke's with Sir Joshua. Burke told origin of "bluestocking." Stillingfleet, grandson of bishop, learned man, had it at Mrs. Montagu's. So this joke began it, and Mrs. Vesey carried it to Dublin, and it has gone

---

[6] Probably the Constable whom the journal (11 May 1783) calls an old friend of Boswell's friend W. J. Temple; possibly the Rev. Thomas Constable, Rector of Sigglesthorne, Yorkshire, who was enrolled in St. John's College, Cambridge, during part of the time that Temple was enrolled in Trinity Hall. Both men were northerners: Constable from Yorkshire, Temple from Northumberland (Berwick-upon-Tweed).

[7] Elizabeth Farren (?1759–1829) was a leading actress in London. Walpole called her the most perfect actress he had ever seen. She later (1797) married the Earl of Derby as his second wife. Mrs. Bach was an opera-singer, the wife of Johann Christian Bach (Johann Sebastian's youngest son by Anna Magdalena, his second wife). She was "first woman" at the opera in London 1766–1772, and quite popular with the royal family. When her husband died in 1782, Queen Charlotte gave her a pension and the money to return to Italy.

[8] The Duke of Montrose. He was in his sixty-ninth year, but had long been blind.

on.[9] Talking of Stuart in India and Brutus, Burke was beginning to defend Brutus.[1] "Come, come," said I, "don't go too far in this cursed Whiggery. You will be back to us.[2] Only black yourself with cork, which will easily wash off; don't dye in Whiggery; don't tattoo." Prince of Wales's buckles. Sir Joshua said, "One cannot help drawing inference." BURKE. "No; won't do." Said I: "You mean to say, 'Ex pede Herculem.'"[3] Langton in middle of ladies: Burke said, "like maids dancing round a maypole."

MONDAY 30 APRIL. My brother David came to breakfast, easy and well. He and I visited Mr. and Mrs. Ward and General Oglethorpe. He went to City, to return to dinner. I to No. 35. Saw her blackguard; [said,] "You're welcome to what you've got. But I swear—no more."[4] Had brandy; a *little* intoxicated.

Called Sir Joshua a moment. A little with Palmeria. Called Burney; not at home. Beauclerk's auction a little, calm. Malone there. Then Dr.

[9] "About this time it was much the fashion for several ladies to have evening assemblies for conversation with literary and ingenious men. These societies were known by the name of *bluestocking* clubs, the origin of which title being little known, it may be worth while to relate it. One of the most eminent members of those societies when they first commenced was Mr. [Benjamin] Stillingfleet, whose dress was remarkably grave, and in particular it was observed that he wore blue stockings. Such was the excellence of his conversation that his absence was felt as so great a loss that it used to be said, 'We can do nothing without the *blue stockings*'; and thus by degrees the title was established. Miss Hannah More has described a *bluestocking club* in her poem [*The Bas Bleu*], in which many of the persons who were most conspicuous there are mentioned" (manuscript of the *Life of Johnson*, paper apart following 8 May 1781).

[1] In 1776 James Stuart (d. 1793), colonel in the service of the East India Company, acting on the orders of the majority of the Council of the Madras Presidency, arrested the Governor, Lord Pigot, and put him under guard. This behaviour might be likened to Brutus's joining the conspiracy against Caesar.

[2] That is, back to Toryism. Boswell was well aware of Burke's inclinations, which later brought forth his strenuous opposition to the French Revolution.

[3] The Prince of Wales (later George IV), at this time eighteen years of age, had been allowed his own establishment at the beginning of this year and had immediately been launched upon the town. Thackeray (*The Four Georges*) says that the Prince signaled his entrance into the world by inventing a very large shoe-buckle. We suspect Thackeray of garbling his source, but shall be unable to offer anything better until we locate that source or some other contemporary report. Meanwhile we venture no guesses as to the inference that Sir Joshua thought so obvious. "Ex pede Herculem" is a proverbial phrase meaning that one can recognize Hercules by the sight of his foot only.

[4] "No. 35" was probably a street number used as a cipher: possibly for the mysterious "Dinah" of the entry for 12 April 1781 above. In 1778, in London, Boswell systematically designated as "No. 36" an old dallying companion (probably Mrs. Love) with whom he had renewed relations.

Johnson's. Met him at the door going to dine with Dr. Douglas. Told him he did not look well today, nor at Academy dinner. Asked if well. He said he was. Went to an ironmonger's near Bolt Court. "Sir, will you let me have a small *poonch?*" Saw him choose one carefully. Then buy a hundred nails. BOSWELL. "What, Sir, are you a great carpenter?" JOHNSON. "It is to nail up my fig tree." "Then," said the man, "here are nails will do better. When I know the purpose, I can fit one." "Ay," said I, "you adapt the fact to the law." Convoyed the Doctor near to Fleet Market. He said nothing and seemed dull.

Then home. Brother with us. He was really agreeable. Was calm and well. Dressed; went to Constable's. Elegant company. Sauntered pleasingly. Aberdeenshire man played Irish bagpipe on stairhead. Saw Highland officer; looked [at his] button: Lord Seaforth's [Highlanders.] Asked name: Macrae.[5] Asked him to go to Lord Eglinton's. By the road, told him my name. Sat at Earl's an hour and half, quite weary. Macrae soon exhausted, [I] vexed at loss of night. At twelve took him to the Mount. Toasted biscuit, brandy punch. There he found Humberston's deaf brother. [They] talked with fingers and I was left out.[6] Pretty night. Went, knocked at Lord Eglinton's door en passant; found him alone after supper. Got brandy punch, and we were truly cordial. Told him of Macrae. EGLINTON, "Where's your friend?" BOSWELL. "At Mount." EGLINTON. "Will you give me leave to send for him?" BOSWELL. "No, no. He'll bring the deaf man with him." We drank till about two, I fancy. Were hearty and well. Talked highly of my wife. I gave her as my toast. He disputed pleasantly whose toast she should be. Came off pretty sober. Walked in street just to take off intoxication. Called Madame de Wurtz.[7] Door not opened. Home safe, but sick.

[5] Kenneth Macrae, a lieutenant in the 78th Regiment of Foot, raised and commanded by the Earl of Seaforth. The officers of this regiment were largely from the Clan Mackenzie, and the men were rude clansmen from the western Highlands and islands, many of them Macraes, who, though not of Lord Seaforth's clan, were yet his "people" (Journal, 1 September 1773) because they lived on his lands of Kintail. It was a group of Macraes in the 78th Regiment who had mutinied in Edinburgh three years before (see above, 22–28 September 1778). In 1781 the regiment was in Guernsey and Jersey. Kenneth Macrae later rose to the rank of lieutenant-colonel, and was Paymaster-General of Jamaica.

[6] Francis Mackenzie Humberston, brother of T. F. Mackenzie Humberston (who was lieutenant-colonel of the 78th Foot), on the death of Lord Seaforth later in 1781 and of his brother in 1783, succeeded to the Seaforth estates and the hereditary chieftainship of the Clan Mackenzie. Though rendered totally deaf by scarlet fever at the age of twelve, he attained the rank of lieutenant-general in the Army and served for six years as M.P. (Ross-shire). In 1797 he was created Lord Seaforth, Baron Mackenzie of Kintail in the peerage of Great Britain.

[7] Unidentified. Probably no better than she should have been.

TUESDAY 1 MAY. Awaked ill. Lay snug till General [went] out. Better. Up and had tea. Called Lord Graham a little; dressing. He was gracious. Crosbie a minute. Then Sir L. Dundas's. BOSWELL. "Do you dine at home?" SIR LAWRENCE. "Yes, and I hope you've come to dine with me." BOSWELL. "Have you no great company?" SIR LAWRENCE. "No; two as honest fellows as in England: Sir Charles Davers and Perry Wentworth." I enjoyed much the grand house and pictures, and was quite happy. Lady Dundas was ill. Charles dined with us. Sir Charles was a hearty Suffolk man who had been in the Army and saw Lord Dundonald killed at Louisbourg. Lives near Mr. Symonds. Said if I'd come down, he'd do his best to entertain me. "Symonds here, I there, the Bishop of Derry there—just a triangle." Said I: "I should like to be the mathematician and describe it; Q.E.D."[8] Wentworth and I had been well acquainted at Newmarket twenty years ago.[9] We were quite cordially gay, and he asked me to his house, not mile off the road between Ferrybridge and Wetherby. Drank a good deal till I found myself unfit for Mrs. Grace's, where I was asked. Had tea comfortably. Then called Dance's,[1] nobody . . .

[EDITORIAL NOTE: More than half of the leaf has been torn off. The censorship is probably explained by a rough note for 1 May which reads, "Breakfast home. Dinner Sir Lawrence's. Evening ranged."]

WEDNESDAY 2 MAY. Maclaurin breakfasted [with] us. Walked with him Lord Graham's, General Oglethorpe's. Called Smith,[2] Langton. Found Ramsay. Glass in Fleet Street. Fanny Bates while he walked.[3] Went in chariot and brought to dinner Dr. Johnson. With us in all, Bishop of Killaloe, General Oglethorpe, Statella, Sir Joseph Banks, Pinto,[4] my

[8] The seats or residences of Sir Charles Davers (Rushbrook), John Symonds (Bury St. Edmunds), and the Bishop of Derry (Ickworth) would form the three points of a triangle with sides of three or four miles each. Boswell had probably referred to Symonds and the Bishop as old acquaintances. He had met them in Genoa in 1765, and had so roused them by his accounts of Corsica that they both visited the island.

[9] Lord Eglinton (older brother of the Lord Eglinton of the present volume) had carried Boswell to the races at Newmarket in 1760, when Boswell had run away to London.

[1] William Dance, musician, was Mrs. Love's son ("Love" was a stage name). His house was presumably the "No. 36" where Boswell had met Mrs. Love in 1778. He does not name her in the present London journal.

[2] Presumably Adam Smith. See below, 29 May 1781, where Boswell uses the style "Dr. Smith."

[3] Ramsay is presumably Allan Ramsay the painter, but we do not know why or where he walked. Fanny Bates is sufficiently explained in the entry for 5 May 1781.

[4] Statella is not certainly identified; he always turns up in Paoli's company. Pinto was no doubt Isaac de Pinto (?1715–1787), a Dutch Jew of Portuguese extraction, who lived in France as well as at The Hague. He was a financier of international reputation, director and annuitant of the East India Company, highly respected for his

brother. With Johnson and Bishop in chariot. Cards and supper, Sir Lawrence's. Wrote letter Lord Bute dated 3.

THURSDAY 3 MAY. Dempster breakfasted with us. With him called Rumbold. Found Mrs. Blair and Mrs. Johnson. By self called Smith. I dined Lord Eglinton's; Crazy Hall. We took much. Told me he had not written in *Public Advertiser* against "Methodist." [5] Amazing *drink*. Sir Lawrence there, said I had cost him £10,000.[6] Said the *best thing* [he could say was] "when will this company dine with me?" Home, I know not how. Had sent letter to Lord Bute; flutter about it.[7]

FRIDAY 4 MAY. Breakfasted Osborn in fever. Lord Ossory's indecision, buckskin breeches. Elegant man Osborn.[8] Then Lord Eglinton's; walked with Miss Wenton. Fanny *Udell*.[9] House of Lords. General Oglethorpe came. Lord Mansfield bowed to him and me.[1] He and I met Burke.

---

publications on economic matters. A strong supporter of Government in the American war.

[5] John Hall-Stevenson, friend of Laurence Sterne, wrote *Crazy Tales*, 1762. The allusion to "Methodist" and the *Public Advertiser* is not explained. Among various pamphlets written against Sterne in 1760 was one entitled *Letter from a Methodist Preacher to Mr. Sterne*. Boswell may have attributed to Hall-Stevenson some reply to this that he had seen in the *Public Advertiser*.

[6] In the election of a Member of Parliament for the Stirling Burghs, autumn 1774, when he campaigned for Lt.-Col. Archibald Campbell and as delegate for Culross cast his vote for Campbell against Sir Lawrence's nominee, Sir Alexander Gilmour. Sir Lawrence may well have spent £10,000 in this election. It was notorious for violence and bribery, and a published letter of Sir Lawrence's shows that he instructed one of his agents to secure votes at any cost. Colonel Campbell's campaign is said to have cost him over £17,000.

[7] "Acquainted with all of your Lordship's sons, intimate with the two eldest, I have never been able to get myself introduced to your Lordship.... When a man has tried the great avenues and found the gates shut, if he is very anxious to get in, he will naturally attempt out-of-the-way paths. It is not from affected singularity but from absolute despair that I venture this chance. If your Lordship is gracious enough to give me leave to wait on you, your Lordship will do a kindness which will be more gratefully felt than any bounty which you conferred while Prime Minister. If otherwise, I shall not be ashamed of what I have done; but, lamenting some strange fatality which counteracts my wishes, shall ever remain, with very high respect, my Lord, your Lordship's most obedient humble servant" (To Bute, 3 May 1781). Bute replied the same day, granting an interview.

[8] Obscure. John Osborn, formerly British Minister at the Court of Dresden (Boswell had met him at Marseilles in 1765) is shown by later references to have been a valued friend of Paoli's. He perhaps related some anecdote indicating the superiority of his own judgement in matters of dress to Lord Ossory's.

[9] Probably two strangers he had struck up conversation with in the street. The first name with some forcing could be read "Benton."

[1] The only part of the day's business that would seem to have been of special interest to Boswell was the hearing of counsel in a Scots appeal: Earl Fife appellant, Lord

Carried to Parsees. Brahmin ill.[2] Lord Eglinton dined with us. Lord Caithness, Aberdeen, Statella. Ranelagh evening. Sir Joseph Yorke, Duke of Queensberry.[3] All well. Mrs. Buller, "Lord Graham's incantations, or rather decantations." She not blue. "Yes, sky-blue." [4] Home with Earl and Macdonald. Above two bottles claret.

SATURDAY 5 MAY.[5] Rose and dressed quickly. Just saw General. Away to Asiatics. Heard by the way there was no review. Knocked at their door, having first walked with a fine woman, well-scented, who went to Mr. O'Beirne's.[6] Went in; saw Mrs. Halhed,[7] who told me they had *waited*,

---

Banff and Peter Garden of Delgaty respondents. Lord Mansfield did not speak. On the previous Tuesday (1 May) Lord Mansfield had made a long and important speech on the question whether an appeal could be taken to the House of Lords from a capital sentence of the High Court of Justiciary, but it does not seem very likely that Boswell got his dates wrong.

[2] Three East Indians who had come to England on a mission from one of the petty princes of India whose throne had been usurped. Their credentials having been tampered with *en route,* they could not be received in any official capacity by the King or the East India Company, but they were lodged in a house in Abingdon Street, received many civilities, and became an attraction for the curious. (They were to have been at a party at the Thrales' on the day that Thrale died.) The names of the Parsees (father and son) were reported to be Manowar Ruttagee and Manowar Cussagee; the Brahmin's as Ramobram. The *Gentleman's Magazine* (October 1781, li. 485) hints that the Brahmin's occasional absence from the group was due rather to "some disagreement among them" than to indisposition.

[3] Yorke was general in the Army and Ambassador at The Hague until the previous December, when hostilities broke out between Holland and Great Britain. Boswell had not seen him since 1764. Queensberry is the 4th Duke, "Old Q." He had succeeded to the title in 1778.

[4] Mary Buller, widowed after two years of marriage to a young Devonshire gentleman, was noted for her learning in Greek and her exploits as a traveller. Her witticism on Lord Graham's "decantations" suggests that she was present at the evening party at Miss Monckton's at which Boswell had disgraced himself (see above, 22 April 1781). She denies being a bluestocking but Boswell emphatically disagrees.

[5] There is also a short note summarizing this day: "Very wild. Lord Bute's dinner, and supper Sir Joshua. O'Byrne and Crew." The combination of names pretty certainly identifies "O'Byrne" as the Rev. Thomas Lewis O'Beirne, naval chaplain, pamphleteer, contributor to *The Rolliad,* and adapter from the French of a comedy, *The Generous Impostor.* Mrs. Crewe "protected" the play when it was acted at Drury Lane in November 1780, and it was dedicated to her and Mrs. Grenville when it was published in 1781. O'Beirne served two viceroys of Ireland as chaplain and private secretary, and was rewarded by the bishopric of Ossory, from which he was later translated to the see of Meath.

[6] See the preceding note. The well-scented woman cannot have been Mrs. Crewe, for Boswell was well acquainted with that lady (see above, 29 April 1781), and she would not have been walking without an escort.

[7] Unidentified; probably the "Asiatics'" landlady.

and were now gone out. So I was so far in a scrape. Then Fanny Bates, pressed. Away to public house; little house [8] and ale. *Then* full Venus de' Medicis. Then *Ray's* (the public house) again. *Charming* cider. Sergeant and two soldiers of Coldstream.[9] "The King [has] been pleased to say ours the cleanest regiment. Every man would get up at six and brush." *Then* Lady Elgin's; Hill, Methodist Member of Parliament, with her. Told me [he was] frightened for me. I said, "No, I'm much of a mystic." Left alone; begged tea. She showed me *Vie et lettres de Gellert.*[1] I was quite in love. Said, "This is too much." Was quite divinely amorous.[2] Then to Bengal lady, Mrs. Spencer. Procured solace.[3] Then John Wilkes, gay and well; remember nothing, except [my] asking, "Why [are you] *acharné* [4] against Paoli?" HE. "Natural 'antipathy of good to bad.' "[5] I. "No, because [he] would not marry Kate Macaulay and call out 'Wilkes and Liberty!' "[6] Told [him I was] going [to call on] Lord Bute. [HE]. "[I] hope you'll lay me at his feet." Walked with Heaton Wilkes.

Then Earl of Bute's. Hall [a] constellation of laced footmen; all glit-

[8] Privy.

[9] The 2nd Regiment of Foot Guards. The regiment was first enrolled by General Monck at Coldstream, Scotland, in the period 1659–1660.

[1] French translation by Mme de la Fite, Utrecht, 1775. Boswell had interviewed Christian Fürchtegott Gellert ("the Gay of Germany") at Leipzig, 5 October 1764.

[2] Lady Elgin (now first mentioned in the existing journal) was the "Miss W———t" (Martha Whyte) whom Boswell at eighteen had been in love with and had hoped to marry. "O Willie! How happy should I be if she consented some years after this to make me blessed!" (To W. J. Temple, 29 July 1758). An orphan with a fortune which rumour set at £30,000, she had married the Earl of Elgin and Kincardine in the summer of 1759, and was now a widow.

[3] The "Bengal lady" was Catherine Soubise, sister of Julius Soubise who in 1784 kept a fencing-school in Calcutta. She had been married to (or had been the mistress of) one Henry Spencer, who in 1778 advertised himself as "Proprietor of a Repository for Gentlemen's Horses." (Information from the files of Dr. J. N. M. Maclean of the University of Edinburgh, who had it from the late Major V. C. P. Hodson, biographer of the officers in the Bengal Army. Since Hodson also called Mrs. Spencer "the Bengal lady," it appears that she was generally so designated.) In Boswell's usage "solace" often has a sexual connotation: "I solaced my existence with them, one after the other" (Journal, 19 May 1763).

[4] Furious.

[5] Pope, *Epilogue to the Satires,* ii. 198 ("The strong antipathy").

[6] Mrs. Catherine Macaulay, the famous female historian, a great republican. Johnson had glanced at her in *Taxation No Tyranny,* and allowed Boswell to tease him about having ruined his chances of making her his wife: " 'You'll never make out this match with Mrs. Macaulay, Sir, since you are so severe against her principles.' JOHNSON. 'Nay, Sir, she is like [Hippolyta] the Amazon; she must be courted by the sword. Though I have not been hard upon her.' BOSWELL. 'Yes, you've made her ridiculous.' JOHNSON. 'That was already done. To make Macaulay ridiculous is like blacking the chimney' " (Journal, 2 April 1775).

ter. Then a man like a Member of Parliament, whom at first I thought
Lord Bute. In to the room. "Come in," said he with gracious invitation.
I saw Charles, [called out,] "My dear Colonel!" [7] "Come," said Lord Bute,
and took me into another room, Charles also. "My Lord," said I, "I'm
very much obliged to you. This has been a siege of Troy: ten years to
get into your Lordship's house." He said, "I wonder Mountstuart did not
bring you." I said, "I suppose he was afraid. He is not afraid to look the
King of Sardinia in the face, but he is afraid of your Lordship."

We talked of the Ministry. I told Dr. Johnson's saying of "[Now]
no Minister but an agent for Administration in the House of Commons." The *Great Man* was pleased with this. He spoke of the Corsicans. I said, "Brave people." He asked me what France had paid for
the island. I said I believed nothing. Genoa had run in debt for garrison-
ing towns.[8]

I asked, "My Lord, I am a very forward fellow. Will you be so good
as tell me, did the blackguard abuse when you was Minister make any
impression upon you?" He answered, "The blackguard? No. But you
know there was [a will] to tear one in pieces." He added that Lord Holland
owned to him he never grew callous, but felt as sore from attacks the last
day of his power as the first. He said, "The people here have talked a
great deal about me. Charles, you was with me when in Rome I read that
I opposed Wilkes's election." [9] (He said at first, "Nothing could induce
you to see an old man going out of life but your love for antiquities.")

I asked Charles how Colonel James was. Said I: "I was angry with
him at first. I thought he had deserted his post. But I find it was necessity. He'd have died if [he had] not come home." [1] Talking, I know

---

[7] Bute's fourth son, later Sir Charles Stuart, lieutenant-colonel in the 26th Foot.

[8] Boswell seems to have been essentially correct. Genoa "consented to the retention of
these places [the towns garrisoned] by France, and the occupation of any other parts
of the island thought necessary for the safety of the French troops. The possession of
the island was to be security for the repayment by Genoa of the money spent in the
occupation. Genoa retained the right to redeem this pledge by paying the costs, and in
the mean time surrendered all claim to sovereignty; but the island was not to be
parted with to any third party.... To put the matter shortly, Genoa pawned Corsica
for eighty thousand pounds" (L. H. Caird, *The History of Corsica*, 1899, p. 162).

[9] Presumably referring to one of the attempts by the electors of Middlesex to re-elect
Wilkes to Parliament, after his expulsion from the House. This was early in 1769,
when Bute was travelling in Italy and France.

[1] Colonel Stuart felt disgraced by his forced return and was deeply contrite because
of the unhappiness he had caused his family. He blamed his illness on his own "great
follies" (letter from him to Mrs. Stuart, 29 March 1781), but there can be no doubt
that he had been very ill indeed. Mrs. Stuart wrote to Boswell on 16 March 1781, "You
will grieve to see how sadly he looks; indeed the West Indies and a long illness, the
consequence of the climate, has made a surprising change in him."

not how, of libraries, I wondered [that] Duke of Argyll, whose heart was set on it, who wrote catalogue with own hand, did not entail it. "No," said Lord Bute, "his wish was to buy books with large margins, and to say, 'They will be good for my executors.'" I told him he was born in Scotland, and (what my old friend and companion abroad, John Wilkes, ten years ago would have given ten guineas [to know]) [record of his baptism "son of] Earl of *Boot.*" [I said,] "An odd man will read odd things. I looked into Register and read century." [2] Said he: "I'm told I was born fifteen storeys high in the Parliament Close. But my aunt, the Duchess of Argyll, believed [I was] born in London."

I said Corsica had furnished [2a] ship-timber and seamen. "Just what we want," said he. "When I went to France, Duke of Richelieu sounded me. I saw clearly we could have stopped it. A threatening word, a look, would have been sufficient." [3] Colonel Charles spoke of my being with Mrs. Stuart some days at Richmond. "You see," said I, "[I] am willing to be *un homme sans conséquence.*" Lord Bute asked me about the wines of Corsica, the population, the size of the people. I mentioned "a little *Account* of it which I published some years ago." He said, "I have read it," or, "I have seen it." I think we talked of my having seen Voltaire and Rousseau. He said he had subscribed to Voltaire's *Works*; never had subscribed to such a book: forty volumes in quarto.

The Scotch bar was mentioned. He asked me if I was at it. I think I had said before I had an excellent wife and five children. I now answered, "Yes, my lord, to get beef for my wife and milk for my children. It is hard work. Sometimes a guinea, sometimes two, for a great deal of writing." His Lordship asked me, when I happened to mention studying in Holland, how long I had been there. I said, "About ten months at Utrecht and The Hague." He said he had been three years in Holland studying civil law and public law at Groningen and Leiden. His uncle [4] made him do this, for then there was a notion that there was nothing to be done without civil law and public law. "I studied them three years, and now don't recollect a word of them." BOSWELL. "Forgive me, my

[2] See for examples above, 12, 13, 14, 17 April, 18 and 21 November 1780.
[2a] That is, would have furnished.
[3] Bute's rather off-hand assessment of the potential success of British intervention would have been quite correct had England in 1766–1768 had a strong prime minister supported by his king. This condition did not obtain. The French timed their movements according to the uncertainty and dissension in the British cabinet. The King was unwilling to risk a major war for the sake of Corsican independence, and the administration was distracted by the Middlesex election-riots and riots in Boston over taxes.
[4] Archibald, third Duke of Argyll, the "boss" of Scotland during Walpole's administration. Argyll had himself studied law at Utrecht.

Lord, for thinking that the civil law may be of use. It is the great source of our law in Scotland, and is indeed mixed with it; and Blackstone has shown that notwithstanding the aversion of the English to it—the 'Nolumus leges Angliae mutari' [5]—a great deal of the law of this country is founded on it.''

He talked of entails, and said he thought them good things. His was an instance of an old estate which had never been entailed. He never should entail it, but he hoped Lord Mountstuart would. I said I had joined with my father in one, "because," I said, "I should have entailed, and why should not he?" His Lordship said he had observed the lawyers were against entails. I smiled and said it was because they made property more permanent and left room for few disputes. His Lordship regretted the old land proprietors of Scotland estranging themselves from their estates. "Now," said he, "Mountstuart has been in Bute, and loves it, as indeed it is the prettiest place I ever saw. But his son has never seen it, and perhaps never will." "Pray, my Lord," said I, "give me leave to ask, when was your Lordship last there?" HE. "Not these thirty years." I. "Allow us to lament. Though the Stuart of Bute is very well as we see him in South Audley Street." He said when I asked him if he had not the Duke of Argyll's library, "Yes, along with my own. A great part of it," said he, "is law, lying in boxes which I have not yet opened."

Talking of Dr. Johnson, I said, "Among other things, my Lord, I have to thank your Lordship for making that great man easy by a pension." He bowed. Then said, "Pray, have they given him anything since?" I said, "No, my Lord." Said he: "I thought they had." I said, "I can assure your Lordship, not a shilling. Yet he has worked hard. But he does not like them. Do you know what he says, my Lord? 'We have no prime minister,' etc." [6]

I do not recollect any more that passed. When I rose to go, I said, "I am much obliged to your Lordship. I shall take the liberty to call again." He said nothing, but bowed courteously. Colonel Charles and I then

---

[5] "We do not wish the laws of England to be changed." In *The Hypochondriack* No. 64 Boswell quotes this famous declaration in the active form (*mutare* for *mutari*) and explains that it was "pronounced with one voice by the earls and barons of the realm when legitimation by subsequent marriage was attempted to be introduced in the reign of Henry III [1236]. Their conduct on this occasion is applauded by Blackstone, who speaks of 'the firm temper which the nobility showed at the famous parliament of Merton.' "

[6] Journal, 14 April 1775. One wonders how much the *et cetera* included. Johnson, speaking at length about Bute, had granted that he was "a very honourable man," but had accused him of bookishness and "an improper partiality to Scotsmen. He turned out Dr. Nicholls, a very capital physician, to make room for Duncan, a very low man who had cured him. Wedderburn and John Home went errands for him. He had occasion for people to go errands, but he should not have had Scotsmen."

walked away as far as the top of Long Acre just for a walk. I was still *elevated.*

Intended to have dined at Jemmy Rudd's, but it was too late.[7] *Wished* to dine with Sir Joshua anywhere. Went to him, and fortunately he asked me to dine with him with Admiral Keppel, etc. But as there were ladies, I must go and have my wig well powdered. I walked then a little in the Square [8] with Lord Dalhousie, then was shaved, powdered, and had shoes cleaned at a barber's in Orange Street. Returned to dinner. Keppel, Erskine,[9] Dick Burke (brother), ditto (son), Mrs. Burke, Mrs. and Miss Eliot, Captain King (who had gone round world),[1] Mr. Brett,[2] Miss Keppel. We soon were jovial, and after dinner Erskine and I kept it up. He repeated his letter to me in Johnson's style and his *Monkey.*[3] Also the fine passage on war from *Falkland's Islands.*[4] Dick Burke said he would not give his humanity credit for it, because it was only to prevent one particular war. But when he wished to support a war, furious. Surely as

[7] See below, latter half of 16 May 1781. What follows to the end of the entry for 5 May is now printed for the first time.

[8] Leicester Square, where Sir Joshua lived.

[9] See above 23 March 1781, n. 10.

[1] James King, astronomer with rank of second lieutenant on Cook's third voyage. He was on shore when Cook was killed in Hawaii, 14 February 1779, and with a few men had to repel the attack of the natives until assistance arrived in the ship's boats. When the second in command died, King brought the *Discovery* home. He was no doubt, like his brother Walker King, a friend of the Burkes'.

[2] Probably Keppel's friend Charles Brett, formerly an officer in the Navy, M.P. for Sandwich, 1776–1780, appointed to the Admiralty Board under the second Rockingham administration, 1782.

[3] The letter in Johnson's style has not turned up among the Boswell Papers, and we do not even know when it was written. It was presumably a parody, but Erskine's own early style, as shown by a pamphlet he published in 1775 while still a lieutenant in the Army, was remarkably stately and polysyllabic. The *Monkey* was a poem which he wrote earlier while stationed at Minorca. Peter, the pet monkey of the Governor's lady, having been doomed by her to banishment, prays to be sent to England. The poem is too long to quote, but may be seen in *Notes and Queries,* 3rd series, 1866, x. 3.

[4] A political pamphlet by Johnson, published in 1771. "The life of a modern soldier is ill represented by heroic fiction. War has means of destruction more formidable than the cannon and the sword. Of the thousands and ten thousands that perished in our late contests with France and Spain, a very small part ever felt the stroke of an enemy. The rest languished in tents and ships amidst damps and putrefaction: pale, torpid, spiritless, and helpless; gasping and groaning, unpitied among men made obdurate by long continuance of hopeless misery; and were at last whelmed in pits or heaved into the ocean without notice and without remembrance. By incommodious encampments and unwholesome stations, where courage is useless and enterprise impracticable, fleets are silently dispeopled and armies sluggishly melted away." In the *Life of Johnson* (Spring 1771) Boswell calls this passage "one of the finest pieces of eloquence in the English language."

much humanity due to our brethren in America as to Spaniards. Drank . . .[5]

SUNDAY 6 MAY. Ill after riot with Keppel. Young Burke breakfasted. Portuguese Chapel, sick but after offertory. Walked into air. Lord Graham's. Langton's. Long offended at imputing hypocrisy.[6] Beauclerk's dogs will be bulls.[7] Mrs. White's. Wrote a deal of Lord Bute. Dined home with Statella. Wrote again. Lecture, three glasses.[8] Miss Monckton's, charming; [said she was] not blue but white. Home with Burke, O'Beirne etc. Bruce Boswell with me a little. Had called Lord Cathcart and seen him and her.

MONDAY 7 MAY. Symptoms of illness. Breakfast Sir Joshua; too late, but Palmeria gave tea, and I read some of Pope. Port Eliot came, and I called out, "Now we're Whig and Tory." He said no sensible man was really a Tory but Dr. Johnson; and as that reputed great man was wrong in the two great points of civil and religious liberty, had some doubt as

---

[5] Catchword at the foot of a recto with blank verso. At least one more page of journal is probably missing, but not certainly so. In his stints of journalizing, Boswell frequently broke off at the foot of a page, even when by so doing he left a sentence uncompleted.

[6] In the conversation of 7 May 1773, when Johnson tossed and gored Langton for introducing the subject of the Trinity. If Johnson imputed hypocrisy to Langton (as reported in the *Life of Johnson*, he seems merely to have taxed him with *gaucherie*), it was for trying to involve him in a wrangle under pretence of seriously seeking his opinion. Langton undoubtedly felt aggrieved for some time, and Boswell tried by letters to cajole him out of his resentment.

[7] "Beauclerk told me that at his house in the country two large dogs were fighting. Mr. Johnson looked steadily at them for a little, and then, as one would separate two little boys who are foolishly hurting each other, he ran up to them and cuffed their heads till he had them asunder from one another" (Journal, 18 October 1773). Langton or Boswell remarks that in the way stories grow unless recorded, the dogs are likely to end by becoming bulls.

[8] Paoli read him a lecture and got him to promise to curb his drinking. Boswell preserved notes of the lecture, headed "General Paoli, Monday morning, 7 May": "Of me he said yesterday, 'Your friends did not think ill of you. I scolded your faults but threw a shining veil over them, covered them with gold lamina.—I will offend you, I will be your friend [I shall offend you, but as your friend it is my duty to do so]. For all my regard, if the King would send you as Secretary with me to Corsica to restore our affairs, I would say, "I will not have him. From his fault I cannot trust him." Cure of this and you will be asked by men in power; it will be their interest. But you must appear [in your better character] to them. They will not draw you from the waves. The malignity of human nature likes to see you struggle. But get to shore; be firm, be able, and they will have you.—Yesterday morning your wit was fine; it was clear, limpid as water, not muddied by porter or wine. Wit of sober man a picture with fine light of Salvator Rosa; wit of wine that with dark shades of some bad painter. Wine a night-piece; sober, with the brightness of day.' "

to his greatness. I said he and Doctor would agree, for Eliot admitted [we should have] king and honour him; nay, had hovered four years before he went into Opposition. I repeated Barnard's verses. Then Dr. Johnson. HE. "I hope you don't intend to get drunk tomorrow as you did at Paoli's." [9] Whig and Tory great armoury.[1] Malone came. Dined Temple. Tea Forbes's. Uneasy when I saw his children to think of my wild life. More ill. Dilly's a little. Alarmed with cold. A. Donaldson's a little. Home; read Pope.

TUESDAY 8 MAY. Called George Byng a moment. Said Wilkes's speeches must be prepared; were built of pebbles. Uneasy for fear of morbus. Breakfasted Dempster late. Saw his brother. Walked out. *Noon Gazette* "calculated for the *meridian* of London." [2] Called Judge Jamieson [3] and sat a little. Called Duke of Argyll, Lord Bute, Duke of Queensberry, Earl of Findlater, Lady Oughton, and sat. Burke just going out. Walked down to House. HE. "Crofts a bad imitation of Johnson: all the warts and contortions without the ———; all the panting and convulsions of the Sibyl without the inspiration." [4] Talked of Whig and Tory. Went to Chancery and King's Bench a little. Gallery House of Commons moment. Then Dr. Johnson; ready. Told how Burke, who lamented the turbulence, said more order, etc., in George II's reign with Whig administration than now: "Who, then, in fault?" Doctor said, "First place,

---

[9] Probably on Wednesday 2 May, the most recent date on which Boswell and Johnson had dined together at Paoli's. Boswell does not report drinking too much on that occasion (he spent the evening playing cards at Sir Lawrence Dundas's), but what Johnson called getting drunk he may have considered no more than normal convivial hilarity. He certainly went to bed at Paoli's very drunk on the evening of Thursday 3 May and probably also on the evenings of Friday 4 and Saturday 5 May.

[1] A cramped interlinear addition: "armoury" may be misread. The reference is no doubt to a remarkably candid and conciliatory definition, "Of Whig and Tory," which Johnson dictated to Boswell, perhaps on this very day. (It appears in the *Life of Johnson* just before a letter dated 2 June 1781.) Boswell, who had complained that, though he was a zealous Tory, he lacked reasons for his faith, perhaps meant that the definition was to him an inexhaustible storehouse of intellectual armour.

[2] A London newspaper (*The Noon Gazette and Daily Spy*) that began publication in 1781. Boswell perhaps now saw this paper for the first time.

[3] Presumably the same as "Old Jamieson" in the entry for 30 May 1781. Jamieson was perhaps nicknamed "Judge" because of his litigiousness.

[4] Herbert Croft (not Crofts), later a baronet, had written the life of Edward Young for Johnson's *Lives of the Poets*. This saying of Burke's appears in the *Life of Johnson* (in the year 1781, *Life of Young*) as "No, no, it is *not* a good imitation of Johnson; it has all his pomp without his force; it has all the nodosities of the oak without its strength.... It has all the contortions of the Sibyl without the inspiration." Boswell presumably took his imperfect note back to Burke for amplification and correction. One change ("force" for "sense") must have been made in the proofs.

Tories, though in opposition, will not go so far as Whigs; more reverence for government. Whigs will try to turn out Tories by every means."

[EDITORIAL NOTE: For the remainder of the day, the journal as now preserved contains only the terse note, "Dined Dilly's." The dinner mentioned so casually was that at which Johnson met Wilkes for the second time. If Boswell had any written account of this dinner before he wrote the first draft of the *Life of Johnson*, it is now missing from his papers. He may have needed no note, having got the conversation sufficiently into his memory by repeating it frequently, as we know he did his now lost conversation with General Burgoyne. (This matter is discussed in the Introduction to *Boswell in Extremes, 1776–1778,* pp. xxi–xxii.) Recopyings of bits at the beginning and end of the conversation and a docket, "Second Conversation between Dr. Johnson and Mr. Wilkes," show that, like the first conversation, it was detached from the manuscript of the *Life* and sent to Wilkes for his approval. We print the draft as it stood before revision.]

On Tuesday 8th May I had the pleasure of again dining with him and Mr. Wilkes at Mr. Dilly's.[5] No *negotiation* was now required to bring them together; for Johnson was so well satisfied with the former interview that he was very glad to meet Wilkes again, who was this day seated between Dr. Johnson and Dr. Beattie. WILKES. "I have been thinking, Dr. Johnson, that there should be a bill brought into Parliament that the controverted elections for Scotland should be tried in that country, at their own Abbey of Holyrood House and not here; for the consequence of trying them here is we have an inundation of Scotchmen who come up and never go back again." JOHNSON. "Nay, Sir, I see no reason why they should be tried at all; for you know one Scotchman is as good as another." WILKES. "Pray, Boswell, how much may be got in a year by an advocate at the Scotch bar?" BOSWELL. "I believe two thousand pounds." WILKES. "How can it be possible to spend that money in Scotland?" JOHNSON. "Why, Sir, the money may be spent in England. But there is a harder question. If one man in Scotland gets possession of two thousand pounds, what remains for all the rest of the nation?" Here again they joined in extravagant sportive raillery upon the supposed poverty of Scotland, which Dr. Beattie and I did not think it worth while to controvert.

The subject of quotation being introduced, Mr. Wilkes censured it as pedantry. JOHNSON. "No, Sir, it is a good thing; there is a community of mind in it. Classical quotation is the *parole* of literary men all over the world." WILKES. "Upon the Continent they all quote the Vulgate

[5] The first dinner (which furnished the most famous passage in the *Life of Johnson*) had occurred on 15 May 1776.

Bible. Shakespeare is chiefly quoted here; and we quote also Pope, Prior, Butler, Waller, and sometimes Cowley."

We talked of letter-writing. JOHNSON. "It is now become so customary to publish letters that in order to avoid it I put as little into mine as I can." BOSWELL. "Do what you will, Sir, you cannot avoid it. Should you even write as ill as you can, your letters would be published as curiosities.

> Behold a miracle: instead of wit,
> See two dull lines by Stanhope's pencil writ." [6]

He gave us an entertaining account of Bet Flint, a woman of the town, who with some eccentric talents and much effrontery forced herself upon his acquaintance. "Bet," said he, "wrote her own life in verse, which she brought to me wishing that I would furnish her with a preface to it (laughing).[7] I used to say of her that she was generally slut and drunkard, occasionally whore and thief. She had, however, genteel lodgings, a spinet on which she played, and a boy that walked before her chair. Poor Bet was taken up for stealing a counterpane and tried at the Old Bailey. Willes, who loved a wench,[8] directed the jury to acquit her, and she was

[6] "Club at the King's Head in Pall Mall that (arrogantly) called themselves 'The World.' Lord Stanhope then (now Lord Chesterfield), Lord Herbert, etc., etc. Epigrams proposed to be writ by each after dinner once when Dr. Young was invited thither. Would have declined writing, because he had no diamond. Lord Chesterfield lent him his, and he wrote immediately [the couplet quoted]" (Joseph Spence, *Observations, Anecdotes and Characters of Books and Men*, ed. J. M. Osborn, 1966, No. 852, i. 343). The lines were ascribed to Pope in *Joe Miller's Jests*, 1742.

[7] This sentence of necessity follows the revised draft. In the first draft Boswell wrote merely, "Bet composed a poem," left three lines blank, and went on. Evidently he was not clear as to what Bet had written or her reason for coming to Johnson, and he sought help, almost certainly from Fanny Burney. A scrap among the Boswell papers, headed "1781. Wilkes's conversation," is apparently his note of what she told him: "Bet Flint came to Dr. Johnson to beg he would write a preface to her life, which she had written in verse, of which he remembered the first four lines as follows:

> When first I drew my vital breath,
> A little diminutive I came upon earth;
> And then I came from a dark abode
> Into this gay and gaudy world."

He printed the verses in a foot-note, with acknowledgement to "a young lady of [Johnson's] acquaintance," substituting "minikin" for "diminutive," either from some other source or by happy conjecture.

[8] "Lord Chief Justice Willes ... was not wont to disguise any of his passions. That for gaming was notorious; for women, unbounded. There was a remarkable story current of a grave person's coming to reprove the scandal he gave, and to tell him that the world talked of one of his maidservants being with child. Willes said, 'What is that to me?' The monitor answered, 'Oh! but they say that it is by your Lordship.' 'And what is that to you?'" (Horace Walpole, *Memoirs of George II*, 1847, i. 89).

acquitted; upon which Bet said with a gay and satisfied air, 'Now that the counterpane is my own, I shall make a petticoat of it.' "

Talking of oratory, Mr. Wilkes described it as accompanied with all the charms of poetical expression. JOHNSON. "No, Sir; oratory is the power of beating down your adversary's arguments and putting better in their place." WILKES. "But this does not move the passions." JOHNSON. "He must be a weak man who is to be so moved."

Mr. Wilkes observed how tenacious we are of forms in this country, and gave as an instance a vote of the House of Commons for remitting money to pay the Army in America *in Portugal pieces*, when in reality the remittance is made not in Portugal coin but in our own specie.[9] JOHNSON. "Is there not a law, Sir, against exporting the current coin of the realm?" WILKES. "Yes, Sir. But might not the House of Commons order our own current coin to be sent into our own colonies?" Here Johnson, with that quickness of recollection which distinguished him so eminently, gave the *Middlesex Patriot* an admirable retort upon his own ground. "Sure, Sir, you don't think a *resolution of the House of Commons* equal to a *law of the land?*" WILKES. "GOD forbid, Sir." To hear what was treated with such violence in *The False Alarm* now turned into pleasant repartee was extremely agreeable. Johnson went on, "Locke observes well that a prohibition to export the current coin is impolitic; for when the balance of trade happens to be against a state, the current coin *must* be exported."

Mr. Beauclerk's fine library was this season sold in London by auction. Mr. Wilkes said he wondered to find in it such a numerous collection of sermons, seeming to think it strange that Mr. Beauclerk should have chosen to have many compositions of that kind. JOHNSON. "Why, Sir, you are to consider that sermons make a considerable branch of English literature, so that a library must be very imperfect if it has not a numerous collection of sermons; and in all collections, Sir, the desire of augmenting grows stronger in proportion to the advance in acquisition, as motion is accelerated by the continuance of the impetus. Besides, Sir" (looking at Mr. Wilkes with a placid but significant smile) "a man may collect sermons with intention of making himself better by them. I hope Mr. Beauclerk intended that some time or other that should be the case with him."

The company gradually dropped away. Mr. Dilly himself was called downstairs upon business. I myself left the room for a little while. When

---

[9] Portugal used the gold it received from Brazil to pay for goods of other European nations. "Almost all our gold, it is said, comes from Portugal" (Adam Smith, *An Inquiry into the Nature and Causes of the Wealth of Nations,* 1776, Bk. IV, ch. 6).

I returned, I was struck with observing Dr. Samuel Johnson and John Wilkes, Esq., literally tête-à-tête; for they were reclined upon their chairs with their heads leaning almost close to each other and talking earnestly in a kind of confidential whisper of the personal quarrel between George the Second and the King of Prussia.[1] Such a perfect easy sociality between two such opponents in the war of political controversy as I now beheld would have been a very good subject for a picture.

Dr. Beattie appeared to Mr. Wilkes in so advantageous a light that he very soon after paid him a visit at his lodgings and sat with him a considerable time.

WEDNESDAY 9 MAY. Sat awhile with General Oglethorpe and took notes of his life.[2] Colonel Howart, an original Tatler, came in.[3] Then for Dr. Johnson; took hackney-coach and we came together. Pinto, Paoli, Gentili. [Johnson said] only, "No, Sir," as to going to Newfoundland.[4] Perry came.[5] Johnson off. Saw him to coach.

THURSDAY 10 MAY. Dined Bishop of Killaloe. Burke's night. Not well.

[1] Frederick the Great was George I's grandson. It was confidently asserted (by Horace Walpole among others) that the quarrel arose because George II destroyed his father's will, which Frederick believed to have contained a large legacy to his mother, the Queen of Prussia, and was rendered inveterate by Frederick's rude and repeated demands for the bequest.

[2] See above, note on 24 April 1779.

[3] Colonel Howart (Howarth would be a more probable spelling) remains unidentified. Boswell probably means that he was much like the character assumed by Steele in the *Tatler*, not by imitation, but naturally so. The *Tatler* in its first number announced an intention of giving from appropriate coffee-houses accounts of gallantry, pleasure, and entertainment; poetry; foreign and domestic news, etc.

[4] Boswell presumably means either that this was the only remark Johnson made, or that it was the only remark of Johnson's that he remembered. The dinner seems to have been at Oglethorpe's. We have found no other mention of this interesting suggestion that Johnson entertained, or was thought to have entertained, a plan of making a voyage to Newfoundland.

[5] George Perry, later called by Boswell "Oriental Perry," is a person one would like to know more about. Langton in a letter to Boswell the previous April or May describes him as being "furnished, by what I can understand, with a larger store of knowledge in Oriental learning, particularly as to the various languages and dialects of those regions than has perhaps yet been attained by an European." Like Sir William Jones, Perry appears to have been a philologist versed in Eastern languages who went out to India to study Sanskrit. A detached note for 13 May 1781 shows that Boswell told Lord Bute that Perry was leaving his family, and that Bute "quoted some Latin verse as to every man living in his own way. Get it." On 4 June 1781 Perry wrote to Boswell from Portsmouth, thanking him for a copy of Boswell's *Account of Corsica*. Boswell endorsed the letter, "Mr. Perry the traveller into the East, when about to sail in 1781. Q? Did he ever return?" We can at least answer that question: he died outside Calcutta in March 1786.

FRIDAY 11 MAY. General objected clothes. Lord Cathcart's breakfast, and tailor came.[6] City and on Change. Had General's coach. Commons a minute. Dined Langton. Beattie home with you. Sir Lawrence's cards; Scotch disgusting. Home before supper.

SATURDAY 12 MAY. With Chevalier Pinto, etc., to Perry's. Then Indians. Then Ulbster's. Wilkes, gay; Miss Wilkes, etc. [Wilkes's] looking-glass; [I said I should] take to Scotland and show, sixpence apiece. WILKES. "But have they sixpence apiece?" Coach to St. Paul's. Not well, but would be hearty with L[ord] M[ayor].[7] Home; powdered wig. Miss Monckton's. Book on dressing hair. Then Sir R. Herries, weary.

SUNDAY 13 MAY. Captain Jardine of the Artillery, who had lost an arm, breakfasted with us. I found him to be a natural son of Sir Alexander's. We were very late this morning. I went for a little while and adored in the Portuguese Chapel. Then called Lord Bute's. Was received, to my agreeable surprise, or relief, as I doubted of being again admitted. Was steadier. Perceived that there was not one bit of lace on the footmen, and that my fervent imagination had gilded them and produced the blaze. Mr. Marsh (his foreign *gentleman*, whose name I was afterwards told by Mrs. Stuart) was very courteous. I stopped a little in the room where I had first seen the Thane, and looked at a pretty good picture of Lord Mountstuart, done at Geneva. Then was ushered into the Earl's interior room. Found him quite alone. "My Lord, I am much obliged to you for letting me in." He was exceedingly courteous, and took me cordially by the hand and asked me how I had been. I said I had a bad cold. He asked me what I did for my cold. I said, nothing. I only lived differently from what I had done for some time since I came last to London. For I had been living two lives, which I found was too much for any one man. I had been living with people who sat up late and people who rose early, and a good deal with Lord Eglinton. "And drinking hard," said he. "Yes, my Lord." BUTE. "Pray, how does Lord Eglinton go on now? He used to take a great deal of exercise." BOSWELL. "He begins now not to be able to walk so much. He rides part of the morning. He is an honest, honourable man. He has acted nobly in paying his brother's debts, which were about £75,000. His brother's personal estate was, I understand, about £25,000. So he took £50,000 upon himself, and I believe next year it will be all paid." BUTE. "But his brother had laid out a great deal of money in raising the value of the estate." BOSWELL. "True, my Lord. It

---

[6] Manuscript, "Gen. objected clothes Ld. Cathcarts—break and Taylor came." We think this means that Paoli told Boswell that he had no clothes suitable for the presentation at Court which Lord Cathcart had arranged (see below, 16 May 1781); that Boswell consulted Cathcart, and sent for a tailor.

[7] Sir Watkin Lewes. Boswell would have found his anti-Ministerial politics congenial.

is now an estate of £12,000 a year actually paid. And it is a very fine place." BUTE. "Are you an Ayrshire man?" BOSWELL. "Yes, my Lord. I have the honour to see the island of Bute every day from the windows of my father's library."

The late Lord Dundonald was mentioned, I think as connected with the Eglinton family.[8] Lord Bute observed what an entertaining man he was, and that he was a bold man at a pretty advanced age to marry a beautiful young woman.[9] His Lordship knew her well and had danced with her. I gave him an account of this Earl's sad situation, and how his mother was distressed by it. His Lordship regretted her being distressed, and said this Earl had project [1] from his father, Tom, who brought up a hundred specimens of silk from Paisley. His Lordship told me that he had received information that Shawfield wished to sell Islay, but asked a price he never would get: £150,000. He said Old Daniel went over to France and gave Lord Kilsyth £200 for a confirmation of his lease of that estate, in case of accidents.[2]

We talked of his son James, and of his having excellent sense but that he must be employed. Said my Lord: "He was once a great Nimrod. I am glad he took to the army. I hope he will make a profession of it. I wish he was a major in an old regiment. His son Jack is the finest boy I ever saw, a boy of uncommon abilities; and James [3] is a fine boy too. I think he'll do very well for the sea." I said, "Mrs. Stuart is leading a most meritorious life at Richmond, without a carriage, one footman, and being governess to her daughters, who are very fine girls. I have observed her hear the lessons on the harpsichord and in French; and if it is not perfect enough, they must go and get it better and come back." His Lordship said nothing, which was not well.

He told me that he did not wish to be Prime Minister, but when Pitt and the Duke of Newcastle went out, he was obliged to take that place. Pitt would not have gone out had he foreseen the successes which

---

[8] Alexander Montgomerie, ninth Earl of Eglinton, father of Boswell's friends the tenth and eleventh Earls, married as his *first* wife Margaret Cochrane, daughter of Lord Cochrane, and first cousin of Lord Dundonald's father. The mother of the tenth and eleventh Earls, however, was their father's *third* wife, Susanna Kennedy, daughter of Sir Archibald Kennedy of Culzean.

[9] He was fifty-three when he married Jean Stuart as his second wife.

[1] A speculative tendency.

[2] Lord Kilsyth was a Jacobite, whose lands were forfeited because of his part in the uprising of 1715. Presumably "Old Daniel" (Campbell of Shawfield) bought Islay in the sale of the forfeited estates and then got a lease from Kilsyth in case his attainder should be reversed.

[3] The future Lord Wharncliffe, who edited the letters of Lady Mary Wortley Montagu (his great-grandmother).

afterwards happened. The Duke of Newcastle wanted a loan of two millions.[4] The King was persuaded to agree to it. But Lord Bute would not go along with the measure, upon which the Duke of Newcastle went out. Lord Bute came in, on an express promise from the King that he should have leave to resign when he had made the peace. His Lordship told me Pitt owned to him that he did not think the demolition of Dunkirk of consequence.[5] But that the nation had such a notion of it, a peace could not be made without it. That upon the same principle a peace could not be made without keeping Canada, and Pitt always said, "We *must* have North America." Lord Bute, however, candidly said that it was not from this consideration only that he acted, for he really did think it best to keep Canada. He was sensible now he was in the wrong. But he did not apprehend that there would be such disturbances in our American colonies. ———, a French author who wrote in ——— and whom his Lordship has since read, says, "Whenever the . . ."

[EDITORIAL NOTE: The account breaks off here at the foot of a full recto with blank verso and a catchword ("the"), but it may well be that Boswell wrote no more of the expanded account. (See above, p. 346 n. 5). We continue with a stray slip and the rough note for the day.]

Lord Bute, when I mentioned Perry's leaving family, quoted some Latin verse as to every man living in his own way. Then met Lord Graham; paid guinea bet.[6] Angry at Douglas.[7] I said I was [a] *very* good man, but did not go to worthy people. LORD GRAHAM. "You only know what a good man is." [8] Ramsay's; Lady Margaret's. Sir Joshua dinner. Dick Burke vulgar and fierce. Lord Mansfield's. When you said, "Father grows old too soon," [he] said, "That very good of you. 'Nec ante tempus patris inquirere annos,' " [9] or some such thing. Miss Monckton. Heavy rain. Sir Joshua supper.

MONDAY 14 MAY. Up in calm spirits. In all forenoon and wrote let-

---

[4] For carrying on the war with France and Spain. Bute wished to conclude a peace. Newcastle resigned as Prime Minister and Bute succeeded him in 1762.

[5] According to the terms of the Peace of Paris (1763), France agreed to dismantle Dunkirk.

[6] Probably that he would not contract gonorrhea. He made such bets in the hope that they would act as a deterrent.

[7] Perhaps because of something Graham told him. Graham's sister, Lady Lucy Graham, Archibald Douglas's first wife, had died something over a year before. See above, 14 February, 24 March 1780.

[8] One of the most profound remarks Boswell ever recorded. A significant writer does not have to be a good man, but he does have to know what a good man is.

[9] "A son should not be in haste to ask how long his father will live" (Ovid, *Metamorphoses*, i. 148, paraphrased).

ters to Temple, etc., and journal. Took salts. But complaint seemed rather worse. Sir J. Dick called. General and Gentili went to review at Blackheath. At five, Sir Lawrence's. Lords Eglinton, Kellie, Sir D. Carnegie, Governor Seton, Colonel Macdonell, Parsons. Lord Eglinton instantly begun on my being ill: Scottish raillery. I evaded. At dinner lived rather well, but shunned the claret. Nothing brilliant [said,] far less discussed. Tea Oxford and Bath Coffee-house. Then (strange) followed in Bond Street fine [woman] (satin skin with blond hair) to Hanover Square. She cried after telling [that] her husband did all he could with his wages. Left her. Lady Margaret, elegant and spirited Montgomerie. Very good evening.

TUESDAY 15 MAY. Perry the orientalist and Ulbster breakfasted with us. I was sickened by Perry's verbiage. Sinclair [1] walked with me to the City. Dr. Johnson not at home. Went to Change. At Guildhall got out Wilkes from Court of Alderman.[2] He, laughing, said, "The gods are listening to our deliberations. Jupiter bends an ear." Then Dilly's a moment. Temple and broke bread.[3] Then to Wilkes's. Told him that though all the Scotch world and half the English believed he had offered himself to Lord Bute, his Lordship had candidly told me not so; and I related what had passed. He was much pleased, and when after dinner I toasted John, Earl of Bute, he drank it, seemingly *de bon cœur*, and said, "You may tell Lord Bute I was in two mistakes. I mistook Lord Temple, and I mistook Lord Bute." [4] Miss Wilkes was very polite and agreeable, but spoke indistinctly. Wilkes talked of my removing to London. I said, "Will you get me causes?" "To be sure," said he. He toasted Dr. Johnson and General Paoli, but spoke against the latter. I told him the General said, "I forgive the father for the sake of the daughter." "You never told me that before," said he. I drank very little. A Mr. Withy, a broker I believe, who had been once imprisoned for bribing at an election, was there. A blackguard-looking man. Wilkes is used to have such about him. He is contaminated. There was only today what Dr. Johnson gives as the character of his conversation: "a general gaiety." I remember nothing particular. (He said I was a dangerous man, because I wrote down con-

[1] Same as "Ulbster": John Sinclair of Ulbster, later a baronet. He too was interested in language. See above, 18 October 1780.

[2] Wilkes was alderman of Farringdon Without, 1769–1797.

[3] Boswell is "keeping his terms" by being present in the commons of the Inner Temple on the last dining days of an Easter term. See also his entry for the day following this.

[4] Apparently, "You may tell Lord Bute that I now find him to have been more candid and generous than Lord Temple, my supposed friend." The reference must be to Wilkes's alleged solicitation of Bute for the governorship of Canada, in return for which he was to discontinue his attacks in the *North Briton.*

versations.) I posted away about six. Took a hackney-coach in Parliament Street. Drove to Covent Garden and got in time to the pit and was much entertained with Macklin's new comedy.[5] Then to Tom Davies's; biscuits and small beer and ale and tolerable chat. I thought it a duty to give him an evening.

WEDNESDAY 16 MAY. Seward and his friend Mr. Freeman, a West Indian (who made no figure at all) breakfasted with us. I then dressed in scarlet with rich buttons. Lord Cathcart's coach came and took me to his house. Saw my Lady. Then came my London *Colonel*,[6] and away we went to St. James's. I liked being thus introduced by my noble cousin, by the heir of line of the family of Auchinleck.[7] Was quite easy amongst the *courtiers*. Lord Willoughby de Broke was in waiting, and he knew me. So I was well. After kissing the King's hand, Lord Cathcart made me place myself close to the door, that the King might speak to me. I was before Lord Camden. I bowed and made an apology. He insisted on my remaining, and said, "I keep as far back as I can." Said I: "I'm sorry for it, my Lord. If the voice of many of us could be heard, it should not be so. Your Lordship will allow us to talk a little metaphorically." He said, "I'm too old a man." [8] The King did speak. But he only said, "You are come to make some stay?" Easy and firm as I felt myself before, the immediate presence of HIS MAJESTY so awed me that I answered, "Yes, *my Lord*." "My Lord the King" is a good ancient expression. But confusion made me forget to say "*Sir*," "My Lord" being the highest denomination of respect to which I am used. I conversed with Chevalier Pinto, Baron Nolcken, and the Ministre de Hesse.[9] Nolcken told me he had made inquiry in Sweden for my relations, but could not discover them, as it is customary to change family names. I wish it may be true that he *has* inquired.[1]

[5] *The Man of the World*, presented in Ireland under the title *The True-born Scotchman* as early as 1766, had up to this time been refused a license in England because of its political implications. The chief character, played by Macklin himself, was Sir Pertinax MacSycophant, a Scottish politician.

[6] Cathcart himself, wearing his uniform as officer in the Coldstream Guards. He was captain in the regiment, lieutenant-colonel in the Army.

[7] Cathcart was directly descended (as Boswell was not) from David Boswell of Auchinleck (d. 1661), the laird who had no sons and left the estate to a nephew. Cathcart's great-great-grandmother was David Boswell's daughter. Boswell had met George III once before, at which time he had been introduced by Lord Eglinton, through Lord Denbigh (*Journal*, 18 February 1766).

[8] Camden, a friend and disciple of the elder Pitt, had been in Opposition since his removal from the office of Lord Chancellor in 1770.

[9] Christian, Baron von Kutzleben.

[1] Boswell managed in 1791 to get in touch with descendants of this branch of the family. They proved to have settled in Germany, not Sweden.

Lord Loughborough acknowledged me by a bow. I went up to him. "I don't know, my Lord, if I may speak to your Lordship. I don't know if I am acquainted with you." [2] Here was an opening for his saying something polite and obliging. But his cold stiffness was quite silent. I went on, "But I would beg leave to ask one question. Lord Bute told me that Dr. Johnson's pension was given at your Lordship's desire. Pray, was there any application on the part of Dr. Johnson, or who first suggested it?" LOUGHBOROUGH. "Why, it is so long ago I cannot exactly say. There was no application from the Doctor himself. There was a consultation among his friends whether he would accept of a pension. It was a very right thing to give it, and it was given in the handsomest manner— as a reward of merit, without any stipulation that he should write." BOSWELL. "Yet he has written a great deal—those political pamphlets." LOUGHBOROUGH. "He'd have written *them* though he had not got his pension." (This was a very good compliment to the Doctor.) BOSWELL. "I believe he would. His old Tory indignation would have made him write." (I afterwards told this compliment to the Doctor in his garden. He said he *should* have written his pamphlets. "All," said I, "but *Taxation No Tyranny*. You'd have let the Ministry and the colonies fight it out." JOHNSON. "Nay, Sir, I should have written that if I wrote any. And they must fight it out at any rate.") I said to Lord Loughborough, "Old Sheridan claims some share in getting Dr. Johnson's pension." LOUGHBOROUGH. "He rung the bell." BOSWELL. "I remember your Lordship on the top of the Cross at Edinburgh, drinking." LOUGHBOROUGH. "You have a memory for bad things." [3] BOSWELL. "No, no, my Lord; the same spirit when well directed—" I told him I had a translation of an ode of Anacreon by his father when at college, very well done.[4] But he expressed no desire to see it. However, though cold he was civil.

I then got into General Paoli's chariot; enjoyed what my own ardent curiosity in going to Corsica and assiduity in writing an account of it had procured me; drove to Nichols the printer and sat a little with him, like a patron of literature, and put him in mind of Dr. Johnson's proof-sheets of the *Prefaces*, which Mr. Nichols had saved for me. Called Dr. Johnson by sending to his house. Not at home. Broke bread in Temple Hall, which fin-

[2] Loughborough was a Scotsman and member of the Faculty of Advocates. He must have pleaded before Lord Auchinleck, and apparently knew Boswell by sight, but there is no earlier record in the journal of their having met.

[3] This particular escapade does not appear to have been otherwise recorded. It could have happened no later than 1757.

[4] Peter Wedderburn was elevated to the bench as Lord Chesterhall. The translation was apparently among those "by young gentlemen when in Regent Scott's class," in the University of Edinburgh, which Boswell read aloud to his father, 22 March 1777.

ished a term. Home and dined, after changing clothes; Statella and somebody else there. Dined short, and away to White Horse Cellar; cold and pain
in stomach. Tasted gin. Got into Richmond stage. A fat fellow and a German who had been servant to George II with me. We stopped at Jamie
Rudd's.[5] I told him I had heard much of him, but had not seen him till
today. The German said, "Mr. Rudd is known, not only in England, but
abroad." We had fine ale. The King was introduced. I told the story of
His Majesty and Sir J. Pringle; what wine he should drink. Said Rudd:
"It would be better for him if he'd drink a couple of tankards of ale or
a pot of porter." "Ay," said I, "he'd govern for himself a little more. Now
there's Lord North who governs him; he drinks a bottle of claret every
night." Said Rudd: "He'd be a damned fool if he did not." There was a
Cheshire cheese in the bar, like a millstone, as one of my companions
said. It was one hundred forty lb. weight. It lasts, I think, three weeks.
It was good. I said, "Mr. Rudd, I am told you have always a good cold
buttock of beef." "Come, Sir," said he, "you shall see. Nay, you shall not
see, but you shall taste." We three followed him to a kind of pantry,
whence he took out a lovely buttock indeed, and said, "Look ye, there's
beef! No king in the world has so good. Nay, 'tis too good for a king."
Then brandishing a knife half a yard long, I suppose, he cut each of us
a piece, which we eat. I said I'd come and dine with him at his own
table, and asked his hour. "At one o'clock, Sir," said he. "Sunday, Wednesday, and Friday are our boiling days, when you may have the beef warm.
On Sunday there is boiled beef with young cabbages from my own garden, a
fillet of veal stuffed, and a plum-pudding." He looked like one of "the
lords of humankind" [6] when he said this. I gave him a hearty shake of
the hand, and said, "I'll be with you." A laced coachman went into the
stage with us. I learnt from him not to pity coachmen in the street at
night. Said he: "I serves now a very good lady, and gets to bed every
night at eleven. But I'd rather be back again to a single gentleman. I
grows too fat. And when one is used to sitting on the box in the night-
time, it is very easy. I have waited seven hours for my master when he
was at the gaming-table." Strange restlessness and discontent of human
nature! I went to Colonel James Stuart's. He was expected tonight, Mrs.
Stuart told me. But he did not come. She and I were friendly as usual.
I confessed my wild life since I was here last, and was calmly consoled.

THURSDAY 17 MAY. Rose with a severe headache, coldness, and giddi-
ness. Breakfast did me some good. Visited Lady Di Beauclerk. Her gay

---

[5] Probably the Red Lion, Putney.

[6] Goldsmith's *Traveller*, line 331. Johnson in the Hebrides (23 October 1773) had repeated the passage "with such energy that the tear started into his eye" (*Journal of a
Tour to the Hebrides*).

conversation did me good. I said gaiety, by making animal spirits well, would cure every complaint. "Every nervous complaint," said she. I complained of Langton's worthy, dull, Lincolnshire-goose justice. "O, Massenberg,"[7] said she. "I have seen them all. One is not to die of these worthy people." "No," said I, "and a sad death: the reverse of

Die of a rose in aromatic pain.[8]

They overlay one." I begged to see a particular painting by her Ladyship from Spenser's *Faerie Queene*, and read the passage: Book 4, Canto 7, §35–36, and looked at the picture and was charmed.[9] I said the representation was such, one could not say whether the poetry was taken from the painting or the painting from the poetry; whether the poetry or the painting was first.[1] Said she: "That is the finest compliment I ever had paid me. I'll write that in a book, as you do." She went in her carriage to the Park with her daughters. I crept down the hill, cold and not well. Was obliged to take peppermint drops and sit by the fire. Aberdeen came for a little. Then came Miss Danby and Mrs. Morris, and dined. I was entertaining. But they were all against me for filling Veronica's head with London finery. Mrs. Morris and I went to town in the chaise which brought the ladies. I had a little gloom by the way.

Went to Mrs. Reynolds's; Dr. Johnson there. Told him we had not met for a week. "Then let us live double." Drs. Beattie and Dunbar were by him. When Dr. Burney came in, the Doctor called out of them, "Two northern lights." Gave us the history of Dr. Thompson,[2] and maintained against Dr. Percy the Bristol poetry neither Rowley's nor Chatterton's, but by some middle man. Bigge was here. I grew better and went home quiet.

FRIDAY 18 MAY. The General and I breakfasted with Ulbster and saw his curious warlike inventions.[3] Oriental Perry there. Then we called

[7] William Burrell Massingberd of Ormsby, Langton's neighbour in the country. He was admitted to the Inner Temple, was High Sheriff of Lincolnshire, 1744–1745, and was no doubt also a Justice of the Peace.

[8] Pope's *Essay on Man*, i. 200.

[9] Amoret awakening in the arms of the squire who had assisted Belphoebe in rescuing her from the clutches of Lust. Lady Diana's illustrations to *The Faerie Queene* appear never to have been engraved. Five of the original drawings (unfortunately not the one that so pleased Boswell) are in the Lewis Walpole Library, Farmington, Connecticut.

[1] Boswell was proud of this compliment, and recounted it later in a letter to Lord Pembroke (30 April 1782).

[2] Thomas Thompson, a popular physician of the forties, who had treated Pope and Fielding. Johnson mentions him in the *Life of Pope*. Vivid (and opposed) evaluations of him will be found in Sir John Hawkins's *Life of Johnson* and Fielding's *Amelia*.

[3] Sinclair was always interested in such matters, and in later years patronized Henry Shrapnel, inventor of the shrapnel shell.

on the Bishop of Killaloe, and I introduced them to Sir Lawrence Dundas, and they saw his pictures; Mr. Lumisden, whom I had engaged to be there, and Burrows going through with us. I then called at some places.[4] The Bishop dined with us. Nobody but ourselves. We were quiet and happy. I walked with his Lordship to his door. Drank tea with Mrs. Burke. Played cards and supped at Sir Lawrence Dundas's. Abyssinian Bruce there, coarse in liquor. Talked of my describing him. He was sure I had meant no offence.[5] My complaint was troublesome.

SATURDAY 19 MAY. Rev. Mr. O'Beirne breakfasted with us. I think I stayed in most part of the forenoon and wrote. Sat awhile at the Mount with Lord Kellie. Called on Seward and went with him to Sir George Baker's. Only Mrs. Horneck and Mr. Weston, a clergyman, there. Took with Lady Baker. Sir George said Dr. Johnson was the greatest creature he had ever seen, and talked with strong admiration of him. Said he had seen Monboddo after a concert was begun hand a lady up the room, turn two gentlemen out of their seats, sit down by the lady, and fall fast asleep. He said Sir J. Pringle had done all that application could do. Was well here. Seward and I called Burke and Sir Joshua; not in. Damp night. Hypped a little. Took him home with me and read him some of my *Hypochondriack*, and we did better than I expected.

SUNDAY 20 MAY. Awaked ill, sick with a headache. Threw up. Rose. Was so giddy and ill, was obliged to go to bed again. Had some coffee. Lay till about three, I think, when I grew better. Dressed and dined calmly amidst several foreigners. Was quite mild. Evening Miss Monckton's. Sir W. Howe and I as usual had a tête-à-tête conversation. We talked of the people of Scotland contrasted with the people of England

---

[4] Probably one of the "places" was Horace Walpole's. On 22 May Walpole wrote to Mason: "Boswell, that quintessence of busy-bodies, called on me last week, and was let in, which he should not have been, could I have foreseen it. After tapping many topics to which I made as dry answers as an unbribed oracle, he vented his errand. 'Had I seen Dr. Johnson's *Lives of the Poets?*' I said, slightly, 'No, not yet,' and so overlaid his whole impertinence. As soon as he could recover himself, with Caledonian sincerity, he talked of Macklin's new play, and pretended to like it, which would almost make one suspect that he knows a dose of poison has already been administered; though by the way I hear there is little good in the piece, except the likeness of Sir Pertinax to twenty thousand Scots" (*Correspondence*, ed. W. S. Lewis, xxix. 144–145).

[5] Boswell had extracted an unwilling interview from Bruce on his return from Abyssinia (1774) and had published it in the *London Magazine*. In it he had applied to Bruce Virgil's line describing Polyphemus: "Nec visu facilis nec dictu affabilis ulli" ("Forbidding in appearance, in speech to be accosted by no one"). At the time Bruce had given strong indications of disliking Boswell.

who are politicians. We talked of married men. The General said he thought a husband quite constant must be a cold companion not worth having, and the best is one who, after being away a while, likes his wife better than any other woman. Talked with Ladies Clermont, Pembroke, Mary Lowther, etc. Lady Craven bid me sit down by her. Asked me if I could keep a secret. Then invited me to a fine small party at her cottage on Wednesday to hear her read a new comedy she had written, and play on the harp.[6] Mr. Corry, Member for Newry, said he'd carry me. All gay to my fancy. Saw Lord Herbert, first time after his travels. Was charmed with the music. Home quiet.

MONDAY 21 MAY. Breakfasted with Bishop of Killaloe. Then in stage to Richmond to find Col. James Stuart. He was gone for London. Enchanted with Sally. Mrs. Stuart and Miss Danby on the Thames. Was taken into the boat a little. Had bread and milk. To town again in stage. Called for Colonel at Sir W. Cuninghame's; gone to dinner. Dined home with General and Gentili only. Went to Dr. Johnson's. Found him with Mrs. Williams. Settled he and I should not go to Club next day but dine with Mr. Allen the printer. In his garden told him how Wedderburn had said he'd have written his pamphlets though he had not had pension. "So I should," said he. "All," said I, "but *Taxation.*" "Nay," said he, "I should have written that if I writ any." "No, no," said I, "you'd have left Ministry to fight it out with the Colonies." "They must fight it out at last," said he. "But I should have always been against rebels." I went to find Col. James Stuart at his brother Charles's. Not there but at Lord Eglinton's. Went to them. Colonel could do little more than curse. Macdonell speechless. The Earl well. I drank some white wine negus and slipped away in reasonable time.

TUESDAY 22 MAY. Breakfasted by appointment with Lord Eglinton, who talked with me of a letter he had received from Coilsfield on the Ayrshire politics. I engaged to write to Sundrum on the subject. I perceived <the folly of> having carelessly talked . . .[7]

WEDNESDAY 23 MAY. Away with Corry to Lady Craven's cottage. Ranelagh night. Lord of Bedchamber.[8]

THURSDAY 24 MAY. With Lord Cathcart to Court. Introduced to

---

[6] *The Silver Tankard,* a musical farce acted at the Haymarket, 18 July 1781.

[7] The rest of the leaf, containing, if full, some one hundred and fifty words, has been torn off. The corresponding rough notes read, "Dined Allen's. Tea Dilly. Supped Allen's. Bishop of Killaloe night."

[8] He went to the Lord of the Bedchamber in waiting for that week (the Duke of Roxburgh) to request that he be presented to the Queen at the drawing-room to be held the next day.

Queen. King [did] not speak. Dined home. Mrs. Vesey's; Miss Luttrell, Bishop of Peterborough. Home with Mrs. Burke, well.

FRIDAY 25 MAY. Townley's with Bishop, etc. Beauclerk's sale. Dr. Johnson, cheerful. Very easy with him. Spoke of Lord Chesterfield's letter. HE. "You shall have it. You shall make one copy for self, one for me." Called Lord Pembroke. Sunday was day fixed to dine with him. With Lord Cathcart on guard, dinner.[9] [Followed] fine girl beyond Westminster Bridge. Ventured again. Vexed. Lord Eglinton's, well.

SATURDAY 26 MAY. Osborn breakfasted agreeably. With him to G. Byng's. To Baldwin's and finished *Hypochondriack*.[1] Dined Dr. Butter's with Dr. Johnson, [my] brother, and Pitt, curate of St. George's. Supped Dean of Carlisle.

SUNDAY 27 MAY. Rose very well. Moffat called and mentioned his poverty. Gave him half a guinea. Called Lord Bute. First said not at home. Then shown into the parlour. Then told not at home. Breakfasted Duke of Montrose's with his Grace and Lord Graham. Duke told two stories of my grandfather: that of his saying to Arniston he was racehorse, etc.; another that a minister's son was enlisted and my grandfather was lawyer to get him off. Nobody would be lawyer for the officer. My grandfather said, "What! shall it be held that putting a guinea into a man's hand makes him a soldier?" The Captain said, "I hope I may be allowed to speak. I wish I had a better fee, but here, Mr. Boswell, are two guineas in the King's name" (offering them). My grandfather drew back. "My Lords," said the officer, "I appeal if the gentleman's gestures are not more convincing than his arguments." He told me how in 1739 as he was riding down to Hampshire, he shot the highwayman, a grenadier of the Guards. Two of them were together. One, a big strong man, was close up with him, going to seize him. He fired and the man fell off dead. His servant, William, called, "Well done, my Lord," "Done!" said he, "I've done what I'm afraid will give me concern for some time." But he had no uneasiness when he reflected rationally on it. William replied, "Damn him, if you had not shot him, he would have shot you." His companion in confusion threw himself off his horse, fell on his knees, and begged quarter. William said, "Shall I take him?" "Why would you take him?" said the Duke. "Let him live and repent." So he got away. I made a good bull today. Talking with Lord Graham, I said if a man lay with my wife,

---

[9] Cathcart had guard duty; Boswell dined with him at the officers' mess.

[1] "It has for some time been a custom with me when I hear one praised as a sensible man to ask this simple question, 'Pray is he a sensible-speaking man or a sensible-acting man?' 'Both is best,' to adopt the vulgar witticism. But surely for the substantial advantage of a man and of his family the latter is preferable" (*The Hypochondriack*, No. 44, on prudence).

I would cut his throat behind his back. Duke sent service to my father. Said he had spirits, but deafness was worse than blindness.[2]

I then adored and was at elevation calmly devout in Portuguese Chapel. Then home and dressed and went to Court. The Queen spoke to me, and said, "Do you make some stay here or go to Scotland?" I answered, "I go to Scotland." The King spoke to me. "Have you been long here?" "Some weeks." "Do you go soon?" "Yes, Sir. I am obliged to go. I practise the law in Scotland." "How long have you done that?" "Some years, Sir. My father is one of Your Majesty's judges." "I know. How does he do? Is he pretty hearty?" "He grows old, Sir. He has laboured very hard." "And he wants to make you labour too." "I was a pressed man into the profession of the law, but I do as well as a volunteer." I admired Mrs. Loraine-Smith. She saw it. She came close to me and said, "I want to get out this way." "Madam," said I warmly, "you may go where you please. You may do what you please, or make any man do what you please." I made room for her to pass. She said, "I'm not going yet" (making a sign that she would wait till the King went away). "I hope," said I, "he shall stay an hour there, that you mayn't go away." We then talked of the appearance of the Court, etc. I was quite in love with her; or, more properly speaking, in admiration. I told Lord Loughborough Dr. Johnson was much pleased with his Lordship's saying he would have written his pamphlets though he had not pension. Said his Lordship: "Johnson could not bend his mind to write anything against his own way of thinking." I talked much with Lord Antrim, who presented me to the Archbishop of York,[3] with whom I talked awhile of Monboddo. Lord Stormont acknowledged me politely. Stopford and I talked awhile, and Lord Beauchamp and I. In short I was quite well and enjoyed Court. I was much taken with the Prince of Wales's pleasing countenance. I thought I could follow him. I walked out, saw Capt. James Erskine, and went home with him to Cleveland Row. Had lemonade and crust. Then in hackney-coach to Lord Pembroke's, with him while he dressed. We were pleasant and easy. Dined Lord Pembroke's. Moment of Claud.[4] Miss Monckton's; Duchess of Portland, Lady Howe, Lady Erskine, etc. Home in Lord Graham's carriage.

MONDAY 28 MAY. To Richmond. Colonel Charles and R. Mackye dined. Called Lady Di. Evening raving against journal.[5]

TUESDAY 29 MAY. Walk to Ham. Colonel sensible. Lord Elphinstone

[2] See above, 29 April 1781, near the beginning. The Duke was now losing his hearing.
[3] William Markham, D.C.L.
[4] He had a momentary meeting with Claud Boswell of Balmuto.
[5] Perhaps Colonel Stuart saw him posting the journal. (Mrs. Stuart certainly had: see above, 26 April 1781.)

and Sir W. [Cunynghame] came. To town for Burke's; too late. Greedy of wine. Home. General Oglethorpe's; Canary restorative. Bishop of Killaloe a little, serious on religion. Covenanted pardon, etc. Burke's a moment, saw him and her; to return at night perhaps. Called Lady Elgin and Dr. Smith. Bishop of Chester's; Nares, Heberden, etc. Dr. Johnson's *Poets*. Chamberlayne, difficulty as to practice. Christian of all men most miserable.[6] Yet a religious life pleasing. Away to Dr. Johnson, mentioned it. Scolded me.[7] Burke's at twelve. Bottle of beer. Bishop [8] there. Burke near two from Lord Rockingham's. BISHOP. "Rest. Oration [to-] day." Walked to his door.

WEDNESDAY 30 MAY. Awaked between seven and eight very well, though I had slept but about five hours. Went into the General's room. Talking of Dr. Johnson, he said, "What is upright is good for supporting a building, but does not ply to other uses." He meant that the Doctor has strong principles but stiff manners. He said I should by my humour and vivacity gain the acquaintance of people of consequence, and then by degrees show them that I have superior talents, so as to make myself of consequence to them. I should compose a speech for Lord Graham or Lord Mountstuart. He was friendly and animating. I breakfasted with Sir Joshua Reynolds comfortably. He expressed a kind wish for seeing more of me before I went to Scotland. There was nobody but Miss Palmer, he, and I; and we were pleasingly social. After breakfast she played on the pianoforte and sung charmingly, and I wrote out for her my ballad on Dr. Barnard's promotion, the first copy given to anybody. Then sat a little with Spottiswoode; left a card for Miss Howe, came home and dressed. Old Jamieson sat awhile with me and growled at the loss of his cause. I told him, whatever I thought as a private gentleman, I could not as a judge give it for him.

Donald Macdonald, my father's old servant, called on me. He was handsomely dressed. He said he came to inquire after his old master; that he had been at Auchinleck when General Paoli was there; [9] that he had come up here with an officer, then had served Squire Page, to whom he was recommended by Mr. Alexander Boswell, Dr. Boswell's son; that service was too hard for him. Mr. Page recommended him to the Bishop

---

[6] 1 Corinthians 15. 19. Paul says in effect that *if there is no life after death*, then Christians "are of all men most miserable." Chamberlayne seems to have removed the proviso. It is perhaps not without significance that he committed suicide the next year.
[7] Boswell repeated Chamberlayne's remarks and Johnson scolded him for countenancing such despondent doctrine.
[8] Barnard.
[9] In the autumn of 1771.

of Salisbury,[1] with whom he had now lived seven years; that he was butler and steward, had thirty-five guineas of wages, but with card-money and vails[2] his place was worth sixty guineas a year; that the Bishop had promised to give him some place, perhaps £50 or 60 a year; that the Bishop was a very old man, and he would live with him till he died; that last year he got a prize of £500 in the lottery, which he had in the three per cents; that he did not know that he had any relations alive, but he intended to go to Scotland with his money. Wished to know if he could do anything for me; he would get me franks if I wanted them. I said I was much obliged to him, but I knew some Members of Parliament who were so obliging as to give me what I wanted. I shook hands with him, rejoiced at his good fortune, wished him all success and happiness, and bid him call on me when I came to London again.

I then drove in the General's chariot to Court. It was a very full levee. The inner room was crowded to the door. Colonel Stopford and I walked in the outer room. At length the King came to the door, and bowed a signal to us in our turns to approach. I stood in some uneasiness lest he should not speak to me, as he first spoke to a gentleman on my left hand and then to Stopford on my right. But he relieved me. When I approached him, the following conversation took place. (I mark it before dinner on my return home.) KING. "When must you be in Scotland for your law?" BOSWELL. "The 12 of June, Sir. Our term begins that day." KING. "Have you practised the law long? Ever since you returned from abroad?" BOSWELL. "Yes, Sir." KING. "Ever since you came from Corsica?" BOSWELL. "Your Majesty is pleased to recollect my having been there." KING. "When did you see General Paoli?" BOSWELL. "I saw him today,

---

[1] John Hume, D.D.

[2] Gratuities given by visitors on their departure to the servants of a house in which they have been guests. By the middle of the eighteenth century it was widely felt that vails were being extorted rather than freely given. The house servants would customarily form a double line at the door at the end of an evening and await their tips. Servants who were not so rewarded would sometimes resort to violence. By this time, there was a graduated scale of proper vails for breakfast, drinking tea, or dinner. Card-money was a sub-division of the vail, left on the table at the end of an evening of gaming to reimburse the servants for the cost of the cards, refreshment, and lights. "*Card-money*, or leaving *twice* or *thrice* as much on the table as the cards used on it are worth, the servant being *supposed* to provide them at *his cost*, as is generally practised. This is well known to be carried much further, where the company play in the *high style*, that is, like *gamesters*, for the servants then pay also for *wax lights*; and sometimes for the *coals* they burn. . . . A *vast number* of people may by this means assemble at a small expense to the host" (Jonas Hanway, *Eight Letters to His Grace ——— Duke of ———, on the Custom of Vails-giving in England*, 1760, pp. 22–23).

Sir. I live in his house." KING. "Do you? That's but fair. I think him a man of an excellent heart." BOSWELL. "He is indeed, Sir; and is always very sensible of Your Majesty's goodness to him. But though Your Majesty is pleased to make him very comfortable as a private gentleman, I, who have seen him in Corsica, am sensible that it is a sad change." KING. "Was it not like to kill him at first? But I believe he is a philosopher." BOSWELL. "He is, Sir. But I remember when he was amongst our mountains (for he came down to us to Scotland), I heard him have this soliloquy: 'Ah, que cela me fait souvenir que je ne suis plus rien.' " [3] KING. "When he saw your hills?" BOSWELL. "Yes, Sir." KING. "He has very good sense." BOSWELL. "He has, Sir. Old Ambassador Keith said of him at my house, 'This is the most sensible man I ever saw.' " KING. "I believe he was a greater politician than a soldier." BOSWELL. "The French have been at great pains to depreciate him as a soldier. But from what I have been informed, I trust he had courage enough" (or "acted very well"). KING. "I don't mean he was deficient. But that his forte was being a legislator— in short, putting law into a people who were law*less*." "Yes, Sir," said I, "and he did it with great ability." After saying that General Paoli had an excellent heart, His Majesty added, "He is a great deal better than the people among whom he was. They were wild" (or some such word). "They were a brave people, Sir," said I. I was exceedingly happy at being allowed thus to talk with the Sovereign. I even felt some allowable vanity. Colonel Stopford said, "You've had a long conversation with the King." "Yes," said I. "He is a very sensible" (or "a very agreeable") "man. I wish to be acquainted with him." I spoke a little with the Bishop of Chester and Lord Stormont and young Charteris, who carried me home to the General's in his coach. I was in very fine spirits, and related to the General all that had passed at Court. Colonel Stopford luckily was not engaged to dinner, so I secured him to be with us. (All this I took care to write before dinner the same day.) Young Burke and Stopford, Statella, etc., dined. Mrs. Bach evening. The Bishop [gave me his] blessing. To Poultry.

THURSDAY 31 MAY. Rose quiet in my city *retirement*. My brother David and Mickle breakfasted. Then called on Dr. Towers; Dr. Watkinson with him. Was very entertaining. Towers said he had a high respect for Dr. Johnson, though he differed from him. I told from the best authority how his pension was given. Watkinson was glad to have this to tell. Mentioned Sheridan ringing the bell, as Lord Loughborough said.

---

[3] "Ah, how all that reminds me that I no longer am anything." A good example of the accuracy of Boswell's memory. He quotes this saying as he had recorded it in his Notes, 9 September 1771, merely substituting "*suis*" for "*vaux*."

"This," said I, "was effectual. He was *the mighty Tom*—'There's ne'er a man will leave his can, etc.' " [4] Talked of Priestley's Necessity. Said I disdained being the finest machine—not a gilded clock with diamond wheels. Saw Wilkes administer justice between master and apprentice, etc. [5] Called a little on Lockyer Davis. Then Tho. Davies, at dinner; tasted his cold roast beef and brandy and water. Proposed to meet with Macklin tonight at supper or tomorrow at dinner. Davies went ambassador; Macklin not at home. But message was left with Mrs. Macklin, and in a little came a note from him that he would with pleasure meet me, and that he would be at Mr. Davies's at eight and adjourn from thence to where we could fix (or some such phrase). My mind got into the old frame as when first in London. Had called Anderson and settled the loan of £500 by me to Bruce Boswell, under the Royal Exchange. Business done very neatly. Called Lord Antrim and left card: "Going to Scotland, but shall be proud to avail himself of Lord Antrim's acquaintance." Called Lord Percy. Then General's; Cavalli there. Lord Bute had sent this morning to know if I was at home. Wrote a card regretting being away to City, and wishing to see him tomorrow. Then hastened to Colonel Stopford, and took him to Mr. Burke's to dine. We waited till about six. But our orator did not come from the House. His lady, son, and brother, and I think Mr. Nugent and Mrs. Champion dined with us. It was very well. We drank tea. Miss Palmer came. Stopford and I walked so far and bid a cordial adieu.

I then went to Davies's; Macklin there. We were very courteous. He said, "Sir, I honour you." In a little we proceeded to the Shakespeare. They called, "Show the Apollo and Daphne." [6] As we walked up to it, Tom Davies

[4] Nobody has ever seemed to think it necessary to gloss Loughborough's remark (see above, 16 May 1781) that Thomas Sheridan's share in getting Johnson's pension was to have "rung the bell." The present passage at least shows how Boswell understood it: Sheridan effectually alerted all Johnson's friends and united them in a drive on Wedderburn; Wedderburn pushed Bute. Confident explanation of Boswell's wit in the present instance must wait on certain identification of his allusions. Two ingenious suggestions have been made to us in the mean time. (1.) *"The mighty Tom"* is Old Tom bell in the tower of Christ Church, Oxford, which towards midnight rings 101 times to call straying students back to the college before the gates are shut; none of the students will leave off guzzling beer till the bell rings. (2.) Thomas Sheridan, who was stage manager of Drury Lane Theatre for his son R. B. Sheridan during 1778–1780 and was of an autocratic disposition, may have called the actors to be ready for their entrances by ringing a bell behind scenes, or even by sending a messenger with a bell to nearby taverns. It should be added in fine that Boswell never demanded that this kind of wit should run on all fours.

[5] London aldermen sit as magistrates.

[6] The Shakespeare was a tavern in the Piazza, Covent Garden, the Apollo and Daphne no doubt one of its private rooms.

before the old genius and I after him, we both at one instant called out, "We have Apollo with us." It was a large, lofty room. We had a bottle of port, and ordered a light supper.[7] Macklin, as well he might, took the lead, and to my surprise talked not merely as a player and one who had seen variety of life, but as a man of extensive reading, strong and clear judgement. He said he was eighty-one, and he talked of something which he had witnessed, saying, "This was seventy years ago." It was curious and agreeable to sit with a man who had played with Wilks, Booth, Mrs. Oldfield, Old Cibber, etc., and was playing yet. I asked him if it was true, as said, that he had abridged his name. He said it was. His name was McLaughlin, and if he could have proved himself to be the identical Charles McLaughlin, the son of his father, he should have had an estate in Ireland. But having left the north of Ireland very young, he could not establish himself to be his father's son. He said he was of Scotch extraction. I asked if he would come to Scotland. Said he: "Will you insure me?" I promised I would. He told us as we walked to the Shakespeare that his *Love à la Mode* was first thought of at his house or lodgings in Great Russell Street (to which he pointed), Sir John Irwin, Dean Marlay, and somebody else whom he named, present. He said he wished to give a true-born Scotsman, a true-born Englishman, a true-born Irishman, and a true-born Welshman. When he gave two Irishmen, a bad and a good, (*where* was this?) the Irish supposed the good character to be meant as the true-born Irishman. But when he gave a good and bad Scotsman, the Scotch supposed the bad to be meant. "They are jealous," said I. Said he: "I have a Scotch lawyer, and I have a Scotch Highlander, an admirable character who has struggled through all difficulties. My original was General Frazer, who was killed at Saratoga, a fine fellow. He was not known to his countrymen. He left them young; and I aim to do honour to my clan (I think he said) and call him the laird of McLaughlin." [8]

[7] The bill for the supper has survived and is printed at the end of this entry.

[8] In trying to make sense of this passage, it should be kept in mind that Macklin was quite old, and had been given to large schemes all his life. *The Man of the World* had originally been called *The True-Born Scotchman. The True-Born Irishman* had been successful in Dublin, but failed in London and was immediately withdrawn (which perhaps accounts for Boswell's ignorance of it). The good and the bad Irishmen are not easy to explain: possibly Murrough O'Dogherty (good) and his wife (bad) in *The True-Born Irishman.* The bad Scotsman is Sir Pertinax MacSycophant and the good is his son Egerton. Macklin left no plays containing a "true-born Welshman," a Scotch lawyer, or a Highlander called the laird of McLaughlin. The confusion in his account of his characters is characteristic of Macklin: he plagiarized his early plays (or portions of them) for his later plays, so that the purity of his ideal national characters was bound to be somewhat muddled.

Bill at the Shakespeare, Covent Garden. Macklin, Tho. Davies, and I at supper, 31 May 1781.[9]

Bread and beer	0. 0. 9
Port	0. 5. 0
Stewed veal, etc.	0. 2. 0
Peas, toast, dressing, and butter	0. 2. 6
Ragout of sweetbread	0. 2. 6
Tartlets	0. 1. 0
Cheese and butter	0. 0. 9
Strong beer	0. 0. 6
Biscuits	0. 0. 6
Wax lights	
Claret	0. 5. 6
	£1. 1. 0
Claret	0. 5. 6
	£1. 6. 6
Waiter	3. 6
	£1.10. 0
10 shillings apiece.[1]	

SATURDAY 2 JUNE. Got up to prepare for setting out. Was somewhat languid, but packed very well. Brother T.D. came; read my *Hypochondriack* on prudence to him. He seemed much pleased with it. He breakfasted and bid adieu. Thought of visiting Lord Loudoun, etc., at other end of town, but perceived time run so fast, resolved against it. Was hurried after all. But happily felt no gulf between London and Edinburgh. Only perceived positive distance, which time and travelling could *certainly* overcome. Should have been with Dr. Johnson at twelve. Did not get to him till one. Found him in his garden, eating oranges in the sun. He took me upstairs, looked at the head for the octavo edition of his *Poets' Prefaces,* and said, " 'Tis surly Sam." [2] Got into hackney-coach and away to Dilly's in excellent spirits. T.D. there waiting to see us set out. Drank lemonade. Then Doctor and I drove away. Mr. C. Dilly came

[9] This heading (an endorsement in the manuscript) is in Boswell's hand, as is also everything below the total of £1. 1*s.* 0*d.*

[1] No entry has survived for 1 June 1781, and the *Life of Johnson* contains no conversation for that date.

[2] Published on 16 June 1781 in four volumes. The head (which is indeed surly) was engraved by Thomas Trotter from Reynolds's portrait of 1778.

in after we were out of the streets where I fancy he supposed himself known. It was a high satisfaction to find Dr. Johnson really with me thus. I slept some, it was so warm. Changed horses at Barnet.

Arrived at Welwyn about five. Dr. Johnson proposed tea. He had read close in Watson's *Chemistry*, Vol. 2,[3] and in *Rasselas*. As concerted with C. Dilly, I slipped away to Mr. Young's, son of Dr. Young; knocked at his door. Thought if received, well; if not, no matter. Housekeeper came. "Is Mr. Young at home?" "Yes, Sir." "Please tell him a gentleman wants to speak a single word to him." Shown into parlour. He and daughter, a young miss, beginning tea. "I beg pardon, Sir; I wish much to see this place if you'll give me leave." YOUNG. "Sir, we're just going to drink tea. Will you sit down?" "I thank you, Sir. But tea is ready for us at the inn. I am come from London. Dr. Johnson is with me. We are going to Mr. Dilly's at Southill" (YOUNG. "I know Mr. Dilly") "and to see Lord Bute's, and then I am to proceed to Scotland. My name is Boswell. I travelled with Dr. Johnson in the Western Islands. We did not think of it, or we might have had a recommendation to you from Mr. Crofts." [4] YOUNG. "Sir, I should think it a great honour to see Dr. Johnson here. Will you give me leave to send for him?" BOSWELL. "No, Sir; if you please, I'll go to him and bring him. He knows nothing of my calling here." He looked *steady*, as the phrase is; quite a country squire with a scratch wig. I went and told the Doctor, who agreed to go.[5] So we drank tea and eat bread and butter, and then walked to Young's. By the way the Doctor asked how he was to return, and on hearing "by the fly," he said, "If I had known there was to be such trouble, I would not have come. I have a great mind to go back." I was uneasy to see him fret. But on his being told a place would be secured in the fly, he said, "Well, well." When I introduced him to Young, he said, "Sir, I had a curiosity to come and see this place. I had the honour to know that great man, your father." Young was bluntly silent. He conducted us through his garden, etc., and we sat in the summer-house and saw the library. Poor collection. Himself had bought the classics. Only the books marked on the back with written numbers were his father's. Dr. Johnson thought him very unknowing, and wondered how he had got such uncouth manners. He said of the Doctor, "He is a great man." The

---

[3] The first two volumes of *Chemical Essays* by Richard Watson, D.D., had just been published. It was to this Richard Watson, then Bishop of Llandaff, that Wordsworth in 1793 addressed the *Apology for the French Revolution* which was found unpublished among his papers.

[4] Properly Croft. See above, 8 May 1781.

[5] Boswell later wrote a second account of this visit, repeating some details of the first version, omitting some, and adding a great many others. It is printed at the end of this entry.

Doctor told that Dr. Young had sent for him to Richardson's and read to him his *Conjectures on Original Composition*. We went to church and saw monument.[6] He offered me very good cider. I accepted. This kept us a little. Mr. Dilly told Dr. Johnson, "Mr. Boswell's wanting a glass of cider." Said the Doctor: "Ay, he's always wanting something." Had it, that I might drink in Dr. Young's house. Said to Mr. Young I should take the liberty to call when passing from Scotland. YOUNG. "I shall be glad to see you, Sir." All well enough.

Drove pleasingly cool to Southill. Squire, Miss Dilly, and Miss Davies, rather interesting. Hearty supper. The Doctor took several strong-ale glasses of syllabub with brandy in it. After supper Miss Dilly asked him what he'd have for breakfast. (I said, "Cold sheep's head?" and told the story at Lochbuie's.)[7] Would he have gruel? I was much diverted. (When I joked with him next morning before he was up about the gruel, he pleasantly evaded me by saying, "You are a judge of oatmeal; go and see if it be good.") He smiled drolly and asked what she took. "Coffee and tea," said she. Said I: "The Doctor is a great coffee-and-tea man." He told me today when he drank very large quantities of tea he took no other liquid, not even water. I went to his room; joked on the odd notions as to what a Doctor must have, and said, "You're Pantagruel." Hoped to be well in spirits in Scotland.[8]

At first when I told him that Mr. Young would be proud to see him at tea, he was rather displeased, and said, "What is the meaning of this? One does not like to accept, nor does one like to refuse." But when I told him I had mentioned we were to drink tea at the inn and would call after, he said, "O, very well," and took his repast heartily. There is just in a line with the door into the garden at Mr. Young's a gravel walk, on each side of which is a row of ——— trees, seven and seven, which Dr. Johnson called a fine grove. They are large and form a canopy at top. They were planted by Dr. Young. Mr. Young remembered them all brought in a cart drawn by one horse. He seemed fond of a deception suggested by Dodsley and put up at the

[6] Which Mr. Young had erected to his parents.

[7] "Before Mr. Johnson came to breakfast, Lady Lochbuie said he was a 'dungeon of wit,' a very common phrase in Scotland, though Mr. Johnson told me he had never heard it. She proposed that he should have some cold sheep-head for breakfast. Sir Allan [Maclean, Lady Lochbuie's brother] was very angry at her vulgarity. 'I think,' said I, 'it is but fair to give him an offer of it. If he does not choose it, he may let it alone.' 'I think so,' said the lady. When Mr. Johnson came in, she called to him, 'Do you choose any cold sheep-head, Sir?' 'No, Madam,' said he, with a tone of surprise and anger. 'It's here, Sir,' said she, as if he had refused it to save the trouble of bringing it. He confirmed his refusal sufficiently; and I was entertained to see the ludicrous cross-purposes" (Journal, 22 October 1773, at Lochbuie in Mull).

[8] The end of the entry as originally written. See the last note but two.

summit of the green field on the other side of the brook Mimram, which runs at the foot of the garden. It is boards painted like a brick summer-house, the door open and a chair seen. "Mimram," said he, "is the name of an Egyptian midwife." [9] Both he and the Doctor called this a river. It is but a brook.

Mr. Young has added to the summer-house a cold bath by enclosing with boards a portion of the brook. In the summer-house is a case with glass panes containing tea-china and another containing a few modern books. On the entablature (I mean the open, thus,[10] of the outer end wall) is "Ambulantes in horto, audiebant vocem Dei," and under it, with reference to the river or brook, "Vivendi recte qui prorogat horam," [1] etc. Young said, "These were my father's inscriptions, and I have not effaced them." I said I was told his father was cheerful. Young said, "He was too well-bred a man not to be cheerful in company, but he was gloomy alone. He never was cheerful after my mother's death, and he had met with many disappointments." Dr. Johnson said afterwards, "This was no favourable account of his father. For it is no credit" (or some such word) "to a man to be gloomy because he has not got preferments enough, nor to have so little acquiescence in the ways of Providence as to continue long gloomy for the loss of his wife. Grief has its time." Young said his father had a subscription of some thousands for his *Universal Passion*, all which he

---

[9] Professor Albrecht Goetze thought that the ultimate source of this remarkable piece of information might have been the sixth-century pseudepigraphic book called *The Cave of Treasures*, a compendious history of the world from the Creation to the Crucifixion. In it the name of the daughter of Pharaoh who brought up Moses is given as Makri, but there are variations of spelling in the manuscripts, and a variant Mamri or Mamre would not be surprising. The mediaeval chronicles contain a good deal of such apocryphal material, but he had not found this particular bit there. In any case, the etymology is purely fanciful.

[10] Boswell has drawn here a small rough sketch which shows that by "entablature" he meant "pediment" and by "under it," "entablature."

[1] The second Latin quotation (properly "Qui recte vivendi," etc.) is Horace, *Epistles*, I. ii. 41–43: "The man who puts off the hour of right living [is like the clown who waits for the river to run out"]; the first is a Romantic perversion of Genesis 3. 8 ("And they heard the voice of the Lord God walking in the garden"). The Latin of the inscription, which is presumably Young's own (the Vulgate text is quite different) means, "As they walked in the (or a) garden, they heard the voice of God." The accuracy of Boswell's report is guaranteed by another made by Young's curate, John Jones (*Correspondence of Edward Young*, ed. Henry Pettit, 1971, p. 600). Sir Herbert Croft in the biography of Young which he wrote for Johnson's *Prefaces to the Works of the English Poets* (paragraph 87) gives the inscription as "Ambulantes in horto audierunt vocem Dei," but there are two independent witnesses against him, and the imperfect "audiebant" is inherently more probable. Young meant a continuing action ("were wont to hear") rather than a single encounter.

lost in the Sea.[2] Dr. Johnson said this was not true. Nobody had ever seen a subscription book. I said to Young, "I should have liked to have seen Dr. Johnson and your father together." "Ay!" said Young with some appearance of emotion. He mentioned Crofts, Junior, and very sensibly said it was wrong in him in *Love and Madness,* which he wrote, to bring in circumstances which he owned were not true. Said I: "Truth and fiction should not be mingled."[3] "No," said Dr. Johnson, "fiction should not be introduced where there is a basis of truth." Said I: "He has mentioned me in that book as attending executions." Said Dr. Johnson: "I talked to him of that, and told him he was mistaken." Said I: "I used to go much, but I've cured myself of it."[4] On the road, talking of publications, the Doctor said, "My opinion, I have found, is no rule for the sale of a book." I asked him if he had been much plagued with authors sending him their compositions to revise. "No, Sir," said he, "I have been thought a sour, surly fellow." "Very lucky for you," said I, "in that respect." I had much internal satisfaction at Young's, thinking that I was actually in the garden of the author of *Night Thoughts,* which made such an impression on my mind in early life; and I had an agreeable association of ideas of all this with my dear cousin and wife, with whom I used to read the *Night Thoughts.* Yet I felt some unreasonable regret in feeling that I might have been here with Dr. Young and seen him just like an ordinary man in many parts of life. There is a picture of him in the parlour which Mr. Young said was a copy by Sir Joshua Reynolds from Ramsay. Dr. Johnson did not believe this.

SUNDAY 3 JUNE. Rose quite well, and had whey, and breakfasted. The Doctor and I and the two Dillys went to church. Mr. Smith read prayers. His nephew preached from John on sending the Comforter.[5] I stayed the Communion and was very devout. Only nineteen communi-

---

[2] That is, the South Sea Bubble. Isaac Reed, in a very useful list of corrections and additions to the *Life of Johnson,* sent to Boswell c. November 1792 and now at Yale, pointed out that the South Sea year was 1720, and that *The Universal Passion* was published in 1726 and 1727.

[3] In the previous year Croft had published a narrative of the murder of Martha Ray (see above, following 10 April 1779) in what purported to be a series of letters from Miss Ray and Hackman. Only a few of them were genuine.

[4] The passage is in a supposed letter from Hackman to Miss Ray, dated 27 June 1777, describing the execution of Dr. Dodd: "Your H. is neither *artiste* nor *amateur* [of executions]—nor do I, like Paoli's friend and historian, hire a window by the year which looks upon the Grassmarket at Edinburgh" (*Love and Madness,* 1780, p. 103). There is no record of Boswell's having attended an execution between 19 April 1779 (Hackman's) and 28 April 1785, but in the latter year he suffered a bad relapse, for he attended at least three more.

[5] John 14.26, 15.26, 16.7. Appropriately, it being Whitsunday (Pentecost).

cants. Mr. Smith wished to have us to tea at his house and sent card. It rained and thundered a good deal this forenoon. I went to the Doctor's room and was not afraid of the lightning, though near. He said I did right to stay the Communion. He had not thought of it.[6] I said, "I'd fain be good, and I am very good just now. I fear God and honour the King; wish to do no ill, and to do good to all mankind." He cautioned me against trusting to impressions. Said there was a middle state of mind between conviction and hypocrisy, of which many were conscious (a fine remark), and that by being subject to impressions a man was not a free agent. If so, he should not be suffered to live. If he owns he cannot help acting in a particular way, there can be no confidence in him, no more than in a tiger. He said, "No man believes himself impelled irresistibly. We know that he who says he believes it, lies." He said that in general no man could be sure of acceptance with God. Yet perhaps some had had it revealed to them. Paul, who wrought miracles, may have had a miracle wrought on himself. Yet Paul, though he expresses strong hope, also expresses [fear] lest having preached to others, he himself should be a castaway.[6a] We talked of Original Sin and the Sacrifice of Christ. I prevailed with him to dictate some sentences to me on the subject.[7] I was in an excellent frame and thought I should preserve it in Scotland. The Rev. Mr. Palmer, Fellow of Queen's College, Cambridge, dined with us.[8] We had a most hearty dinner, and the Doctor was much pleased. He said that he had not observed that men of great fortunes got anything extraordinary that makes happiness. What had Duke of Bedford? What, Duke of Devonshire? The only instance he knew of a manly enjoyment of wealth was Jamaica Dawkins, who, going to Palmyra and hearing it was infested by robbers, hired a troop of Turkish horse to guard him.[9]

[6] That is, had not made previous preparation.

[6a] I Corinthians 9. 27.

[7] They appear in the *Life of Johnson* under the record for this day.

[8] Thomas Fyshe Palmer soon after this became a Unitarian, renounced his prospects in the Church of England, and became minister of a Unitarian society in Dundee. In 1793 he attended a meeting of the Friends of Liberty in that city and revised the draft of an address to the public complaining of the heavy war taxation and advocating universal suffrage and short parliaments. The authorities, who had been thrown into a state of frenzy by the Reign of Terror in France, indicted him for treason and sentenced him to seven years' transportation. In spite of the efforts of Fox to obtain reversal of the sentence, he was sent to Botany Bay and served his full term. In 1800 he combined with others to purchase a vessel for trading on the way home. After a series of misadventures, they put in at an island in the Marianas, then under Spanish rule, where they were treated as prisoners of war. Palmer was attacked with dysentery and died at Guam on 2 June 1802. Two years later his body was exhumed by an American captain and taken to Boston for burial.

[9] James Dawkins (1722–1757), born in Jamaica, was an ardent Jacobite and just as

Mr. Palmer wished better provision made for parish clerks. The Doctor approved, and said he should be a man who could make a will or write a letter for anybody in the parish.

I mentioned Monboddo's opinion that the Egyptians were woolly blacks. Mr. Palmer said, did it appear from the mummies? Dr. Johnson approved of this test.[1]

We went and saw the church. The Doctor would not go down to the Torrington burial-place, though open and light. He has a strange horror for dead bodies and tombs. We drank tea at the Vicar's, our ladies with us. Miss Davies was really elegant, I thought.

Doctor said, when I observed thieves timorous, "No wonder; afraid of being shot getting into a house, and hanged getting out."

Told us at night he had once written six sheets in one day: forty-eight quarto pages of a translation of Crousaz on Pope, published by itself in 1740 or 1741.[2] He'd be glad to see it now. And he wished he had copies of all pamphlets written against him, as it is said Pope had.

He said he took to Dr. Gibbons, and said to Mr. Dilly, "I shall be glad to see him. Tell him if he'll call on me and dawdle over a dish of tea in an afternoon, I shall take it kind."

When the cards of invitation for tea came from Mr. Smith's and were delivered by Squire Dilly, he said, "We must have Mr. Dilly's leave. We cannot leave your house, Sir, without your permission"—very polite, though formal. I said, "Has any man the same conviction of the truth of religion that he has in the common affairs of life?" He said,

---

ardent an enthusiast for antiquity. On a journey to "the most remarkable places of antiquity," from which he carried off a great number of sculptures and artefacts, Dawkins hired "an escort of the Aga [of Hassia]'s best Arab horsemen," which increased his caravan "to about two hundred persons" (Robert Wood, *The Ruins of Palmyra*, 1753, unpaged address of the Publisher to the Reader, and p. 34).

[1] Monboddo's notion was borrowed from Herodotus (Bk. II, ch. 104). One of the editors of Herodotus answers Palmer's query: "The mummies have always been found to possess straight hair, and ... in the paintings the Egyptians are represented as *red*, not black" (J. W. Blakesley, *Herodotus with a Commentary*, 1852–1854, i. 239 n. 293).

[2] *A Commentary on Mr. Pope's Principles of Morality, or Essay on Man, by Mons. Crousaz*, duodecimo in 328 pages, printed for publication in 1739 but perhaps withdrawn; reissued with the date 1742. In the *Life of Johnson* Boswell reduced his substantially correct "translation of Crousaz on Pope, published by itself in 1740 or 1741" to "translation from the French," no doubt, as Dr. Powell suggests, because he had never come upon but one translation of Crousaz on Pope of that date, and he knew that that, though sometimes attributed to Johnson, was actually by Elizabeth Carter. (Johnson's pamphlet is surprisingly rare.) Boswell also omitted his "forty-eight quarto pages," presumably because those words were an interpolation of his own, and would have been correct only if the book was in quarto.

"No, Sir." I mentioned that the Bishop of Killaloe maintained there was merit in faith. "Why, yes, Sir," said he. "Were hell open before him, no man would take a fine woman to his arms. We must, as the Apostle says, live by faith, not by sight." He made a good distinction at Mr. Smith's as to forgetfulness being a man's own fault. "To remember and to recollect are different. A man has not the power to recollect what is not in his mind. But when a thing is in his mind, he may remember it." The remark was occasioned by my leaning back on a chair which I had perceived to be broke on leaning on it a little before. Said he: "It's being broke was certainly in your mind." [3]

MONDAY 4 JUNE.[4] On Monday 4 June we went to Luton Hoo to see Lord Bute's magnificent place, for which I had obtained a ticket. As we entered the park I talked in a high style of my old friendship with Lord Mountstuart and said, "I shall probably be much at this place." The Sage, aware of human vicissitudes, gently checked me. "Don't you be too sure of that." He made two or three peculiar observations, as when shown the botanical garden, "Is not *every* garden a botanical garden?" When told that there was a shrubbery to the extent of several miles, "That is making a very foolish use of the ground. A little of it is very well." When it was proposed that we should walk on the pleasure-ground, "Don't let us fatigue ourselves. Why should we walk there? Here's a fine tree, let us get to the top of it." But upon the whole he was very much pleased. He said, "This is one of the places I do not regret coming to see. It is a very stately house indeed. In the house magnificence is not sacrificed to convenience, nor convenience to magnificence. The library is very splendid, the dignity of the rooms is very great, and the quantity of pictures is beyond expectation, beyond hope."

It happened happily without any previous concert that we visited the seat of Lord Bute upon the King's birthday. We dined and drank His Majesty's health at an inn in the village of Luton.

---

[3] Boswell in this passage can hardly have done justice to Johnson's powers of succinct and precise definition. Some of the difficulties disappear if one assumes that Johnson is giving the word "mind" the sense it bears in the expression "to have in mind," that is, to have something within the area of one's current mental attention. Having in mind is a matter of will. A man cannot by an act of will recollect instantly what has somehow passed out of "mind," but he can and should *keep* in mind matter of quite recent observation that might affect his behaviour. Surely, however, Boswell did in fact forget, and what one forgets is not at that moment in the "mind." The last sentence would seem more properly to have read "The fact that the chair was broke was certainly in your mind a few moments ago, and you should have kept it so."

[4] If there ever was a journal entry for 4 June 1781, it has not survived. The account that follows is taken from the first draft of the *Life of Johnson*.

TUESDAY 5 JUNE. At breakfast between eight and nine, Dr. Johnson was pleasant. I said Mr. C. Dilly was resolved not to marry a pretty woman.[5] Said he: "It is foolish to resolve against marrying a pretty woman. No, I'd rather marry a pretty woman, unless there are objections to her. A pretty woman may be foolish. A pretty woman may be wicked. A pretty woman may not like me. But there is no such danger in marrying a pretty woman as is apprehended. She will not be persecuted if she does not invite persecution. A pretty woman, if she has a mind to be wicked, can find a readier way than another; and that is all."

We had Mr. Dilly's chaise to Shefford. He courteously returned him thanks for all his favours. At Shefford we had tea and bread and butter again. I asked if it would not be rational for me to get into the great circle of life if I could. He said yes. I said my wife was very willing to come to London. She thought it would be of great advantage for the education of the children. That her son would have a better chance of being a great man. But that I would make him retain at the same time an affection for the old rock.[6] "That," said the Doctor, "you could not." Said I: "He would go to Scotland every year." Said he: "As Lord Bute does." Said he: "As an Englishman, I should wish all the Scotch gentlemen to be educated in England. Scotland would become a province. They'd spend all their rents in England." I was sorry to part with him. I was affectionate towards him. The Bedford coach came. He embraced me and said, "Fare you well. GOD bless you for Jesus Christ's sake." I paid half a guinea for his seat, saying that if I had had my own coach, he should have had it, and this was cheaper. He was alone, and drove off. (I mentioned my being plagued with narrowness, and how Lord Mountstuart made me give two pauls [7] instead of one, to give me the faculty of parting easily with money. "He was right," said the Doctor.)

I drove back to Southill; wrote journal a little till the two Dillys were ready. Then they and I set out in the chaise for Bedford. Stopped at Mr. Nesbit's, who showed us several pictures of his own painting. He had dined with me at Sir Joshua's; had been intimate with him, Goldsmith, etc.[8] His grandfather, he said, was a Scotsman from the Border. Arrived at Bedford; the old bridge and St. Mary's Church the first objects. Drove to the Swan. Were accosted by Smith the chaplain, then by ———— Smith,

---

[5] None of the Dilly brothers, nor their sister Martha, ever married.

[6] The Castle of Auchinleck.

[7] Or paoli, an obsolete Italian silver coin worth about fivepence sterling.

[8] Probably John Nesbit, Justice of the Peace and Deputy Lieutenant for Bedfordshire, who died at Cotton End (on the road between Shefford and Bedford) in 1783. He is presumably the "Mr. Nesbitt" who sat to Reynolds in 1759 and 1761, and also the Nesbitt mentioned in Goldsmith's verses beginning "Your mandate I got."

who asked us to dine with the Corps. Squire Dilly was a man of consequence here. Several officers asked him to dine with the mess. This was what I wished. Walked to the bowling-green, on top of what was the old fort. Fine views of the country from it; extraordinary. Walked on and looked at the Moravian manufactory at the head of the town.[9] Called on Rev. Mr. Macaulay, who was ill and confined to the house. Then down the High Street. I liked to see the signposts hanging in the old way. It gives a crowded variety to a street.[1]

SUNDAY 10 JUNE. (Writing Monday 18.) Visited Dr. Webster. Was agitated when again in the house where I had seen the poor Colonel so often, but behaved decently.[2] The Doctor supported himself by GOD's grace wonderfully well. I went to his seat forenoon and afternoon, and he to the elder's seat.[3] Mr. Peckwell preached in the forenoon. Mr. Kemp in the afternoon, an affecting funeral conclusion. The text, ———. I cried much, and most of the congregation shed tears. I shook hands with Mr. Kemp after church, thanked him, and desired to be better acquainted with him. My wife and I dined with Dr. Webster between sermons. In the evening visited Sir John Pringle; found him better than I expected. Drank tea with him. Called Evory and fixed next day at eleven to go and wait on Captain Macbride.[4] Home and heard the children say divine lessons comfortably.

MONDAY 11 JUNE. (Writing on Tuesday the 19.) Met Evory at Edinburgh at eleven, after having visited Dr. Webster and Commissioner Cochrane. Walked with him to Leith, and went so far in a boat towards Captain Macbride's ship, when we heard he was at land; took places in the fly and followed him to town; met him in Princes Street; found him to be a pleasant, clever, fine fellow. Walked half-way back to Leith with him. Engaged him to dine with me on Thursday. Dined and drank tea at the Commissioner's with Dr. Webster. Drank rather too much, to be comfortable with His Holiness. Was somewhat uneasy at night.

TUESDAY 12 JUNE. (Writing on Tuesday the 19.) Went to the Lord President's and paid my respects. Was free and easy among the judges.

[9] A Moravian congregation had been established at Bedford in 1745. The "manufactory" was perhaps operated by the women of the community, who engaged in embroidery and tambour work.

[1] If any entries were written for 6–9 June, they have not survived.

[2] Lt.-Col. James Webster was mortally wounded at the battle of Guilford Courthouse, 15 March 1781, where he commanded a brigade. The news had only recently reached England.

[3] At the Tolbooth Church, of which Dr. Webster was Minister.

[4] Captain (later Admiral) John Macbride was one of Mrs. Boswell's Irish cousins (his mother was a Boyd). At this time he was in command of the frigate *Artois*, convoy to the Baltic trade.

Felt luckily a kind of avidity for practice in the Court of Session. Dr. Webster and Commissioner Cochrane dined and drank tea with us at our country-house.[5]

WEDNESDAY 13 JUNE. (Writing on Tuesday the 19.) Dined at the Hon. A. Gordon's on a family dinner. Drank tea with Mr. George Wallace, after which he and I visited Sir John Pringle and walked in the Meadow with him and his dull women, Miss Hall and Miss Gray.

THURSDAY 14 JUNE. (Writing on Tuesday the 19.) Captain Macbride, the Hon. A. Gordon, Evory, Sibthorpe, the Lord Provost,[6] Major Montgomerie dined with us at our town house. All went on well. My dear wife was happy to see her Irish cousin, and I to show a connexion of hers any civility in my power. Our four eldest children came in after dinner. We drank tea. At night, eat strawberries with Lady Colville.

FRIDAY 15 JUNE. (Writing on Tuesday the 19.) Got what little business I had in the Court of Session managed for me, and my wife and I and Miss Grant (Dr. Grant's daughter), Veronica, Phemie, and Sandy got into a hackney-coach, which came for us about six in the morning, and drove to Leith, taking with us the Lord Provost, Hon. A. Gordon and his Countess, and other ladies; or rather being joined by them. Evory and Sibthorpe also joined; and away we sailed in two boats sent by Captain Macbride to his ship, the *Artois*. I was pleased to see my children sail for the first time. It was a charming day. We had a good breakfast, saw all parts of the ship, then sailed to a three-decked ship, the *Princess Amelia* (Captain Macartney),[7] Sir Hyde Parker being with us all the time, and saw her well. Then sailed back again through the numerous fleet of merchantmen bound for the Baltic, back again to Leith. My wife and children were sick returning. I was entertained with this naval sight, but was also shocked to see such a number of men shut up in a state little better than dogs in a kennel, with the addition of horrible dangers. I did not like to think of the *system of things*. My spirits were not as when in London. Edinburgh operates like the *Grotta del Cane* on my vivacity.[8] I dined at the Lord Provost's with Admiral Parker[9] and all the navy cap-

[5] At Drumsheugh. Mrs. Boswell must have moved the family in his absence.

[6] David Steuart.

[7] Captain John Macartney was killed two months later in the action with the Dutch at Dogger Bank. See below, 13 August 1781.

[8] Boswell had visited the Grotta del Cane, near Pozzuoli, when he was in Italy in 1765. A dog was used to demonstrate the effects of the suffocating vapour (carbon dioxide) which collected along the floor: hence the name.

[9] Vice-Admiral Hyde Parker (later a baronet), in command of the squadron. Sir Hyde Parker, mentioned earlier, was his son, knighted for his exploit of opening the North River, New York, in 1776. He was in command of the frigate *Latona*.

tains, Hon. A. Gordon, Sir W. Forbes, Sir P. Ainslie, etc. Lived freely, but not to excess.[1]

[TUESDAY 19 JUNE.] . . . in Captain Macbride's cutter, which was manned for me, and thus did I sail to the *Latona* and visit Sir Hyde Parker and the company on board of him. Sir Hyde came with me to the *Artois*. After an uneasy sail back to Leith, I went home with Lady Colville to dinner. The Scottish vulgarity of manners and censorious cast of her and Lady Anne and Andrew disgusted me. I drank tea at home; then went to town and dictated some. Was uneasy at night that my indisposition did not seem abating.[2]

WEDNESDAY 20 JUNE. (Writing on Thursday the 21.) Was still languid and without relish of life. However, I said nothing, but attended the Court of Session, dictated wonderfully well, dined in town by myself on a broiled chicken, and in the evening sat a long time with Sir John Pringle, whom I found quite alone.

THURSDAY 21 JUNE. (Writing on Monday the 25.) The day passed in dullness as usual. I sat some time with Sir John Pringle at night.

FRIDAY 22 JUNE. (Writing on Monday the 25.) Drank a dish of tea at Lord President's in the morning. Such a day as this may be simply recorded *ditto*. George Wallace's observation is very just: that one is quite a different animal in Edinburgh and in London. Was at the concert.

SATURDAY 23 JUNE. (Writing on Monday the 25.) When I got to my town house, Captain Macbride called on me to make an apology that he could not go to Drumsheugh this morning to see my wife. I know not well how the forenoon loitered away. I dined at Dunn's Hotel in St. Andrew's Square with the Admiral and several officers both of the Baltic and Jamaica squadrons. Had no *gaieté de cœur*. Was very sober; drank tea with them. Went home quiet.

SUNDAY 24 JUNE. (Writing on Tuesday the 26.) My wife and I and three eldest children walked decently from our country-house to the New Church and heard Dr. Blair. Lord Kames stumbled at the foot of the stair which leads up to the lords' loft, and fell on the pavement, by which he cut his forehead and three of his fingers a little. I visited him afterwards, and found him not a bit disconcerted. I dined by special invitation with the Admiral and the captains of the squadron—a turtle feast, eighteen in

---

[1] Two pages, containing the entries for 16, 17, 18, and part of 19 June, have been removed. See below, 16 July 1781 and n. 5.

[2] The usual "morbus," which he had brought home from London. Boswell has inked out the greater part of this sentence, and of that in which he passes such harsh judgement on the Kellie family.

company. I drank more today than I had done for some time, and was a little disturbed. Drank tea, and at ten visited Sir John Pringle.

MONDAY 25 JUNE. (Writing on Tuesday the 26.) Was somewhat uneasy from the small excess of yesterday. Sir Hyde Parker and Captain Macbride called on me, and I went with them to Dr. Grant's and heard Miss Grant play. My wife dined with me in our town house. Worthy Grange arrived today. I drank tea with him, and was consoled and revived by his sensible, cheerful, friendly conversation.

TUESDAY 26 JUNE. (Writing on Tuesday 3 July.) Admiral Parker, Sir Hyde, and Captain Macbride, Sir W. and Lady Forbes, Mrs. Dundas of Arniston and Miss, and Miss Grant passed the evening with us and supped. My wife and I lay in town.

WEDNESDAY 27 JUNE. (Writing on Tuesday 3 July.) I had visited Sir John Pringle yesterday forenoon. This day I dined on board the *Latona*; Sir Hyde Parker, the Admiral, Captain Macbride, Lord Balcarres, and several ladies and gentlemen there. It was now a fair wind for the Baltic fleet. So they were all afloat while we were on board, as was the *Latona*. It was a fine animating scene, and I really liked the sea today. Captain Napier had two boats which took us to Leith. I drank more today than was good for my health. But it strengthened my spirits. I was glad to be again in my garden at night.

THURSDAY 28 JUNE. (Writing on Tuesday 3 July.) My wife and I dined at Sir W. Forbes's, where some of the captains of the Jamaica fleet were expected but by mistake did not come. We stayed tea. Balmuto walked out with us and supped.

FRIDAY 29 JUNE. (Writing on Tuesday 3 July.) Captain Courtnay, of my friend Colonel Stuart's regiment, who had come home in the Jamaica fleet, had called on me on Tuesday. He and Grange dined with us today at our country-house. He stayed tea. Lady Colville and Lady Anne Erskine were then with us. I walked into town with him. Visited Sir John Pringle, a pretty long tête-à-tête.

SATURDAY 30 JUNE. (Writing Tuesday 3 July.) This was a very poor week of practice as a lawyer. I got only one guinea. I thought that my having little practice would make my removing to London more rational. Sir John Pringle and Miss Gray and Surgeon Wood dined and drank tea with us at our country-house. Sir John sauntered with me in my garden pretty placidly, and I liked it. He pressed me to go home with him, saying it would do him more good than anything else. So I went from sincere gratitude; and we talked a long time tête-à-tête. I was near growing too violent against his Arian notions. His despondency and weariness hurt my spirits. I had no vivid enjoyment.

SUNDAY 1 JULY. (Writing Tuesday the 3.) Lay long in bed agreeably. It was a showery forenoon. The children said divine lessons. My wife and I walked in to the New Church afternoon, and then dined and drank tea with Sir J. Pringle; Dr. Hope's family there.

MONDAY 2 JULY. (Writing on Wednesday the 4.) Dictated pretty well. Dined by myself in town. Grange walked out with us at night and supped.

TUESDAY 3 JULY. (Writing on Wednesday the 4.) Lost two causes: one before Lord Braxfield and one before the Lords. I was quite clear I was in the right in both, and was really hurt to find justice so ill administrated. Worthy Grange walked out with me to Sir Alexander Dick's, who had been ill of his annual asthmatic complaint and really in danger, but was now better. I was uneasy to think I had not visited him since my return from London. But my apology was soon accepted. I had little relish of existence, and was perpetually thinking of this, and wearying. Baron Maule had died last night. As he had been a man whom in my early years I had viewed in a grand style, I was saddened by such a memento of the *end* of human consequence.[3] Visited Sir John Pringle at night. Mr. George Wallace with him.

WEDNESDAY 4 JULY. (Writing on Tuesday the 10.) Was not at all in good spirits. My dear wife persuaded me to go out with her to dinner. I was so much pleased with my garden and children that I grew pretty easy and indulged tranquillity instead of going into town to labour. Lady Ainslie drank tea with us, and carried my wife and me to town in her coach. After dictating some, I think I went to Sir J. Pringle's.

THURSDAY 5 JULY. (Writing on Tuesday the 10.) Existed drearily. Dined by myself. My father came to town this afternoon. Visited him in the evening. He did not attack me on having gone to London. But was quite indifferent. His women were disagreeable as usual.

FRIDAY 6 JULY. (Writing on Tuesday the 10.) My father did not come to the Court. I dined with him. But was fretted to find him show me no affection. I dictated pretty well. Drank tea with Grange. Visited Sir J. Pringle.

SATURDAY 7 JULY. (Writing on Friday the 13.) Mr. Stalker, the English master, dined with us and stayed tea. Miss Susie Dunlop drank tea. I was easy, without much relish of life. Sauntered all the evening. Had visited Sir John Pringle in the forenoon.

SUNDAY 8 JULY. (Writing on Friday the 13.) Was at the New Church

[3] John Maule of Inverkeillor, one of the barons of the Court of Exchequer in Scotland. In July 1764, while on his travels in Germany, Boswell thought himself "a kind of Baron Maule. I will take care to have all the elegancies of life." As he became more convinced that hypochondria is ill health, he "resolved to live like Baron Maule" (Journal, 10, 28 July 1764).

forenoon and afternoon. Dined at my father's between sermons. Walked home to tea with my wife. It came on a heavy rain. So I did not get to Sir John Pringle's. The children said divine lessons.

MONDAY 9 JULY. (Writing on Wednesday the 18.) Dictated pretty well. Mr. Lawrence Hill and Mr. Lawrie dined with us in the country. At night visited Sir John Pringle.

TUESDAY 10 JULY. (Writing on Wednesday the 18.) Nothing to remark but that life was dull. I had a little satisfaction this session in resuming my occupation of copying from the records of the Privy Council. I was now troubled with a kind of inflammation in my eyes. I dined at my father's. He was quite indifferent.

WEDNESDAY 11 JULY. (Writing on Wednesday the 18.) Dined at my father's; Sir John and Sir James Pringle there. It was dull. Visited Sir John at night.

THURSDAY 12 JULY. (Writing on Wednesday the 18.) My wife and I and our three eldest children dined and drank tea at my father's. He was, I fear intentionally and perversely, neglectful of us. I forget whether I visited Sir John Pringle. P.S. No. I played cards and supped at Sir William Forbes's.

FRIDAY 13 JULY. (Writing on Wednesday the 18.) Dined at Mr. Maclaurin's with Sir John Pringle, Lord and Lady Macdonald, Mr. George Wallace, Dr. Adam Smith, Mr. Baron Gordon, etc. Was now, on account of my inflamed eye, on a vegetable and water regimen. Had no relish of life. Maclaurin and I walked with Sir John in the Meadow and went home with him. Maclaurin confessed his doubt, or rather belief, that there would be no future state. He expressed himself curiously: "I might flatter you, Sir John" (as if he himself had no concern in the matter). "But I really think we have no reason to expect a future state. It is a beautiful fancy. But what right has man to it?" and said that thinking on the subject made men mad or whimsical like Lord Kames or Lord Monboddo. Sir John said he should talk with men like his father, who was a rational Christian. It was unpleasing to hear Maclaurin express his infidelity. But he had not studied the subject.

SATURDAY 14 JULY. (Writing on Friday the 20.) My wife and I and our three eldest children dined at Prestonfield by special invitation. I was soothed by worthy Sir Alexander's placid old age, but my inflamed eye hurt my spirits.

SUNDAY 15 JULY. (Writing on Friday the 20.) Took salts for my eye. The children said divine lessons. I stayed at home all day and read reviews, and was tolerably easy, though dejected.

MONDAY 16 JULY. (Writing on Friday the 20.) My eye continued painful. I had to dictate a good deal. Was in town all day, and had the room much darkened. Dictated none, but wrote *The Hypochondriack* No. 46.[4] At night had a *happy* reconciliation.[5]

TUESDAY 17 JULY. (Writing on Monday the 23.) Nothing worth recording.

WEDNESDAY 18 JULY. (Writing on Monday the 23.) My eye was still very uneasy.

THURSDAY 19 JULY. (Writing on Monday the 23.) My eyes became wonderfully better today. I had washed them with a water sent me by Mr. Wood, the composition of which I know not, and with vitriol water sent me by Mr. George Wallace; and every night I had bread steeped in water and put between the folds of a cambric handkerchief laid upon them. They had both been uneasy. I dined at my father's either today or yesterday. My spirits were better as my eyes grew well.

FRIDAY 20 JULY. (Writing on Monday the 23.) Dined at Mr. George Wallace's with Sir John Pringle, Maclaurin, etc. No animated conversation, but very tolerable talk. I drank some glasses of claret. Mr. Wallace and I walked with Sir John in the Meadow.

SATURDAY 21 JULY. (Writing on Monday the 23.) My eyes were quite well. Grange dined with us. A large company of children. Old Lady Wallace and Miss Dunlop drank tea. I went to Sir John Pringle's in the evening, and enlivened him more than I have done since he came last to Scotland. His nephew Sir James Pringle, Mr. George Wallace, and I eat cold meat with him. Grange and I visited Mr. John Syme in the Sanctuary today.

SUNDAY 22 JULY. (Writing on Monday the 23.) Was in pretty good spirits; free from fretfulness, though not vividly happy. Heard Dr. Blair in the forenoon. Dined at my father's between sermons. Observed that he avoided speaking on religion. Sir John Pringle indeed told me the other day that he had tried two or three times to bring him upon that subject. "But he always escaped me," said Sir John. In the afternoon it was exceedingly warm, and I was quite languid. I resolved to go home to my country-house and be calm with my children, and perhaps find my wife, who for some days was troubled with a cold, which gave me some apprehension. When I got home I found that she and Veronica and Phemie were gone to church in town. I had my two sons to walk with me and eat gooseberries in the garden, and go half-way to town to meet their mother and sisters; but we did not meet them. I was in a quiet, placid frame. When all the family was assembled, we had tea most agreeably. Old John Boswell, who had arrived the night before from London, came to tea. After which

[4] On children and their education.
[5] With his wife, who had been cool to him because of his rakish behaviour in London.

he and I walked in the garden, and I got into a comfortable Auchinleck frame. It is in vain to investigate ideas and feelings of this kind. They are as immediate as the tastes of different substances. I went to Sir John Pringle's in the evening. Nobody there but Dr. Adam Smith. I had read today some of Lord Kames's book on education, and I talked slightingly of it. Smith said, "Every man fails soonest in his weak part. Lord Kames's weak part is writing. Some write above their parts, some under them. Lord Kames writes much worse than one should expect from his conversation." David Hume, he told us, observed, "When one says of another man he is the most arrogant man in the world, it is meant only to say that he is very arrogant. But when one says it of Lord Kames, it is an absolute truth." Smith said *The Elements of Criticism* was Lord Kames's worst work. "They are all bad," said he. "But it is the worst." He said *taedium vitae* was a particular disease. I fear it is general. His conversation was *flabby*, as Garrick said of it.[6] The children said divine lessons well today.

MONDAY 23 JULY. (Writing on Thursday the 26.) News came to me this forenoon that Sir Adam Fergusson was arrived, having been appointed a Lord of Trade, so that there was to be a new election for Ayrshire. It fluttered and vexed me that a man whom I disliked so much should be so lucky, and that by the sudden vacancy the roll of electors would just be in his favour as before. Craufurdland, Fairlie, Grange, Old John Boswell, Mr. Matthew Dickie, and Mr. Walker his clerk, dined with us in the country. I drank port and water, and was pretty comfortable. After tea I walked in with such of the company as stayed. I had nothing to dictate. Grange and I supped at Mr. John Gordon's, Writer to the Signet, with Dr. Beattie.

TUESDAY 24 JULY. (Writing on Thursday the 26.) We were asked to dine at my father's. My wife, Veronica, Phemie, and Sandy went. I sent word that I was engaged, for I could not bear the triumph which I supposed he and his women would express on Sir Adam Fergusson's success. I went to the race at Leith in Old Erskine's chaise, little Sandy, my son, with us. I was really entertained. I called on Sir John Pringle, intending to have dined with him, but he was engaged out. I came to the (writing on

[6] "Smith was a man of extraordinary application, and had his mind crowded with all manner of subjects; but the force, acuteness, and vivacity of Johnson were not to be found there. He had book-making so much in his thoughts, and was so chary of what might be turned to account in that way, that he once said to Sir Joshua Reynolds that he made it a rule when in company never to talk of what he understood. Beauclerk had for a short time a pretty high opinion of Smith's conversation. Garrick after listening to him for a while, as to one of whom his expectations had been raised, turned slyly to a friend and whispered him, 'What say you to this?—eh? *flabby*, I think' " (*Life of Johnson*, note by Boswell to Langton's Johnsoniana, 1780).

Saturday the 28) Cross and sauntered. Followed Lord Eglinton and Fairlie to the Earl's lodgings, where was Mr. Wauchope, and there we talked of the election. I adjourned with Fairlie to Wauchope's, where we dined; and having considered the state of the roll, a very sensible letter from Lord Loudoun, and a very well-written one from Lord North asking of Lord Eglinton as a great favour to suspend his political operations and permit Sir Adam Fergusson to be rechosen at this time without opposition, we sent a joint letter to Major Montgomerie giving it as our opinion that it would be best to make a virtue of necessity. We were quite sober today. Sir John Pringle was next day to go on a jaunt to the west country.

WEDNESDAY 25 JULY. (Writing on Saturday the 28.) Went to the race in Lady Colville's coach with her three nieces [7] and my three eldest children. Sat on the coach box while the horses ran, and was pretty well amused. Dined at home. It rained pretty heavily about dinner-time, and I felt such uneasy sensations as I have had in wet weather in the country. Dictated some in town in the afternoon.

THURSDAY 26 JULY. (Writing on Saturday the 28.) My left eye was a little sore this week. Sir Charles Preston dined and drank tea with us. I was in a most listless state; felt no pleasure in life, nor could imagine any. My fancy roved on London and the English bar, yet I had faint hopes of happiness even in the metropolis, which I dreaded would pall upon me; and I thought it would be wrong to desert Scotland. In short I did not know what to do. I had more business as a lawyer these three weeks than the Session at first seemed to promise. But the embarrassed state of my affairs and my father's indifference distressed me. I came to our town house a little; was indolent. Went out again.

FRIDAY 27 JULY. (Writing on Saturday the 28.) Went to the race with Maclaurin in his coach. Was sadly dispirited; thought myself insignificant and subjected to a wretched destiny. Had no clear thoughts of anything, no consoling pious feelings. Had been with Lord Eglinton once since Tuesday. Went to him today near three and had a consultation on the election with his Lordship and Mr. Wauchope, an express having brought letters from Major Montgomerie and Mr. Hamilton of Sundrum. Had some pleasure in observing the Earl's sense and spirit, but was saddened by speculative clouds composed of the uncertainty of life, the forgetfulness of things years after their happening, and such dreary truths. Wondered how I had ever been active and keen in anything. Went and dined with Mr. Wauchope to concert again what should be written to Major Montgomerie. I myself wrote him a friendly letter recommending a cessation of arms at this time, when he could not succeed, and might

[7] See above, 4 December 1780, n. 1.

obtain from Administration what he wished by not opposing. I was grievously hypochondriac in the evening. Went early to bed and fell soon asleep.

SATURDAY 28 JULY. (Writing on Tuesday the 31.) Got up so well that I eat an egg and two rolls and butter to breakfast. Was pretty well in the Court of Session; called on Lord Eglinton, visited Dr. James Hunter with him, and saw him take his chaise and set out. I felt a warm kindness for him and a sort of pity that he had lost the election. Grange dined with us in the country. It rained a good deal in the afternoon. When it faired, I walked into town, was shaved and dressed, and went to sup with Lord Kames; but finding company was to be there, I did not go in, but walked quietly home. I borrowed today out of the Advocates' Library, David Hume's *Treatise of Human Nature*, but found it so abstruse, so contrary to sound sense and reason, and so dreary in its effects on the mind, if it had any, that I resolved to return it without reading it.

SUNDAY 29 JULY. (Writing on Tuesday the 31.) Grange and I walked out to Duddingston and heard the apostolic Mr. William Bennet lecture on the miracle of Cana in Galilee, and in good plain terms inculcate the truth of our Saviour's divine mission. We were calmly happy. Lord Abercorn and his brother Dr. Hamilton, prebendary of Salisbury, and Mr. Burgess, Lord Somerville's brother-in-law, being all decently in church, confirmed the good frame. We were afterwards quite pleasant, eating gooseberries with the young folks in the garden at Prestonfield in warm sunshine. We dined comfortably with worthy Sir Alexander, who was remarkably well and walked agreeably with us. I then paid a visit to my father, whom I had not visited since the Ayrshire election was again in agitation. Not a word was said of it, and he was very well with me. I had a satisfaction in observing his steadiness even in old age. Went home and heard the children say divine lessons very well.

MONDAY 30 JULY. (Writing on Tuesday 7 August.) Dictated some, tolerably. Dined at my father's with Dr. Webster and Commissioner Cochrane. Drank just enough to wish for more. Called at Maclaurin's. He was at Lord Macdonald's. Called there. Found them two at claret. Drank some, and stayed tea. Was a little intoxicated.

TUESDAY 31 JULY. (Writing on Tuesday 7 August.) I think I dined quietly at my father's. In the evening DOUGLAS, Lord and Lady Macdonald, etc., played cards and supped with us in town. I drank moderately. My wife and I lay in town.

WEDNESDAY 1 AUGUST. (Writing on Wednesday the 8.) Our three children came in early and breakfasted with us, and we also dined in town. I was in poor spirits. In the evening was at St. John's Lodge at the entering of the Hon. George Cochrane.

THURSDAY 2 AUGUST. (Writing on Wednesday the 8.) Was quite restless and uneasy. Dined at my father's; Philip Dundas there.

FRIDAY 3 AUGUST. (Writing on Wednesday the 8.) Dined at my father's. Nobody there. One of these days my wife and I paid a visit at Mr. Hugh Maxwell's, where I had not been for several years, I know not why. His mother was now with him, and had called on us. We also paid visits at Lord Macdonald's, Captain Frazer's, and Robert Boswell's. I supped at Lord Kames's, but was very dull and unhappy.

SATURDAY 4 AUGUST. (Writing on Wednesday the 8.) Why keep a journal of so "weary a life"? I yesterday spoke to Lord Advocate of Major Montgomerie, and his Lordship frankly agreed to assist him in getting a battalion to go to the East Indies. This pleased me; and as he asked me to come and take mutton and claret with him, reminding me that I had said in London that was the best way to keep up old friendship (which however I had not exactly said), I resolved to be well with him. The young Campbells dined with us today, as usual on Saturday. I was in the humour of drinking wine with pleasure, and took more than half a bottle of white wine. I then went over to Lady Colville's, and her brother Andrew and I drank a bottle of port. His sensible, firm manner of talking of low spirits, which he had sadly experienced, did me some good. I drank tea there too. I then called on Sir John Pringle, who had returned two days ago, but he was not at home. Then Lord Kames's; not at home. Could not be without some company. Took Grange and Mr. James Loch to sup with me in the country. I took only buttermilk.

SUNDAY 5 AUGUST. (Writing on Wednesday the 8.) Got up better. Veronica went with me to the New Church in the forenoon. A Mr. Moncrieff preached. I was insipid but not unhappy. Veronica and I walked out again to dinner. It was a very warm day. My wife went to church in the afternoon. I stayed at home with the children, who said divine lessons; but I had too little authority over them. Sandy had not been very well for some days. I felt something agreeable from knowing that it was the Sacrament Sunday in the West Kirk parish and observing a great number of people going to church. I wished that my wife and I had attended it. I supped at Sir John Pringle's with Mr. George Wallace and Mr. Brand, an English clergyman, just returned from travelling with Sir James Hall.[8] Was pretty well.

MONDAY 6 AUGUST. (Writing on Wednesday the 8.) Went to hear the examination of the High School, which pleased me. Had met Major

---

[8] Sir James, a nephew of Sir John Pringle, was the first geologist to apply directly the test of laboratory experiments to geological hypotheses. His travels were devoted to geological study.

Montgomerie returned from Ayrshire, and informed him of Lord Advocate's good intentions. Appointed to meet the Major at the Cross at one and inform him when we could see the Advocate together. His Lordship was at the High School examination, and appointed two o'clock. I went with the Major. But my spirits were so woefully sunk, I could hardly open my lips. We walked a little in the Meadow. I was somewhat shocked with the idea of the honest Major's going to such a distance from his wife and children, and into the dangers of war. But he was keen for it. So I was satisfied. Lord Advocate engaged to write that very night both to the Secretary at War [9] and to Lord North's secretary, and said it was a shame the Major had not got a battalion before. I dined at my father's; Commissioner Cochrane, Balbarton, etc., there. I was dull, but, I cannot tell how, am easier there when in wretched hypochondria. I drank tea with Grange. I was quite feeble and sunk at night, and could not sleep for some time from thinking drearily of Hugh Montgomerie's going to the East Indies.

TUESDAY 7 AUGUST. (Writing on Monday the 13.) Was in a dull state. Took Mr. Lawrie out to dinner. Sauntered and stayed tea, placid enough. Returned to town and dictated pretty well.

WEDNESDAY 8 AUGUST. (Writing on Monday the 13.) Dined at Mr. Maclaurin's; Lady Wallace, Lord Monboddo, Lord Ankerville, etc., there. Drank pretty liberally and was cheered. Stayed tea. At night, just as Maclaurin and I were preparing to go to Sir John Pringle's, Lady Wallace returned and brought Lord Maitland. We sat down to cards, and played till near one. I lost and was vexed. I would not stay supper, but walked home in a disagreeable feverishness. But this occasional sally into the agitation of fashionable life made me view with satisfaction that domestic tranquillity which had appeared insignificant and wearisome.

THURSDAY 9 AUGUST. (Writing on Monday the 13.) Cultivated the feeling which last night's excess had given me. Dined at my father's; Balmuto and Robert Boswell there; an unpleasing scene. Supped at Sir John Pringle's. Felt going out at night, now that it was dark, disagreeable. Met Lord Braxfield in the Meadow as I was going to Sir John's. He said, "It's a cursed business, ours." I was mischievous enough to join with him, and say, "You labour hard and get no thanks." I had now lost all relish for the Court of Session, and could not think of being a judge there but merely with a view to have an annual income to assist my family and an occupation only better than being idle. I languished for London; yet feared I should not be able to rise to any eminence there. Sir John Pringle said to me one day this summer, "I know not if you will be at rest in

[9] Charles Jenkinson, later Earl of Liverpool.

London. But you will never be at rest out of it." I felt a kind of weak, fallacious attachment to Edinburgh. But I considered, "I hope to be in Heaven, which is quitting Edinburgh. Why then should I not quit it to get to London, which is a high step in the scale of felicity?" I thought I might try the English bar and be sent down a baron of exchequer. In short I was very wavering.

FRIDAY 10 AUGUST. (Writing on Tuesday the 14.) Was rather better. Mr. Solicitor-General, Colonel Craufurd of Craufurdland, and Mr. Robert Dundas dined with us in the country. I was steady and relished company and good wine. They drank tea. I had visited Sir John Pringle in the forenoon.

SATURDAY 11 AUGUST. (Writing on Tuesday the 14.) Rose quite well. I have not been so since my return from London. I relished everything, even the Court of Session. I however was not displeased that it rose today. There was something comfortable in the prospect of being for some time free from any fixed attendance. My wife and I and our four eldest children dined and drank tea at my father's. I wearied heavily. Went home at night, met Grange, took him back and had just a social bottle of cider.

SUNDAY 12 AUGUST. (Writing on Tuesday the 14.) It was a very wet day. So I stayed at home all the forenoon and heard the children say divine lessons. Mr. Sibthorpe, who was going a jaunt to England next day, came out and dined. I sat a little, and then walked to town, being engaged to dine with Sir John Pringle. I wished to be at public worship, but was too late either for kirks or chapels. Went to the Quakers' Meeting built by Mr. Miller; only twelve present. All silent. I had calm meditation. Then dined at Sir John Pringle's. Thought I would try if I *could* be saturated with wine there. Drank six glasses in the time of dinner and three large draughts of port and water, which, with the few glasses after dinner, made me warm and hearty. After tea I walked with him, Sir James Hall, etc., who dined with him; and then walked home, where I found Mr. Nairne, who supped with us.

MONDAY 13 AUGUST. (Writing on Tuesday the 14.) Intended to have gone to Sir Alexander Dick's with Sandy and Grange. But when we got to town, it rained so hard we could not go. Grange dined with us in the country and drank tea. I grew weary, walked to town, heard the dreary news of Admiral Parker's engagement with the Dutch.[1] Called a little at my father's. Went home.

---

[1] On 5 August, on the Dogger Bank. Parker's squadron, coming south with a convoy of two hundred merchantmen, met a Dutch squadron convoying their merchant fleet to the north. There was heavy loss on both sides, but the action was indecisive. Parker was dissatisfied with the support he had received from Lord Sandwich, and resigned

TUESDAY 14 AUGUST. (Writing on Monday the 20.) Dined at my father's with Commissioner Cochrane, played whist, and drank tea. Was dull.

WEDNESDAY 15 AUGUST. (Writing on Monday the 20.) Grange and Sandy and I walked out to Prestonfield. There came on such a rain that we stopped above an hour in Sharp's coachyard in the Pleasance. Mr. Bennet was at Prestonfield, so we had a most comfortable day. I shunned the execution of Daniel Mackay for stealing from the post-house, though I felt an inclination to see it.[2] Sandy rode home. I was dreary at night, thinking of the execution.

THURSDAY 16 AUGUST. (Writing on Monday the 20.) Was languid and sauntering. Could not write a *Hypochondriack*. Resolved to make an essay published before serve for No. 47.[3] Might have forced myself to write, but thought it as well to adopt a good essay. Had Mr. Lawrie out to dinner.

FRIDAY 17 AUGUST. (Writing on Monday the 20.) Was wretchedly low-spirited. Called at my father's a little. Had no pleasure at all but from my senses. Grew better before dinner. Sir Alexander and Lady Dick, Miss Dick, Miss Annie, Miss Peggie, and Mr. Robert and worthy Mr. Bennet dined with us at our country-house. I relished it excellently and was quite well for the time. They drank tea.

SATURDAY 18 AUGUST. (Writing on Monday the 20.) Lord Herbert had been several weeks in Scotland. I had seen him at Leith Races, and said I would soon wait on him, understanding that he was quartered at Dalkeith. I was miserable to think I had delayed so long to pay my respects to the eldest son of Lord Pembroke, who is so good to me. I therefore mounted a good hack this morning after breakfast and rode almost to Dalkeith, but met a dragoon who informed me Lord Herbert was quartered at Linlithgow.[4] The exercise on horseback did me good. I grew manly. I went to Moredun. Mr. Baron Stewart[5] was not at home, but I met him on the road and went back, walked with him round his villa, dined heartily, and he and I drank four bottles of claret, the last

---

his command. In 1782, under the new Ministry, he accepted appointment as commander-in-chief in the East Indies. His ship, the *Cato*, was lost on the voyage out with all on board.

[2] Mackay had been tried and convicted 29 July in the High Court of Justiciary for the theft of a letter containing bank-notes, taken from the General Post-Office, Edinburgh, where he was an under-porter.

[3] He chose a facetious essay, "The New Freezing Discovery," first printed in the *Public Advertiser* for 2 June 1770.

[4] Lord Herbert was at this time captain in the 1st Regiment of Dragoons.

[5] David Stewart Moncrieffe had recently succeeded John Maule as baron of exchequer.

of which I called for. Was afterwards sorry for this excess. When I got home, found Veronica had been ill, thrown up, and spit a little blood and was feverish. I grew intoxicated somewhat.

SUNDAY 19 AUGUST. (Writing on Wednesday the 22.) Had been ill most part of the night, and was vexed to think that I had indulged in such excess in the company of an old, foolish, vain creature with whom I could have no rational society. Buttermilk and tranquillity made me pretty well in the forenoon, the children saying divine lessons, and Veronica being much better; but I was sadly frightened about her. I dined with my family, was at afternoon service in the New English Chapel, drank tea at my father's, and sat part of the evening at Sir John Pringle's.

MONDAY 20 AUGUST. (Writing on Wednesday the 22.) Was listless and depressed. Grange dined with us, and he and I walked about Sunbury. Mrs. Jeweller Kerr and Miss Kerr drank tea with us. I had some relief in having old ideas revived by her. Grange walked to town with me. I supped at my father's, who was to go west on Wednesday. I was dreary while I thought of his age.

TUESDAY 21 AUGUST. (Writing on Wednesday the 22.) Was exceedingly sunk, and could see no comfort. I could not call up my principles of religion. All was darkness and uncertainty. Yet I prayed to GOD as a Christian morning and evening amidst all this gloom. Yesterday and today I dictated so much of a law paper, but with no animation. Dr. Dunbar of Aberdeen called on me in the forenoon with a small parcel of MS. of *Prefaces to the Poets* which he had brought me from Dr. Johnson. I could with difficulty keep up any conversation with him, but thought myself obliged to ask him to dine with me next day, and he accepted. I dined at my father's very dully, and took leave of him. He expressed no wish to see me at Auchinleck, and was silent when I said I intended to be out soon. I was so melancholy that I saw little difference between age and youth. I called on Dr. Gillespie; then sauntered uncertain and uneasy as I used to be when at the College. Drank tea at Sir John Pringle's and walked in the Meadow with him and some ladies, very dully. At night felt the blessing of having a cheerful wife.

WEDNESDAY 22 AUGUST. (Writing on Friday the 24.) Last night had a card from Lord Graham inviting me to meet him at Bothwell Castle, but in terms by no means such as I liked, because he put it on being *diverted* with my company. I hesitated however whether or not I should go, and at last resolved not. I was very low-spirited today; and during this late fit, there has come into my mind the horrible thought of suicide. It was most effectually checked by thinking what a triumph it would afford to my enemies, or rather enviers, and how it would hurt my children. I had *some* rationality therefore in store. Dr. Dunbar's dining with me had appeared a heavy task. Sir John Pringle said very well, "Have somebody with him with whom you are easier. Dilute him." I had Grange; and, most unexpectedly, I was very well.

THURSDAY 23 AUGUST. (Writing on Friday the 24.) It rained all day. I did not go to town, but read some of the *Arabian Nights* to Veronica, and was entertained, though my attention was not seized as it was in my early years by tales. I was upon the whole pretty easy. Lady Colville invited us all today to tea. We went and were comfortable. I know not how it happened, but I had a complete relief from melancholy for an hour or two, and enjoyed some of Dr. Johnson's *Lives of the Poets* fully. We played a rubber at whist. My wife, who had been a little hoarse for some time, spit some blood, which alarmed both her and me. I persuaded her to go to bed early. She said my father and I were quite different. My spirits required agitation, no matter by what. His did not. I was brandy kindled, the flames of which, if not stirred, went out. He was a good coal fire, which burnt steady.

FRIDAY 24 AUGUST. (Writing on Thursday the 30.) Went uninvited to dine with Sir John Pringle. Found it was not *the thing*, as the saying is. Miss Hall went home with me to tea, as Sir John was going out. In the evening I was restless. Walked into town, intending to sup at Princes Street Coffee-house. But luckily changed my mind and came home.

SATURDAY 25 AUGUST. (Writing on Thursday the 30.) It was a very wet day. But I passed it very easily. My wife was no longer ill, which was a great comfort. Veronica and Phemie read each a chapter in the Bible to me, which they now generally do every morning. Veronica played on the harpsichord, and I read the *Arabian Nights' Entertainments*, which engaged me more the more I read. In the evening I went to Sir John Pringle's as a recompense for disturbing him yesterday at dinner. Drs. Black, Hutton, and Rutherford,[6] and Hamilton of Bangour came and all stayed to his cold meat. We were pretty cheerful. It was fair at night.

SUNDAY 26 AUGUST. (Writing on Thursday the 30.) It was a good forenoon. I attended divine service at the Old English Chapel, and was well pleased with Mr. Bell's sermon. Went home to dinner. It was a very wet afternoon. The children said divine lessons. I was very placid.

MONDAY 27 AUGUST. (Writing on Thursday the 30.) It rained all day. I passed the day as I did Saturday, and was easy. I was however somewhat vexed to be sensible of supine indolence. But I recollected my late dreary state, in which all seemed gloomy; so that ease was to be prized.

TUESDAY 28 AUGUST. (Writing on Thursday the 30.) It still continued to rain. Indeed, I do not remember such a continuance of wet

---

[6] Sir Walter Scott's uncle.

weather about Edinburgh. It grew fair after twelve. I walked into town, but was listless. Came home to dinner, and passed the afternoon tolerably. Read more of the *Arabian Nights* and some of Erskine's *Principles*, and played at catch-honours and birkie [7] with Veronica and Phemie. Was charmed with Veronica's playing on the harpsichord. At night my dear wife talked seriously of our state in this world; that we ought to be submissive and trust in GOD, and not inquire eagerly into futurity. This seemed sensible, but humbling to an aspiring philosophical curiosity. It however pleased me at the time.

WEDNESDAY 29 AUGUST. (Writing on Thursday 6 September.) I recollect nothing of this day. P.S. Lady Frances Montgomerie and Grange dined.

THURSDAY 30 AUGUST. (Writing on Thursday 6 September.) I recollect nothing except a deal of thunder at night.

FRIDAY 31 AUGUST. (Writing on Thursday 6 September.) My wife and I dined, drank tea, and played at cards at Dr. Grant's. There was a very high wind at night.

SATURDAY 1 SEPTEMBER. (Writing on Thursday 6 September.) Went to Sir John Pringle's in the evening. Nobody but Sir James Pringle there. Eat cold meat and drank port cordially.

SUNDAY 2 SEPTEMBER. (Writing on Thursday the 6.) Thought the New Church had been opened again, after having been shut on account of being painted, but it was still locked. Went to Barclay the Berean's meeting and heard him pray and lecture drearily and wildly.[8] It was hearing a sect somewhat new to me. But he differed little from the Glassites. I was shocked that the chapel at the foot of Carrubber's Close, where I first was charmed with the Church-of-England worship, should be debased by such vulgar cant.[9] It was a fine day. I dined at home between sermons. Went in the afternoon to the West Kirk and heard Sir Harry Moncreiff. Lady Colville and Lady Anne Erskine drank tea with us. I went to Sir John Pringle's and eat cold meat. Dr. Black and several more

[7] "Catch-honours" was a simplified form of whist; "birkie" the same as "beggar-my-neighbour," a children's card-game.

[8] He had been extremely popular in the parish of Fettercairn, where he had been assistant to the minister, but his antinomian doctrines were obnoxious to the Presbytery, who refused him a certificate of character. This refusal, being sustained by the Synod and the General Assembly, debarred him from holding any parish in the Church of Scotland.

[9] Temple took Boswell to his first Church-of-England worship at this chapel, probably on Christmas Day, 1755. It was a "qualified" chapel, that is, one served by priests in English or Irish orders conducting themselves without obedience to the bishops of the Episcopal Church in Scotland. Its meeting-place had been built as a theatre by Allan Ramsay, finished in 1737 and closed almost as soon as it was opened.

were with him, and he was more cheerful than usual. He was to set out for London and Bath on Tuesday, being weary of Scotland.

MONDAY 3 SEPTEMBER. (Writing on Thursday the 6.) Went in a post-chaise with Colquhoun Grant and dined at Arniston, to pay a visit to the President after his late illness and before his going to Buxton. It was just an Arniston day. Twenty-two men, women, and children dined, and there was much hearty laughing and drinking. I was in pretty good spirits. It rained much. I came home somewhat intoxicated.

TUESDAY 4 SEPTEMBER. (Writing on Thursday the 6.) Though I was not sick, I awaked with a severe headache and lay till two, so that I did not get to see Sir John Pringle. It rained a good deal. I got up quite relaxed and unhappy. Passed the afternoon listlessly.

WEDNESDAY 5 SEPTEMBER. (Writing on Thursday the 6.) It was a pretty good day, but I was as languid and dreary and fretful and as much unconnected, as it were, with the comfort of real life as can be imagined. My dear wife walked into town with me and cheered me. Grange dined with us. I sunk again after dinner; did not know what to do. Was vexed at my silly wretchedness. Walked to town with him. Had resolved to go in the Ayr fly for Auchinleck on Friday. Was advised by Commissioner Cochrane to stay till the weather was more settled. Having a *Hypochondriack* to write before I went, thought I would not go till Tuesday. Felt a strange confusion and hurry in the view of moving only for a few weeks to Auchinleck. Drank tea with Grange. Grew somewhat better. Was pretty well at night.

THURSDAY 6 SEPTEMBER. (Writing on Monday the 10.) Visited Mr. Solicitor at Murrayfield. Sir Walter Montgomerie-Cuninghame and Grange dined with us. I supped at Dunn's Hotel with Lord Graham and Douglas. Was moderate. I played first a rubber at Old Lady Grant's.

FRIDAY 7 SEPTEMBER. (Writing on Monday the 10.) Sir Walter did not come to us, though he said he would. Mr. Sibthorpe and Grange dined with us. I supped at Mr. Ilay Campbell's with Lord Graham and Douglas, etc. Was moderate. Had an alarm that little Jamie might have water in his head, as he used to wake in the night and complain of pain in his head. But I hoped this was only apprehension in his mother and me. He was now a delightful child.

SATURDAY 8 SEPTEMBER. (Writing on Monday the 10.) Sir Walter came to us after breakfast and walked into town with me. I fixed to go to Auchinleck on Tuesday, and took a ticket in the Ayr fly. Sir Walter said he would meet me that day at Auchinleck. Grange dined with us today. I walked to town in the afternoon and sauntered. Visited Old Lady Grant for a few minutes. Lady Wallace took me home with her for a little. Was fond as usual, without regard.

SUNDAY 9 SEPTEMBER. (Writing on Monday the 10.) Heard Mr. Walker in the New Church in the forenoon; respected his decent manner and seriousness, but had too much philosophy for his orthodoxy. Had not an unpleasing sensation of wonder as to what *may be* the real result of this dubious, changeful state. My wife was at the West Kirk. I dined comfortably at home, and drank some port comfortably. I have relished my wife and children and the comforts of life very much for some days. Should I not be content with such enjoyment? The children said divine lessons in the afternoon. After tea I went to town, visited Lord Macdonald, and walked a good while with Major Montgomerie. Then came to Grange's and put the finishing paragraph to a *Hypochondriack* on dreaming, in which I indulged an agreeable superstition.[1] I had written it during these three days with satisfaction. I was really very well just now, though my existence would not bear an analysis so as to appear to advantage in description. My notions are too high.

MONDAY 10 SEPTEMBER. Went in to town early and talked with Major Montgomerie about his getting a battalion. Lounged most of the forenoon. Grange walked out and dined with us. Commissioner Cochrane drank tea. I went to town again to see that nothing was forgot before my going to Auchinleck.

TUESDAY 11 SEPTEMBER. Had slept very little for fear of sleeping too long. Got up before three. Got in good time to the fly. Had for companions Miss ——— Hamilton, niece to Coilsfield, going to Ayr, old and ugly but conversable, and a very pretty-looking, pleasing woman who went as far as Carstairs, and whom I fondled, I think, too much. I did not know till afterwards that she was married. Got to Cumnock about three. Was struck with wonder at finding myself so soon removed from what used to appear at such a distance. Dined there and had Logan, Old John Boswell, James Johnston, and Mr. Millar, Mr. Dun's assistant, to drink a glass of wine. It was a fine warm day. Came out at Ochiltree and walked to Auchinleck in good time to tea. Went to the Old Castle with James Bruce, and felt for the first time the agreeable wonder of coming from Edinburgh in a day.

WEDNESDAY 12 SEPTEMBER. Walked with James Bruce round all

---

[1] "In my opinion, the operations of the soul in sleep, like those when we are awake, are sometimes entirely its own, and sometimes, though rarely, are influenced by superior intelligence.... That the interpretation of dreams was a science very carefully studied by certain wise men in some of the ancient nations is too well attested to be denied; and supposing the means of acquiring it to be now withheld, that would neither disprove its having once existed, nor convince us that it will not exist again" (*The Hypochondriack*, No. 48).

the Tenshillingside plantations. In the afternoon went out to shoot partridges with Sandy Bruce. Got none.

THURSDAY 13 SEPTEMBER. Dr. Gillespie and I and John Samson, miller at Ochiltree, were out shooting partridges all forenoon in the Mucklewood. I fired once, but did not hit.

FRIDAY 14 SEPTEMBER. Walked about in the forenoon. After dinner walked to Mr. Dun's and drank tea.

SATURDAY 15 SEPTEMBER. Went to Sundrum. Rode about his Place [1a] and saw a great deal done. No company there. Drank a bottle of claret and was very well. The weather was hitherto dry and warm, and the country was very agreeable.

SUNDAY 16 SEPTEMBER. It was a wet day. I felt somewhat dreary. The family stayed at home. I read one sermon of Mr. Zachary Boyd's to my father and Dr. Gillespie in the forenoon, and another and the *aucht* sermon of Mr. Pollok,[2] a shocking piece, together with some of the Bible, to them and the ladies after dinner. Not a soul had been here since the family came last but Mr. Auld and Mr. Young at the time of the Sacrament, and Bruce Campbell with George and David one day. I was in a state of insipidity.

MONDAY 17 SEPTEMBER. Bruce Campbell and his wife and eldest son, George and David, and Mr. Connell of Sorn came to dinner. It seemed a great company. Mr. Connell went home after dinner. The rest stayed all night. I had no enjoyment of life, but I was free from uneasiness. My father seemed very dull, but not uneasy. In the forenoon I read some of Monboddo on language.

TUESDAY 18 SEPTEMBER. Bruce Campbell, etc., stayed all day. Mr. Shepherd, Minister at Muirkirk, dined.

WEDNESDAY 19 SEPTEMBER. Bruce Campbell, etc., went away. Dr. Gillespie and I walked over and visited Mr. Reid. Found him somewhat more failed than I had observed for years, being thinner and duller of hearing. He told me my grandfather had always a heaviness about him. We were wet going and coming. In the afternoon talked of a future state with Dr. Gillespie till I grew somewhat gloomy. Was sadly sunk.

THURSDAY 20 SEPTEMBER. Had dreamt that my dear wife was married to somebody else; yet I had a confused notion that she had been my wife. She looked smart and engaging as Miss Peggie Montgomerie. Resolved when awake to pay her all possible attention. I was quite vexed in

1a Not the whole estate but Sundrum House and its surroundings.

2 "Eighth." Mr. Pollok (whom we have not identified) presumably used the Scots ordinal himself. It perhaps indicates that, like Zachary Boyd, he flourished in the seventeenth century.

my sleep at the thought of having lost her. Intended to have gone to Eglinton or towards it. But it rained in the morning. The day proved pretty good. Prepared for going. Fingland dined. Got into stout spirits. Was hurt however by the coldness of my father and his women's venom.

FRIDAY 21 SEPTEMBER. After breakfast set out for Eglinton. Stopped at the laird of Fairlie's. Heard the Earl was in Fife. Dined and stayed all night. Craufurdland there. Drank too much.

SATURDAY 22 SEPTEMBER. Awaked ill. Went in the forenoon to Lady Crawford's; her son, Captain Hamilton, and cousin, Miss Jeanie, there. Comfortable living.

SUNDAY 23 SEPTEMBER. Read three of Mr. Steele's sermons.[3] Strange, bouncing pieces. The Countess carried me in her coach to Irvine Church in the afternoon.

MONDAY 24 SEPTEMBER. Rode over to Eglinton. No news of the Earl. Went to Irvine. Visited old Mrs. Rutherfurd, who said she was quite willing to die. Called on Mr. G. A. Cuninghame. Not at home. Mr. John Hunter came to dinner at Lady Crawford's and stayed all night.

TUESDAY 25 SEPTEMBER. Breakfasted at Fairlie. Nobody there. Was to have been with Colonel Craufurd at dinner, but heard he was to dine at Fairlie. Rode back to Bourtreehill and went with Mr. John Hunter to dine at Greenvale. Rode in by Doura; Sir Walter not at home. Poor-looking place. Fine day. Greenvale looked very pretty. Miss Fergussons of Doonholm there, and Mr. G. A. Cuninghame, who had followed me from Bourtreehill. Had hesitated and wished as to going to Dunlop. But found I had not time. Was determined to go next day with Mr. John Hunter to Lord Cassillis's. Was pleased at Greenvale, as Miss Peggie Montgomerie was revived to me. Went back to Bourtreehill at night. Heard by the way that Lord Eglinton was to be home that night. So I could not go to Lord Cassillis's. Was quite comfortable at Bourtreehill.

WEDNESDAY 26 SEPTEMBER. Captain Robert Hamilton and I rode to Eglinton. The Earl out a-hunting. Joined him in Irvine Muir. Had two short chases of hares, but did not kill any of them. Nobody with us at dinner but the Baron of Lochrig.[4] Drank much, as usual. I do not recollect how, talked of a future state. The Earl professed a positive disbelief of it. I tried to argue against him, but in vain. I was shocked and somewhat dreary. But a quantity of wine deadened uneasiness. Played *vingt-et-un* about an hour. Supped at ten. Attempted to drink more, but could do little. Grew sick and went to bed in a pretty confused state.

THURSDAY 27 SEPTEMBER. Awaked very ill. Had coffee in bed. Lay

[3] Richard Steele (1629–1692), nonconformist divine.
[4] Matthew Arnot Stewart.

till twelve. Then rode to Lady Crawford's, and grew better. Back again to dinner; the same company with the addition of Mr. Haddow. Drunk port and was pretty well, and held out the whole course of a day; viz., dinner, *vingt-et-un*, and supper.

FRIDAY 28 SEPTEMBER. Breakfasted with Lady Crawford; called at Fairlie and Caprington for a little. Saw only Lady Betty. Came to Loudoun and dined comfortably; only the Earl and Douglas, his factor. Was sickly at first, but recovered. After a bottle of port apiece, drank with cheerful ease, the Earl asked if I'd have another. "Do you wish it, my Lord?" "Yes, I wish it." "I own *I* do. Thank you, my Lord, for *birling* a wish." [5] I was really happy here. Rode briskly to Auchinleck. Had fine weather almost all this jaunt.

SATURDAY 29 SEPTEMBER. A wet dull day. No company came.

SUNDAY 30 SEPTEMBER. It rained some. Went to church in chariot with Miss Boswell and Dr. Gillespie. Mr. Millar did me good by a sermon on Psalm 73, last verse. In the evening read to father and Dr. G. the last discourse of Robert Fleming, V.D.M.[6] Father said tonight, "I am not able now to go about here. You must do it." I said I would do my best if he gave me power. "Then," said he, "begin tomorrow." The Doctor seconded.

MONDAY 1 OCTOBER. Nothing to mark but a wet day.

TUESDAY 2 OCTOBER. Had a long walk with James Bruce and with Dr. Gillespie, and made a report to my father of what I thought should be done.

WEDNESDAY 3 OCTOBER. Set out about eight for Cumnock to take evidence in a Submission [7] between Logan and Mrs. Johnston. Rode in by the Mill of Auchinleck and saw some good houses, newly built by the miller. Breakfasted at Cumnock with Mr. John Boswell, his wife, and daughters, all but Jeanie, who was not at home. Employed all the forenoon in conversing with Logan and Mrs. Johnston and taking what evidence I could find. Was sound and well. Took Mr. Boswell with me to dine at Mr. Dun's, where we were truly comfortable. Examined the parish register for the preceding year, and paid Mr. Halbert 6/3 for recording the deaths.[8]

THURSDAY 4 OCTOBER. Mr. Bruce Campbell came and dined. I was in good spirits.

FRIDAY 5 OCTOBER. Was to return to Edinburgh. Breakfast was early

[5] "For satisfying a wish with liquor."

[6] *Verbi Dei Minister* ("minister of the word of God").

[7] A contract between two parties agreeing to refer the dispute to others for arbitration, and to be bound by their decision.

[8] See above, 2 September 1780.

on purpose for me. Mounted the young horse between eight and nine. Rode down to the Old House, that I might go from *the green* of Auchinleck to Edinburgh in a day. Was in an excellent frame. William Lennox took my portmanteau on another horse. Found the Ayr fly waiting for me at Ochiltree. Had a good journey in. My companions, a woman from Ayr and a son of Mr. Farquhar Kinloch's. On arriving at my house of Drumsheugh, to which I walked from Bristo Port, found my dear wife ill, she having had a miscarriage. This gave me uneasiness. The children however were well, and she was better.

SATURDAY 6 OCTOBER. (Writing on Friday the 19.) Grange and the young Campbells and Miss Nancy Grant dined with me. Upon a message from Commissioner Cochrane, I drank tea with him.

SUNDAY 7 OCTOBER. (Writing on Friday the 19.) Stayed at home in the forenoon. Went in the afternoon to the New English Chapel. Drank tea with Mrs. Mingay, Dr. Webster not at home.

MONDAY 8 OCTOBER. (Writing on Friday the 19.) Mr. Sibthorpe dined with me. I was already indolent and relaxed more than at Auchinleck.

TUESDAY 9 OCTOBER. (Writing on Friday the 19). Prepared for the press Answers for Commissioner Cochrane.[9] Dined at his house with Dr. Webster and Dr. Blair.

WEDNESDAY 10 OCTOBER. (Writing on Friday the 19.) Mr. Sibthorpe introduced to me a young neighbour of his from Ireland, come to study here, the second son of Sir Patrick Bellew. I had them and Grange out to dine and drink tea with us. My wife came to the table today. Commissioner Cochrane called after dinner, but would not stay tea.

THURSDAY 11 OCTOBER. (Writing on Friday the 19.) Was amused yesterday by having a hogshead of claret bottled, and today by having it put into a catacomb. Was very listless.

FRIDAY 12 OCTOBER. (Writing on Friday the 19.) Sandy rode and Veronica and Phemie walked with me to Prestonfield and dined. They were the worse for coming home in the night air.

SATURDAY 13 OCTOBER. (Writing on Friday the 19.) The young Campbells dined with us. I drank tea at Mr. George Wallace's and had some good talk.

SUNDAY 14 OCTOBER. (Writing on Friday the 19.) New Church forenoon and afternoon. Dined at Dr. Webster's. Miss Wardrop went to my seat in the afternoon. Tea Dr. Webster's; curious. The children said divine lessons.

---

[9] This cause has not been traced. Quite probably the Commissioner was cited in his official capacity.

MONDAY 15 OCTOBER. (Writing on Friday the 19.) Should have written a *Hypochondriack*. But could not. Resolved to make an old essay serve.[1] But could not find a motto. Was very insignificant. Lady Colville and her sister were very uneasy from a letter mentioning that Lord Kellie was ill at Brussels. I drank a little port with them after dinner. In the evening, as for some nights past, played at commerce [2] with the children.

TUESDAY 16 OCTOBER. (Writing on Friday the 19.) Happily found a motto for my old essay in Holyoke's *Dictionary*, and was content.[3] Dined at Dr. Blair's with Dr. Webster, Commissioner Cochrane, and Mr. Blair, the advocate. Drank too much. His Holiness was obliged to go away rather early to meet a party at Walker's tavern. Good Dr. Hugh proposed that he and I and his cousin should take one bottle. We did so. The claret was excellent. I was pleased to find they could both trace themselves from a fifth son of the laird of Blair. I walked to town a good deal intoxicated. Had worthy Grange with me till I wrote to Dilly and sealed up my *Hypochondriack*. Supped at Dr. Webster's. He not in. Nobody but Mrs. Mingay and Mr. Macpherson. Was not pleased with myself. Was in bad frame at home.

WEDNESDAY 17 OCTOBER. (Writing on Friday the 19.) Was very ill in the night and morning, but could not blame myself. Veronica made me a very good answer today, when I asked her in the usual way if her sister's getting more sugar almonds than her made her poorer. "Yes,"

[1] An essay on identification by numbered buttons, first printed in the *Public Advertiser* for 22 January 1768. "For instance, a *lawyer* is never esteemed till he has been of so many years standing at the bar; I would therefore have the gentlemen of the long robe to wear upon their buttons the number of years which they have served in their profession. . . . I know not how the *divines* ought to be numbered, whether according to the plurality of their benefices, according to the books they have written, or according to the disappointments which they have suffered. I think it would not be amiss to number our preachers according to the length of their sermons; so that upon seeing a clergyman enter a church, we should have no more to do but to cast our eyes on his buttons, to be informed how many minutes his discourse is to last. The only danger would be that many of the audience, on observing the number on a preacher's buttons to exceed twenty-five, might be apt to go away and disturb the congregation" (*The Hypochondriack*, No. 49).

[2] Commerce is a game in which exchange or barter is the chief feature. It had apparently been a fashionable favourite at card assemblies five years earlier, but soon became a children's game.

[3] The quotation from Flavius Vegetius Renatus he found in Thomas Holyoke's *Lexicon Philologicum et Dictionarium Etymologicum*, 1677. This passage explains the source of much of the obscure learning in the series: Boswell, as one might have expected, found many of his learned mottoes in the passages quoted by dictionaries to illustrate usage. Here he merely looked under the article *numerus*.

said she, "it makes me poorer than her." I grew better, walked to town, dressed, and had worthy Grange to accompany me almost to Prestonfield, where Sir Alexander and I and the Rev. Mr. Bennet got into the Knight's coach and drove to Lord Somerville's, where we were to dine by appointment. Sir Philip Ainslie was there, and talked with a lofty vivacity which was very entertaining and gained much upon Sir Alexander. Mr. Wauchope of Niddrie and a young midshipman were there. My heart warmed to be again here, where in the late Lord's time I was so happy. This Lord, though very silent, seemed very well pleased to see us, and all was elegant. He promised to dine with me before he went to London. I hoped to bring about a cordiality between us.[4] Sir Philip carried me to town. We were quite sober, which was agreeable. I sat a little at his house, and then at Lady Macdonald's. Was in better humour than ordinary; something in London spirits. When I got home, heard Lord Kellie was dead. Was somewhat agitated by the news.[5]

THURSDAY 18 OCTOBER. (Writing on Friday the 19.) Lord Kellie's death kept my mind from stagnating. Lady Colville did me the honour to send a letter, announcing it, to copy, and to let me know that perhaps she would have more occasion for my assistance. I wrote at her desire to Captain James Francis Erskine and to Lord Eglinton. Had Mr. Stobie, in his way to Auchinleck, and Grange to dine with us. In the evening wrote to my father, James Bruce, and Dr. Gillespie, with a degree of application and ease which gave me satisfaction. Had talked to Mr. Stobie of several things about the estate of Auchinleck. Had been somewhat gloomy since I last came home, contemplating my father's death and my insufficiency for representing our ancient family. I however hoped to do well, and thought that probably hypochondria made me think the duty more difficult, and myself more unfit, than was really just.

FRIDAY 19 OCTOBER. (Writing on Tuesday the 30.) I remember

[4] The "late Lord" (who died in 1765) had been Boswell's first patron and encourager, and had stood model to him in a number of important ways. "Let me here express my grateful remembrance of Lord Somerville's kindness to me at a very early period," he wrote in the *Life of Johnson* (1781, foot-note to discussion of the *Life of Pope*). "He was the first person of high rank that took particular notice of me in the way most flattering to a young man fondly ambitious of being distinguished for his literary talents."

[5] Thomas Alexander Erskine, sixth Earl of Kellie, Boswell's distant cousin and a brother of his close friend Andrew Erskine and of Lady Colville. Boswell had been acquainted with him for years, and by 1762 knew him well enough to borrow money from him at the races: "I felt a strong regard for him and was pleased at the romantic conceit of getting it from a gamester, a nobleman, and a musical composer" (Journal, 20 October 1762).

nothing except that I drank tea with Mrs. Jeweller Kerr and had my mind furnished with old ideas.

SATURDAY 20 OCTOBER. (Writing on Tuesday the 30.) Nothing to mark.

SUNDAY 21 OCTOBER. (Writing on Tuesday the 30.) Stayed at home in the forenoon. Heard Dr. Blair in the afternoon. The children said divine lessons. Little Jamie could now answer the first six questions of the *Mother's Catechism.*[6]

MONDAY 22 OCTOBER. (Writing on Tuesday the 30.) Walked to Craighouse and breakfasted with Lord Covington, whom I had not seen for many months. He was grown very dull of hearing, and gave me a discouraging view of life and old age and human existence. He said his memory was failed, and that the mind and body failed together; and he seemed to acquiesce in that dreary notion, without hope of restoration. And he said when one looked back on life, it was just a chaos of nothing. He however was not cast down, and said he would meet Maclaurin and me at a party at cards. I walked to town and found Dr. Webster had been in quest of me to go with him to dine with Lord Advocate. I dressed, and we drove to Melville Castle. The Advocate said he was very glad to see me, and all went on cordially. He mentioned after dinner an anecdote of me for which he said he had frequently given me credit: how last spring in London, when he had got the better of me in the Ayrshire election, I came up to him and said that our families had long been friends; that somehow he and I had taken different lines, but that should be no more. In short, he made a very good story of it for me; better, I am sensible, than the reality. And we now agreed that we should henceforth be well together. We had no strangers at table; just his old uncle and brother and Blair the advocate and Dr. Grieve of Dalkeith, and we drank liberally. When the Doctor and I were taking our chaise, Lord Advocate came and said to me, "It never does to go against old connexions. It never succeeds." "Why, my Lord," said I, "I will not say that. You have been very fortunate. But it never *should* succeed." His making up thus to me showed a generosity of mind in his prosperity; and perhaps he may be of essential service to me yet. He had a good effect upon me after Lord Covington's languor. He appeared all life and activity. I told him Lord Covington's reflection on life. It struck him at first. He seemed to shudder. It was like throwing cold water on hot iron to give Lord Advocate in all the glow of his prosperity a glimpse of the sad indifference of old age, which, if he should live, he himself was to feel. The difference be-

[6] By John Willison; first published in 1731.

tween the two was like Horace's "intererit multum," etc.; the Advocate "adhuc florente juventu fervidus." [7] He said, "I shall take care that *my* life shall not be a chaos of nothing" (dashing high-flavoured claret into his glass). Dr. Webster and I jogged quietly to town, and I went home to Drumsheugh.

TUESDAY 23 OCTOBER. (Writing on Tuesday 6 November.) Nothing to mark.

WEDNESDAY 24 OCTOBER. (Writing on Tuesday 6 November.) Nothing to mark.

THURSDAY 25 OCTOBER. (Writing on Tuesday 6 November.) Have only to mark that Grange dined with us.

FRIDAY 26 OCTOBER. (Writing on Tuesday 6 November.) Had Mr. Martin Lindsay to look at my garden at Drumsheugh and advise me what I should get done to it. He and Grange dined and drank tea with us. I was in a comfortable frame.

SATURDAY 27 OCTOBER. (Writing on Tuesday 6 November.) Nothing particular to mark.

SUNDAY 28 OCTOBER. (Writing on Tuesday 6 November.) Stayed at home in the forenoon. Heard Mr. Walker in the afternoon. It was wet and dull. Called on Grange, and he and I drank a couple of bottles of Teneriffe [8] cordially. We enjoyed this much. But it was not right to take it on Sunday, for it disturbed me so much that I was not in condition to hear the children say divine lessons. Poor Phemie had been ill since yesterday with a feverish disorder.

MONDAY 29 OCTOBER. (Writing on Tuesday 6 November.) Had been uneasy all night, and awaked ill. Grew better. Went to town, dressed, and attended Hunter-Blair's election dinner in the Assembly Hall. [9] Was not gloomy. But felt a cold indifference. Got next to Maclaurin. He was not jovial and went away early. I joined a jolly set gathered about Colonel Hunter, and grew brisker. After much solicitation I sung *Sir Dilberry Diddle* better than I ever did, having first made a speech that I hoped none of the gentlemen of the Edinburgh Defensive Band would suspect any ridicule upon *them*. (I had seen this band with great satisfaction per-

[7] "It makes a great difference [whether a god is speaking or a hero, a ripe old man or] one still in the flower and glow of youth" (Horace, *Ars Poetica*, 114–116).

[8] Canary wine.

[9] James Hunter-Blair had been elected M.P. for Edinburgh to succeed Sir Lawrence Dundas, who died 21 September. He was later created a baronet. "This day came on the election of a Member of Parliament.... Mr. Hunter-Blair afterwards gave an elegant entertainment to the Members of Council and a great number of other gentlemen and principal citizens in the Assembly Hall" (*Edinburgh Evening Courant*, 29 October 1781).

form their exercise last week on Heriot's Work bowling-green.) I then was called up to Hunter-Blair's right hand, and by various requests was induced to sing *Twa Wheels and an Axletree*.[1] I had no vivid enjoyment, but just moved along the tide of life. I got up and was pleased with a hunting-song, and wished there had been more tonight, in honour of the great Hunter at my hand; and I gave this toast: "May the Hunter of Edinburgh prove a mighty Nimrod in the House of Commons." This had an admirable effect. The deacons,[2] etc., got up on their feet and drank it. I kept myself quite sober, and got home between ten and eleven.

TUESDAY 30 OCTOBER. (Writing on Friday 9 November.) I took a ride in the forenoon with Sandy round about Dalry, Bells Mills, etc., which made him very happy. Went to town in the evening and saw my father, who arrived about five o'clock. Found him in his ordinary way of late, and rather more kindly.

WEDNESDAY 31 OCTOBER. (Writing on Friday 9 November.) Poor Phemie had been ill since Saturday of a cold and pretty high feverishness. I went into town, and got a message from my wife to get either Mr. Wood or Dr. Gillespie for her. I carried out Mr. Wood to dinner. Miss Annie Boswell was there. He thought Phemie in no danger. As a message had been also left for Dr. Gillespie, I resolved that he should come, but as it was a bad afternoon, I walked in with Mr. Wood to stop him from coming till next day. We sat down with him and drank a little port. I was alarmed about poor Phemie, and vexed that I had ever shown more fondness for Veronica, so as to hurt Phemie's spirit at all. I stayed tea at Dr. Gillespie's. Commissioner Cochrane was ill of a fever and really in danger. Dr. Gillespie had been with him in the forenoon and was to go again at seven. I accompanied him in the Commissioner's chaise and found the old gentleman in bed, quite lean and pale, but retaining his spirit. I really was sorry for him, and uneasy at the thought of one whom I had so long known being carried off and seen no more in his life. I went to my father's with Dr. Gillespie and supped. I found it proper to be well with Gillespie.

THURSDAY 1 NOVEMBER. (Writing on Friday the 9.) I should have marked that since the accounts came of Lord Kellie's death, my wife was exceedingly attentive to Lady Colville and Lady Anne Erskine, and I called several times on Andrew, whom I found more affectionate than I supposed him to be. He took my visits kind. I dined today at the Rev. Dr. Hunter's with Hunter-Blair, etc. Was not vivid, but liked to be at the Professor of Divinity's.

[1] "A nonsensical Scotch song" (Journal, 13 February 1775) of Boswell's own writing; *Sir Dilberry Diddle* may have been his too. Neither is known to have survived.

[2] Presidents of the incorporated crafts; *ex officio* members of the Town Council.

FRIDAY 2 NOVEMBER. (Writing on Wednesday the 14.) We came to our town house. The change was comfortable. I dined at my father's with my two sons. I visited Commissioner Cochrane in the forenoon, who was better.

SATURDAY 3 NOVEMBER. (Writing on Wednesday the 14.) Nothing particular to mark except that I drank coffee at Mr. Solicitor's; Dr. Cullen there.

SUNDAY 4 NOVEMBER. (Writing on Wednesday the 14.) Was too late for church in the forenoon. Visited my father between sermons. Heard Dr. Blair in the afternoon. In the evening the children were all indisposed but Veronica, who said divine lessons.

MONDAY 5 NOVEMBER. (Writing on Wednesday the 14.) Dined at my father's; Balbarton, Dr. Webster, and Dr. Gillespie there. Got just as much claret as to give me a relish for it (not quite half a bottle or at least not more). Called on Maclaurin, who hospitably produced claret, and he and I drank a bottle apiece most socially. I only regretted his infidelity. It hurt me.

TUESDAY 6 NOVEMBER. (Writing on Wednesday the 14.) I recollect nothing particular except that Captain Scott of the Forge dined.

WEDNESDAY 7 NOVEMBER. (Writing on Wednesday the 14.) Maclaurin and I were to have gone out to Lord Advocate's at Melville Castle. But heard he was in town. Dr. Webster insisted I should dine with him, as he had some good claret which would be gone. I did so, and we took a bottle apiece. In the evening I was agreeably surprised with a visit from my brother John, who had returned from Moffat last night. He was well dressed, and behaved wonderfully well. He supped, and he and I drank a little mountain comfortably. I thanked GOD for the happy change.

THURSDAY 8 NOVEMBER. (Writing on Wednesday the 14.) Was at the New Church forenoon and afternoon, it being the Fast Day before the Sacrament. I had little feeling, but was decent. Mrs. Mitchelson dined with us between sermons. My brother John drank tea with us. He and I visited our father together, and then supped at Dr. Webster's comfortably.

FRIDAY 9 NOVEMBER. (Writing on Wednesday the 14.) My brother John supped with us, and was really companionable in a grave style. I was however under restraint with him. Mr. George Wallace sat an hour with us in the evening.

SATURDAY 10 NOVEMBER. (Writing on Wednesday the 14.) Visited my father. My brother John and I walked out and visited Commissioner Cochrane. Was at the New Church in the afternoon. Kept quiet at home all the evening.

SUNDAY 11 NOVEMBER. (Writing on Thursday the 22.) Attended the New Church and took the Sacrament, but without fervour. Miss Preston dined with us between sermons. The children said divine lessons in the evening.

MONDAY 12 NOVEMBER. (Writing on Thursday the 22.) Heard Sir Harry Moncreiff in the New Church. Visited my father. Dined with Dr. Webster, etc., at the Rev. Mr. Kemp's (the first time of my being there). Drank too much port. Supped with Dr. Webster.

TUESDAY 13 NOVEMBER. (Writing on Friday the 23.) Had been ill last night from drinking too much port, and was still so much indisposed that I wished to lie in bed; but got up to make my appearance in the Court of Session. Thought it dull and poor.

WEDNESDAY 14 NOVEMBER. (Writing on Friday the 23.) Nothing recollected except waiting on the Lord President in the morning.

THURSDAY 15 NOVEMBER. (Writing on Friday the 23.) Nothing to recollect except that either last night or this (last, I am pretty sure) I supped with Lord Kames. Nobody there but Mr. Russell, the surgeon, who seemed to be of more pleasing manners than young men about Edinburgh usually are. I found my Lord dictating to his clerk a proposal to give premiums for planting oaks near the banks of the Great Canal.[3] He was as entire in his faculties as ever I knew him, and so was Mrs. Drummond. I supped well, as I always do there. We had no conversation to be registered.

FRIDAY 16 NOVEMBER. (Writing on Friday the 23.) My wife and I, Veronica, Phemie, and Sandy dined at my father's.

SATURDAY 17 NOVEMBER. (Writing on Friday the 23.) Had laboured for some days under an impotence of mind, so that I could not write No. 50 of *The Hypochondriack*. This day wrote it all but a little.[4] The Lords altered their interlocutor in the simple question as to a paragraph in the *Edinburgh Gazette* being published *animo injuriandi* against the Edinburgh Procurators, or Solicitors, before the inferior courts. It vexed me that the judges of this country should be so wavering, and I feared too a mixture of partiality.[5] My brother John dined with us today with

---

[3] The thirty-eight-mile canal connecting the Forth and the Clyde, constructed 1768–1790. Work on it was suspended, 1775–1786, but the eastern portion had been finished before the interruption.

[4] On learning. Boswell leans heavily on Cicero's *Pro Archia*, and ends with assurance of the longevity of scholars: "For the comfort of the studious, I can with pleasure mention that I have seen a table of longevity, lately drawn up by a curious gentleman, consisting of three columns: one of kings, one of poets, and one of philosophers; and it appears that the poets lived many years more than the kings; but the philosophers, whose application must be allowed to be the greatest, lived many years more than either the poets or the kings" (*The Hypochondriack*, No. 50).

[5] The term "solicitor" had not previously been much used in Scotland. Lawyers qualified to plead cases in court were styled *advocates*; lawyers who drew legal docu-

the young Campbells, the first time of his seeing them. He was really conversable with me, and he and I drank a bottle of mountain. What a comfort was it to have a social afternoon with a brother who had been so long insane! He stayed tea.

SUNDAY 18 NOVEMBER. (Writing on Friday the 23.) Stayed at home in the forenoon. Heard Dr. Dick in the College Kirk in the afternoon. Was troubled with dreary doubts. Miss Macredie drank tea with us. The children said divine lessons.

MONDAY 19 NOVEMBER. (Writing on Friday the 23.) Dined at my father's (whom I have visited several times not mentioned); the laird of Logan, Dr. Gillespie, and Mr. Stobie there. For some time past had been in sad spirits, having little value for anything. Drank a bottle of sherry. Was a good deal intoxicated, though I concealed it well. Supped at Lord Kames's; Captain Home of Ninewells [6] there. Was better in spirits.

TUESDAY 20 NOVEMBER. (Writing on Friday the 23.) Last night, after a long interval (ever since I was last in London), I got a letter from my friend Temple, which I kept till this morning, and opened it when I was at breakfast and calm. [7] It did me good, but had not so vivid an effect

---

ments and were qualified to manage cases in the superior courts were styled simply *writers*; while lawyers who were qualified to practise only in the inferior courts were styled *procurators*. The Society of Procurators of Edinburgh had recently obtained a royal charter in which at their request their ancient style was changed to that of "solicitors," no doubt because "procurator" was too close in sound to "procurer." The *Edinburgh Gazette* (28 April 1780) had thereupon published a sarcastic paragraph saying that the caddies or *"running stationers"* of the City "in imitation...of an *equally respectable* society" were applying for a charter granting them "the sole privilege of PROCURING, in the most extensive sense of the word." The Society of Solicitors (formerly Procurators) prosecuted Thomas Robertson, the publisher of the *Gazette*, for *animus injuriandi* ("intent to injure"). Boswell was advocate for Robertson. The Lord Ordinary had found in favour of the Society, but his interlocutor was reversed by the Inner House. The Society (as Scots law permitted them to do) petitioned the Lords for a review. At this stage (4 June 1781) Boswell had persuaded Johnson to dictate an extended argument which he included verbatim in his Answers for Robertson. On 17 November 1781 the Lords, with no new evidence before them, reversed their own judgement, and fined Robertson £5 sterling with costs of suit.

[6] David Hume's nephew. David had changed the spelling of the family name.

[7] "You think I prefer the company of a good-humoured, sensible neighbour to the gaiety and poignancy of professed wits and authors. I confess I do so. The former amuses, the other irritates me; the one wishes to please or inform, the other to shine and to sparkle. Besides, nothing can be more disagreeable than the impatience of persons of the latter description to outdo one another; they are not content with being simple and just and true, but writhe and distort their imaginations to produce somewhat singular, far-fetched, and generally absurd and ridiculous. There is a clergyman here, about twenty miles distant, whom I sometimes see, who has learning,

as his letters have had in earlier years. I dined at the Hon. A. Gordon's; his mother, Lord Haddo, and Mr. James Dallas, Writer to the Signet, there. Was hearty and in momentaneous spirits and drank a good deal, thinking of the old friendship between the late Earl of Aberdeen [8] and my grandfather. Played brag and whist, supped and played again; sat till two in the morning. Lost a little at cards; was much intoxicated.

WEDNESDAY 21 NOVEMBER. (Writing on Wednesday the 28.) Was so ill that I could not get up till late. Luckily had nothing to do in the Court of Session. However, I grew better, and went down to it a little. Dined and drank tea at Dr. Webster's with Lord Banff and his brother David,[1] Sir John Belsches, etc., comfortably.

THURSDAY 22 NOVEMBER. (Writing on Wednesday the 28.) Balbarton and Mr. Evory dined and drank tea with us. I visited my father before dinner.

FRIDAY 23 NOVEMBER. (Writing on Wednesday the 28.) Dined at my father's; Phemie and Sandy, Dr. Gillespie and Mr. Stobie there. Stayed and played whist and drank tea. Felt myself well employed in contributing to divert my father, whose bladder complaint was since autumn last so increased that he required the catheter three times a day, and when he took exercise had bloody urine, so that he kept the house close. I was tenderly affected with his situation, for all his coldness.

SATURDAY 24 NOVEMBER. (Writing on 3 December.) I recollect nothing but visiting Lady Colville in the forenoon and having Mr. Sibthorpe, Dr. Gillespie, etc., at dinner.

SUNDAY 25 NOVEMBER. (Writing on 3 December.) Was at New Church all day. Drank tea at Commissioner Cochrane's. Visited my father both forenoon and evening. The children said divine lessons. Was happy on this anniversary of my marriage day.

MONDAY 26 NOVEMBER. (Writing on 3 December.) Dictated part of a Petition for Robertson, the printer,[2] and was pretty well. Sent for my brother John to tea. He came, and was social enough.

TUESDAY 27 NOVEMBER. (Writing on 3 December.) Dined at my father's; Mrs. Boswell of Balmuto and Mr. Claud there. Mr. and Mrs.

---

sense, and candour, and whose conversation (from the sample I have had of them) I infinitely prefer to that of all your modern Johnsons and Goldsmiths. If your London parties in general resemble that we once had at your friend Langton's, I am not mortified to think I am banished so far from them" (From Temple, 6 November 1781).
[8] Gordon's father.
[1] Ogilvy.
[2] See above, 17 November 1781. The Lords declined to consider the cause further.

Macredie drank tea with us. I had today a disagreeable struggle in endeavouring to settle an exchequer process against my father about his carriage duty,[3] while Claud and John Stobie wanted to push it on. They had my father biased for it, so that I could not move him. The Hon. A. Gordon and I supped at Lord Kames's cheerfully.

WEDNESDAY 28 NOVEMBER. (Writing on 3 December.) The Hon. A. Gordon called at my father's while I was there in the forenoon. Commissioner Cochrane was there for the first time since his illness.

THURSDAY 29 NOVEMBER. (Writing on 3 December.) My client, Mr. Mercer of Lethendy,[4] insisted on entertaining me in the evening with a glass of claret at Walker's tavern. I went at six. Had heard he was an extraordinary character. Found him naturally and habitually odd, and also somewhat in liquor, so that he was very curious company. He had wild fancies and odd gestures, but was withal a man of sense and a Latin scholar. Mr. Mitchell, writer in Perth, his country agent, was with him. We made claret circulate very briskly. Mr. Robert Boswell joined us for some time, he being his agent in the process in which I am his lawyer. I grew jovial and somewhat extravagant, and being remarkably strong in head at the time, drank freely and humoured my client, who after every sentence or two sung *The Humours of the Glen*, without words. After Mr. Robert Boswell went away, we got in Walker, the landlord, who drank a little with us. It was a very singular scene. I had asked my client to sup with me tonight, but luckily he could not. I engaged him and Mitchell to dinner next day, Mr. Robert Boswell being to be with me. About ten my client was carried off in a chair. Mitchell and I sat a few minutes after him, and thought ourselves very sober, though eight bottles of claret were drank, besides part of a bottle of Madeira, which Mr. Mercer, as having been in America, called for.[5] I walked home; and though flustered, did really imagine that I was not much intoxicated.

FRIDAY 30 NOVEMBER. (Writing on 3 December.) Awaked very ill, but grew better, and was in the Court of Session at nine. At one saw the Edinburgh Defensive Band exercised on Heriot's Green, and Mr.

[3] We have been unable to find anything further about this process.
[4] In 1778 the Justices of Peace of Cupar had pronounced John Duff to be unemployed and disorderly, thus making him liable to be impressed into military service, though at the time he was employed as Mr. Mercer's servant. Mercer and Duff prosecuted the Justices for damages and expenses. For a full narrative of the cause, see Appendix B at the end of this volume. Also see below, 5 December 1781.
[5] Because of restrictions imposed by the mother country, the American colonies could trade directly with the Madeira Islands, but not with Continental Portugal or France. Consequently Madeira was much more drunk in America than either claret or port.

Crosbie appear for the first time as their lieutenant-colonel. At dinner Mr. Mercer, my client, having been drinking in the forenoon, was much in the same state as when I first saw him last night. Mr. Robert Boswell, wife and sisters, and Mr. and Mrs. Cannan, and Mr. Mitchell were with us. I was sorry that I had with too much openness described him to some of my brethren in the forenoon, for a client's oddities should not be exposed. Sandy Gordon came and sat awhile with us after dinner to see him. But he sunk into inarticulate drunkenness very soon, and insisted to be handed to his chair by his counsel. He however kept his old spirit; for on the stair he muttered, "Pro rege et patria." The account of Lord Cornwallis's surrender came today.[6] It pleased me much, as I trusted it would at length put an end to the American war. Mr. Gordon insisted on my coming to his house to make up a party at whist. When I went, I found a party without me; and as my feelings on public affairs were very different from theirs, I did not stay supper. I did not go to the meeting of Freemasons today, having been at it with Lord Balcarres last year.[7]

SATURDAY 1 DECEMBER. (Writing on the 3.) Restrained my joy on Lord Cornwallis's surrender, not to give offence. But it inspirited me, in so much that though for some time I have been quite lazy in the morning, relaxed and unable to rise, I this day sprung up. I called on my father before dinner for a little. Then Mr. George Wallace and I walked out to Prestonfield, where my son Sandy was before me, having walked out at eleven. We were very comfortable, and we had the coach to town. I went and supped at my father's. I was a little heated with wine. He had his old republican humour, reading the King's speech: "What a clattering's this —*my* forces! I think he might have said *ours.*" [8]

SUNDAY 2 DECEMBER. (Writing on 3.) Stayed at home in the forenoon. Heard Mr. Walker in the afternoon. The children said divine lessons. Mr. Boswall of Blackadder,[9] whom I had not seen for two years (I think), called and supped with us very agreeably. I was pretty well, though my enjoyment was not vivid.

MONDAY 3 DECEMBER. For many nights past I have rather been dis-

---

[6] At Yorktown, on 19 October, to Washington and Rochambeau.

[7] On this day (St. Andrew's Day, the regular date for the election of Grand Officers), Lord Balcarres was re-elected Grand Master. Boswell probably means no more than that he felt justified in absenting himself, having done his duty the previous year.

[8] "It is with great concern that I inform you that the events of war have been very unfortunate to my arms in Virginia, having ended in the loss of my forces in that province" (the King's speech, dated Westminster, 27 November 1781, *Scots Magazine*, November 1781, xliii. 562).

[9] Alexander Boswall, "the Nabob."

turbed in my sleep by confused dreams, except one night when I had a pleasing interview with my amiable friend Mrs. Stuart and Colonel James. I am too fat at present. My belly is more swelled than I ever remember it; and perhaps my humours are gross. I have a torpidity of mind that I have not often experienced. I have not "a lively hope of immortality." [1] It occurred to me today that perhaps a man is immortal or not as he happens to die in a dull or a lively frame. I have often been an immortal soul. At present it seems to me that I am not of celestial fire. I am quite sensual, and that, too, not exquisitely but rather swinishly. My wife and I and our three eldest children dined at my father's and drank tea; an ungracious scene. Last week I called on Sir W. Forbes, who had read forty of my *Hypochondriacks* and liked them; said there were many original thoughts, and always a good tendency. He is to give me remarks on each.[2] I just lounged today. Only studied a long cause. For the first two weeks of this Session got only one guinea. Was desponding, but too dull to feel much. Last week got seven.

TUESDAY 4 DECEMBER. (Writing on the 6.) Miss Susie Wellwood dined and drank tea with us. I did little today.

WEDNESDAY 5 DECEMBER. (Writing on the 6.) This day to my agreeable surprise the Court of Session determined my client Mercer of Lethendy's cause for him. I was clear he should gain it, but had experienced such a procedure upon it before that I had no hope but in an appeal.[3] I was pretty keenly agitated, which I had not been for many weeks. I dined with my client at Mr. Robert Boswell's, but kept myself sober. Supped at Lord Kames's with General Gordon of Fyvie, his brother Alexander, Miss Jardine, etc. Lord Kames drank after the ladies were gone, "Good rest to us all with Miss Jardine." "I fancy," said I, "there would not be much rest with her. It would be old Hardyknute's rest:

---

[1] 1 Peter 1. 3–4: "a lively hope by the resurrection of Jesus Christ . . . to an inheritance incorruptible and undefiled, and that fadeth not away."

[2] Boswell was no doubt thinking that he might collect the series in book form when it was completed, and had decided that a volume-division at the fortieth number would be appropriate. (He had printed No. 50 by this date, and was to continue the series to No. 70.) We should no doubt recognize the copy that Forbes read (and later Lord Kames: see below, 23 and 29 July 1782) in a volume at Yale which consists of the first forty monthly numbers torn from the volumes of the *London Magazine* in which they appeared, with corrections and some revision in Boswell's hand. Another similar set at Yale presents something of a puzzle. It is practically complete and is also corrected and revised by Boswell, but the corrections and the revision appear to have been made independently of the set with forty numbers.

[3] The Lords awarded Mercer and Duff £40 and expenses of suit. But this was not final. See below, 2 and 22 January 1782.

Full seventy years he now had seen,
With scarce sev'n years of rest." [4]

My Lord seemed a little stunned by this, as if a joke upon himself, which was certainly not meant. But he soon plucked up spirit and said for himself, "Old Hardyknute would do as well as any of you." [5] Dr. Walker at Moffat walked up the street with me, and gave it as his opinion that Lord Kames would live long yet.

THURSDAY 6 DECEMBER. On the night between the 27 and 28 November last I dreamt in so lively a manner of Mrs. Stuart that next day I wrote to her of it:

MY CHARMING FRIEND,—Last night I dreamt that I was a good while in company with you and Colonel Stuart; and thus by the benignity of my guardian angel, or a particular sunshine of fancy, enjoyed a happiness which I cannot at present have when awake. Have you not felt that any person or circumstance of which you have had a pleasing dream has been exceedingly agreeable, more so than ever, while the impression remained upon the mind, unruffled by the rude course of life? I feel this with a fond serenity at this moment. I have an eager wish to be with you, and would value a letter from you in a peculiar manner. Be kind enough to write to me as soon as you can. How fortunate should I be should a sympathetic power have affected you in the same manner at the same time.

The rest of my letter was expressing my wish to obtain what would enable me and my family to live in London. By strange supineness this letter lay till this day that I sent it off. Being of a dreaming nature, it had slept in my drawer. I told her so in a postscript. Called on my brother John in the morning. Had him at dinner and Mr. Lawrie. Was indolent and did no business. Was at a consultation at eight, this week being pretty prosperous. Went and supped at my father's. He was in a quiet state of failure. I was in a state of indifference.

FRIDAY 7 DECEMBER. (Writing on Friday the 14). Dined at the Hon. A. Gordon's with Lady Wallace, General Gordon, etc. Was very gay. He and Shawfield and Craufurdland and Maclaurin played cards and supped with us.

SATURDAY 8 DECEMBER. (Writing on the 14.) There was a debate in the Faculty of Advocates whether we should oppose Mr. John Wright's

[4] Lines 3–4 of *Hardyknute: A Scottish Fragment*, circulated as an ancient ballad, actually the composition of Elizabeth, Lady Wardlaw (1677–1727).

[5] Rather coarse jesting, considering that Miss Jardine was to become his daughter-in-law in less than a year.

petition to come among us, he being of low origin and gaining his liveli-
hood as a teacher of law and mathematics. I was keen for him, being of
opinion that our Society has no *dignity*, and must receive every man of
good character and knowledge. There was a vote, and the party for him
carried it by *ten*. Dr. Gillespie accompanied me to Prestonfield for the
first time. He and Sir Alexander took much to one another as physicians.
Veronica, Phemie, and Sandy were with us. We dined and drank tea. My
wife was very ill with a cold since Thursday.

SUNDAY 9 DECEMBER. (Writing on the 14.) Went to the New English
Chapel in the forenoon and heard prayers read by Mr. Cleves,[6] a clergy-
man famous for elocution. He pleased me much. I did not greatly admire
Dr. Dechair's preaching, whom I heard today for the first time. I heard
Dr. Blair in the afternoon. The children said divine lessons. I visited my
father in the evening, and supped at Dr. Webster's with Mr. Moodie at
Riccarton [7] and Mr. John McLure.

MONDAY 10 DECEMBER. (Writing on the 14.) Dictated well. Dined
at Balmuto's, where Lord Monboddo and Dr. Gillespie were introduced
and took well to each other. Mr. David Erskine too was there. We had
really a good afternoon, without drinking too much. I was in such spirits
that I chose to end the day socially; so supped at Lord Kames's with Dr.
Blair and Mr. and Mrs. Morehead. Walked home in hearty vigour. Was in
danger from dalliance in the Luckenbooths,[8] but shunned it.

TUESDAY 11 DECEMBER. (Writing on the 14.) The day went on tolerably. I visited my father. Grange, who returned from the country only
yesterday, supped with us.

WEDNESDAY 12 DECEMBER. (Writing on the 14.) Dictated well, and
was as busy at night as I ever have been as a lawyer. Mr. Alexander

[6] Properly Cleeve.

[7] The minister of the parish, pilloried by Burns in *The Holy Fair*:

> Now a' the congregation o'er
> Is silent expectation;
> For Moodie speels [enters] the holy door
> Wi' tidings o' damnation:
> Should Hornie, as in ancient days,
> 'Mang sons o' God present him,
> The vera sight o' Moodie's face
> To's ain het hame had sent him
> Wi' fright that day.

[8] A range of heavily-eaved buildings in the thoroughfare of the High Street, parallel
to St. Giles's Church, from which they were separated by a gloomy lane only wide
enough for foot-passengers. The buildings dated from the reign of James III, and the
name came from their being booths that could be closed or locked, as distinguished
from the open booths which at one time lined the street on both sides.

Walker, who came late to consult me, supped with us, along with Mr. Lawrie, whom I now have seldom at meals.

THURSDAY 13 DECEMBER. (Writing on the 14.) Awaked this morning remarkably well. Had a good dream in the night of being in company with a steady English counsellor, with whom I had a good deal of conversation which animated me, as the English character so agreeably does; and I recollected distinctly a peculiar phrase which he used: that a man should acquire "preciseness and peremptoriness of mind." It was well dreamt. I was in strong spirits all day, and was sensible that a great deal of my unhappiness is mere cloud which any moment may dissipate. I thought that at any period of time, a man may disencumber himself of all the *accessories* of his identity, of all his books, all his connexions with a particular place, or a particular sphere of life; and retaining only his consciousness and reminiscence, start into a state of existing quite new. That therefore I should be more *myself* and have more of the "mihi res non me rebus submittere."[9] Dictated a great deal, and when weary went and supped at my father's.

FRIDAY 14 DECEMBER. (Writing on the 19.) Nothing to record.

SATURDAY 15 DECEMBER. (Writing on the 19.) There was a debate in the Faculty of Advocates whether we should give our approbation to the scheme of the magistrates for removing the slaughter-houses a mile from the Cross. I alone opposed it, from a principle of *justice* to the fleshers, and, I will own, at the same time from a wish to appear the champion even of *that* corporation. It is wonderful to what keenness I worked myself up.[1] Mr. Moodie, Minister of Riccarton, my brother John, Painter Donaldson, etc., dined with us. I was a staid, sensible man today, but drank too much wine. I visited my father in the evening; and then being heated wandered in the street, but did no harm. Called on Matthew Dickie, who had the gout.

SUNDAY 16 DECEMBER. (Writing on 19.) Heard Dr. Blair in the forenoon and Mr. Walker in the afternoon. This day the custom of having only one discourse in the forenoon was introduced into the New Church. I visited Dr. Webster in the afternoon. The children said divine lessons in the evening. Grange supped with us. I drank too much, and being . . .[2]

---

[9] "[I try] to subdue the world to myself, not myself to the world" (Horace, *Epistles*, I. i. 19).

[1] Boswell always showed strong indignation at any proposal to abrogate long-standing property rights without compensation. It was this, more than anything else, that caused him to oppose Fox's East India Bill and Wilberforce's bill to abolish the slave trade. See his *Letter to the People of Scotland*, 1783, and the *Life of Johnson*, 23 September 1777.

[2] Boswell inked out the first four words of this sentence. Six pages of the manuscript,

[SATURDAY 29 DECEMBER.] . . . my straitened circumstances and my father's unkindness. There is something quite inexplicable in the human mind. I this day under all these evils felt a spring and a manly vigour. I visited Laird Heron at Clarke's Hotel, my former house in Chessel's Buildings.[3] I heard from Mr. Hunter-Blair this forenoon so good an account of the comedians that I resolved to go at night to *The Beggar's Opera*, inhale London cheerfulness, and be of service in dissipating my wife's gloomy apprehensions. There was but a very thin house. I took my place in the pit, got in at the song " 'Tis woman that seduces," [4] and really had the same pleasure that I used to have at seeing *The Beggar's Opera* in my youth. Charles Crookshanks appeared unexpectedly to me in the pit, and I sat by him. I came home enlivened.

SUNDAY 30 DECEMBER. (Writing on Tuesday 8 January 1782.) At home forenoon calm. Grange and I walked out to Prestonfield and dined comfortably. Returned to tea and found Dr. Webster. The children said divine lessons. I had not been at my father's since the disagreeable scene on Monday. But Mrs. Boswell of Balmuto having been taken ill today in church, I paid him a visit in the evening, thinking he might be softened. Grange supped with us. I read one of Mr. Carr's sermons out.

MONDAY 31 DECEMBER. (Writing on 8 January 1782.) Commissioner Cochrane called and told me he had seen my father, but that before he came, Lady Auchinleck had settled with him that I should have my £100 of arrear; and he said I should thank her. My wife was still very ill. My brother John and Grange dined with me today. My wife did not come to dinner. John drank tea with us.

---

containing the entries from the 17th to the 28th, have been removed. Among other matter lost was presumably a record of a "disagreeable scene" at Lord Auchinleck's on Monday 24 December. See below, 30 December 1781.

[3] Where Boswell and his wife lived from May 1770 to May 1771.

[4] Boswell comes in on the second scene of Act I.

1782

TUESDAY 1 JANUARY. (Writing on Tuesday the 8th.) I felt nothing particular on the beginning of a new year. My mind was depressed with anxiety about my wife. After breakfast I had a message from my father to come to him. I went; and he and I and John Stobie went into his bedroom, where he told me that he had once resolved not to give me the £100, but he was now to do it. But that he declared upon his honour that if I ever again exceeded my income, he would give me no more. I calmly mentioned that this £100 was a part of my income. Stobie said *my Lady* insisted on it. When we went into (writing on 9 January) the drawing-room, my father mentioned his giving me the £100. I said to *her* I believed I was obliged to her. She answered no. She never interfered. (An assertion not *exactly* the thing that *is*.) [5] "I'm sorry for it," said I. "Why?" said she. "Because," said I, "I'm glad when there's any good." "That would not have been good," said she. Since she chose to *deny* her influence, I had no more to say. I came home and dined, the young Campbells with us, and returned to my father's and drank tea.

WEDNESDAY 2 JANUARY. (Writing on 9 January.) Dictated all day Answers for John Duff and his master Lethendy.[6] Was in able spirits for business, though sadly uneasy about my dear wife. Miss Betty Dick came to be some days with us.

THURSDAY 3 JANUARY. (Writing on the 9.) Dictated also this day the same paper, having given in a note of apology to the Lord President's box for not being ready on this day as ordered. Mr. Lawrie had gone to the country and thoughtlessly stayed too long.

FRIDAY 4 JANUARY. (Writing on the 9th.) Was amused with correcting the proof-sheets of my paper, and was pleased with my own performance, regretting however that my abilities were confined to so narrow a sphere. My wife's illness confined me to town this vacation, so that I was disappointed of an excellent visit to Shawfield with Sandy Gordon and Maclaurin, the former of whom called on me the evening that he returned,

[5] "He [the Houyhnhnm who was Gulliver's master] replied that I must needs be mistaken or that I *said the thing which was not*. For they have no word in their language to express lying or falsehood" (*Gulliver's Travels*, Part IV, ch. 3).
[6] The Justices had appealed the decision of 5 December 1781.

and the other a day or two after. Their cheerfulness relieved my dreary, anxious depression. I was also disappointed of a visit to Valleyfield and Alloa, and to Sandy Gordon's at Rockville. These three days I was not out of my house.

SATURDAY 5 JANUARY. (Writing on the 9.) Walked out as far as Bristo Port with Dr. Gillespie. It was a damp day. Felt a pain in my bowels. Drank one glass of wine at dinner. Had a visit of Major Brown in the forenoon. Had my brother John at tea.

SUNDAY 6 JANUARY. (Writing on the 9.) Stayed at home all day, my bowel complaint continuing. Read Bryant's *Address to Priestley against Philosophical Necessity*. Had this day so clear a head and so stout an understanding that I did not fear this subject which has often distressed me; and I studied it with a firm ease. I liked part of Bryant's treatise, but wondered to see inconsistencies which so able a scholar unconsciously uttered, particularly on prescience. The children said divine lessons. I read to my wife two of Carr's sermons. Dr. Webster drank tea.

MONDAY 7 JANUARY. (Writing on the 10.) Was still indisposed a little. The young Campbells dined with us. Heard a debate in the Midlothian County meeting about erecting a turnpike on the road to Musselburgh. Lord Advocate was in the chair. After the meeting rose, he shook hands with me cordially, and promised that if he could, he would dine or sup with me before he went to London, and would let me know when. My dear wife desired me to ask him. I had resolved to have no company as long as her illness continued. She had no spitting of blood. But had a severe hollow cough in the night-time, unless when quieted by laudanum, and sweatings every night. Also at times during the day heats all over her body and a quick pulse. Also swellings in her legs; and she was very, very thin, and had pains shooting through her neck and breast. All these symptoms might be nervous. But both she and I dreaded the consumption, the fatal disease of her family. The apprehension of losing her and being left with five young children was frightfully dreary. All my affection for her and gratitude to her, and the consciousness of not having acted as her husband ought to do, overwhelmed me; and several times I cried bitterly, and one night lay long awake in misery, having wild schemes of desperate conduct floating in my imagination upon supposition of her death. The consideration of her cold, unworthy treatment by my father added much to my distress. It hurt me deeply to think that she should have been my wife only during my narrow and dependent state, and not have lived to be lady of Auchinleck. My views of futurity too were dim. In short I was very wretched. Miss Betty Dick left us this forenoon. I prayed to GOD in his mercy to restore my wife to health.

TUESDAY 8 JANUARY. (Writing the 10.) I sat a good while with Sir

William Forbes at his counting house, and talked of religion and Fate and Free Will with an easy firmness quite different from the feeble melancholy with which I have conversed with him in that place on those subjects. For distress had given a kind of fever to my mind that produced a temporary strength. I often *wonder* what will be the view which one shall have at last when fairly in another state of being. I visited my father before dinner. But found such indifference that I did not stay. My bowels too were still not right. Grange supped with us and I took a little port negus. My wife was better.

WEDNESDAY 9 JANUARY. (Writing on the 15.) I think I was at home all day. At tea my wife said, "What will you give me for a letter?" I guessed it was from Doctor Johnson. A kind letter it was. My heart was comforted and my spirits raised by it.[7]

THURSDAY 10 JANUARY. (Writing the 15.) Before I was out of bed, had a message that Lord Kellie was come and asking me to dine with him today at Lady Colville's.[8] I hastened out to breakfast, and was quite easy with him as an earl. I walked to town with him. Lady Dundonald, whom we had not seen since her son Charles was killed,[9] had kindly offered a visit to my wife. We begged that she and her sons George and Andrew would dine with us today, which they did and stayed tea. It was comfortable, nobody else being of the party. Her behaviour was like that of a Roman matron. Grange supped with us. I drank more wine today than for many days before.[1]

TUESDAY 22 JANUARY. (Writing on the 23.) I omitted to mention on Friday that Baron Sir John Dalrymple, who has several times flippantly told me that "we never meet" (though he published a scurrilous pamphlet against Lord Barrington and then refused a challenge from his Lordship, which I think should exclude him from the company of every gentle-

---

[7] Not, at first glance, a spirit-raising letter: "My health has been tottering this last year; and I can give no very laudable account of my time. I am always hoping to do better than I have ever hitherto done. My journey to Ashbourne and Staffordshire was not pleasant; for what enjoyment has a sick man visiting the sick?—Shall we ever have another frolic like our journey to the Hebrides? I hope that dear Mrs. Boswell will surmount her complaints; in losing her you would lose your anchor, and be tossed, without stability, by the waves of life. I wish both her and you very many years, and very happy. For some months past I have been so withdrawn from the world that I can send you nothing particular. All your friends, however, are well, and will be glad of your return to London" (From Johnson, 5 January 1782).

[8] Archibald Erskine had succeeded his brother as seventh Earl of Kellie.

[9] At Yorktown, where he was aide-de-camp to Cornwallis, 18 October 1781 (the day before the surrender).

[1] Eight pages of the manuscript, containing the entries from 11 to 21 January, have been removed.

man),[2] came up to me again, and with his usual pertness said, "How d'ye do? We never meet. We're wearing out of acquaintance. What's the meaning of it?" I answered, "I'm afraid Lord Barrington would take it amiss." And left him. This was well done. Yet I know not if anybody shuns him, except Lord Monboddo because he praises David Hume extravagantly. This day Duff and Mercer's cause came on. The Lord President did me the honour to praise my Answers for them from the Chair. "They are drawn with moderation, precision, and firmness. I have not seen a paper that pleased me more." I was very agreeably solaced with this praise. No philosophy can resist such a solace. But such is the discontent of my disposition that I was vexed such a display of my abilities had not been made in London. I gained my cause finally, but by one vote. Lord Monboddo had altered his opinion. I was truly alarmed at the danger the cause was in. It was comfortable to have it made *certain* at last, unless the Justices should appeal.[3] Having been informed by Mr. George Wallace that Sir John Pringle was taken very ill, I went out and visited Miss Hall, his niece, and found it to be too true, and that there was no hope of his recovery. I then visited Sir James Hall and his tutor, the Rev. Mr. Brand. Then Mr. Daniel, then Mr. Sibthorpe, whom I had visited some days ago, he being confined by indisposition. Sir Charles and Miss Preston and Surgeon Wood dined with us. Major Brown of Knockmarloch forwardly made his way upstairs after dinner and broke in upon Sir Charles, Mr. Wood, and me, sitting comfortably. We soon ended drinking wine and went to tea. Mr. Wood had brought accounts of Sir John Pringle's death. I was somewhat struck, but not with near so much sensibility as some years ago would have been the case. I was a very little heated with wine. My wife with much propriety prevented me from going to my father's and

[2] Sir John Dalrymple, Bt., one of the barons of exchequer, wrote *Three Letters to the Right Hon. Viscount Barrington* (1778), to which a fourth letter was added in the second edition (1779). This pamphlet, a medley of complaints, accuses Barrington, the Secretary at War, of sabotaging a corps, raised at Dalrymple's insistence, of which his brother William was commandant, and also of treating his brother Samuel, a captain in this corps, with brutality. The pamphlet's tone and content seem to merit a challenge: "If D'Estaing's fleet has, at this hour, passed the line, it is *you* and *you* only, who have lost the West Indies to England" (Letter I, pp. 6–7); "Woe to that country, in which the necessities of state are in such hands as yours, obliged continually to yield to the punctilios of office!" (Letter I, p. 24).

[3] The Justices did not appeal, but Mercer did. See below, 5 June 1782, in Editorial Note following 15 May 1782. Copies of all the printed papers submitted by Boswell to the Court of Session in this cause are preserved in the Signet Library, Edinburgh. We print as Appendix B at the back of the present volume an abridged text of the Answers which the Lord President praised so highly. We should have liked to print the whole, but it runs to thirty-six closely printed quarto pages. Boswell received three guineas for writing it.

announcing to him the death of his old friend, who was just two months younger than himself. She said it would be hollowing Mortimer in his ear.[4] I went and sat a little with worthy Grange. At night had again enjoyment.[5]

WEDNESDAY 23 JANUARY. (Writing on the 28.) This day I lost Garrallan's cause against Lord Dumfries, about a march-dike.[6] I thought the Lords wrong and was vexed. Grange dined with us. I drank tea at my father's, who seemed little moved by Sir John Pringle's death. He informed me that he had bought a house in the New Town. I found out afterwards that there had been a secret combined exertion to make him do this. Commissioner Cochrane, Claud, and Stobie had all aided the Lady on Monday the 14, and carried the point. I apprehended that the liferent, if not the property, would be settled on her. I was vexed and irritated, but resolved to be quiet.

THURSDAY 24 JANUARY. (Writing on the 28.) Visited Sir James Pringle and Miss Hall. Dined at the Lord President's; the Duchess of Buccleuch and Lady Frances Scott, Mr. Baron Norton, Dr. Hugh Blair, etc., there. The President himself was wonderfully jovial, and he and his company drank a great deal. He talked to me of John Duff's decision. I observed it turned all upon Lord Ankerville. He said, "It did so. And I don't know if you would have had Ankerville if he had not dined here the day before. I fixed him. I said, 'Ankerville, we have that case of the recruit tomorrow. We'll never alter *that*.' 'No,' said he, 'we'll never alter *that*.' " I was struck with the strange *management* of justice in this country. I came home in a chair a good deal intoxicated. Grange supped with us.

---

[4] *1 Henry IV*, I. iii. 218–221:

> He said he would not ransom Mortimer,
> Forbade my tongue to speak of Mortimer;
> But I will find him when he lies asleep,
> And in his ear I'll hollow "Mortimer!"

[5] Boswell inked out this sentence. The next to the last word is somewhat doubtful.

[6] Garrallan, owned by Patrick Douglas, a surgeon, adjoined the much larger property of the Earl of Dumfries. A "march-dike" is a boundary wall. Douglas had agreed to the construction of a stone dike on the line between the two properties, he to pay half the costs; but when the work was completed and the bill presented, declared that he had authorized only a short stretch of wall, not one for the entire march; furthermore, that the wall was badly built and the charge excessive. Boswell, having lost the cause three times before the Ordinary (Lord Kennet) has now lost it before the full bench, to whom he had addressed a long Petition on 11 December 1781. We find no record that Boswell made any further appeal. Patrick Douglas's daughter and only child married Hamilton Boswell, son of John Boswell ("Young Knockroon"). Lt.-Col. John Douglas Boswell, W.S., who purchased Auchinleck House from Lord Talbot de Malahide, was their grandson and representative.

FRIDAY 25 JANUARY. (Writing the 28.) Awaked exceedingly ill. However, I went to the Court of Session, and dined with Dr. Gillespie in company with Lieutenant Bligh, who had gone round the world as Master of Captain Cook's ship, the last voyage.[7] Maule of Panmure [8] and Mr. Macredie were there. I have not had so good a day since I left Dr. Johnson, we had so much good conversation. I drank wine and water, and came home sober and placid. Mr. Daniel sat a little with us in the evening.

SATURDAY 26 JANUARY. (Writing the 28.) My dear wife has for some days been a good deal better. She had an excellent night, and awaked well this morning. Miss Dick came in Sir Alexander's coach and conducted me and my three eldest children and Mr. George Wallace to Prestonfield, that the worthy Knight and Mr. Wallace and I might lament together the loss of Sir John Pringle. Sir Alexander was quite placid and gay, though he regretted his old friend. I felt Sir John's death more gloomily today than at first. It impressed me with the vanity of human life very sadly. Mr. George Wallace came home and supped with us soberly. I liked his variety of knowledge, but was uneasy to think of his want of belief; though to do him justice, he does not offensively obtrude it. It hurt me to be conscious that if I were strictly interrogated as to my own precise articles of faith, I should appear very unsettled.

SUNDAY 27 JANUARY. (Writing 6 February.) Heard the celebrated orator Mr. Cleeve [9] in the New English Chapel in the forenoon. Felt his manner as too theatrical. Heard Dr. Blair in the afternoon. The children said divine lessons very well. I am not sure whether I was at my father's. I think I supped there.

MONDAY 28 JANUARY. (Writing on 12 February.) Grange dined with us. Mrs. Thomas Boswall, to whom I had paid a visit lately, supped, having called in the evening.

TUESDAY 29 JANUARY. (Writing 12 February.) Dined at Dr. Webster's with Sir Charles and Miss Preston, Mr. Seton on Leith Walk's family, etc., an excellent dinner and enough of claret. Being pretty well warmed, I was foolishly amorous, but shall register no more. Went to a concert for the benefit of the music of the Defensive Band. Was noisy. Got

---

[7] The now famous William Bligh of the *Bounty*. (Boswell spells the name Blyth, which may represent the actual pronunciation. In the *Journal to Stella* Swift has the spelling Blith for the same name.) He had taken part in the battle on the Dogger Bank (see above, 13 August 1781), and in September of this year was to sail for Gibraltar with Lord Howe.

[8] Boswell *hoped* he would be "of Panmure," but the Court of Session ruled otherwise. See below, 1 March 1782.

[9] See above, foot-note on 9 December 1781. This time Boswell spells the name "Cleives."

General Mure Campbell and Colonel Craufurd to go and sup at Fortune's. I drank negus, and we parted about twelve.

WEDNESDAY 30 JANUARY. (Writing 12 February.) Had been restless all night. Was ill in the morning and lay all forenoon, as the Court did not sit today. Rose, and *thought* solemnly of this anniversary,[1] though I did not keep it publicly. Dined at Lord Monboddo's with Mr. Bligh, the circumnavigator, Dr. Gillespie, etc.; drank port and water, had good conversation, and came home well.

THURSDAY 31 JANUARY. (Writing 12 February.) Sir Charles and Miss Preston played whist and supped with us comfortably.

FRIDAY 1 FEBRUARY. (Writing the 12.) Grange dined with us. I know not what days I visited my father this week.

SATURDAY 2 FEBRUARY. (Writing the 12.) Walked out with my brother John and showed him our country-house at Drumsheugh. Sandy was with us. They returned to town, while I paid a visit to Lady Colville and Lord Kellie. John and Grange dined and drank tea with us. John drank rather too much. He was more sulky than usual today. I was heated with wine and was foolishly licentious in Liberton's Wynd with the landlady, whom I had never seen before. Would not with P.C., as now married.

SUNDAY 3 FEBRUARY. (Writing the 12.) Was at the New Church in the forenoon. Miss Susie Dunlop, who had come to town last night, dined with us between sermons. I kept her till afternoon church was out, and then went home with her and visited Old Lady Wallace. Was foolishly licentious same as last night. Was dull in perception as to morality in one point. The children said divine lessons. Felt myself in no pleasing state. Visited Lord Eglinton in the forenoon.

MONDAY 4 FEBRUARY. (Writing the 12.) Colonel Craufurd took a family dinner with us. Shawfield and Mrs. Campbell played whist and supped with us. In the forenoon I waited on the Lord President; found him ill with a cold and depressed, so that he was more mild and kindly than when in high spirits. I went on purpose to have a confidential conversation with him about (writing on the 17 February) my situation with my father. He gave me the same advice that Lord Advocate did: just to be quiet and say nothing. I suggested a doubt whether deeds executed by him would stand. The President said, "That is an inquiry which I wish may be prevented," or words to that purpose. He said that many days my father did not know what was going on in the Court. "He had" (said his Lordship) "flashes of understanding. I alwise[2] knew when he

---

[1] Of the execution of Charles I.

[2] See above, 24 March 1780, n. 10.

understood." In short it appeared to me that the President thought him in a state of incapacity. "James," said he, "the best thing that can happen to him is to die quietly." It shocked me to hear a man whom my father all along considered as his great friend speak thus of him without any tender regret; and the general dreary view of death hung upon my mind. I then visited my father for a little. Colonel Craufurd called at my house before dinner, and very easily agreed to take a family meal with us. In the evening Shawfield and Mrs. Campbell played at whist and supped with us in a cordial way.

TUESDAY 5 FEBRUARY. (Writing the 18.) I recollect nothing to register.

WEDNESDAY 6 FEBRUARY. (Writing the 18.) I recollect nothing to register.

THURSDAY 7 FEBRUARY. (Writing the 18.) This was the Fast by Proclamation.[3] Before knowing it was so, I had engaged Lords Eglinton and Kellie, Lady Colville, and Lady Anne Erskine to dine with us. I was very well pleased that we had them on this day, as I cannot join in imploring Heaven's blessing on the arms of the present Administration. We had an excellent dinner, choice wines, and the best company. The two Earls had never met till now, and they took to one another much. My dear wife was now much better, though this forenoon she was alarmed with spitting a little blood. The two Earls and I sat till half an hour after nine. I was a good deal intoxicated.

FRIDAY 8 FEBRUARY. (Writing the 18.) I got up really very well. Mr. Fairlie of Fairlie, Colonel Craufurd, and Knockroon supped with us soberly.

SATURDAY 9 FEBRUARY. (Writing the 18.) I dined at Lady Colville's; nobody there but her Ladyship, Lady Anne, and Lord Kellie. He and I drank our claret very cordially. When I got to town I was a good deal heated, and went grossly to Liberton's Wynd. Thought meanly of myself.[4]

SUNDAY 10 FEBRUARY. (Writing the 18.) Was at the New Church forenoon and afternoon. Dined at my father's after sermons. The children said divine lessons. It was a snowy day.

---

[3] "We, taking into our most serious consideration the just and necessary hostilities in which we are engaged, and the unnatural rebellion carrying on in some of our provinces and colonies in North America, and putting our trust in Almighty God, that he will vouchsafe a special blessing on our arms both by sea and land, have resolved, and do, by and with the advice of our Privy Council, hereby command that a public fast and humiliation be observed" (dated 20 January 1782, *Scots Magazine*, January 1782, xliv. 51).

[4] Boswell inked out this sentence and the preceding.

MONDAY 11 FEBRUARY. (Writing the 18.) Mr. John Boswell (Senior), Grange, Mr. Matthew Dickie, and Colonel Craufurd dined with us. Knockroon came in after dinner and took a glass. We were hearty but sober. I supped at my father's.

TUESDAY 12 FEBRUARY. (Writing the 18.) I recollect nothing to register. My life seemed to me very insignificant.

WEDNESDAY 13 FEBRUARY. (Writing the 18.) A very cold day. Was shocked by seeing the procession of Wilson Potts, late Commander of the *Dreadnought* privateer of Newcastle, going to Leith to be executed.[5] Fell into a wretched melancholy and was hopelessly gloomy. Had engaged (after once refusing) to dine today at Lady Colville's with company, Lord Kellie having come to me himself and said it would be good if I would come. I was now sadly averse to go. However, I went. Hon. A. Gordon and his lady, Mr. Irvine of Kingcausie, etc., there; and such was the simple effect of good meat and drink that I had not half dined till I was quite well. I drank till well warmed, played whist, and returned to town in high spirits. Called in Forrester's Wynd and sat with a strange woman, I dare say half an hour, but without any folly.

THURSDAY 14 FEBRUARY. (Writing the 18.) Wrote No. 53 of *The Hypochondriack,* I believe entirely.[6] Was in tolerable spirits. I have omitted to mention that one day I had a visit from General Mure Campbell and Sir James Pringle; and another day Dr. John Erskine paid us a forenoon visit and was comfortably social. And on the forenoon of the 7th I wrote to Temple, which did me much good.

FRIDAY 15 FEBRUARY. (Writing the 18.) Did very little. I was indolent, yet uneasy that I had no distinguished occupation. Supped at my father's. He appeared somewhat kindly to me tonight, which warmed my heart.

SATURDAY 16 FEBRUARY. (Writing the 18.) Was in exceeding good spirits, just from some better state of my blood. Dined at Lady Colville's, the last day of Lord Kellie's being in Scotland, or rather at his sister's, before his return to his regiment in Ireland. Just he and I and the ladies as last Saturday. I insisted on a peremptory bottle of claret and was quite as I could wish, pleasing myself that the Earl of Kellie and the laird of Auchinleck would pass many good days together. Returned to town a

---

[5] He was found guilty of having robbed a Danish vessel on the way to Iceland of 20,000 crowns. Since Denmark was a neutral country, this constituted piracy. The jury had recommended mercy on the ground that Potts was drunk when he committed the crime, and that he delivered up the money as soon as he recovered his senses. The sentence directed that, as a pirate, he be hanged at Leith, within the flood-mark.

[6] On words.

good deal intoxicated. Was foolishly licentious with landlady.[7] Was sulky and violent at home. Sir Walter M.C. supped with us.

SUNDAY 17 FEBRUARY. (Writing the 26.) Was at New Church in the forenoon. The children said divine lessons. Sir Walter M.C. and Grange supped with us. I sat a good while with Lord Kames, who had been ill, which kept me from church in the afternoon. Between sermons took Sir Charles Preston to visit my father. I was surprised when Sir Charles thought him better than when he visited him two years ago. I did expect he would have been a witness to his failure, though I said nothing of this to Sir Charles. I am now by mistake mentioning what Sir Charles observed next day as if it had been on this. I should have had some uneasiness at letting my father's failure be seen had I not considered that the interest of *the family* required me to take precautions against imposition being practised upon him. My disappointment in Sir Charles's opinion struck me a little as if I had been in the wrong. But Sir Charles has little discernment. Sir Walter M.C. dined with us after sermons. Lady Auchinleck whispered my father, and he asked Sir Charles to dine next day, and me to come along with him.

MONDAY 18 FEBRUARY. (Writing the 26.) Dined at my father's with Sir Charles Preston, Dr. Gillespie, Mr. Stobie. Drank a bottle of claret and some port and white wine. Was cautious and grave, but warmed and intoxicated. Had heard today that Old Balbarton had been ill for some time and had delayed too long to call Dr. Gillespie, who told me he had no hopes of his recovery. This agitated me. I went from my father's and called on Balbarton; found him in bed, distressed with strangury,[8] dropsy, and asthma. He had the same countenance of tranquillity that he used to have, and shook hands with me cordially. I told him I did not hear till today of his being ill, and found fault with him for not sending for me. He was all his life modestly shy as well as indolent. He said to me, "It 'ill no do wi' me now"—plainly letting me know he was sensible he was dying. I immediately started the subject of a future state. He said Ovid gave a beautiful description of transmigration. He did not know but it might be true. At any rate he said it would be quite different from anything we had ever . . .[9]

[TUESDAY 19 FEBRUARY.] . . . I walked with Grange to Duddingston Loch and saw a number of people skating. Went to Prestonfield and dined cordially. Grange and I returned to town to tea. Colonel Craufurd came in again from Ayrshire tonight, and we had a consultation at

---

[7] Boswell inked out this sentence.

[8] A disease of the urinary organs characterized by slow and painful passage of urine.

[9] Two pages of the manuscript, containing the rest of the entry for the 18th and the beginning of the 19th, have been removed. See below, 27 February 1782.

Crosbie's on Gemmill's cause against him, which was to come on next day.[1] I went to take Hunter of Thurston's house in St. Andrew's Square, my wife having liked it. I looked at it with her in the forenoon. But I found it was already taken. I had brought my mind to remove to the New Town, as better for the health of my wife and children, and as I should be near to my father in his new house. I paid a visit at Old Lady Wallace's and prevailed on Miss Susie Dunlop to sup with us. Was gay. Grange and I called at Balbarton's on our return to town. But his nephew told us he was so ill we could not see him.

WEDNESDAY 20 FEBRUARY. (Writing the 27.) Colonel Craufurd won his cause unanimously, which animated me. I called on Balbarton in the forenoon, but was told he died last night. Was struck much. Dr. Gillespie told me Balbarton gave his dying testimony that I was the best man of the name. The Doctor mentioned my father. Balbarton said he was a good man for himself. Sir Walter M.C. and his man of business, Mr. Andrew Blane, dined with us, and we talked of his affairs. But he was too wise in his own conceit.[1a] I drank rather too freely with them for my weak head. Grange supped with us, and he and I drank three bottles of strong ale. I insisted on it. I loved it at the time. But it intoxicated me. In the forenoon Grange and I visited M. Dupont and Miss Scott, and I was at the opening of Balbarton's repositories.

THURSDAY 21 FEBRUARY. (Writing the 27.) Awaked exceedingly sick. Rose; was obliged to go to bed again. Grew better and drank smoked milk.[2] Resolved not to be one day absent from the Court this Session. So got up and went to it. The Lords were up. But Lord Hailes was still sitting in the Outer House, so I had an opportunity of appearing in wig and gown. Had a cold and hoarseness. Dined at my father's and drank a

[1] Colonel John Walkinshaw Craufurd of Craufurdland had, with some neighbouring landowners, accused and attempted to bring to trial Thomas Gemmill and Peter Gemmill his father for the crime of poaching. The accused poachers had met with some of their neighbours to settle upon a plan of defence, and the same night an "incendiary letter" had been found in the avenue leading to Colonel Craufurd's house. Some time later a building belonging to the Colonel was burned to the ground. The first trial (29 January 1781) charged the Gemmills with the writing and sending of an incendiary letter. Boswell served with Maclaurin and Crosbie for the prosecution and presented the testimony of engravers (who appeared for the prosecution as handwriting experts) that Thomas Gemmill had written the letter. The jury, however, returned a verdict of "not proven." Gemmill thereupon sued Craufurd in the Court of Session for damages and expenses, on the ground that the prosecution in the Court of Justiciary was "groundless and oppressive."

[1a] Proverbs 26. 5, 12.

[2] Several popular medicinal recipes of the eighteenth century call for milk darkened over a fire.

little port. His lady ill. Just he and I and old Miss Boswell at dinner. Called a little on Maclaurin. Drank tea with Mrs. Boswell of Balmuto; just she and Miss Menie at home. Felt comfortably and somewhat consequentially, for they thanked me for my visit. Was not well at night. Sir Walter and Grange supped. I would not drink.

FRIDAY 22 FEBRUARY. (Writing the 27.) Was better. Sir Walter's horses had been arrested at Calder. He had tried to borrow money here (£20 would have done) to relieve them, but could not get it. He resolved to ride home to Doura and bring it. I did not offer him a loan, as he has shown no anxiety to repay me what I have already advanced, as he went against my warm wishes at last election, and as I thought his being obliged to take so much trouble would make him think. Yet I had a good deal of uneasiness on his account. Away he went. At two I attended Balbarton's funeral. It made a dreary impression upon me. The day was very cold, and my mind relaxed and gloomy.

SATURDAY 23 FEBRUARY. (Writing the 27.) Mr. Kentish, a young student of physic from Yorkshire recommended to me by Squire Godfrey Bosville,[3] Mr. Lawrence Hill, and Dr. Gillespie dined with us. I was calm in spirit, but drank so much as to be uneasy. I had been vexed that I had not sooner shown civility to a young man so well recommended to me. But I am very slow and awkward in doing these things.

SUNDAY 24 FEBRUARY. Was at the New Church forenoon and afternoon. In the afternoon Dr. Blair preached very well on the last verse of the 17 Psalm, displaying the agreeable hopes of a blessed future state. He reserved till another opportunity the time when it was to take place; viz., "when I awake." I shall be curious to hear him on this. I doubt he is not divine enough to enter into the disquisition whether the soul at death passeth immediately into a new state of existence, or if it sleepeth till the General Judgement. My family was now quite an hospital; Sandy and Veronica were not recovered from the measles, and our other three children were taking them. Some divine lessons however were said. Lord Kames had been in the Court of Session for a little yesterday. I went to him this evening and had I fancy about an hour's conversation by ourselves. I found his principles very lax, and was convinced he was not a

---

[3] "Surely a correspondence should be kept up among kindred, and the fortune of physic promoted. The bearer is come to improve in that science and is the second I have noticed to you on that subject, though the first being of our own family you was equally interested to show him civility with myself. This (William says, who is more acquainted with him than I am, for they are intimate) . . . is a very ingenious young man" (From Godfrey Bosville, 29 September 1781). Kentish went on to receive an M.D. at the University of Edinburgh, and was admitted a licentiate of the College of Physicians of London, 30 September 1790.

Christian. Was dissatisfied with him. Supped there; Miss Carre of Nisbet and Miss Grizzy and nobody else. He was feeble and silent, and coughed hardly.

MONDAY 25 FEBRUARY. (Writing the 27). Dined and drank tea at Lady Dundonald's with Sir Charles and Miss Preston. Was in a good frame, and had a portion of my old feelings in the late Earl's time. Drank as much as to intoxicate me somewhat.

TUESDAY 26 FEBRUARY. (Writing the 27.) Sir Walter M.C. had returned last night with money. He and I dined at my father's. Was somewhat intoxicated, and had almost gone to a tavern with Sir Walter and drank more. I am really in a state of constant, at least of daily, excess just now. I *must* pull the reins. But I feel my dull insignificance in this provincial situation. I have even little employment as a lawyer, and my mind is vacant and listless till quickened by drinking. I called at Liberton's Wynd, but was not licentious. Sat awhile with the Hon. A. Gordon. Came home restless. Sir Walter supped with us. I have been so lazy all this Session that I believe I have not been out of bed any one morning before eight. But I have not had that relish of bed which I have sometimes experienced, my mind not being at ease but fretted by my situation, so ill-suited to my aspiring views. Sir Walter supped with us.

WEDNESDAY 27 FEBRUARY. (Writing 4 March.) Sir Walter and Grange dined with us. I do not recollect anything more except that either yesterday or today I left this my journal lying open in the dining-room while I went downstairs to look for some book or paper, and my dear wife having taken it up, read the account of my life on Monday the 18, with which she was shocked, and declared that all connexion between her and me was now at an end, and that she would continue to live with me only for decency and the sake of her children. I was miserably vexed and in a sort of stupor. But could say nothing for myself. I indulged some glimmering of hope, and just acquiesced in my fate for the present. I was still heated with wine.

THURSDAY 28 FEBRUARY. (Writing 4 March.) Dined at home with my wife and children in bad spirits. After dinner went down to Grange, and he and I drank a bottle of port, which did me some good. Called at Liberton's Wynd, being anxious lest conception might have taken place. Could not learn as yet. Was not licentious. Played cards and supped at Old Lady Wallace's. Sir Walter came to supper. I just drank wine enough to warm and invigorate my frame.

FRIDAY 1 MARCH. (Writing the 4.) Yesterday and today I attended the pleadings in the cause between the heir male of the family of Panmure and Lord Dalhousie and his second son, the disponees of the late Earl, concerning two baronies (£9,000) and some leases claimed by the former.

This day the Court determined it. I thought I saw a visible bias in favour of Lord Dalhousie, and indeed I could not help thinking I was right. Lord Alva alone was for the heir male for the lands and money and everything. Lord Braxfield supported his claim to the leases, and it carried for him. The President was keen against him and said, "I will try to find law." I was warmly zealous for the heir male.[4] I dined at my father's, this being his birthday, on which he entered on his seventy-sixth year. Old Mrs. Boswell, Miss Menie, and Mr. Stobie were there, but no notice was taken of *the day*. Lady Crawford came to town today. I paid her a visit in the evening. Sir Walter and Grange supped with us. I was still in such a state that I heated myself somewhat.

SATURDAY 2 MARCH. Dined home with Lieutenant. Tea Miss Gray, Sir James Pringle. System of manners.[5] Lady Crawford a little.[6] Supped S. Mitchelson's. Much claret.

SUNDAY 3 MARCH. Home after five.[7] Rose not very uneasy. With Grange to New Church. Home and to bed. Evening father's with Lieutenant.

MONDAY 4 MARCH. Dined father's with Lieutenant. Lady Crawford and Bourtreehill [8] supped with us.

TUESDAY 5 MARCH. Called father's a little. At Lady Crawford's a little. Supped Lord Kames's with Charteris. Heard him against Beattie for attacking D. Hume, which I contradicted. He told of Hume resolving never to write against religion.

WEDNESDAY 6 MARCH. Mr. Lawrie dined. At Lady Crawford's a little. Wife there. She supped with us. Visited father.

THURSDAY 7 MARCH. Clerk Matthew, etc., dined. Not intoxicated. Called Lady Crawford's. Not in. Snowy night. Did not go to Lord Kames's, though on road.

FRIDAY 8 MARCH. Great day of Baron McLaren and Dunn's ball.[9]

---

[4] See above, 25 January 1782. The "heir male" was Thomas Maule, a lieutenant in one of the six companies of Invalids stationed at Plymouth.

[5] Unexplained. Presumably a topic discussed.

[6] Lady Crawford (Mrs. Boswell's close friend) appears to have been making a three-weeks' visit to Edinburgh, and Boswell is unusually attentive to her because his wife is not able to go abroad much.

[7] He no doubt got to playing cards and played till dawn. His journal (21 October 1775, 1 March 1777) records other indecently extended Saturday-night bouts of cards in which Samuel Mitchelson, Jr., took part.

[8] See above, 20 February 1781, n. 8a.

[9] Unexplained. We believe the name in this spelling occurs nowhere else in Boswell's journal. Scots peers were never styled "Baron"; the universal style for the first grade of the Scots peerage was "Lord." Judges of the Court of Exchequer were styled

SATURDAY 9 MARCH. *Rec.*[1] Early at father's, then Lady Crawford's tea. Then Parliament House a little, very well. It rose. Dined home with Grange. At *Recruiting Officer* with Duchess.[2] At Princes Street Coffee-house with Sir Charles.

SUNDAY 10 MARCH. Had Grange in my seat to hear Dr. Blair in afternoon. He and Sibthorpe dined. Supped Lady Crawford's. π.

MONDAY 11 MARCH. Dreadful storm of snow. Grange dined with us. Strange's ball.[3] Supped Maclaurin's, etc.

TUESDAY 12 MARCH. Sadly vexed.[4] Dined father's, Claud and Doctor [5] there. A little port. Restless. Called Lord Loudoun. S. Gordon, Dr. Webster all out. With honest Grange, mountain. Visited S. Gordon and Lord Loudoun. Supped Lady Crawford.

WEDNESDAY 13 MARCH. Lady Crawford visited wife forenoon. I visited at father's. Lord Loudoun and John Hunter supped.

THURSDAY 14 MARCH. Fast. Church all day.[6] Father's a little.

FRIDAY 15 MARCH. Wrote No. 54.[7] Lady Crawford dinner and tea. Lieutenant not well. With him both forenoon and evening.

SATURDAY 16 MARCH. Finished No. 54. Church. Captain Campbell, 92,[8] called. Father's a little. Coffee-house with Dr. Gillespie.

SUNDAY 17 MARCH. In good sound frame.[9] But regretted not Church of England. Evening father's with Lieutenant. Father shook hands with me in stair.

MONDAY 18 MARCH. Nothing to mark but visiting Lady Crawford and Lady Elphinstone with Captain Campbell (92), and Bourtreehill.

"Baron," but in 1782 none of the exchequer judges was named McLaren. In Scots feudal law, all who held immediately of the Crown were designated barons, whether nobles or commoners, but as a contemporary social style this sense of "Baron" would have been quaint or jocular. (Compare Boswell's own "Baron Boswell" or Scott's "Baron Bradwardine.") James Dunn kept a fashionable hotel in St. Andrew's Square.

[1] Added above the line. Probably the start of a second recording of his attendance at the performance of George Farquhar's *Recruiting Officer* on the evening of this day.

[2] Puzzling. The only duchess with whom Boswell was ever on terms of familiarity was the old Duchess of Douglas, who died in 1774. Perhaps the Duchess of Buccleuch, whom he had met at the Lord President's on 24 January 1782, had made up a party to attend the play.

[3] A dancing-master named David Strange lived in Toddrick's Wynd (*Edinburgh Dictionary*, 1778–1779).

[4] Unexplained. Probably over something that had happened the previous evening.

[5] Probably Dr. Gillespie.

[6] In preparation for the Sacrament.

[7] Of *The Hypochondriack*, the first of two papers on religion.

[8] Of the 92nd Regiment.

[9] His state of mind on receiving the Sacrament.

They and Colonel Craufurd and Miss Dunlop supped. Wife all afternoon with Lady Crawford.

[Boswell to Burke] [1]

Edinburgh, 18 March 1782

My DEAR SIR,—I promised to trouble you with a letter in favour of the Corporation of Butchers (or *Fleshers* as we emphatically call them), who have been long in possession of shambles in this city, but are threatened to be set adrift by an Act of Parliament. I was the only member of my own Society, the Faculty of Advocates who as an *antistes justitiae* [2] opposed a resolution for *unconditional* proscription. [3] I enclose a newspaper in which you will find my reasons. I was once going to advise them to present an address in favour of the American war, making an offer of their *knives* and fortunes, which might have secured the Ministerial party. But as they happen to have *justice* on their side it is my opinion they will have a much better chance with Mr. Burke and his friends; and therefore I presume to recommend them to you.

Will you now, my dear Sir, give me leave to apply to you on my own account? I allow that I have no other right to do so, but that *imperfect right*, as we lawyers speak, [4] arising from your having shown me much kindness upon every occasion, which naturally founds an expectation of more. When a lady disappoints such an expectation, she is called a jilt. I believe there is no particular epithet for a friend who does so. I am also aware that fancy grafted on a good stock of self-opinion produces fallacious blossoms in many cases both of love and friendship. But I will venture to trust to those which your beams have cherished in my mind.

When I was last in London, you asked me on one of our pleasant evenings over your home-brewed, "how I *could* live in Edinburgh?" I answered, "Like a cat in an air-pump." [5] In short, in so narrow a sphere, and amongst people to whom I am so unlike, my life is dragged on in

---

[1] The manuscript of this letter and also the manuscripts of those of 18 and 30 April following are in the Fitzwilliam Papers and are published by permission of the Earl Fitzwilliam and his trustees and the Director of Sheffield City Libraries.

[2] An expert in justice.

[3] See above, Saturday 15 December 1781.

[4] A right is perfect or imperfect in legal parlance as its scope is clear, settled, determinate, or is vague and unfixed.

[5] This evening Boswell spent with Burke seems to be otherwise unrecorded. "For want of other patients, [they] amuse themselves with the stifling of cats in an air-pump" (Addison, *Spectator*, No. 21).

> Like cats in air-pumps, to subsist we strive
> On joys too thin to keep the soul alive
>
> (Edward Young, *Love of Fame*, Satire V, ll. 177–178).

languor and discontent. What more years may do I cannot tell. But as yet I do not feel myself a bit easier. I explained to you in confidence my hopes of obtaining by Lord Mountstuart's interest some place of such an income as to enable me to keep house in London. But alas!

> Eheu fugaces, Postume, Postume,
> Labuntur anni! [6]

And I see no prospect of my wish being accomplished. His Lordship has assured me that he is not well with the present Ministry. Pray would he be better with another? Pray is there not now a certainty of a change, upon which a numerous variety of arrangements will take place? May I not now assure myself that you are near your apotheosis, as poor Goldsmith said of you *poetically* several years ago; for experience proved that his eye was only "in a fine frenzy rolling." [7] If it is now to be real, may I not desire to be remembered by you? I ardently wish for occupation of more consequence than drudging at the bar in Scotland; and I think I should be very happy in exerting what talents I have under your auspices.

The late Sir John Pringle said to me last autumn when he was here, "I know not if you will be in rest in London. But you will never be at rest out of it." And I recollect Dr. Johnson observing one day at Sir Joshua Reynolds's upon the subject of a London life "that every body is at rest in its proper place. They who are content to live out of London have minds fitted for it." [8] Pray be good enough to afford me a little consideration, and tell me as a philosopher and friend if my restlessness out of the great scene of exertion be not "the divinity that stirs within me" [9] and points out the line I should take? Would there not be something generous in your giving me your aid to attain greater happiness? You told me £600 a year would defray the difference between keeping house in London and in Edinburgh. How shall I contrive to get £600 from Govern-

---

[6] "Alas, O Postumus, Postumus, the years glide swiftly by" (Horace, *Odes*, II. xiv. 1–2, trans. C. G. Bennett, Loeb ed.).

[7] Unexplained. Goldsmith in his known poems nowhere predicts Burke's "apotheosis," and it may well be that by *"poetically"* Boswell meant "enthusiastically; unrealistically." The present letter serves to remind us how many of the good sayings current in the Johnson circle Boswell did *not* get into his journal. See the note following this. "In a fine frenzy rolling" is *Midsummer Night's Dream*, V. i. 14.

[8] Boswell recorded Sir John's remark in his journal, 9 August 1781 ("*at* rest in London," see above), as having been made "one day this summer." We have been unable to locate Johnson's either in the journal or the *Life of Johnson*. If, as seems likely, Sir John's remark was prompted by Boswell's report of Johnson's, 30 March 1781 (see that date above) would be an appropriate date for Johnson's, though Boswell failed to record it then.

[9] Addison, *Cato*, V. viii. 7, "me" for "us."

ment? Would the King, with whom I related to you an excellent conversation, but of himself transplant me into a better climate, how pleasant would it be! But I wish not to indulge romantic visions. I am advancing to be called to the English bar, as another string to my bow. In short, I am eagerly looking out.

In the mean time, I have an aged father whom it is my pious wish as well as my interest to please; and as he disapproves of my going to London without a sufficient reason, I beg to hear from you whether my being upon the spot this spring may not be of some advantage to me. The *noctes cenaeque deum* [1] which I enjoy there are a sufficient reason in my own mind. But you can understand at once that something else must weigh with him.

You will be pleased to present my best compliments to Mrs. Burke and to your son when he returns, as I presume he is now upon the circuit.

I trust this letter to your goodness and honour. To have its contents mentioned to anybody might hurt me essentially. I ever am, my dear Sir, with very high esteem, your obliged and affectionate humble servant,

JAMES BOSWELL.

I send you a pamphlet written by me upon the administration of criminal justice in Scotland, to which I wish your attention to be directed. [2]

TUESDAY 19 MARCH. Uneasy with last night's cups. Was to have dined at father's with wife. Had not nerves on hearing number there. Lady Crawford went. Home calm. Charity Assembly at Dunn's at night. Whist and lost.

WEDNESDAY 20 MARCH. Dined at father's, only he and Lady A. Played whist ill. He said in his old style, "James, d'ye work at this for siller?" Horatius Cannan at tea and consultation. Supped at Baron Gordon's with Maclaurin. Whist.

THURSDAY 21 MARCH. Breakfasted with President tête-à-tête. He spoke of father's being duller, but said, "He may live a long time." Had seen him that morning. Soup at Maclaurin's. Then with him, Donaldson printer. Called Mrs. Scott and Miss Sally Craufurd. Douglas was to dine. Dined with Maclaurin. Spoke of his want of principles. He said steel to back. Sent for to Douglas. More claret. Then in high spirits. Supped home with Sir Charles, etc. Intoxicated and, it seems, harsh.

FRIDAY 22 MARCH. Very ill. Lay till dinner-time. Had Colonel Craufurd, calm. Supped Old Lady Wallace's.

SATURDAY 23 MARCH. Very well. Visited Mrs. Dundas, then father,

[1] "O nights and suppers of the gods" (Horace, *Satires*, II. vi. 65).
[2] *Letter to Lord Braxfield*, 1780.

who was cold and dull. Then Maclaurin. Had lost young son. Visited Sir William Forbes, Nairne, Mrs. Young, Colonel Craufurd, etc., dinner. Resolved not to go to play.

SUNDAY 24 MARCH. Home forenoon. Afternoon New Church *with wife*. Dr. Blair. Visited father. Supped Dr. Webster's. Told me of five years ago imagining himself failed.

MONDAY 25 MARCH. Visited Lady Macdonald. Walked with George Wallace. Full of new Ministry.[3]

TUESDAY 26 MARCH. Visited father. Dined Sir A. Dick's with George Wallace.

WEDNESDAY 27 MARCH. George Preston with us morning. Maclaurin called. Had him to dine. Spoke of being Under-Secretary. His infidelity disagreeable. Went to Baron Gordon's, whist. Lost, was uneasy. Spoke of joy on wife's recovery. He laughed *incredulus*. Disliked him. Felt myself young.

THURSDAY 28 MARCH. Very well. Dined and tea, I and wife, Dr. Webster's. Company of friends: Sir Charles, etc. Cordial. Then foolish engagement for weeks. Then folly. Johnston. Then father's, Grange supped.

FRIDAY 29 MARCH. (Good Friday.) Called and disentangled from foolish engagement. Blackfriar Wynd Chapel, devout. Grove preached. Then father's. Wife and two sons there. He pleased more than ordinary. Said of Jamie, "That's a dear creature." Back to prayers. Then walked in King's Park and Piazza. Home. Coffee. Calm, supped.

SATURDAY 30 MARCH. Too late for prayers. I and all children and Grange to Drumsheugh. Delightful day. Visited Lady Colville. Dr. Gillespie, etc., dined. Visited father. Found them in the old way.

SUNDAY 31 MARCH. Old English Chapel all day. Nairne supped.

MONDAY 1 APRIL. Dined Dr. Bell's. Letter from Dr. Johnson.

TUESDAY 2 APRIL. Father's a little. Dined P. Ramsay's with Webster, etc.

WEDNESDAY 3 APRIL. Father's a little. Supped with him. Sat with Grange a little.

THURSDAY 4 APRIL. Father's a little with wife and children. Walked to Leith with H. Erskine. P. Ramsay's dinner. Dunn's at night. Agitated about new Ministry.

FRIDAY 5 APRIL. Called father's. Had Lady Macdonald, etc., supper.

SATURDAY 6 APRIL. Breakfasted Lady Anne Erskine. Dined John Hunter's with Sir W. Maxwell, etc. Liberton Wynd.

---

[3] North's administration had fallen on 20 March 1782. See below, 29 July 1782.

SUNDAY 7 APRIL. New Church all day. Father's between sermons. Divine lessons. With Dempster evening. Saw him weak and indifferent, was vexed a little. π.

MONDAY 8 APRIL. Grange dined with us.

TUESDAY 9 APRIL. Still idle. Dined father's. Drank too much. Was heated. Dr. Gillespie told me of his filing [4] breeches. Grange walked out with me. Met Abercrombie. Happy evening over punch. Thought of first wishing to be advocate from paper of his.[5] Too free, horrid at home.

WEDNESDAY 10 APRIL. Very ill. Public at Dunn's. Quite sunk. Afraid of virus. Miserable. Wife had heard neighbour in Liberton Wynd.

THURSDAY 11 APRIL. A little better. Called father's. Very idle. Supped with Sundrum.

FRIDAY 12 APRIL. Still very idle. Walked in New Town with my sons. Called Sundrum and Old Lady Wallace. Fear of virus went off. Had Lieutenant at dinner, but drank no wine. Tea Old Lady Wallace and introduced George Wallace. Supped father's.

SATURDAY 13 APRIL. Hon. A. Gordon called. Went with him to Maclaurin's. Then walked in New Town with Maclaurin. Very idle. Dined home. Again afraid of virus. Supped father's.

SUNDAY 14 APRIL. Took physic. Lay in bed all day and read Priestley's second volume of *Institutions on Truth of Christian Religion*. Less in it than I expected. But had my degree of faith somewhat confirmed. Read Mandeville against charity schools. Able, lively sophistry. Sure wrong, though could not detect. Still afraid of virus. Was in miserable hypochondria. Saw my ambitious views in London all madness. Vexed at being neglected by Burke. Thought I'd indulge a proud distance and just be an old Scottish baron and Tory. A slumber in the afternoon produced shocking melancholy. Up to tea. A *little* better. Thought myself unworthy of valuable spouse. Was quite sunk. To bed without supper. Divine lessons.

MONDAY 15 APRIL. Still uneasy. Wrote *Hypochondriack* No. 55 agreeably.[6] Grange dined with us. Was at my father's at night during supper, but took nothing.

TUESDAY 16 APRIL. Still uneasy. Dined and drank tea at Horatius

---

[4] Soiling. ("File" is the verb corresponding to the adjective "foul." It survives in present-day use in the compound "defile.")

[5] The Abercrombie whom Boswell most frequently mentions is Alexander, but he was a solicitor (Writer to the Signet), not an advocate. Perhaps George Abercromby of Tullibody, advocate, formerly Professor of Public Law in the University of Edinburgh. Two years older than Lord Auchinleck, he lived to be ninety-five, dying Father of the Bar in 1800. General Sir Ralph Abercromby was his son.

[6] A second paper on religion.

Cannan's. Sir John Gordon of Afton and lady and many more whom I rarely can meet there. Lady Gordon talked of a young sea-officer that would strain his little understanding to converse with her. Tasted a very little port wine. Visited father. Then home. Found Sandy Cuninghame returned from America far gone in a consumption. Melancholy sight.[7]

WEDNESDAY 17 APRIL. Visited father forenoon and Maclaurin. Home all day after. Yesterday and today read Priestley's third volume. Thought it flimsy.

THURSDAY 18 APRIL. Visited Shawfield forenoon. Was in sauntering humour, applying my mind strongly to nothing. Got into good spirits, imagining not *virus* but only gleet from hard drinking of punch on Tuesday the 9th. Sandy Cuninghame came to dinner and stayed rest of the day. Had Shawfield and Mrs. Campbell, Mr. Baron Gordon, and Maclaurin at whist and supper. Drank only water. Was too high-spirited. Had visited father and Maclaurin in the evening. Was told by Maclaurin of the death of Sir James Dunbar, Judge Advocate.[8] He advised me to write up soliciting the office. I wrote to Lord Pembroke, Burke, and Dempster.[9] Was placid tonight from the resolution to be very good. Called father.

[Boswell to Burke]

Edinburgh, 18 April 1782

MY DEAR SIR,—Although I am hurt by your neglect of an anxious confidential letter which I wrote to *my friend Edmund Burke* on the 18 of last month, I will not let the pride of an old baron prevent me from soliciting *Mr. Paymaster-General*[1] for his interest to obtain for me the office of Judge Advocate in Scotland, which is just now become vacant by the death of Sir James Dunbar. I understand it must be filled up by one of our Faculty of Advocates, of which Society I was the single man who at any of our meetings openly avowed a detestation of the measures of

[7] Mrs. Boswell's nephew, the third of the Cuninghame boys. He was captain in the 76th Foot.

[8] A civilian lawyer (an advocate) whose special responsibility was the conduct of courts-martial. The salary was £180 a year.

[9] The manuscript of the letter to Burke is in the Fitzwilliam Collection of the Sheffield City Libraries. The letter to Dempster is not known to have survived, but a copy of that to Pembroke, dated 22 April, is at Yale.

[1] As stated above, North announced the end of his administration in the House of Commons on 20 March 1782. Burke was not given a Cabinet post in the succeeding Rockingham administration. He was not necessarily disparaged by not being given a Cabinet office. The Paymaster-Generalship was the highest-paid appointment the new Government had at its disposal, and Burke may have preferred money to power. The Cabinet was known 26 March and the Treasury appointments shortly thereafter.

the late Ministry against our brethren in America. The Lord Advocate, who is our Dean or President, will candidly attest this.

But I trust much to your private friendship; and I hope you will lose no time in taking the proper steps. As it is in the military department, I suppose General Conway will have the disposal of it. But you will know well what is to be done. The post is just going off, so I have only time to subscribe myself still affectionately yours,

JAMES BOSWELL.

FRIDAY 19 APRIL. Much in same way as yesterday. Visited father.

SATURDAY 20 APRIL. Sundrum, lady, and daughter dined. Visited father.

SUNDAY 21 APRIL. New Church all day. Children said divine lessons. Visited father.

MONDAY 22 APRIL. Wavered as to *virus*. Visited father. Grange dined with us.

TUESDAY 23 APRIL. Got up early to go to Rockville with Maclaurin. Dear wife gave me breakfast. Bid adieu to Grange, thinking he was to go to country before I returned. More breakfast with Maclaurin. Went in his coach with him. Disappointed on finding in the boasted East Lothian no inns for many miles and scarcely a tree or a hedge. Corned the horses at Drem, a little village. Got to Rockville before dinner and had rubber. Mr. Swinton at North Berwick and Mr. Murray the parish minister and old Miss Duff there. I drank only water. Whist evening, I won.

WEDNESDAY 24 APRIL. Nobody but ourselves. Whist and brag all day. I liked this life. We lived comfortably. I was in such spirits over water after dinner that both Gordon and Maclaurin said they never would ask me to drink wine again.

THURSDAY 25 APRIL. Got up early. Drove in good spirits. Breakfasted at Prestonpans. Came to town. Met worthy Grange in street, not yet gone. He dined with us. Evening father's.

FRIDAY 26 APRIL. Dined Commissioner Cochrane's by invitation. Brother John there. He and I walked to town. Letters from Lord Pembroke and Dempster: nothing to be done about Judge Advocate's place. Was fretted at this, and no answer from Mr. Burke. Father's evening.

SATURDAY 27 APRIL. Wife and three eldest children and I dined father's. First time wife dined there since illness. Virus gone. Supposed only gleet.

SUNDAY 28 APRIL. New Church all day. Sat a little with Sandy Cuninghame. Evening father's.

MONDAY 29 APRIL. Read George Wallace on Scottish peerage. Much entertained. Out in Sir A. Dick's coach to Prestonfield, Lady Dick ill. Mr.

Bennet and Surgeon Russell there. In fine spirits by water-drinking. All this week cold weather. On return home, letter from Mr. Burke enclosing one from General Conway. Burke as friendly as I could wish. Wife pleased. She said [it showed what] interest [I had]. Maclaurin said I'd get *this* office or an equivalent. Went to father's. Saw no opportunity to mention letter; read it after to Dr. Gillespie. In fine frame. So well now that ventured π. Wife wonderfully good.

[Burke to Boswell]

Charles Street, 23 April 1782

MY DEAR SIR,—Don't censure me too harshly for not answering your very kind and obliging letter. I protest I had not time for it. Alas! in that letter you much overrate my power of serving my friends; you cannot overrate my disposition to please or to arrange [2] them. I have served the public for seventeen years with great fidelity and labour, and just at the decline of my life there comes to me a temporary office of some emolument, considerable expense, and no power. I have the long arrear of all the obligations and kindnesses that I have received as a charge upon any little interest I may be able to obtain. My friends in power have come in with equally long claims upon them, with a divided patronage, and a reduced establishment. If I could serve you, I tell you in sincerity that the bringing you to a residence here would be no mean bribe to me. But what I can do I will upon all occasions where I am free. I lost not a moment's time in applying to General Conway. You have a copy of what I wrote to General Conway and my answer that you may see my diligence at least in obeying your commands. I conversed also with Mr. Fox on the subject, who has very kind wishes for you. I am ever, my dear Sir, your most faithful and obedient humble servant,

EDMUND BURKE.

[Enclosure. Edmund Burke to General Henry Seymour Conway]

Charles Street, 23 April 1782

MY DEAR SIR,—Business somewhat urgent prevents me from waiting upon you, as I intended to do this morning to solicit you in favour of a friend of mine in Scotland, who wishes to succeed Sir James Dunbar as Judge Advocate. . . . Mr. Boswell, son of the judge of that name . . . is a lawyer

[2] Used here, it would seem, in the sense "accommodate," "please." This is one of the meanings of French *arranger*, from which the English word is derived. As the *Oxford English Dictionary* remarks, "arrange" was "a rare word until modern times; not in Bible 1611, Shakespeare, Milton's poetry, or Pope." Burke was the first to use the verb in two of the senses the *Dictionary* records. Apparently he also introduced the word in this further French meaning as well.

of ability and of general erudition, and the pleasantest and best-tempered man in the world. I believe this office is in your gift as Commander-in-Chief. I am sensible that I take a great liberty in asking for it, but I do not hesitate to promise you that when he has an opportunity of coming to thank you for your protection, you will have no cause to repent of having attached to you so agreeable a man as Mr. Boswell. You will pardon this freedom with your usual kindness. I have the honour to be with very real esteem and regard, my dear Sir, your most faithful and obedient, humble servant.

[Second enclosure. Conway to Burke]

Little Warwick Street, 23 April 1782
DEAR SIR,—I had this moment the favour of your letter recommending Mr. Boswell for the place of Judge Advocate in N. Britain, now vacant. Some particular circumstances prevent my being able to give any positive answer at present, though you may be assured that both the quarter from whence the recommendation comes and the person so favoured with your good opinion and so distinguished incline me much to wish it were in my power immediately [to] determine as you desire. I am, dear Sir, with the greatest truth and esteem, your most faithful and obedient servant,
H. S. CONWAY.
Rt. Hon. Edm. Burke, Esq.

TUESDAY 30 APRIL. Walked about forenoon. Dined at father's and played cards. Communicated letters from London showing what interest I had. Father was pleased.

[Boswell to Burke]

Edinburgh, 30 April 1782
MY DEAR SIR,—The real kindness, the active benevolence of your friendship for me which I have now experienced, is pleasing beyond expression. I used to say that I was never sure of your being a very happy man till I was admitted familiarly to your house and saw how agreeably you lived with your endearing connexions of wife and son. I am now satisfied that you are a very, very good man. Be assured that your goodness is fully felt by me, and that if ever an opportunity shall occur, you shall find me warmly grateful.

To have such a character from Mr. Burke as you have been pleased to give of me in your letter to General Conway is to have a pearl of great price.[2a] I sincerely thank you; and I shall be ambitious to preserve it. Although your application for me at this time should not prove successful,

2a Matthew 13.46.

I am as much obliged to you as if I had obtained the office; and I shall upon any future opening freely solicit you.

Let me now, my dear Sir, most sincerely congratulate you on your promotion and most chiefly on the power which I trust it will afford you of doing a great deal of good to the British Empire. When more important objects are settled, I shall take leave to suggest some particulars which I am persuaded would tend to make North Britain both happier in herself and a better sister to South Britain. For my own part, I much approve of what you once suggested to me, that both parts of the Island should be founded into one mass. . . .

I regret much that I am not in London this spring. But as my father is as much pleased as he now can be in his decline with your friendship for me, your writing to me to come up, when the practice of the law here will allow me, will secure me his approbation of my paying you a visit. . . . I am sure you will approve of my anxious, my almost childish care to humour an aged parent.

I am much flattered by Mr. Fox's kind wishes. I beg you may present my best respects to him. I have the honour to be, my dear Sir, with the highest admiration, your much obliged and affectionate, humble servant,

JAMES BOSWELL.

WEDNESDAY 1 MAY. Nothing to remark particularly except that Alexander Cuninghame dined, and Miss Susie Dunlop drank tea. Visited father.

THURSDAY 2 MAY. Breakfasted Lady Colville's in fine spirits. Visited Dr. Blair, confined with gout. Talked of Lord Kames. Got him to promise subscription to Tho. Davies.[3] George Wallace came in. Walked with him in Meadow. Dined with him; Sir James Grant, General Fletcher, the Craigs of Riccarton, etc., there. Was gay upon water. Walked with him in New Town. Supped father's. He was in shocking humour. Said, "Have you seen your wife the day?" As if I rarely saw her. Mentioned my intention to go west on Tuesday. Miss Boswell asked if I was to be at Auchinleck. I said yes. Lady Auchinleck said, "Ye'll get cold quarters there." Dr. Gillespie, when we came away, talked with wonder of their conduct, and advised me to stay away a day and just to leave them to themselves and see if they would have the civility to write out and order things to be comfortable for me.

FRIDAY 3 MAY. Walked about. Had Mr. Sibthorpe at dinner. Walked to Restalrig and drank tea with Lord Covington. Was much pleased.

SATURDAY 4 MAY. One day this week visited George Drummond of Blair and talked to him of his father's improprieties. Promised to show

---

[3] To Davies's forthcoming *Dramatic Miscellanies*, published in 1783.

him his father's life before publication. This day visited father a little. Was told in street by Dr. Gillespie that Mark Pringle had got Judge Advocate's office.[4] Was a little disappointed, but soon recovered. Called on Mr. George Wallace, and wondered at his knowledge. Carried him home to dine with me in a friendly way; Dr. Gillespie and my brother John with us. We were very social. After tea, walked with Mr. Wallace in Abbey and St. Anne's Yards, and on Castle Hill. Listened to his Shenstonian reveries,[5] and tried to banish them. Did not like his violent resentment against the Arniston family.

SUNDAY 5 MAY. Little James was in kirk for first time; in New Kirk. When the minister spoke of "the Father," he spoke out, "He should not say 'Father.' He should say 'God.' " Walked to Duddingston Kirk, Sandy with me. Saw man on fine horse. Asked Sandy if he'd like to ride such a horse. He said, "I would not like to ride on Sunday except to the kirk." Happy dining at Prestonfield. Looked over some of Sir Alexander's letters. Home happy. Sibthorpe and Bellew tea. Divine lessons. Visited father.

MONDAY 6 MAY. Called at father's. Was told by her I should have bad quarters at Auchinleck, etc. (Note of it apart.) [6] Told it to Maclaurin and to Mr. Lawrie. Was quite hurt. Resolved not go till Friday. In coach with Sir W. and Lady Forbes to Lady Colville's. Dined and drank tea. Had Dr. Gillespie a little at night, and got good, spirited counsel from him how to act.

TUESDAY 7 MAY. Up in good calm spirits. Called. Found *noverca* alone. SHE. "What, not gone?" I. "No. I think I could not well go after what you told me yesterday." (Repeated what she had said.) "I thought my father's son might have been at least as well taken care of as Mr. Stobie." She was fluttered, and I think for the first time I saw her blush. SHE. "What was I to do? What was I to order?" I. "You know that best." SHE. "You might have ordered what you pleased." I. "I should not have presumed. I should have expected common civility." SHE. "You seem not to think it necessary to acknowledge my Lord or me. If you had asked if there would be proper accommodation for you—" I. "I mentioned my going. I resolved to say nothing about my accommodation, but leave that to you." SHE. "I only meant to put you on your guard in case you had taken people there." I. "I certainly should not have done that. So far from

---

[4] Mark Pringle, who was admitted advocate in 1777, was a good deal younger than Boswell. He was heir to the M.P. from Selkirkshire, and probably got the appointment through the influence of Henry Dundas and the Earl of Buccleuch.

[5] Presumably reveries in praise of "the peace of solitude, the innocence of inactivity, and the unenvied security of a humble station" (Johnson's *Life of Shenstone*).

[6] This seems to have disappeared.

inviting, I have begged people not to come, even when the family was there; and far less would I invite when the family is not there." SHE. "There is a way of asking company not to come which may make people ridiculous." I. "One does not know what to do." SHE. "It is plain enough what to do when there's kindness." Father came to door. She went and told him. He came in. She said with a sneer, "I've been telling him you're angry I did not make preparations." I. "I am not angry now. I was angry. I thought my father's son might have been as well taken care of as Mr. Stobie." Father stood by fire and said nothing. Before he came in, she said, "What's all this now? You said nothing yesterday." I. "I was angry yesterday. I don't like being angry, and I went away till I should cool." She was so plausible and my feelings are so tender that I declare I was sorry for her, and thought she *might* not intend any ill. But on recollection I saw her devilish insolence. Visited David Erskine and wife for first time. Out to Prestonfield, fine. Read many of Sir Alexander's letters; dined. My dear wife came. I was quite charmed.

WEDNESDAY 8 MAY. Yesterday and today should have written letters and *Hypochondriack*. Was in sauntering humour. Did not go to father's. Wrote notes for No. 56.

THURSDAY 9 MAY. Instead of writing *Hypochondriack,* looked among old journal, etc., and was unwilling to begin, so that I resolved to write it in country. Mr. George Wallace sat awhile with me. I drank tea at father's. His *women* never said a word about my accommodation at Auchinleck, or indeed my being to see it. He was mild and even kindly, and bid me see how many larches were cut, and seemed willing to purchase Haugh multures. When I went away, he took me by the hand, *like* a father, and said, "Fare you well, my dear James." My heart was warmed. I was in the evening hurried as usual before a journey.

FRIDAY 10 MAY. Set off in the Ayr fly at four in the morning, Miss Craufurd and Mr. Hall my partners. A good day. Conversation went on well. At Cumnock found Old John Boswell and Mr. Dun waiting for me, and several offerers for Chisholm's farm. Dined. Found myself abler to talk about setting my land than I apprehended. Engaged to be at Auchinleck manse next evening, when offerers might come to me. Mr. Dun and I walked over and were just in time to meet Effie Rule's [7] burial. I carried from the corner of the enclosure next the church. Was glad to meet a number of the tenants and observe their cordial attachment to our family. Was confirmed in my opinion that an affectionate tenantry is better than a high rental. Beheld with solemn emotion our family vault, my *long home*. [8] Was not shocked at the thought of death. Had the

[7] David Boswell's nurse. See above, 25 August 1780.

[8] Ecclesiastes 12. 5.

comfortable hope of future happiness. My mind was sound and piously calm. Had a hospitable reception at my old governor's at the manse. Was satisfied with myself. Was *content*, as the French say.

SATURDAY 11 MAY. After breakfast Mr. Millar walked with me to Auchinleck. My heart warmed as I viewed the scenes of my early years. But I declare I am happier now than when I was a boy. I felt a kind of exultation in the consciousness of a line of ancestors, and in the prospect of being *laird* myself, and ruling over such a fine Place and such an extent of country. Found James Bruce pretty well again. Surveyed the hedges, etc., with more *attention* than I used to do. I hope in time to understand country affairs moderately well. Returned to the manse to dinner. My temper was so sweet just now that I was amused with the perverse treatment of the present, and thought it would make my future independence more agreeable by comparison. Craigdarroch, for whom I had sent an express, dined with us and assisted me in setting my farm in the afternoon to James Weir, who came with Old John Boswell.

SUNDAY 12 MAY. Was pleased to be in our parish church. Mr. Millar, by a hint from me yesterday, preached again his sermon on the last verse of the 73 Psalm, on which I heard him with much satisfaction last autumn.[9] I resolved if I should live to be Patron, he should be Minister of Auchinleck. But I intended to say nothing of it to him in the mean time. In the afternoon he preached well on "Commune with your own hearts."[1] Knockroon came to us in the evening from Ayr. We conversed rationally. I felt none of that restlessness and fretfulness which has often disturbed my peace. I had No. 56 of my periodical paper to write out tonight from notes, as I was to go to Craigengillan's next morning, and it would not be in time if not sent by Tuesday's fly. I felt a reluctance to begin. But when once set to it, my notes pleased me; other thoughts occurred, and I was upon the whole in a very good frame. I finished my essay just about three in the morning, and went to bed satisfied.[2] Had no anxiety about my dear wife and children. Was well in body and mind.

MONDAY 13 MAY. Fingland, whom I had asked to be my guide through the moors, came to breakfast. It was highly agreeable that I could have such extent of thinking and reading in my last night's essay, and accommodate myself easily to ordinary chit-chat. Knockroon and James Johnston, who joined us at Cumnock, gave me a convoy half-way to Berboth. It was a fine shining day, and the moors looked pleasing. I was fond of a *following*, and felt a degree of consequence in having people ready to accompany me on my way. Got to Berboth in good time to din-

[9] 30 September 1781.
[1] Psalms 4. 4.
[2] On penuriousness and wealth, one of Boswell's favourites in the series.

ner. Found Craigengillan neither sick nor sorry, but *himself,* in good health and spirits, though one arm and one leg were so hurt by a fall down his stair that he could not move himself, and had been confined to bed five weeks, which he never had been before for four-and-twenty hours, as he told me. I had a great deal of jocular rattling with him, intermixed with solid advice about my farm and country affairs in general. It was a month this day since I tasted any liquor stronger than tea. My spirits were pure as crystal. I had conversation enough with Mrs. McAdam and the young ladies.

TUESDAY 14 MAY. Rose well as I could wish to be. Had more hearty conversation with the laird. Set out after breakfast. Saw old Mr. McMyne at Dalmellington. Called on his son at the manse, which was preparing for his reception.[3] Fingland was seized with a fit of the gravel and could not go on. With Thomas Edmondson's help, got my way to Cumnock. It was a windy, wet forenoon. Found Garrallan and the two John Boswells at Swan's. They dined with me, and James Johnston came in after. I drank tea with Mrs. Boswell. Got back to Mr. Dun's at night. Found Mr. Gillies of Kilmaurs there.

WEDNESDAY 15 MAY. Awaked ill with a headache. But resolved to pay visits and return, as the *set* of Dalblair was not yet finished. Knockroon came to breakfast. He and I rode by the Mill of Auchinleck to Barquharrie and found Mr. Reid wonderfully well, though last winter he had been distressed with a cough and failure of eyesight. I perceived a difference in his way of thinking of death from what there was at one of my visits to him within these few years. He then said that it had been observed old men were willing to die, but for his part he was as unwilling as ever. Now he said he would [wait][4] patiently till his change came, which showed that life was rather a burthen to him. He however conversed cheerfully, and told me that he never knew my grandfather much in liquor but twice: once when he had supped at a tavern with Arniston, and once when in Lady Betty's absence he had Duncan Forbes, Arniston, and a good many more supping in his house. "The keys were left with me," said Mr. Reid, "and I thought I should be affronted. I was once going in to have told them they had sat long enough." My headache continued, and I imagined it might be owing to my having lived too low for a month, and that there might be vapours in my stomach. So drank a little both of whisky and of strong ale. Felt a cordial glow. Knockroon rode with me by Trabboch to Sundrum. Major Montgomerie of Boreland there. Comfortable. Tasted liquors. Went at night to Coilsfield. Played

[3] The Rev. Duncan McMyne, minister of the parish, had been Boswell's classmate in the University of Edinburgh. His father was the parish schoolmaster.
[4] Word omitted inadvertently.

brag and lost above £4, which really vexed me. Drank gin and water, and was social and externally well.

[EDITORIAL NOTE: "After this comes a slip of paper containing very short notes—the bones of my life from May 16 till June 9, inclusive." On 17 May Boswell visited General Mure Campbell, now Earl of Loudoun, at Rowallan, and went on for a visit with Sir Walter Montgomerie-Cuninghame at Doura. On the 21st he returned to Edinburgh, where he was kept busy for some days with causes in the General Assembly. On 1 June he inspected Lord Auchinleck's new house in the New Town. On 5 June he learned that John Duff, the five-foot-two serving-man whose adjudication to be a soldier he had worked so hard to prove illegal and oppressive, had died, and that Duff's master, Charles Mercer of Lethendy, planned to appeal for larger damages than the Court of Session had awarded him. At present we lack all information about the circumstances of John Duff's death, but he presumably died in America, possibly in military action. (The 76th Highland Foot fought with Cornwallis and surrendered with him at Yorktown, 19 October 1781. If Duff survived Yorktown, he probably died in prison camp.) Boswell wrote to Mercer on 5 June: "I have this day read with great pleasure your letter to Mr. Robert Boswell authorizing him to appeal the cause against Aldie, etc., the Perthshire Justices. The death of poor John Duff makes the cause more interesting, and it will be proper that his nearest in kin be parties to the Appeal, for which there will be full time, as it cannot be taken till next session of Parliament. But independent of that, I think that the liberty of the subject on this side of the Tweed and your honour and dignity as a gentleman, circumstanced as you are, render it a cause of such consequence that the elusory [4a] judgement of the Court of Session ought not to be permitted to pass without correction and amendment by the more liberal tribunal of the House of Lords, before which, if I am alive, I shall be proud to continue my most zealous exertions to obtain exemplary justice; and I cannot doubt of success.—Hoping to drink a bottle in triumph with the Chief of the Mercers under his own roof, I am. . . ." The Appeal did not come up in the House of Lords till 1785, and will be reported at the proper dates in the volume succeeding this.

When the journal resumes, Boswell is at Valleyfield, where he and Veronica had gone on 6 June.]

MONDAY 10 JUNE. Awaked a good deal heated. But rose pretty well. An exceeding wet day. Made an index to Douglas's *Baronage* so far as Sir

---

4a Evasive.

Charles has it; I think to the 400 page.[5] Miss Preston in bed with the influenza.[6] Lived moderately today, and felt no *taedium*. Walked a little in the evening when dry. Was tenderly uneasy at the thought of leaving Veronica next morning. Poor little thing, though wishing to stay, she came once back at night and said "Good night" (second time), and another time, "Papa, write to me."

TUESDAY 11 JUNE. Awaked well. Rose before six. Had Sir Charles's chaise to the North Ferry. Met there with Mr. Joseph Monro, and he and I crossed in a yawl together. Breakfasted at the Halls, and went to Edinburgh in the fly in excellent spirits. Found my wife ill with the influenza. Visited my father at night. He shook hands with me. I supped with him and drank some port wine to preserve me from the infection of the air, or whatever other cause.

WEDNESDAY 12 JUNE. (Writing Tuesday the 18.) Waited on the Lord President at his levee the first day of the Summer Session. Was in excellent spirits, and felt myself really superior to the mere men of this narrow country. Walked after the Court rose with Mr. John Swinton and Mr. Henry Erskine in the Meadow. Visited my father in the evening. Was really sound in body and mind. Went to Lord Kames's with intention to sup. Baron Dalrymple came, and though the creature (after my speech to him about Lord Barrington) asked me to come and see his new house, which made me relent, I went away to shun him. I told Mrs. Drummond warmly Lord Dumfries should not have his road.[7]

THURSDAY 13 JUNE. (Writing on Tuesday the 18.) Waited on Lord President this morning; was admitted into his study, and spoke with him confidentially about my father. He wished my father to be at Auchinleck, but wisely observed that as his physician was against it, I should not interfere for his going; because if he should be the worse for it, there might be reflections. We went up to the drawing-room, and I made tea for him. I renewed my invitation, and he promised he would dine with me one day this Session.[8] A number of people came. Wight told that Lord Covington had been very ill the day before, was left speechless and without hope of recovery.[9] The President instantly with a shake said (or roared rather)

[5] See above, 16 October 1778.

[6] Of which there was an epidemic all over Europe. The disease seems to have affected nearly everyone, but caused few deaths.

[7] See above, 2 November 1778, 2 September 1780.

[8] Boswell had invited the Lord President to dine early in April, but he had sent his regrets.

[9] Lord Covington recovered from the stroke (see below, 24 and 31 July 1782), but died the following November.

in a high key, "Send awa' your express, Johnny Swinton!" "Indeed, my Lord," said I, "he may send a cloak-bag horse (writing 19 June) if he pleases, for he is very sure of the gown;—a heavy Merse nag." "With a long tail, James," said he. "Ha! ha! ha!" "Now," said I, "here is a striking proof how a Lord of Session is lamented when he dies. The first thing is a joke about his successor." I then told the noted story of Lords Kames and Covington on Lord Pitfour's death.[1] I continued to enjoy wonderful spirits. In the Parliament House, Old Erskine, Sandy Gordon, and I found ourselves in glee together. Said I: "We three are well. Are we engaged to dinner?" They said, "No." "Why then," said I, "will you two take a leg of roast mutton with me?" Erskine answered, "Accursed be he by whom it is denied." I sent to my wife that two gentlemen were to dine, and I sent for MacGuarie, who was now in town, and I asked David Cuninghame. I went with Gordon and visited Lady Aberdeen and her young ladies, and there I asked Lord Haddo and Sir John Scott. Gordon and I then visited my father for a little. Bringing such a company suddenly was not fair to my wife. But she acquitted herself wonderfully. There was an excellent dinner and plenty of good claret, and every man at the table was blood. I liked Sir John Scott as the representative of Balweary. Old Erskine rashly said that he had heard there was a custom among the lairds in the Western Isles to keep a dunkerer,[2] a teaser, for their ladies. MacGuarie denied it. "What, Sir," said Erskine, "did you never hear this before?" "No, Sir," said the old chieftain pretty sternly, "I think I hear it soon enough now." "Are not the women cold?" said Erskine. "No, Sir," said MacGuarie; "and if you have a curiosity to try, I think you have no time to lose." This was very well. I got them kept in good humour. I was in as high roaring spirits as ever the late Dundonald was, with more genius. I went with Lord Haddo, Gordon, and Sir John Scott to Dunn's Hotel to sup with Bargany,[3] whom I had visited

---

[1] This does not appear to have been recorded.

[2] This word is missing from the standard dictionaries, but the gerund of the corresponding verb, "duncarring," is defined as "buggering" in *A New Dictionary of Terms Ancient and Modern of the Canting Crew*, by E. B., Gent., London, 1699, sign. E. "Teaser" survives as a breeder's term: "an inferior stallion or ram used to excite mares or ewes" or "an imperfect ram which is allowed to run with the ewes." Edward Burt records the same legend in his *Letters from a Gentleman in the North of Scotland*, but not of the Hebrides: "They tell you that some of the lairds in the Islands of Shetland ... hire a domestic by the half-year, or by the quarter, just as they can agree, whose business is to put an instrument in order when the laird has an inclination to play upon it, but if he attempts to play a tune himself, he is sure to be discarded" (Letter XXV).

[3] John Hamilton (born Dalrymple) of Bargany, advocate, M.P., Wigtown Burghs, 1751–1768, brother-in-law of Col. Hugh Montgomerie.

in the morning. Met there Lord Cassillis, for whom I had called, Countess of Dumfries and Stair,[3a] etc. Played at brag. Lost a pound and was vexed.

The time, O ye muses, was *heavily* spent.[4]

Rarely does one both dine and sup happily the same day. But I did not get drunk.

FRIDAY 14 JUNE. (Writing the 19.) Awaked sick and uneasy. However, Sandy Gordon prevailed with me to dine with him, and we called on MacGuarie and had him with us. I resolved to be home soon and not to play cards. However, I was warmed while MacGuarie stayed. And after he went away, I played whist and brag and supped and played again, Bargany and Hew Dalrymple of North Berwick having come, and I lost £2.14. I came home at two in the morning, really miserable, but manfully determining to bear my game misfortunes, and never again to play but for trifles, and not at all at brag.

SATURDAY 15 JUNE. (Writing the 19.) There was no meeting of the Court of Session today, the Lords having adjourned till Tuesday.[5] I went out a little, and the rest of the day wrote a good part of No. 57 of *The Hypochondriack*. David Cuninghame passed the evening with us.

SUNDAY 16 JUNE. (Writing on the 19.) Imagined I was taking the influenza. Lay in bed till about one. Had excellent spirits. Sandy was very attentive to me. I read today Bruce's *Inquiry into the Cause of the Pestilence*, as there was an alarm that the influenza was growing into it in London. I was really entertained with his collection of facts and plausible conclusion, and wondered how a leather-merchant in the *Bow* could make such a book.[6] Balmuto drank tea with us. William Lennox brought inquiries about us from my father's. I took him into a room and examined him as to my father's state of memory and other particulars. Found him very distinct; desired he might not leave my father, and bid

---

[3a] Alexander Gordon's wife.

[4] Adaptation of John Byrom's pastoral, *Colin and Phoebe*:

> My time, O ye Muses, was happily spent,
> When Phoebe went with me wherever I went.

[5] "On Friday June 14 the Court of Session adjourned to the Tuesday following, several of the Lords being absent, and so many of them affected with the influenza . . . that there was no probability of a sufficient number of their lordships being able to attend next day to constitute a quorum. An instance of an adjournment of the Court of Session by themselves has not happened in the memory of man, if ever any such event took place" (*Scots Magazine*, July 1782, xliv. 388, which proceeds to draw on "a curious manuscript in the possession of James Boswell, Esq., advocate").

[6] Alexander Bruce first published this book in 1759. We have found no more information about him than Boswell gives.

him be careful to observe and remember, as he might be perhaps called upon.

MONDAY 17 JUNE. (Writing the 19.) Was better. Had still wonderful spirits. Finished my *Hypochondriack* No. 57.[7] The Earl of Kellie called. I asked if he would eat a part of a fine roasted hare without ceremony. He agreed, and we were really cordial. I walked with his Lordship to the New Town, visited my father, and took bread and butter and port and water. Lady Auchinleck and some of the servants having the influenza, it seems there was no meat supper of any kind. There was a wonderful importance about the sickness in *their* house. My father was very unsocial. He had the influenza a day or two when it first began in Edinburgh. I came home and eat my egg cordially.

TUESDAY 18 JUNE. (Writing the 19.) Still in wonderful spirits. Felt myself easy and *above* the Court of Session. Why cannot such spirits always last? For I now have as full satisfaction in my own existence as Mr. Burke has, only that I wish for greater objects. But I am quiet when I consider that during my father's life, I *cannot* have them. I sat an hour with Sir William Forbes in high happiness and read to him my 56 *Hypochondriack*, with which he was much pleased. Lady Margaret Macdonald, who had come to Edinburgh last night, drank tea with us. I accompanied her to Dunn's Hotel to Sir John and Lady Anstruther, with whom she had come and with whom she went this night to Fife.

WEDNESDAY 19 JUNE. (Writing on Friday 28.) Dined at my father's; Lady Auchinleck not at table. He said very little. I drank seven or eight bumpers of port, which intoxicated me somewhat. My head was stuffed, and I had a little of a headache. In short, I apprehended I was taking the influenza, which was now raging. I sat a little with Maclaurin, who was ill. Drank tea with Mr. George Wallace. Supped at Old Lady Wallace's by earnest invitation of Miss Susie Dunlop, whom I had visited in the forenoon and had a kind of quarrel with. I met there the beautiful

---

[7] "I hope none of my pious readers ... are troubled with scrupulous fears of riches, from misapprehending temporary precepts, adapted to the early state of Christianity. ...To be *'rich in good works,'* is above all to be desired and endeavoured. But riches, in the common acceptation of the word, are necessary in order to enable us to do good. ... I am only giving money fair play amongst the pursuits of this life. If it shall be objected that we cannot carry it with us when death comes, the answer is, that neither can we carry with us our books or our pictures, our houses, our gardens, our lawns, or our groves, of all which we may, without offending against religion, be pleasingly fond, and that without such fondness the lives of all but pure mystics, who it is meant should be few, would be passed in torpid inutility" (*The Hypochondriack*, No. 57, the second on wealth).

Captain Parkhurst of the 25.[8] I was in gay spirits, but cold, and more affected with symptoms of influenza. Drank a good deal of port to keep off the infection.

THURSDAY 20 JUNE. (Writing the 28.) Awaked hot and profusely sweating, with a violent headache; in short with the influenza. Lay all day in great pain.

FRIDAY 21 JUNE. (Writing the 28.) Continued just as ill as yesterday. If I but raised my head from the pillow, it grew quite giddy. But I resigned myself to my fate, Mr. Wood assuring me I had only to sweat. I drank a deal of tea and water gruel and bitter-orange and water.

SATURDAY 22 JUNE. (Writing the 28.) Had a miserable night of pain and sickness and distress of mind; for my dear wife, who had taken too much exercise during the late hot days, had a violent coughing between three and four, and spit up a great quantity of blood. She was much alarmed. I was so too. But without emotion; for I was so overcome by the effects of the influenza that if she had been carried dead from my side, I could not have stirred. Mr. Wood was called about seven. He made her remove to the drawing-room and have her bed there for better air. I lay all day. Sandy Gordon paid me a short visit. I was in a sad state, but not hipped.

SUNDAY 23 JUNE. (Writing 3 July.) Was somewhat better. Rose about noon, I think, and sat awhile by my wife. The children said divine lessons. I missed my sweet Veronica.

MONDAY 24 JUNE. (Writing 3 July.) I have a particular journal of my wife's illness.[9] So shall not be particular as to it here. I was now free from influenza, but it had flown out on my lips all up to my nose,[1] and made me a fright.

TUESDAY 25 JUNE. (Writing 3 July.) Wife much as yesterday. I dictated a law paper.

WEDNESDAY 26 JUNE. (Writing 3 July.) I dictated another law paper; a good part of one. My time passed not unhappily. Hypochondria never assaulted me. I was less frightened for my wife than upon former occasions, except in solitude when night and darkness came.

THURSDAY 27 JUNE. (Writing 3 July.) I was awaked early yesterday

[8] All we know of the beautiful Captain is that his name was George, that he became captain on 3 July 1781, and his name does not appear in the Army List after 1783.

[9] It extends from 22 June to 11 November.

[1] "An eruption about the nose and lips was not uncommon" (Edward Gray, *An Account of the Epidemic Catarrh of the Year 1782*, first published in 1784, reprinted in *Annals of Influenza*, ed. Theophilus Thompson, 1852, p. 123).

morning, my wife having been worse. This last night she had also been much distressed. She was ordered by Mr. Wood to be kept very quiet. She had read *Rasselas* this week. She now wished to have *Tom Jones*, which she had never read. She knew Fielding by *Joseph Andrews*, from the manner.[2] I read to her. Finished my law paper.

FRIDAY 28 JUNE. (Writing 3 July.) My wife was rather easier. I read more of *Tom Jones* to her. Mr. Baron Norton, to whom I had applied for an Exchequer pension for the aged daughters of the late Sir Harry Wardlaw,[3] recommended to me by Sir Charles and Miss Preston, called on me this forenoon and most obligingly promised me the utmost he could give: viz., £10 per annum whenever there should be an opening by death. His *English* cast of conversation revived me, and I was pleased that I had it in my power to obtain such a favour.[4] Dr. Gillespie was confined, I think since Tuesday.

SATURDAY 29 JUNE. (Writing 3 July.) My confinement was unlucky in session time. But there was no help for it, and I did not fret. Yesterday and today the Court of Session did not sit for want of a quorum. This pleased me. I should have liked a surcease of justice till I was well again. I did not think of its being of any hurt. And indeed I doubt if it would have been of much hurt. The day passed much as yesterday. *Tom Jones* entertained both my wife and me. I was more entertained than her, having a warmer fancy. But I did not admire the work so highly as when I heard it read in the year 1761 by Mr. Love, the player. I made excerpts from it now. This week I was visited by Old Erskine, by Messrs. Maclaurin and George Wallace twice, by Sir Alexander Dick, by Sir W. Forbes twice, Mr. Hunter-Blair, Mr. Macredie; by Messrs. Blane, Matthew Dickie, and Robert Boswell on business, and by Mr. James Baillie, who drank tea with me; also by Commissioner Cochrane and Dr. Webster, and by Sir Walter and David Cuninghame. To the credit of George Campbell I must register that when he found his aunt ill, he wept a great deal.

SUNDAY 30 JUNE. (Writing 4 July.) My wife was rather better today. I read some of the Bible, and of Heylyn's *Discourses* to her, particularly about John the Baptist and in favour of a *call* which some have to retire-

---

[2] Perhaps Boswell means that his wife did not know who wrote *Tom Jones*. He could have been suggesting books for her, and she had read his first selection, *Rasselas*; now his second is *Tom Jones*. As soon as he begins to read it to her, she recognizes the style as Fielding's.

[3] Not the husband of the putative author of *Hardyknute* but his nephew, who had died in February of this year. The pensions were granted by 18 July.

[4] "His Majesty gives a bounty of £2,000 per ann. to be distributed by the barons to such poor persons as they judge proper" (*Royal Kalendar for the Year 1782*, p. 244).

ment.[5] The children said divine lessons. My mind was calm. Phemie went to Prestonfield yesterday.

MONDAY 1 JULY. (Writing the 4.) I had nothing to trouble me about myself but the remains of a scurf on my lips, which was wearing away. My wife was a good deal better. Phemie came home.

TUESDAY 2 JULY. (Writing the 4.) My wife continued to be a good deal better, which cheered me finely. During the course of last week my spirits had been wonderfully good, owing, I suppose, to my light diet and tasting no fermented liquor. I had even flights of fancy in the view of my being a widower. These shocked me afterwards. But, as Milton says, "Evil into the mind," etc.,[6] I put down a fair transcript of the phases of my mind. Either yesterday or today my brother John visited me of his own accord. He had been with me last week on my sending for him. This day Mr. Andrew Lumisden, who had called before, sat a long time with me in the forenoon and gave me a most engaging account of M. de Buffon's way of living. He had been three months last summer at his *château*. The day went on easily. Worthy Grange, who arrived last night, visited me today.

WEDNESDAY 3 JULY. (Writing the 4.) My dear wife was worse. Dr. Gillespie visited her this forenoon. I had visits of Hon. A. Gordon, Sir W. Forbes, and Mr. George Wallace either today or yesterday; also of Commissioner Cochrane and Mr. Stobie; of Mr. Maclaurin today. I finished *Tom Jones*. My wife disliked Fielding's turn for low life, and did not think even his Sophia quite refined. She suspected Miss Bridget to be Jones's mother from the time that the account of her death is told. That was truly penetrating, or rather sagacious. Last week I read Towers's defence of Mr. Locke, Blackstone on the King's right (and admired him, only saw him evading the Revolution) as also some of the *Anatomy of Melancholy*, that amazing aggregate of learning; also some of Pilrig's *Philosophical Essays*, new.[7]

THURSDAY 4 JULY. (Writing the 5.) This day also my dear wife was worse. Though I keep an exact journal of the changes of her distress, I find her being so interwoven with mine that she must appear in my

[5] John Heylyn (?1685–1759), a mystical divine. His *Select Discourses* were first published in 1749.

[6] *Paradise Lost*, v. 117–119:

> Evil into the mind of God or man
> May come and go, so unapprov'd, and leave
> No spot or blame behind.

[7] Joseph Towers's pamphlet was a reply to *Civil Government* by Josiah Tucker, Dean of Gloucester, which attacked the political principles of John Locke. "Blackstone on the King's right" is in the famous *Commentaries* (Bk. I, ch. 3). "Pilrig's" name was John Balfour, the title of his book properly, *Philosophical Dissertations*.

own diary also. Worthy Grange visited me twice today. In the forenoon I was visited by Lord Kellie, Commissioner Cochrane, Mr. Lumisden, Major Preston, and Matthew Dickie upon business, and in the afternoon by Horatius Cannan. I had been visited since I was ill by Mr. John Young and by Mr. McNab, clerk to Mr. David Erskine, upon business. Mr. Maclaurin did for me what I have done for him by appearing for me at the bar. I dictated law papers with satisfaction. I made a good many excerpts from *Tom Jones*. My wife disliked Fielding's turn for low life, as I have observed yesterday. But it is human nature. She has nothing of that English juiciness of mind of which I have a great deal, which makes me delight in humour. But what hurts me more, she has nothing of that warmth of imagination which produces the pleasures of vanity and many others, and which is even a considerable cause of religious fervour. *Family*, which is a high *principle* in my mind, and genealogy, which is to me an interesting amusement, have no effect upon her. It is impossible not to be both uneasy and a little angry at such defects (or call them differences); and at times they make me think that I have been unlucky in uniting myself with one, who, instead of cherishing my genius, is perpetually checking it. But on the other hand, I consider her excellent sense, her penetration, her knowledge of real life, her activity, her genuine affection, her generous conduct to me during my distracted love for her and when she married me, and her total disinterestedness and freedom from every species of selfishness during all the time she has been my wife. And then I value her and am fond of her, and am pained to the heart for having ever behaved in a manner unworthy of her merit. I also consider that a woman of the same imagination with myself might have encouraged me in whim and adventure, and hurried me to ridicule and perhaps ruin, whereas my excellent spouse's prudence has kept me out of many follies, and made my life much more decent and creditable than it would have been without her. She was very apprehensive today and sadly dejected. She read some of Lord Lyttelton's *St. Paul's Conversion*, which she praised, but said it occurred to her as a temptation of the devil that perhaps (as Festus said) Paul was mad, and all might be delusion. She thought his boldness at the time of the vision extraordinary. She has always a dreary terror for death. Indeed he is the King of Terrors. She said yesterday it was desirable to live long for one reason: because old people come to be as little afraid of death as children are. Balmuto visited me this evening. The prospect of going out again was not pleasing to me. I find the life which I now lead, upon the whole, the most agreeable to me. I am calm, I am heavenly-minded. Shall I end my days in a convent? This often seems probable to me. My dear wife's illness was more distressing to me that I reflected she had never had the advantages to which the match she had made entitled her, my father having kept me upon a small allowance, and he and his women having treated her with shameful coldness. When I thought she might perhaps die before my coming to the estate of Auchinleck, which would place her in a situation which she so well deserves, I was grievously vexed; and as a wife is to be preferred to a father, especially when he lives only to continue the harsh and unjust power of a stepmother, I could not help viewing his death as a desirable event. I know not what to think of this. Certainly the death of a father *may* be a desirable event. It is nice to determine in what cases. A son should be able to give strong reasons. I have given mine; and I do not see as yet that I am in the wrong. It is not on my own account that the wish rises. It is a wish formed upon the principle of choosing the least of two evils. In my devotions during this alarming illness of my dear wife, I earnestly beseech GOD to restore her to health; and I vow that with the aid of His grace, which I earnestly implore, I shall maintain a conduct becoming a Christian. *That* I am bound to do at any rate. I know it, yet there is something natural in vowing upon an occasion of deep concern; and this vow may do me good.

FRIDAY 5 JULY. (Writing the 11.) Time passed very well. I read over the letters which I wrote to my friend Grange at different towns abroad, and was much pleased with myself. He visited me today. I have nothing particular to mark. I keep a journal of my wife's illness. I was less alarmed now.

SATURDAY 6 JULY. (Writing the 12.) My lips, which had been quite crusted with eruption, were now almost quite clean, the scurf having gradually come off. Mr. Lumisden visited me this forenoon, and Sandy walked with him to Prestonfield. He visited me again in the evening, as did Mr. George Wallace and Grange.

SUNDAY 7 JULY. (Writing the 12.) This day passed so smoothly that I recollect no trace of it.[8] I had omitted to make the children say divine lessons till they were in bed. Recollecting this, I hurried to the nursery, and to keep up the good custom uniformly, made them say shortly. Grange visited me, as did Mr. John Hunter, who asked me to be judge of Lord Loudoun's roup.[9]

MONDAY 8 JULY. (Writing the 12.) Got myself fully shaved and dressed, and my coat on for the first time since my illness. My brother John visited me in the forenoon. In the afternoon I ventured out. The town had a strange appearance to me. My head was giddy, and I walked

---

[8] "13 [July]. I now recollect I abstracted from Priestley's *Institutes of Religion*"— BOSWELL.

[9] Sale, auction, in this case of farms.

feebly. I went by the timber bridge for shortness and privacy,[1] and reached my father's. Found him and his lady and Commissioner Cochrane at whist, and Dr. Gillespie reading the *London Chronicle*. The unfeeling reception (at least it seemed so) after my illness and such anxious distress in my family, quite shocked me. My father had never visited us all the time, though he had been once at Commissioner Cochrane's, and this very day at the Countess of Sutherland's. I blamed the woman who "girds him—leads him whithersoever she willeth," a very good application by our minister, Mr. Dun, to my father's old age, of what Christ says of St. Peter.[2] I went up to my father and offered him my hand, which was accepted awkwardly. He never asked me about my illness, nor did he open his mouth about my wife, till after a long time he said, "Is your wife bravely the day, James?" I calmly answered, "She is rather better." I tried to get him to buy the farm of Willockshill next day at Lord Loudoun's roup. But he avoided it, and said he had no money, nor he believed would have money. "What," said I, "will you not have £400 in a year or two years?" "What if I die?" said he, with a kind of angry tone. "Any of us may die," said I. "Hoot!" said he, as if despising an attempt to seem insensible of his being near death or in danger of it soon, at least much more than most of us. I drank tea with them, and then went with the Commissioner in his chaise and was set down at the West Port, having driven round the Castle.

TUESDAY 9 JULY. (Writing the 16.) I went to the Court of Session. I felt a languor which was not unpleasing; perceived a kindness of inquiry in some, which was a cordial, and a total inattention in others, which gave me a just view of how little consequence an individual is. My wife was better. I had good accounts yesterday of Dr. Johnson from Mrs. Thrale.[3] I was judge this afternoon of Lord Loudoun's roup.

WEDNESDAY 10 JULY. (Writing the 16.) My dear wife was so much better today that she went out and took an airing in a chaise. While she was out, my father and Lady Auchinleck called, for a wonder. I got them

---

[1] Either a temporary structure at the site of what was to become the Earthen Mound or the beginnings of the Earthen Mound. It ran from a point near James's Court, across the North Loch to Princes Street.

[2] John 21. 18. ("When thou wast young, thou girdedst thyself, and walkedst whither thou wouldest: but when thou shalt be old, thou shalt stretch forth thy hands, and another shall gird thee, and carry thee whither thou wouldest not.")

[3] "The account ... of Dr. Johnson alarms me to the heart; and you, whose veneration and affection for him are in unison with mine, will conceive what I feel.... It will be doing me a kindness, which I shall most gratefully acknowledge, if you will be pleased once a week to let me know by a single line how he recovers" (To Mrs. Thrale, 25 May 1782). Mrs. Thrale replied on 3 June and 4 July 1782; Boswell sent grateful thanks on 9 July 1782.

upstairs with me for a short and cold visit. Yesterday and today I dictated a paper in the cause, Walker against Young, in which the Lords and Mr. Russell, the accountant, were all egregiously wrong; and I thought I demonstrated they were so.[4]

THURSDAY 11 JULY. (Writing the 16.) I had a degree of vertigo and weakness about me. But I took special care of myself. Grange and I and Phemie went out in Sir Alexander Dick's coach and dined at Prestonfield; nobody there but Mr. Andrew Lumisden, who was very entertaining. We walked in the garden, and sat down; and Grange and I agreed we were now as happy as we had ever been in our lives, and looked up to the skies with hope of permanent felicity. When I came home I found Lord Pembroke had called. I hastened out to find him. Met him near Miln's Square (a rainy night), frank and pleasant as ever. But he was to lie at Dalkeith. Was going to Ireland and then to return here. Met also Colonel Hugh Montgomerie, who had called on me. Was cordial with him after his recovery. My wife rather low today.

FRIDAY 12 JULY. Time went on placidly. I had little business in the Court of Session this summer. But I did not fret. My wife was this evening so well that she thanked GOD she was quite a different woman from what she had been lately. I visited Lord Loudoun.

SATURDAY 13 JULY. (Writing the 16.) My wife and I and Sandy and Phemie and Grange went out in a landau and looked at Mr. Scott's

---

[4] This cause turned on an interesting legal point too complicated to be presented fully in this edition: the proper times of year for collecting the rents of a miller, whose income, unlike that of most tenants of an estate, came not from a crop planted by himself but from multures (shares of all the grain he ground at his mill). William Elder, tenant in the mill of Stonehaven, Kincardineshire, having become insolvent, his affairs had been settled, with payment of ten shillings in the pound, by two trustees, William Young, sheriff-clerk of Kincardine and factor for Elder's landlord, Lord Elphinstone (the principal creditor) and James Wood, farmer in Fetteresso, to whom Elder owed £100. Wood later fell out with Young, and John Walker, tenant in Acquhirrie, to whom Elder had owed a small sum, obtained an assignment of Wood's claim, joined it to his own, and brought suit against Young for an accounting. Boswell was counsel for Walker, who by this time had lost his cause twice before Lord Elliock (25 February 1780, 17 January 1781), and at least once before the whole Court (3 July 1781). At that point the cause is very fully documented by four printed papers preserved in the Signet Library, Edinburgh: a Petition by Boswell for Walker (12 July 1781, nineteen pages), Answers for Young by George Buchan Hepburn (31 July 1781, eighteen pages), Replies for Walker by Ilay Campbell (12 October 1781, twenty-four pages), and Duplies for Young by Hepburn (21 November 1781, ten pages). The cause is valuable to biographers of Boswell because it enables them to compare Boswell as a lawyer with "the first writing lawyer at [the Scots] bar" (*Journal,* 27 August 1774), writing in the same cause and treating almost exactly the same evidence. Though Campbell's paper is unquestionably the better of the two, Boswell's stands the comparison very well.

house and garden on the road to Prestonfield, thinking to take it for the rest of the summer. It pleased her much. Lord Loudoun paid me a visit, and my wife also saw him. Grange dined with us. He and I saw the Defensive Band exercise on Heriot's Green. There I met Raasay, who I heard from Lord Loudoun was in town. I paid a visit to Captain and Mrs. Mingay. Dr. Webster was at Lord Leven's. I saw Miss Wardrop, whom I had met on the Castle Hill, unexpectedly in town for a day or two.

SUNDAY 14 JULY. (Writing the 16.) My wife was more uneasy today. I went to the New Church in the forenoon, Grange in my seat. Dr. Andrew Hunter preached. I was in firm spirits. Visited Raasay. Dined at my father's, where I had not been since Tuesday, as I was yet so tender in my feelings that I could not bear the coldness and harshness. Miss Peggie had been at Balmuto a forthnight or so, the old lady having been ill. The Commissioner dined today. Lady A. went to church in the afternoon. He and I sat the afternoon chiefly with my father, who said almost nothing today. I came home to tea. These two Sunday mornings I have made Sandy repeat to me the history of the lairds of Auchinleck, that he may hold the family in some degree sacred. I was pleased today when I told him the story of an old man warning James IV not to go to Flodden, and how some thought it a man in a venerable dress and some an angel or a ghost, he took the superstitious alternative.[5] He and Phemie

---

[5] "The King came to Lithgow, where he happened to be for the time at the Council, very sad and dolorous, making his devotion to God, to send him good chance and fortune in his voyage. In this meantime there came a man clad in a blue gown in at the kirk door, and belted about him in a roll of linen cloth; a pair of brotikings [buskins] on his feet, to the great of his legs; with all other hose and clothes conform thereto: but he had nothing on his head, but syde [long] red-yellow hair behind, and on his haffets [cheeks], which wan [reached] down to his shoulders; but his forehead was bald and bare. He seemed to be a man of two-and-fifty years, with a great pike-staff in his hand, and came first forward among the lords, crying and speiring [asking] for the King, saying he desired to speak with him. While, at the last, he came where the King was sitting in the desk at his prayers; but when he saw the King, he made him little reverence or salutation, but leaned down groffling on the desk before him and said to him in this manner as after follows: 'Sir King, my mother hath sent me to you, desiring you not to pass at this time where thou art purposed; for if thou does, thou wilt not fare well in thy journey, nor none that passeth with thee. Further, she bade thee mell [meddle] with no woman, nor use their counsel, nor let them touch thy body, nor thou theirs, for if thou do it, thou wilt be confounded and brought to shame.' By this man had spoken thir words unto the King's grace, the evening-song was near done, and the King paused on thir words, studying to give him an answer; but, in the meantime, before the King's eyes, and in the presence of all the lords that were about him for the time, this man vanished away, and could no ways be seen or comprehended, but vanished away as he had been a blink of the

and Jamie said divine lessons in the evening. I paid a visit at Belleville. Lady Dundonald was ill, but I saw Lady Elizabeth Heron. At night my wife was hoarse and feverish and dejected. I thought that my sleeping with her might soothe her, and lay down by her. But she felt herself too much heated, and coughed much; so I rose and went to my own bed downstairs. I was alarmed about her.

MONDAY 15 JULY. (Writing the 17.) On Saturday and Sunday I read a curious little book called *A Two Years' Journal in New York*, written by C. W., A.M., who went out chaplain to the Governor in 1678.[6] It is wonderful how much substance may be contained in a few sheets. Abridging is an excellent art. I really believe that a folio might be boiled into a small duodecimo. Newbery's little books for children have epitomized *Tom Jones* and other works to admiration. I walked out today to Scott's house and met my wife; Dr. Gillespie, etc., there. She was now unwilling to take it. I dined at my father's to meet the Commissioner. I drank small beer and two glasses of port, one mixed with water. I felt even this instigate my rage for intoxication, so I "put a knife to my throat."[7] I must mention something in favour of my father today. I had yesterday asked him to let me have Skene's *Acts of Parliament* with Fountainhall's notes.[8] He declined it. Today he remembered my request and said I might send for the book. How much is it to be lamented that he is so deficient in tenderness, in the "charities" of relationship and of social intercourse![9] But am I not in some degree so myself? I came home to tea, after attending the judicial sale of Fetteresso, etc.[1] I was in a state of listlessness tonight, without being uneasy. Colonel Montgomerie visited me in the forenoon. I called on Lord Advocate. Met him in George's Square, and was told by him of his preferment.[2]

TUESDAY 16 JULY. (Writing the 18.) My words to the Quick March

---

sun, or a whip of the whirlwind, and could no more be seen" (Robert Lindsay of Pitscottie, *The History of Scotland*, 1728, as quoted in Scott's *Marmion*, IV. xiv note).

[6] Charles Wolley, the author of this book, graduated B.A. from Cambridge in 1674 and was the first clergyman of the Church of England to hold a charge in the province of New York. His journal was first published in 1701.

[7] "Put a knife to thy throat, if thou be a man given to appetite" (Proverbs 23. 2).

[8] Sir John Skene's *Laws and Actes of Parliament* was published in 1597. The notes by Sir John Lauder (Lord Fountainhall), who died in 1722, must have been in manuscript.

[9] *Paradise Lost*, iv. 756–7:

> Relations dear, and all the charities
> Of father, son, and brother.

[1] The mansion-house of a forfeited Scots estate, formerly the property of the Marischal family.

[2] Explained in the next entry.

by Mr. Muschet for the Edinburgh Defensive Band was this morning published by George Reid *for the small price of one penny,* and sold at the Parliament House. I felt a little awkward at this, though I really liked the *War Song,* as I entitled it; for though too high perhaps in panegyric, it pleased Crosbie and many of the band, and I did mean it as an exaggerated eulogium, a caricatura compliment.[3] It was *omnia magna loquens,*[4] and there were good verses in it. It is curious how one may be in some measure hurt by the censure of the lowest creature, though one knows it to have no kind of judgement in the matter which it censures. I experienced this today when Robert Jamieson, the Writer to the Signet, told me the song was "too severe," and when I contradicted him, maintained the composition was bad. An insect's sting will be felt. One has only to avoid insects. Lord Advocate, to whom a King's Messenger had come from Lord Shelburne on Sunday with an offer of the Signet for life and being Treasurer of the Navy, was in the Court of Session today in a coloured coat and bob-wig. I asked him if I could have ten minutes conversation with him before he set out for London, which he was to do in a day or two. (Writing the 21.) He said he would speak with me now, upon the benches. So he walked up, I following him; and there we sat in the sight of the crowd in the Outer House, who wondered and conjectured while we talked seriously and confidentially. I told him I was much obliged to him for his letter.[5] That I was doing very well here, but I wished for something better. "You would have something in the other end of the island," said he. I said yes. But I consulted him if my wish was irrational and ought to be checked. He said no. I told him that I had been so often amongst the people there, I felt myself so much at home there, I had such a desire for something upon a larger scale and being connected with matters of consequence, that I was very desirous of being

[3] This song, which was printed as a broadside, is reproduced as one of the illustrations of the present volume, following p. 250. The piece is one of Boswell's rarest publications; indeed, his copy at Yale is at present the only one reported.

[4] "Putting everything in grand style" (Horace, *Satires,* I. iii. 13).

[5] Boswell had written to Dundas on 20 April 1782 that he had been "fortunate enough to become convinced that politics was the strongest poison to the human mind, and would insensibly instigate excellent men to do very wrong things. I excused your Lordship's ardent ambitious conduct. I upon my honour forgave you." He then asks Dundas "to give me your kind assistance, and . . . your able advice in my endeavours to obtain promotion." Dundas replied (12 May 1782) that he "never felt a moment's resentment from the estrangement of your friendship from me, and the moment you showed a disposition to return to it, the business was done upon my part. . . . You will be satisfied how readily I adopt the principle of your letter." But he failed to say that he would do anything to help Boswell obtain promotion.

employed in London. I said I had no right to ask him but old hereditary friendship and our early friendship; but would he have his thoughts (or think) of me, and see if something could be procured for me? He said he would. He added that it would require time to consider deliberately and give his advice. He would be down again in September. I said I intended being in London when the Session was up. He said, very well, we could talk there. He told me that he *knew* Burke wished to assist me. I had mentioned this; and I concluded from what he said that Burke had expressed himself warmly to him. I was pleased in thinking I had now another string, and that a strong string, to my bow. This forenoon, or another forenoon early in this week, Lord Pembroke honoured me with a visit, and was pleasant and easy.

WEDNESDAY 17 JULY. (Writing the 23.) I recollect nothing particular.

THURSDAY 18 JULY. (Writing the 23.) My wife went in a chair to my father's. I met her there, and afterwards walked with her on the pavement in the New Town. The coldness at my father's was shocking. The chariot was at the door, yet there was no offer of it to her. It was a bright, sunny forenoon.

FRIDAY 19 JULY. (Writing the 23.) Grange and I dined at Prestonfield by special invitation. But we were not so happy as we could wish, there being a collection of females. Mr. Lumisden visited me today.

FRIDAY 19 JULY.[6] (Writing the 27.) I recollect nothing particular. I keep a journal of my wife's illness, and therefore mention it only when there is some remarkable variation.

SATURDAY 20 JULY. (Writing the 27.) This day I read Phillips's *Election Cases*, Vol. I. Went and drank tea with Lord Covington. I have marked what passed on a separate paper, being a slip of materials for his life.[7] I visited my father as I returned.

SUNDAY 21 JULY. (Writing the 27.) Having long wished to read calmly with Mr. Andrew Lumisden his accurate and classical account of Rome and its environs, I had appointed this forenoon for it at his suggestion. I in general wish to keep Sunday with a good degree of strictness; not from express obligation, but from an opinion of its being expedient and advantageous to do so. But I thought the study of Rome might be indulged on that day. So I went to his lodgings in the back part of Miln's Square, and we sat about three hours. I was quite cheerful and manly, and relished what I read as much as I did the specimen

[6] Boswell inadvertently wrote two entries for this day.

[7] None of Boswell's materials for the life of Lord Covington have been recovered. It is doubtful that the project advanced beyond the collection of materials.

of the work which I had read at Rome seventeen years ago.[8] This was very agreeable. We stopped at Praeneste, now Palestrina, and deferred going farther till after the Race Week, during which he said he would be dissipated. Grange was in our seat in church in the afternoon, but we had no satisfaction, the minister who preached being without eloquence of any kind. I went after much solicitation and by my wife's desire to dine at Old Lady Wallace's to meet Lord Loudoun. In the evening I walked with my wife in Lord Chief Baron Ord's garden. She was much worse today and thought herself gone, so that she cried when Mr. Wood was with her. I met him in the New Town and talked with him about her. He could not conceal his apprehension of her being in danger, so that I was woefully alarmed. He said the best thing for her was change of air and exercise, and if she could be persuaded to it, a southern climate. Even England, he thought, might be of benefit to her if her mind would give her to it. I regretted her having nothing of my roving disposition. There was in the midst of my anxiety and shooting pains of grief a sort of agitation that rather gave a kind of pleasure. The children said divine lessons.

MONDAY 22 JULY. (Writing the 27.) Dined at my father's; the Commissioner, Lieutenant,[9] etc., there. My father was in bad frame. I had visited the Commissioner at the Custom House in the forenoon, and he found fault plainly with the treatment which I suffer. I paid a visit to Miss Gray about five o'clock, she having been with my wife in the forenoon and complained that I had been long without seeing her. Her uncle, Dr. Steedman, was with her. I claimed merit with her as one of Sir John Pringle's representatives. "Sir John," said I, "is now in commission." This was a good allusion to the seals being in commission when there is no Chancellor.[1] I could not stay tea, having a consultation at home. My dear wife was wonderfully better today. She walked on the Castle Hill and in the Castle with me and Jeanie Campbell, and was refreshed and amused, and looked like herself again, like Miss Peggie Montgomerie. She received a visit from Lord Kellie after she came home. I walked with his Lordship to the end of the bridge. I slept with my wife tonight. π. It was a renovation of felicity.

TUESDAY 23 JULY. (Writing the 29.) This morning (I believe) visited

---

[8] When Boswell had first become acquainted with Lumisden, then serving as secretary to the titular James III, the Old Pretender. Lumisden's *Remarks on the Antiquities of Rome and Its Environs* was not published till 1797.

[9] John Boswell.

[1] When the Lord Chancellorship is for any reason in abeyance, the seals are commonly put in the hands of several commissioners who exercise the authority of the office as a group.

Lord President at breakfast. Grange dined with us. One evening last week I visited Lord Kames and read to him two of my *Hypochondriacks*: Nos. 45 and 46. He was much pleased with them and agreed to revise some more numbers. So I sent him yesterday the first forty. So long ago as 1762, as appears from my journal at the time, he recommended to me to write essays of that kind.[2] I put him in mind of this; and as I had never since my return from abroad communicated any of my writings to him, I thought I would pay him a compliment now. His criticisms might do me some good. After dinner today Grange and I walked down to Leith sands in our usual way to see a race. Surgeon Wood joined us. I was in strong spirits, which I never recollect to have been at the time of the races, hypochondria being by some curious periodical influence always with me at that time. I got up to the magistrates' scaffold at the distance post and saw the whole round very well. There was an excellent match between a horse of Duke Hamilton's and a mare of a Squire Wetherell's for the King's Purse. I was entertained much, though a little disturbed by the thought that the poor animals suffered. I must not forget to remark that while I was confined, Alexander Macphail, a desperate Highlander who had employed me in a cause which I afterwards found out to be absolutely untenable, after my engaging to do what I could for him, said to me in the true wild tone, "Well, I'll give you as little trouble as possible. But at the same time, I'll put my weight upon you—under GOD." I again slept with my wife. π.

WEDNESDAY 24 JULY. (Writing the 31.) I went with Mr. Maclaurin in his coach and paid a visit to Lord Covington in the forenoon. We found him walking in his garden, and he stated a plea he had against Mr. Baron Gordon, holding Mr. Maclaurin by the neck of his waistcoat, with all the recollection and keenness he had ever shown at the *fore bar*.[3] It was about dung and furniture bought from him at Craighouse. He grew so warm he once swore by his Maker (pronouncing the awful name). He took himself, and said "Beg pardon for swearing." My wife went in a chair to Lady Colville's; drank tea. I met her there. The ladies only at home. Grange supped with us. I was very well. π.

THURSDAY 25 JULY. (Writing the 31.) I wish much to abbreviate this my journal when there is no particular that merits being fully

---

[2] "He said that he thought me well calculated for writing lively periodical papers, and insisted that I should begin at Kames to do something in that way; and said he should assist me and put me upon a method of improving. He told me that he had once a scheme for the publication of a work of that kind at Edinburgh, but found a want of witty and humorous writers, which he said Captain Erskine and I would sufficiently make up" (Journal, 14 October 1762).

[3] That is, as an advocate.

recorded. I dined today at Commissioner Cochrane's with Dr. Webster. I drank one glass of port and some port and water. My wife came and drank tea. I supped at my father's. He was in a pretty good frame, though dull. One evening this summer he observed to me that I was sadly fallen out of business, for he seldom saw my name at printed papers. As my *noverca* was present, I waived the subject. But it hurt me. I however observed that a man could not solicit business. π.

FRIDAY 26 JULY. (Writing the 31.) I was in a roving frame and wished to dine at Lady Colville's with Lord Kellie. Lady Anne happened to call. Phemie and I walked out with her. I had a good day of it. No company there. But, for the first time since I had the influenza, I drank a good many glasses of wine: two or three of port, and a third share of two bottles of claret. This disturbed me considerably. The Earl and the ladies went to town. I took a long walk in the garden and round the place with my old friend Andrew, who told me that all he wished was to pass his time agreeably, but it was hard he should be miserable from some disorder in his stomach, or some other unknown cause. That he had been quite well for some time last winter in London. But, he knew not how, had grown dreary again. On comparing notes, I found he differed from me in this: that he at no time had any ambition or the least inclination to distinguish himself in active life, having a perpetual consciousness or imagination that he could not go through with it. Whereas I have a restless wish for distinction in England, in short on a great scale. When I came home I found a letter from Temple after a long silence. I would not open it while disturbed by wine.

SATURDAY 27 JULY. (Writing the 31.) Read my old and most intimate friend's letter with calm satisfaction at breakfast over tea, and was comforted to find myself extended into Cornwall. Was at the funeral of a Miss Graham from Inverness on the invitation of Mr. William Graham, son of Colonel Gordon Graham. I make it a rule never to refuse an invitation to a funeral unless I am either particularly engaged in business or very ill. I dined quietly at home. In the afternoon I read to my wife Michael Ramsay's letters to the Countess of Eglinton, giving an account of her son, the late Earl, while upon his travels. I got them from the Countess, together with some of the Earl's, one or two of which I also read to my wife. It was a very wet afternoon, which damped my spirits; and I felt a flat indifference while perusing accounts of what was now as if it had never been.

SUNDAY 28 JULY. (Writing the 31.) Went to the New English Chapel and was pretty well, though not fervent, having bowel pains. Lady Colville had invited me to dinner with her today to meet Lord Glencairn. I went to excuse myself, both as not being well and as being unwilling to dine abroad on Sunday. It was remarkable that Mr. Fitzsimmons preached on "Remember the Sabbath day to keep it holy." But she would not let me off. So after paying a visit to my wife (to whom her Ladyship has been exceedingly attentive, calling often, and sending different things from her garden), she carried me out in her coach. It proved a very tolerable day, and would have pleased me enough had not Robert Arbuthnot, whose manner offends me, been there, he having a permission to dine there every Sunday. I drank a good many glasses of wine without being anyhow hurt by it. In the evening the children said divine lessons.

MONDAY 29 JULY. (Writing the 31.) I was engaged as sole counsel in an Advocation before the Court of Justiciary to try whether two young men could be tried before the Sheriff of Midlothian on a libel concluding for corporal punishment, without a jury. It was an important question, and there was to be a hearing upon it next day. I shall never forget the obliging behaviour of Mr. Morthland, my brother advocate, who had been on the same side of the same question at the Glasgow Circuit last autumn. I had asked his assistance. He called himself this forenoon and put all his authorities that he had collected into my hands. There was a liberality and obliging attention in this which gave me much pleasure. I dined at my father's with Dr. Webster, etc. He was more kindly to me than usual, expressing a wish that I would dine with him on Wednesday and meet Lady Margaret Macdonald. But I was engaged at Lord Covington's. I drank tea with Lord Kames. I had sent him the first forty of my *Hypochondriacks,* hoping to have some criticisms from him. He had read them. But he was much offended that in my essay on war I had taken no notice of what he says on that subject in his *Sketches.*[4] He said he thought it supercilious; and he returned my essays without giving me any remarks. He talked a little with me on the

---

[4] Boswell's position, stated in *The Hypochondriack* No. 3 (December 1777), was that "war is followed by no general good whatever.... The evils of war, upon a general view of humanity are ... a mere loss without any advantage." He denied even that wars were necessary to keep population within bounds. Kames, answering his own rhetorical question: "Manifold indeed are the blessings of peace; but doth war never produce any good?" comes up with a number of positive answers: "Barbarity and cruelty give place to magnanimity; and soldiers are converted from brutes into heroes." He saw a much greater danger in luxury produced by wealth (a fruit of peace): "A slow poison, that debilitates men and renders them incapable of any great effort.... In a word, man by constant prosperity and peace degenerates into a mean, impotent, and selfish animal. An American savage, who treasures up the scalps of his enemies as trophies of his prowess, is a being far superior." He also makes a strong case for war as a reducer of excess population: "It serves to drain the country of idlers, few of whom are innocent, and many not a little mischievous" (*Sketches of the History of Man,* 1778, Bk. II, sk. vi).

question concerning a jury trial. When he went out in his carriage with Mrs. Drummond, I sat awhile with his clerk, who frankly expressed a very bad opinion of him, and promised me anecdotes of him. I asked Mrs. Drummond with wonder how she married him. She said if she had known she was to be heiress of Blair Drummond, she probably would not have married him. But she had but £1,000 fortune, no better offer appeared, and he was a rising man. Lord Graham, on whom I had not called, sent me an invitation to sup with him tonight. I hesitated, as he had not called on me. But I resolved to go. Sundrum called on me this evening and I walked with him to the New Town. We met Colonel Montgomerie, went home with him, and talked a little on the Ayrshire politics. I was languid. At Lord Graham's there was a choice company: Douglas, Campbell of Calder, Sir Gilbert Elliot, young Scott of Harden, Lord Haddington—not a man except myself who was not a Member of Parliament or a peer; and *I* was an old baron, *moi*. I had one good image: that Burke's indignation when the Members were leaving the House while he was relating the reasons of his resignation was like that of a man at the fatal tree whom the crowd should leave just as he is making his last speech and dying words: "What! Will you not stay and see my execution?" [5] But upon the whole, I was not well, though not near so ill as I have been on many occasions, my spirits having been better this summer than I almost ever remember them. But the *tone* of my speaking amongst so many English accents seemed uncouth. I thought I should not make a good figure in Parliament or at the English bar. We were sober. I got home before one. Slept alone, as my wife was quiet.

TUESDAY 30 JULY. (Writing 6 August.) The slight irregularity of supping out and sitting a little late last night had hurt my nerves so that I was a good deal afflicted with hypochondria today, which I had not felt for a considerable time. I recollect nothing more. My dear wife comforted me.

WEDNESDAY 31 JULY. (Writing 6 August.) Maclaurin, Cullen, and I dined at Lord Covington's and found him wonderfully well. He had on his wig, and was absolutely better company than I ever saw him. The Rev. Mr. Bell of the English Chapel was the only other guest. It was really striking to observe Mr. Alexander Lockhart when past fourscore. He told us that Sir John Stewart of Grandtully had made a bargain with a Jew in London for a loan of £500, to be repaid at the death of his brother,

---

[5] Rockingham, appointed Prime Minister in March 1782, lived only to 1 July, whereupon Lord Shelburne became Prime Minister. Burke, following the lead of Fox and other members of Rockingham's party, refused to support Shelburne and resigned his office as Paymaster of the Forces.

Sir George. They met at a tavern to finish the transaction. The money was lying on the table. Sir John said to the Jew, "You have a good bargain, friend, for my brother has had a palsy in one side this year past, and one foot in the grave." "Say you so?" said the Jew (drawing the money to him), "then I'm off. For I knew a man who had a palsy in one side who lived ten years." To hear a man who was lately given over thus joking on mortality was most curious. We soon went to whist. My Lord was as keen as ever he was in his life. I lost fourteen shillings, which vexed me. I am determined never to play for more than a shilling, and very seldom.

THURSDAY 1 AUGUST. (Writing the 6.) I was pretty well today. I drank tea with my brother John. Grange was there. It was very comfortable. I went to my father's at night. He spoke of poor John with contemptous [6] disgust. I was shocked and said, "He's your son, and GOD made him." He answered very harshly, "If my sons are idiots, can I help it?" I supped with him, and was patient.

FRIDAY 2 AUGUST. (Writing the 6.) Dined at Mr. George Wallace's with Colonel Fletcher Campbell, the Hon. A. Gordon, and the Rev. Mr. Britton. Mr. Baron Norton could not be with us, as he was kept in Exchequer by a trial. Colonel Campbell, for the first time in my presence, was an excellent companion; well informed, able, lively. [7] My spirits were moderately good. We sat till near ten, but I did not drink to excess. I did not feel the love of wine.

SATURDAY 3 AUGUST. (Writing the 6.) Dined with Mr. David Steuart, Writer to the Signet, at Newington, the very house where our family lived in 1745. [8] I went early, that I might walk about the place, where I had not been for thirty-seven years. I was in a calm, pleasing frame, and though I had a very imperfect reminiscence of the (writing 7 August) particulars, I had much satisfaction in surveying the spot. I went into a park which I clearly recollected, and lay upon a little green rising ground where I had lain when a child; and for a few moments I was as calm and gentle as at that time. Lady Maxwell of Pollok, who had visited my wife and on whom I had called, Stewart Shaw, Nicolson, and Maclaurin dined here. We were sober. Nicolson entertained me with his usual sallies and quotations from plays. I was much more sedate than when I formerly

[6] See above, p. 21 n. 6.

[7] According to James Paterson's article on him in *Kay's Edinburgh Portraits*, he was vain of the fact that he had studied at St. Andrews, and usually interlarded his speech with scraps of Latin in the manner of the Baron of Bradwardine. He addressed everybody indiscriminately as "my dear."

[8] This was probably during the Highland occupation of the City. The house appears to have been the one known in the nineteenth century as West Mayfield House.

associated with him. He considered me as a departed genius and said, "I respect your memory." I came home to tea and found Miss Dunlop. π.

SUNDAY 4 AUGUST. (Writing the 7.) Was at the New Church in the forenoon and heard Dr. Blair, but not with much edification. Sandy was with me. Between sermons Dr. Gillespie, who visited my wife, begged I would dine with him and meet Mr. MacDougall from the East Indies, whom I had known as Mr. Wood's prentice, who had done well there as an army surgeon, but was obliged to come home on account of his health. I agreed. The Doctor and I walked on the Castle Hill, where we were joined by Mr. George Chalmers, who never fails to give one information. I walked down to the King's Park; then to Mr. Miller's Quaker Meeting, and had calm meditation. Dined cheerfully at Dr. Gillespie's, and was entertained with MacDougall's accounts of India. Visited my father. The children said divine lessons. Grange supped with us.

MONDAY 5 AUGUST. (Writing the 7.) Dined at Captain Engineer Andrew Frazer's with Sir Alexander, Lady, Miss, and Captain Dick, Mr. Andrew Lumisden, Mr. Wauchope of Edmonstone, etc. Had unaccountably been very little with Frazer, my early acquaintance. All was elegant. I drank a good deal of wine, and was happy, though not exquisitely. I called at my father's, and fortunately the ladies were engaged with a Miss in the parlour; so I had my father for about a quarter of an hour by himself, and found him calm and even somewhat kindly. Dr. Gillespie had told me in the strongest terms that exercise hurt him. I mentioned this when I asked if he was going to Auchinleck. He said it was not true; and he said he intended to go to Auchinleck. Therefore the Doctor was deceiving me in order to keep my father in Edinburgh, or my father was so much failed as to forget what recently affected him. I suspected the first. I took this opportunity of telling him that I was now upon good terms with Lord Advocate, and that he had promised to assist me. I found my father's notions of me unhappily very poor. The ladies came. I sat a little and went home. Found Lady Margaret Macdonald and Lady Frances Montgomerie. Insisted on their supping with us. I was a little heated. π.

TUESDAY 6 AUGUST. (Writing the 13.) I recollect nothing [9] except paying a visit to Mr. A. Donaldson, who was just come from London.

WEDNESDAY 7 AUGUST. (Writing the 13.) I recollect nothing but Grange dining.

THURSDAY 8 AUGUST. (Writing the 13.) I recollect nothing but at-

---

[9] The words following "I recollect nothing" in this and the two following entries were later additions.

tending a proof about a freedom [1] of Prestwick, and supping at my father's.

FRIDAY 9 AUGUST. (Writing the 13.) Dined at Lady Colville's by particular invitation. Just the ladies and Andrew and Lord and Lady Binning and Miss Scott (Cadie); an easy, cheerful day. But I had no high relish of life. Lord Binning and I called on Lord Justice Clerk, who was returned from France and Italy. He was not at home. I supped at Mr. John Gordon's of Balmuir with Dr. Beattie, Grange, and a good many more; so that there was no good comfortable conversation. I had drank tea at Sir William Forbes's with Dr. Beattie one of these days, and had some talk that pleased me.

SATURDAY 10 AUGUST. (Writing the 13.) The Session rose. I felt nothing particular. Mrs. Mitchelson and Grange dined with us, as did the young Campbells. Lady Colville came in her coach and took my wife and me and Sandy and Jamie out to tea. The boys were delighted, running about in the garden and fields. It vexed me that they were banished from Auchinleck. I was very well this evening. Supped at my father's. π.

SUNDAY 11 AUGUST. (Writing the 13.) Went to the New English Chapel in the forenoon. Felt an unpleasing indifference, and thought that if I were to become a constant attendant there, I should experience insipidity and perhaps disgust. Mr. Nairne and I were engaged to dine with the Solicitor at Murrayfield. We first visited Dr. Beattie, and were well with him; then Lady Colville, and walked with her in her garden. Then went on to Murrayfield by a very pretty walk along the Water of Leith, and over walls, so as to have a straight road. The Solicitor first entertained us by giving us full freedom to pull cherries off six trees richly loaded. Then there was old brandy, then a good hearty dinner, and then abundance of wine. Mr. Menzies of the Customs, Mr. Andrew Stewart, Junior, Mr. Carnegie the advocate, and a Mr. Anderson from London were there. We were exceedingly jovial. The two last went away earlier than the rest of us. We drank till between nine and ten. I was much intoxicated, and having insisted to walk to town, fell and hurt my hands; after which Mr. Menzies took me into his chaise, in which he had Mr. Nairne. I came out at the foot of the West Bow. Mr. Nairne walked with me to the head of James's Court. I then wandered about an hour in the street, but most fortunately met with no strong temptation, so got home clear. Mr. Kentish obligingly endeavoured to see me home. But I cunningly evaded. I was quite unhappy to find myself again in such a brutal state, after a full Session of sobriety. I was vexed that I had em-

---

[1] A share of common land.

ployed Sunday so ill, and that my children had not said divine lessons. I resolved to be more strictly upon my guard. I was very sick. I went to my own bed.

MONDAY 12 AUGUST. (Writing the 13.) Mr. James Baillie had been anxious last night to have me to write a paper for him this forenoon. He called this morning between eight and nine. I begged to be allowed to repose till ten. I then rose. Was curious to think that I was instantly to write upon a case of which I then knew nothing. I soon understood it, and had the paper done to my satisfaction before dinner, though I had made my appearance at the High School examination and the review of the Defensive Band. I was however sadly uneasy. Worthy Grange consoled me. He dined with us, and the young Campbells came in after. I was quite dislocated in mind. I paid a visit to Lord Elliock, whom I had not visited since my marriage. Found him alone; was cordially received, and had a scene of old Scottish sense and anecdote over a dish of tea. My visit was partly on Grange's account, that my Lord, as a Director of the Royal Bank, might get things made easy to him as one of Mr. David Armstrong's cautioners,[2] which his Lordship, who expressed a regard for Grange, obligingly engaged to do. I had spoke of it to him before. Then visited my father. Then found Dr. Beattie by himself at Walker's Hotel, and had an agreeable conversation with him, in which he told me many particulars of his private interview with the King.[3] He told me a striking anecdote of Dr. Johnson, to account for his being often unwilling to go to church. He mentioned to Dr. Johnson his being at times troubled with shocking impious thoughts, of which he could not get rid. "Sir," said Dr. Johnson, "if I was to divide my life into three parts, two of them have been filled with such thoughts." Dr. Beattie told me he once kept a journal for two years. But he found it to be so trifling that he burnt it, when under some apprehension that he was going to die. I regretted that my wife's indisposition had prevented me from having him at my house this time. He was to go north again next day. I came home better, and returned to my wife's bed. We were to go to Valleyfield next day if good. Strange as it may seem, even the thought of that small change of scene occasioned a degree of hurry and agitation in my spirits. I had the *Hypochondriack* No. 59 to write, and knew not well how, though I had fixed on flattery as the subject. This forenoon I had a note from Lord Hailes, to whom I had sent No. 40, "that it was a good essay, and gave an air of novelty to a threadbare subject." This encouraged me.[4]

[2] Sureties.

[3] Beattie was granted a pension of £200 on 20 August 1773, and on 24 August was privileged to talk for an hour with the King and Queen at Kew.

[4] The greater part of a leaf of the manuscript, containing the whole of the entry for

[WEDNESDAY 14 AUGUST.] . . . in her breast. On my <return home, I found> she had spit a good deal of blood. <I was> not so much alarmed as before. I thought she might have occasional fits of it.

THURSDAY 15 AUGUST. (Writing the 16.) The day was damp and uncertain. My wife was a little better. I was still low-spirited. I finished my *Hypochondriack*. Visited Maclaurin before dinner. Grange dined, and I eat cheese and drank strong ale. Still I was dull. Had a short meeting with David Cuninghame in the evening. Supped at my father's. He was harsh.[5]

SUNDAY 18 AUGUST. (Writing the 21.) Heard Dr. Blair lecture on Christ's transfiguration. He did not do so well as I could wish. He might have been solemnly philosophical on the subject of apparitions. I remember Dr. Johnson once observed that so many thousand years had elapsed and it was not yet settled whether a ghost had ever appeared; the belief of the affirmative was universal, but it had never been proved. *This* of Moses and Elias is a proof. But perhaps he did not mean to include sacred history in his remark.[6] I dined by special invitation (writing the 22) with Commissioner Cochrane, who had returned yesterday from his jaunt to see Craigengillan with Dr. Webster. Dr. Gillespie was there, and we were social over old rum punch sweetened with marmalade of oranges. We stayed tea. As Dr. Gillespie and I walked together into town, he assured me that my father had not recollected when he said exercise [did not][7] hurt him; for that any motion, even walking round St. Andrew's Square, occasioned bloody urine. He said my father showed no more signs of religion than a stock or a stone, and that I must not expect his temper to soften as he grew older and more afflicted with his disorder, but on the contrary. He told me Lord Justice Clerk spoke to him warmly of me and my family not going to Auchinleck, saying, "How different is my situation with my son. His happiness is my happiness. We have no divided interests. What an appearance has it to the world that Mr. Boswell and his family do not go to Auchinleck. I have a great regard for Lord Auchinleck's family. I wish I could do anything to make things better." There was a benevolent effusion in all this which pleased me

---

[5] 13 August and nearly all of that for 14 August, has been removed. The words within angular brackets are conjectural restorations. The reason for the censorship is not apparent.

[5] The entry for 16 August, which was written on the verso of the mutilated leaf mentioned in the note preceding this, has completely disappeared. All of the entry for 17 August is missing except for bits of two unidentifiable letters and the character π with which it ended.

[6] Johnson's observation is reported in the *Life of Johnson*, 31 March 1778.

[7] An inadvertent omission.

much, and I resolved to be cordial with the worthy Justice. Dr. Gillespie
called with me and visited my wife. After he went away, I found myself
in a good frame, and went to see my father. But was at once damped by
his coldness and the devilishness of his women. The children said divine
lessons. I had worthy Grange to sup with me on moorfowl and Malaga.
I was comfortable. π.

MONDAY 19 AUGUST. (Writing the 22.) It was so uncertain a day
that Mr. Wood was against my wife's setting out for Valleyfield. I dined
at my father's with Commissioner Cochrane, Dr. Webster, Dr. Gillespie,
and David Cuninghame. A very disagreeable scene of ill humour in my
father happened after dinner. For all the money that is spent by his
women, there is a meanness at his table in grudging claret, which very
seldom appears. When Dr. Webster is there a bottle is set down to him;
and as it is a great chance no more will be allowed, I generally never
take any of it. Today I chose a glass of it, and said easily, "Doctor, will
you give me a glass of your wine?" He made me welcome, to be sure. As
I was taking the bottle to me, my father said with a snarl, "That's Dr.
Webster's bottle, man." "I know," said I. "But the Doctor makes me
welcome, and I like to take a glass of claret when I'm with a man who
can afford it. But if it is disagreeable to you, I shall not take any of it."
He was ashamed when I thus spoke out. But he looked displeased. I
repeated, "If it is disagreeable to you that I should drink claret, I shall let
it alone." He wished to have the meanness concealed, and said, "Never
fash [8] your head." So I drank claret. Lady Auchinleck called for another
bottle of claret. This roused him, and with a vengeance he filled my glass
with sherry. I was stunned, and hesitated for a little what to do. I once
thought of instantly leaving the company. But I luckily restrained myself;
said, "It's all one"; and then putting some claret into my glass, said, "I'll
make burgundy of it." After this the other bottle of claret was decanted;
I partook of it as if nothing had happened, and he was quiet. It was
really wretched treatment. I went with David Cuninghame to Robert
Boswell's, and we walked round St. Andrew's Square on the gravel walk,
talking of raising money to pay David's lieutenancy; [9] and then drank tea

[8] Bother.

[9] In the spring of 1779, David Cuninghame had purchased a commission as lieutenant
in the Second Regiment of Dragoons ("the Greys"). Having failed by two urgent letters
to persuade Boswell to stand security for him for the sum of £250 or to enable him to
borrow the money in some other way, he remained three years afterwards in debt for
£230 to Capt.-Lt. John Nesbitt of the Greys, and Nesbitt was pushing him for payment. It may be that Nesbitt himself was being pushed for the price of his own
promotion to captain-lieutenant, which occurred on the same day that David was
commissioned. Boswell's conference with Robert Boswell probably means that David

at Robert's, where I had not been for a long time. I then went home. My dear wife was hurt by my father's treatment of me and thought I should have instantly resented it, because submitting to it seemed mean. She said, "If a father slaps his son in the face, when he is a man, the son ought not to bear it peaceably." I was much disturbed reflecting on it. But her temper is keen; and the Commissioner convinced me next morning that I did well not to take notice of it. Lady Colville, Lady Anne Erskine, and Miss Susie Dunlop visited my wife this evening. I walked home with Miss Dunlop, that is to say, opposite to her door; and then I sat a little with Colonel Montgomerie, who was ill of a cold, and told me he hated himself and everybody else. Such was his fretfulness; and I felt myself superior to him at the time. In the forenoon I met Andrew Erskine on the Bridge, who told me it was impossible to be happy upon a system. I am not sure if he is right. He said if he could have been a very eminent man, he would have liked it. But he was sure he never could. So he desired only ease. I insisted he should have cultivated his poetical talents. He said he never could have been great, and he did not care for being like Pomfret or others whom I told him I would like to be. But surely the higher a man is in point of eminence, the better, though he should not be among the most eminent. I was restless this night.

TUESDAY 20 AUGUST. (Writing the 22.) It was so wavering a day that we were doubtful whether to set out. I sat awhile with Sir William Forbes at his counting-house, where I find a never-failing source of good conversation, mixed with some local and personal prejudices, but all good-natured. Between twelve and one we resolved to go. Had a fine day till we came to the Queensferry (Halls), when it began to rain. Two rascals of boatmen eager for a speedy fare assured us the rain would be nothing. So we went into their yawl and set off. But it came on the heaviest shower that I ever remember. My wife was sadly frightened, though by means of greatcoats I and my servant kept her almost quite dry. We were obliged to turn back. I never shall forget this scene. She was quite gone, and I was in a kind of despair. It soon grew fair, and she had spirit enough to go on board again. She looked charming. We got safe over. Dined ill. But drove briskly to Valleyfield. She had spit a little blood at the North Ferry. Found a cordial reception. Veronica was grown a good deal bigger, but had a coarse appearance and the Fife accent. I was glad to have my wife fairly here, to have a trial of the country.

WEDNESDAY 21 AUGUST. (Writing the 23.) Mr. and Mrs. Wellwood,

---

was begging them to lend him the money out of the funds of George James Campbell of Treesbank, whose tutors they were.

Mrs. Agnes Preston (the aunt), Colonel Robert, Major George, Sir Charles, and Miss Preston were our company last night. This was a fine day. My wife, who had not rested very well, walked out. It was a fine day. I was charmed with her looks; quite the lady. I was merely sensual for the time, having no intellectual object agitating me. Eat well, but drank moderately. In the evening read in Mosheim's *Ecclesiastical History* an account of the Arminians and Quakers.[1] Wondered how the human mind could be fully occupied by small differences in opinion. π.

THURSDAY 22 AUGUST. (Writing the 23.) A fine day again. My wife walked out, as I did both yesterday and today several times; and this day I wrote some journal and copied some journal of my tour with Dr. Johnson, written last year, to have it on paper of the same size with the rest. Captain Thomas Maitland, Mr. George Bruce from Culross, young Dundas of Blair, and Captain Wellwood came to dinner. Were [I][2] to describe characters and mark reflections, I might fill sheets with the history of one day. I led the same life as yesterday; without lively existence, but well enough.

FRIDAY 23 AUGUST. (Writing the 24.) Mr. Wellwood, as we walked out, mentioned Edwards on irresistible grace[3] and Lord Kames on necessity. I dislike the subject, unless when I am in full spirits to assert my *freedom*. It is curious to think that the most inconsiderable human being may analyse the mind of the greatest. A Presbyterian minister in an obscure parish may speculate on the *motives* of Burke, and be *clear* that he is a *machine*. This is a provoking thought. To be considered as a *mere machine*, or a *reprobate from all eternity*, even by a creature whom one despises, cannot but hurt one, while there is a *possibility* that the creature may be in the right. And there is not *absolute demonstration* to the contrary. It was a fine day. My wife mounted a little Galloway, and though she had not been on horseback for twelve years, rode with ease, and looked so genteel that I was as much in love with her as a man could be. The ladies and gentlemen (except Mr. Wellwood) walked over to Torry. My wife rode to it. She then rode several times along the new road into Valleyfield, I sometimes walking at her horse's feet, sometimes waiting till she rode on briskly and returned to me. She was much enlivened by this; said it was life for her; got into good spirits, and talked of riding at Edinburgh every good day. She rode today above two hours, and a good

---

[1] Johann Lorenz von Mosheim's book was published in 1737–1739. A translation by Archibald Maclaine (no doubt the work Boswell was reading) appeared in 1765.

[2] An inadvertent omission.

[3] Probably Jonathan Edwards's famous treatise, *A Careful and Strict Inquiry into the Modern Prevailing Notions of ... Freedom of the Will*, 1754. The book has some running titles that employ the word "grace."

many miles. His Holiness Dr. Webster arrived before dinner, which added much to the social scene. My wife was well at dinner. But in the afternoon she grew uneasy and spit some blood mixed with matter, coughed severely, and felt the pain between her shoulders very painful. She was sadly cast down, and I was sadly alarmed. I spent a great part of the evening in my own room, writing a continuation of my journal during Dr. Johnson's Highland journey. I recollected wonderfully.

SATURDAY 24 AUGUST. (Writing the 27.) My wife was pretty well, but rain and wind prevented her from getting out. I wrote a good deal of the journal with Dr. Johnson. It pleased me much to revive the scenes. In the evening there was a great storm. π.

SUNDAY 25 AUGUST. (Writing the 27.) The day was good, though there fell some heavy showers. Sir Charles, the Major, and I walked to Culross, Dr. Webster being to preach. It was curious to see him in the pulpit where he had first preached as minister about forty-nine years ago, having been settled here in 1733. He gave us two short sermons on "the good old way," inculcating the comfort of religion above all other things. I was in a placid frame. When I got to Valleyfield, I found that my wife had spit a good deal of blood. This was very discouraging. But she grew better. Just after dinner David Cuninghame arrived, having come over in impatient anxiety about getting a loan to pay his lieutenancy, no letter having yet come for me from Lieut.-Colonel Home, to whom I had written for advice as to his continuing in the Dragoons.[4] I was somewhat disconcerted by his coming upon me thus abruptly, and told him after a long dialogue that I would not agree yet to his getting the loan. He turned about and was going away hastily. I believe I should have brought him back. But Sir Charles came out and insisted on his coming in. He was so much hurt that he for some time could not show his face, but walked on. I joined in asking him to stay. When I saw his face, I perceived him in tears. Poor fellow! my heart suffered for him, and I at once resolved to do all in my power to get him made easy. He was persuaded to come in to the company and to stay till next morning. Sir Charles's humane hospitality was truly amiable. I was so much affected

---

[4] See above, note on 19 August 1782. Boswell had written on 16 August 1782 to Lt.-Col. David Home, second in command of the Greys, attributing David's predicament to the confusion of his brother Sir Walter's affairs, and soliciting Home's advice as to David's exchanging out of the Greys, thereby getting money enough to pay his debts while still retaining his rank in the line. David, he said, was exceedingly averse to this and wanted to remain in the Greys, "being confident that he has a good prospect of promotion without purchase." Home (letter dated 24 August) declined to give David advice, but said that in his opinion the chances of getting promotion in the Greys without purchase were "too remote for my eye-sight to stretch their length."

with seeing a young man, well-born, in such difficulties that I drank a good deal of whisky shrub punch,[5] and was a little heated. I then told David Cuninghame that I would write next day to Robert Boswell to let him have the loan.[6] Veronica said divine lessons. Dr. Webster, who had dined at Blairhall, returned at night and said prayers. I drank various liquors at night and had rather too much.

MONDAY 26 AUGUST. (Writing 13 September.) This day and the two next I group together. On one of them Major Preston and I walked to Culross, and I visited Mr. Thomas Bruce and Bailie Johnston, and called on Bailie Bald,[7] Mrs. Jean Erskine, and Clerk Ireland, and would have called on Bailie Halkerston, but met him walking. Dr. Webster was not well, and his spirits were low. I talked a little with him on religion. He admitted we could not account for GOD's permitting evil; and that *prescience* for *certain* was equivalent to a *decree*. In short he depended on *grace*; in which I agreed with him. On Wednesday I drank so much at dinner as to be warmed or indeed heated, and somewhat intoxicated; and at supper I drank more and increased the heat and intoxication, and talked a great deal in an idle, jocular, impolite strain. Little did I apprehend that my honoured father was then lying on his death-bed!

[EDITORIAL NOTE: The fully written journal was discontinued at this point, and the special journal of Mrs. Boswell's illness gives no information for 27 and 28 August beyond the statement that she was at Valleyfield on those days. For the week beginning with 29 August, Boswell kept rough notes, which he has endorsed, "Notes of journal at the time of my honoured father's death."]

THURSDAY 29 AUGUST. Awaked, not well. Up. [Set off] with Sir Charles; [he said] road to Dunfermline like a *march* in America. Just before roads parted, [came] caddie on horse with letter express. Knew at once father ill. Was not shaken. Into chaise; agitated curiously. Over with Calder, and to town. Rather wished it over, yet tender.

---

[5] A punch made with lemon or orange and sugar.

[6] He and Robert Boswell allowed David to borrow £230 from his cousin, George James Campbell of Treesbank, for whom they were tutors. As suggested above (16 August 1782), this was probably what David had been begging them to do all along. The action seems of questionable propriety on Boswell's part, but we are glad to report that George did not suffer because of Boswell's softness of heart. A settlement of 1790 indicates that George got his principal (£230) plus interest from 1782 (£87. 14s. 2d.).

[7] MS., *Baads*. If it were not for the "s," the two spellings would be equivalent, for "bald" was pronounced "bawd," and Boswell's "aa," as appears from other passages in the journal, represents the vowel of "law," not that of "father."

Dressed at home. Then over. Was told by R. Boswell of illness particularly. Went upstairs. Miss Peggie: "Don't go in hastily; not an agreeable sight." Went in. He took no notice as I passed, curtains open. Went round; she sitting by curtains. Shook hands. I asked if in pain. "Has the pains" (or "struggles" or some such word) "of dissolution on him." Her hardness was amazing. I wished to go near. She said, "It will confuse his head. Don't torture him in his last moments." I was benumbed and stood off. Wept; for, alas! there was not affection between us. Went backwards and forwards. Commissioner came; was affected, but with spirit. I went home and took coffee. Quite confused. Over again; just as before. Claud came. [Father] did not know *him.* Commissioner to tea [with] Miss Hogg. Dr. Cullen came: "All we can do is make [him] easy." Wife came. Went to her. Stayed home while she went and paid visit, but to no avail. When she returned, I went. Lady Auchinleck, [when I asked to] see if he could speak, [said,] "There's all that remains of him." Wished to stay all night. Miss Peggie like a devil. Went home to bed.[8]

Raised. Went back. Women servants gathered. Miss Peggie: "Come and see." [He was] very low. Stayed in room. She [9] carried off, Robert Boswell attending. Miss Peggie's flutter shocking. Strange thought: "Still alive, still here! Cannot he be stopped?" Breathing [grew] high, gradually ceased. Doctor closed eyes. Miss Peggie's exclamations. Up all night. Young sent for. Breakfasted next morning. Sent for Commissioner; consultation about burial. Over to wife: had spit blood. Grange, I think, dined. [Some time] writing letters in giddy state. At night looking at his Skene,[1] [from] affection and nervousness cried and sobbed.

SATURDAY 31 AUGUST. After a sleep was better. Saw the irrationality of grieving. At home all day writing. Evening went over. Lady Auchinleck had said she would see me. I said too late.[2] Supped with Balmuto, Miss Boswell, Mr. Stobie. Was calm and *retenu.* Inventory of presses at Auchinleck read to me. I was hurt to think how easy all might have been made without death. Had visit of Sir W. Forbes today. Told R. Boswell [I] did not take kind his concealment.[3]

SUNDAY 1 SEPTEMBER. Was really well. Sir Alexander and Lady Dick

---

[8] Friday 30 August begins somewhere near this point.
[9] Lady Auchinleck.
[1] See above, 15 July 1782.
[2] Too late in the evening for an interview that was bound to be difficult.
[3] Robert Boswell had drawn and witnessed the Trust Disposition which gave Lady Auchinleck liferent of the new house. Boswell had expected this (in fact, he had feared she might be given the house outright), but perhaps felt that Robert Boswell should have told him about the disposition as soon as it was made.

came. Went over. Was taken up to Lady Auchinleck. Doleful-like, really. Told her all should be decent. I could say little. She spoke of three generations being sober, etc.; hoped would continue. Wished me to take W. Lennox.[4] [I said] I thought she had wished Sandy. SHE. "*Me*? I've thought of nothing. My mind just a vacancy." I said I wished she would mention everything she chose. I would endeavour—mumbled. She said she believed me; and the more so that I would find all right, or some such phrase. She grew moved, and we went away. Had asked Mr. Ilay Campbell to come to me. He came kindly, and talked accurately of all particulars. Drank tea with Commissioner. Sorry for him. Told him what [my] debt was.[5] He surprised; wished he had known, to tell father. Told him of wife's good conduct. Evening a little at father's after visit from Nairne and Dr. Gillespie. Tried π, [but thought,] "What! when he who gave you being is lying a corpse?" Checked.

MONDAY 2 SEPTEMBER. Breakfasted early; agitated [but] rather well. Douglas Mill, calm.[6] Wondered at my being so steady.

TUESDAY 3 SEPTEMBER. Came along well.[7] Mr. Dun, etc. met. James Bruce affected. I again cried. Dinner. Walk, Old House. [Opened] repositories. High feelings.

WEDNESDAY 4 SEPTEMBER. Beautiful day. James Bruce said, "My

---

[4] That is, to continue him as coachman.

[5] Boswell wrote out a "State of My Affairs" on 1 September 1782. His largest debts were £2,000 to Mr. Kerr of Blackshiels, secured by his lands of Dalblair, and £500 to Alexander of Mackilston, by personal bond; Dalblair he thought adequate to offset both these. He had borrowed £500 from the Town of Ayr to enable Alexander Cuninghame to get his lieutenancy, but he held Alexander's personal bond for the amount. He owed various smaller sums totalling £1,456, but estimated his funds in addition to Dalblair and Alexander Cuninghame's bond to amount to £1,013. Though he was paying or bound to pay interest on nearly £4,000, his own comfortable kind of book-keeping made him only £443 in debt.

[6] The funeral cortège (the hearse accompanied by two mourning-coaches for "gentlemen" and their "servants") sets out from Edinburgh and spends the night at an inn on the road. The "gentlemen," besides Boswell and his brother John (see the end of the entry for 4 September), certainly included Claud Boswell and probably Robert Boswell. T. D. Boswell should of course have been of the party, but in order to have him present the funeral would have had to be delayed a week or more.

[7] The company breakfasted at Muirkirk and the cortège arrived at Auchinleck House perhaps by noon. From that time on till late afternoon of the next day Boswell would have been almost constantly engaged in receiving the gentry of Ayrshire, most of whom would have called to pay their respects and some of whom would have remained overnight. It was Mrs. Boswell's, not Lady Auchinleck's, place to preside as hostess, but she being ill the caterer from Ayr who was providing the entertainment had probably engaged a "sewer" to direct details of the hospitality. Lady Auchinleck had completely effaced herself and had remained in Edinburgh. Boswell was in complete charge of all the funeral arrangements ("Told her all should be decent").

Lord was always fortunate." Told me when he [8] was ill in 1765 his [9] wife was in the room, and he [8] did not know it. He [8] said to my mother, "I am going, GOD knows where." Bruce Campbell, son, and young Campbells came early.[1] Was in agitation all the forenoon, and rather awkward with the company. Lord Dumfries very attentive. Went to barn and drank health of tenants.[2] Dinner very decent. But I was confused in mind and somewhat dreary. Funeral very decent. Felt manly all the way to church, and acquiesced in the course of things. [When I was] carrying [father] to vault, was *carried* myself. Wandered; was in the state which I suppose a man going to execution is. Hardly was sensible of what was around me. Saw mother's coffin. Helped to deposit father. Then into our loft. Was affected much, and cried. Sanders Pedin perceived it and retired. Was grieved to think how long he had been in the hands of the Philistines. Away to Douglas Mill. Do not recollect what day, had argument with Balmuto [3] on his [8] being failed when he made fictitious votes. Balmuto *really* or affectedly denied, and said, "Because against *you*." "No," said I; "because against *himself*." Maconochie supped with us.[4] I kept perfect sobriety. Was still serious and tender. John behaved very well.

[Johnson to Boswell]

London, 7 September 1782

DEAR SIR,—I have struggled through this year with so much infirmity of body and such strong impressions of the fragility of life that death, wherever it appears, fills me with melancholy, and I cannot hear without emotion of the removal of anyone whom I have known into another state.

Your father's death had every circumstance that could enable you to bear it; it was at a mature age and it was expected; and as his general life had been pious, his thoughts had doubtless for many years past been turned upon eternity. That you did not find him sensible must doubtless grieve you; his disposition towards you was undoubtedly that of a kind, though not of a fond, father. Kindness, at least actual, is in our power, but fondness is not; and if by negligence or imprudence you had extinguished his fondness, he could not at will rekindle it. Nothing then

---

[8] Lord Auchinleck.

[9] Bruce's.

[1] After the Treesbank boys (the "young Campbells" here mentioned) and the Lainshaw children, the Campbells of Barquharrie were Lord Auchinleck's nearest relations in Ayrshire.

[2] The caterer had provided a cask of rum for this observance. See the summary of his bill, below, at the end of the text.

[3] Clear evidence that Claud Boswell went down and returned in the mourning-coach.

[4] Alexander Maconochie was Douglas's principal man of business.

remained between you but mutual forgiveness of each other's faults and mutual desire of each other's happiness.

I shall long to know his final disposition of his fortune.

You, dear Sir, have now a new station, and have therefore new cares and new employments. Life, as Cowley seems to say, ought to resemble a well-ordered poem; [5] of which one rule generally received is that the exordium should be simple and should promise little. Begin your new course of life with the least show and the least expense possible; you may at pleasure increase both, but you cannot easily diminish them. Do not think your estate your own while any man can call upon you for money which you cannot pay; therefore, begin with timorous parsimony. Let it be your first care not to be in any man's debt.

When the thoughts are extended to a future state, the present life seems hardly worthy of all those principles of conduct and maxims of prudence which one generation of men has transmitted to another; but upon a closer view, when it is perceived how much evil is produced and how much good is impeded by embarrassment and distress, and how little room the expedients of poverty leave for the exercise of virtue, it grows manifest that the boundless importance of the next life enforces some attention to the interests of this.

Be kind to the old servants and secure the kindness of the agents and factors; do not disgust them by asperity or unwelcome gaiety or apparent suspicion. From them you must learn the real state of your affairs, the characters of your tenants, and the value of your lands.

Make my compliments to Mrs. Boswell; I think her expectations from air and exercise are the best that she can form. I hope she will live long and happily. . . .

I received your letters only this morning. I am, dear Sir, yours, etc.,

SAM. JOHNSON.

[Boswell to Johnson]

Auchinleck, 1 October 1782

MY DEAR SIR,—I came to this place, with my wife and children, on Wednesday the 18 September and took possession of the seat of my ancestors on Dr. Johnson's birthday. This was no conceit of my superstitious mind: it accidentally happened by our being kept a day longer at Edinburgh

---

[5] *Ode upon Liberty*, ll. 111–115:

> If life should a well-ordered poem be,
> In which he only hits the white
> Who joins true profit with the best delight,
> The more heroic strain let others take;
> Mine the Pindaric way I'll make.

by bad weather. But I own it pleases me that it has so happened. I hovered here in fluttering anxiety to be with you till Tuesday the 24; and on that day, though my dear wife had the night before a disagreeable return of her spitting of blood and was very uneasy to think of my going away, I set out. I felt myself drawn irresistibly. I imagined I could neither act nor think in my new situation till I had talked with you. I lay that night at an inn two stages off, with intention to get next morning into a fly which crosses the country there from Glasgow to London by Carlisle. But before it came up, I was stopped by an express that my wife had been seized with her alarming complaint of spitting of blood more violently than ever and that she entreated I might return. I hastened home again; and the agitation of her spirits being calmed, she has ever since been pretty easy. But that calm she owes to you. For while I was still intent on flying away to you, your most excellent letter forcibly dissuading me from *deserting my station* arrived, and at once settled me.[6] My words on reading it were, "Well, he is a most wonderful man! He can drive me to the end of the world or confine me in a dungeon." My wife was so affected by your letter that she shed tears of grateful joy, and declared she would write to you herself. Accordingly you have enclosed the spontaneous effusion of her heart, which I cannot doubt will interest you. There is much tenderness in the passage where she bids you "remember that delays are dangerous in her complaining state of health." [7] I love and value her as much as ever husband did wife; and I should upbraid myself for having resolved to leave her, had it been with any other purpose than to be with You. I flatter myself with hopes that her complaint is not of a consumptive nature. She is quite averse to travelling. The most attentive care therefore must be taken of her at home. Ease, cheerfulness, light diet, fresh air, and gentle exercise may by God's blessing re-establish her health.

Now that I allow myself to look into the affairs of the estate, I find that my presence here is essentially necessary, there being several farms to let. But as I am very ignorant myself of country concerns and have very different opinions given me, I am perplexed how to act. I must do as well as I can at first and get more knowledge gradually. I am as sober as you could wish me to be. It was my determination that I should maintain the decorum of the representative of Auchinleck; and I am doing so.

[6] Not the letter preceding this but another written some two weeks later. Boswell excerpted only a brief paragraph from it (not including this phrase) in the *Life of Johnson.*

[7] Mrs. Boswell's letter is unfortunately lost. (Boswell printed no part of it in the *Life of Johnson.*) She had in an earlier letter invited Johnson to Auchinleck, and is telling him now that her health is such that he cannot safely postpone his visit if he wishes to see her.

Could you not without risking any injury to your health come to us here this month? Or if that is too much, may we not meet only for two days at one of the stages on the west road? In two days a fly takes me to Doncaster; in three to Stilton. Could you not come to a middle place between these? Six days' absence may be allowed me without uneasiness. My earnestness to see you this year is very strong; and we could discuss more in an hour's conversation than in a great deal of writing. Decide, I pray, as to this, and fix any day you please if you can gratify me. If you cannot, I depend on full answers to all the questions I have to put.

In the mean time, I am undecided as to the way in which it is proper for me to behave to my *noverca*. That she is *injusta* is but too clear.[8] From my father when his faculties were sadly decayed she has instead of £150, the jointure in her contract of marriage, contrived to obtain lands now worth £325 yearly, a house worth £100 yearly, and the property of the furniture in it reckoned worth £1,000, which at double interest for her life is £100 a year more—nay, the bygone or past rents of her jointure lands, which from the indulgence of this family to the tenants will be about £500. Is not this an exorbitant plunder? Should I attempt, by a proof of my father's incapacity and of his avowed sentiments as to moderate jointures when his mind was unimpaired, attempt to set aside the deeds, which would be an indelicate, though a justifiable, suit, or shall I just acquiesce? But her greediness is not what hurts me most. I think with regret and indignation of her totally estranging my father from me and my family; and I find a large collection of family letters, particularly a most affectionate and pious correspondence between my grandfather and grandmother for many years, has been destroyed, though carefully bound up by my father for preservation. I suppose she has either destroyed it herself or persuaded my father that his son was unworthy to have it. She was cutting a valuable wood before it was ripe. She was letting leases at low rents, for what we call *grassums* or entry-money. In short, she was doing all she possibly could to hurt my interest so that if my father had lived a few years longer, I should have had but the skeleton of an estate. I have as yet behaved to her with wonderful decorum. I have been mindful of the divine precept to forgive even until seventy times seven. But it strikes me also that there is a weakness, a silliness, in not at least breaking off all intercourse with so bad a woman. The distinction between the good and the bad will be confounded if they are treated alike well. I beg to have your counsel at large upon this. The Lord Advocate, who is at the head of my father's executors, is of opinion that she might have had more. But that is only saying that my father was entirely under her influence.

[8] See above, p. 154 n. 7a.

When you have answered this, be so good as burn it. Indeed I have for many years so opened to you all my heart in our correspondence that I depend on your friendship to burn all my letters or to take care that in case of your death they be delivered to the representative of this family at the time.

Once more allow me to press upon you my earnestness to see you this year, and be assured that it is not possible for one man to have a higher regard for another than I at all times have for you.

The expression of my being *good* referred to the kindness which I felt at the time towards all about you, even for a person who you have convinced me is not very worthy.[9] I ever am, my dear Sir, your much obliged and affectionate humble servant,

JAMES BOSWELL.

Pray present my best compliments to Mrs. Thrale. Do not think it a wild imagination that I may one day have the pleasure of seeing her here.

[EDITORIAL NOTE: "All the funeral expenses are in this bundle" says a note by Boswell on a band of paper enclosing a thick sheaf of folded bills. The charge borne by Lord Auchinleck's personal estate for his obsequies amounted to nearly £300, almost a fifth of his annual rents.[1] The bills not only speak eloquently of the heir's determination to do the thing handsomely, they even hint at that recklessness of expense which was likely to overtake the frugal Scots generally when they had occasion to bury a laird. The two-day provision of catered funeral meats and drinks at Auchinleck House was hardly on the scale which completed the ruin of the Master of Ravenswood, but it serves to show how little Sir Walter Scott needed to heighten fact to produce that fine fiction.[2] A summary of the bills follows, for the most part in their own words.]

30 Aug.	To Alexander Allan, cloth merchant, Parliament Square, Edinburgh. 11½ yards grey cloth,[3] 14 yards shalloon; 3 cocked hats; 7½ yards crape; 3 pairs hose; 3 pairs gloves

£11. 0s. 8d.

[9] Mysterious. Perhaps Mrs. Desmoulins.

[1] The funeral expenses came ultimately out of Boswell's own pocket, for he was heir to the remainder of his father's estate after payment of bills and legacies.

[2] *The Bride of Lammermoor*. For some indication of what the funeral of one of Lord Auchinleck's tenants would have cost, see in the Introduction to *Old Mortality* the authentic bill for the funeral charges of Robert Paterson, who died in 1801. Though undoubtedly frugal (the total was £2. 1s. 10d.) the outlay included thirteen shillings for bread, cheese, rum, and whisky.

[3] Cloth for the mourning-suits for coachman and footmen mentioned in the next entry.

31 Aug.	To George Jolly, tailor, Jolly's Entry, Canongate, Edinburgh.[4] 3 suits of mourning for coachman and footmen; 51 big and 6 dozen small buttons; silk and twist; buckram binding and thread; 5 pockets for each frock and vest; pockets and worsted garters; green linen sleeve-linings; 7½ yards serge flannel[5]	£3. 8s. 0d.
30 Aug.	To Alexander Stoddart & Co., cloth merchants, Bridge Street, Edinburgh. To Lady Auchinleck for servants, 70¼ yards brilliant [6]	£4. 13s. 8d.
2 Sept.	To Hart & Co., no address, presumably Edinburgh. To Lady Auchinleck for the servants, 9¼ yards muslin; ½ yard do., tape and bobbin; making and washing 3 aprons; do. 3 handkerchiefs; do. 6 pairs frills; do. 3 caps; 8½ yards ribbon; 37/8 yards cambric; making and washing 6 pairs weepers; [7] do. 6 cravats; 3 pairs gloves; 2¼ yards cambric; 3/8 yard India twill; making 6 stocks; 9¾ yards mode; [8] 11½ yards linen; [9] 4½ yards love; [1] 8 do.; 24 do.; 6 do.; 3¾ yards silk ribbon; 4 yards silk ribbon; pasteboard, wire, and making 3 bonnets; do. 3 cloaks	£12. 19s. 4d.
2 Sept.	To Robert Hart, no address, presumably Edinburgh. Lady Auchinleck, making a crape night-gown [2] and petticoat with a flounce for one of the servants; body linen, whalebone, cord front [3] and a lace; making 1 ditto; [4] body linen, etc.; making 1 ditto; body linen, etc.	£1. 11s. 6d.

[4] See the facsimile of Boswell's *Excellent New War-Song*, above, following p. 250.
[5] Probably twilled flannel.
[6] A kind of silken fabric.
[7] White linen or muslin borders (cuffs) on the sleeves of mourning coats and dresses.
[8] A thin, light, glossy black silk; short for "alamode." An English product, officially encouraged to compete with crape, which had to be imported from Italy.
[9] MS., "lining," but in these bills the specific *kind* of fabric is mentioned, not its use. Robert Hart's bill, which follows this (see n. 3 below on this page), has the spelling "linning." Since speakers of all ranks "dropped their g's" in the eighteenth century, "linning" would have indicated the same pronunciation as now.
[1] A kind of thin silk fabric used for ribbons. Short for "love-hood."
[2] What would now be called a dressing-gown.
[3] The materials for making a bodice ("body"), lined with linen, stiffened with whalebone, and laced in front. (MS. spelling "linning" here could possibly mean "lining," but probably does not. The import would be the same.) Since the word "lace" is specifically used for the means of bringing the two sides of the "front" together, "cord" is presumably a fabric. We find "Janus cord" defined (example, however, dated 1867) as "a black rep of wool and cotton, the fine cord showing equally on both sides. Much used for mourning" (C. W. Cunnington, Phillis Cunnington, and Charles Beard, *A Dictionary of English Costume*, 1960, p. 259).
[4] The bill is clumsily made out. Hart made identical outfits for *three* women servants.

2 Sept. To John Hendrie, merchant, Ayr.[5] 6⅞ yards fine
black cloth; 6¾ yards shalloon; 5¾ yards plaiding;[6]
4 yards stenting [7] and pocketing; 1½ yards buckram;
7 oz. thread; 4 yards [8] stay-tape; 3 dozen big and 4
dozen small buttons; 1⅜ yards fustian; 1 pair knee-
garters; 22 yards crape; 21 drop [1] silk and twist; 16¾
yards broad black mankie; [2] 1 pair black out-sized
stockings; 2 pairs do.; 3½ yards Italian hat crape;
4 yards black ribbon; 2 yards linen; 2 yards muslin;
2 yards do.; 1¼ yards do.; 2 handkerchiefs; 2 do.;
2 pairs gloves; 2 hats; 16 yards black flannel; [3] 2
women's gloves; 2 pairs black buckles; 12 yards tape;
paid for making a suit of clothes   £17. 13s. 9d.

1, 2, 3, 4,   To money given out about Lord Auchinleck's
6, 7 Sept.,   funeral by James Bruce. To an express to Ayr for
8 Oct.   Mr. Wharton, vintner; spirits to men at opening the
burying-vault; a man warning tenants to burial; 1
quire mourning-paper and a stick black wax; 1 pair
moorfowl and six pairs partridges; 2 pairs mourning-
shoes for myself and son Alexander; an express from
Ayr with sundries; five gallons ale from Ochiltree for
burial-service; expenses for men and two carts at
Ayr, with ropes; making servant-maids' caps, aprons,
and petticoats, etc.; to the poor about this time;
returned with Ochiltree mort-cloth for the use of the
poor; [4] expense of two men and carts taking Mr.

---

[5] The former bills were for mourning for Lord Auchinleck's servants in Edinburgh; this is for those at Auchinleck House. Hendrie made up one suit of men's mourning clothes, but the women's mourning clothes seem to have been made up in Auchinleck House.

[6] Twilled woollen cloth, the fabric of which plaids are made, in this case presumably solid black or in black and white check.

[7] Material for stiffening.

[8] We emend the manuscript, which quite clearly reads "hd." "Hand," a linear measure of four inches, seems to have been used solely to indicate the height of horses from a time much earlier than this quotation. In any case, sixteen inches of stay-tape (corset-lace) is impossibly short measure and the unit price of a penny (present in the bill but omitted in our transcript) seems expensive for four inches. See the next to the last item in the bill.

[1] An obsolete Scots weight equal to one sixteenth of an ounce.

[2] A kind of glazed worsted fabric. Short for "calamanco."

[3] MS., *Blak Flennall.*

[4] Bruce borrowed the pall from Ochiltree parish to cover the coffin, either because Auchinleck parish had no pall or the Ochiltree pall was finer. Rental would hardly have been expected (Lord Auchinleck was a heritor of Ochiltree parish), but Bruce sent half a guinea for charity.

Wharton's things to Ayr; to women assisting at
preparing and cleansing House, waiting on the cook,
from the 31 Aug. to 7 Sept.; to Andrew Morton,
mason, widening the catacomb [5] and sundries in
burying-vault; to Alexander Pedin, wright, painting
aisle door of kirk [6] and other doors black, mending
trap-door into the burying-vault; to James Wilson,
tailor, making a suit men's mournings; two
women's gowns; mounting the kirk-loft, pulpit, and
precentor's desk with black cloth; to my own and
horse expense at Ayr settling accounts	£5. 12s. 5d.

2 Sept.	To William Gibb, merchant in Mauchline, 9½
dozen shortbread; caraway; 4 pecks [7] plum cake	£3. 2s. 0d.

2 Sept.	To Robert Wharton, vintner, Ayr. To entertainment
at Auchinleck House, 2 days (£50); [8] to claret, 6 doz.;
to Madeira, 2 doz.; to port, 8 doz.; to sherry, 2 doz.;
to rum, 1 cask; to porter, 6 doz. in bottles; to candles,
8 lbs.; to 1 doz. glasses; to brockage, including a
server; [9] to carriage and package of wines, etc.; to
servants' expenses, with horse and chaise-hires; to
dittos wages per Mr. Boswell's order	£94. 18s. 4d.

2 Sept.	To James Cummyng, herald-painter, painting a
funeral escutcheon of 16 branches; [1] 5 yards black
calico; 2 papers of large corking pins [2]	£8. 17s. 2d.

2 Sept.	To Young and Trotter, upholsterers and cabinet-

[5] The stone niche or cell in the burial-vault into which Lord Auchinleck's coffin
was to be inserted. The "widening" shows clearly on the outside, where the niche is
closed with a rectangular slab of stone. Lord Auchinleck's coffin was over-size, as
befitted his status.

[6] The burial-vault, as explained above (p. 234 n. 1), is under the floor of the old
church, then in use but now abandoned and a ruin. Entrance to the vault was
originally through the church pavement, but in the first half of the seventeenth
century the vault was sealed at the top and new access provided by constructing a
lateral wing to the church ("the aisle of Auchinleck"). Inside this, steps (usually
covered by a trap-door) led down into the vault. The aisle opened into the church, and
contained an elevated seating-area ("loft") for the Auchinleck family.

[7] He presumably provided only the mixed dry ingredients, and the "cake" was made
up at Auchinleck.

[8] We have generally reported only the totals of bills, but as this item accounted for
more than half of the present one, we think it well to state it. It presumably covered
the cost of some of the food served and all the charges for service.

[9] "Breakage, including a salver or tray." "Brockage" in this sense is Scots.

[1] The coats of arms of the families of Lord Auchinleck's parents, grandparents, and
great-grandparents. It would presumably have been mounted over the entrance to
the Boswell aisle and then hung up in the church.

[2] Pins of the largest size.

makers, Princes Street, Edinburgh, to a coffin
covered with fine black, run within and lined with
crape, and inscription plate; a suit of superfine grave
clothes; a hearse with best pall-cloth [3] with 6 horses
from Edinburgh to Auchinleck and back, 4 days out;
2 mourning-coaches ditto; 12 pallbearers' cards; 2½
yards black cloth; 1 packing box for escutcheon; [4]
tolls of hearse, coaches and horses going and
returning; bills on the road at Little Vantage,
Carnwath, Douglas Mill, Muirkirk, etc.; best hearse
mort-cloth; [5] an express sent with the escutcheon;
2 ushers who went from Town to Auchinleck;
2 ditto who went to Gorgie; 6 horse-hires to
Auchinleck; 2 horses to Gorgie; [6] drink money to the
coachman; Mr. Young's attendance, 4 days; 2 bearers
who put the coffin into the hearse; messages, etc.   £72. 7s. 6d.

                                    Total   £236. 4s. 4d.

(If one adds the £50 for mournings allowed to Lady Auchinleck by Lord Auchinleck's will, the total comes to nearly £300.)

[3] MS., "Pal" (a later insertion in a very cramped space). Presumably a large pall draping the hearse on the outside. The charge for the hearse was £12. 12s. 0d., not including horse-hire nor a "hearse pall-cloth." See the next note but one.

[4] The total to this point is £43. 3s. 7d. The remainder of the bill (£30. 0s. 2d.) bears the sub-heading "Cash Paid Out."

[5] The "pall-cloth" mentioned above draped the hearse on the outside; the "mort-cloth" covered the coffin inside the hearse. The "pall-cloth" was part of Young and Trotter's own funeral equipment, but they apparently rented the "mort-cloth" from a parish or guild in Edinburgh, for the charge (£2. 2s. 0d.) is entered under "Cash paid out." At Auchinleck the Ochiltree mort-cloth was presumably substituted for the one Young and Trotter had brought.

[6] Gorgie on the Water of Leith, then a hamlet, is a little over a mile south-west of Edinburgh on the road to Auchinleck. Two hired ushers on horseback accompanied the cortège as far as Gorgie and then turned back; two other ushers went on with the hearse and two mourning-coaches to Auchinleck.

APPENDIX A

The Cause of Crosse against Marshall

[See above, 6 October 1778]

COPIES OF BOSWELL's printed Information (10 October 1778, seventeen pages) and of a later Petition for Marshall by the counsel for Marshall, Robert Cullen (2 February 1779, fourteen pages) are preserved in the Signet Library, but being *ex parte*, they leave the motives of the litigants and even some of the facts somewhat less than clear. It was a foolish cause, illustrating strikingly the pertinacity with which some Scots litigants, in their determination to win "an honourable victory" (the words are quoted by Cullen from Crosse's Information), were capable of pressing actions involving ridiculously small sums of money. William Crosse, retired merchant in Glasgow, paid an artist five guineas for painting a miniature in water-colours of one Mrs. Rowand, with whom he was carrying on an intrigue. She got the miniature into her possession, but by his account only on loan. John Marshall, also a merchant but a younger man than Crosse, warned Rowand, his first cousin, of his wife's improper connexions, and she left her husband, going first to Edinburgh and then to London. This naturally caused gossip and scandal, and several men, including Crosse, were publicly mentioned as having been her lovers. Before Mrs. Rowand decamped, according to Marshall's version of events, she summoned him and gave him the miniature, behaving as though it were her own property, and alleging that she wished him to keep it as a remembrance of her and to enlist his good services for her child, whom she was leaving behind. Marshall took the picture home, but at once thought better of the arrangement and took it back to Mrs. Rowand. When she found him firm in refusing to keep it, she suggested that he destroy it, and they both defaced it by rubbing it with a wetted finger. Crosse was furious at Marshall and appears to have sent him a challenge, which Marshall declined. ("In his Condescendence he . . . alleged that he 'had demanded *every* mode of reparation from Mr. Marshall to no purpose,' the insolent meaning of which was *studiously* made sufficiently plain by putting *every* in italics"—Boswell's Information, p. 14.) He then took the only legal course of redress open to him by suing Marshall before the magistrates of Glasgow for £5. 5s., the value of the picture, plus £2 for damages and expense of process, asserting that Marshall had destroyed his property, knowing it to be such. His hope, apparently, was to convict Marshall of falsehood and perjury in public estimation, if not in the eyes of the law. But Marshall escaped all examination of the facts by a plea in law: even if Crosse had established his ownership of the picture originally, he had not established it for the time at which the picture was destroyed; hence his action was irrelevant. The magistrates (1 August 1777) "assoilzied" (acquitted) Marshall on this plea, and later found him entitled to ten shillings in expenses. In reply to a Petition from Crosse, they adhered to their interlocutor, but reserved Crosse a right to demand the picture or its value "on proper authority from Mrs. Rowand, to whom the pursuer gave or lent the picture, and who was in possession thereof at the time libelled." Crosse appealed both decisions to the Court of Session, where he was represented by John Morthland, advocate, and in a Condescendence given in to the Lord Ordinary (Lord Gardenstone) demanded that the facts at issue be referred to Marshall's oath. Marshall's counsel continued the plea of irrelevancy ("with learning and ingenuity," according to Boswell), but Lord Gardenstone was not satisfied, and on 15 July 1778 took Marshall's deposition. This was not at all what Crosse had hoped for. He had urged that the deposition be taken in Glasgow, where he could be sure of large attendance of his acquaintances "come," as he was reported to have once said, "to hear the defender . . . swallow the picture and perjure himself." On 22 July Lord Gardenstone assoilzied Marshall in the action for destruction of property, but asked for further debate as to expenses. On 31 July, "in respect of the particular circumstances and conduct of the parties in the cause," he took the question of expenses to report to the full Court, appointing Informations to be lodged in the Lords' boxes on 10 October 1778. According to Cullen's Petition of 2 February 1779, Boswell's Information for Marshall was ready at the appointed time, but as the Information for Crosse was not obtained until 15 December, the cause lay over. By his Petition Cullen demanded redress for "many injurious reflections thrown out upon" Marshall in Crosse's Information. The outcome of the cause has not yet been ascertained.

APPENDIX B

[See above, 28–29 June, 1 July 1780 in Editorial Note following 19 June 1780; 29 November, 5 December 1781; 22 January 1782; 5 June 1782 in Editorial Note following 15 May 1782. Boswell's paper has been abridged by unreported omission of words, phrases, sentences, and paragraphs; but except for the editorial summaries within square brackets, everything given here is Boswell's own words in his word-order.]

3 January 1782

ANSWERS for John Duff, late servant to Charles Mercer of Lethendy, Esq., and the said Charles Mercer, Esq., for his interest, Pursuers, to the Petition of William Mercer of Aldie, David Kinloch of Gourdie, John Stewart of Stenton, and others, Justices of Peace and Commissioners of Supply for the County of Perth.

Judges, supreme and subordinate, are unquestionably entitled to all due respect in their different departments; and nothing is more unworthy of a good subject or more prejudicial to the comfortable order of civilized society than an indecent rashness in censuring those who fill the seats of justice. There is, it must be confessed, a too general propensity in mankind, especially in the inhabitants of a narrow country, to rail, or at least to murmur, against sentences as unjust because they are disagreeable. It is only from men of enlarged minds and conscientious thinking that a fair estimate of the characters of judges is to be expected.

These considerations it is expedient, doubtless, to keep in view when forming an opinion upon the conduct of any persons whose conduct in the capacity of judges is called in question. But at the same time it must be allowed that judges are subject to human passions like other men, so that it is a possible case that they *may* be guilty of wilful oppression and injury. And surely oppression, under colour of law, is most dangerous and most grievous.

In times of great exigency, the Justices of Peace and Commissioners of Supply have been empowered to sit as a court to judge concerning the lives and liberties of their fellow subjects, by determining that some of them shall be compelled to serve in the Army; and happy would it be if their determinations had never been intentionally wrong.

In the eighteenth year of His present Majesty's reign, an act was passed, commonly known by the name of the Comprehending Act, by which the Justices of the Peace and Commissioners of Supply were appointed to co-operate in making a speedy and effectual levy of able-bodied men by adjudging such persons to serve His Majesty as soldiers as the Legislature deemed fit for that purpose.

But as such a measure, however necessary, is in this free country a matter of much prudence and delicacy, the Act of Parliament very studiously and very carefully expressed a variety of exceptions, so that the powers of the Commissioners acting under it might be so limited as to prevent any danger of arbitrary tyranny. The general scope of the statute was that such persons only should be impressed as were a burden to the community, by being idle and disorderly without having any settled way of living.

It might have been hoped that such excellent instructions would have had a good effect upon the dullest and most rugged Commissioners, so that no instance would have appeared of any of the King's subjects being grossly injured in the execution of this act. Instances, however, did occur in different parts of the kingdom; and the respondents were unfortunate enough to experience a most flagrant and audacious abuse of it by the petitioners.[1]

The respondent, Mr. Mercer, is a gentleman possessed of £500 a year of landed property in the county of Perth, and by good economy is happily free of debt, so that he is as independent as any private gentleman whatever. He is also one of His Majesty's Justices of Peace; and to this hour he has not been able to discover any just cause of offence ever given by him to any of the gentlemen of the county where he lives. Mr. Mercer is the heir male of the family of Aldie, and consequently the true feudal representative. The gentleman who enjoys the estate, through a female succession, and carries the name of that family may perhaps be displeased that the respondent does not choose to acknowledge him as his Chief, but most certain it is that for many years Mr. Mercer of Aldie, though nephew to the respondent and his next heir, failing his own brother and sister, has not been in speaking terms with him. Mr. Kinloch of Gourdie, though the respondent's cousin and his very near neighbour,

---

[1] When this cause first came on in the Court of Session, John Duff and Charles Mercer were the pursuers (plaintiffs) and the Justices of the Peace (William Mercer and others) were the defenders (defendants). At the stage the cause has now reached, judgement has been given against the defenders, who have reclaimed (appealed) to the same court in a printed Petition; Boswell, as counsel for John Duff and Charles Mercer, has replied with the present printed Answers. In the Answers, John Duff and Charles Mercer, though occasionally referred to as "the pursuers," are generally styled "the respondents"; the Justices are generally referred to as "the petitioners," less commonly "the defenders."

has involved him in a variety of lawsuits within these last ten years and been on a dry and distant footing with him. The respondent is sorry to say that, whether from the influence of these gentlemen over others or from groundless prejudice independent of that influence, he has been unlucky enough to become an object of spleen and pique to a good many country gentlemen in the county of Perth. To this unhappy ill will he ascribes the very extraordinary conduct of the petitioners, who on the 10th of September 1778 did without evidence, without the form of trial, and in direct contradiction to the most capital exceptions in the Act of Parliament, adjudge John Duff, his faithful and approved servant, to be a soldier.

Your Lordships will easily figure how much surprised and confounded both of the respondents were by this sudden sentence; but in order that it might be rescinded, a Reclaiming Petition was given in, along with which was produced a certificate from his master that he was neither idle nor disorderly, but always behaved well and was employed in all his ordinary work, but particularly at his corn-harvest.

The petitioners appear to have been somewhat startled and to have hesitated a good deal, for they delayed the consideration of the Petition from time to time; but at last, upon the 4th of February 1779, they resolved to run all hazards and therefore refused the Petition and adhered to their former judgement.

A Bill of Suspension was presented [to the Court of Session in Edinburgh], complaining of this sentence, but as there was then a judgement of this Court finding it incompetent for your Lordships to review the proceedings of Commissioners acting under the aforesaid Act of Parliament, it was refused by the Lord Covington on the 19th February 1779, without Answers; and a few days thereafter John Duff was dragged out of the country and embarked for America as a private soldier in Colonel Macdonell's regiment,[2] to one of the officers of which he had been delivered.

[Application for redress was continued in the form of an action of damages before Lord Westhall as Ordinary. Lord Westhall called for Memorials and then made avisandum to (took the opinions of) the other Lords. On 15 June 1779 the Lords pronounced an interlocutor assoilzieing (acquitting) the defenders and finding them entitled to expenses. The pursuers reclaimed, with a fuller recital of circumstances; the defenders gave in Answers with more allegations against John Duff's character; the pursuers petitioned to be allowed to reply; and on 3rd August 1780 the Lords by interlocutor remitted the cause to the Lord Ordinary (Lord Westhall again), who allowed this time a proof at large, again

[2] The 76th Regiment of (Highland) Foot.

ordered Memorials, and again made avisandum to the Lords. The Lords on 5 December 1781 found the adjudication of John Duff arbitrary and oppressive and therefore found the Justices liable in £40 sterling as damages to John Duff, also finding the Justices liable in expenses. The defenders reclaimed, their Petition was appointed to be answered, and the present Answers were submitted. Boswell's first article, presented at great length and supported by numerous citations from the Proofs (here largely omitted) was that the Commissioners showed ill will in the manner in which they got John Duff before them. They maintained that they could have had no *animus injuriandi*, because they did not know that he was to appear before them on 10 September 1778. No warrant, they maintained, was issued by the Justices and Duff received no citation from them; he appeared voluntarily to give evidence in favour of two men charged with rioting.]

This argument is exceedingly plausible, but unfortunately for the petitioners it is clearly not true. [Boswell cites passages from former papers of theirs in which they admitted both to a warrant and to a summons.] This contradiction, however, is not the worst of it, for your Lordships' attention is now to be humbly entreated to a strong circumstance of malice prepense which escaped the attention of their counsel till now.

The ill will of Mr. Mercer of Aldie and Mr. Kinloch of Gourdie towards Mr. Mercer has already been pointed out. It is indeed notorious to the whole neighbourhood. Mr. Mercer of Aldie appears to have been exceedingly active in this oppressive affair and seems to have had a pride in sitting preses of [presiding at] the meeting which affronted his uncle and adjudged poor Duff. Mr. Stewart of Stenton entertained a resentment against John Duff, who had formerly been his servant. Margaret Reid, page 8 H of the Pursuers' Proof, depones "that she was one day going to Dunkeld, and upon the way fell in with a man who was going the same road, and they travelled so far of the way together. Depones, that person asked where she stayed? and she informed him that she stayed with Mr. Mercer at Pittendrich. Upon which this person said to her that there was one John Duff there also concerning whom he had heard Mr. Stewart of Stenton say that he would be upsides with him and would have him made a soldier; and the reason of Mr. Stewart's saying so was that one time, upon Mr. Stewart's striking John Duff with a horsewhip, John Duff had offered to strike Mr. Stewart again."

Your Lordships see then that there was in Aldie and Gourdie an enmity against Mr. Mercer, and in Stenton an enmity against John Duff, so that in the assemblage of Commissioners two different currents of enmity met, and there is no wonder that their united force went beyond all bounds of law, reason, and humanity.

The *preparation* for the business, however, had something of the dark machination of a conspiracy, for it *is* true that John Duff was insidiously cited as a witness notwithstanding that a warrant had been issued against him as an alleged rioter. They knew that if notice was given to him of an intention to make him stand trial for his character and liberty, he would have come so well prepared that it would have been impossible for them to have touched him. Therefore the warrant which would have put him upon his guard was *secreted,* and he was served with a simple citation as a witness, that he might come before them suspecting no evil, and be catched unawares.

And that the Justices well knew that John Duff was to be before them on the 10th of September, and that it was resolved that he should then be adjudged, is undeniably certain from the circumstance that the strange letter against him from one Mr. Bisset, a minister, was in readiness that day, was produced in court, and was inserted *verbatim* in the record of their proceedings, so that while care had been taken to prevent poor Duff from having any evidence in his favour, evidence to his prejudice, such as could be had, was cut and dry in the pockets of his and his master's enemies.

Was it well, then, in these gentlemen, sitting in the character of judges, to lay such a stress upon a letter so obtained? And when your Lordships find that so much evil intention and machination in some of the petitioners has been actually traced, is it unfair, is it uncharitable, to presume that a great deal more is latent and appears only in its effects? Sensible of their tortious conduct, the petitioners, in the course of their process, have twisted and turned their defence, sometimes one way, sometimes another, being altogether at a loss to palliate an arbitrary and oppressive sentence, which, when they pronounced it, they flattered themselves was not subject to the review of your Lordships.

Your Lordships have read the words of the sentence adjudging John Duff, and the respondents trust you have read them with indignation, because they purposely described John Duff as Mr. Mercer's servant in order to insult that gentleman. Stenton, perhaps, might have been satisfied to have had Duff adjudged, no matter upon what grounds, if he were but "upsides with him." But others were not satisfied with this alone. Mr. Mercer, his master, must also suffer "the whips and scorns o' the time," "the insolence of office." [3] And it must be proclaimed that being *his* servant was no protection, was no better than being a vagrant or any other obnoxious character. It was said that by inserting that insulting designation they "very properly intended to distinguish between a servant *de*

---

[3] *Hamlet,* III. i. 70 ("scorns of time"), 73.

jure and a servant *de facto,* and to declare that though Duff was *then* in the service of Mr. Mercer, they neither did nor could acknowledge him to be his *legal servant,* because he was actually the engaged servant of another man." But as some stress is still laid upon an allegation that John Duff was at the time the engaged servant of Mr. Bisset, the minister, it is proper to bring that matter again under the view of your Lordships.

Charles Fenwick depones, Pursuers Proof, p. 8 C, "that Mr. Bisset and John had agreed to take trial of one another." Agreeably to this, Robert Monro, *ibid.,* p. 3 D, depones "that John Duff told the deponent that he had not undertaken Mr. Bisset's work but for a trial and until Mr. Bisset should be otherwise provided." And it appears by Charles Fenwick's oath, *ibid.,* p. 8 E and F, that the cause of John's leaving Mr. Bisset was his insisting upon unreasonable services; for "he wanted him to thresh the beasts' meat before daylight and then to do the out-works through the day, which John said he was not fit for." Such was all the "right, title, or pretence" which Mr. Bisset had to claim John Duff as his servant.

If they had intended or wished to act fairly, why did they not send to Mr. Mercer, their neighbour and brother justice, and desire to know from him the character of this young man, his servant? The answer made to this question is a gross aggravation of the injury already committed, for it is said in plain terms that "Mr. Mercer kept no society with any of the other gentlemen in the country, either in a public or private capacity, nor indeed with any but his servants and some of his tenants, so that an application to him would have in reality been no better than an application to Mr. Duff himself." This scandalous averment is notoriously false. Mr. Mercer disdains to say more to the petitioners. But he humbly begs the protection of the Court; and trusts that your Lordships will order this impertinent calumny to be erased from the record.

The sentence first pronounced, then, being utterly destitute of any just foundation, your Lordships will be pleased to observe what was the conduct of the petitioners upon the merits of the case being brought under their view, which was done as soon as their unworthy intentions were discovered. [Boswell reviews at length the Petition given in to the Justices asking reversal of their action on the grounds that John Duff was not within the description of the Act. "He was the engaged servant of Mr. Mercer, and actually serving him at the time, and at his harvest; and his master is willing to attest his good behaviour. Besides, he is only five feet two inches high." Along with the Petition was a certificate from Charles Mercer, testifying to his employment.]

Had the petitioners apprehended that their conduct would have come under the review of your Lordships, the respondents will venture to say it was morally impossible that they could have disregarded this Petition and certificate. But although they were so exceedingly hasty in pronouncing sentence against John Duff, they were as dilatory in resolving whether they should do him justice in setting aside their sentence, for they delayed the matter, meeting after meeting, without assigning any reason whatever. Mr. Mercer's agent attended three times, and Mr. Mercer himself, together with his agent, attended at last with witnesses ready to support Duff's character if necessary, but all in vain. The petitioners turned a deaf ear to every remonstrance and obstinately adhered to their cruel sentence.

An *animus injuriandi*, therefore, in this case is very apparent from the conduct of the petitioners, which can admit of no other explanation. The exceptions in the Act of Parliament were plain, even to the meanest capacity; and had they been less so, the petitioners, one of whom was a Writer to the Signet,[4] were not so stupid and ignorant as totally to misunderstand all of them. Your Lordships are to balance the probability between stupid ignorance and wilful wrong.

It is hardly decent in the petitioners to tell your Lordships on p. 12 that "it has been clearly instructed [5] by the depositions of the masters he had formerly served, the servants who were in the house with him, and others who had the best cause of knowledge, that in place of the sober, industrious servant Mr. Duff is represented to be on the part of Mr. Mercer, he is in fact a disobedient and disorderly servant, a turbulent and quarrelsome companion, and an idle, restless, troublesome fellow to everyone within his reach."

It would be very improper to trespass upon your Lordships' time by again going through the different particulars of the Proof which your Lordships considered so lately. The respondents would be ashamed to enumerate and refute the paltry particulars which the defenders have been in a world of pains to collect from the confused recollection of former years.

Neither do the respondents imagine it will be necessary to trouble your Lordships with many words in answer to the ingenious attempt in this Petition to divide the clause in the Act of Parliament which points out the persons over whom alone the Legislature gives the Commissioners authority: *viz.* "all able-bodied, idle, and disorderly persons who cannot upon examination prove themselves to exercise and industriously follow some lawful trade or employment, or to have some substance sufficient

[4] John Smyth of Balharry. The full list of the petitioners (nine in number) appears in the printed Summons, 8 March 1779, of which a copy is preserved in the Signet Library, Edinburgh.

[5] Proved.

for their support and maintenance." The petitioners affect to think that this clause describes *different* characters of men, whereas the pronoun *who* puts it beyond a doubt that the meaning of the clause is to describe the persons so particularly that an arbitrary exercise of the statutory power may be prevented as much as is consistent with the possibility of executing the Act.

The respondents do deny that there is the smallest pretence under the Act of Parliament for adjudging any man to be a soldier *in modum poenae*.[6] But miserable would be the state of the country if the vague description alone of being idle and disorderly should without any exception whatever put every one of His Majesty's subjects in the mercy of any three Commissioners, for that number is a quorum.

A man's idleness or industry in his profession depends often more upon others than upon himself. Many an ingenious and active man repines in indolence for want of employment. How many physicians, nay, how many lawyers, feel the truth of this remark! A gentleman's servant, who certainly follows a lawful employment, is idle or industrious according as his master chooses; and it is well known that many gentlemen's servants are hired for the purpose of lounging half their time in genteel attendance. If, therefore, John Duff had been, with his master's approbation, as idle as the petitioners have endeavoured to represent him, they could not have adjudged him. He was Mr. Mercer's approved servant, and that was enough. At the same time, your Lordships have it now proved that John Duff, instead of being idle, was industrious, for he not only attended on his master's person but cheerfully put his hand to any kind of work. And in particular when he was summoned before these Commissioners he was working at his master's corn-harvest, which is of itself an express and positive plea of exception, specified in the Act of Parliament.

That John Duff was employed at his master's corn-harvest, not occasionally but as a constant labourer, insomuch that it was necessary to have a man in his place when he went before the Justices as a witness, has been so completely proved that the petitioners no longer attempt to contest it. All they can do is to have recourse to subtleties and objections in form, which the respondents will be pardoned to say are unbecoming in country gentlemen, from whom plain honesty and candour should be expected. They tell your Lordships that "when Duff was first adjudged, no such defence was then offered for him." Alas! what do they mean? They *know* that when Duff was first adjudged, he was adjudged as a man knocked down behind his back, without having the least notion that any such thing was intended, so that he could neither offer this de-

---

[6] As punishment (for unlawful behaviour).

fence nor any other. He attended as a witness. To his astonishment, he received sentence of adjudication. Should not the petitioners be ashamed to argue upon want of proof when Duff was first adjudged? But when his Reclaiming Petition was given in, did he not undertake to give their Honours satisfaction in every respect *if allowed?* Why, then, did they not hear him? Why did they not give him an opportunity of demonstrating to them that he was neither within the letter nor the spirit of the Act? Along with his Petition was presented a certificate from Mr. Mercer, his master, as a Justice of Peace, that he was employed at his corn-harvest. The petitioners tell your Lordships that this certificate was not also subscribed by a minister and elder, as the Act of Parliament directs. Was that a sufficient reason for paying no regard to it? Were they sitting as judges to take a catch of such an omission? Well must they have known that the subscriptions of a minister and elder would be adhibited as soon as that omission was observed; and accordingly your Lordships have read in the former papers a certificate, perfectly formal, subscribed by Mr. Mercer as a Justice of Peace, the Reverend Mr. Williamson, Minister of Lethendy, and James Smyth, an elder of that parish. If the petitioners had been pressed in point of time to fix the fate of John Duff, if they had been so eager to send him directly to the wars that they could not stay to have an informality rectified, there might have been some appearance of an excuse but, so far from being in a hurry, they put off the determination of the affair for months. They "shook, but delayed to strike." [7]

That John Duff was not of the stature required by Act of Parliament but only five feet two inches and one eighth is proved by Mr. Williamson, who measured him (Pursuers' Proof, p. 4 C) and by Margaret Reid who saw him measured (*ibid.*, p. 2 D).

The petitioners affect to treat this exception very lightly and tell your Lordships that "the Legislature surely did not mean that the Commissioners were to have a measuring-rod constantly with them." That the Legislature meant to have its own exceptions observed ought not to be controverted, and the Commissioners are to take proper means for having the exceptions ascertained. Accordingly at Perth and many other places, the Commissioners had a measuring-rod; and certainly either they or the officer appointed to attend them should have one. The exception of size is as clear in the Act of Parliament as the exception of age, which is never disputed. No discretionary power is left to comprehend persons under five feet four, but it is provided in direct terms that the Commissioners shall not adjudge any man who is under that size.

Upon this point, too, as upon the point of profession or employment

[7] *Paradise Lost,* ii. 492.

we are barred from indulging speculation. A man above the age of forty-five may be as stout and as able to serve His Majesty as a much younger man; and a man under five feet four may make as good a soldier as one who is taller, but there is no licence here for theoretical heads. It is upon law, upon a British statute, that the question is to be decided, and it is enough to say *ita lex scripta*.[8]

It is asserted by the petitioners that "as soon as the Act of Parliament in question was published, they issued their precepts to the constables and other proper officers, enjoining them to search for, apprehend, and bring before them all such persons as they should judge to fall under the description of the statute." If this account which the petitioners give of themselves were true, what is the meaning that care was taken not to issue any precept to the constables of the *parish of Lethendy*?

Does it not betray a consciousness in the petitioners that circumvention was their aim, and that Mr. Mercer of Lethendy should not have it in his power to guard against the plot by which he was to be robbed of a favourite servant?

There is another remarkable circumstance to which your Lordships will be pleased to attend, which is that if the petitioners were so very active and zealous as they boast to have been, it is wonderful that the precepts which they issued were altogether ineffectual; for it is a certain fact that not a single man of the whole district over which they act was adjudged as a recruit except the respondent John Duff.

Supposing that being guilty of a riot or breach of the peace were a good ground for adjudication, or could be believed by the petitioners to be a good ground, even that did not appear against John Duff. Duff's behaviour in the market of Meikleour is now proved to have been such as rather to recommend him for his good nature than to stigmatize him as a culprit. [Boswell quotes from the Pursuers' Proof depositions reporting that while the disturbance was going on in the market, John Duff was standing by, looking on and speaking to John Scott, constable; that Peter Scott, John Scott's brother, came from behind and pushed him over into the gutter; that John Duff thereupon in a threatening manner lifted up a staff in his hand and said that if he had him in a convenient place, he would pay him for it. That John Scott touched him and told him he was under arrest, and he made no resistance; that he was seen afterwards in the market behaving in a peaceable manner and that he returned home sober.]

Upon what grounds was it then that the petitioners adjudged John Duff? Let their own last Memorial tell, p. 4: "The riot in the market was

---

[8] So the law is written. ("We must be content with the law as it stands, without inquiring into its reasons"—H. C. Black, *Law Dictionary*, revised 4th ed., 1968, p. 966.)

a very inconsiderable part of the dittay [9] against him. A letter was produced from Mr. Bisset, a clergyman in the neighbourhood, claiming Duff as his servant, and acquainting the Commissioners that he had deserted his service and had been protected by Mr. Mercer. Duff's character and behaviour in the country was notoriously known to be bad, and many of the Commissioners themselves were personally in the knowledge of a number of facts proving him to be a nuisance to the neighbourhood and an idle and disorderly person in the most extensive sense of the words."

Whatever liberties the petitioners might have ventured to take *before* the Proof, it is truly presumptuous in a high degree to make such averments *after* the Proof. It is very material to observe that even upon the supposition of Duff's ever being Mr. Bisset's engaged servant, the engagement is alleged to have been at Martinmas 1777 and would have been at an end long before the time when this foolish claim was mentioned, for the next term, *viz.* Whitsunday 1778, was past many months before the period of John Duff's adjudication.

Now that a proof at large has been taken, a proof granted by the Lord Ordinary so broad and extensive as not to be limited on any point, the respondents desire to know where is the variety of culpable articles? Where are the different misdemeanours, the number of facts, the bad character and behaviour of John Duff to be found? And what is there in any degree to support this alleged personal knowledge?

The petitioners having totally failed in supporting their sentence of adjudication what opinion can your Lordships form but that it proceeded from bad motives? And though the petitioners will not confess it, the respondents cannot help feeling an irresistible impression that the petitioners struck this audacious and cruel stroke in the pride of their hearts, believing themselves to be supreme and their sentence final.

[The petitioners cannot shelter themselves under the refusal by the Court of Session of John Duff's Bill of Suspension because that refusal happened *after* their sentence of adjudication was passed. That the Bill was not refused by the Court upon the merits of the question is shown by the fact that Lord Covington, who refused the Bill, was first of the Lords to give his opinion in favour of the respondents when the cause really came before the Court. It is not incumbent upon the respondents to point out previous malice in every one of the petitioners; indeed, it is not incumbent on them to detect previous malice in *any* of the petitioners. "An *animus injuriandi* is to be inferred from what is done. If one man attacks another and knocks him down, he cannot plead that he was not guilty of a wilful wrong."]

[9] Indictment.

Having done, then, with these lesser matters, the respondents beg leave again to direct the attention of the Court to the general view of the case. That John Duff was grievously injured and his master affronted and put to a very disagreeable inconvenience by having a good and necessary servant illegally dragged away from him between terms cannot be denied; and this being the case, is it not reasonable and just that the petitioners should make reparation?

[The Roman Civil Law, Title *Ad Legem Aquiliam*, cited with Voet's commentary.]

The Act says that no person who is not idle and disorderly shall be adjudged, but John Duff was certified to be neither idle nor disorderly. The Act says that no person who follows a lawful employment shall be adjudged, but John Duff followed a lawful employment, being at the time the actual and approved servant of a gentleman of £500 a year and a Justice of Peace in the county. The Act says that no man who is under the size of five feet four inches without the shoes shall be adjudged, but John Duff was only five feet two inches. And the Act says that no person working at corn-harvest shall be adjudged, but John Duff was actually working at his master's corn-harvest and carried from thence before the Commissioners.

How is it possible then to prove that there was wilful injustice if such an accumulation of real evidence, arising from direct opposition to the provisions of the Act of Parliament, is not to be held as sufficient? In all questions upon the Act 1701, there is no room left for alleging the want of an *animus injuriandi*, because certain penalties are specially annexed to certain particulars; and although there is not the same advantage given to the subject in the Act now under consideration, judges in interpreting it should, it is humbly thought, proceed upon the liberal principle of redressing an injury which appears to have been committed against the clearest light.

Although neither the law of England nor the decisions of the courts there are strictly speaking of authority in the courts of this country, yet your Lordships, it is not doubted, will always have some regard to judgements pronounced in England, upon a British statute which is common to both countries; and therefore the respondents shall again lay before your Lordships the noted case determined in the Court of King's Bench on the 25th April 1780.

[David Wilmot, Esq., Justice of Peace for Middlesex, severely reprimanded and fined £100 for falsely imprisoning Joseph Lister, fellowship porter [1] of the City of London, as acting under the late impress act.]

---

[1] A member of the "fellowship" of the Porters of Billingsgate, a guild having certain monopolies in the City of London.

Your Lordships are now fully possessed of this cause. It is a cause exceedingly interesting to the respondents. It is also very important as a precedent, that the country in general may know that the liberty of the subject under a British statute is held equally sacred and equally under the protection of the courts of law by your Lordships as by other judges, and that the same redress for arbitrary oppression is to be had on this side of the Tweed, as on the other.

In respect whereof, etc.

JAMES BOSWELL.

INDEX

This is in general an index of proper names with an analysis of actions, opinions, and personal relationships under the important names. Buildings, streets, and other locations in Edinburgh and London are listed under those headings. Observations or opinions on a person are always listed under the name of that person and usually under the name of the person who is quoted or cited. For example, John Wilkes's comment on David Garrick is under Wilkes as well as under Garrick. In the index article on Samuel Johnson his opinions on various people are listed alphabetically in Part III. Details of Boswell's personal and social relationships are indexed under the names of people concerned. That is, Boswell's relationship with his father, Lord Auchinleck, is indexed under Auchinleck, not under Boswell. Part II of the article on Samuel Johnson is an analysis of Boswell's relationship with Johnson. Sovereigns appear under their Christian names; noblemen and Lords of Session under their titles. The titles given in the index are those proper to September 1782. Maiden names of married women are given in parentheses. Titles of books are listed under the name of the author. Abbreviations used are D. (Duke), M. (Marquess), E. (Earl), V. (Viscount), B. (Baron), Bt. (Baronet), Kt. (Knight), W.S. (Writer to the Signet), JB (James Boswell), SJ (Samuel Johnson).

Index

Johnson, Samuel (*continued*)

poonch, 325, 337; *woonce,* 326; angered by Mrs. Hall and Mrs. Williams, 326; calls Miss Monckton a dunce, 329n.4; attends Royal Academy Dinner with Dr. Beattie, 331–335; looks ill, 334; buys nails, 337; his attitude towards war discussed, 345–346; Eliot of Port Eliot doubts his greatness, 346–347; no sensible man really a Tory but SJ, 346; Langton offended by his imputations of hypocrisy, 346 *and n.*6; and Beauclerk's dogs, 346 *and n.*7; second dinner with John Wilkes, 348–351; tells story of Bet Flint, 349–350, 349n.7; tête-à-tête with Wilkes good subject for a picture, 351; Wilkes toasts, 355; Sir George Baker admires, 360; has always been against rebels, 361; pleased by Loughborough's remark about his political pamphlets, 363; Paoli's remarks on his principles and manners, 364; Dr. Towers has a high respect for, 366; eating oranges in his garden, 369; "Surly Sam," 369 *and n.*2; visits Edward Young's house with JB, 370–371, 371–373; a great coffee-and-tea man, 371; his horror of dead bodies and tombs, 375; wishes he had copies of all pamphlets written against him, 375; pleased with Luton Hoo, 376; his health, 456 *and n.*3; mentioned, 46n.8, 63, 69, 79, 80, 151n.1, 220n.9, 281n.1, 291n.10, 312, 422, 474, 475

II. *Relations with JB:* letter to JB, text, 479–480; letters to JB, mentioned, quoted, 122, 135, 139, 199 *and n.*9, 240, 283n.5, 435; letters from JB, text, 101–102, 145–148; 480–483; letters from JB, mentioned, quoted, xxvii, xxix, 49, 122, 139, 233n.5, 257, 480; introductory account of, 1; JB's verses on supposed nuptials of SJ and Mrs. Thrale, xvii, 316, 318; tour of the Hebrides, 53n.3; JB meets him in London, March 1779, 56, March 1781, 292; angry with JB for writing with anxiety about him, 56; ridicules JB's Scotticisms, 61; JB compares him with Fielding, 64; JB collects material on, 83, 298 *and n.*3, 470; accepts JB's puns, 84; comment on JB's sore foot, 101; JB's experiment to see if SJ will write to

him first, 121–122; angry because JB does not write to him, 135; JB resolves to read *Rasselas* once a year, 122; JB consults him on guardians for his children, 139–140, 162; "Aliis laetus, sapiens sibi," maxim, 141, 147; JB at Lichfield, visits SJ's friends, 145–147; says JB never left a house without leaving a wish for his return, 146, 308; SJ has made JB unhappy in ordinary company, 184; at Auchinleck, 196n.7; rebukes JB for complaining of melancholy, 199; JB sends him *Letter to Lord Braxfield,* 209; JB rewrites his journal on tour of the Hebrides, 232 *and n.*4; David says he bewilders JB, 247; JB quotes SJ's sayings to Dr. Gillespie, 247; JB wants to meet him at York, 257; JB shocked to think that he must die, 273; JB meets unexpectedly in Fleet Street, 292; tells JB, "I love you better than ever I did," 292; thinks JB acted rightly about his brother's settlement, 293; gives JB original copy of *Lives of the Poets,* 293–294, 294n.9; JB tells him he might have been kinder to Gray, 295 *and n.*3; refuses to discuss Liberty and Necessity with JB, 297; JB mentions his "scale of liquors," 300 *and n.*9; advises JB on how to argue before the Ayrshire election committee, 304; JB and others amused by, 317–318, 328–329; scolds JB, 318, 364 *and n.*7; SJ and JB discuss *being called,* 325; catches JB stealing out, 326; JB imagines himself a match for, 329–330; JB tells him he doesn't look well, 337; JB brings to dine at Paoli's, 338; chastises JB for drinking too much at Paoli's, 347 *and n.*9; he and JB have not met for a week, 359; he and JB decide not to dine at The Club next day, 361; promises JB a copy of Lord Chesterfield's letter, 362; at Southill and Welwyn with JB, 369–377; cautions JB against trusting to impressions, 374; bids farewell to JB, 377; dictates argument for JB's Answers for Robertson, 407n.5; JB comforted by letter from, 419 *and n.*7, 481; Mrs. Thrale sends JB a good account of his health, 456 *and n.*3; JB takes possession of Auchinleck on birthday of, 480; his advice to JB on management of his estate, 480; JB asks